Finding Meaning

Finding Meaning

An Existential Quest in Post-Modern Israel

Edited by

OFRA MAYSELESS

University of Haifa

and

PNINIT RUSSO-NETZER

Achva Academic College
University of Haifa

OXFORD

UNIVERSITY PRESS

OXFORD
UNIVERSITY PRESS

Oxford University Press is a department of the University of Oxford. It furthers
the University's objective of excellence in research, scholarship, and education
by publishing worldwide. Oxford is a registered trade mark of Oxford University
Press in the UK and certain other countries.

Published in the United States of America by Oxford University Press
198 Madison Avenue, New York, NY 10016, United States of America.

Library of Congress Cataloging-in-Publication Data
Names: Mayseless, Ofra, editor. | Russo-Netzer, Pninit, editor.
Title: Finding meaning : an existential quest in post-modern Israel /
edited by Ofra Mayseless, Pninit Russo-Netzer, University of Haifa.
Description: New York, NY : Oxford University Press, 2022. |
Includes bibliographical references and index.
Identifiers: LCCN 2021024161 (print) | LCCN 2021024162 (ebook) |
ISBN 9780190910358 (hardback) | ISBN 9780190910372 (epub) |
ISBN 9780190910389
Subjects: LCSH: Meaning (Psychology)—Israel. | Group identity—Israel. |
National characteristics, Israeli.
Classification: LCC BF463.M4 F56 2021 (print) | LCC BF463.M4 (ebook) |
DDC 155.8/95694—dc23
LC record available at https://lccn.loc.gov/2021024161
LC ebook record available at https://lccn.loc.gov/2021024162

DOI: 10.1093/oso/9780190910358.001.0001

1 3 5 7 9 8 6 4 2

Printed by Integrated Books International, United States of America

Contents

PART VI. CONCLUSION

Contributors

Uriel Abulof, PhD
Associate Professor
School of Political Science, Government
and International Affairs
Tel Aviv University, Ramat Aviv, Israel
Cornell University
Ithaca, NY, USA

Ayman K. Agbaria, PhD
Senior Lecturer
Leadership and Policy in Education
University of Haifa
Haifa, Israel

Benjamin Beit-Hallahmi, PhD
Professor Emeritus
Department of Psychology
University of Haifa
Haifa, Israel

Tzlil Ben-Gal, MA
School of Communication, Faculty of
Social Sciences
Bar-Ilan University
Ramat-Gan, Israel

Batia Ben-Hador, PhD
Senior Lecturer
Economics and Business Administration
Ariel University
Ariel, Israel

Uzi Ben-Shalom, PhD
Associate Professor
Department of Sociology and
Anthropology
Ariel University
Ariel, Israel

Eyal Doron, PhD
Researcher and Facilitator
Interdisciplinary Center, Herzliya
Herzliya, Israel

Adi Duchin, Phd
Instructor
Faculty of Education,
University of Haifa
Haifa, Israel

Hagar Hazaz-Berger, PhD
Postdoctoral Fellow at Bar Ilan
University Department of Sociology &
Anthropology
Bar Ilan University
Ramat Gan, Israel
Hebrew University
Jerusalem, Israel

Menachem Keren-Kratz, DMD, PhD
Independent Scholar
Jewish Studies
Ramat Ha-Sharon, Israel

Sawsan Kheir, MA
Double Degree PhD Student
Department of Psychology
University of Haifa
Haifa, Israel

Udi Lebel, PhD
Associate Professor at the School of
Communication
Senior Research Fellow at the Begin-
Sadat Center For Strategic Studies
Bar Ilan University
Ramat Gan, Israel

Sami Mahajnah, PhD
Beit Berl College
Kefar Sava, Israel

Ofra Mayseless, PhD
Full Professor; Head of the Center for the
Study of Human Spirit
Faculty of Education
University of Haifa
Haifa, Israel

Mohanad Mustafa, PhD
Senior Lecturer
Department of History and Department
of Society and Culture
Beit Berl College
Kefar Sava, Israel

Nurit Novis-Deutsch, PhD
Lecturer
Department of the Learning Sciences
The University of Haifa
Haifa, Israel

Peter Nynäs
Professor
Faculty of Arts, Psychology and
Theology
Åbo Akademi University
Turku, Finland

Michal Pagis, PhD
Associate Professor
Department of Sociology and
Anthropology
Bar-Ilan University
Ramat Gan, Israel

Yuval Palgi, PhD
Associate Professor
Department of Gerontology
University of Haifa
Haifa, Israel

Samuel (Muli) Peleg, PhD
Director
Oranim International
Oranim College
Tivon, Israel

Tomer Persico, PhD
Visiting Assistant Professor
Department of Near Eastern Studies, and
the Berkeley Institute for Jewish Law and
Israel Studies
University of California
Berkeley, CA, USA

Pninit Russo-Netzer, PhD
Senior Lecturer and Researcher
School of Advanced Studies
Achva Academic College
Arugot, Israel
Head of the Compass Institute for the
Study and Application of Meaning in life
Research Fellow
University of Haifa
Haifa, Israel

Marianna Ruah-Midbar Shapiro, PhD
Professor
Zefat Academic College
Safed, Israel

Dov Shmotkin, PhD
Professor Emeritus
School of Psychological Sciences
Tel Aviv University
Tel Aviv, Israel

Avihu Shoshana, PhD
Full Professor
Faculty of Education
University of Haifa
Haifa, Israel

Amit Shrira, PhD
Professor
Interdisciplinary Department of Social
Sciences
Bar-Ilan University
Ramat Gan, Israel

Hadas Wiseman
Full Professor
Faculty of Education
University of Haifa
Haifa, Israel

PART I
INTRODUCTION

1

The Israeli Scene as a Case Study of Processes of Search for Meaning in Life in a Post-Modern and Globalized World

Ofra Mayseless and Pninit Russo-Netzer

Search for Meaning in Life in a Post-Modern Sociocultural Context

This book offers an academic inquiry on contemporary processes of the search for meaning in life in a post-modern context, with a focus on the Israeli cultural scene. Constructing or finding meaning in life is considered to be fundamental to human existence (Batthyany & Russo-Netzer, 2014; Frankl, 1963; George & Park, 2016; Mayseless & Keren, 2014; Russo-Netzer, 2018; Russo-Netzer, Schulenberg, & Batthyany, 2016; Steger, 2012; Wong, 2012). Such meaning reflects individuals' search to understand and organize their experience in a coherent manner, achieve a sense of their own worth and place (e.g., an identity and a sense of belonging), and recognize the things that matter to them (e.g., have purpose in life). When such meaning in life is adopted, individuals often feel that their life transcends their transitory existence and hence matters (George & Park, 2016). Viewed as a uniquely human quality (Emmons, 2003; Frankl, 1963) that enables people to interpret and consolidate their experience in the world (Steger, 2009), meaning has gained a growing degree of scientific attention within the psychological field. For example, several components of meaning have been identified (George & Park, 2016; Martela & Steger, 2016), the distinction between search for meaning and having meaning in life has been delineated (e.g., Steger, Kashdan, Sullivan, & Lorentz, 2008a), and the importance and centrality of meaning in life to individuals' well-being and functioning has been established (e.g., King et al., 2006; Park, 2010; Steger, 2012).

Ofra Mayseless and Pninit Russo-Netzer, *The Israeli Scene as a Case Study of Processes of Search for Meaning in Life in a Post-Modern and Globalized World* In: *Finding Meaning.* Edited by: Ofra Mayseless and Pninit Russo-Netzer, Oxford University Press. © Oxford University Press 2022. DOI: 10.1093/oso/9780190910358.003.0001

The construal of meaning in life by individuals is a psychological process, yet it is intimately linked to the cultural context and historical period in which individuals live (Leung, Chiu, & Hong, 2011; Hicks & Routledge, 2013). The social and cultural contexts often offer and sometimes impose narratives, expectations, norms, and values that individuals can align with in their search for coherence, value, and purpose (Hicks & Routledge, 2013). Processes of globalization and neo-humanism challenge the meaning and security individuals find in their national or religious identity. Such processes appear to delegitimize the national and patriotic bases which grant a sense of meaning as part of a collective, advocating instead an individualistic, capitalistic perspective together with the virtue of seeing oneself as a citizen of the world (Navarro, 2007; Soederberg, Menz, & Cerny, 2005; Yeates, 2002). This may lead to diverse reactions, with some individuals and cultural groups, mostly from high socioeconomic statuses subscribing to the ideological legacy of globalization and adopting neo-humanistic perspectives; others turning instead to espousing extreme nationalist identities or radical religious worldviews; and yet others disengaging and adopting a more escapist and relativistic perspective on life, morality, and identity (Featherstone, 1990; Jasko, LaFree, & Kruglanski, 2016; Kinnvall, 2004).

Such processes of search for meaning in life are further affected not only by the grand post-modern perspective but also by the interplay between the specific culture in which an individual lives and that individual's personal pursuit of meaning in his or her life (Chao & Kesebir, 2013; Steger, Kawabata, Shimai, & Otake, 2008b). This book utilizes Israeli culture as a case study to learn about processes related to search for meaning in life in a post-modern and globalized world (Chao & Kesebir, 2013). The book sheds light on these processes in the Israeli cultural scene. It offers new insights with regard to our innate need for meaning and to how it materializes in a post-modern and globalized cultural context that intensifies such searches. The Israeli cultural scene thus serves as a magnifying glass for unravelling a variety of significant contemporary manifestations of the human "will for meaning" (Frankl, 1963), a fundamental motivation for finding meaning in life.

The Israeli Cultural Scene

Established in 1948, Israel is a young and small country, both in size (8,367 square miles/21,671 square kilometers) and in population (about 8 million people). Israel is a Western liberal democratic state containing a complex mosaic of religious and secular policies and institutions (Cohen & Susser, 2000). Only about 20% of Israel's Jewish population consider themselves religious, whether Orthodox (10.0%) or Ultra-orthodox (8.8%). Traditionalists make up about 40% of the Jewish population, and they appear to value religion as a culture and tradition but do not uphold religious precepts (*mitzvot*). The majority of the Jewish population, about 42.5% (Central Bureau of Statistics, 2013), identify themselves as secular in the sense of not belonging to a religious community and not observing traditional rituals. To the Israeli Jewish secular population, Judaism is experienced as more of a national than a religious identity (Ezrachi, 2004). Furthermore, the lack of a clear separation between religion and state in Israel leads to the dominance of religious laws (*halakha*), customs, and symbols in a variety of spheres. This state of affairs often evokes resentment and hostility toward religiosity among the more secular and traditionalist population (Pelleg & Leichtentritt, 2009) as it is perceived as involving an element of coercion.

Since the establishment of the State, Israeli society has undergone significant economic, political, and social changes, gradually moving from a collectivist orientation toward individualistic values; changing from old hegemonic groups to new ones (Mautner, 2011); struggling with large waves of immigration and with the occupation of the West Bank and Gaza Strip, with its large population of Palestinian Arabs; and becoming more pluralistic, fragmented, and decentralized (Kenny-Paz, 1996; Sharabi & Harpaz, 2007). For example, a major change can be seen from the hegemony of the founders of the state of Israel who were mostly of Western origin (e.g., Europe and America) and were mostly secular and socialists, to the hegemony of more right-wing politics and stronger focus on Jewish religious tradition in its diverse forms. Concurrently, the Israeli scene is characterized by fragmentation, and several cultural groups (e.g., right-wing settlers, neoliberals, religious and Ultra-orthodox Jews) passionately vie to become the hegemonic voice, and these groups as well as others (e.g., Muslim Arabs and Mitzrahi ethnic Jews mostly immigrating from Arab countries) also compete to have their voice and, in particular, their narrative heard and adopted by Israeli society.

The schism can be seen along several divides, although these often do not show clear demarcation and have murky boundaries. These include schisms between the political left, which advocates the importance of compromise on land to achieve just and sustainable peace with Palestinian Arabs, and the political right, which pushes toward annexation of the West Bank and is often associated with religiously based justifications for this act; between neoliberal and free-market economy and welfare state supporters; between Ashkenazi Jews (of European/American descent) and Mizrahi Jews (of Middle-Eastern/African descent), where the latter challenge the hegemony and dominance of the former in the narratives of the nation as well as in the nation's power positions; and between humanistic and human rights activists and nationalists (Azoulay & Ofir, 2008; Bar-Tal & Schnell, 2012; Barzilai, 1997; Rabinowitz, 2000; Ram, 1999, 2013).

As a Western society, Israel has also seen its fair share of contemporary trends and experienced the processes of globalization and individualism as well as the rise of a consumer culture (Ben-Porat, 2013). These processes were accompanied by weakening trust in other sources of security, such as political leaders, the nuclear family, and religious institutions (Canetti-Nisim & Beit-Hallahmi, 2007).

Consequently, a variety of historical, social, and cultural contexts contribute to the complex and multifaceted character of Israeli society and position it as a unique setting for the manifestation of meaning-making processes. Its uniqueness can be reflected in three central characteristics, each contributing to the intensity and prominence of the processes of searching for life's meaning and purpose.

1. *Existential focus.* A unique contextual characteristic of Israeli society stems from the prominence of existential threats and the salience of death and mortality. This is related to the acknowledgment of the fragility of life among Israelis in light of the collective trauma and legacy of the Holocaust and other experiences of persecution throughout the past 2,000 years. But it is also related to the ongoing shared experience of existential threats due to terrorist attacks and wars in a country constantly exposed to the danger of armed clashes with its neighbors and terrorist acts within its borders (Mayseless & Salomon, 2003; Reich, 2018). The small population, as well as the close familiarity among Israelis; intense media focus on terrorism and armed clashes; and compulsory military service for Jews at the age of 18 expose almost every Jewish Israeli home to such existential concerns. This shared experience of imminent existential threats raises critical questions concerning meaning, ethos, and mortality and often leads to a search for meaning (Vess, 2013).

2. *Predicament of identity.* Israel is a nation of immigrants. The large majority of its Jewish citizens are either immigrants themselves or the
second or third generation of immigrant families. Israel thus includes
an intricate, rich, and complex mélange of cultures, rituals, and identities that appears to split the country into "cultural tribes." These include the Arab minority in Israel (about 20% of its population, not
including the West Bank), Jews of Ashkenzi and Mizrahi origin, and
cultural groups divided by level of religiousness despite sharing a basic
legacy and identity as Jews: secular, traditionalist, religious, and Ultra-
orthodox Jews. Within this vibrant multicultural new nation, individuals often struggle with the construction of their identities while
answering questions related to the meaning of their lives at three main
levels: the personal ("who am I?"), the communal ("where do I belong?"), and the cultural ("what is the value of my life as part of this
nation?").

3. *Co-existence of core dialectic worldviews.* Israeli daily life touches on
several passionate and salient dialectics that often require individuals
to take a stand. These relate to a strong ambivalence toward religion
and toward Orthodox Judaism in particular, along with the realization
that Israel as a Jewish state rests on a Jewish legacy which, at its core,
is religious. Such a dialectic tension toward Judaism characterizes a
large number of Israelis. A similar dialectic tension exists between the
adoption of an individualistic perspective that accords with the values
of other Western societies, including the free market neo-liberal paradigm, and the established communal and familial setting in Israel
with its socialist and welfare overtones. In the latter, individuals feel
bound by their responsibility and commitment to their family, friends,
and, in particular, the state, and they expect the state to provide them
with economic security and affordable housing. Another dialectic tension relates to the political left, characterized by pro-compromise with
Palestinians attitudes regarding the land, versus the political right, characterized by pro-annexation of the occupied territories, attitudes which
often rely on religious justifications. These three dialectic tensions are
highly salient in Israel and instigate a search for meaningful answers
with respect to a person's values, moral stand, faith, and identity.

Taken together, this collective alert to existential threats, uncertainty, and
instability, coupled with the transition to new hegemonies and a deepening

of social, cultural, and ideological crises of identity and belonging, has insti-gated the search for a variety of alternative sources of meaning and has resulted in an increased interest in and a move toward spiritual, metaphys-ical, and radical venues of meaning in Israeli society (Beit-Hallahmi, 1992). This intense and vibrant scene is described in this volume at the macro, con-ceptual, and descriptive levels as well as at micro levels that include the em-pirical exploration of various subcultures of Israeli society as well as different age groups.

Building on the extant literature, this volume offers a much-needed and thus far neglected perspective on the human search for meaning in the post-modern context by focusing on one noteworthy culture (Israel) and examining a variety of manners in which these search processes mani-fest within this culture as well as how they are affected by its character-istics. The volume provides a multifaceted and nuanced picture of such processes within one overarching cultural context. Despite its small size and population, Israel continuously attracts international attention. This is due to a variety of reasons, among which are its status as a Jewish state in the Holy Land, a land and legacy significant to millions of people world-wide; the unabating violent conflict with its neighbors, and its economic success story in agriculture and industry (e.g., being a "start-up nation"). For people who are specifically interested in Israel as a nation and culture, the volume provides an in-depth, timely, and innovative perspective on major processes of the search for meaning characteristic of Israeli society, thus contributing to a better understanding of its contemporary cultural climate.

In addition, this volume highlights the centrality of the human search for meaning in human experience, offers new understandings of the variety of ways through which people express their search for meaning in life, and provides a better understanding of such endeavors at the cultural level, at the psychological level, and at the intersection of the cultural and personal levels. It underscores the importance of examining searches for meaning within the cultural context in which they take place.

Content and Structure

This volume includes 18 chapters by distinguished researchers from different disciplines including psychology, religious studies, anthropology, cultural studies, sociology, education, and political science. It has six parts, including this Introduction.

Part II, "A Quilt of Perspectives of the Israeli Scene: Start-Up Nation, Multicultural, and Trauma and Bereavement Struck," includes three chapters that shed light on three core aspects of Israeli society, which will also resonate in other chapters. Chapter 2, by Eyal Doron, grapples with the quandary of how, despite all its tensions and socioeconomic gaps, most of Israel's citizens have a deep sense of connection and meaning. His suggestion underscores the importance of historical heritage, its "start-up nation" present, and the unique Israeli free spirit and self-expression. Chapter 3, by Hagar Hazaz-Berger presents a case study of the Rothschild encampment during the Summer 2011 Social Protest that underscores processes of "multitopia"—where ideological cracks in the Zionist utopia and Israeli society gave rise to individual processes of search for meanings reflecting the need to find personal utopias and identities through spiritual practices and by the deconstruction and reconstruction of social categories. Chapter 4, Udi Lebel and Tzlil Ben-Gal, sheds light yet on another major discourse in Israeli society, that of the national bereavement discourse, the meaning it gives to Israeli people, and the centrality of existential concerns both national and individual in Israeli culture.

These chapters thus underscore three major scripts that give Israelis a sense of meaning, a *unique cherished and valuable national and historical identity* (past and present), *individualistic freedom to shape one's meaning in life*, and *salient death awareness that can serve a purpose*.

Part III includes four chapters that delve more specifically into developmental issues and specific case studies under the heading of "Developmental Processes and Challenges in the Israeli Search for Meaning."

Chapter 5, by Samuel (Muli) Peleg, presents an in-depth case study of a small but influential group of youth in Israel—the Hilltop Youth in the West Bank. By adopting an extremist and messianic religious perspective (often also observed among youth in other cultures), defying current political and religious structures, and embracing violent activities, they create for themselves and others, often more passive observers and older, a new and liberating meaning.

Chapter 6, by Benjamin Beit-Hallahmi, sheds light on yet another unique case study, the Physical Immortality group. Despite the group's declared focus on denying death, it appears that for participants—mostly wealthy and successful followers in their middle adulthood years who were also habitual joiners of self-enhancement groups—it served as a venue of support, belonging, and positivity.

Chapter 7, by Amit Shrira, Yuval Palgi, and Dov Shmotkin, takes a look at yet another age group: older adults. The chapter underscores the frequency of trauma-related events in the lives of older adults in Israel (e.g., Holocaust, terrorist attacks, wars) and relies on several conceptualizations as well as a number of studies to underline the central role that meaning in life plays in their coping with the double challenge of aging (universal) and traumatic adversity (more specific to the Israeli scene).

The final chapter in this part, Chapter 8, by Adi Duchin and Hadas Wiseman, again focuses on a unique case study of Holocaust survivors (now in their 70s and 80s) who have written memoirs read by family members. The chapter underscores the significant role of intergenerational processes, especially between Holocaust survivors and the third generation (grandchildren) as central to creating a shared narrative and legacy that provides integrated meaning for family members and highlights the variability among families in this respect.

Together the chapters highlight the centrality of age and generational cohort in facing challenges related to meaning in life within the unique Israeli culture, underscoring both universal and distinctly Israeli/Jewish aspects. These chapters further highlight two other scripts that give Israelis a sense of meaning, *an extreme messianic religious perspective, belonging and being supported by groups or family*, and, again, the script that underscores the centrality of *trauma and death that can be meaningful*.

Part IV, "Struggling for Identity," includes five chapters that look at different subcultures in Israeli society and their attempts to form an identity and a cultural narrative that can give them clarity and belonging, well-being, and a sense of worth within the post-modern context and the Israeli cultural scene. Chapter 9, by Uriel Abulof, looks at the current situation of Zionism, which led to the establishment of Israel as a state and was central in the identity and meaning of its citizens. The chapter contends that nations need existential legitimation, or "nomization," which can boost the nation's resilience, and the author suggests that, based on analyses of social and political processes, currently, Zionist "nomization" is not as strong and clear as it used to be and hence the national "politics of fear" is closer to anomy.

Chapter 10, by Avihu Shoshana, looks at ethnic and socioeconomic class identities (both relevant to power status) among Jews in Israel, with a focus on Mizrahim (of Middle-Eastern/African descent). The chapter underscores the centrality of class, ethnicity, and their interplay in adopting identity scripts (e.g., focus on ethnic or class identity) that provide individuals with meaning and personal value.

Chapter 11, by Ayman K. Agbaria, Mohanad Mustafa, and Sami Mahajnah, focuses on the Arab minority in Israel and identifies three narratives in the Arab politics of belonging. These narratives reflect a search for meaning and a political vision to reconcile the entangled relationships and contradictions between their Palestinian nationality, Israeli citizenship, and religion of Islam in Israel. The chapter further analyzes how these three narratives of politics of belonging—the romantic, the practical, and the visionary—are expressed among Arab political and Muslim religious actors.

Chapter 12, by Menachem Keren-Kratz, focuses on Haredi (Ultra-orthodox) women. This chapter discusses the historical background of Haredi women's status in Israel and highlights their current agentic pursuit to answer their intrinsic need for a meaningful life and self-fulfillment in spheres such as their own family, the workplace, their free time, and also in their public and political representation. The chapter underscores that, for them, such pursuits are in conjunction with their intrinsic adherence to Jewish Haredi identity and tradition.

Chapter 13, by Michal Pagis, focuses on a distinct, high-profile, and growing group of individuals whose interest led them to Buddhist thought and practice and in particular Vipassana practice. The chapter highlights that, through meditation, Israelis find an embodied anchor for selfhood, shift away from local social embeddedness, and find meaning in life. This meaning relies on a humanistic-based identification with humanity at large—a universal nonlocal existence, one that transcends the hectic and difficult local life in Israel.

Together, the chapters highlight a variety of scripts—narratives of identity and belonging that provide individuals with meaning and personal value and are deconstructed, reconstructed, and also adopted by individuals from a variety of subcultures in Israel. Some are more visionary in their content, and others may emphasize well-being; some rely heavily on the past and on tradition; while others focus on the present and on practices.

Part V focuses on a central dimension in processes of search for meaning in life: "Between Religiosity and Secularism." This part includes four chapters that discuss the place and significance of religiosity, spirituality, and secularity in processes of search for meaning in life among Israelis. Such issues have already been underscored using a variety of perspectives in previous chapters as well (e.g., Chapter 5 on the Hilltop Youth and their extreme messianic religious orientation, Chapter 7 on older adults in Israel and the significance of spirituality and religion as sources of meaning, Chapter 11 on the Arab minority in Israel and the centrality of Islamic perspectives of belonging, and Chapter 12 on Haredi women). In this part, the chapters specifically center on the dimension of religiosity/spirituality and secularism.

Chapter 14, by Tomer Persico, looks at the burgeoning scene of contemporary spirituality in Israel and, as in Chapters 3 and 9, underscores the decline of the secular Zionist meta-narrative. The chapter discusses a strong tendency among those active in this scene to go back to Judaism as a source of meaning, but it also underscores that they do so using a post-collectivist, individualistic ethos. Such a process is conceived in the chapter as involving a renovation and restructuring of Judaism, often by creating an individual, autonomous, tailor-made Judaism which is itself seen as a new form of secularization.

Chapter 15, by Marianna Ruah-Midbar Shapiro, looks at the same scene of contemporary spiritualities and discusses another prevalent and significant phenomenon—that of turning to the Far East and Asian traditions as a source of meaning. The chapter underscores that this process involves an imagined East where Israelis (and other Westerners) selectively choose what they take from Eastern culture and embrace reverence toward this imagined East. When returning to Israel, Judaism also becomes an object for projections, and individuals redesign Judaism to be exotic, incorporating New Age values that lend them meaning in life.

Chapter 16, by Udi Lebel, Batia Ben-Hador, and Uzi Ben-Shalom, presents a case study of rabbinic seminars for noncombat officers who experience alienation in their military work environment. The chapter highlights how the seminar has succeeded in infusing meaning in these soldiers' lives and military service by infusing in them a Jewish-spiritualistic discourse and language that combines New Age motifs with Judaism and how such seminars promote a modern hegemony of religion in the army and draw participants closer to the Jewish-nationalist discourse that provides them with a strong sense of meaning, mission, and recognition.

Chapter 17, by Nurit Novis-Deutsch, Peter Nynäs, and Sawsan Kheir, examine university students from three faith traditions in Israel: Jewish, Muslim, and Druze. The chapter underscores the importance of culture in sanctioning meaning-making paths or narratives. For example, secular Muslims and Druze often expressed a sense of meaninglessness, whereas

Jewish seculars expressed high levels of purpose-making based on social action. In accordance, Muslims were most engaged in religious meaning-making as a source of meaning and Jews were least engaged.

Together, the chapters in this part, as well as others in the book, underscore the centrality of religious and spiritual narratives in current searches for meaning in life in Israel. The chapters further underscore that often such religiosity or spirituality is custom made and includes a renewed combination of tradition with New Age perspectives, individualistic concerns of self-agency and self-fulfillment, and secular individualistic undertones.

Part VI comprises one chapter by Pninit Russo-Netzer and Ofra Mayseless (Chapter 18), "Meaning in Life at the Crossroads of Personal Processes and Cultural Crisis," which provides a conceptual overview of the volume and addresses the main characteristics of the interplay among context, culture, and personal processes of meaning-making.

Taken as a whole, the volume's chapters highlight how a culture challenged by current and past existential threats, an identity predicament, and a core ambivalence in general worldviews engenders deep, lively, and powerful processes of meaning-making that rely on a large number of potential narratives of meaning.

References

Azoulay, A., & Ofir, A. (2008). *This regime which is not one: Occupation and democracy between the sea and the river (1967–).* [Hebrew]. Resling.

Bar-Tal, D., & Schnell, I. (Eds.). (2012). *The impact of lasting occupation: Enduring challenges and emerging answers.* Oxford University Press.

Barzilai, G. (1997). Between the rule of law and the laws of the ruler: The Supreme Court in Israeli legal culture. *International Social Science Journal, 49*(152), 193–208.

Batthyany, A., & Russo-Netzer, P. (2014). Psychologies of meaning. In A. Batthyany & P. Russo-Netzer. (Eds.), *Meaning in positive and existential psychology* (pp. 3–22). Springer.

Beit-Hallahmi, B. (1992). *Despair and deliverance: Private salvation in contemporary Israel.* SUNY Press.

Ben-Porat, G. (2013). *Between state and synagogue: The secularization of contemporary Israel.* Cambridge University Press.

Canetti-Nisim, D., & Beit-Hallahmi, B. (2007). The effects of authoritarianism, religiosity, and "New Age" beliefs on support for democracy: Unraveling the strands. *Review of Religious Research, 48*(4), 369–384.

Central Bureau of Statistics. (2013). Statistical abstract of Israel 2013—No. 64. https://www.cbs.gov.il/en/publications/Pages/2013/Statistical-Abstract-of-Israel-2013-No64.aspx

Chao, M. M., & Kesebir, P. (2013). Culture: The grand web of meaning. In J. Hicks & C. Routledge (Eds.), *The experience of meaning in life* (pp. 317–331). Springer.

Cohen, A., & Susser, B. (2000). *Israel and the politics of Jewish identity: The secular-religious impasse.* Johns Hopkins University Press.

Emmons, R. A. (2003). Personal goals, life meaning, and virtue: Wellsprings of a positive life. In C. L. M. Keyes & J. Haidt (Eds.), *Flourishing: Positive psychology and the life well-lived* (pp. 105–128). American Psychological Association.

Ezrachi, E. (2004). The quest for spirituality among secular Israelis. In U. Rebhun & C. I. Waxman (Eds.), *Jews in Israel: Contemporary social and cultural patterns* (pp. 315–328). Brandeis University Press.

Featherstone, M. (Ed.). (1990). *Global culture: Nationalism, globalization and modernity (Vol. 2).* Sage.

Frankl, V. E. (1963). *Man's search for meaning: An introduction to logotherapy.* Washington Square Press.

George, L. S., & Park, C. L. (2016). Meaning in life as comprehension, purpose, and mattering: Toward integration and new research questions. *Review of General Psychology, 20*(3), 205–220.

Hicks, J., & Routledge, C. (Eds.). (2013). *The experience of meaning in life.* Springer.

Jasko, K., LaFree, G., & Kruglanski, A. (2016). Quest for significance and violent extremism: The case of domestic radicalization. *Political Psychology, 38*(5), 815–831.

Kenny-Paz, B. (1996). Israel towards the year 2000: A changing world. In M. Lisk & B. Kenny-Paz (Eds.), *Israel towards the year 2000* (pp. 408–428). Magnes. [Hebrew]

King, L. A., Hicks, J. A., Krull, J. L., & Del Gaiso, A. K. (2006). Positive affect and the experience of meaning in life. *Journal of Personality and Social Psychology, 90*(1), 179–196.

Kinnvall, C. (2004). Globalization and religious nationalism: Self, identity, and the search for ontological security. *Political Psychology, 25*(5), 741–767.

Leung, A., Chiu, C-Y., & Hong, Y-Y. (Eds.). (2011). *Cultural processes: A social psychological perspective.* Oxford University Press.

Martela, F., & Steger, M. F. (2016). The three meanings of meaning in life: Distinguishing coherence, purpose, and significance. *Journal of Positive Psychology, 11*(5), 531–545.

Mautner, M. (2011). *Law and the culture of Israel.* Oxford University Press.

Mayseless, O., & Keren, E. (2014). Finding a meaningful life as a developmental task in emerging adulthood: The domains of love and work across cultures. *Emerging Adulthood, 2*(1), 63–73.

Mayseless, O., & Salomon, G. (2003). Dialectic contradictions in the experience of Israeli Jewish adolescents. In F. Pajares & T. Urdan (Eds.), *International perspectives on adolescence* (pp. 149–171). Information Age Publishing.

Navarro, V. (Ed.). (2007). *Neoliberalism, globalization, and inequalities: Consequences for health and quality of life.* Baywood Publishing.

Park, C. L. (2010). Making sense of the meaning literature: An integrative review of meaning making and its effects on adjustment to stressful life events. *Psychological Bulletin, 136*(2), 257–301.

Pelleg, G., & Leichtentritt, R. D. (2009). Spiritual beliefs among Israeli nurses and social workers: A comparison based on their involvement with the dying. *OMEGA-Journal of Death and Dying, 59*(3), 239–252.

Rabinowitz, D. (2000). Postnational Palestine/Israel? Globalization, diaspora, transnationalism, and the Israeli-Palestinian conflict. *Critical Inquiry, 26*(4), 757–772.

Ram, U. (1999). The state of the nation: Contemporary challenges to Zionism in Israel. *Constellations, 6*(3), 325–338.

Ram, U. (2013). *The globalization of Israel: McWorld in Tel Aviv, Jihad in Jerusalem.* Routledge.

Reich, B. (2018). *Israel: Land of tradition and conflict.* Routledge.

Russo-Netzer, P. (2018). Healing the divide through wholeness: Holding on to what makes us human. *International Journal of Existential Positive Psychology, 7*(2), 17.

Russo-Netzer, P., Schulenberg, S. E., & Batthyany, A. (Eds.). (2016). *Clinical perspectives on meaning: Positive and existential psychotherapy.* Springer.

Sharabi, M., & Harpaz, I. (2007). Changes in work centrality and other life areas in Israel: A longitudinal study. *Journal of Human Values, 13*(2), 95–106.

Soederberg, S., Menz, G., & Cerny, P. G. (Eds.). (2005). *Internalizing globalization.* Palgrave Macmillan.

Steger, M. F. (2009). Meaning in life. In S. J. Lopez & C. R. Snyder (Eds.), *Oxford handbook of positive psychology* (2nd ed., pp. 679–687). Oxford University Press.

Steger, M. F. (2012). Experiencing meaning in life: Optimal functioning at the nexus of spirituality, psychopathology, and well-being. In P. T. P. Wong (Ed.), *The human quest for meaning* (2nd ed., pp. 165–184). Routledge.

Steger, M. F., Kashdan, T. B., Sullivan, B. A., & Lorentz, D. (2008a). Understanding the search for meaning in life: Personality, cognitive style, and the dynamic between seeking and experiencing meaning. *Journal of Personality, 76*(2), 199–228.

Steger, M. F., Kawabata, Y., Shimai, S., & Otake, K. (2008b). The meaningful life in Japan and the United States: Levels and correlates of meaning in life. *Journal of Research in Personality, 42*(3), 660–678.

Vess, M. (2013). Death, the need for unambiguous knowledge, and the construction and maintenance of multi-level meaning. In J. Hicks & C. Routledge (Eds.), *The experience of meaning in life* (pp. 271–283). Springer.

Wong, P. T. (2012). Toward a dual-systems model of what makes life worth living. In P. T. P. Wong (Ed.), *The human quest for meaning* (2nd ed., pp. 3–22). Routledge.

Yeates, N. (2002). Globalization and social policy: From global neoliberal hegemony to global political pluralism. *Global Social Policy, 2*(1), 69–91.

PART II
A QUILT OF PERSPECTIVES OF THE ISRAELI SCENE

Start-Up Nation, Multicultural, and Trauma and Bereavement Struck

PART II

2

The Meaning of Life Through Israeli Eyes

Happiness and Creativity in the Restless Start-Up Nation

Eyal Doron

Introduction

Daily life experience in Israel is characterized by day-to-day tension and absence of calm. Despite this situation Israel consistently achieves high ranking on the World Happiness Index. On the other hand, Israel is ranked third among countries of the Organization for Economic Cooperation and Development (OECD) in its poverty rate and is in the top third of countries in income inequality. This is but one example of the many paradoxes that Israeli reality reflects. Does Israeli society, which is small yet typified by dramatic social and economic gaps, enable the majority of its citizens to achieve a fulfilling, meaningful, and happy life?

In this chapter I suggest that active citizenship in the "startup nation" of Israel provides Israelis with a deep sense of worth, significance, and meaning because it connects its residents, in the most profound way, to the basic myth of the Jewish people: being part of a special "chosen" nation that has to prove its talent, its ability to invent, and its unique creativity. This view of the few against the many, and of the few acting for the benefit of the many, has also shaped Israel's education system. As early as second grade, a select few (1–3%) are defined as gifted. These super groups are placed in a separate, well-planned program, usually only one class per city. In line with this Israel produces an enormous number of prestigious award laureates and boasts achievements in science, the arts, medicine, agriculture, and cyber and high-tech ("islands of excellence"). This striving for excellence cannot be separated from the sense of emergency that accompanies daily existence in a small country surrounded by enemies. The sense of emergency and stress intensifies due to the strong sense, felt by most Israelis in the past several

Eyal Doron, *The Meaning of Life Through Israeli Eyes* In: *Finding Meaning*. Edited by: Ofra Mayseless and Pninit Russo-Netzer, Oxford University Press. © Oxford University Press 2022. DOI: 10.1093/oso/9780190910358.003.0002 decades, that, unfortunately, there is no one with whom to negotiate peace "on the other side."

In this chapter I present and analyze the various elements comprising what is defined as a "special compensation mechanism" that enables the average Israeli, who observes the chosen few and the extraordinary who act in the name of all Israelis, to feel a profound ability for self-expression, uniqueness, and meaning.

I further delve into the narcissistic-like quality of the individual versus his near-total emotional involvement in any extreme situation pertaining to "the whole country." The outcome is a very unique life model in which striving for a true sense of meaning and obsessively focusing on innovation and creativity come together powerfully.

The presented model is key to understanding the state of Israel as a laboratory of restless innovation, a kind of national accelerator, but at the same time also as a place with unique perceptions of happiness and meaning of life.

The Few Against the Many: The Few in the Name of the Many

Born in the Startup Nation

I'm on my way to one of those prestigious, glittering fundraising events. The guests are members of a leading Israeli hospital's donor association, mostly older wealthy people. The man speaking before me is a renowned surgeon who delivers the opening address. He does not wait very long before shooting off a barrage of data about Israel's amazing level of innovation. The facts are truly impressive: Israel is ranked first in the world for startup companies per capita (Senor & Singer, 2011), third in number of companies traded on NASDAQ after the United States and China (McKenna, 2017), fifth in patents filed per capita, and first in medical device patents per capita (USPTO).[1]

The surgeon's style is sharp and confident, his slides are full of graphics, his speech direct and a bit arrogant. I step up right after he finishes his talk,

---

[1] Ministry of Economy and Industry—Invest in Israel (n.d.). https://investinisrael.gov.il/ExploreIsrael/sectors/Pages/sectors.aspx

knowing that I'm expected to continue the enjoyable and inspiring tone of the evening. He immediately becomes engrossed in his cellphone (out of courtesy, he sits in the audience rather than rushing out).

I address him, making him raise his head. "An impressive lecture," I say. The graphs about the state of Israel in relation to the world are really astonishing. The question is: Which Israel do you want to talk about—the 3% who are moving ahead at full steam, or the enormous gaps between them and everyone else? For every metric of excellence at the top of these tables, there are other metrics where Israel lags far behind: it is ranked third among the OECD countries in its poverty rate, it is in the top third of countries in income inequality, and very near the bottom in representation of women in politics (OECD, 2017). Israel is ranked next to last in education among the OECD countries (Ben-David & Kimhi, 2017). The investment in early childhood education (ages 0–3) is approximately one-third of the average in the Member States. The occasion requires that we not turn this place into a battleground, but the question lingers. How can we really describe today's Israel? "You saved a good friend of mine who was given no chance of survival," I tell the professor, getting him to raise his head from his cellphone once more in order to look at me. "But maybe it is precisely for the sake of this excellence that we have an obligation to enable more and more people to participate in the celebration of Israeli creativity."

Does Israeli society, which is small yet typified by dramatic social and economic gaps, enable the majority of its citizens to achieve a fulfilling and happy life? The reality presents fascinating paradoxes, one example of which is Israel's consistently high ranking on the World Happiness Index (more on this later). The Israeli reality reflected in European Union reports does not necessarily reflect the surprising life model, with its complexities and myriad inner contradictions, that actually exists on the ground.[2]

We will attempt to interpret and understand how Israeli reality enables each of its participants to gain a sense of compensation and a sense of meaning and uniqueness.

---

[2] Google, Amazon, Apple, Facebook, and Microsoft are some of the companies with research and development centers in Israel.

Excellence Against All Odds

I was born in the state of Israel, and today I live in the Startup Nation. My parents were born in Tel Aviv, a city that sprang up from desolate sand dunes to become a modern, teeming metropolis. For many years I lived in my "bubble"—an Israel that was secular, modern, abundant in technology, ambitious, and entrepreneurial. But, in fact, each Israeli tribe lives in its own bubble: national-religious, Ultra-orthodox, Druze, Israeli Arabs (if they agree to be defined thus), residents of Israel's geosocial periphery, residents of the large cities, or people who live on kibbutzim. Active citizenship in the Startup Nation of Israel connects its residents, in the most profound way, to the basic myth of the Jewish people: being part of a special nation that has to prove its talent, its ability to invent, and its unique creativity. Israel is a small country that produces an enormous number of prestigious award laureates and boasts achievements in science, the arts, medicine, agriculture, and in cyber and high-tech. A select few conquer the summits on Israel's behalf, spurring its economic growth and its success in the world. The flip side of the race to excellence and of nurturing outstanding people, as stated, is the creation of social and economic gaps, which makes one wonder.

Part of the Jewish-Israeli story has always been the story of the few against the many and of the few acting for the benefit of the many. Excellence against all odds, victory with insufficient tools, means, or starting conditions, with no help from most of the world's nations—all these are an inseparable part of the Jewish people's ethos through the generations. That is what happened in the battle between David and Goliath in the Valley of Elah. Time and again, the Israelis send chosen representatives to succeed and win in their name. It is no coincidence that Israelis excel in individual sports such as judo and windsurfing—events in which only one athlete participates.

Interestingly, despite the fundamental difference between the population that serves in the army and the Ultra-orthodox (who do not), the ideal of individual excellence is highly congruent with the Ultra-orthodox ethos. Tens of thousands of members of these communities look up to sages and prodigies in learning; these are the geniuses of their generations, experts in the Torah, who are assured of particularly advantageous marriages. I recently gave a talk at a conference attended by a thousand Ultra-orthodox women that was part of an attempt by government authorities to integrate them into the labor market so that their husbands could continue to study. "You are daughters of kings" (a biblical reference), the Chief Rabbi of Jerusalem told them, heaping praises on them for enabling their husbands to sit and learn undisturbed. Despite the great diversity that is visible to the eye in Israel among Ultra-orthodox, religious, and secular people, the greatest appreciation is given equally to those who demonstrate original thinking. They are declared geniuses due to an innovative interpretation, a groundbreaking religious ruling, or for coming up with a solution to a specific problem. From this standpoint, Gil Schwed, CEO of Check Point, an Israeli cyber company that has become a global icon, is admired by a similar standard, exactly like the late Rabbi Ovadia Yosef, who is renowned for his original and daring religious rulings, which include permitting the remarriage of widows of Israeli soldiers who fell in the Yom Kippur War and whose burial place is unknown (according to religious law, these widows could not remarry as long as there was no evidence of their husband's death).

The Local Educational Model for Excellence

This view of the few against the many and of the few acting for the benefit of the many has also shaped Israel's education system, tipping the scales in favor of educating for excellence. As early as second grade, all children in Israel undergo standardized tests whose purpose is to identify gifted children. Most children are told, even before they reach third grade, that they are "ordinary" and not special, while a select few (1–3%) are defined as gifted.

It is fascinating to compare the Israeli view with that of two dominant concepts of education systems: Finland and China. Finland is seen by many as the capital of global education since 2000, with the PISA tests ranking its pupils' achievements first in the world (PISA, 2018; the PISA tests compare 15-year-old pupils from dozens of countries by their performance levels in science, math, and English). Despite Finland's impressive accomplishments, it strives to fulfill, first and foremost, the fundamental principle of social equality, which has informed the establishment of free, high-quality public schooling. This is precisely why Finland does not try to identify gifted pupils; the idea is to enable everyone to attend a good school, even if this means that there are no excellent schools. Officially, Finland has no private schools, no standardized tests that compare different schools, and the classrooms include every type of education from first grade onward: vocational, academic, and special education. Israel, on the other hand, sorts pupils into different tracks: special education, standard education, and special courses for pupils who are destined to sit for their final math exams as early as tenth grade and begin attending university. From there, the path proceeds toward specialized army service, where they will be recruited to elite, secret intelligence units, supervise espionage and surveillance programs, or work in technological development. Their next station will be a startup company that courts them. The army, which in the past delayed the self-actualization process, has become a shortcut to extraordinary success at a particularly young age. Some Israeli startup companies try to identify talented people as young as 16 or 17, as do the various army units. Jewish mothers, who once wanted their sons to be doctors or pilots, now hope their children will serve in a prestigious intelligence unit, far from the battlefield and close to opportunities for self-fulfillment.

The other leading concept of education is represented by Asian education, and Shanghai education in particular with its high worldwide scores in mathematics. Pupils from China or South Korea strive for the highest possible grades and, as early as sixth grade, begin planning for college entrance examinations that will determine their academic future. Their supreme goal is to attain the highest possible grade and a higher average than their classmates, which translates to endless marathons of practice and revision. It is all about scholastic achievement and getting the highest score. After visiting China, you only begin to slightly understand the intimidating competition every young Chinese person is facing with countless young people like them. The Israeli model of excellence, by comparison, is again different. It strives for a way of thinking that sparks the imagination. In the language of the *beit midrash*, or Jewish study hall, such thinking is known as *ipcha mistabra* (literally, "on the contrary")—a type of thinking that serves well in the ranks of Israeli intelligence or in startup companies. Complex models of what is now referred to as "innovation" or "disruptive innovation" have found expression for generations in the sources of Jewish thought, such as the Talmud or Jewish mysticism, which emphasizes thinking from unexpected angles of contemplation or putting together elements that have not been linked before. This extraordinary aspiration to excellence, which arouses such amazement, is also somewhat linked to pride and the desire to prove oneself. Israeli thinking does not believe in low volume. It strives for peak experiences, like the courageous spirit of the Israeli fighter pilots, or that of Israeli chefs, who gain the world on a platter when they serve combinations of foods and spices that no one has ever thought of before.

The Collective and the Individual: Israeli Happiness

The Dramatic Shift

The example that illustrates the transition from the dream of the collective or community way of life to the age of the individual is clearly evident in what happened to one of Israel's best-known marvels: kibbutzim. In the state's early days, like-minded people who were imbued with a specific vision formed communities based on the idea of communal life. The members of these communities shared their property and even raised their children in a communal children's house. The children were separated from their parents from an early age (many of these children admitted years later that they ultimately paid an emotional price for this). The members of the kibbutzim, who worked in farming and manual labor, enlisted in elite army units—all in order to fulfill the Zionist dream of making the desert bloom. They hoped to build a utopian society, which indeed became a well-known global brand for many years. In their heyday, the kibbutzim attracted volunteers from all over the world, and the young, tanned kibbutznik—male and female alike— became a symbol of youth and vitality.

Just a few decades later, most of the kibbutzim fell into financial difficulty. Most were privatized, and the idea of communal life fell by the wayside. By contrast, a few kibbutzim experienced an extraordinary degree of economic prosperity. It is fascinating to discover that the success of the latter was usually due to one person who thought differently and took everyone in a new direction. In most cases, it was an enterprise that was established on the kibbutz and slowly became a source of income for all its members. This is what happened with Netafim, for example, a company that bears the name of the kibbutz where it began; it produces drip-irrigation sprinklers for more than a hundred countries all over the world. Another example is Kibbutz Sasa's armor protection enterprise, which turned the kibbutz's 100 members into millionaires. I met some 20 kibbutz secretaries who told me the same story: one of the members came to them with an idea for changing the whole way the kibbutz worked and make money before it would be too late. It was hard to believe prophecies of doom while the kibbutzim were doing so well, but as one kibbutz secretary told me: "On the 1% chance that there was something in it, I funded his research." It seems that two people are required: one to come up with an idea, and one to believe in him.

One way or another, the kibbutz vision of the commune and the collective collapsed, bringing in stories of success thanks to individuals. The experience of the kibbutzim cannot be detached from the spirit of the time or from the political and general changes that have taken place in Israel. Yet the process that the kibbutzim underwent symbolizes a growing trend in Israel of admiring and appreciating the few who conceived a project, took a chance, and achieved financial success. The few against the many in battle—or, more precisely, the few who think in a different way, thus saving the many who follow the strict, misleading way of thinking.

The kibbutz ethos took on a completely different form and symbolized the breakdown of Israeli society into sectors and subsectors (as articulately described by Israeli sociologist Daniel Gutwein). The state's role as a supportive system was replaced by various politicians representing subsectors and their narrow interests. The aspiration to fulfil the collective vision of the wandering nation's salvation in its own land was replaced by various narrower aspirations—each sector and its chosen few. Given this state of affairs, it is even more intriguing to understand the unique model of satisfaction, of connection and local belonging that took shape in the young state.

If this is how things are, then we should be grappling with a disturbing question: Is Israel a country that promises a sense of a fulfilling, meaningful life only for a select few? Surprisingly, and as we shall see, life in Israel, with all its complexity, succeeds in providing most citizens with a deep sense of connection and meaning despite the enormous socioeconomic gaps between population sectors.

Eleventh on the World Happiness Index

Israel has ranked eleventh on the World Happiness Index time and again (Helliwell et al., 2018). This statistic is astonishing in light of the state of Israel's existential situation, the tension that constantly accompanies life in Israel, and the gaps and tensions between the various elements of Israeli society. Israel's fairly low ranking on the Global Trust Index and its relatively high ranking on the Corruption Perceptions Index (CPI) are also worthy of note.[3] Still, Israel persistently precedes countries such as Germany, the

---

[3] The Global Trust Index questionnaire asked: Do you agree with the statement that most people can be trusted? In 2004, 23 percent of Israelis agreed with that statement. Israel is ranked in the lower fourth. In Finland, by comparison, 58 percent agreed with the statement, and in Norway, 73 percent

United States, the United Kingdom, and France. The mystery dissipates when we examine the question that the World Happiness Index uses in its inventory.

The questionnaire is based on one main item: Please imagine a ladder, with steps numbered from 0 at the bottom to 10 at the top. The top of the ladder represents the best possible life for you, and the bottom of the ladder represents the worst possible life for you. On which step of the ladder would you say you personally feel you stand at this time? (Also known as the Cantril Ladder.) There is something about this question that pushes respondents to consider and evaluate their life in a comprehensive and inclusive way. Unlike a questionnaire about satisfaction, in which people are asked if they felt positive or negative experiences over the past week, this index directs their attention to evaluating life holistically and skips over the memory of yesterday. The Cantril Ladder invites us to consider our lives on a deep level, beyond the day-to-day tension and absence of calm. Above all, the poll with its ladder refers to a definition of happiness as deeply meaningful, not as a momentary feeling of enjoyment or satisfaction regarding the routine of life.

In the experiment I conducted in conjunction with the Ministry of Science to mark the state of Israel's seventieth anniversary, it was noted that the average happiness grade in Israel was almost identical to that of the World Happiness Index (7.3 in our experiment, compared with 7.2 in the Gallup Poll; Ministry of Science and Technology, 2018). In accordance with the mood indicated in the majority of studies, it might have been expected that married people would be happier than single people in Israel, too. As a rule, the picture that emerges is similar to that in the United States or Europe regarding the connection between life choices and the chance of increasing one's happiness level. It appears that average Israelis feel a relatively strong degree of belonging and spend their life as part of a social network and a strong family. Israelis never stop complaining and venting all the way to happiness. From this perspective, perhaps, the constant venting about "where we live" only proves the level of the relationship, belonging, and emotional connection to the country.

agreed with it (The World Values Survey, 2014). In the Corruption Perceptions Index (0 to 100), only twelve countries got a grade above 80. Israel, with a passing grade of 62, is in 32nd place in the general ranking (CPI: Corruption Perceptions Index, 2017).

Interim conclusion: Israeli society encourages excellence on the part of individuals and does not necessarily place emphasis on equal conditions and opportunities. The ethos of gifted pupils in education, select individuals in the army, and a select few in the job market, has become the leading story of the state of Israel with the passage of time. On the other hand, average Israelis feel that they have a chance to live happily, that they are connected to a network of family and close friends, and that they have a deep emotional connection to the country. The reality is one of extremes. From this standpoint, Israelis are always "members of the gang" and "a tribe," yet, at the same time, they are fans of a few glittering stars who will pull everyone else upward. It still seems that these are not enough to reach the topmost rankings on the World Happiness Index.

Outlines of a "Compensation Mechanism"

We need to try to understand how the unique structure of Israeli society serves as a sophisticated compensation mechanism that provides each of its members the possibility to feel meaningful and important. The question remains unanswered: Where do the average Israeli's desires and aspirations find expression? What gives average Israelis a sense of freedom and self-expression in a society that admires high achievers and seems to neglect and ignore all the rest?

Examination of the unique structure within which Israeli society conducts itself reveals a unique combination of circumstances, the outcome of which is a kind of compensation mechanism: a framework that enables the average Israeli who functions as an observer of the extraordinary who are extolled to feel profound feelings of meaning, belonging, freedom of expression, and a sense of his own uniqueness.

We shall attempt to describe and refine the three main elements of this unique mechanism, which correspond on an everyday basis with a special sense of continuity between past, present, and future; belonging to a special elite group that affords an opportunity to deviate from the self; a sense of opportunity for extensive, almost boundless, self-expression; and the constant necessity for survival in the face of threatening danger. Combined, these elements create a unique framing within which most Israelis feel a profound sense of meaning and involvement.

I Am Jewish and a Member of a Chosen People

For most average Israelis, the sense of "chosenness" is associated, first and foremost, with the fact of belonging to a "chosen people." Throughout history, the identity of "being Jewish" has been associated with belonging to a formidable and highly regarded isolationist people, but also to a persecuted, beaten, and battered people that arouse jealousy and hatred. The Jewish ghetto of the Diaspora continues to exist today in different places around the world, and Judaism makes it very difficult for anyone wishing to convert and join its ranks. Belonging to the Jewish people is charged with historical memories of hardship and displacement, and, in this respect, the Land of Israel is "The Promised Land." It is the land of milk and honey that was given to Abraham the Patriarch and promised to the chosen people. The Patriarchs of the Jewish people are buried in Nablus and Hebron (which many call the "occupied territories"). The sociopolitical discourse is constantly intertwined with the question of the state of Israel being first and foremost Jewish or the state of all its citizens, and recent legislation in the Knesset (Israel's legislature) seeks to establish Israel's incontrovertible Jewish character. Even among Israelis who define themselves as secular, the majority are what is known as *masorti*, or traditional. The links and affinity between Judaism and the average Israeli's everyday life are evident everywhere.

Belonging to the Jewish people is a characteristic that is present to a greater or lesser degree and that ties Israelis to the consciousness of a persecuted people that never relinquished its identity. For many Israelis, this identity is an inseparable part of the meaning they attribute to their choice to live a life filled with tension and danger in the state of Israel. But the reward is clear and tangible—belonging to a select group that has made a historic decision, upholds an ancient historical dictate, and devotes itself, fully understanding the price entailed, to settling the Holy Land. Some live this idea to the full, every day, while others actually experience its full force when traveling around the world and representing, at times inadvertently, the Jewish people. I recall a trip to Europe during Yom Kippur (Day of Atonement, the holiest day in Judaism, traditionally observed by fasting). My fellow travelers expected me to fast, and I was left with no choice. In practice, belonging to the chosen Jewish people provides a sense of weightiness and meaning that is difficult to avoid. Thus, from the outset, every Jew in Israel gains a sense of uniqueness and value by their very membership in Judaism and the meaning it symbolizes—a chosen people spreading light unto the nations.

I Am Israeli and a Citizen of the Proud and
Independent Startup Nation

If for some Israelis the sense of belonging to the Jewish people is on an unconscious level, the identity of being a citizen of the independent state of
Israel is emotional, alive, and beats in the heart of every Israeli. In total contrast to the helpless, persecuted Diaspora Jew, the image of the strong and
capable new Israeli appears in the late 20th century, an Israeli who can stand
up for himself and defend himself. Here, the sense of "chosenness" is considerably heightened and is validated virtually every day, both at the existential-
military level—a small country that can overcome its enemies—and in its
renewed version of becoming a prominent and distinctive startup nation.

Where Does All This Come From?

Among the formative experiences of my youth there were two annual media
events, both of which marked memorial days: National Memorial Day and
Holocaust Remembrance Day. All the television channels were filled with
special commemorative programming. Holocaust Remembrance Day
recounted disturbing revelations of atrocities committed by the Nazis and
about Jews who had gone to their bitter fates "like sheep to the slaughter." The
Jewish community debated this subject openly in the early days of the state,
and traces of this dispute ("how can we make sure it never happens again?")
have not entirely vanished. The last surviving participant in the Warsaw
Ghetto Uprising, Simcha Rotem, died recently. This revolt was one of the
rare and extraordinary examples of Jewish heroism and resistance against the
Nazis. For the past two decades, the broadcasts on Holocaust Remembrance
Day have included a speech by the Israeli Chief of the General Staff from a
podium in Poland or a flyover of Israeli aircraft led by the commander of
the Israeli Air Force: a symbol of the current military power of the Jewish
state as opposed to the Jews' helplessness less than a century ago. Even if it
sounds less elegant and up to date, any attempt to ignore the connection between the "national memory" and the question of "Israeli meaning of life" is
misleading. In this context the national obsession with innovation and technology all but guarantees our notion of "it will never happen to us again."

The second day of commemorative broadcasts, Memorial Day for
fallen soldiers and civilian victims of terrorism, is filled with touching and

disturbing films in memory of soldiers who fell on the battlefield, young people full of charm who died before their time. This blood-drenched history permeates every Israeli's very being. Israeli intellectuals from the liberal camp have written a great deal about the need to disengage from the memory of the Holocaust and begin living in a "healthy" manner, to heal from the sense of Israeli victimhood or as a constantly self-justifying occupier. Israeli society currently perceives such views as "extreme left," and a strong sense of being-in-the-right typifies most layers of Israeli society. The present generation of Israeli leaders grew up in a reality wherein the belief that Israel could reach agreement with its neighbors was lost. Irrespective of the degree of justice of this feeling, the Israeli story of the past several decades is one of "there's no one to talk to, and no one to trust." Most Israelis view the Palestinian leadership as untrustworthy, unstable, and dangerous.

In other words, and to continue our discussion, there are no "others" that need to be taken into consideration or with whom it is possible to build a relationship or a system of expectations. This sense of emergency also shapes, or justifies in retrospect, the disregard for small, unimportant, everyday sensitivities toward others in everyday life. Would you stand in line politely if you felt that your very existence might be threatened at any moment? In this respect, discussions about an agile, innovative organization that always has to remember the threat to its existence are the staples of Israeli mentality. This is not always conscious, but it is always there, seething and simmering in the background. In this context, we might wonder about the extent to which this day-to-day experience shapes the spirit of Israeli creativity. Is it our neurotic reality that gives rise to projects and inventions?[4]

The "Digital Hope"

It seems that, in the Israeli mindset, the only way to live and thrive is to be stronger and more excellent than ever or to connect to the enlightened world in any way apart from the geographical continuum in which the state of Israel is "stuck." The longing for the digital world is particularly inspired by a sense that the physical space is limited, hostile, and lacking in options. It

---

[4] In this context, it is interesting to note the contradiction between two leading global indices: The Global Entrepreneurship Index (GEDI, 2018), where Israel is ranked high in various metrics, on the one hand, and the poor achievements in the PISA index on the other.

is no coincidence that Israel excels in the hidden codes of the virtual world, since its reflection matches the way it sees itself much more than it does in the Middle East in which it is trapped. This feeling of being a small country that has to take its fate into its own hands is linked to the experience of traveling the length or breadth of Israel. Inhabitants of the United States, Germany, Saudi Arabia, or China will find it difficult to understand this, but the feeling that you have traversed your entire country in just 3 or 4 hours of driving pervades you. The phrase, "We got there so quickly," is uttered anew almost every time you travel to a particularly distant destination, from one side of the country to the other. There are hardly any spaces where you can get lost. After Israel's mythical victory in 1967 (which brought with it control over the territories), Yuval Neria wrote about how the country had expanded infinitely, describing excitement over the fact that now there was somewhere to go. "The horizon was, for the first time, open and wide" (Neria, 1989).

The crowded geographic space and the constant discourse of existential danger create tension. From this perspective, Israel's behavior resembles the psychology of a minority. It is very similar to that of the Korean, Indian, or Chinese minorities who came to Britain or the United States and felt that they had to excel and stand out. Israel, however, behaves like a minority in its own country, feeling that it has to excel, constantly aspiring to uniqueness and sustaining a sense of emergency. From this perspective, we may define the Israeli spirit as one of constant "disruptiveness."

Short-Term Perspective

Does an intensive reality like this inevitably lead to better results? In the short term, I think it does. The accompanying sense of emergency in the background emphasizes improvisation, initiative, and creativity. The result of all these is expertise in the short term and considerably less emphasis on the long term (in this respect, Israel may be more suited to the new world). Most Israeli high-tech companies symbolize the excellence of relatively short sprints. This perspective is foreign to Western thinking. Thus, for example, Ángel Gurría, chairman of the OECD, explains his fear of a future lack of investments in Israel. Israel, he warns, must contend with changing demographics and start making long-term plans and some difficult decisions (Sahar, 2016). The average Israelis want everything right here, right now. Local history has already proved to them how fickle everything is.

The breakthrough models of disruptive innovation, which emphasize the need for rethinking and warn organizations and corporations against rigid, stagnant thinking, describe an almost constant situation in many Israeli companies. The output is higher, the discussion more personal, and few are the times when mid-level managers are afraid to express their opinions near the CEO. But restraint and politeness, and a certain level of caution, have other advantages that sometimes are also frequently lost: a larger variety of opinions and respectful listening, more humility and attentiveness, meticulousness and considered judgment. It is hard to imagine entrepreneurship remaining successful over time without thoroughness and precision at work. Strict procedures ensure greater promise of continuity, stability, and precision over time. On rare occasions, the Israeli spirit of spontaneity, improvisation, and resourcefulness combine with strict systems that create an exceptional result—as in Israel's air force, high-tech companies, and biotech industry.

One result of all this are islands of excellence set against extensive erosion and a deterioration in service (groundbreaking surgeons vs. public hospitals that are collapsing under their burdens; schools that win almost every global competition in robotics or mathematics vs. a cracked and crumbling public education system). Exceptional examples of Israeli excellence combine audacity and extraversion, entrepreneurship and directness of method, attention to detail and meticulousness. This is a select minority on whom the state's reliance—as well as this minority's own distance from the average Israeli—is growing.

Another result is a deep sense of being part of an elite group known as "the Startup Nation."

The average Israeli feels an inseparable part of a small country that, against all odds, manages to survive, excel, and lead. A large proportion of Israelis sacrifice valuable time in military service, and some have suffered personal loss. The constant sense of emergency (realistic to a greater or lesser degree) accentuates this shared identity and mutual connection. The distinctiveness and uniqueness resulting from the sense of belonging to a chosen people are accorded a modern context of being part of a wondrous nation that repeatedly proves its abilities as a technological, innovative, and creative wonder in a desolate and dangerous wilderness. The headlines report security alerts or rocket attacks in Israel's south virtually every day—or, alternatively, Israel's latest high-tech exit. Everything is intermingled and exists in a single crowded space—one of shared dangers on the one hand, and shared successes on the other. The sense of belonging and meaning of each member of the group is very intense: I am Israeli, and a citizen of the proud and independent Startup Nation.

A Self-Expression Mechanism and Disregarding the Other at an Everyday Level

So far we have identified two essential cornerstones of the unique compensation mechanism we are attempting to outline here—a mechanism that ensures a profound sense of uniqueness and meaning for every member of Israeli society, a society whose leading ethos is excellence and focusing on the chosen few, rather than genuine and deep equal opportunity. We have discussed the element of belonging to the Jewish people, chosen to spread light unto the nations, a people that have been cast for this historical role by their God, and, in the past 70 years, the special sense of belonging to an independent nation capable of overcoming the enemies surrounding it, a nation that, for the first time in its history, is defending itself independently of others and becoming a proud Startup Nation. These two elements are present, to a greater or lesser degree of awareness, in every Israeli's consciousness. Added to the national-religious and historical contexts is a fascinating element that represents the Israeli culture created in the nascent state. This element completes the unique compensation mechanism created in Israeli society.

We shall attempt to describe and analyze how Israeli culture enables relatively extensive self-expression at an everyday level; a culture that at times sanctifies *chutzpah* (audacity), directness, and certain narcissistic characteristics and at times seems to embrace disregard for the needs of others or the public space.

It is interesting to observe that in the experiment we conducted, a clear connection was found between Israelis' sense of personal control over their lives and their level of happiness. The respondents answered the following question: "From 1 to 7, to what extent are the occurrences in my life the result of my choices and actions?" Clearly, the more we feel that the events in our life are the result of our choices and actions, the greater the chance that we will feel happy (Verme, 2009). The majority of respondents reported a sense of control over their lives despite reports describing a society typified by considerable social and economic gaps.

A certain sense of control over one's surroundings and life gains particularly interesting expression in Israel. There is a fascinating paradox here that requires explanation: the average Israeli can admire a unique individual on the stage or the chosen few during prime time, but a moment later feels that he deserves and has to receive special attention himself. His sense of control and uniqueness must be satisfied. I apologize in advance for the rough generalizations I am making, but from the outset this kind of discussion employs generalities and generalizations. Thus, with all due caution, it may be stated that what emerges is an image of Israeli *chutzpah*, but of a very special dialectic kind, of a person who can simultaneously admire others for their peak performance and, a moment later, demand respect, without one taking away from the other. This image of the Israeli could be termed "audacious admirer." This elusive description begs illustration, and I believe I may have found a way. The fact that the average Israeli is an "audacious admirer" manifests in his physical living environment.

A direct and somewhat harsh result of the individual's sense of uniqueness in Israel is their self-centeredness in their own homes, coupled with their indifference to their everyday environment. A glaring reflection of this is the architecture of the Israeli street, which faithfully represents local priorities. Israelis may devote their savings to remodeling their kitchen to the most advanced standard while leaving the entrance of their building in an almost complete state of neglect. This disregard for the public space is an odd continuation of the Jewish shtetl in Europe or the streets of the Ultra-orthodox city of today, both neglecting and avoiding investment in the environment. The religious world scorns engagement with the physical world since doing so runs counter to its emphasis on spiritual life. This neglect of the public space stems from a basic lack of awareness and disrespect.

I have wandered the streets of Amsterdam, Paris, or Berlin in amazement, enjoying the harmony of colors and architectural styles of the buildings that make up street life. The buildings are decorated in complementary colors, and the residents of Paris or Rome often sacrifice their own comfort to live in unrenovated buildings in order to preserve their historic character. The Israeli street conveys a message that is almost the opposite: Virtually every building is in a different style, with no attempt to create a connection or continuity with the adjacent buildings. It is astonishing, each time anew, to see an Israeli apartment building in a well-maintained neighborhood with all the air conditioner motors hanging outside between windows amid a tangle of pipes and with no attempt whatsoever at an aesthetic solution. Even in apartment buildings that do maintain a garden at the entrance, the façade is invariably covered with an unsightly web of air conditioner pipes. Israel's climate is indeed unbearably hot and humid, but no one seems to have given any thought to dealing with home cooling systems in a way that is considerate of the shared space.

Personal comfort seems to be a supreme value that takes precedence over almost any other limiting norm. Common manifestations of this include vocal self-expression outdoors, lack of restraint or consideration for others in the public sphere, and honking the horn as soon as the traffic light turns green, amazed that someone in the car in front is slowing you down . . . as if they have the right to be there in the first place!

One only needs to witness the dynamic of waiting at the door of a busy restaurant or in line at the bank, post office, or any government office to understand the unique sense of control the average Israeli expects to have or, more accurately, is afraid of losing. An altercation can erupt within minutes if one of the people waiting in line feels hard done by because someone has jumped the queue. The average Israeli wants everything right here, right now. Much has been said about "Israeli *chutzpah*" or lack of humility. There is a great deal of "freedom" in the way the average Israeli behaves and reacts (in some places it would be considered rudeness).

All this does not prevent Israelis from rushing to help a neighbor in time of need, the same people whose entire existence they basically ignore in day-to-day life. In what sometimes seems to be a form of "narcissistic behavior," they act alone and in charge, but in the next moment they may leap to rescue and protect the people around them. The experiment we conducted confirms the connection between helping others and an increase in the level of happiness, which is parallel with other countries. Israeli society places considerable importance on helping others in distress, sometimes even to the point of self-sacrifice, yet devotes much less thought to day-to-day generosity toward others in general.

One of the arguments I am raising here is that this free spirit and *chutzpah* of the individual, coupled with the tendency for self-sacrifice in extreme cases, is the background for the emergence and growth of Israeli innovation. This attitude to life is part of the impetus of Israeli entrepreneurial groups that bring with them unprecedented, obsessive, and restless energy alongside sacrifice for the benefit of an extreme objective that they have defined together. From the moment the setting is defined in which the startup has determined to operate in the world, it will strive tirelessly for achievements and ignore customary or accepted norms of behavior in that particular field. In our terms, it constructs for itself its building and personal design and ignores everyone and everything else. The justification for the absence of self-restraint and etiquette corresponds with the sense of emergency that always accompanies the life of every Israeli. And it is impossible to truly talk about the meaning of life through the eyes of Israelis without discussing the sense of emergency that has accompanied their existence since time immemorial.

Conclusion

The Meaning of Life Through Israeli Eyes

"There is no place like Israel," says the man sitting next to me in the café. He left Israel 25 years ago and has never come back except to visit. His accent is almost completely American, and he will soon be running to catch his return flight to Los Angeles—but not before announcing once more, out loud, "There is no place like Israel." It is uniquely Israeli to be nostalgic about Israel even when you have lived elsewhere for decades. I recall to this day a tour that an American Jew living in Los Angeles gave me. We wandered through the city's streets and passed by Chinatown, Koreatown, and Little Italy. Every state and mini-state had a symbolic presence of its own. There was no "Little Israel." My host, an older and highly experienced man, shared an astonishing fact with me: the American immigration authorities were having difficulty granting American citizenship to Israelis, a process that requires a declaration of loyalty to the United States. "They know that Israelis are loyal to their own country first of all. Unlike the Chinese, Korean, or Italian immigrants, they came here to get rich, and they plan to go back home as soon as they can, even if it never happens." I have thought about this conversation for many years. I think it represents the world of internal contradictions in which Israeli society lives—an almost symbiotic emotional involvement with the country and a desire to flee to a more comfortable and saner country that allows them to develop economically; constant complaints about Israel alongside strong identification with it. Israeli mentality is rife with strong contradictions: between conservatism (more than 58% of Israelis define themselves as at least "traditional"; Central

Bureau of Statistics, 2009) and daring and provocative thinking; between a sense of power and a sense of lack and weakness; between a sense of strength and a sense of being a small country surrounded by enemies; between devotion to family and tribe and foreignness in the commonly shared space; and the constant conflict between brilliance and carelessness. In his book, *Creativity: Flow and the Psychology of Discovery and Invention*, renowned psychologist Mihaly Csikszentmihalyi describes creative people as people of contradictions, and the spirit of the average Israeli definitely matches this description to a tee (Csikszentmihalyi, 1997).

Above all is the principal contradiction: the image of the "audacious admirer," a kind of narcissistic quality of the individual encapsulating fear for their personal freedom versus their near-total emotional involvement in any extreme situation pertaining to "the whole country." They envy Western Europe with its excellent organization and aesthetics, the wide open spaces of the United States, the exotic character of South America, and the Ganges River and mass meditation workshops—but before and above all else, they are bound up with Israel in every atom of their being. A select few are sent to gain victory in the name of everyone and enable the continued existence of the myth of the People of the Book and the Chosen People. The life identity of Israelis and their sense of meaning is a fact of their being part of the best team around, even if they spend their life sitting on the bench. But, paradoxically, the Israeli semi-chaotic social order enables everyone to experience much more than their "15 minutes of fame" on the field.

Israeli culture and society present a unique mechanism that is full of fascinating paradoxes. All the elements we have mentioned come together to form a compensation mechanism that enables each of the participants to feel a special sense of blending, of being part of some-thing bigger than life, something with a charged historical continuity, alongside the possibility for self-expression that sometimes borders on what seems like disregard for everyone else and the norms of consid-eration for one's surroundings. Belonging to the chosen people, being a member of an independent state that has become a prime startup na-tion, combined with everyday behavior that sanctifies extreme freedom of expression for every individual—these form a unique combination of ostensibly contradictory elements that together create a unique Israeli response to the profound need we all have for a sense of meaning and reason in our life.

Highlights

- Life in Israel, despite all its complexities, tensions, and socioeconomic gaps, succeeds in providing most of its citizens with a deep sense of connection and meaning.
- The average Israeli feels a part of a special nation that has to prove its talent, its ability to invent, and its unique creativity.
- The Israeli model of excellence strives for a way of thinking that sparks the imagination. Complex models of what is now referred to as "innovation" or "disruptive innovation" have found expression for generations in the sources of Jewish thought.
- The unique structure of Israeli society serves as a "special compensation mechanism" that provides each of its members the possibility to feel meaningful and important. This mechanism includes three elements: the Jewish past and the sense of "chosenness," the "start-up nation" present and excellence against all odds, and the Israeli free spirit and *chutzpah* which allow every individual the opportunity for extensive self-expression.

References

Acs, Zoltan & Szerb, László & Lafuente, Esteban & Lloyd, Ainsley. (2018). The Global Entrepreneurship Index 2018. 10.1007/978-3-030-03279-1.

Ben-David, D., & Kimhi, A. (2017). *Shoresh research paper: An overview of Israel's education system and its impact.* Shoresh Institution for Socioeconomic Research.

Central Bureau of Statistics. (2009). Population by religion and population group. https://www.cbs.gov.il/en/subjects/Pages/Population-by-Religion-and-Population-Group.aspx

Csikszentmihalyi, M. (1997). *Finding flow: The psychology of engagement with everyday life.* Harper Perennial.

Helliwell, J., Layard, R., & Sachs, J. (2018). *World happiness report 2018.* Sustainable Development Solutions Network.

Inglehart, R., C. Haerpfer, A. Moreno, C. Welzel, K. Kizilova, J. Diez-Medrano, M. Lagos, P. Norris, E. Ponarin & B. Puranen et al. (eds.). 2018. World Values Survey: Round Six—Country-Pooled Datafile. Madrid, Spain & Vienna, Austria: JD Systems Institute & WVSA Secretariat. doi.org/10.14281/18241.8

McKenna, J. (2017). Israel is a tech titan. These 5 charts explain its startup success. https://www.weforum.org/agenda/2017/05/tiny-israel-is-a-tech-titan-these-5-charts-explain-its-startup-success

Ministry of Science and Technology. (2018). *The big happiness experiment.*

Neria, Y. (1989). *Fire.* Kinneret-Zmora-Bitan Dvir.

OECD. (2017). Social and welfare statistics. http://www.oecd.org/Israel

PISA. (2018). Web site. http://www.oecd.org/pisa

Sahar, L. (2016). OECD report: Israel is corrupt, poor and happy. https://www.ynet.co.il/articles/0,7340,L-4760070,00.html

Senor, D., & Singer, S. (2011). *Start-up nation: The story of Israel's economic miracle.* Little, Brown & Company.

Verme, P. (2009). Happiness, freedom and control. *Journal of Economic Behavior & Organization, 71*(2), 146–161.

3

Multitopia

Searching for Meaning in the Rothschild Encampment During the Summer 2011 Social Protest

Hagar Hazaz-Berger

It's almost midnight. Several people are part sitting, part lying down around the tent, others join slowly while others leave. A worn-out table offers cups, cookies, and snacks. Eddie plays the guitar while Avishag is humming quietly. This casualness of sitting on couches that must have forgotten their original colors, in front of a boulevard-turned-home, excites me. Dali and I go on talking in this eclectic atmosphere. She tells me she arrived at the encampment by chance; she's between jobs and trying to figure out what she wants in life. I listen to her and the music in the background: "I've been here for a month, trying to figure out what this all means and how this protest can help me find myself again," she says and falls silent. I look at her, wondering what is it that she's trying to find. My mind drifts to my own situation, and then Lea starts singing. Her hypnotic voice brings everything together, lends meaning to those fractions of seconds. (August 2011)

This field diary excerpt represents a typical evening in the Rothschild Boulevard encampment in the heart of Tel Aviv, the main encampment in the social protest of summer 2011. The excerpt relates a casual conversation between myself and 32-year-old Dali, who had stumbled on the encampment by accident and found it a perfectly appropriate space for the search for meaning.

The nature of social protest fields as reflective spaces is largely neglected by literature. Instead, the prevalent research discourse tends to examine them as macro socioeconomic-political processes (Della Porta & Diani, 1999; Goodwin & Jasper, 2003). The 2011 global protest wave was treated in the same way (e.g., Abellán, Sequera, & Janoschka, 2012; Glasius & Pleyers, 2013; Gledhill, 2012; Köksal, 2012; Mavrommatis, 2015; Morell, 2012; Pickerill et al., 2016; Razsa & Kurnik, 2012). Few studies of social protests have

Hagar Hazaz-Berger, *Multitopia* In: *Finding Meaning*. Edited by: Ofra Mayseless and Pninit Russo-Netzer, Oxford University Press. © Oxford University Press 2022. DOI: 10.1093/oso/9780190910358.003.0003 touched on the individual and identity processes (Gusfield, 2009; Melucci, 1988, 1996a), and even those have made little reference to the intersubjective aspect of the protest and processes of self-search and search of meaning. Local studies on the 2011 protest in Israel also focused on economic (Ram & Filk, 2013; Swirski, 2013; Yonah & Spivak, 2012), gender (Herzog, 2013), or class aspects (Rosenheck & Shalev, 2013). The present study contributes to the literature by focusing on processes of reflection and search for meaning within the field of a social event, examining them at the micro level.

In this chapter, I discuss the search for personal meaning among participants of the 2011 social protest, with special focus on the Rothschild encampment. The much-spotlighted Tent Protest started on July 14 of that year as a demonstrative act by a young female Tel Avivian whose rent was raised sharply by her landlord. She went to the boulevard, hammered a spike, and erected a tent as a rent-fee housing protest. More people joined her that very day, erecting tents in streets and public gardens in the Rothschild Boulevard area and elsewhere in Tel Aviv and the rest of the country. For 3 months, Israel became a veritable encampment: anyone who had anything to say, to protest against, was out in the streets—private individuals with an axe to grind as well as political and nonprofit organizations. They were all out to shout for social justice. The protesters' two main demands of the government were affordable housing and a lower cost of living.

The Rothchild encampment was populated by people of various ages, class, gender, and origin and somewhat represented a "microcosms of Israeli society," as described by one of my informants. According to various publications, while the encampment was on site, it hosted around 800 people who spent a night or longer there, while thousands of others went from and through it every day. In this sense, Rothchild Boulevard mirrored local Israeli society at the heart of the most global city in Israel.

In this chapter, I will try to discover

- How did the space created at the heart of Tel Aviv during the summer of protest serve the search for meaning?
- What was the effect of spending time in the encampment on the construction and deconstruction of identities, as well as the reconstruction of social categories?
- And what were the practices used by the residents in these processes?

In what follows, I show that much can be learned from the "meaning-searchers" participating in my study about societal processes in Israel, which can be examined in the context of the weakening link to identity and place discussed by Zygmunt Bauman (2000), as well as to the sense of constant threat experienced by individuals in the post-modern world (Beck, 2008). Spaces such as the encampment generate change, as suggested by 33-year-old Spiritual psychotherapy student Adam: "Rothschild is the cesspool—everything passes through here and spills from here into the Israeli psyche. . . . If . . . you look at Israeli society from a bird's eye view, I think that if you look at it from space, you will see Rothschild today" (August 2011). In this quote, Adam linked the events in Rothschild to Israeli society as a whole. He later added: "Rothschild was a generator, a mind-transformer. This was the purpose, to open the mind. . . . And from now on, this is the face of what you don't want to see . . . our reflection towards ourselves." Through the encampment and people like Adam, I will shed light on questions of meaning and personal identity and the future of Israeli society.

The first section presents the theoretical background and reviews relevant literature on social protests, the quest for meaning and post-modern identity, and describes the study's methodology. Next, I describe the encampment as a unique "wondering space," as I call it, and examine its structure as a social field affording the search for meaning. In the third section, I discuss three search-for-meaning practices enabled within the wondering space: spiritual discourse, blurring and ignoring social categories, and structuring a post-modern identity. I examine the materials collected in the field in the context of the search for meaning through the lens of each practice. Finally, I discuss the various issues with reference to Israel's cultural evolution from the Zionist vision[1] to the present, exploring the ways in which this personal analytic reflection of social processes changes the social and cultural discourse in Israel and the effect of this discourse on mainstream Israeli society in the 21st century.

Literature Review

Society in Crisis

In 2011, Israel faced an extreme financial and social crisis. Israel had originally been established as a welfare state, then passed through neo-liberal

---

[1] Zionism, the ideology of creating a national home for the Jewish people, which led to the establishment of Israel in the mid-20th century.

processes. These, along with the global financial crisis of 2008, created occupational insecurity, rising house prices, and a general sense of helplessness, which led to the 2011 social protest.

Social Protest

Up until the early 1950s, protests were seen as social movements acting against an existing social order (Della Porta & Diani, 1999; Goodwin & Jasper, 2003; Meyer, 2004). Goodwin and Jasper (2003) offered the most comprehensive definition: "Protest refers to the act of challenging, resisting, or making demands upon authorities, powerholders, and/or cultural beliefs and practices by some individual or group" (p. 3).

The 1960s saw the rise of new social movements that advocated different types of protest (Fisher & Kling, 1994), blurring the distinction between the public and private spheres. Whereas in the past, struggles revolved around class, religious, or political conflicts, the new social movements were inspired by the belief that change is possible in *any* area in life. Therefore, their fields of interest were extensive and covered all aspects of sociocultural life.

These movements are informed by post-materialistic values such as environmental protection and well-being. They condemn capitalism and its outcomes and focus on formulating a collective identity while giving space to the individual, thereby challenging the discourse of former protests by promoting global issues that affect local problems (Gusfield, 2009). Thus, the individual member of the new social movement not only protests against the collective identity, but is also influenced by their own personal identity and seeks to include issues involving quality of life, self-discovery, and the search for meaning in the protest discourse (Della Porta & Diani, 1999; Melucci, 1996b, 1997).

Accordingly, the focus of literature has shifted from the concrete issues driving the protest to the protesters' personal stories (Polletta, 2006, 2008) and emotions (Collins, 2011; Young, 2011), exploring processes affected by the individual protester's personality that are linked to the broader social context. Consequently, we now have a better understanding of the central role played by today's social protests in changing the perceptions and beliefs of society (Gamson, 1995; Goodwin & Jasper, 2003), but also—and more importantly for our current purposes—of how they enable self-search (Snow & McAdam, 2000).

In Israeli history, social protests were clearly meaningful in shaping society and raising awareness of social gaps (Dahan Kalev, 1999; Korazim & Benish, 2011). As indicated earlier and further discussed later, the 2011 summer protest brought to the fore profound changes in the individuals who make up Israeli society and highlighted the need of those individuals to take advantage of the collective protest space for a personal search for meaning, making it a phenomenon worthy of scholarly attention.

Search for Meaning

Frankl (1946) wrote that the individuals' most basic motive is to find meaning in life through insightful understanding of their life experiences. Existential questions[2] that preoccupy every person worldwide inevitably resonate in social protests, particularly when their concrete triggers and "official" causes are ambiguous and not fully understood or relevant to each and every participant.

This ambiguity is a result of the transformation in the character of social protests in the West and is deeply related to the broader historical trends of the collapse of modernity and the rising popularity of the New Age[3] worldview (Heelas, 1996). The search for alternative meaning and the unsatisfactory results of this search are responsible for the nagging sense of discomfort plaguing the individual in post-modern societies (Bauman, 1991; Fromm, 1941). The demise of modernity led to a split, multifaceted, post-modern identity following the collapse of clearly defined concepts and systems (Bauman, 2000). Beck (1992) associates this meltdown of the old social order with individual risk: we are all constantly fighting for (mental) survival— constantly searching for answers. The uncertainty regarding a single truth seeps in deeply and leads to a spiritual journey and greater openness to foreign religions and creeds. These journeys are deeply personal and lead individuals away from the collective by rejecting those cultural norms the young searchers have been raised to uphold (Heelas, 1998). The search is for one's authentic self (Taylor, 1991).

---

[2] The existentialist approach stresses that philosophy starts with the living, feeling, active individual, and raises questions about the absurd, free will, meaning, and loneliness.

[3] *New Age* is an encompassing term for numerous spiritual and semi-religious theories and movements that focus on the search for spirituality and an alternative lifestyle.

The shattered identity motivating this search seeks self-synthesis (Holland, 1997). Social protests offer a solid platform, a reliable basis for (re)defining the identity of the people within their space in relation to other group members (Abrams & Hogg, 1990; Tajfel & Turner, 1986). Similarly, Breakwell (1986, 1992) argues that identity is dynamic and always interacts with a social context—whether concrete or imagined. In a similar vein, Melucci (1988) claims that only a society or a group enables people to construct their identity consistently, expressively, and reflexively. Accordingly, the search for meaning in a group involved in a social event transcends the protest's concrete role (Melucci, 1996b) and connects the event to the individual struggling with existential questions.

Hence, our perception of social protests was also changed in the post-modern era; this perception was subjectified and individualized, as shown by Reger, Myers, and Einwhhner (2008), who suggest that protest is a means to constructing identity through social activity or activism. Styker, Owens, and White (2000) also describe this identity search in social protests and the "inside-out" process, discussing the ways of constructing the self through activism and the id motivation to participate in a protest.

Method

The study is based on "urgent ethnography" (Hazaz-Berger, 2018)—a methodology which focuses on sudden and unexpected fields that emerge from an emergency event with no predefined beginning or end. Thus, time is a crucial dimension in the process of data collection because the event can end quickly, as is the case of this protest. I entered the field and started field diaries, conversations, interviews, many open-air small-talks, and participant observations of various protest events during the encampment's 3-month lifecycle, adding interpretations on the go. I relied on the *grounded theory approach* (Strauss & Corbin, 1998), a qualitative method that enables researchers to understand the world and its sociocultural meaning as it is constructed by its participants without imposing their own perspective (Glaser & Strauss, 2009; Strauss & Corbin, 1990, 1998).

This kind of research requires us to consider interpretation acts as multi-dimensional, ambiguous, complex, and dynamic and extract narratives from the field of research (Van Manen, 1997, 2002). We must acknowledge that the participants live within an ambiguous and ambivalent discourse and that their lives are part of their social context (Bruner, 1995; Denzin, 1989).

The material was systematically content-analyzed using the Narralizer qualitative analysis software that helps to code information segments into themes. These themes were then used to make sense of the personal narrative as a complex cultural text that combines individual, collective, and intermediate meanings in an attempt to clarify its significance in reflecting cultural and social processes in contemporary Israeli society and particularly the sectors represented at the Rothchild encampment.

The Rothschild encampment was used as a platform for the search of meaning and self-determination and for discoveries about the meaning of life, jobs, romantic relationships, beliefs, tendencies, local and global citizenship, and more. It was a sphere that allowed its participants to leave their daily routine behind and focus on internal processes, sometimes by talking to others and sometimes through an internal monologue. They were able to reflect on their social and personal life decisions from a distance without having to travel physically for a long period, as so many young Israelis do. The ethnography was conducted from the day the first tent was pitched on July 14, 2011, until the encampment was dispersed in early October of that year.

The Wondering Space

Rothschild Boulevard was a unique space that enabled the protesters, on the one hand, to undergo processes related to their participation in a broad social movement and, on the other hand, to wonder, wander, and linger—to reflect on their non-protest lives and search for meaning. I coined the term *wondering space* to refer to this search-for-meaning arena shared daily by thousands of encampment residents.

As one of them described it, life in Rothschild meant taking the time to "sit in the morning and look at the passing cars, at the parents running around with their children, the newsboys, the waiters waking up in the restaurants—the life that used to be mine a second ago, and now I'm watching them, thinking about my life and how they're passing by before my eyes" (Noga, 29, student). Noga provides a tangible description of looking out of the tent into the mundane world outside. From the space of wondering, daily activities seem mechanical, routine, and, above all, meaningless.

As suggested by Coral (25, acrobat) the Boulevard's physical location helps connect the protester both to the here-and-now and to conflicts and wonderings related to completely different contexts: "The most important things in the city happen in this boulevard. . . . It's not that I couldn't travel to India and search for myself. But no. No more running away. Like, if I had a fight with my mother, should I go away and find the solution elsewhere? It's all here. Being here really enables me to do some serious work." For Coral, the encampment's central location provides a strategic advantage. The uniqueness of this wondering space lies in its daily clash with the metropolitan mundane. This is a far cry from the "classic" transitional sphere, as Turner (1969) suggests, where the individual breaks away from their natural environment and seeks answers in exotic otherness.

The wondering space thus has a therapeutic potential, and the option afforded by the boulevard's centrality of smoothly moving in and out of it at will—and looking out both ways—enhances its uniqueness as a platform for reflection. Barry (58, ex-theater actor) has benefitted greatly from this potential. " I was an actor all my life, and then I decided to make money. . . . This protest is a gift to me. I can keep working, spend time with my son, and come back here in the morning, meet more people, open up to ideas, to different mentalities. To be part of this process, for me, involves a self-discovery no therapist has ever been able to give me."

Barry did not suspend his nonencampment life, only added the wondering space as an element that allowed him to look inside. For him, being in the encampment means relating to others and benefitting from alternative ideas that help him reflect on life while being on the move. And, as in therapy, he could go in and out. Lacan (1970) likened this to a Möbius strip, where the patient can be both inside and outside at the same time. The familiar space of Rothschild Boulevard allowed its environment (friends, relatives, geographical surrounding, language, practices, etc.) to become an integral part of the process experienced by its residents.

By being reflective of both the social fracture that led to the 2011 protest and the individual ambiguity of its post-modern participants, the Rothschild encampment represented Israeli society as a whole, as well as individual urban life in the 21st century. It is therefore no surprise that many of my interviewees spoke about their need for space to reflect on capitalist daily realities—experiences that lead people to an ongoing search for meaning.

Spontaneous, transparent, transient, flexible, and familiar—this was the Rothschild encampment wondering space. People arrived there independently, mostly intuitively, without preparation, to take part in a social field constrained physically and temporally but much less so conceptually—and therefore conducive of the individual search for meaning. Unlike such searches in other fields, this one was primarily designed to achieve a political purpose. It was both artificial and detached from daily life, while at the same time serving as a living space that used the geography of a workaday business and entertainment hub for a discourse concerning questions that are usually relegated to the margins of daily life or to the therapist's clinic. In such a space, people can search for configurations of life and meaning, wonder and reflect, and reinvent themselves. We will now examine the practices through which people have searched for meaning.

First Practice: Spiritual Discourse

The wondering space was opened at the heart of a protest that called for social change but—typically post-modern—became fragmented into shards of meanings. Thus, the campers found themselves in a discourse with themselves and others about meanings, knowledge, feelings, and visions. Each in their own way tried to see how the meditative New Age glossary could provide an answer to an inner self searching for meaning. Many talked about adopting various spiritual practices. Adam described it as follows:

> And most importantly, I brought myself here . . . this is like my redemption. . . . Here I pitched my tent, I created my home, in the place where the universe told me, come, let's see what you've got . . . let's see how you do it. I created my boundaries, my place, with other people . . . who tested my boundaries and I came . . . and said, listen up guys . . . everything anybody does here, like, affects the Israeli mind. And this, this is my gift to myself because no other school would have given this to me . . . I was chosen to come here . . . the chosen one. A huge gift.

Beyond participating in the protest, Adam used the encampment for his internal search. He used the spiritual discourse to connect his personal search to Israeli society's and emphasized that everything that occurred in the wondering space was part of that discourse. Gil (36), a marketing freelancer, reinforced this fact by arguing that the processes in the encampment

were part of ongoing, long-term processes that Israeli society has been going
through.

> If you asked me two weeks ago . . . what I'm doing here, I'd have told you
> that this country is so messed up, something's gotta change. . . . It's an inner
> voice that started talking to me slowly, like what am I, anyway. And all of a
> sudden all this has meaning, it's bigger than us—to transform our tribe, we
> have to look deeper inside.

Gil described the encampment as a container that enabled his search to proceed within a definite social structure, a search he could have never under-
taken where he came from. He associated his individual search for meaning
with the "tribe" to which he belongs—Israeli society—thereby highlighting
the point that individual transformation is the first step in societal transformation. The latter is necessary, he argued, because "we have lost our way.
What we've been promised no longer exists."

Hemi (38), who works in advertising, expressed a similar sentiment: "I
served in the military, in a combat unit. . . . I travelled abroad [after his military service, as many Israeli Jews do], I studied, but all this doesn't matter—
it's not only the money, there's no future. We're lost, each to himself." Hemi
emphasized his need to belong to Israeli society and pay his dues, but, on the
other hand, he described himself as part of a lost generation of disoriented
individuals who have little hope for the future, regardless of the economic
difficulties that triggered the protest. Loneliness and alienation are creating
the common feeling of being lost. The encampment allowed him to reinforce
his links to his society and surroundings.

One of the solutions for this sense of isolation is the search for different meanings. As 23-year-old Tom, a communication and film student,
relates:

> I'd like to connect to the real me . . . we have strayed so far from ourselves
> that I'm searching for myself with the Breslovs [an Ultra-orthodox Hassidic
> sect active among secular Jews]. . . . That's why so many here are attracted
> to all those spiritual movements, it's like, there's something greater than
> ourselves.

Tom's words indicate that the spiritual meanings out there meet a deeper
need of finding herself, despite being aware at the same time of their illusory

nature, which actually pulls her away from herself. She admits her attraction to the Breslovs, but at the same time wonders whether they have the answer.

Bennie (37, freelancer) also talked about the sense of meaninglessness in life, offering an even more distrustful view of external sources of meaning. He described the protest as a social field allowing him to connect to his personal search, adding,

> We need to have something to hold on to in order to believe in our existence. But come on, really, you have to hold on to yourselves—there's nothing out there, we were born alone, and we will die alone . . . everybody has "seen the light," has "awakened"—come on now, you just found another drug to put you to sleep—that's the illusion of meaning.

Bennie believes that this "illusion of meaning" is designed to prevent individuals from searching within themselves, from raising existential questions of loneliness and finality that have no real answer. His solution is internal reflection, with each holding on to his subjective take on the meaning of life. For him, all the rest really does not exist; it is nothing but a failed attempt to find some sort of organizing structure outside.

As indicated by these statements, the use made by many protest participants of New Age concepts reflects a passion for individual spiritual change and awakening. The catchwords thrown around the boulevard, "mindfulness," "seeing the light," "a protest of love" all came from the spiritual glossary, but, instead of being empty slogans, they slowly seeped into the daily lives of these people. Although each was located differently on the spectrum between self-realization and social change, they all sought for the one through the other and dreamed of both.

It was precisely in this space of social protest that more room was opened for accepting and containing multiple identities that had little to do with traditional social movements, but more with spirituality. As indicated by Shai (37, farmer), issues that used to be relegated to the margins of social protests have become central. These, he stresses, "are actually very wide margins and they're part of this protest." Shai voiced the need felt by many Israelis—not only activists—to search for meaning, perhaps due to the growing irrelevance of Zionism in the post-modern era. Thus, the wondering space allowed many to wander around an "identity supermarket" and be both passive and active in their search for meaning within the broader context of social protest. By searching for spiritual-personal meaning while being part of a group and a social field, the subject gets closer to herself or himself through sociocultural relationships and dialogue with significant others.

The wondering space was fertile ground for reflection. It gave people the opportunity to taste something of the variety of beliefs, religions, and political currents flowing into the encampment. Many individuals found themselves reinforcing their previous identities, while others took advantage of this opportunity to doubt their credos and find psychological peace in a new home. Be that as it may, many sought spiritual discourse out of the desire to find their "inner self."

We might wonder whether the New Age discourse and search for truth in the encampment served as little more than a "spiritual bypass," defined by John Welwood (1984) as enabling spiritual training, on the other hand, while at the same time preventing us from truly looking into our feelings, traumas, and needs. Paradoxically, the encampment brought participants closer to their selves while at the same time providing an easy alternative for a truly painful and productive quest for meaning.

Second Practice: Blurring and Ignoring Social Categories

Another solution to the problem of lost meaning that preoccupied the protest participants was to blur, ignore, and even eliminate the sociological categories with which they had arrived. Marcel Mauss (1985) describes this practices as *games of categories*—shedding the persona and getting closer to the self. By shedding categories such as gender, class, ethnicity, or generation, the participants were able to give their lives a different meaning of their own choosing, independent of any external imposition—all thanks to the liminal nature of the wondering space.

Shai summed this up succinctly when he said that

In the encampment you realize it doesn't matter who and what you are— we're all in this together. There are no age, class, or ethnic differences here. The boundaries have been broken, and here . . . we can create a new world— one where we, and nobody else, we are the people of the world.

Yochai (41, businessman and soundman) reflected a similar notion: "I'm a soldier of the revolution just like everybody else. . . . We've been raised to think in terms of religious-secular. . . . Arab–Jew. You ask me what I see?

I really think we have to create a new nation here." Yochai reference to the protest as a revolution empowers it to challenge the very foundations of Israeli society and recreate it anew, free of categorical distinctions. Part of this desire to create a new nation is motivated by the wish to discard inherited stereotypes that led to social gaps and conflicts.

Dori, a 28-year-old student, adds the important aspect of "committing category suicide" (paraphrasing Freire, 1978).

> I feel no need to stand with a flag here and flaunt my manhood or my whiteness. . . . Beyond the fact that this helps me position myself with reference to the Other, it means nothing to me. Even this ongoing discussion about Zionism is irrelevant to this revolution as I see it. . . . We want to generate change, but a deeper one, that touches precisely those points that make us human.

Dori would rather discard all categories and their associated narratives, including the Zionist one, in accordance with the post-modern tendency to consistently steer clear of fixed narratives. Eddie (29, musician), who owns a private sound company, concurs: "I believe each person's identity, everyone's . . . is made up of many things. . . . You cannot reduce a person by saying that he's a Jew and that's that. That's his identity. Or say he's a Christian, or an Arab, or an Israeli."

This practice enables the participants to position themselves at the front of society without being shackled by categories such as gender, race, or class and thereby become new citizens who are ostensibly not committed to any overarching narrative. Photography student Sivan (29) had this to say:

> As a former Kibbutznik,[4] I can say that the [Zionist] discourse of "building the country" can no longer provide the exclusive answers to daily realities in Israel—we must let it go.

Sivan likens the Zionist narrative to an obsolete technology. As the new citizen, she also wants to be a *tabula rasa* and reinvent herself by using a new and more effective person.

---

[4] A kibbutz is a form of collective settlement unique to the Zionist movement, a combination of Zionist and socialist values (Spiro, 1963).

This "category-cidal" practice complements the previous one of using the spiritual discourse. Both set local social categories aside and supersede them with universal dimensions related to the subjective experience of the individual within the social field. A third practice used in the wondering space to search for meaning does not involve discarding categories but re-examining their potential uses to structure a subjective experience.

Third Practice: Constructing a Post-Modern Identity

The third practice, of re-examining and restructuring social categories rather than ignoring them, has three manifestations. The first is holding on to categories commonly considered contradictory.

Laurie (27, student) was shifting between categories. A religious woman who had moved to Tel Aviv to pursue a musical career, she explained,

> Where I came from, you are not allowed to sing. . . . In Tel Aviv, it was the first time I felt I could be a singer and also live a religious life. . . . The fact that I sing doesn't make me less religious.

In Ultra-orthodox Jewish society, a woman may not sing in front of men ("woman's voice is nakedness"). Thus, Laurie's chosen career challenged and crossed traditional categories. She did not abandon either category, but rather tried to reassemble them to build something new, despite their apparent contradiction. Thus, one of the practices of searching for meaning by constructing an identity is to use social categories but also try to combine and integrate them despite apparent or commonly perceived contradictions between them.

A second manifestation of this practice is rejecting dichotomies. This was apparent mainly in discussions of religious and political issues. Whereas in the Israeli political scene, the right and left are sharply divided, the boulevard's wondering space enabled protesters to transcend this dichotomy. Michelle (36, unemployed) said "I see who [in politics] serves my needs. . . . For years I've been anti-left, and here comes MP Shelly Yachimovich [of the Labor Party]. . . . It's like every word she said came right out of my gut."

Avishag (32, waitress) referred to the religious–secular dichotomy when she discussed the difference between her personal religious tendency and her feelings toward the religious community: "I find myself relating to many things [in Judaism], and I also take them forward in terms of the way I see things. . . . It's OK to say that religion is beautiful and that I believe in God, but I don't like the religious people." This denial of dichotomies, this recategorization, enables Avishag to maintain identity flexibility and keep her faith while rejecting a religious establishment often seen as overpoliticized and corrupt.

A third manifestation of this practice is to keep using the category but re-shape it according to the individual's subjective preferences. The three major categories relevant in this context are gender, ethnicity, and nationality. For example, Adva (37), who works in insurance, felt sexually liberated by the encampment: "I've been living with Gilead for over 5 years, and it's nothing compared to living here with other men, women . . . it opens you up to all sorts of experiences . . . it wakened a lot of dormant things in me."
Adva tries to restructure the boundaries of her sexual preferences and her ideas about monogamy. She expands the category of sexual intimacy by suggesting that one can remain intimate with another but also enjoy sex with other partners, not only of the other sex.

Zehira, a store vendor in her fifties, referred to her ethnicity: "As a 'white' Moroccan, I can manage everywhere . . . but I can tell you that my ethnicity is actually what I feel inside." She considers herself as having a fluid ethnic iden-tity and thereby redefines it as not just positioned in-between, but as some-thing she herself constructs.

As another example of the third manifestation, Danny (35, freelancer) refers to the nationality category: "I'm moving to Berlin. . . . I'll be a much better Zionist there. My Zionism means doing what's good for me. And it's not only within the borders of our country." Danny redefines the boundaries of his national identity, thereby enabling even those leaving the country—often frowned upon by Jewish nationalists—to remain Zionists.

Hitherto we have characterized the wondering space as one which has facilitated practices of searching for meaning: using spiritual discourse, ignoring and blurring social categories, and constructing a post-modern identity. Each practice, in its own way, illuminates a unique perspective of the Rothschild campers' search for meaning and self. In the following discussion,

I examine what may be learned about 21st-century Israeli society from the use of these practices.

Discussion

The main character in Woody Allen's *Annie Hall* says: "My only regret in life is that I'm not somebody else." Many things have changed since 1977, and, by 2018, the character would probably have said: "My only regret in life is that I'm not somebody else, whoever that may be." This chapter focuses on the Rothschild encampment in the social protest of summer 2011 as a field of individual search for meaning. This search sheds light on broader processes in Israeli society and even more broadly on the quest for meaning in a post-modern world.

Using varied ethnographic materials collected in the temporal field of the main encampment in Rothchild Boulevard, Tel-Aviv, I tried to pinpoint the role of the encampment in the participants' quests for meaning, the impact on reconstruction of social categories, and the practices used by the campers in these processes.

Faced with the permanent sense of uncertainty in the broader space around them, the protest participants took advantage of their wondering space and used spiritual discourse, blurred social categories, or reconstructed them to find meaning in life. In the protest field, participants could reflect on their lives and identities on a daily basis and explore the multiple, albeit ambiguous, options offered by the post-modern era. The wondering space was to them a quasi-therapeutic setting.

The existential questions they grappled with were raised in the context of a social event and reflected the fundamental change undergone by Israeli society—from a collective and intensely ideological Zionist society to one where that single overarching dream gave way to a multiplicity of mutually exclusive ideas, beliefs, and lifestyles, all left for the individual to choose from. The therapeutic setting in the boulevard was also ideal for coping with that fragmentation of faith.

In *Paths in Utopia*, Martin Buber (1949/1996) wrote about the attempt to design a utopian society here and now and related it to the socialist ideal and its adoption by the Zionist ideology. Over the years, Buber's utopic hope, or vision, began to shatter, and he expressed his deep disappointment with what the utopia actually turned out to be.

More recently, *Trouble in Utopia*, by Moshe Lissak and Dan Horowitz (1989) described the schisms in an Israeli society that has failed to mature into a utopia. Lissak and Horowitz identified five main schisms: national, religious, political-ideological, socioeconomic, and gender. These are all obstacles undermining the utopia, which was illusory to begin with. This utopia, they wrote, was founded on discrimination of other national and ethnic groups and used an extreme version of the "melting pot," one designed to melt identities away by excluding or eliminating them. With so much left outside the pot, Zionism lost its status as the collective dream.

The 2011 protest is a major milestone in the process that had begun with the utopia described by Buber, continued with the fracturing and fragmentation described by Lissak and Horowitz, and culminated in the Rothschild encampment with its multicultural, pluralistic discourse offering a variety of individualized options. The Israeli protest resembled other concurrent protests in Egypt, Spain, and elsewhere, most of which had to do with the desire to change the system of government, establish a democracy or express distrust in representative democracy, and call for equal distribution of resources. In Western countries, people protested against the failure to realize the neo-liberal promises of globalization, while using neo-liberal tools to form a heterogeneous platform of demands. The common element in these protests was the lack of a single concrete position or objective, in maintaining ideological ambiguity, an independent agenda, and the abandonment of the quest for a single utopia.

My study suggests that, in the Rothschild encampment, a third evolutionary stage has been reached: *multitopia*. The Greek word *utopia* may be translated as "the best place" or "nowhere," and the word is used to refer to a hypothetical, ideal society. Utopia offers an escape from this world's troubles to a better place (Kanter, 1972). The idea behind *multitopia* is that the same space allows ambiguously related or even opposing forces to operate at the same time and manage the mosaic of multiple utopias without excluding or "melting" any. The multitopian whole is greater than its utopian parts.

The multitopia is a natural extension of the post-modern discourse, with its emphasis on multivocality and acceptance of a variety of ideas and opinions (Jameson, 2002). Just as the post-modern discourse percolated into everyday life, so did it affect the way people protest. The protest is no longer clearly defined and focused on a single issue but is rather a potpourri of voices calling for a better life. And, unlike previous utopias such as Zionism, the multitopia is a field of searchers where the group setting is the ideal context for a basically individual search.

As Gil (36) described,

> Everyone came here to establish their own independent state as they
> see fit. It's a microcosm of our country, of living in this world. You can't
> follow one thing, but we all believe in living together inside that great
> diversity that was created here. . . . As for me, I came here to get in
> touch with myself. In the tent on the right, there's a couple who lives
> in a tent in the wild and wants to spread the message of loving nature
> and living in harmony with the Earth, and down there lives a guy who
> believes in returning to the barter system. What brings them all to-
> gether is the knowledge that what we have now is rotten, and that it
> must be changed.

This quote illustrates the Babylonian discourse of the Rothschild multitopia,
a hodgepodge of perspectives on questions in a variety of areas in a setting
conducive to dialogue free of the conventions of the world outside and open
to the infinite possibilities for individual choice of a better world. As Jameson
put it, "Utopias are non-fictional even though they are also non-existent"
(2004, p. 12).

Within that multitopian space, there is enough room for *identitopias*—
independent utopias where each member of society finds their own
meaning. In the tent protest of 2011, Rothschild Boulevard functioned
as a true multitopia. The three practices discussed—spiritual discourse,
ignoring social categories, and identity construction—served the same
search for identitopias within a multitopia. The path to a better world could
be a tent in the desert, conversations with divinities, reducing the rent, returning to an old spirituality, or coming up with a new one. The Rothschild
Multitopia was emblematic of a new form of protest, diverse but united in
the belief that reality is not enough, that the utopia promised has failed, and
that a new multipolar world must be created.

This study suggests that Israeli society has turned from one that
melts or glues its members together to one that tries to remove the artificial glue, searing its exposed skin, deepening its multicultural character to become multitopian. Future studies may address the question of
whether this third stage would simply fragment society or allow all its
members to unite in a single geographical space where every utopia can
be realized.

Highlights

- This chapter explores the questions of searching for personal meaning in a social event, focusing on a central encampment in Tel-Aviv during the summer 2011 social protest in Israel.
- People who came to the encampment were raising questions and looking for meaning in a space that allowed them to temporarily wonder outside of their normal life, a space I describe as a "wondering space."
- The search for personal meaning in a social event can provide insights about the cracks in the Zionist utopia, reflecting the need to find personal utopias. This situation is described as "multitopia."
- Multitopia is defined as a multiutopian sphere where every subject is looking for their own personal meaning, trying to bridge the ideological cracks in Israeli society.
- The wondering space has therapeutic potential, and the option afforded by the boulevard's centrality of smoothly moving in and out of it at will—and looking out both ways—enhances its uniqueness as a platform for reflection.
- Faced with the permanent sense of uncertainty in the broader space around them, the protest participants took advantage of their wondering space and used spiritual discourse, blurred social categories, or reconstructed them to find meaning in life.
- Within that multitopian space, there is enough room for *identitopias*— independent utopias where each member of society finds their own meaning.
- This study suggests that Israeli society has turned from one that melts or glues its members together to one that tries to remove the artificial glue, searing its exposed skin, deepening its multicultural character to become multitopian.

References

Abellán, J., Sequera, J., & Janoschka, M. (2012). Occupying the Hotelmadrid: A laboratory for urban resistance. *Social Movement Studies, 11*(3-4), 320–326.

Abrams, D., & Hogg, M. A. (1990). Social identification, self-categorization and social influence. *European Review of Social Psychology, 1*, 195–228.

Bauman, Z. (1991). *Modernity and ambivalence.* Cornell University Press.

Bauman, Z. (2000). *Liquid modernity.* Polity Press.

Beck, U. (1992). *Risk society: Towards a new modernity.* Sage.

Beck, U. (2008). *World at risk.* Polity Press.

Breakwell, G. M. (1986). *Coping with threatened identities.* Law Book Co. of Australasia.

Breakwell, G. M. (1992). Processes of self-evaluation: efficacy and estrangement. In G. M. Breakwell (Ed.), *Social psychology of identity and the self-concept* (pp. 35–55). Surrey University Press.

Bruner, J. (1995). The autobiographical process. *Current Sociology, 43*(2), 161–177.

Buber, M. (1949/1996). *Paths in Utopia.* Syracuse University Press.

Collins, R. (2011). Focus of emotional attention. In J. Goodwin, M. Jasper, & F. Polletta (Eds.), *Passionate politics: Emotions and social movements.* (pp. 27–45). University of Chicago Press.

Dahan Kalev, H. (1999). Patterns of oppression in Israel: The case of the Wadi Salib rebels. *Theory and Criticism, 12-13,* 31–44. [Hebrew]

Della Porta, D., & Diani, M. (1999). *Social Movements: An Introduction.* Blackwell.

Denzin, K. N. (1989). *Interpretive biography.* Sage.

Fisher, R., & Kling, J. (1994). Community organization and new social movement theory. *Journal of Progressive Human Services, 5*(2), 5–23.

Frankl, V. (1946). *Man's search for meaning.* Goodreads.

Freire, P. (1978). *Pedagogy in process: The letters to Guinea-Bissau.* Seabury Press.

Fromm, E. (1941). *Escape from freedom.* Henry Holt & Co.

Gamson, J. (1995). Must identity movements self-destruct? A queer dilemma. *Social Problems, 42*(3), 390–407.

Glaser, B. G., & Strauss, A. L. (2009). *The discovery of grounded theory: Strategies for qualitative research.* Transaction.

Glasius, M., & Pleyers, G. (2013). The global movement of 2011: Democracy, social justice and dignity. *Development and Change, 44,* 547–567.

Gledhill, J. (2012). Social protest movements in the 21st century. *Social Movement Studies, 11*(3-4), 342–348.

Goodwin, J., & Jasper, J. M. (2003). *The social movement reader: Cases and concepts.* Blackwell.

Gusfield, J. R. (2009). *New social movements: From ideology to identity.* Temple University Press.

Hazaz-Berger, H. (2018). *Multitopia Rothschild: Thoughts on postmodern identity in a space of wondering* (doctoral dissertation). Hebrew University of Jerusalem.

Heelas, P. (1996). *The New Age movement: The celebration of the self and the sacralization of modernity.* Blackwell.

Heelas, P. (1998). *Religion, modernity and postmodernity.* Blackwell.

Herzog, H. (2013). A generational and gender perspective on the Tent Protest. *Theory and Criticism, 41,* 69–96. [Hebrew]

Holland, D. (1997). Selves as cultured: As told by an anthropologist who lacks a soul. In R. D. Ashmore & L. Jussim (Eds.), *Self and identity* (pp. 160–190). Oxford University Press.

Jameson, F. (2002). *A singular modernity: Essay on the ontology of the present.* Verso.

Jameson, F. (2004). The politics of Utopia. *New Left Review, 25,* 35–54.

Kanter, R. M. (1972). *Commitment and community: Communes and utopias in sociological perspective.* Harvard University Press.

Köksal, I. (2012). Activist intervention: Walking in the city of London. *Social Movement Studies, 11*(3-4), 446–453.

Korazim, Y., & Benish, A. (2011). The governance of protest: Vikki Knafo and the single mothers' social protest in Israel. *Jerusalem Papers in Regulation & Governance, 40.*

Lacan, J. (1970). *The languages of criticism and the sciences of man: The structuralist controversy.* Johns Hopkins Press.

Lissak, M., & Horowitz, Z. (1989). *Trouble in Utopia.* SUNY Press.

Mauss, M. A. (1985). Category of the human mind: The notion of the person, the notion of the self. In M. Carrithers, S. Collins, & S. Lukes (Eds.), *The category of the person: Anthropology, philosophy, history* (pp. 1–25). Cambridge University Press.

Mavrommatis, G. (2015). Hannah Arendt in the streets of Athens. *Current Sociology, 63*(3), 432–449.

Melucci, A. (1988). Getting involved: Identity and mobilization in social movements. In B. Kalandermans, H. Kriesu, & S. Tarrow (Eds.), *From structure to action: Comparing social movement research across cultures* (Vol. 1, pp. 329–348). Jay Press.

Melucci, A. (1996a). *Challenging codes: Collective action in the information age.* Cambridge University Press.

Melucci, A. (1996b). *The playing self: Person and meaning in the planetary society.* Cambridge University Press.

Melucci, A. (1997). Identity and difference in a globalized world. In P. Werbner & T. Modood (Eds.), *Debating cultural hybridity: Multi-cultural identities and the politics of anti-racism* (pp. 58–69). Zed Books.

Meyer, D. S. (2004). Protest and political opportunities. *Annual Review of Sociology, 30,* 125–145.

Morell, M. F. (2012). The free culture and 15M movements in Spain: Composition, social networks and synergies. *Social Movement Studies, 11*(3-4), 386–392.

Pickerill, J., Krinsky, J., Hayes, G., & Gillan, K. (Eds.). (2016). *Occupy! A global movement.* Routledge.

Polletta, F. (2006). *It was like a fever: Story telling in protest and politics.* University of Chicago Press.

Polletta, F. (2008). Culture and movements. *Annals of the American Academy of Political and Social Science, 619*(1), 78–96.

Ram, U., & Filk, D. (2013). The rise and fall of the social protest. *Theory and Criticism, 40,* 1–10. [Hebrew]

Razsa, M., & Kurnik, A. (2012). The Occupy Movement in Žižek's hometown: Direct democracy and a politics of becoming. *American Ethnologist, 39*(2), 238–258.

Reger, J., Myers, D. J., & Einwhhner, R. L. (2008). *Identity work in social movements.* University of Minnesota Press.

Rosenheck, Z., & Shalev, M. (2013). The political economy of the 2011 protests: A class and generational analysis. *Theory and Criticism, 41,* 44–68.

Snow, D., & McAdam, D. (2000). Identity work processes in the context of social movements: Clarifying the identity/movement nexus. In S. Stryker, T. J. Owens, & R. W. White (Eds.), *Self, identity, and social movements* (pp. 41–67). University of Minnesota Press.

Spiro, M. E. (1963). *Kibbutz venture in Utopia.* Schocken.

Strauss, A., & Corbin, J. (1990). *Basics of qualitative research: Techniques and procedures for developing grounded theory.* Sage.

Strauss, A. L., & Corbin, J. (1998). *Basics of qualitative research: Techniques and procedures for developing grounded theory* (2nd ed.). Sage.

Styker, S., Owens, T. J., & White, W. (2000). Social psychology and social movements: Cloudy past and bright future. In S. Stryker, T. J. Owens, & R. W. White (Eds.), *Self, identity, and social movements* (pp. 1–17). University of Minnesota Press.

Swirski, S. (2013). The middle class needs to take control of its money: On the crisis of the Western middle class. *Theory and Criticism, 41,* 147–163. [Hebrew].

Tajfel, H., & Turner, J. C. (1986). The social identity theory of inter-group behavior. In S. Worchel, & W. G. Austin (Eds.), *Psychology of intergroup relations* (pp. 7–24). Nelson-Hall.

Taylor, C. (1991). *The malaise of modernity.* House of Anansi Press.

Turner, V. W. (1969). *The ritual process.* Penguin.

Van Manen, M. (1997). *Researching lived experience: Human science for an action sensitive pedagogy.* Althouse Press.

Van Manen, M. (Ed.). (2002). *Writing in the dark: Phenomenological studies in interpretive inquiry.* Althouse Press.

Welwood, J. (1984). Principles of inner work: Psychological and spiritual. *The Journal of Transpersonal Psychology, 16*(1), 63–73.

Yonah, Y., & Spivak, A. (2012). *To do things differently: A model for a well-ordered society.* Hakibbutz Hameuchad. [Hebrew]

Young, M. P. (2011). A revolution of the soul: Transformative experience and immediate abolition. In J. Goodwin, M. Jasper, & F. Polletta (Eds.), *Passionate politics: Emotions and social movements* (pp. 99–135). University of Chicago Press.

4

Yearning for Meaning

Israeli Terror Casualties' Families Community and the National Bereavement Discourse

Udi Lebel and Tzlil Ben-Gal

Introduction

Recent years have seen a growing number of communities in Israeli society lobbying for institutional and national recognition of the trauma and loss experienced by their members as an integral part of Israel's struggle for independence and security. These communities include, for instance, veterans who fought in the Red Army during World War II and made *Aliya* (immigrated) to Israel requesting that a monument be built in their honor and that their fight against the Nazis be officially recognized as part of the struggle that ultimately enabled the establishment of the State of Israel. Ethiopian Jews who made *Aliya* to Israel demanded that their relatives who died during the long journey from Sudan be named on a monument in Mount Herzl in Jerusalem—Israel's national commemoration site—and that they be treated as having sacrificed their lives for the Zionist cause. In fact, these two communities attempted to promote a new framing for their sacrifice or loss. In the first example we see an attempt at a reframing of soldiers recruited to fight in a war on behalf of the Soviet interest as citizens of Eastern European countries as having fought as Jews against Hitler for the Zionist cause. And in the second example—an attempt at a reframing of Ethiopian Jews who died while immigrating to Israel in order to be saved from a life of poverty and violence in Ethiopia as being an integral part of the Zionist migration waves into Israel and as having knowingly attempted a dangerous and difficult journey so as to fulfill the Zionist cause.

There is no disputing the fact that the ability to ascribe meaning to loss and trauma is a typical rehabilitative resource. We wish to propose here that one of the ways of producing it and successfully ascribing it to the experience

Udi Lebel and Tzlil Ben-Gal, *Yearning for Meaning* In: *Finding Meaning*. Edited by: Ofra Mayseless and Pninit Russo-Netzer, Oxford University Press. © Oxford University Press 2022. DOI: 10.1093/oso/9780190910358.003.0004 of sacrifice is achieved by an act of reframing. In this chapter we illustrate the links between the *framing theory*, the theory of *meaning-making* in particular, and the field of rehabilitation and trauma in general. We do this by studying a specific community: families of Israeli terror casualties.

Framing theory is traditionally linked to the study of communication and rhetoric. It focuses on the ways in which language defines the reception of reality and the psychosocial attitudes toward it.

The theory of meaning-making, stemming from rehabilitation disciplines, focuses on the positive impact of sense-making and productivity in the wake of trauma and loss and the ways of coping with it and even recovering and growing as a result.

Much has been written on states and societies coping with the "new wars" era, in which the battlefield occurs within cities and the victims, as well as many acts of heroism, no longer involve combat soldiers but civilians.

We wish to contribute to a further related perspective—that of the field of collective memory, victimology, and death studies—and to specifically discuss the efforts of new communities to demand recognition of their sacrifice, thus enabling them to ascribe meaning to their trauma by reframing the death and loss of their loved ones from a personal framing to a national one.

In the "post-modern condition" (Lyotard, 1984) of the nation state, "new" voices demand to be included in collective memory and gain recognition as having also taken part in the national project, whether as its victims or its heroes (Orr, 2001). In the contexts of wars and military conflicts, these are normally groups of civilians wishing to gain recognition for their suffering, sacrifice, and contribution to national resilience. They wish to be recognized alongside the "military voice" that has gained exclusivity in national Israeli memory and in the official memorialization of the modern-heroic era which only allows military soldiers and casualties to attain collective meaning for their sacrifice and loss.

In Israel, following the 1993 Oslo Accords and more so as of the Al-Aqsa Intifada (2000), society was exposed to recurring organized terror attacks against civilians and to warfare by the Israel army against terror organizations whose main method of operation was targeting missiles against the Israeli rear. The many families of Israelis killed and wounded in these attacks began to function as a "memory community" (Assmann, 2010) with the aim of including their loved ones among the country's national fallen—a category referred to as "Israeli casualties of war." To achieve this aim, the families acted to reframe the deaths of their loved ones in a way that would match the meta-frame ascribed to fallen soldiers in this category, one always exclusively limited to army and security organizations casualties. This new framing perceives the death of these civilians as having taken place under productive and heroic circumstances, thereby offering a collective meaning for their death.

Purpose, Structure, and Methodology

This chapter discusses a phenomenon which the writers believe will continue to expand in the future as increasingly fewer military soldiers die in operational or heroic circumstances, and, in parallel, a growing number of casualties killed under operational-heroic circumstances are not soldiers. This would of course further deepen the polemic on the identity of casualties to be included in the "Israeli casualties of war" category and of those positioned on the heroic ethos, thereby granting meaning and a range of rehabilitative resources to bereaved families who will gain recognition, acknowledgment, and an organized and institutionalized allocation of national meaning to their loss.

We propose the framing theory as a methodological tool for analyzing qualitative texts to identify an ideal practice of a "loss community" or "memory community" wishing to attain meaning for its loss. We also wish to present the collective memory challenges of the new wars and post-heroic warfare era by looking at a unique community—families of civilians who were murdered in terror attacks in Israel.

We will show how attempts to ascribe meaning to bereavement dictate death reframing efforts. We will also show how, in the Israeli case—even in the post-heroic era—militarism as an ethos and the Ministry of Defense as an institution continue to serve as the ultimate providers of meaning and granters of hero-framing. This, in turn, frames them as holders of a cultural and rehabilitative function which is no less crucial than its military and security one.

Based on the study of the development of new subcultures in the business, academic, cultural, or political spheres (Lee & Tan, 2017), the current study analyses communal discourses while investigating the remarks and actions of central representative figures in the examined communities. In the words of renowned community discourse scholar Wellman, these central figures can be perceived within the "as if" realm, because they represent all participants of their discursive community (Wellman, 1988) and are perceived by their counterparts as expressing the "authentic and representative voice" of the community (Fraser, 1990).

The current study uses the *discourse frame analysis* method (Snow & Benford, 1992) commonly used for investigating the discourses of new social movements. This methodology involves the analysis of correspondence, protocols, media interviews, policy documents, and more.

Our investigation of the public discourse within bereaved communities includes two "counter discourse communities" (Wang, 2016), Israeli Terror Casualties' Families on one side and the community of military bereavement organizations on the other. Our underlying methodological assumption defines each "bereavement community" as a discursive community holding relatively homogenous values and interpretations that form the "narrative ID" of its members in a way that is dichotomous to that of "the other group" (Spector-Mersel, 2010).

The term "boundary work" is a well-known phenomenon within loss communities, acting to reduce or expand the limits of the social-cultural-emotional framework serving as their preferred "emotional space" (Sawicka, 2017). In our case, this is the attempt by the Terror Casualties' Families community to remove the symbolic boundary between it and the military casualties' families' community. It is an attempt to reposition (Kalafatis, Tsogas, & Blankson, 2000) the term "terror casualty" (or, to be precise, "the Jewish terror casualty") whom the Zionist imagination does not perceive as belonging to the "heroics and sacrifice" arena of Zionism, side by side with fallen soldiers, who are perceived, although not always justly, as having entered this category due to objective circumstances.

The first part of the chapter will discuss meaning as a rehabilitative resource among those who have experienced loss and trauma. By examining the relationships among "positive framing" of loss, the ability to ascribe it the required meaning, and social activities carried out by communities, we identify those communities which the modern-heroic meaning regime has left outside of this framing.

The second part will discuss the Israeli case, in which the Ministry of Defense, backed by military logic, has exclusively framed military and security forces' casualties as pertaining to a community that upholds social meaning for its loss by a range of practices.

In the third part we present our case study: the activities carried out by families of Israeli terror casualties to revise the framing of the death of their loved ones so that it matches the framing previously defined as exclusively dedicated to military casualties. We also present efforts by the loss communities of Israel's military and security institutions to prevent this process of reframing of terror casualties and their acceptance as a part of what is known in Israel as "Israeli casualties of war"—those whose families form a community that possesses a class consciousness, with their loss being granted meaning in an organized and institutionalized manner mainly via acts of commemoration of their loved ones and rehabilitation for their families.

Finally, we present an overview of quantitative data illustrating the transformation in the profile of Israeli fallen soldiers in terms of the circumstances of soldiers' deaths and, in parallel, in the extent of civilian deaths in the post-heroic era, and the achievements of the community of terror casualties' families in their efforts toward a reframing of the loss of their loved ones.

The chapter concludes with insights on the psychosocial link between framing and a sense of meaning, relevant to Israeli society as well as to other post-heroic arenas.

Meaning as a Rehabilitative and Public Resource

In his eulogy to the fallen soldiers of Athens, Pericles said to their parents

> You know that your dead have passed away amid manifold vicissitudes; and that they may be deemed fortunate who have gained their utmost honor, whether an honorable death like theirs, or an honorable sorrow like yours, and whose share of happiness has been so ordered that the term of their happiness is likewise the term of their life . . . and be comforted by the glory of those who are gone"
>
> (Pericles' Funeral Oration, Thucydides'
> History of the Peloponnesian War)

Pericles made it known among the Athenian public and among bereaved parents in particular that their sons had died a meaningful, productive, and heroic death, granting them, as well as their parents, public acceptance and recognition. While it is doubtful that Pericles had consciously relied on sociotherapeutic concepts, his words seem to have been written with an understanding of the fact that ascribing meaning to loss is a strong rehabilitative resource. Current research on coping with loss and trauma has shown that the inability to ascribe them with meaning is expressed in an overtendency for posttraumatic symptoms (Park & Ai, 2006), a destabilization of the family unit (Murphy et al., 1984), deteriorated health (Davis, Wohl, & Verberg, 2007), and "mental defeat" syndrome, which involves a tendency for confusion, detachment, and the adoption of dysfunctional beliefs (Dunmore, Clark, & Ehlers, 2001). Conversely, the ability to frame trauma as meaningful and to ascribe meaning and productiveness to loss has been identified as promoting greater well-being and as contributing to a reduced rate of pathologies and an accelerated recuperation (Park & Ai, 2006). Recent studies on posttraumatic growth have identified the ability to ascribe meaning to trauma as one of the central variables that may promote it (Park & Ai, 2006). This has been found to be increasingly important among parents coping with the death of a grown child (Cordova et al., 2001; Tomich, Helgeson, & Nowak, 2005). In fact, all of these studies can be grouped into a single discipline entitled "posttraumatic growth" (Gerrish, Dyck, & Marsh, 2009).

Among the various types of loss, the loss of a grown child has been identified as the most difficult to cope with (Stroebe & Schut, 2001), mainly due to its diverse components: it is a parental loss of a child, and it is usually a sudden (Neimeyer, Prigerson, & Davies, 2006) and violent (Rynearson, 2006) death and therefore difficult to ascribe it meaning (Gillies & Niemeyer, 2006; Matthews & Marwit, 2006). Hence the importance for bereaved parents to accumulate meaning from as many sources as possible (Gillies & Niemeyer, 2006). In their paper "Community as a Key to Healing After a Death of a Child," Hastings and her colleagues describe the rehabilitative value of the ability of bereaved parents to connect to a collective sense of meaning and to a social discourse that frames their loss as productive to the community, which in turn provides organized sources of community support and recognition (Hastings, Musambira, & Hoover, 2007). We have found that even in very small communities, the very fact that the community's discourse frames the loss as meaningful gives solace and relief (Rudrum, 2005).

Meaning Through "Positive Reframing"

What is that sense of meaning which mourners need so much? How can they feel its presence? What would express it? In fact, that valuable sense of meaning is expressed by the framing of trauma and loss. The mourners' framing is achieved by their becoming a part of "the community's story" and their departed loved ones being seen as "the community's fallen" (Mathes, 2006).

Neimeyer was among the first to contribute to an understanding of the relationship between the framing of loss and the structuring of trauma within an effective narrative envelope (one that provides meaning) and the ability to cope and recuperate (Neimeyer, 1998, 2006; Neimeyer & Stewart, 1996). In the context of loss and bereavement, this involves a sociotherapeutic process taking place in the public space, one meant to affect the community's rhetoric and from there to penetrate the individual's sense of self and personal experience (Kromer-Nevo, 1999). Reality and narrative are intertwined, and, in fact, "what is not integrated into the Narrative is not experienced in the first place" (Kromer-Nevo, 1999, p. 285).

Bandler and Grinder (1982, p. 2) defined reframing as "the change of the frame used by the individual to perceive an event, in order to change its meaning," thereby clarifying the importance of the reframing technique as "when the meaning changes, the individual's response and behavior will also change." In other words, the reframing process involves the creation of an alternative, preferred story, which is in fact a preferred alternative reality or "a place to stand in" (White, 2005)—a reality that improves the effectiveness of the individual's ability to cope with trauma (White, 2005). As proposed by Watzalwick et al., the reframing technique involves replacing one's conceptual and emotional approach toward the experiencing of an event with another frame that is better suited to the "facts" of that concrete situation and, as a result, changes the entire meaning ascribed to the event (Watzalwick, Weakland, & Fisch, 1974, p. 211). James Coyne's pioneering study exposed the effectiveness of the reframing technique in this therapeutic practice by showing how reframing leads to a shift in perspective and to attaching a more positive connotation to events or behaviors so as to change the meaning ascribed to them, thereby enhancing our ability to cope (Coyne, 1985).

These conceptions have been validated by studies showing that the more "positive reframing" is attached to difficult experiences, the more a person's ability to cope, extent of recuperation, and individual growth are enhanced. "Positive reframing" has been linked to lower incidence of depression and to a sense of coherence—two central challenges for those experiencing trauma or loss (Lambert & Mallett, 2007). Moreover, a correlation was found between "positive reframing" and a sense of life satisfaction (McCullough, Emmons, & Tsang, 2002), improved self and group image (Clarke, 1998), and an enhanced sense of well-being expressed, among other things, by a reduced need to see physicians and less complaints of routine health issues (Lambert & Mallett, 2007).

Social Activism for Positive Framing

In many cases the ability to reframe trauma or loss requires social action. This concept corresponds with the "politics of recognition," a process described by Taylor while illustrating how individuals or communities aiming to achieve a positive reframing need to act toward the redrafting of the historical narrative of their community (Taylor, 1994) so that the majority of the community can adopt a narrative in which they would find their valued place. The "politics of recognition" relies on what "dialogism," by which the person is in constant dialogue with his surroundings, and his consciousness is a product of this dialogue. Thus, the identity of the individual or of a community would only be complete if externally validated, and the individual would be able to view himself through the social mirror in the way in which he aspires to be seen. As long as the positive frame is limited to the individual and does not achieve wide public reception, the individual is not able to enjoy the framing nor its rehabilitative resources. This is why communities who feel that their trauma is perceived within what Gamson has coined "injustice frames" (Gamson, 1992) may act in a way that we can refer to as "discursive activism" to reframe their loss or mourning within the wider community to which they pertain (Desrosiers, 2015; Gamson, 1995).

"Meaning Ascribing" Regime in the Post-Heroic State

In the combat culture of the 20th century, military casualties have been framed as "operational heroes" (Dew, 2014), their death perceived as having taken place in a combat setting under necessarily operational circumstances. Therefore, and due to the fact that combat took place far from society, the deaths of most fallen soldiers were framed within what Ben-Ari defined as "good military death" (Ben-Ari, 2005): a heroic, mean- ingful death, deserving of recognition, and therefore granting the family of the fallen soldier unique symbolic capital that is often converted into an ethical status that grants them an "entry ticket" to participation in public discourse (Eyre, 2007).

But, as of the end of the previous millennium, when the military conflicts encountered by most of the world's democracies became post-heroic—in "small wars" or "new wars"—increasingly, soldiers are no longer in mortal danger, and, alongside the few who are physically present in combat areas (mostly special unit forces), most combat soldiers consist of local militia forces or security contractors (Lebel, 2016). Hence, the combat zone is expected to include a declining number of soldiers belonging to the combating nation because, in these "new war" confrontations, the enemy's violence is targeted at civilians (Cronin, 2013).

Moreover, coping with the challenges of combat increasingly becomes the duty of civil organizations responsible for combating terror as well as handling and protecting the attacked civil society. This leads to the fact that, even among the fallen who have died in operational and heroic circumstances, there are increasing numbers of nonmilitary deaths. This has resulted in families of civilian victims acting to demand a collective meaning to their loss, alongside "victim capital" (Halvorsen, 2001) and sometimes even "heroic capital" (Hensell & Gerdes, 2017), a meaning enabled by a change in the meta-frame that organizes the memory and commemoration discourse that has, until now, kept heroism and sacrifice as the exclusive arena of military soldiers (Morgan, 2009).

What, therefore, may be felt by families whose loved ones have died not in a military setting, but, in their eyes, in identical or similar circumstances, or in circumstances of national meaning which do not fall short of that of military soldiers? These may include families of security guards, rescue organizations personnel, or brave civilians who gave their lives to prevent a terrorist from carrying out a mass murder. Are these families destined to remain, alongside their fallen, in their anonymity only because their loved one did not die while serving in the military? At the same time, they may perceive their reality as "relative deprivation" (Gurr, 1970) because in their eyes the death of their loved one corresponds with what Weaver referred to as "same death, different framing" (Weaver & Heartz, 1999). This is "disenfranchised grief"—not in the way in which Doka (1989) defined it, as a dichotomous perception of grief which may be recognized or concealed, but in the way in which Robson and Walter (2013) perceived it, as a continuum consisting of recognition and rights granted to the griever.

The Israeli Case: The Ministry of Defense as an
Institutional Framer

In Israel, eligibility for immediate organized national meaning for loss depends on the deceased being recognized as an "Israeli casualty of war," a status that manifests itself, from an organizational viewpoint, in the family being cared for by the Ministry of Defense's Rehabilitation Division. In such cases the Ministry of Defense is also responsible for commemorating the deceased. Thus, a seemingly technical-institutional decision—whether a bereaved family would be cared for by the Ministry of Defense or by the National Insurance Institute—in fact dictates whether the deceased would be commemorated on the private or public level, whether their family would gain national and collective recognition for its loss, or whether the family's bereavement would be confined to the private arena and any commemoration efforts would depend on the family's own initiatives. In the context of loss, the Ministry of Defense functions as an *institutional framer*, marking all of the bereaved families handled by it as having a loved one who has died under productive, heroic circumstances, and providing them with support, recognition, and public meaning for their loss. All families of deceased soldiers receive such framing and therefore gain an Ascription Status—resulting from the very fact of their belonging to the Ministry of Defense—rather than an Achievement Status—which is granted based on meritocratic principles to those who actually functioned in operational circumstances (Bruce, 1992).

This dichotomy is backed by legislation dictating that recognition of deceased soldiers as "Israeli casualties of wars" and their families as bereaved families would be handled by the Ministry of Defense's Rehabilitation Division and that this status would be granted to anyone killed during or as a result of his or her military service in the Israeli Defense Forces (IDF) or in a number of parallel security organizations. Even if the death occurred during military service but under completely civilian circumstances (e.g., during army leave), the soldier is still recognized as a fallen soldier and the inscription on the grave reads "Killed in the line of duty" (Katz, 2007). This legislation, unique to Israel, stems from Israeli soldiers' Ascription Status and the fact that the families of the fallen are cared for by the Ministry of Defense rather than, as is the practice in other countries, by civil authorities (Unger, 2010). These families gain precedence over bereaved families who are not cared for by the Ministry of Defense in three main aspects, each of which contributes to the ascription of meaning to their loss.

1. *Commemoration.* The commemoration of fallen soldiers ensures their "social revival" within the national story as expressed in the physical space of the nation (Mathes, 2006). Renowned military historian J. Winter wrote that, beyond the educational-propagandist value of monuments and commemoration initiatives, they also have a rehabilitative value in that they "help the bereaved recover from their loss" (Winter, 1995, p. 95).

   Fallen soldiers acknowledged as such by the Ministry of Defense are commemorated—according to national, municipal and military laws—in national commemoration publications and on the website of the *Yad LaBanim* soldiers' commemoration organization, in *Yad LaBanim* centers around the country, and in municipal monuments built in towns and cities. In parallel, they are commemorated by their military corps, brigade, and command, as well as by the youth movements they belonged to and by other commemoration initiatives organized by nongovernmental organizations, including memory books, sports competitions, scholarships, etc.

   The Public Council for Commemorating Soldiers plans Israel's collective military memorialization and commemoration policy. The council, unique to Israel, is run by bereaved parents who organize various initiatives and ceremonies that are budgeted by the government and aimed at commemorating fallen soldiers throughout the year. Its main task is the organization of Israel's official Memorial Day, which by law is an inseparable part of the Israeli calendar and in fact is the "holiest" day in Israel's civil religion (Liebman & Don-Yihia, 1983). It is a day of national ceremonies and memorials to fallen soldiers, attended by senior army commanders and parliament members. This is in addition to individual memorial services held for each soldier on the anniversary of his or her death.

2. *Rehabilitation.* The Ministry of Defense's Rehabilitation Division is the most budgeted welfare and rehabilitation organization in Israel. Each bereaved family is allocated a casualties officer who accompanies them personally. There is funding for personal and group therapy, as well as financial benefits in many areas (purchasing vehicles, apartments, vacations, recreation and culture, academic studies, and more). Contrary to the bureaucratic rehabilitation process in the National Insurance Institute, this is a highly effective and proactive rehabilitation process as well as being more financially rewarding (Gal, 2002). It

covers a wide range of occupational, familial, and communal rehabilitative initiatives.

By law, the Ministry of Defense's Rehabilitation Division takes care
of families of fallen IDF soldiers, as well as of casualties of a small
number of additional organizations who are, following legislation, included in the "Israeli casualties of war" category: the Prison Service,
the Mossad, the Israel Security Agency (*Shin Bet*), Israel Police, Israel
Border Police, the Knesset Guard, and the South Lebanon Army,
emergency squads, as well as soldiers who died while in pre-military
courses and those who died in the pre-state era as underground resistance warriors fighting for national independence (Ministry of
Finance, 2018).

3. *Discourse.* The Israeli national discourse is a tool for reproducing collective meaning ascribed to soldiers' deaths. It is a comprehensive framing
   that perceives all military losses as having occurred under heroic and
   productive circumstances, which in turn enables collective justification for the allocation of their families to the Ministry of Defense and
   hence to prioritized rehabilitation and commemoration, a fact which
   in itself defines the context of the lives lost. Since the establishment of
   the state, the Israeli bereavement discourse emphasized the fact that
   these deaths took place under extraordinarily heroic circumstances.
   For instance, many commemoration books published by the Ministry
   of Defense during Israel's first decades as a state included a quote by
   well-known Jewish author Shai Agnon addressing parents of fallen
   soldiers and explaining to them why there is meaning to their loss: "You
   should find solace in the fact that your son has died a hero" (1950, as
   cited in Zamir, 1952). Similar thoughts are expressed in the letter issued every year by the Minister of Defense to families of fallen soldiers.
   In 2017, the minister wrote that the state of Israel is secure thanks to
   its fallen soldiers who fought "with courage, self-sacrifice and devotion" (Minister of Defense, 2017). The special *Izkor* (remembrance)
   prayer devised for Memorial Day is intended to remember "the loyal
   and the brave, the soldiers of the Israel Defense Forces . . . who have
   given their lives in the wars on the establishment of Israel." One of the
   most well-known sayings in Israel is "In their death they ordered us to
   live," which often adorns covers of memorial books or monuments for
   fallen IDF soldiers. This collective framing is based on a general conception among the Israeli public, as found in public opinion polls, that

the vast majority of the IDF's fallen soldiers died in operational-combat missions (Nuttman-Swartz et al., 2010).

There is wide social acceptance of the meta-frame and its hegemonic representation of the military casualty in a way that is not necessarily realistic (Parry & Doan, 1994). The role of the Ministry of Defense as a framing institution is similar to the way in which Azulai presents the allocation of symbolic capital by elite art galleries. These galleries grant their artists symbolic capital expressed by a public ranking of their work as being of high artistic value and therefore worthy of praise and approval (Azulai, 1992). Hence, it is not the profile of the gallery's clients that is responsible for its prestige, but the very belonging to the gallery—the institution—that is the source of the client's prestige, as described by Goffman in his treatise on the concept of class status (Goffman, 1951). In the Israeli context, cultural militarism defines civil hierarchy and, in our case, even meaning and rehabilitation, as explained so well by Kimmerling: "As a class, echelon, group or person gain proximity to 'security' areas—they come closer and closer to 'holiness'" (Kimmerling, 1993, p. 130).

Case Study: Israeli Terror Casualties' Families and Their Struggle to Connect to a National-Collective Meaning

Since the establishment of the state, Israeli Terror Casualties' Families have protested their inferior status and the fact that the general public has failed to recognize their loss. During a 1982 Knesset hearing on the matter, a manager in the National Insurance Institute rehabilitation division testified as follows: "These people live in a constant sense of discrimination resulting from the very fact that they are handled by the National Insurance Institute. Despite all we do for them, they cannot get over the feeling of being second class citizens. This of course makes our work much more difficult, as even the best service cannot diminish their bitterness and sense of discrimination" (Knesset, January 21, 1982).

Israeli Terror Casualties' Families protests of the fact that they belong to the National Insurance Institute rehabilitation division rather than to the Ministry of Defense do not stem from their wish to improve the quality of the services and benefits given to them, but rather their exclusion from belonging to the meta-frame granted to those being handled by the Ministry of Defense. Proof of this is the policy implemented in 1970, when it was decided that the exact same benefits granted to families of fallen IDF soldiers would be granted to terror casualties' families. These benefits, which include financial compensation, royalties, pension, eligibility for medical and psychological care, rehabilitative-occupational support, and more, were compared to those granted by the Ministry of Defense to families of IDF casualties (Rimmerman & Araten-Bergman, 2010, p. 256) and the only remaining difference between the two categories of casualties is on the symbolic level.

This sense of deprivation is the result of a conscious, premeditated policy implemented by Israeli decision-makers. Knesset member Eliezer Shostak explained the reasoning behind the rehabilitation policy that he and his colleagues have devised: "There is something in the State of Israel that grants special eligibility to serving in the IDF, more than any other casualty, even those injured in hostilities . . . there is a psychological matter of eligibility in IDF service and being injured or killed while serving in the IDF more than anywhere else. This is how the State has perceived this issue. There is special treatment and eligibility resulting from service in the IDF and being injured in war" (Shostak, 1973). Nearly a decade later Knesset member Shevach Weiss also expressed very similar thoughts when explaining the unique mechanism for supporting families of fallen IDF soldiers: "The tendency is not to use social considerations, but symbolic ones" (Knesset, May 10, 1982).

Moment of Change: Social Activism for National Ascription of Meaning

The moment of change in the effectiveness of the "voice" of Israeli Terror Casualties' Families was the signing of the Oslo Accords (in 1993), after which the Israeli rear became exposed to an unprecedented intensity and scope of terror attacks. Since then, terror hitting civilian populations in cities west of the Green Line has become one of the country's greatest and most devastating challenges. The number of people who lost a child, spouse, parent, or sibling in a terror attack grew exponentially, resulting in, for the first time in the history of the state, the establishment of an organized group of Israeli Terror Casualties' Families, which soon became a memory and policy community with a huge presence in Israel's social discourse.

Many murderous attacks resulted in the deaths of soldiers and civilians alike, leading to a differential status of recognition of people killed in the exact same situation: soldiers and their families immediately gained the unique status, allocation of meaning, and national recognition reserved for soldiers, while the families of civilians killed in the same attack remained devoid of these resources. The result was an enhanced sense of relative deprivation (Gurr, 1968) and the onset of collective action (Sandler, 1992) to rectify the situation. Such action was further enhanced following the start of the Al-Aqsa Intifada, with its rise in the frequency of terror and a resultant growing sense of deprivation. Between 2000 and 2004, more than a thousand Israelis were murdered, 70% of them civilians ineligible for the framing granted to the 30% killed while belonging to the military institution (Rimmerman & Araten-Bergman, 2010, p. 253).

Our calculations, based on official data from the Knesset's Research and Information Center (Shahak, 2017), led to the finding that between 1987 (the onset of the first intifada) and 1992 (inclusive), 230 Israeli civilians (not belonging to the country's security forces) were killed in hostilities. If we deduct the 95 who were killed in 1991 during the Gulf War (Bar-Moha, 2001), there remain 135 civilians killed. Hence, in 6 years an average of 22.5 civilians died each year as a result of hostilities.

However, during the period between 1993 (in which the Oslo Accords were signed and the Palestinian Authority was established) and 2005 (including that year, during which Israel retreated from the Gaza Strip), Israel faced its strongest terror wave until then from the Palestinian side. This situation resulted in the need to develop relevant defense doctrines and empower the civil population. During this period, 1,071 civilians (not belonging to the country's security forces) were murdered—an average of 82.38 civilian deaths per year as a result of hostilities over a period of 13 years, an increase of 366.13% compared to the previous period examined.

Since 1993 (including that year) until 2017 (including that year), 1,342 Israeli civilians (not belonging to the country's security forces) were murdered in hostilities—an average of 53.68 deaths per year. Hence, as of the Oslo Accords and the establishment of the Palestinian Authority, until 2017—a period of 25 years—the number of Israelis murdered in hostilities increased by 238.57%, thereby transforming casualties' families into a substantial group of people that communicates internally and grants its members a unique identity and community consciousness. This has also led to the establishment of the Organization of Victims of Hostilities, a representative organization acting on behalf of the families in the public arena. In turn, this community of families has been transformed from a memory community to a policy community as the organization began to represent their aspirations in the political and security arenas.

Loss Reframing Activities

The families of terror casualties began to promote narrative themes that would frame their loved ones alongside the IDF's fallen soldiers and themselves alongside the IDF's bereaved families who are handled and rehabilitated by the Ministry of Defense. They acted to clarify the reasoning behind their refusal to be positioned differently by becoming a part of the national heroics granting its members collective meaning for their loss.

To identify these themes and reasoning, we observed and accompanied the community of families of terror casualties in a number of ways. First, we studied the many archived files containing correspondences between bereaved parents and decision-makers, between themselves, and between them and current and past public figures. Some of these documents are private, held by active bereaved parents who opened their homes to us. Others can be found in public archives such as the State Archive, the Knesset Archive, or Media archives that we visited.

Our second research was via in-depth interviews which we held with many of the bereaved families operating within the studied community. These interviews contributed on an informative as well as a narrative and phenomenological level to our understanding of the motivations and interpretations among bereaved families toward the public policy that they aim to change.

Our third methods was to review many relevant legislations, court rulings, and social policies as expressed in policy documents, protocols, and other texts found in public archives, and especially at the National Insurance Archive in Jerusalem, the Ministry of Defense's archive at Tel Hashomer, the Knesset archive in Jerusalem, and press archives.

We analyzed all of these texts, whether formal texts that we collected or texts transcribed by us during interviews, using the discourse frame analysis method (Fairclough, 2003), which allowed us to identify psychocultural themes attesting to the narrative components behind the social change initiative under analysis. These identified themes transform the analyzed community and its members into a homogenous "discourse community" (Kent, 1991) that uniformly perceives reality and, in this case, its eligibility to be seen as equals with families of fallen IDF soldiers, without distinction, as families whose loved ones sacrificed their lives and died in a national, patriotic, heroic context, and whose pain and loss must be marked, recognized, and commemorated.

Using this method, we were able to identify three themes in their struggle.

Zionism and the Civil Battle Heritage

The families explained that since the beginning of modern Zionism, civilians had been a part of the national story of sacrifice. They argued that "Anyone living in this country is part of the national struggle . . . the thing that unifies us here are the circumstances of our lives rather than whether we did or did not wear a uniform at a certain moment" (Amior, 2011). This is an attempt to rectify what is perceived as the history of Zionist sacrifice so that it is not imagined as being only the result of the work of uniformed soldiers. In the words of Smadar Haran-Kaizer, whose husband and daughter were murdered by a terrorist, "All that we ask is that the part of the civilian fallen be recognized in the historical, collective and personal memory, with an understanding that these civilians are a part of the struggle for the revival of Israel" (Haran-Kaizer, 1998b, as cited in Lebel, 2013). They aimed to convince others that, in parallel to the military story, there is a "civil battle heritage" that has been silenced: "Since pre-State times until now our daily lives have been disrupted by terror attacks and severe hostilities. We, the casualties of these hostilities, our children, our spouses, our parents and other family members, have served as murder targets just because we are citizens of this country" (Haran-Kaizer, 1997, as cited in Lebel, 2013).

The New Wars Take Place in the Rear

A second theme that the families of terror casualties attempted to instill is that the "new wars" take place in the rear. Therefore, a "war" should not be perceived as necessarily taking place outside the country's borders, and lives lost in urban shopping centers should not be excluded from the concept of battle or war. As expressed by Dov Kalmanovich, who was wounded in a terror attack during the first Intifada and headed the organization representing the families of casualties, "The history of the national struggle is changing before our eyes. No longer classic wars against armies that kill soldiers, but against terrorists that kill civilians. The enemy has intentionally directed its war against the civil population and in doing so has converted it into a fighting population" (Amior, 2011). They asked that the Al-Aqsa Intifada, which resulted in hundreds of deaths, be officially recognized as a war. As written by three fathers whose children were murdered in a terror attack in Haifa: "Does the fact that 75% of casualties in the past three and a half years have been civilians mean that this period of time would not be called a war? . . . Why are the State's institutions refraining from defining the time we are living in as 'the war of the rear'?" (Zur, Mendelovich, & Carmi, 2006).

We, Too, Are Soldiers

As a product of the two previous themes, the families strived to change the way in which the image of the soldier is portrayed in the Israeli discourse. Again and again they showed that their loved ones, similarly to soldiers fighting a war, did not die passively nor did they find themselves caught in the site of the terror occurrence from other than national motivations. In a letter to Minister Moshe Katzav, then head of the ministerial committee for symbols and ceremonies, Smadar Haran argued that "The death of a great many of the fallen in hostilities and terror attacks was neither incidental nor arbitrary. Many of them were living in settlements to which they were sent by the State's settling institutions and its authorized bodies in order to form and determine the borders of the State of Israel in their presence. . . . They should not be seen as passive victims but rather as active participants in the struggle for the establishment of the State and its safeguarding. Many have paid with their lives the price of the State's decision not to relinquish its principles in the face of terror" (Haran-Kaizer, 1998a, as cited in Lebel, 2013). She further argued that often the unarmed civilian is required to cope with harsher circumstances than are soldiers: "Civil resistance is different than the heroism of battle . . . many have met the enemy face to face and empty handed." In fact, the families of terror casualties demand recognition for achievement rather than ascription reasons because, in contrast to military casualties, they necessarily endured a trying experience and among them there are none whose loved ones were killed in circumstances other than national. Hence, in their eyes, this is a civic heroic that should be recognized: "We, who do not retreat from the lines of confrontation and frontier settlements; who continue to ride busses and attend street markets, who refuse to give in to fear, who understand that where the spirit is not trampled, the power of terror is diminished; we know that this is the essence of the spirit of coping and civic heroism" (Haran-Kaizer, 1998a, as cited in Lebel, 2013). The use of the term "soldiers" to describe their loved ones is a type of reframing that grants meaning to the loss forced on these families. A "soldier" is one whose death was forced upon him as part of a national story—not as an individual but as a representative of a community who sees him as having sacrificed his life for it. It is a narrative envelope that grants meaning infused with relief and support. The mother of a daughter killed in a terror attack said "We tried to think of her as a soldier, although she had not yet been drafted. A soldier who had fallen in the unending war between the people of Israel and those plotting against our existence" (Elichai, 1982).

The Gatekeepers of Hegemonic "Loss—Regime" and the Monopoly of Meaning Following Loss

The coalition formed to counter these claims by the families of terror casualties included heads of military bereavement organizations, members of the National Council for Commemoration of Soldiers, Knesset Members, Ministry of Defense personnel, and current and veteran senior army officers whose common interest was to maintain the exclusivity of the framing of the "Israeli casualties of war" category as consisting exclusively of those who lost their lives as soldiers and, in doing so, to maintain the monopoly on eligibility for gaining collective meaning for the loss of family members. The themes promoted by this coalition served to reproduce the hegemonic representation of Israel's fallen soldiers as having necessarily died under operational, heroic, productive circumstances.

A senior Ministry of Defense official insisted on the need to maintain the distinction between civilian and soldier: "We view the question of who wore a uniform and who did not as an educational and moral matter of the utmost importance . . . those who wear the uniform must be respected and the only way to do so is by ensuring a clear distinction between the memory of IDF casualties and that of all others" (Amior, 2011). The same message was voiced by many Knesset members, from the political left and right alike, such as Knesset member Tamar Gozanski: "This is an educational message: were you wearing a uniform, or not, were you protecting your country and died, or were you unlucky to be in a certain place and you died? . . . if we blur these boundaries, we undermine our beliefs" (Amior, 2011). A central difference between civilian and soldier, as expressed by officials, is that fallen soldiers who are commemorated are only those whose deaths were characterized by productiveness and heroism—a death having allegedly taken place in the battlefield, during combat, while consciously risking one's life. As can be clearly seen from the words of the head of the IDF Widows Organization at the time: "The soldiers were called to battle knowing that they might not return home. They set out to fight to protect the people and the State. In terror attacks innocent civilians were walking in Jerusalem . . . and a murdering terrorist came and killed them. How can this be a part of the heroism of Israeli casualties of war? The war in Dizengoff vs. the war in the battlefield? These are incomparable . . . how can we compare our fallen soldiers to a person killed in a café?" Many officials define the difference between civilians and soldiers by a meta-frame that frames every fallen soldiers as having necessarily knowingly risked his life in action: "It is difficult to refer to the three women who sat in Café Apropo as 'warriors'" said Knesset member Shaul Yahalom. "There should be no mixing between people who served for their country and in their death ordered us to live, and those who, despite all our sorrow, were walking in the street and found their death" explained the chairman of the *Yad LaBanim* organization. "It is impossible to compare a warrior to a person walking the street when an atrocious terrorist exploded a bomb that caused his death. He did not volunteer to risk his life, he did not volunteer to serve . . . he is in another framework and thus deserves another treatment," said professor of philosophy Asa Kasher, himself a bereaved father of a soldier and the writer of the IDF's first code of ethics (Keidar, 2006).

Image Versus Reality

However, in reality, a study of IDF casualties points to a different reality than the heroic, combatant, and productive image that most people hold. As Israel increasingly advances into a reality of the new wars and post-heroic challenge, the number of IDF soldiers serving in combat positions has been steadily declining. In 2010, only 20% of serving men were serving in combat roles (Arad, 2010), a fact that clearly impacts the circumstances in which soldiers die. Between 1990 and 1999, only 14% of the soldiers killed and recognized as IDF casualties died in "operational action," a category that also includes soldiers killed in weapons accidents, training accidents, terror attacks, or tragedies such as fires, road accidents, etc. A committee appointed to examine data from 2000 to 2009 found that 20% of soldiers deceased during these years were killed in operational action, while the rest died from illness (44%), suicide (15%), and other causes (Goren, 2014). A review of

2006–2015 conducted in another study found similar figures: during these years, only 18% of deceased soldiers were killed in operational action, while 23% committed suicide, 21% died of illness, and 13% died in road accidents during leave. If we look only for deaths that occurred during battle—which is in fact the category that defines heroic death—we see that only 18% of all soldiers who died during these years died in action (Yoeli & Yoeli, 2017).

Loss Reframing Steps

The work of Israeli Terror Casualties' Families toward reframing the loss of their loved ones has led to considerable achievements that, although they did not result in their inclusion in the Israeli casualties of war meta-frame, did in fact promote a positioning within the continuum between anonymous civilian casualties and public ones framed by the security forces. These steps can be defined as *loss reframing steps*, mostly expressed in the institutionalization of ceremonial practices held in parallel with those pertaining to IDF casualties and their families. These "reframing steps" described here consist mostly of decisions reached by a public committee headed by former Supreme Court Judge Yaacov Melz (Melz Committee, 2000) appointed in 1998 to form the memorialization and rehabilitation policy for terror victims and their families (Government Decision 4505, st/120, November 26, 1998) alongside a number of additional policy initiatives developed in later years. It should be noted that the committee itself consisted of a majority of representatives from military bereavement organizations and the security establishment.

1. *Ceremonies.* As of 1999, it was decided that 1 hour before the opening of the official national ceremony commemorating Israel's casualties of war—a ceremony broadcast live on national TV and radio—a ceremony would be held to commemorate terror casualties. In parallel to the Minister of Defense honoring the ceremony commemorating Israel's casualties of war with his presence, it was decided that the ceremony to commemorate terror casualties would be held in the presence of the Minister of Welfare (Government Decision 4902 st/123, March 11, 1999). In 2000, it was decided that the Minister of Defense and the Prime Minister would also be present in this ceremony and that it would be held at 13:00 hours (Government Decision 1587 st/39, April 27, 2000).

2. *Funerals.* IDF soldiers are buried in a military ceremony, accompanied by a military guard and a predefined military ceremony. In funerals to terror casualties, it was decided that government ministers would be present, but with no official army or security forces presence. It was further decided that the graves of terror casualties would be provided by the state and would have a uniform design, similar to graves of IDF soldiers, but without the army emblem.

3. *Names of the fallen.* Every fallen IDF soldier is commemorated in the *Izkor* book, a collection of biographies and photographs of the fallen, published once every few years by the Ministry of Defense. In addition the name and details of each fallen soldier can be seen on the website of *Yad LaBanim* in the soldier's home town or city, and his picture is displayed on the commemoration walls of these local branches. In addition, as of 1994, slides with the names of all IDF fallen soldiers are consecutively shown on a special TV channel throughout Memorial Day. For terror casualties it was decided that parallel but separate steps would be taken: their names would also be collected and commemoration books would be published with their photographs and a number of biographic details about them, but these would be produced by the National Insurance Institute and would have a cover of a different color than the cover of the *Izkor* books in memory of the fallen soldiers. Their names would also be displayed on Memorial Day. However, they will not be chronologically fitted in between the names of IDF soldier but shown separately afterward. The most meaningful decision was to change the official name of Memorial Day, and here, too, the differentiation between the two bereavement communities became clear: from "Memorial Day for the Fallen Soldiers of Israel" to "Memorial Day for the Fallen Soldiers of Israel and Victims of Terrorism." This was to the detriment of the families of terror victims who would have preferred the name not be changed but rather that their loved ones would be recognized as an integral part of the group "Israeli casualties of war," thereby defining the struggle of the rear as a "war" and comparing the sacrifice made by soldiers to that demanded of civilians. The request by the families to establish museums in memory of their loved ones, similarly to *Yad LaBanim* branches to be found in every city, were not accepted, nor was their request to allocate special cemetery plots for the casualties, similarly to military plots established in cemeteries around the country.

4. *Terror victims' families.* To the detriment of the families, they were not recognized as part of the families eligible for rehabilitation by the Ministry of Defense, but remained under the responsibility of the National Insurance Institute. However, at the institute, they were separated from departments managing families who experienced loss under civil circumstances such as work accidents, road accidents, or murder, and they began to be handled by a newly established department: the Victims of Hostilities division, dedicated to accompanying families of victims murdered by terrorists. A slow process led to these families receiving the same social benefits as families of fallen soldiers. For instance, only in 2010 were they allowed official leave of absence from their work places on Memorial Day, just like families of fallen soldiers.

5. *Commemoration of victims.* Similarly to the central memorial site dedicated to IDF fallen soldiers inaugurated in 2018 at Mt. Herzl in Jerusalem, which had been a work in progress for decades and which commemorates the names of all IDF fallen soldiers, in 1997, the Israeli government decided on the establishment of a "Central memorial site for civilians having fallen in hostilities and terror attacks, as a sign of solidarity with their families and a monument to those murdered by atrocious terrorists, in the State's struggle against terror" (Government Decision 1549, st/28, February 5, 1997). While representatives of the IDF's bereavement organizations were thankful that terror victims were not to be included in "their" memorial site, they protested the use of the word "fallen," which they argued should be used only to describe soldiers. This and similar debates postponed the establishment of the site. Moreover, the Melz Committee, whose recommendations were later adopted by the Israeli government, stated that an initiative should be embarked upon to identify the names of all terror victims (contrary to IDF fallen soldiers; up to that time there had been no organized and comprehensive registry) and that these names would be engraved on a separate memorial wall to be erected at Mt. Herzl (Government Decision 4505, st.120, November 26, 1998). The families of terror victims were disappointed by the decision to maintain the separate memorialization and even petitioned the Supreme Court to force the state to include their loved ones in the military casualties commemoration site, but the court rejected their demand (Supreme Court ruling 3017/12, 2013) and the site remained

and will remain in future a space exclusively commemorating fallen
IDF soldiers.

Conclusion

As the political struggle in the region gradually transforms into a "new war"
taking place mainly in the civil rear, the number of terror victims in Israel
has steadily increased. As tragic as this is, the growing presence of families of
victims and the growing public exposure to the fact that the heroism of the
post-heroic era takes place in the rear have enabled this community to more
effectively promote its aspirations by transforming the official treatment of
their loss and obtaining recognition and appreciation comparable to that
given to families of fallen soldiers (Lebel, 2013, Lebel, 2014(.

To obtain the resource that they value most—national meaning for their
loss and trauma—the families of terror victims did not ask to establish a
unique or separate victimized identity for themselves but rather to be perceived as an inseparable part of the "families of Israeli casualties of war," a
community recognized by the Israeli public as holding a meta-frame that
leads to the perception of their loved ones as having died during productive
operational action (Nuttman-Shwartz et al., 2010). However, this perception is very far from the reality in which slightly fewer than 20% of all fallen
soldiers actually die in operational or combat circumstances (Lebel, 2013).

The quest for meaning is also expressed in the very fact that the families of
terror victims were disappointed with proposed legislation that would ensure
they receive financial benefits and support identical to those given to parents
of fallen IDF soldiers, the only difference being that they would be provided
by institutions that are not part of the Ministry of Defense. In Israel the ultimate meaning of loss is granted based on belonging to the category of "Israeli
casualties of war" and being handled as a family by the Ministry of Defense,
which in turn serves as a sort of "gallery" that attests to the aesthetic value of
the works of art displayed in it based on the very fact that they are displayed
there. Hence, the institution marks its customers as being perceived under the
meta-frame that grants them national meaning.

The families' attempts to "enter" the same meta-frame as families of fallen
soldiers were supported by the fact that, gradually, the Israeli public began
to realize that not all those framed as fallen soldiers actually died under
circumstances that justify such framing. There is a parallel action here—an

attempt to reframe the death of their loved ones while in parallel casting doubt on the moral eligibility of those who have achieved this framing and have been granted national meaning to their loss.

This can be further explained based on the insights made by Gamson and Lasch, who investigated the circumstances in which governments respond to policy demands on welfare matters. They found that these demands are adopted when they correspond with what they referred to as a "meta welfare package" (Gamson & Lasch, 1981). Clearly, as long as the new wars continue to take place, increasing numbers of nonmilitary groups are expected to demand recognition, appreciation, and national meaning to their sacrifice for civic strength and national security.

From the viewpoint of the investigative discourse on rehabilitation from loss and, most of all, on that of obtaining a "sense of meaning" (Oishi & Diener, 2013), in this chapter we attempted to expand the theoretical psychosocial field to include theories on discourse. Furthermore, we attempted to discuss the mutual effects between the sociocultural level and the individual-therapeutic one on matters involving rehabilitation and recuperation from loss. This is a further example of effective sociotherapeutic (rather than psychotherapeutic) interventions following trauma (Jeansen et al., 2015). This approach may serve to improve an individual's condition following interventions carried out within the public discourse and, most importantly, in the community as part of a growing school of thought on the formation of a discursive narrative and rehabilitative-therapeutic process (Waters, Holttum, & Perrin, 2014). Finally, we have raised a number of basic insights pertaining to the growing body of knowledge on the sociology of meaning (Neimeyer, 2001; Saito, 2014) that are yet to find their worthy place in the social study of rehabilitation from loss.

Highlights

- The many families of Israelis killed and wounded in organized terror attacks against civilians in the aftermath of the Oslo Accords and the 2000 Intifada began to function as a "memory community" aiming to include their loved ones among the country's national fallen—a category referred to as "Israeli casualties of war"—and then as a policy community as their organization began to represent their aspirations in the political and security arenas.

- In Israel, a seemingly technical-institutional decision—whether a bereaved family would be cared for by the Ministry of Defense or by the National Insurance Institute—in fact dictates whether the deceased is commemorated on the private or public level.
- Families of "Israeli casualties of war" gain precedence over bereaved families who are not cared for by the Ministry of Defense in three main aspects, each of which contributes to the ascription of meaning to their loss: commemoration, rehabilitation, and discourse.
- The families of terror casualties began to promote narrative themes that would frame their loved ones side by side with the IDF's fallen soldiers and themselves alongside the IDF's bereaved families who are handled and rehabilitated by the Ministry of Defense.
- They acted to clarify the reasoning behind their refusal to be positioned differently by becoming a part of the national heroics granting its members collective meaning for their loss.
- The coalition formed to counter these claims by the families of terror casualties aimed to maintain exclusivity of the framing of "Israeli casualties of war" as consisting exclusively of those who lost their lives as soldiers and, in doing so, to maintain the monopoly on eligibility for gaining collective meaning to the loss of their family members.
- The work of Israeli Terror Casualties' Families toward reframing the loss of their loved ones has led to considerable achievements or *loss reframing steps*, mostly expressed in the institutionalization of ceremonial practices held in parallel with those pertaining to IDF casualties and their families.

Acknowledgments

The authors wish to thank Ms. Yael Nachumi for her contribution to the manuscript. Her professional editing and insightful comments were a valuable contribution to its maturation and finalization. big thank you to the editor of Oxford Publishing Ms. Poonguzhali Ramasamy for her professional and kind work and supervision in producing the chapter. Our utmost gratitude is extended to Judith Levy, Eyal Hanan, and the workers of the archives in which we collected a vast amount of documents: the National Security Archive, the

Knesset Archive and the Archive of the Maariv daily newspaper. We wish to thank Ms. Tikva Levi from the Israeli National Security for her assistance, to, Ms. Esther Gliechman—The Bar-Ilan University Social Science' Library Manager, for her great support in the era of covid-19, and finally—as always— a huge Thank you Ms. Osnat Cohen, the Director Division Of Hostile Action, the Israeli National Security: On constant sensitivity, professionalism, and understanding the importance of research in shaping social and national policy.

References

Amior, H. (2011, May 6). One for all. *Israel Today*. [Hebrew]

Arad, B. (2010). *Israeli professional army*. The Jerusalem Institute for Market Research. [Hebrew]

Azulai, A. (1992). On the possibility of existence of critical art in Israel and its condition. *Theory and Criticism, 2*, 89–117. [Hebrew]

Bandler, R., & Grinder, J. (1982). *Reframing: Neuro-linguistic programming and the transformation of meaning*. Real People Press.

Bar-Moha, Y. (2001, March 6). Due to a missile attack on Israel. *Haaretz*. https://www.haaretz.co.il/misc/1.684354. [Hebrew]

Ben-Ari, E. (2005). Epilogue: A "good" military death. *Armed Forces and Society, 31*(4), 651–664.

Bruce, J. (1992). The university, democracy and the challenge to meritocracy. *Interchange, 23*(1-2), 19–23.

Clarke, G. (1998). Non-governmental organizations (NGOs) and politics in the developing world. *Political Studies, 46*(1), 36–52.

Cordova, M. J., Cunningham, L. L. C., Carlson, C. R., & Andrykowski, M. A. (2001). Posttraumatic growth following breast cancer: A controlled comparison study. *Health Psychology, 20*(3), 176–185.

Coyne, J. C. (1985). Toward a theory of frames and reframing: The social nature of frames. *Journal of Marital and Family Therapy, 11*(4), 337–344.

Cronin, B. (2013). Reckless endangerment warfare. *Journal of Peace Research, 50*(2), 175–187.

Davis, C. G., Wohl, M. J. A., & Verberg, N. (2007). Profiles of posttraumatic growth following an unjust loss. *Death Studies, 31*, 693–712.

Desrosiers, M. E. (2015). Tackling puzzles of identity-based conflict: The promise of framing theory. *Civil Wars, 17*(2), 120–140.

Dew, A. J. (2014). Inspirational, aspirational and operational heroes: Recruitment, terror and heroic conflicts from the perspective of armed groups. In S. Scheipers (Ed.), *Heroism and the changing character of war* (pp. 237–250). Palgrave Macmillan.

Doka, K. (1999). Disenfranchised grief. *Bereavement Care, 18*(3), 37–39.

Dunmore, E., Clark, D. M., & Ehlers, A. (2001). A prospective investigation of the role of cognitive factors in persistent Posttraumatic Stress Disorder (PTSD) after physical or sexual assault. *Behaviour Research and Therapy, 39*(9), 1063–1084.

Elichai, H. (1982, July 14). Letter to the editor. Haaretz.

Eyre, A. (2007). Remembering: Community commemoration after disaster. In H. Rodríguez, E. L. Quarantelli, & R. R. Dynes (Eds.), *Handbook of disaster research* (pp. 441–455). Springer.

Fairclough, N. (2003). *Analyzing discourse: Textual analysis for social research*. Routledge.

Fraser, B. (1990). An approach to discourse markers. *Journal of Pragmatics, 14*(3), 383–398.

Gal, G. (2002). The indemnification principle in the social security system for people with disabilities in Israel and its implications. *Work, Society and Law, 9*, 115–143. [Hebrew].

Gamson, W. A. (1992). *Talking politics*. Cambridge University Press.

Gamson, W. A. (1995). Constructing social protest. In H. Johnston & B. Klandermans (Eds.), *Social movements and culture* (pp. 85–106). University of Minnesota Press.

Gamson, W. A., & Lasch, K. E. (1981). *The political culture of social welfare* (CRSO Working Paper Num. 242). Center of Research on Social Organization, University of Michigan.

Gerrish, N., Dyck, M. J., & Marsh, A. (2009). Post-traumatic growth and bereavement. *Mortality, 14*(3), 226–244.

Gillies, J., & Niemeyer, R. A. (2006). Loss, grief and the research for significance: Toward a model of meaning reconstruction in bereavement. *Journal of Constructivist Psychology, 19*, 31–65.

Goffman, E. (1951). Symbols of class status. *British Journal of Sociology, 2*(4), 294–304.

Goren, A. (2014). *The public committee for assessing eligibility for support from the rehabilitation divisions*. Prime Minister's Office, Jerusalem. [Hebrew]

Government Decision 1549 (st/28), February 5, 1997. [Hebrew]

Government Decision 1587 (st/39), April 27, 2000. [Hebrew]

Government Decision 4505 (st/120), November 26, 1998. [Hebrew]

Government Decision 4902 (st/123), March 11, 1999. [Hebrew]

Gurr, T. R. (1968). A casual model of civil strife. *American Political Science Review, 62*, 1104–1124.

Gurr, T. R. (1970). *Why men rebel*. Princeton University Press.

Halvorsen, R. (2001, November 2-4). *Active citizenship and social mobilisation among social security claimants in Western Europe* [Conference presentation]. COST A13 Conference on Social Policy, Marginalization and Citizenship, Aalborg University, Denmark.

Hastings, S. O., Musambira, G. W., & Hoover, J. D. (2007). Community as a key healing after the death of a child. *Communication and Medicine, 4*(2), 153–163.

Hensell, S., & Gerdes, F. (2017). Exit from war: The transformation of rebels into post-war elites. *Security Dialogue, 48*(2), 168–184.

Jansen, S., White, R., Hogwood, J., Jansen, A., Gishoma, D., Mukamana, D., & Richters, A. (2015). The "treatment gap" in global mental health reconsidered: Sociotherapy for collective trauma in Rwanda. *European Journal of Psychotraumatology, 6*(1), 1–6.

Kalafatis, S. P., Tsogas, M. H., & Blankson, C. (2000). Positioning strategies in business markets. *Journal of Business & Industrial Marketing, 15*(6), 416–437.

Katz Y. (2007). *Heart and stone: The story of the military tombstone in Israel 1948–2006*. Ministry of Defense Publishing House. [Hebrew]

Keidar, N. (2006, May 1). *Wars of bereavement* [documentary film]. Yes Docu Channel. [Hebrew]

Kent, T. (1991). On the very idea of a discourse community. *College Composition and Communication, 42*(4), 425–445.

Kimmerling, B. (1993). Patterns of militarism in Israel. *European Journal of Sociology, 34*, 109–202.

The Knesset. (1982, January 21). Protocol of the Labor and Welfare Committee Meeting, the 10th Knesset, Knesset Archive. [Hebrew]

The Knesset. (1982, May 10). Hearing on the Local Authorities Law—waiver of municipal tax to soldiers injured by war and to police forces. [Hebrew]

Kromer-Nevo, M. (1999). What's your story? *Society and Welfare, 19*(3), 282–301. [Hebrew]

Lambert, P. and Mallett, R. (2007). Introduction: The heroisation-demonisation phenomenon in mass dictatorships. *Totalitarian Movements and Political Religions, 8*(3-4), 453–463.

Lebel, U. (2013). Unrecognized loss—anti-hegemonic bereavement and a renewed framing of trauma: The relative deprivation experience of families of terror victims in Israel. In H. Shanun-Klein, S. Kreitler, & M. Kreitler (Eds.), *Thanatology: The study of loss, dying and bereavement: Selected topics* (pp. 207–242). Pardes Publishing House. [Hebrew]

Lebel, U. (2014). "'Second Class Loss': Political Culture as a Recovery Barrier? - Israeli Families of Terrorist Casualties and their Struggle for National Honors, Recognition and Belonging", *Death Studies, 38*(1), 9–19.

Lebel, U. (2016). Casualties. In P. Joseph (Ed.), *SAGE encyclopedia of war: Social science perspectives* (275–276). Sage.Lebel, U. (2016). "The 'Immunized Integration' of Religious-Zionists within Israeli Society," *Social Identities* 22(6), 642–660.

Lee, A. V. Y., & Tan, S. C. (2017). *Temporal analytics with discourse analysis: Tracing ideas and impact on communal discourse*. In LAK '17 Proceedings of the Seventh International Learning Analytics & Knowledge Conference (pp. 120–127). Simon Fraser University of Southern Queensland.

Liebman, C. S., & Don-Yehiya, E. (1983). *Civil religion in Israel*. University of California Press.

Lyotard, J. F. (1984). *The postmodern condition: A report on knowledge*. University of Minnesota Press.

Mathes, C. (2006). *And a sword shall pierce your heart: Moving from despair to meaning after the death of a child*. Chiron Publications.

Matthews, L. T., & Marwit, S. J. (2006). Meaning reconstruction in the context of religious coping: Rebuilding the shattered assumptive world. *Omega, 53*(1–2), 87–104.

McCullough, M. E., Emmons, R. A., & Tsang, J. (2002). The grateful disposition: A conceptual and empirical topography. *Journal of Personality and Social Psychology, 82*, 112–127.

Melz Committee. (2000). *The Committee for Commemorating and Rehabilitating victims of terror and hostilities and their families, headed by retired Supreme Judge Jacob Melz*. The Prime Minister's Office, Jerusalem. [Hebrew]

Minister of Defense. (2017). *Letter to bereaved families from the Minister of Defense*. IDF Archive.

Ministry of Finance. (2018). *Budget Proposal for fiscal year 2019: Security—Unclassified matters* (Book 30). Jerusalem. [Hebrew]

Morgan, P. (2009). I was there too: Memories of victimhood in wartime Italy. *Modern Italy, 14*(2), 217–231.

Murphy, R. (1984). The structure of closure: A critique and development of the theories of Weber, Collins, and Parkin. *British Journal of Sociology, 35*(4), 547–567.

Neimeyer, R. A. (1998). *Narrative strategies in grief coping*. McGraw-Hill.

Neimeyer, R. A. (2001). *Meaning reconstruction and the experience of loss*. American Psychological Association.

Neimeyer, R. A. (2006). Complicated grief and the quest for meaning: A constructivist contribution. *Omega, 52,* 37–52.

Neimeyer, R. A., Prigerson, H. G., & Davies, B. (2006). Mourning and meaning. *American Behavioral Scientist, 46,* 235–251.

Neimeyer, R. A., & Stewart, A. E. (1996). Trauma, healing, and the narrative employment of loss. *Families in Society, 77,* 360–375.

Nuttman-Shwartz, U., Lebel, U., Avrami, S., & Volk, N. (2010). Perceptions of suicide and their impact on policy, discourse, and welfare. *European Journal of Social Work, 13*(3), 1–18.

Oishi, S., & Diener, E. (2014). Residents of poor nations have a greater sense of meaning in life than residents of wealthy nations. *Psychological Science, 25*(2), 422–430.

Orr, J. J. (2001). *The victim as hero: Ideologies of peace and national identity in postwar Japan*. University of Hawaii Press.

Park, C. L., & Ai, A. L. (2006). Meaning making and growth: New directions for research on survivors of trauma. *Journal of Loss and Trauma, 11,* 389–407.

Parry, A., & Doan, R. E. (1994). *Story re-visions: Narrative therapy in the postmodern world*. Guilford Press.

Rimmerman, A., & Araten-Bergman, T. (2010). Victims of hostile acts in Israel and the United States: Comparable policy review. *Journal of Comparative Policy, 12*(3), 251–274.

Robson, P., & Walter, T. (2013). Hierarchies of loss: A critique of disenfranchised grief. *Omega, 66*(2), 97–119.

Rudrum, D. (2005). From narrative representation to narrative use: Towards the limits of definition. *Narrative, 13*(2), 195–204.

Rynearson, E. K. (Ed.). (2006). *Violent death: Resilience and intervention beyond the crisis*. Routledge.

Saito, C. (2014). Bereavement and meaning reconstruction among Japanese immigrant widows. *Pastoral Psychology, 63*(1), 39–55.

Sandler, T. (1992). *Collective action: Theory and applications*. University of Michigan Press.

Sawicka, M. (2017). Searching for a narrative of loss: Interactional ordering of ambiguous grief. *Symbolic Interaction, 40*(2), 229–246.

Shahak, M. (2017). *Data on Israeli casualties of war and victims of hostilities 1947–2017*. The Knesset, Research and Information Center, Knesset Archive. https://www.knesset.gov.il/mmm/data/pdf/m04124.pdf [Hebrew]

Shostak, A. (1973). *Knesset Protocols 1973*. Knesset Archive. [Hebrew]

Snow, D. A., & Benford, D. B. (1992). Master frames and cycles of protest. In A. D. Morris & C. M. Mueller (Eds.), *Social movement theory* (pp. 122–151). Yale University Press.

Spector-Mersel, G. (2010). Mechanisms of selection in narrative identities claims. In L. Kasen & M. Kromer-Nevo (Eds.), *Data analysis in qualitative research* (pp. 63–96). Ben Gurion University of the Negev. [Hebrew]

Stroebe, M. S., & Schut, H. (2001). Meaning making in the dual process model of coping with bereavement. In R. A. Neimeyer (Ed.), *Meaning reconstructing and the experience of loss* (pp. 116–134). American Psychological Association.

Supreme Court ruling 3017/12. (2013). The Organization of Victims of Hostilities vs. the Prime Minister and others, February 4, 2013. [Hebrew]

Taylor, C. (1994). The politics of recognition. In A. Guttmann (Ed.), *Multiculturalism: Examining the politics of recognition* (pp. 25–73). Princeton University Press.

Tomich, P., Helgeson, V., & Nowak, V. (2005). Perceived growth and decline following breast cancer: A comparison to age-matched controls 5 years later. *Psycho-Oncology, 14*(12), 1018–1029.

Unger, Y. (2010). *Does the extent of support of military casualties depend on the circumstances of the injury?* Research and Information Center, the Knesset. [Hebrew]

Wang, L. (2016). Counter-discourses and alternative knowledge. *Journal of Inquiry and Action in Education, 7*(1), 18–35.

Waters, K., Holttum, S., & Perrin, I. (2014). Narrative and attachment in the process of recovery from substance misuse. *Psychology and Psychotherapy, 87*(2), 222–236.

Watzlawick, P., Weakland, J. H., & Fisch, R. (1974). *Change: Principles of problem formation and problem resolution.* W. W. Norton.

Weaver, H., & Heartz, M. (1999). Examining two facets of American Indian identity: Exposure to other cultures and the influence of historical trauma. *Journal of Human Behavior in the Social Environment, 2*(1–2), 19–33.

Wellman, B. (1988). Structural analysis: From method and metaphor to theory and substance. In B. Wellman & S. D. Berkowitz (Eds.), *Social structures: A network approach.* (pp. 34–67). Cambridge University Press.

White, J. (2005). *Global media: The television revolution in Asia.* Routledge.

Winter, M. J. (1995). *Sites of memory, sites of mourning: The Great War in European cultural history.* Cambridge University Press.

Yoeli A., & Yoeli Y. (2017). The budget book revealed: Almost a quarter of IDF casualties - due to suicide. *Srugim*, April 29, 2017. https://www.srugim.co.il/174066-%25D7%2597%25D7%259C%25D7%259C%25D7%2599- %25D7%25A6 %25D7%2594%25D7%259C- %25D7%2591%25D7%2592%25D7 %259C%25D7%259C- %25D7%2594%25D7%25AA%25D7%2590%25D7 %2591%25D7%2593%25D7%2595%25D7%2599%25D7%2595%25D7%25AA. [Hebrew]

Zamir, A. (Ed.). (1952). *After the death of heroes.* Personal publication. [Hebrew]

Zur, Y., Mendelewitz, Y., & Kerman, R. (2006). The disappearance of mention of civilian victims from the public discourse. *Maamarim* website: www.mamarim.co.il\565454\ tzur;kjghi. [Hebrew]

PART III

DEVELOPMENTAL PROCESSES AND CHALLENGES IN THE ISRAELI SEARCH FOR MEANING

5

In Search of Meaning and Holy Redemption

The Case of the Hilltop Youth in the Occupied West Bank

Samuel (Muli) Peleg

Introduction: A Meeting at a Jerusalem Courthouse

As a young teaching and research assistant in the Hebrew University of Jerusalem, I was asked to cover the trial of the so-called Jewish Underground in the summer of 1984. Twenty-seven Jewish settlers, some of them very prominent members of their communities, were accused of the most severe crimes in the law books: murder, attempted murder, causing grievous bodily harm, and membership in a terrorist organization. Eagerly, I entered the Jerusalem Courthouse on the first day of the proceedings at the exact moment the defendants were ushered in by their prison guards. One after another, chained to one another by their ankles and wrists, the bustling group was momentarily halted to alert the judges of their arrival.

I took advantage of the surprising opportunity and advanced toward defendant number 3, Shaul Nir, whom I knew briefly through a neighbor who grew up with him in Netanya. The prisoners were guarded so sparsely anyone could have approached them in that moment. I stood face to face with Nir, who was accused of killing three Palestinian students in the Islamic College in Hebron. "Shaul," I asked him, vacillating between being a friend-of-a-friend and a researcher of political violence, "what's going to happen to you now?" "Don't worry," reassured me the handcuffed murderer with a broad smile, "the people are with us." Nir was 24 at the time, and he was sentenced to life in prison, a sentence that was controversially commuted three times by then President Herzog. He was released along with his colleagues after serving less than 7 years.

Samuel (Muli) Peleg, *In Search of Meaning and Holy Redemption* In: *Finding Meaning.* Edited by: Ofra Mayseless and Pninit Russo-Netzer, Oxford University Press. © Oxford University Press 2022. DOI: 10.1093/oso/9780190910358.003.0005

This odd brief conversation at the entrance of the Jerusalem Court of Justice aptly reflects one of the strongest motivations to join an extremist group and become violently active: the need for group support, approval, and reverence. I was not the only guest at the Courthouse that morning. It was packed with the defendants' extended families, friends, and colleagues from the embracing settlers' community. The atmosphere was cheerful as greetings and encouragements filled the air. At times, it looked and sounded like a huge picnic with fathers handing out sandwiches and mothers consoling toddlers. Nothing resembled a situation in which cold-blooded killers were about to be sentenced for the crimes they committed. For Nir and his friends, the occasion was an invaluable opportunity to present their worldview and justify their deeds, broadcast live to the entire nation and abroad. The public exposition of their position reveals another motivation crucial to extremists: obtaining vindication and recognition of their unattended needs.

The Case of the Hilltop Youth: Extremism Unbound

This chapter highlights extremism and radicalization of youth as a quest for meaning and purpose in life. The analysis probes the motivations and incentives that attract young activists to radical ideologies, rebellious lifestyles, and violent behavior. The Jewish Underground was a forerunner that stirred inspiration and excitement among younger generations of mavericks and eccentrics who, just like the convicts of the early 1980s, felt that, due to what they perceived as severe social and political circumstances, they must diverge from the mainstream of Religious Zionism and establish their own unique version of Jewish redemption. These circumstances, as these disaffected young adults interpret them, are the fear of losing the holy lands of their forefathers in any future peace process with the Palestinians and the impotence of the Israeli authorities to curtail Palestinian violence. More broadly, they challenge the ability and sincerity of the Zionist State, which is largely secular, modern, and Westernized to ever implement their vision of a Jewish theocratic kingdom (Aldrovandi, 2014; Pedahzur & Perliger, 2009).

The media termed them the "Hilltop Youth," referring to their geographical locale—the desolate hills and knolls of Judea and Samaria, in which they concentrated in makeshift communities and in total defiance and disregard for Israeli law or the indigenous Palestinians. Although the radicalization process of these young religious Zionist activists stems from a confluence of political, historical, cultural, and religious incentives, this chapter brings to the fore the sociopsychological enticement of young militants searching for meaning, a sense of belonging, and a sense of purpose in a precarious age of tumult and uncertainty. They are motivated by an acute feeling of estrangement and depravity that urges them to establish a new collective identity and a new social grouping.

The determination of the deprived and their disillusion with the system's ability to accommodate them create a kind of "affinity of the unprivileged," which gathers them into consolidated subsystems, thereby challenging the original super system, the state. The deprived discover their primordial, unencumbered connections and begin to be aware of their power versus the state's formal-juridical ties. These groups, which congregate around organic and ascribed parameters, not achieved ones, are identity groups of a special kind, the revitalized identity group kind (Peleg, 2003). A revitalized group is an extremist group motivated by the force of a desire to rebuild the whole complex of social and political relations around it, holding to a holistic point of view of a better future, in contrast to the depressive present situation. Hilltop Youth defiance is by no means a unique phenomenon to Israel or to Judaism. It is a case study of an extreme maverick group with a deep conviction to uproot the status quo due to their moral superiority over everyone else. Similar unconditional fervor propelled and galvanized extremist groups in disparate countries and cultures at various times. Unwavering zealots such as the KKK, the Red Brigades, the Taliban, or the Alt Right, despite vastly dissimilar beliefs and motivations, are motivated by a tenacious quest for meaning with dire political circumstances far beyond their own personal transformation.

Their estrangement is further augmented by a profound feeling of victimization. Some young religious Zionists perceive themselves as the victims or dupes of the Zionist state. Seventy years of independence and 120 years of Zionism have not mitigated the inherent tension in the heart of the Israeli Jewish population regarding such fundamental precepts as the nature of their state, their society, and their mission. During the seven decades of statehood, the cleavages gradually deepened as an intrinsic incongruity between religious and secular visions of redemption became intolerable. The tension between the preferential status of Jews and the democratic equality of all citizens stood out from the outset and generated two competing images of Zionism: Israeli nationalism and Jewish nationalism (Kimmerling, 1999; Ram, 1999; Ravitzky, 1996).

Thus, the initial grievance of religious Zionism emerged from a sense of deception: they relinquished conservative Judaism, which rejected Zionism as interference with God's planning, in favor of an activism they thought would precipitate redemption. But, to their dismay, the biggest realization of the venture they embarked on—the inception of a Jewish state—was snatched out of their hands by nonbelievers. While the old generation of religious Zionists seemed obsequious, their mostly *Sabra* (Isreli born) posterity felt betrayed and anxious to change their predicament. This sense of alienation peaked with the jubilation of the 1967 War and the ensuing disillusionment of the 1973 war. Gush Emunim, the ideological precursor to the Hilltop Youth (unlike the Jewish Underground, its activist inspiration), was born as the Settlers' Movement, defying and daring the Israeli government with every move. Their major task had been ensuring and accelerating the pace of settlements in Judea and Samaria (Peleg, 1997).

Half a century has elapsed since the Block of the Faithful first launched their indelible effort. But the passage of time transformed them from rebels to mainstream and from mavericks to establishment functionaries. The Hilltop Youth, born and bred on the Gush's legacy, felt betrayed: they experienced the same fears their predecessors felt, but, in their perception, the Block's veterans became part of the problem. And the major problem now has become the Zionist state: not the Palestinians, not the peace camp, and not the Labor Party, but the state itself. What the Hilltop Youth envision is a theocratic polity, a renewed Kingdom of David in Judea and Samaria (Feige, 2009; Friedman, 2015). This is their sense of purpose, their reason of being. Everything that stands in the way of this aspiration is an enemy. All in all, their activists number several dozens of tenacious and unwavering true believers who reside in improvised dwellings in the deserted hills of the West Bank. They challenge the authority and rules of the state and perceive the confrontation with the authorities as part of the cosmic struggle between good and evil. It is also a part, they believe, of the inevitable Pangs of the Messiah experience, harbinging his immanent arrival. The rebellious spirit of the Block of the Faithful was conferred to the Hilltop Youth, but they expanded it beyond militant political opposition to an all-out rejection of the system.

From the agent perspective, the Hilltop Youth represent a relentless search for meaning and purpose in the wilderness of secularism, modernism, and materialism. Forsaken by their disappointing role models, they ardently seek a new direction for fulfillment, a sense of accomplishment that would cultivate their collective identity and self-esteem. Their reclusive state of being is akin, in their eyes, to the living style of the biblical prophets or the Tribes of Israel when they first inherited the Land. For these young extremists (ages range from 13 to 23), this is an initiation ceremony, a coming of age, becoming part of the army of redeemers. This is a tremendous spiritual and self-transcendent undertaking in which they are unified with God and nature on the top of those barren hills. They take pride in their naturalist, nativist, and self-sufficient existence, nourishing and cherishing a pristine, almost primordial persistence. But they are far from being a bunch of innocent "peaceniks": their political agenda, galvanized by messianic militancy, is set for an ultimate collision course with the Israeli government.

The next section supplies the broader context for the Hilltop Youth phenomenon as religious Zionist youngsters on a quest for new horizons or a new set of norms and rules to redefine their society. It attempts to highlight the theoretical underpinnings of the search for meaning qualified by two parameters: acute change of circumstances and the age group of the meaning seekers. Both are germane to the example of the Hilltop Youth.

The Correlates of Seeking Meaning: Shifting Circumstances and Youth

The search for meaning in life has long been a distinctive desire of people all over the world. Since psychiatrist Viktor Frankl masterfully articulated the concept in his seminal work *Man's Search for Meaning* (1964), the saliency of this pursuit has intensified due to the vagaries and vicissitudes of the modern and post-modern world (Bauman, 2001a, 2001b, 2002, 2003, 2006). These uncertainties accrued because of a combination of weakening traditional bases of meaning such as family, community, and religion alongside rampant tendencies of individualism that encouraged self-efforts in discovering personal meaning. Those two opposing trends were further augmented by the disillusion of progress and knowledge as supplying happiness and rationale for the human experience. Instead, angst and insecurity generated by the complexity of a multilayered reality and overbearing information took over, rendering the quest for meaning increasingly urgent (Crawford & Rossiter, 2006).

If, as Frankl staunchly believed, the search for meaning is a fundamental human drive that constitutes the essence of being human, then this is a

perpetual and ongoing task. Similar thoughts are echoed in Maslow's famous hierarchy of needs (1943, 1954), in which, above the basic needs of
physiology and safety, there are the psychological and self-fulfillment needs
of belonging, esteem, and self-actualization. These upper level wants drive
and stimulate the exploration of meaning. However, not all people are engaged in the pursuit of meaning in their lives, and even those who are do
not indulge in it to the same extent, scope, and intensity. Thus, if the urge for
meaning is generic, what accounts for those differences? Are there times or
circumstances that are more acute and susceptible, perhaps more ripe and
suitable, for a conscientious journey into the significance of human existence? Is there a relevant or appropriate age that lends itself more eagerly to
such a tremendous undertaking?

As this chapter suggests, the answer to both these queries is affirma-
tive: there are possibly typical conditions and circumstances that expedite
the search for meaning, and there is a specific age that is more predisposed
toward embarking on an expedition for new values and morals. More specifically, a search for meaning becomes more pertinent and valid once existing
meanings—narratives, images, or associations—are in crisis or threatened. It
is more likely that the "truth-seeker" population would be composed of relatively young participants, anxious to find order and stability in a crumbling
world and optimistic or naïve enough to trust that their mission is feasible
and imminent.

Change in Circumstances and Age as
Propelling the Search of Meaning

Sudden or unexpected shifts in circumstances or certain age susceptibility are by no means the only catalysts to embark on a quest for meaning.
However, in the case of the Hilltop Youth, due to the acute turbulence in their
hitherto secure and stable environment and, obviously, due to their young
age, these two correlates—severe variations and adolescence—become strik-
ingly influential.

Change of Circumstance
Change of circumstances is most intensely felt when an entire culture is
undergoing a transformation of norms and values. When a whole universe
of symbols, rituals, attitudes, and references is shaken and conventional

truths and ultimate convictions gravitate, people desperately seek out reassurances. A scramble for solid veracities and comforting certainties begins. All-encompassing narratives and large-scale validities are in widespread demand. Absolute accounts and mythologies that are difficult to refute are vehemently and excitedly adopted (Janoff-Bulman, 1992; Madsen et al., 2001; Ruthven, 2004).

The collapse of familiar structures of truth leaves individuals puzzled and insecure. If truth becomes harder and harder to ascertain, the onus of finding alternatives falls on the individual. Lacking the capacity to investigate what was previously handily supplied, the individual must arduously carve her or his access to symbol resources, cultural references, and venues of dialogue through contact with others. Faith-based communities, with their protected reservoirs of indisputable belief, are the natural havens to absorb the disconcerted. They furnish and cultivate a shared code of meaning so severely lacking at this precarious time of turmoil. These close-knit communities offer a base platform of certainty within safe controlled spaces, in which shared omnipotent truth, vouched for by the word of a charismatic leader and the sense of fellowship of being among kindred spirits, gather individuals together. This procedure of finding reassurance within a community yields "a group closing in upon itself and falling back on 'bunker values' or 'refuge identities,'" (Hervieu-Léger, 2006, p. 68). Giddens's *existential isolation* reflects a similar notion, which is less a corollary of "a separation of individuals from others [than] a separation from the moral resources necessary to live a full and satisfying existence" (1991, p. 9).

Grappling with a godless and individualistic order or worse, the predicament of drifting in a normative void with contingent values and relative standards is conceivably very troubling and disheartening for true believers to cope with. Under such conditions, seeking new and fulfilling meaning becomes a life-saving enterprise. A major priority of this pursuit is how to counter the ominous agnosticism of meaning fueled by cultural post-modernity: Can a reliable meaning be established in the face of rampant qualms and relativism? In such a fluctuating landscape of meanings, what are the nature and role of truth? Does truth still matter? The post-modern uncertainty about meaning beckons an anchor to steady the course of a turbulent journey. Three significant parameters of meaning—a sense of identity, a sense of purpose, and a sense of belonging—lose their orbit and go haywire under such conditions. This is the definitive breeding ground for venturing a meaningful change.

Age

George Bernard Show once lamented that "Youth is such a wonderful thing. What a sin to waste it on children." Sociologists have translated this unfortunate mismatch as youth's immaturity and moral imbalance that leads to reach wrong conclusions and a wish to fervidly act upon them. Jack Goldstone, a leading scholar of political activism and violence, argues that youth have played a prominent role in political violence from the English Revolution to the Revolutions of 1848 and that the existence of a "youth bulge"—an exceptionally large youth cohorts—has historically been associated with times of political unrest (1991, 2001). Moller has associated economic depression plaguing German youth in the Weimar Republic with the upsurge of Nazism in Germany in the 1930s (1968, pp. 240–242). Other scholars identified young males as most likely to engage in criminal activities (Neapolitan 1997, p. 92; Neumayer 2003, p. 621) and political violence (Elbadawi & Sambanis 2000, p. 253; Mesquida & Wiener, 1996). Some have attributed the belligerence of young adult males to high male sex hormone levels (Goldstein, 2001; Hudson & den Boer, 2004, pp. 193–195). Whatever the reason, the connection between adolescence and extremism is thought-provoking and tenable.

Various scholars representing disparate approaches of developmental psychology found search for meaning as the central and most perplexing developmental task for young people (Mason, 2006; Webber, 2002). Some scholars link this task with hope and the feeling that the future is bright and that goals are feasible (Bronk et al., 2009; Burrow, O'Dell, & Hill, 2010; Feldman & Snyder, 2005). Kroger (2003), relying on Erikson's notion of life cycles and *emerging adulthood* (Erikson, 1959; Erikson & Erikson,1997), focuses on identity and how it is shaped by young adults. Expanding on Erikson's observations, she suggests that identity is molded by a fusion of a person's psychological needs and social recognition and attention within a specific historical context. That is, one's quest for identity becomes a priority at the interface between internal urges and external conditions such as instability and crisis (Cote & Levine, 2002; Shotter & Gergen, 1989).

Essentially, young people in modern societies find themselves in a quandary: the culture around them extols individualism. So does the commercial world, which promotes individualism as a marketable commodity. But disproportionate individualism might lead to loneliness and isolation, emasculate a sense of community, and generate excessive pressure on adolescents to reconcile between those two incompatible orientations.

Such characteristics of young adults—immature life scheme, rebellious-ness, alienation, the urgent need for an alternative support group, and vac-illating between individualism and group support, independence and dependence—coalesce into a profile of tenuousness and insecurity that might yield intemperate and unrestrained behavior. In its more militant and defiant facet, the juvenile mindset and inclinations were referred to as a *sub-culture of resistance* (Foucault, 1975; Hebdige, 1979; Muggleton & Weinzierl, 2003; Skott-Myhre, 2008). Eric Hoffer (1967) recognized this fragility in his astute observation of the tumultuous 1960s: "If a society is to preserve sta-bility and a degree of continuity, it must learn how to keep its adolescents from imposing their tastes, values, and fantasies on everyday life."

The combination of dire circumstances and young age can indeed be vul-nerable to extremist mindsets and rebellious deeds. But is religion a pro-pitious setting for this precarious meeting between a rapidly changing environment and a volatile age cohort? Can faith be the stronghold, the cata-pult, and the reassurance for a restless and uncompromising pursuit? If so, in what ways does it harbor the true believers and supply them with sustenance and hope?

Religion and the Search for Meaning

Religion as a whole, as an impeccable system with symbols, images, rituals, moral codes, and behaviors, offers a coherent and comprehensive universe of meaning. It has an omnipotent creator, linearity, clear dichotomies of believers and infidels, virtues and vices, and, most of all, a perfect antithesis to the ambivalent and morally dubious modern and secular world. There is no relativity, contingency, or speculation in religion. Meaning is not ephem-eral or capricious; it is permanent, everlasting, perpetual, and hence, uplifting and empowering. In short, religion is a bountiful source by which to discover and embrace alternative meanings of life. Sociologists and anthropologists of culture and religion such as Campbell, Shils, Parsons, Geertz, and others have analyzed religion as a system of meanings fraught with unique terminolo-gies, narratives, images, codes, and symbols. Inspired by Parsons and Shils's (1951, 2007) cultural approach to the study of religion, Geertz highlights reli-gion as denoting "an historically transmitted pattern of meanings embodied in symbols, a system of inherited conceptions expressed in symbolic forms by means which men communicate, perpetuate and develop their knowledge about and attitudes toward life" (1973, p. 89). Later in his classic book he adds that the religious perspective is a particular way of looking at life, a particular manner of construing the world (1973, p. 110). Religion as a framework that structures all aspects of life is consuming and all-encompassing. It is so imposing and substantial that "men have earnestly affirmed and contradicted almost every idea and form of conduct" in its name (Johnson, 1959, p. 47).

Yet the pursuit of meaning does not have to be religious or violent. It can assume other courses, such as embarking on a new professional career, joining a thrilling book club, discovering an unknown frontier, or volunteering for a noble social cause. The specific case of the Hilltop Youth describes fanatic youngsters who turn to religion and violence in pursuit of significance and purpose. Why? What might render a blend of religiosity and radicalism the fulcrum of a juvenile search of meaning?

Perhaps it is the intrinsic nature of religion, where the propensity to extremism and dissent coexists with the craving for guidance and unity; the yearning for redemption and harmony with the penchant for contention and violence (Clarke, 2017; Selengut, 2017). It is this Janus-faced disposition of religion—the unifier and the divider—that makes it conducive for seeking meaning through defiance and vehemence (Peleg, 2003). The fundamental reading of religion, the absolute and unequivocal, instills affirmation and verification in impressionable young hearts. To the loyal disciples, it promises transformation from dissatisfaction to fulfillment, or at least an earnest attempt to do so. Wallace suggests that the historical origin of most religious movements has actually been in revitalization movements torn or split from their parent religion after failing to invigorate it from within. As such, religion is a very appropriate backdrop for enticing and energizing. As he describes it, all religions are "relics of old revitalization movements, surviving in routinized forms in stabilized cultures, and that religious phenomena per se originated... in the revitalization process—i.e., in visions of a new way of life by individuals under extreme stress" (1956, p. 268).

Still, religious convictions, even the most ardent and devoted, are not instantaneously tantamount to aggression and ferocity. The relationship between religious belief and violent lawlessness needs to be more profoundly probed. In essence, there is a cognitive incongruity in this association: How can the notion of religion, the definitive perception of the good, be so intimately entangled with vigor and brutality? For the current generation, this is not merely a philosophical contemplation but a daily callous reality, nourished by ruthless and bloody religiously motivated global violence. It is further enhanced by a long and gory history of religious wars with a horrific human toll, which continues almost unabatedly from the days of the Scriptures to the Twin Towers and the appalling atrocities of ISIS. This legacy instigates a genuine sense of bewilderment and incomprehension: Is this nexus between religious beliefs and forceful behavior inherent to the content or structure of faith, and, if so, in what way? If violence is not intrinsic to spiritual convictions and devotion, then who created such an affinity and for what purpose (Peleg, 2012)?

In Israel, religious protagonists play in the political arena and they seek political goals. They utilize religious terminology and symbols to mobilize supporters. The Settlers' Movement has always used messianic visions and images of imminent redemption to entice and inveigle their followers. Promoting political goals by religious means has been usefully depicted as the *politicization of religion*. At its heart lies the age-old quest for power disguised as a sacred mission of the pious to stave off the forces of evil. However, in a fascinating reversal of the traditional wisdom, Antoun (2001), Juergensmeyer (2004), Lindstad (2006), Herriot (2009), and Ivanescu (2010), among others, pointed out an opposite trend—the *religionization of politics*. In this inverted relationship, the language and symbols of politics are utilized to advance religious goals. Missionary leaders, avid proselyters, and campaigning shamans exploit the political arena to recruit masses for their religious crusades and holy confrontations. There they use political catchphrases and slogans to generate images of good versus wickedness, the faithful and the infidel, and the relentless tenacity worthy of the eternal cosmic collision between the forces of good and all the rest (Appleby, 2000; Gopin, 2000; Juergensmeyer, 2004; Rapoport, 1984; Sprinzak, 1991).

As it swells and intensifies, it becomes the religionization of life, not merely of politics. The religionized life and mundane reality generate an inconsistency that must be resolved. The incongruity between the law of God (natural law) and the law of the land (positive law) was one of the major incentives galvanizing the Hilltop militants into action. They regarded the secular law as temporary and expedient until it collided with their faith; then the former became an obstacle to be swiftly, strictly, and totally (i.e., violently) removed. Unrestricted faith comes to the rescue by invoking violence as a potent tool, encouraging and spurring "the need, the duty, indeed the divine command to slay the Amalekites, to stone the sinner, to put heretics to the torch, nonbelievers to the sword. From these passions, from the wounds of these severances, great streams of blood have flowed" (Isaacs, 1975, p. 153).

Roots of Lawlessness: The Inspiration of the Hilltop Youth

The Hilltop Youth case study is emblematic of adolescents seeking for new and provocative meaning in a transcendent and spiritual fashion. Adolescents are caught between existential needs of autonomy and independence, on the one hand, and the pressure to conform to societal norms and doctrines, on the other (Muncie, 1999; Vigil, 1988). The strenuous transition from childhood to adulthood is structured by societal norms and traditions that dictate stages, directions, and pace, including various thresholds marked by symbolic ceremonies and initiation rites (Barry & Schlegel, 1980; Turner, 1997). However, during times of turmoil and upheaval, such as those experienced in the aftermath of the disengagement from Gaza in the summer of 2005 and the clash over Amona in the winter of 2006, this journey to maturity and ripeness becomes more intense and ferocious "since the social anchor, which is meant to assist the adolescent in the search for his/her identity, is less stable and may leave the youth, who is on a journey towards maturity, bereft of the support and comfort of the clear social models provided by the previous generation" (Friedman, 2015). The social system that was supposed to supervise, mitigate, and smooth their passage to adulthood was rejected by these youngsters due to its perceived failures and incapacities. Unabated and unrelenting, the graduation process persisted, albeit in drastic and sweeping routes, with a new agenda, role models, and ambitions.

Unlike other rebellious youth operating in different social and cultural contexts, the rebellion of the Hilltop Youth in Judea and Samaria was not instigated by socioeconomic deprivation or colonial oppression. It was chiefly an acute distrust of the political and social situation augmented by a fierce sense of national-religious superiority and entitlement. As Friedman (2015) notes, "The combination of these two elements comprises the significant components that influence the construction of a fundamentalist protest which finds expression in innovative positions presented to society by these young people." Their breakaway from their former ideological and religious background—namely, the Settlement Movement and Gush Emunim as its activist compass, as well as from the Israeli establishment—is not only symbolic, psychological, and emotional. It is also physical and geographical. They have selected and delineated an exclusive behavioral space for themselves, their own little kingdom, in which they exercise an austere and nativist lifestyle, coupled with a biblical-style dress, a cultural affinity to nature, and a stern practice of fundamentalist Halachic law (Kaniel, 2004). The

Hilltop Youth used to have a role model, a movement to emulate, and heroes to worship. That movement was Gush Emunim (*the Block of the Faithful*) and its idols, the pioneers and outlaws who deserted comfort and security to illegally and brazenly settle the land taken by Israel in the 1967 War. The Hilltop Youth is composed of second- and third-generation settlers, the offspring of Gush's activists.

However, there is a major difference between the two generations: Gush Emunim still saw the state of Israel and its government as a legitimate source of power and authority, even at times of heightened tensions and severe disagreements with it. The Gush operated within what Shelef (2010) calls an "evolutionary model" of playing simultaneously within and outside the political system. They brilliantly mastered the corridors of power as well as the barricades of extra-parliamentarism. In their calculated long-term ambition to keep the West Bank and Gaza under Israeli control, Gush Emunim leaders meticulously adapted themselves to shifting political circumstances by positioning themselves as a political balancing tip. But for that they occasionally paid the price of muting their real demands: "Gush Emunim's engagement in politics, specifically its desire to ensure Israel's hold over the territories . . . unintentionally led to the institutionalization of the truncated map image of the homeland" (Shelef, 2010, p. 78). The radicalized successors of the Gush would have none of that: they would drop out of the Israeli political system altogether.

Early dissenters from the Gush Emunim's strategy were leaving their mark in the early 1980s with the aforementioned Jewish Underground and other, small-scale unrestrained violent deeds against Palestinians. One of the most dangerous of these groups, more so in its fervid ideology that in its actual deeds, was the movement of the Temple Mount. In his insightful study of this group, Inbari (2009) proclaims that they still exist on the fringes but are exerting growing influence on mainstream religious Zionism as well. Gradually but surely, the author admonishes, these trends and moods penetrate and radicalize the entire political scene. Although currently marginal on the Israeli political scene, Inbari nevertheless cautions about the movement's "inherent potential for subversion and violence" and their creeping influence on the broader religious population since their moral and stimulating influence far exceeds their inner circles. Religious messianism and fundamentalism is contagious.

Similarly to Rapoport (1984), Sprinzak (1991), and Peleg (1997), Inbari believes that the growing appeal of religious extremism in Israel is due to a theological crisis, or a failure of faith, as he terms it, which forms the stimuli for the expansion of extremism and radicalization. He observes a "psychological dissonance" (p. 53) experienced by the religious Zionists between their desired and actual realities. The crisis has been developing gradually, from the missed opportunity to inherit the biblical contours of the Promised Land after what religious Zionists believed to be a divine intervention in the triumph of the 1967 War, the affliction of the 1973 Yom Kippur War, and the following concessions of the peace treaty with Egypt (1978), the Oslo Accords (1992), the Geneva peace proposal (2003), and, ultimately, the disengagement from Gaza in 2005. All these hardships, the religious fundamentalists believe, are meant to test their resilience and loyalty to their faith, and, hence, their reaction is to strengthen their radical approach of activism and their tenacity to pursue the most maximalist goals.

The religious Zionist establishment is caught in a "Messianic dilemma" that curbs its capacity for marginalizing zealots: it is very difficult for them to negate or annul a basic premise of their own thought—messianic salvation. The extremists demand religious perfection, and how could the official leadership reject such a claim? Thus, half-heartedly they tacitly accepted the radicals in their midst hoping that militancy would not blow over in their faces. The Temple Mount activists, on the other hand, maintain a "very delicate balancing game" (Ibid, p. 48): they walk a very fine line between what is forbidden and what is permitted. Hence it is still funded by the religious establishment but it is not a part of it and cannot be coerced or preempted by it. This situation is convenient for the religious authorities as well because they can continue supporting the Temple Mount institute while publicly and officially denouncing its extreme actions.

As the millennium drew to a close, Religious Zionism found itself on the brink of an unprecedented ideological crisis. Its leaders could not ignore the "Messianic dilemma" any longer. The invigorated young generation was pushing to a significant junction of decision: either to rigorously educate Zionist seculars about the meaning of "true Zionism" or divorce from Zionism, which had really been secular to begin with and thus mistaken and misguided. The latter option, the post-Zionist option, was espoused by the maverick and eccentric zealot Yehuda Etzion. Etzion, whose inexorable fanaticism led him to become defendant number 2 of the infamous Jewish Underground culprits list and jail, is perceived as a prophet and a revered role model among the young generation of religious Zionists. As such, he has become untouchable, and the religious establishment is disinclined to ostracize him and the views he expresses. Disregarding extremism in their midst has become even more alarming for religious Zionism when Etzion and others inspired by him began promoting an all-out confrontation with the Israeli government, criticizing the religious establishment's refusal to enter the Temple Mount as preventing an effective struggle against the state (Inbari, 2009, p. 54).

The real concern is how widespread is this trend of religious radicalization epitomized by Jewish militant messianism that was once considered hallucinatory and far-fetched? How effective are its exponents, and what is their future potential? Inbari frames it in operational terms.

> In what circumstances can the movement no longer maintain its position of reconciliation vis-à-vis the world and must it move to a mode of assault? In what conditions can the movement no longer conform to the secular regime? (Inbari, 2009, p. 164).

His answer is not comforting: more and more of the religious Zionist camp experience "a religious crisis due to the government's decision to uproot settlements. As a result, theocratic and revolutionary sentiments can find roots within the hearts of many followers" (p. 165). Instead of being marginalized, the extremists became catalysts who radicalized the mainstream. They became pioneers who tested the possibility boundary, the tolerance of the religious establishment, and, ultimately, the state. Meanwhile, on the sidelines, adolescents who were soon to pack up their knapsacks and run to the hills were admiringly listening and taking notes.

The Hilltop Youth: The Advent of a Movement

A systematic in-depth analysis of the Hilltop Youth phenomenon is yet to be written due to its relatively short duration. Early attempts to theoretically grapple with this subject were made by Feige (2009), Friedman (2015), and Kaniel (2004). Most of the scant material written on the maverick youngsters is to be found in newspapers and magazine articles by reporters and commentators. This doesn't mean it is trivial or inconsequential. On the contrary: it gives the reader a visceral and raw glimpse of the worldviews and living conditions of these juvenile eccentrics dissidents.

One of such stirring account came from Tomer Persico, a scholar of religions who wrote about his encounter with the hilltop youngsters in the Israeli newspaper *Ha'aretz* in January 2016. Persico observes a romantic streak in the adolescents he met in the barren land of Judea. He found their rebellious spirit to be driven by a search for authenticity: the need to be more righteous than the previous generation. The existing system of rules and regulations they grew out of is weak, they maintain. It stifles their creativity, uniqueness, and truth. It subdues genuine identity, and therefore it must be dissented. Such were the exemplifying themes Persico identified with the activists he met: nativity, the search for self, desire to get closer to nature, disdain from the pleasures of modernity, and living on the edge. One youth is quoted as admitting that he was nourished in the bosom of religious Zionism, but he grew to despise it as obsolete, irrelevant, and detached from the new devout experience of cultivating the land, herding sheep, self-sustenance, and unit pride. Finally, a surprising revelation "the Ultra-Orthodox model of creating an uncompromising autonomy within the godless Israeli State, fit us like a glove." This is an astounding statement from the progeny of religious Zionism who traditionally disassociated themselves from the anti-Zionist and obstinate Ultra-orthodox.

A couple of months earlier, in another Israeli newspaper, an interview was published with a 26-year-old Hills resident, Eliashuv Har-Shalom (Eldad, 2015). He expressed similar ideas about breaking away from mainstream Zionism and heralding a new and more authentic path to the Jewish redemption. His precise words are stark and harsh:

There [were] always those who sacrificed themselves on the altar of truth, ready to pay the price, and these fellows are ready to pay the price. But the question is: Where does this place us as a society? We are not "wild weeds," we are fruit-giving trees. You raised us. Suddenly you are dissociating yourselves from us? Suddenly we are not part of you?

Then he pinpoints his anguish and bitterness at specific antagonist. The "you" becomes clear and indisputable.

What is Zionism? We don't know what "Zionism" means anymore. I understand the people who distance themselves from the term, because now it's like being "next to" or "just like" the real thing. I know what Zionism used to be—draining swamps and Beit Hadassah in Hebron. But if being a Zionist is to apologize for your very existence, *then there's a question whether I am a Zionist.* Today we are spitting in the face of Zionism. True Zionists would not have turned "nationality" into asterisks on the ID card. (emphasis added)

A New Sense of Meaning

The fervor of the Hilltop Youth is prodded by their yearning for a self-expression that deviates from and disassociates with their larger community. In fact, the very departure from the embrace of religious Zionism is the main feature of their newly established identity. They fortify and embellish their novel affiliation and sense of meaning by blatantly disentangling themselves from the "mothership" of the institutionalized settlers' establishment and venture the iconoclastic pastures of anti-Zionism as reflected by the state and government of Israel and everything symbolizing them, including Israeli law, policies, and the military. The isolation of these militant youngsters on the top of desolate mounts, sometimes under deplorable condition, is not merely physical but symbolic and spiritual. Detached and remote from the excesses of modern life but also from the yoke of their former familial, communal, social, and educational obligations, they are free to celebrate and nourish their rebellion in purity and harmony with their environment. Under such terms they can earnestly "consider themselves to be the only ones who are truly faithful to Torah and God" (Persico, 2016).

It is important to note though, that the revolt of the Hilltop Youth is against their educators but not against their education. The values, beliefs, and "truths" they were taught—ardently settling the Holy Land of the Forefathers, strict halakhic observance, and superiority over the nonbelievers, especially the Palestinians—are enthusiastically kept, only in a more passionate and un-adulterated manner, as they claim. In light of ominous developments around them, such as the secularism and modernity that compromise the resolve of Israel, democratic institutions and procedures which intervene with and undermine God's plan for the Chosen people, and the political concessions of giving up on what they deem as holy territories that herald the advent of the Messiah, the zealotry of the Hilltop Youth is invigorated and revitalized almost to the point of complete rupture from Israeli society.

The hilltops of Judea and Samaria began to be populated by renegade youngsters veering off their peer groups' and regular youth movements' camping and hiking tracks in the early years of the new century. However, the trigger event that rendered these groups of "weirdos," as the media and the public referred to them, operative in organized violent and illegal activities was the Israeli evacuation of the Gaza Strip in August 2005. Prime Minister Sharon's policy of disengagement from Gaza meant not only the complete withdrawal of the Israeli army but also the removal of all Jewish settlements. Although the Religious Zionist establishment, inside and outside the institutional political system, vowed to thwart the plan by invoking massive protest in the streets, the departure from Gaza occurred with relative tranquility. This event was a traumatic turning point for young idealists of the Settlement Movements who couldn't comprehend how could such calamity, as they understood it, happened under the auspice of their own government and military. The catastrophe of the disengagement indicated something else, something more severe and long-term from the radical young settlers' perspective: religious Zionism's failure to infiltrate the hearts and minds of most Israelis. At the time of its implementation, the disengagement initiative won relatively high approval rates among Israelis, around 70% (Pan, 2005).

Additionally, the fairly smooth undertaking of evicting nearly 9,000 people from their homes alarmed the settlers and made them fear that their deterrence power had worn out. Despite a highly invested and rigorous campaign on their part, the ideological settlers' camp failed miserably in mobilizing the critical mass of Israelis to stop the Gaza retreat. The exhilarating hopes for debilitating civil disobedience to erupt along with considerable conscientious objection campaigns among Israeli soldiers to refuse orders faded rapidly (Weisburd & Lernau, 2006). An unsettling and dreadful realization began to sink in that a terrible precedent had been set for Israeli decision-makers to authorize a later withdrawal from the West Bank due to the empowering consent they witnessed with the Gaza disengagement experiment. This was a doomsday scenario that accelerated and expedited extremist tendencies, especially among splinter groups that were disillusioned with the mainstream Settlers' Movement as being too idle, conservative, and acquiescent to begin with. The rift with the traditional leadership of the Settlement Movement became unbridgeable. The young radicals disavowed themselves from their allegiance to the "elders." They despised their strategy of trying to befriend the secular Israelis and charm them into acceptance. The positive slogans that the settlers' campaign used, such as "we have love, and it will triumph," were defeatist and counterproductive (Feige, 2009, p. 256). In this foreground of despair, fear, and profound disappointment from the

Israeli-Jewish populace, a spirit of rejuvenation and reconstruction was born based on denunciation and refutation of the old along with a spiritual journey to discover new and exciting meanings of Judaic revival. A revival that meant going back to the times of the profits and kings of Judea, of the judges and hermits, who roamed the inhospitable hills and deserts abided only by God and the Torah, not by politicians and public opinion. The immediate goal of the now full-fledge rebellious camp was to do whatever it took, violence included, to prevent the next pullout from the historical heritage bequeathed to them through the generations.

It became clearer to the Israeli policy-makers and the general public that new political players had joined the public arena and that their methods, unlike Gush Emunim's, were exclusively extra-parliamentary, illegal, and illegitimate. The Israeli government realized it had to assert control over groups that no longer respected the state or traditional settler leadership. The challenge of the Hilltop Youth loomed even larger because "mainstream Israeli society has become more apathetic than ever about the fate of the Palestinians. Negotiations between Israel and the Palestinians remain deadlocked, and even their meaningful resumption, let alone success, seems unlikely in the near future. [Under such circumstances], the Israeli government . . . feels little political or diplomatic pressure to confront the extremists" (Byman & Saches, 2012).

The first opportunity to announce their existence as an organized political actor came to the Hilltop Youth shortly after the disengagement from Gaza. In February 2006, the government was preparing to demolish several houses at the illegal outpost of Amona, near the Palestinian town of Ramallah. The post was erected without legal authorization, in violation of Israeli law. Although only nine structures were destroyed in Amona, the incident escalated to a major violent clash between resisting youth and police forces (Myre, 2006). The difference from the relatively quiet and much larger in scope retreat from Gaza only six months earlier was in "the casting": the leaders during this resistance episode were young activists who rejected the "Old Guard" rabbis' reticence in confronting the government (Nir, 2011, p. 7). They successfully amassed and encouraged thousands of activists to violently oppose a large force of Israeli police officers, pelting the officers with rocks, bricks, and metal bars. Hundreds of settlers were injured, as well as scores of police officers, many more than those injured during the Gaza disengagement (Myre, 2006, p. 12). This was the initiation ceremony of the Hilltop Youth into the Israeli political scene, and they made it with a big bang.

Four days after the event, on February 5, the Head of the Shin Beit (Israeli Internal Security Agency), Yuval Diskin, warned the Israeli Cabinet ministers that he was witnessing a "process of rift" between the settlers and the state. He noted that some of the settlers had carried signs that read "In war we will prevail," and "It is Jews who build and Israelis who destroy" (Sofer, 2006). In the insurgents' eyes, although the Amona standoff culminated in the failure of not being able to save the settlement, in the long-run, it was a resounding success. As one of the leaders of the Amona resistance and Parliament Member Uri Ariel later wrote in an article published in the national religious daily *Hatzofe*: "A Defeat That Is All Triumph" (Ariel, 2007).

The logic for this inverse reading of the actual events was simple: the vehement opposition of the Hilltop Youth created a precedent that deterred the government from further dismantling illegal posts. Ariel keenly observed that "the form of the battle in Amona has presented the military and the police with an intolerable price-tag" (Ariel, 2007). Amona became a symbol of determination and readiness to sacrifice for the cause and supplied dozens of renegade youth, disheartened and adrift from their former ideological haven, with a new and enlivening breakthrough to live for. In the following years, impromptu camps of young activists mushroomed all over the West Bank. Their locations were not accidental: they sprang strategically and systematically around illegal settlement posts to resist and obstruct any attempts to remove them. They became a very efficient and dynamic small-scale army consisting of scores of young militants who found their destiny in hindering the policies of their own state. As time elapsed and atrocities continued with impunity, hilltop extremists felt invincible. According to Israeli human rights organizations, "of 781 incidents of settler abuse monitored since 2005, Israeli authorities closed the cases on over 90% of them without indictment" (Byman & Saches, 2012).

Promptly, invigorated by their accomplishments and encouraged by their new generation of extremist leaders, the young activists moved from defensive resistance and protective strategies to the attack. To amplify their deterrence approach, some young militants began to avenge any efforts to curb Jewish settlement activities by hurting Palestinians or damaging Palestinian property. At times, Israeli police officers and soldiers and even left-wing intellectuals and reporters were threatened and physically attacked. At the scenes of these attacks, graffiti insignia denoting the perpetrators were left, echoing the Ariel's warning from his article: *Price-Tag*.

Conclusion

The search for meaning intensifies in times when meaning is deemed obscure or lost. Thus, it is imperative to probe the context in which such endeavor emerges. Throughout this chapter, the pursuit of meaning and purpose were mentioned together, as one undertaking. However, they are not synonyms. According to Damon, Menon, and Bronk (2003), purpose is a "stable and generalizable intention to accomplish something that is at once meaningful to the self and leads to productive engagement with some aspect of the world beyond the self." There is an important distinction here between meaning as internally and individually motivated and purpose as externally and socially motivated. In other words, *purpose* signifies an intention to operate on a larger scale beyond the self, in pursuit of a larger cause on behalf of others. Consequently, if looking for meaning might be a common undertaking among individuals beginning their life journey, assuming purpose is more ambitious and includes a desire to have an impact on the broader world. This passion is a formidable motivational force for purposeful individuals.

Viktor Frankl (1964), analyzing it as part of a high-level belief system, identified purpose as that which enabled people to endure hardships and as playing a significant role in overcoming life's challenges. This is particularly resonating with regards to youth: Erikson (1968) finds that purpose helps young people successfully navigate and resolve their identity "crises." Other studies echoed similar findings, such as a strong correlation between a sense of purpose and collective moral action (Noblejas de la Flor, 1997; Shek, Ma, & Cheung, 1994) and with greater commitment to social and political activities (McAdams, 2001).

The case of the Hilltop Youth demonstrates a vigorous blend of meaning and purpose: an individual pursuit of identity and content coupled with the shouldering of social roles and responsibilities bestowed by a higher being or a social group. This is a commanding combination since it brings together an inexorable and indomitable sense of agency (will) along with group allegiance and guidance (way). Bronk et al. in their study of purpose in three different age groups summarized this.

> Having an identified purpose might prove unavailing if one lacked knowledge of how to enact one's purpose or if one lacked the requisite sense of Agency to pursue it. In other words, having the "will" may be important, but knowing "the way" may be decisive. (2009, p. 501)

The Hilltop youth militants have the will and they were bequeathed a way. They have perceived the evacuation from Gaza as a manifest failure of the old guard's approach. Not only was the state of Israel no longer a vehicle of redemption; it had actively rolled back the most important project of contemporary Jewish religious nationalism: settling the Land of Israel. The settlers felt doubly betrayed by the sense that the government failed to reintegrate them properly into Israel, devoting inadequate resources to their relocation and, in their eyes, essentially neglecting them after the withdrawal ended.

Faced with what the radical settlers saw as a choice between the state and the settlements, they picked the latter. To stave off another disengagement of any kind, they resolved to retaliate against any attempt by the Israeli government to crack down on the movement—hence the birth of the Price-Tag attacks. In this climate, the traditional leadership of the Settler Movement and the authority of the Israeli government are less relevant than ever.

"Price Tag" became a code name for a series of violent, criminal acts of vigilantism, carried out by young illicit agitators who sought to destabilize the precarious situation in the West Bank and demonstrate the feebleness and incompetence of the government, as well as of their own social system, to master their irreverent behavior. In their audacious behavior, the Hilltop Youth relied on a new kind of religiosity they carved for themselves: the kind of fundamentalism that goes literally back to the roots of a pristine and humble existence. They reshaped and reconstructed their self-image as the "new settlers" who find their spiritual place in the "wilderness" of Judea and Samaria (Friedman, 2015; Sheleg, 2000). They earnestly hope that by their activism and militancy they will prepare the ground and thus advance the cataclysmic "end of days" collision. Then, and only then, the Messiah will return and reestablish the Kingdom of David. These self-proclaimed redeemers have managed to compensate for the emptiness in their hearts with the most fulfilling and worthy endeavor of all: expediting divine redemption by removing some of the earthly obstacles in its path. This is a tremendous undertaking: daunting but also empowering, emboldening and uplifting. It is a heartening and strengthening task emblematic of people who seek and find identity and purpose in life; a sense of fulfillment that can explain the broad smile on the face of a convicted killer.

Highlights

- The Hilltop Youth epitomize a revitalized extremist group driven by a fervent desire to usher in a holistic new future on the ruins of what is perceived by them as a totally failing system.
- Such an extreme maverick group with a deep conviction to uproot the status quo due to its moral superiority over others can be found in disparate countries and cultures at various times.
- The Hilltop Youth's specific rage was initially incurred by their frustration and disillusionment with the Zionist state that, in their view, betrayed Jewish redemption by becoming secular, modern, and conciliatory toward Palestinians.
- This chapter provides a psychological explanation of the Hilltop Youth's anguish and violent activism, beyond the familiar political and religious narratives. The group represents a relentless *search for meaning and purpose* in defiance of secularism, modernism, and materialism. As such, they ardently seek a new direction for fulfillment, a sense of accomplishment to bolster their collective identity and self-esteem.
- It is surmised that there are possibly typical conditions and circumstances that expedite the search for meaning and that there is a specific age group that is more predisposed toward embarking on an expedition for new values and morals.
- Certain interpretations of religion offer an ample setting for seeking meaning. The fundamental reading of religion, the absolute and unequivocal, instills affirmation and verification in impressionable young hearts. It encourages transformation from dissatisfaction to fulfillment.
- The Hilltop Youth adhered to the most extremist and zealous religious interpretation. They applied their messianic conviction to their activism against Palestinians in the West Bank and, through their violent activities, created a new and liberating meaning for themselves.

References

Aldrovandi, C. (2014). *Apocalyptic movements in contemporary politics: Christian and Jewish Zionism.* Springer.

Antoun, R. (2001). *Understanding fundamentalism: Christian, Islamic, and Jewish movements*. Rowman and Littlefield.

Appleby, S. (2000). *The ambivalence of the sacred*. Rowman and Littlefield.

Ariel, U. (2007, January 22). A defeat that is all triumph. *Hatzofe*.

Barry, H., & Schlegel, A. (1980). Early childhood precursors of adolescent initiation ceremonies. *Ethos, 8*(2), 132–45.

Bauman, Z. (2001a). *Community: The search for security in today's world*. Polity.

Bauman, Z. (2001b). *The individualized society*. Polity.

Bauman, Z. (2002). *Society under siege*. Polity.

Bauman, Z. (2003). *City of fears, city of hopes*. Goldsmith's College.

Bauman, Z. (2006). *Liquid times: Living in an age of uncertainty*. Polity.

Bronk, K. C., Hill, P. L., Lapsley, D. K., Talib, N., & Finch, H. (2009). Purpose, hope, and life satisfaction in three age groups. *Journal of Positive Psychology, 4*, 500–510.

Burrow, A., O'Dell, A., & Hill, P. (2010). Profiles of a developmental asset: Youth purpose as a context for hope and well-being. *Journal of Youth and Adolescence, 39*(11), 1265–1273.

Byman, D., & Saches, N. (2012). The rise of settler terrorism: The West Bank's other violent extremists. *Foreign Affairs, 91*(5): 73–86.

Clarke, S. (2017). *Competing fundamentalisms: Violent extremism in Christianity, Islam, and Hinduism*. John Knox Press.

Cote, J., & Levine, C. (2002). *Identity formation, agency, and culture: A social psychological synthesis*. Erlbaum.

Crawford, M., & Rossiter, G. (1996). The secular spirituality of youth: Implications for religious education. *British Journal of Religious Education, 18*(3), 133–143.

Damon, W., Menon, J., & Bronk, K. C. (2003). The development of purpose during adolescence. *Applied Developmental Science, 7*(3), 119–128.

Elbadawi, I., & Sambanis, N. (2000). Why are there so many civil wars in Africa? Understanding and preventing violent conflict. *Journal of African Economies, 9*, 244–269.

Eldad, K. (2015, November 12). Hilltop youth: "We are not 'wild weeds', you raised us." *Ma'ariv*.

Erikson, E. (1959). *Identity and the life cycle*. International Universities Press.

Erikson, E., & Erikson, J. (1997). *The life cycle completed: Extended version*. W. W. Norton.

Feige, M. (2009). *Settling in the hearts: Jewish fundamentalism in the occupied territories*. Wayne State University Press.

Feldman, D. B., & Snyder, C. R. (2005). Hope and the meaningful life: Theoretical and empirical associations between goal-directed thinking and life meaning. *Journal of Social and Clinical Psychology, 24*, 401–424.

Foucault, M. (1975). *Discipline and punishment: The birth of the prison*. Random House.

Frankl, V. (1964). *Man's search for meaning: An introduction to logotherapy*. Hodder and Stoughton.

Friedman, S. (2015). Hilltop youth: Political-anthropological research in the hills of Judea and Samaria. *Israeli Affairs, 21*(3), 391–407.

Geertz, C. (1973). *The interpretation of cultures*. Basic Books.

Giddens, A. (1991). *Modernity and self-identity: Self and society in the late modern age*. Stanford University Press.

Goldstone, J. (1991). *Revolution and rebellion in the early modern world.* University of California Press.

Goldstone, J. (2001). Demography, environment, and security. In P. Diehl & N. Gleditsch (Eds.), *Environmental Conflict* (pp. 84–108). Westview.

Gopin, M. (2000). *Between Eden and Armageddon: The future of world religions, violence, and peacemaking.* Oxford University Press.

Hebidge, D. (1979). *Subculture: The meaning of style.* Routledge.

Herriot, P. (2009). *Religious fundamentalism: Global, local, and personal.* Taylor & Francis.

Hervieu-Léger, D. (2006). In search of certainties: The paradoxes of religiosity in societies of high modernity. *Hedgehog Review, 8*(1-2), 59–68.

Hoffer, E. (1967). *The temper of our time.* Buccaneer Books.

Hudson, V., & Den Boer, A. (2004). *Bare branches: The security implications of Asia's surplus male population.* MIT Press.

Inbari, M. (2009). *Jewish fundamentalism and the Temple Mount: Who will build the third temple?* State University of New York Press.

Isaacs, H. (1975). *Idols of the tribe.* Harper and Row.

Ivanescu, C. (2010). Politicized religion and the religionization of politics. *Culture and Religion, 11*(4), 309–325.

Janoff-Bulman, R. (1992). *Shattered assumptions: Towards a new psychology of trauma.* Free Press.

Johnson, P. (1959). *Psychology of religion.* Abingdon Press.

Juergensmeyer, M. (2004). Is religion the problem? *Hedgehog Review, 6*(1),1–16.

Kaniel, S. (2004). The Hilltop Settlers: Are they biblical sabras? In A. Cohen & I. Harel (Eds.), *Religious Zionism in the age of change* (pp. 533–558). Mossad Bialik [Hebrew]

Kimmerling, B. (1999). Religion, nationalism, and democracy in Israel. *Constellations, 6*(3), 339–363.

Kroger, J. (2003). Identity development during adolescence. In G. Adams & M. Berzonsky (Eds.), *Blackwell handbook of adolescence* (pp. 207–225). Blackwell.

Lindstad, G. (2006). *Religionization of politics—does it affect the development and practice of human rights?* (unpublished master's thesis). University of Oslo.

Madsen, R., Sullivan, W., Swidler, A., & Tipton, S. (Eds.). (2001). *Meaning and modernity: Religion, polity, and self.* University of California Press.

Maslow, A. (1943). A theory of human motivation. *Psychological Review, 50*(4), 370–96.

Maslow, A. (1954). *Motivation and personality.* Harper.

Mason, M. (2006). *The spirit of Generation Y: Summary of the final report of a three year study.*

McAdams, D. P. (2001). The psychology of life stories. *Review of General Psychology, 5*(2), 100–122.

Mesquida, C., & Wiener, N. (1996). Human collective aggression: A behavioral ecology perspective. *Ethology and Sociobiology, 17*, 247–262.

Moller, H. (1968). Youth as a force in the modern world. *Comparative Studies in Society and History, 10*, 238–260.

Muggleton, D., & Weinzierl, R. (Eds.). (2003). *The post-subcultures reader.* Berg.

Muncie, J. (1999). *Youth and crime.* Sage.

Neapolitan, J. (1997). *Cross-national crime: A research review and sourcebook.* Greenwood.

Neumayer, E. (2003). Good policy can lower violent crime: Evidence from a cross-national panel of homicide rates, 1980–97. *Journal of Peace Research, 40*, 619–640.

Nir, O. (2011). Price tag: West Bank settlers' terrorizing of Palestinians to deter Israeli government law enforcement. *Case Western Reserve Journal of International Law, 44*, 277–289.

Noblejas de la Flor, M. A. (1997). Meaning levels and drug-abuse therapy: An empirical study. *International Forum for Logotherapy, 20*, 46–51.

Pan, E. (2005, August 8). Q&A: The Gaza withdrawal. *The New York Times.* http://www.nytimes.com/cfr/international/slot2_080805.html

Parsons, T., & Shils, E. (2007). *Toward a general theory of action: Theoretical foundations for the social sciences* (3rd ed.). Transaction Publishers.

Pedahzur, A., & Perliger, A. (2009). *Jewish terrorism in Israel.* Columbia University Press.

Peleg, S. (1997). They shoot prime-ministers too, don't they? Religious violence in Israel: Premises, dynamics and prospects. *Studies in Conflict and Terrorism, 20*, 227–247.

Peleg, S. (2003). If words could kill: The demise of discourse in the Israeli public space. *State and Society, 2*(3), 421–444.

Peleg, S. (2012). The consuming fire: The uneasy nexus between religion and violence- a review article. *Politics and Religion, 3*(3), 16–22.

Persico, T. (2016, January 1). The Hilltop youth are not rebels; they are merely looking for their lost authenticity. *Ha'aretz.* http://www.haaretz.co.il/magazine/the-edge/.premium-1.2825905. [Hebrew]

Ram, U. (1999). The state of the nation: Contemporary challenges to Zionism in Israel. *Constellations, 6*(3), 325–338.

Rapoport, D. (1984). Fear and trembling: Terrorism in three religious traditions. *American Political Science Review, 78*, 658–677.

Ravitzky, A. (1996). *Messianism, Zionism, and Jewish religious radicalism.* University of Chicago Press.

Ruthven, M. (2004). *Fundamentalism: The search for meaning.* Oxford University Press.

Selengut, C. (2017). *Sacred fury: Understanding religious violence.* Rowman & Littlefield.

Shek, D. T. L., Ma, H. K., & Cheung, P. C. (1994). Meaning in life and adolescent antisocial and prosocial behavior in a Chinese context. *Psychologia: An International Journal of Psychology in the Orient, 37*(4), 211–218.

Shelef, N. (2010). *Evolving nationalism: Homeland, identity, and religion in Israel 1925–2005.* Cornell University Press.

Sheleg, Y. (2000). *The new religious people; A contemporary look at the religious community in Israel.* Keter. [Hebrew]

Shotter, J., & Gergen, K. (1989). *Texts of identity.* Sage.

Skott-Myhre, H. (2008). *Youth and subculture as creative force: Creating new spaces for radical youth work.* University of Toronto Press.

Sofer, R. (2006, February 5). Shin Bet: Extremist settlers not marginal. *YNET News.* www.ynet.co.il/articles/0,7340,L-3211299,0.html.

Sprinzak, E. (1991). *The ascendance of Israel's radical right.* Oxford University Press.

Turner, V. (1997). *The ritual process: Structure and anti-structure.* Walter de Gruyter.

Vigil, J. (1988). Group processes and street identity: Adolescent Chicano gang members. *Ethos, 16*(4), 421–445.

Webber, R. (2002). Young people and their quest for meaning. *Youth Studies Australia, 21*(1), 40–43.

Weisburd, D., & Lernau, H. (2006). What prevented violence in the withdrawal from the Gaza Strip: Toward a perspective of normative balance. *Ohio State Journal on Dispute Resolution, 37*, 52–53.

6

The Meaning of Denial

Lessons from Immortality Dreams

Benjamin Beit-Hallahmi

This chapter examines a group known as Physical Immortality, which many considered more bizarre than other belief minorities because it promised its adherents eternal life in the same physical body they were inhabiting in this world. My observations of the group and its members taught me that while the beliefs were indeed unusual, the members were ordinary and normal. It turned out to be an early manifestation of New Age activities in Israel. The group did not develop a distinct identity in its members, which was one reason for its decline.

December 1988

Let me start with a scene I witnessed.

"What are 50,000 shekels [\$31,000] compared with eternal life? These people have given you the gift of eternal life, and you haggle over how much money you should give them?" The time was December 1988. The speaker was an energetic, handsome man in his late forties, addressing an audience of about 150 people in a hotel conference hall. It was the culmination of a weekend gathering for believers in physical immortality, the survival of the human body into an unlimited future life. The Immortals, those who believed they would live forever, were celebrating their triumph over death and giving thanks and money to the individuals who were leading them toward the next 3 billion years of their lives. Was this fantastic interaction part of a movie? No, it was real, and I was there to witness it. Did all in attendance believe in overcoming death? This is one of the issues to be discussed in this chapter.

The Immortals group was started in Scottsdale, Arizona, in the late 1960s by Charles Paul Brown (1935–2014), a former minister and nightclub singer.

Benjamin Beit-Hallahmi, *The Meaning of Denial* In: *Finding Meaning*. Edited by: Ofra Mayseless and Pninit Russo-Netzer, Oxford University Press. © Oxford University Press 2022. DOI: 10.1093/oso/9780190910358.003.0006

They have been known as People Forever International, the Eternal Flame Foundation, the Arizona Immortals, People Unlimited, the Forever People, or, most recently, People Unlimited, and they are "dedicated to building a deathless world." The group was sometimes known as CBJ (Chuck, Bernie, and Jim) where C stands for Charles Paul Brown, B for BernaDeane (1937–), and J for James Russell Strole (1950–).

Brown grew up in Bakersfield, California, and moved to Los Angeles in the 1950s with dreams of becoming a nightclub singer. In the spring of 1960, Brown reports having a vision of Jesus Christ together with the revelation of physical immortality as a reality, or "cellular awakening." The group's doctrine is connected to Christian theology and states that "death is actually a fabrication or lie imposed on our minds and bodies by a ruling death consciousness in order to control the species of man and keep him in eternal bondage . . . there will never be lasting peace on earth until the LAST ENEMY OF MAN, WHICH IS DEATH is abolished . . . most religions believe that physical immortality will eventually take place in the bodies of mankind upon the earth. However, it is always projected into some future dispensation due to misconceptions and religious dogmas. We feel the time IS NOW for an immortal species of mankind to be birthed upon the planet."

According to Brown, Jesus Christ, of Christian mythology, was a real person whose mission was to bring humanity physical immortality, but his work was somehow aborted. Chuck Brown proclaimed a naturalistic, biological, discovery and presented it in a secular context. This presumably biological theory is a departure from the tradition of religious immortality discourse. The group's discourse includes references to "reprogramming" the body's cells, which would lead to an immortal body. The secret of immortality was in a conscious decision made by a person and affecting all body cells. Cellular "reprogramming" would actually lead to a new human species, one liberated from the burden of dying. The Immortals would lead changed humanity to a new future.

Following Brown's death in 2014, the group known as People Unlimited changed its tune and emphasizes "longevity" events (People Unlimited Inc., 2014).

How could anybody believe in the delusion of physical immortality? Could one's conscious decision affect body cells? The idea that our wishes determine the reality around us is absurd or psychotic. Global life expectancy in 1900 was 31 years, and today it is around 73 years. Does anybody really think that this has happened because of moods or wishes? Biomedicine has brought about a real revolution, extending life expectancy globally by decades, and this has not come about through consciousness, but through the application of chemistry and physics. The belief that changed the world was about the value of carefully collecting data and conducting experiments in order to develop new medical technologies.

What Chuck Brown offered was a frontal attack on death, one that would replace all cultural traditions. The elimination of death, humanity's greatest triumph, would be realized without religion. While paying respect to Christian mythology, he eliminated the need for proclamations of faith or rituals.

Very few people have indeed been ready to take the Immortals' message seriously. Despite the content of the message, which could not be more positive, most humans exposed to it remain indifferent or dismissive. Anybody claiming to offer humanity such a total triumph over death would be suspect.

In contrast, culturally learned religious beliefs will not be considered psychotic, no matter how absurd they are (Beit-Hallahmi, 2010). Most believers inherit identity, beliefs, and practices from their parents, with no reflection, thinking, or choice. New religious ideas, or secular ideas challenging conventional beliefs, are judged differently. If you have inherited the belief in immortality from your parents, then it's not a matter of choice. If you have chosen a new kind of immortality claim, then you are going to be regarded differently.

In fact, some would regard Physical Immortality as another scam, one of many in the salvation market. I have witnessed strong reactions from people who described Chuck, Bernie, and Jim as phony scammers. In 1992, I showed a video recording of Bernie making the case for physical immortality to a group of American undergraduates. Within minutes, they protested loudly and demanded to stop the screening. Their unanimous judgment was that Bernie was a fake, a fraud, which they spotted right away. This incident was unlike anything I experienced before or after.

While the group was initially registered in Arizona as a religious foundation, free of taxation, in 1996, People Unlimited Inc. was incorporated as a profit-making, self-development and coaching business. During the December 1988 weekend meeting, I heard one of the founders, Jim (James Srole), in conversation with followers admit that the group was registered as a religious charity only to avoid taxes because its message was secular. Criticism in the media in the early 1990s led the leaders to change its status.

Twenty-first-century technology makes available to us many recorded and televised appearances by group leaders and their followers. Larry King hosted them on CNN in 1991, and Jerry Falwell joined the conversation.[1] You can watch the leadership CBJ in 1992,[2] and a solo appearance by Bernie is available.[3]

Chuck Brown was a prophet without honor in his own country. His message of physical immortality gained very few followers in the United States or in other countries. Why hasn't humanity flocked to Chuck's call? It seemed that people were satisfied with conventional religious ideas about surviving death. Humans are obsessed with death and with the denial of death and are attached to the ways in which they habitually protect themselves from reality.

There was only one country where Chuck found many who were willing to listen. The Israel branch of the Immortals, known locally as Physical Immortality, turned out to be the largest in the world.

Revisiting 1988

How did I happen to spend time with the Immortals? The research that led to the book *Despair and Deliverance* (1992) started in 1979. It involved meeting with followers, seekers, and those offering salvation; collecting media reports, which in those days meant hundreds of newspaper clippings; and attending meetings and events.

Friends and colleagues came to know of my project and kindly offered help in the form of personal accounts or valuable materials. One day in 1987, my friend N told me about a new group. She also handed me a newspaper clipping, convulsing with laughter. Some people were crazy enough to believe in living forever, and they were holding open meetings. I saved the clipping and remembered the story.

A few months later N informed me that she had become a committed member of Physical Immortality and invited me to join her in attending a meeting. I became a regular visitor and discovered that some of the Immortals were individuals I had known for years. The group leaders were friendly and open. They allowed me to attend all activities, even though I made clear to

---

[1] See https://www.youtube.com/watch?v=gAUtR-oAGOU
[2] See https://www.youtube.com/watch?v=IUWMLjsQJ2g
[3] See https://www.youtube.com/watch?v=P-sM9T4iV2w

them that I was there only as an observer. That is how I ended up spending at least 150 hours watching the Immortals and listening to them. I joined the followers sitting in the circle and passing on the microphone. When my turn came, I remained silent. I once even signed, by mistake, the attendance list, and so my name appears on one list of the Immortals.

My attendance at the meetings during a period of 6 months in 1988–1989 was a chance to observe directly one form of private salvation. In writing this chapter, I have been revisiting the case and the 1992 book. Recalling the events that took place almost 30 years ago was aided by notes I made then, many documents, audio recordings, and video tapes. This was also an opportunity to revise and critique what I wrote in the book then. It helped me realize that my conceptualization was in need of refinement. With hindsight and much rethinking, I will offer some hypotheses about seeking, joining, believing, and belonging.

Immortality Dreams

An adult human being, or even any person over age 12, is expected to realize the finality, irreversibility, and universality of death (Beit-Hallahmi, 2011), but eternal life is humanity's fondest wish. All religions claim to transcend nature by denying the reality of death. William James stated that "Religion, in fact, for the great majority of our own race, means immortality and nothing else" (James, 1902/1961, p. 406).

An instance of how the belief in an afterlife may provide relief from depression was given by Leo Tolstoy in 1869. He described one of the characters in *War and Peace*, as he coped with despondency.

> If there is a God and future life, there is truth and good, and man's highest happiness consists in striving to attain them. We must live, we must love, and we must believe that we live not only today on this scrap of earth, but have lived and shall live forever. (Tolstoy, 1869/1966, p. 340)

In understanding cultural coping with death we turn to *terror management theory* (TMT). It "posits that the juxtaposition of an instinctive desire for life with an awareness of the inevitability of death in an animal instinctively programmed for self-preservation and continued existence creates the potential for paralyzing terror. This potential for terror is kept under control by a dual-component cultural anxiety buffer consisting of self-esteem and faith in one's cultural worldview" (Dechesne et al., 2003, p. 723).

Despite the reality of death and an impersonal, chaotic, universe humans love the illusions of structure, order, meaning, and immortality. Religions offer various forms of immortality delusions (Beit-Hallahmi, 2010). The Christian claim is "For God so loved the world, that he gave his only begotten Son, that whosoever believeth in him should not perish, but have everlasting life" (John 3:16).

Most common is the belief that the human soul is immortal, less common is the idea that a living leader is immortal, and the least common is the belief that all members of a group are immortal. In most traditions, including Christianity and Judaism, universal immortality will be our lot following the coming of the Messiah (the Second Coming in Christianity), a new cosmic order, resurrection, and Judgment Day. Until then, most religions promise immortality to the soul, sometimes involving reincarnation, imagined as a curse in some traditions.

Beliefs in the survival of the physical body have been promoted in some religious groups, in addition to legends about people who have never died. Those who never die are exceptional, saints and Messiahs, but most traditions tell us that we may eventually join their number.

Some leaders offer ideas about human evolution toward perfection and immortality. Aurobindo Ghose (1872–1950), known as Sri Aurobindo, is known for his conception of supraconsciousness, the final stage of human evolution, which will overcome material life and individual consciousness. This level will be achieved only by a small elite, the kernel of a new human race (McDermott, 1963).

Christianity in the United States has spawned some death-defying religious groups in which believers handle venomous snakes and (more rarely) drink poison. A few believers die, but most survive such practices, regarded as the best proof of faith (Hood & Williamson, 2008; Williamson & Hood, 2015).

Some modern groups (Transcendental Meditation, Osho Meditation) promise longevity, and some groups describe longevity as a step on the road to immortality. The Black Hebrews, an Afro-American Jewish group founded in Chicago in the 1960s, proclaims longevity and immortality. Their leader has been quoted as speaking about "phasing out death." With a view toward such longevity, presumably, group members do not consume meat, dairy products, tobacco, sugar, or alcohol.

Father Divine (1880–1965), who was the leader of an African American movement known as the Universal Peace Mission Movement, promised his followers everlasting life: "many of us who are in this place will never lose the bodies we now have. God is here in the flesh, and he is never going away from us, and we will remain here forevermore. This is heaven on earth" (Fauset, 1944, p. 105).

One of the historical sources of the Physical Immortality idea is the 19th-century New Thought movement in the United State. It was a "mind healing," "positive thinking" movement, inspired by the work of Phineas Parkhurst Quimby (1802–1866). "Free Thought" groups held national conventions in the United States starting in 1894. The International Metaphysical League was started in 1899, the National New Thought Alliance in 1908, and the International New Thought Alliance was founded in 1914.

The New Thought doctrine is summed up in the belief in "the infinitude of the Supreme One, the Divinity of man and his infinite possibilities through the creative power of constructive thinking and obedience to the voice of the Indwelling Presence which is our source of Inspiration, Power, Health, and Prosperity."

Healing through the power of mind and the ultimate sovereignty of the mind over material reality were the cornerstones of the movement's ideology. Later on, an emphasis on the attainment of financial prosperity and the elimination of "unreal" poverty through "mind power" was added (Meyer, 1980).

What is unique about the Physical Immortality message? It is the clearest denial of death, with no technical interruptions such as burial and resurrection. Being an Immortal and believing in eternal life should mean a totally transformed outlook on one's life, a total liberation, and a triumph over all frustrations and sufferings.

Leaders and Followers

Here is what I reported in *Despair and Deliverance* (1992, p. 162):

> Immortality was started in 1988 by an Israeli couple, Raya and Shmuel Ben Dror, who met the leaders of the Eternal Flame in Britain. It was love at first sight, and the Ben Drors decide to bring the message to their homeland. Within a few months, they gathered around them scores of followers, some of them personal friends, relatives, and business associates. The Ben Drors

do not represent the oppressed and downtrodden by any means. Raya Ben Dror is the heiress to a significant fortune. Her husband is a successful businessman in his own right. Many of the people they have led in the immortality faith are well to do. It isn't clear if all the members in the group, which meets at least twice a week, really believe in physical immortality, but they are all attracted to the incredible optimism which such a faith reflects. The group's meetings are devoted to mutual criticism, testimonials ("how life has changed since I became physically immortal"), and mutual support. The group leader, Raya Strauss Ben-Dror, is a woman of immense wealth and energy (Bin-Nun, 2006). In 2017 she received an honorary degree from Tel Aviv University, honoring her many philanthropic activities (Tel Aviv University, 2017).

The group became known in the Israeli media as Physical Immortality and was a topic of frequent reporting in the 1990s. The term "physical immortality" became part of the Hebrew language, according to two online dictionaries.[4]

Here are some brief portraits of followers.

- E was a well-known and talented artist, constantly self-promoting, who held a number of leadership positions in several organizations. In the 1980s, she used to describe herself as a student of the Kabbala and peppered her speech with "As the Kabbala states...."
- J, around 40, was a successful businessman, whose investment in a canning plant was in danger. Participants were half-jokingly urged to buy his products. When the plant closed, J's personal wealth was not affected.
- S, late thirties, was one of the group's leading members. Tall, handsome, and friendly, he was a natural leader. S was immensely wealthy, but never showed off. While his wealth was primarily inherited, he was also a busy entrepreneur, involved in major projects all over the country.
- Z was one of the oldest followers. She was a heavy smoker and missed meetings because of hospitalizations for cancer treatments. She died

[4] Academic Dictionary entry: http://hebrew.enacademic.com/71775/%D7%A4%D7%99%D7%96%D7%99%D7%A7%D7%9C_%D7%90%D7%99%D7%9E%D7%95%D7%A8%D7%98%D7%9C%D7%99%D7%98%D7%99
Almaany Dictionary entry: https://www.almaany.com/en/dict/en-he/%D7%90%D7%99%D7%9E%D7%95%D7%A8%D7%98%D7%9C%D7%99%D7%98%D7%99/

within a few months, and this is interpreted as the result of her not fully embracing death-rejecting consciousness.

- F was a 52-year-old judge and legal counsel with a successful public service career who later created his own meditation technique.
- K was a single woman with a PhD, holding a responsible position in a large corporation. She admitted to being a serial joiner who had experienced various other groups such as est.
- N, the woman who introduced me to the group, was a successful psychotherapist with offices in two cities and little formal training. Her MA was in social science. She was a lively, energetic single mother in her late thirties.
- L, 50 years old, was an editor, writer, and successful translator of bestsellers and New Age and self-help books from English. She started her career and established herself following the suicide of her husband, a leading financier accused of improprieties, in 1984. L was one of the public faces of Physical Immortality in the media.
- Y, 41 years old (in 1988), is listed in the Hebrew Wikipedia as the spokeswomen for Physical Immortality as of 2018. She was a successful journalist and best-selling author who gained international attention in 1982 after she had interviewed Yasser Arafat during the Israeli invasion of Lebanon. She also authored a book about Raya's family, one of the wealthiest in the country, which included a few paragraphs dealing with Physical Immortality.

The Group Experience

The group leader, Raya Strauss Ben-Dror, is a woman of immense wealth and energy (Bin-Nun, 2006). In 2017 she received an honorary degree from Tel Aviv University, honoring her many philanthropic activities (Tel Aviv University, 2017).

Raya was in charge at all meetings, shaping the group culture. Her main task was to teach the followers how to be Immortals. The meetings I attended turned out to be an endless cycle of grievances, criticism, and support in response to complaints from depressive individuals who were reporting on everyday difficulties, triumphs, and mostly failures. Some of the followers sounded discouraged despite their worldly success.

To reports of distress, Raya responded angrily. "How can an Immortal be bothered by what his mother-in-law says? As a Physical Immortal, you should not be like that. Take hold of yourself!" Followers would join in criticism and support. The interaction would be very brief, and in 5 minutes a follower would report on an event during the past week, receive criticism or support, or both, and the microphone would move on to the next person in the circle.

If Raya inspired awe rather than love and was sometimes aggressive and always tough, Shmulik, her husband, while only second in command, was consistently warm and accepting. His sensitivity was proved to me when I invited a friend, A, to join me at one of the meetings. It turned out that A and Shmulik had met 40 years earlier. Shmulik not only remembered A, but made an incredibly insightful comment about his personality.

Offering support was needed time and again because followers did not learn the proper role of being an Immortal. The terminology of "energy" (both physical and psychological) was used often during the meetings. As a belief system (or as a biological theory), the Immortality doctrine is extremely simple. What was promoted was not only personal optimism, but superiority feelings. The implications of the absurd immortality message were explicitly taught. Any Immortal was separate from the rest of humanity and superior to mere mortals.

Not only does the Physical Immortality idea express an extreme degree of optimism, but the conversations during the meetings reflected other forms of positive thinking. In addition to death, wealth was very much on followers' minds. They were being invited to "prosperity workshops" which, according to the sales pitch, located the source of personal poverty in an individual's unfortunate tendency to project "negative energy" toward financial resources. The solution was, naturally, learning how to send some "positive energy" toward the fortune waiting to be collected. There was no evidence of anybody becoming wealthier after attending these workshops. The fact that some in the group were immensely wealthy was never discussed openly but was a reality all were aware of.

Positive thinking played a major role in testimonials. Thus, E told the group how she could not afford to travel to the upcoming Immortals gathering in Scottsdale, Arizona. Then, her positive thinking paid off, the universe smiled, and she discovered a cheap flight that made the trip possible.

The group process took a surprising turn when a leading member confronted and challenged Raya. This remarkable incident had to do with the permanent war situation in Israel. On December 9, 1987, the Palestinian uprising, soon to be known as the Intifada, started. It ended only on September 13, 1993, when Israel and the Palestinian Liberation Organization (PLO) signed a mutual recognition agreement. This period of more than 5 years involved daily acts of violence all over the country, with unending tension that affected the collective mood. My participation in the Immortals meetings coincided with these developments, which were on everybody's mind. Politics and current events were never mentioned during meetings. Then one evening, S, one of the leading members, decided to raise the issue. "Something enormous is happening around us. Why are we ignoring it?" This was the only time the group culture was challenged. Raya silenced him right away. "We are immortal. We don't need to pay attention to such events." As this incident demonstrates, group culture was moving from denying death to denying current suffering and uncertainty.

On another occasion, it was Raya who rebelled against Chuck. During one meeting, Raya, quite emotional, cried out "Chuck says there is no God, but you should know that there is a God!" There were no reactions.

Periodically, Chuck, Bernie, and Jim would travel to Israel to tend the flock and collect some money because they relied on donations from followers to survive.

The money raising I witnessed in December 1988 was the culmination of the weekend event. It took place on Saturday night (when the weekend ends in Israel) following presentations by Chuck, Bernie, Jim, and some members. Chuck even graced the occasion with his singing, and I was not impressed.

Because the group in Israel and its local leaders attracted much media attention, we have many recordings of their televised appearances. In one brief video clip, the leaders, Shmulik and Raya, explained that living forever meant taking responsibility for one's life. Members who had died failed to do that. The TV host asked about Chuck, Bernie, and Jim, who had flown in from Arizona, and discussed everyday dangers. "Weren't you worried about their safety?" "They have danger sensors, and know how to deal with it."

The clip demonstrates how nonmembers expressed appreciation for the likability and infectious optimism radiating from the followers.[5] Numerous video recordings include both television appearances and clips produced by

---

[5] See https://www.youtube.com/watch?v=vvm_IpBBkLw

the group. They provide one source of data for exploring the group's message and culture.[6]

Because the Immortals enjoyed being together, the idea of living together in several high-rise buildings in Haifa was seriously discussed during the meetings. A specific location was selected, and Immortals who were involved in construction business corporations spelled out the details. The figure of 3 billion years came up quite often, but the plan never materialized.

After the mid-1990s, the group started declining, as fewer and fewer followers were showing up at the weekly meetings. Raya became devoted to a reputed messiah named Nir Ben Artzi, who was becoming known among Orthodox Jews in Israel (Berkowitz, 2017). According to media reports, Raya donated tens of millions of shekels to this Messiah (Mizrahi, 2011).

In the 21st century, the Immortals did not completely disappear, and, as of 2013, Bernie and Jim were still offering weekend workshops in Israel. L and Y are still mentioned in the media as representing the group.

The Meaning of the Search

On page 176 of *Despair and Deliverance* (1992) I presented five ways of defining personal distress:

Organic: Source of distress is to be found in invisible organic disequilibrium. Change will be affected by a change in diet, exercise, or special healing.

Psychological: Source of distress is to be found in invisible psychological disequilibrium. Change will occur through psychotherapy.

Religious: Source of distress is in the individual's alienation from invisible cosmic powers, which control the universe. Change will come through creating a psychological tie with those powers.

Occult: Source of distress lies in a variety of visible and invisible forces (e.g., planets, witchcraft). Change will come through knowledge and manipulation of forces.

Political: Source of distress is in the social divisions of power existing around the individual. Change will come through changing these divisions.

[6] See https://www.youtube.com/watch?v=_Mpf3YaV5Ho; https://www.youtube.com/watch?v=MrNZ1eimGis; https://www.youtube.com/watch?v=DO3i05RsWDs

The seekers I described in the book experienced distress and could choose one of the five ways to deal with it. The assumption was that belief systems are available to seekers, and a match between a seeker and a system leads to commitment. The five options are real, and some individuals can become strongly committed to only one. Strict loyalty exists in religious groups, of course, or in secular individuals who would reject any organic, occult, or religious explanations for distress or for its relief. In others, loyalty operates because of emotional attachments to other followers, without any ideological commitment.

Today, looking closely and with hindsight at individual behavior, I believe that the assumption of discontinuity and disconnection among the five options is, for many individuals, unfounded. As we attempt to understand the experiences of seekers, dabblers, and joiners, we tend to search for a clear division of actions and motives. However, their world is very different from the researchers' world. Individuals don't behave and don't classify their behavior according to the division just presented, even though it is based on valid observations.

How much do the seekers differentiate among solutions to distress? What we can call the *continuity assumption* proposes that, psychologically, from the viewpoint of seekers and believers, boundaries are irrelevant. The process of developing commitment is identical, whether the belief system is secular or religious. From the seeker's point of view, in times of crisis and personal difficulties, choice is not important.

If we evaluate meanings, or perspectives for action, from the actors' point of view, it is clear that they do not seek consistency and are untroubled by contradictions. Their only approach is one of pragmatism or of following "what works." For them, there was only one road to salvation: whatever felt good and offered relief to the self. They could use astrology or palm reading to test suggestions that had come up during psychological treatment.

Secularization and the triumph of individualism in modern societies led to individualized belief systems in which personal autonomy plays a big role (Beit-Hallahmi, 2015). Individuals are free to follow their own whims in choosing beliefs and practices. The language we hear in the context of both secular psychotherapy and religious conversion is that of personal self-discovery and not of obedience to doctrine. We can speak of an a la carte religion or belief system. A person may combine astrology, reincarnation, and Judaism in their own individual belief complex.

Belief, Recruitment, and Commitment

Does commitment arise out of the acceptance of group beliefs? When joining a new belief group, we can assume that there is a critical element of openness to certain beliefs, accompanied by exposure, growing commitment, and support by significant others and group structure.

A rarely examined notion assumes that members of belief communities support and hold the group's tenets of faith. In reality, we find a continuum of belief commitments, with core members loyal to the doctrine, and marginal members, who are not invested in any beliefs. If group beliefs are radically deviant, as in the case of the Immortals, followers must be strongly committed.

In fact, I suggest that loyalty, membership, and cohesion are affected less by specific beliefs and more by strong attachments. The search for meaning and the content of a belief system are less important. It has been noted that preexisting social networks are crucial in recruitment to membership in new belief groups (Marwell, Oliver, & Prahl, 1988) and that involvement develops from the "interaction of individual level biography, networks, and situational context" (Viterna, 2006, p. 3). Another factor is close relationships with members. Members are often pulled into groups by spouses, lovers, friends, or relatives (Beit-Hallahmi & Argyle, 1997).

How do individuals join belief minorities? It is often assumed by observers that recruitment into minority movements means accepting certain beliefs, while in reality primary group attachments play a major role (Snow, Zurcher, & Ekland Olson, 1980). Researchers of religious movements have found that personal attachments create new and committed relationships. Individuals often follow their close friends on their private salvation trek. The group may have a strong hold on them because what they do have is attachment to another person, rather than a conviction in some abstract faith. The attachment may not be to a charismatic leader, but to a close friend who introduced them to the group and now stands by them (Ebaugh & Vaughan, 1984). Women are more likely to join through a social network, while men are more independent seekers (Davidman & Greil, 1993).

The brief description of the Immortals in the 1992 book already raised the question of belief. My observations of the Immortals (and other groups), and especially my conversations with members, showed that many, possibly a majority, enjoyed the experience and the company but did not take group beliefs seriously. For example, V and D, who attended the Immortals weekend event, were two single women in their thirties and best friends. They saw each other almost every day and went on vacations together. The Immortals weekend was for them another kind of outing. It was clear that they did not share any of the beliefs, but enjoyed being in the group and meeting new people. V told me that she was there only because of D, her best friend, even though she was having a good time.

It was clear that many who came to Physical Immortality were following close friends who had shared with them earlier experiences in meditation, est, etc. Some followers regarded Immortality as another "therapy" and stated that the positivity really changed their outlook on life.

Who Were the Seekers and Joiners?

Research has shown that the lack of constraining attachments and commitments or fewer other competing attachments or commitments will lead to joining salvation groups. It has often been stated that adolescents and young adults are most likely to join salvation groups. In Physical Immortality, this was clearly not the case. Most participants were men and women in their forties and older, many with established careers and families. There was a majority of single women among the Immortals, most with successful careers. Some of those in attendance were millionaires, and others, while less wealthy, held positions of influence. Most members were middle-class.

In modern societies, there is a population of seekers who are open (or vulnerable) to accepting new self-definitions or, at least, new ways of looking at the self. What has been called "hunger," which pushes seekers forward, combines with various environmental stresses to lead to an openness or even commitment (Beit-Hallahmi, 1992). Seekers, who are open to the idea of joining a religious or secular salvation group, naturally experience some psychological distress, which creates their hunger (Beit-Hallahmi, 2015).

Were the Immortals real seekers? In the 1992 book, I mentioned one real seeker who was visiting all the religious groups he could find and listening to their messages so that he could eventually decide which one to join. Such serious seekers are rare. Most of those who attended the Immortals' meetings were not true seekers, but habitual joiners or dabblers.

What were the followers looking for? We can consider the search for meaning in the case of the Immortals. Were the Immortals on a search for meaning? In my conversations with followers, it was clear that they didn't even search for immortality.

Many Immortals mentioned their experiences in other salvation and New Age settings, such as channeling, the "alternative medicine" options of homeopathy, shiatsu, or Reiki, yoga, several meditation groups, est, I AM (an est imitation that was successful in Israel in the 1980s), Dale Carnegie, Gurdjieff, tantra weekends, and rebirthing (known in Israel as "rebirssing"). These experiences were discussed and recommended during meetings.

Some of those involved could be described as dabblers, a term sometimes used in the context of the New Age (Woodhead, 2010). This term is not used here in any derogatory sense, but denotes the serial joiners as opposed to devotee or committed member who remain loyal to one group and one identity.

In the followers' own framing, their search was for belonging, acceptance, hope, and joy. It seems that members were not sure if they cared about meaning and purpose, but in the Immortals' meetings they enjoyed the warm, even manic, atmosphere; the connections with friendly peers; and the support from the leaders. For some of them, the idea of belonging to a superior group of Immortals might have had a positive effect on the self.

The Search for Meaning

A common response to death and disasters is "It doesn't make sense," and this response is often followed by attempts to replace meaninglessness with biographical or cosmic significance, most often following religious traditions (Neimeyer, 2000). Janoff-Bulman (2010) suggested that assumptions about the benevolence of the impersonal world, chance, and self-worth are shattered by personal trauma.

Hundreds of studies discuss meaning in life in the face of real adversity, crisis, and failure. Dying of cancer is one condition often discussed, when approaching death pushes both the patient and caregivers to seek meaning (e.g., Collie & Long, 2005). Most discussions of the search for meaning are rather vague. Psychological studies on the search for meaning have attempted to flesh out what has become a modern mantra, but this turned out to be quite a problem.

Attempts to sum up psychological research on meaning in life have been less than enlightening (Brown & Wong, 2015; Heintzelman & King, 2014; Park, 2010). One problem is assessment. How do you ask about meaning in life? In a global study, meaning in life was assessed by the following item: "Do you feel your life has an important purpose or meaning?" (Oishi & Diener,

2014). One leading researcher, Michael Steger, presented an instructive TED talk on "What Makes Life Meaningful."[7] His talk emphasizes "making a difference" and individualism. The sources of meaning, according to the talk, are purpose and significance. Steger is the author of the Meaning in Life Questionnaire, which has been used often (Steger et al., 2006). What should be noted is that 5 out of 10 items in this questionnaire deal with a search for meaning.

Do individuals search for meaning? Or, better yet, who are the individuals who search for meaning? "People theoretically experience the presence of meaning when they comprehend themselves and the world, understand their unique fit in the world, and identify what they are trying to accomplish in their lives. Thus, people are thought to be motivated both to have and search for meaning in life. However, people vary in the degree to which they actively search for meaning" (Steger, Kashdan et al., 2008, p. 200). In fact, the search for meaning may be an indication of unhappiness (Baumeister, 1991; Klinger, 1998).

Schimel (1973) stated that "the quest for identity and meaning can be seen as an index of pathology. When the processes of maturation that optimally go on outside of conscious awareness become a matter of continual conscious scrutiny, concern and implementation, there is the strong suggestion that something is amiss. It is the continuous preoccupation with, rather than the fact of, a concern with identity that is the index of difficulty" (p. 407). In studies looking at individuals, personal and cultural differences were uncovered. Steger, Kashdan et al. (2008) found positive correlations of search for meaning with neuroticism (.18) and anxiety (.20).

At the same time, Baumeister stated that "Desperate people do not ponder the meaning of life. When survival is at stake . . . life's meaning is irrelevant. The meaning of life is a problem for people who are not desperate, people who can count on survival, comfort, security, and some measure of pleasure" (1991, p. 3).

It is assumed that meaning is tied to well-being, but cross-cultural comparisons showed that search for meaning was negatively related to presence of meaning and well-being in the United States, but positively related to these variables in Japan (Steger, Kawabata, et al., 2008). Oishi and Diener (2014) examined wealth and meaning in life across 132 nations. While life satisfaction was substantially higher in wealthy nations than in poor nations,

---

[7] See https://www.youtube.com/watch?v=RLFVoEF2RI0

meaning in life scores were higher in poor nations than in wealthy nations because people in those nations were more religious.

The hope engendered by religious faith may be an important factor mediating the association between religion and well-being and helps individuals suffering from depression. Religion may also offer help through denial and positive illusions, which are helpful in some situations, but not all (Shedler, Mayman, & Manis, 1993; Taylor & Brown, 1988). Belief in an afterlife, which reduces the terror of death, will influence emotional well-being (Dechesne et al., 2003). The belief that the world is just, part of most supernaturalist systems, enables individuals to confront the physical and social environment as though it were stable and orderly (Beit-Hallahmi, 2015).

Could denial be a source of meaning? The meaning of denying death is clear, and most religions have been doing it for millennia. Claiming an immortal soul and thus denying the annihilation of our individual consciousness is something humans have embracing for more than 100,000 years.

A Broader Perspective

Despair and Deliverance: Private Salvation in Contemporary Israel (1992) looked at four roads to private salvation: the return to Judaism, new religious movements (NRMs), secular psychotherapy, and occultism. The theoretical explanations in the 1992 book focused on the notions of stress, collective crisis, growing individualism, and the trauma of the 1973 War. Other factors considered in the book included stress caused by social fragmentation, urbanization, economic change, and alienation.

The 1992 book described significant developments in Israeli culture, including the four salvation options, which differed in the quality of commitment they require. Two major (and seemingly paradoxical) changes were noted. First, a movement of return to Orthodox Judaism and, second, the appearance of NRMs. Another major change in the culture since the 1970s has been the growing prevalence and popularity of secular psychotherapy, which has broken world records in terms of participation rates. In addition to these developments, the acceptance of occultism in various guises had grown among Israelis of all backgrounds.

Examining what I have called *private salvation* can proceed at several levels. The first level of approaching the phenomenon is psychological. Looking at individual behavior, what we encounter are private salvation narratives, or autobiographies of conversion. Had we looked at Israeli culture around 1960 or 1970, such narratives were quite rare. Today they are commonplace.

The historical trauma of the 1973 War appears to be the starting point for an Israeli Great Awakening, but the impact of this trauma is differential, modified by social background variables. The trends noted then have continued, as Israelis faced political crises through the decades between 1970 and 2020. Collective crises, such as the First Intifada (1987–1991), the Rabin assassination in 1995, and the Second Intifada (2000–2004), were accompanied by individual reports of miraculous changes, "healings," etc.

The role of the state in Israel is central and unique, and one road to private salvation (i.e., Orthodox Judaism) is clearly privileged, enjoying legitimacy and state material support, while others are discouraged. This is tied to a massive Judaization of Israeli culture, noted already in 1992 (Cahaner & Leon, 2013; Deshen, 2018; Persico, 2014; Sharabi, 2012, 2014; Sharot, 1999). The dominance of Judaism in Israeli culture has significantly increased since 1973 and even more clearly after 1992 (Ariel, 2010; Werczberger & Azulay, 2011).

Hegemony and state intervention clearly do have their limits. Both Jehovah's Witnesses and Messianic Jews, to name the most notable groups, survive and flourish despite the state's apparent wishes. They represent the most successful new religions in Israel, but constitute a small minority.

The rise of private salvation movements has been occurring at the same time as the decline of collectivism. Buttressing the self, observed among the Immortals and many others, became not only legitimate, but a desirable and commendable goal. Within this broader perspective, where should we locate the Immortals? Why should we be going back to this historical episode? Are there lessons to be learned or generalizations to be garnered?

Conclusion

Predicting, explaining, or postdicting the success of any idea, leader, or organization is impossible. A unique combination of factors accounts for the rise or fall of a religion, a business, or a political party. Over the past 50 years, when researchers have written about future prospects of religious or political movements, the results have been resounding failures.

Thus, the disappearance of Messianic Jews has been predicted by several researchers, but they are doing better than ever. Many other groups, considered solid successes, have disappeared without a trace. In Israel of the 1970s, as well as in the United States, everybody knew about the Guru Maharaj Ji and the Divine Light Mission. Few remember them today. Transcendental Meditation was an astounding success in Israel starting in 1973, with tens of thousands joining. The organization survives, but has lost its prominence.

In the United States, the Jesus Movement of the 1970s seemed set to capture a permanent place in the culture, with hundreds of communes popping up all over the country, but by the 1980s it became a fading memory (Ellwood, 1973; Eskridge, 2013). In Israeli society, political parties could serve as a good analogy to salvation groups. Since 1949, when the first parliamentary election was held, there were more than 100 political parties, which, after being represented at the Knesset, have disappeared completely. While only historians and political experts remember their names, studying their ideological trajectories is directly relevant to Israeli politics in the 21st century.

The Immortals' relative and temporary success in Israel, compared to their total failure to gain attention elsewhere, calls for an explanation. Some suggested that it indicated the presence of total despair among some Israelis, leading to a willingness to clutch at absurd straws. We also can point to a general climate and a broad openness to ideas that made possible the salvation movements active after 1973.

The Immortals presented to the world a startling claim about eternity, but made no demands for the new identity that many salvation groups require of members. Raya tried to build on it and create identity and loyalty but failed.

Despite their beliefs, which most would consider absurd or crazy, the Immortals were never a marginal group in Israeli society. While the group was small, it attracted extraordinary (and extremely friendly) media attention, as shown earlier. During the 1990s, the term "Physical Immortality" was a household word in Israel. What created their improbable popularity was first their message of positivity. The group did not present any challenges to mainstream Israeli identity. It was basically conformist in its emphasis on material success and individualism. If you came to the meetings, you met individuals who were ambitious, confident, successful, and competent. Sitting next to you would be men who were entrepreneurs and senior civil servants and women who independent and ambitious. What they reflected was the neo-liberal discourse, which was gaining dominance in Israel at the time (Simchai & Shoshana, 2018; Wood, 2016).

Discussing the Immortals, we can point to a clear continuity with other options for psychological self-improvement. It turns out that the group was truly representative of developments in Israel between 1980 and 2020.

As mentioned earlier, many Immortals discussed past and concurrent involvements with other salvation and New Age settings, such as "alternative medicine," meditation groups, est, I AM, Dale Carnegie, Gurdjieff, and rebirthing. If we look at Israel in the 21st century we find the same practices attracting many. Est in its various forms and fora continues to find clients (Melchior & Sharot, 2010; Rubinstein, 2005). What we can observe is a seamless continuity between the Immortals and some cultural ("New Age," "spirituality") practices in the 21st century.

Physical Immortality membership was never defined by exclusivity. There was never a demand for identity change or a transformed way of life. The Immortals were not defined by a hunger for salvation (Beit-Hallahmi, 1992) or a search for meaning; what united them was an openness that led them to dabble in Vipassana, Tantra, est, meditation, or "alternative medicine." While seemingly deviant, it was never marginal, despite the delusional nature of its beliefs. Even those beliefs were no more delusional than those of all religions. Its popularity stemmed from the nature of its membership and its continuity with other New Age manifestations.

In the 21st century, references to the Immortals are found in the discourse shared by the dabblers in New Age and Spirituality and those offering New Age workshops (Gazit, 2008). Certain enterprises, such as rebirthing and "prosperity workshops" still advertised themselves in 2015 as being connected to Physical Immortality (Barzel Cohen, 2015).

Developments in Israel since the 1990s in the practices and beliefs that had defined the cultural milieu of the Immortals followed similar changes in Western countries. Western researchers who in the 1990s reported enthusiastically about a New Age revolution (Heelas, 1996) wrote 10 year later about a Spirituality revolution that involved the same population groups (Heelas & Woodhead, 2005). Both New Age and Spirituality offer personalized supernaturalism (Streib & Hood, 2011) as "every individual . . . might create his own cocktail of Christian devotion, Buddhism, and belief in astrology" (Tschannen, 1991, p. 401). In Israel we can substitute Jewish for Christian, but the process is identical.

"Spirituality" has been described as "the individual using whatever ideas, beliefs and practices feel right to the individual, and the authority of religious institutions, especially those of the world religions, is distrusted"

(Walter, 2012, p. 132). In Israel, the same vision has been prevalent among the middle-class, Western population that gave us the Immortals (Simchai, 2014; Simchai & Keshet, 2016; Werczberger & Huss, 2014).

Research since the 1980s has found that the typical New Age follower is a middle-aged woman (Driskell & Lyon, 2011; Farias, Claridge, & Lalljee, 2005; Heelas & Woodhead, 2005; Streiker, 1991). Streiker (1991, p. 50) stated that the "New Age . . . is largely of, by, and for women." Similarly, research on "spirituality" shows that women make up the majority of followers, and Mencken, Bader, and Kim (2009, p. 77) suggested that "[s]pirituality may be perceived as a form of femininity." Eighty percent of those involved as either practitioners and clients in what has been called *self-spiritualities* are female (Heelas & Woodhead, 2005; Woodhead, 2009). The majority of those involved in New Age and spirituality in Israel, just as in other Western countries, are women. So was the majority of the Immortals. Women are also the majority of customers for "alternative medicine" products, a major component of New Age praxis in Israel, as elsewhere (Shmueli, Igudin, & Shuval, 2010; Simchai & Keshet, 2016).

To some observers it seems that Israel in the 1980s and Israel today have offered individuals a bewildering array of choices. Under such conditions, what may lead an individual to any particular commitment?

The same question has been asked about individuals who changed their life course during various historical periods. St. Augustine, known for his conversion to Christianity and his confessions, lived between 354 and 430 CE, and the same question has been asked about him. "Given all the choices, religious and intellectual, available to Augustine in the fourth century, why did he make the ones he did? What factors, environmental and personal, affected his choice?" (Fredriksen, 1978, p. 208). This was more than 1,500 years ago! So, an embarrassment of riches in life choices has characterized cultures since ancient times.

In modern society, despite pluralism in terms of identity choices, most individuals do not get involved in private salvation groups. Individuals have some choices in all cultures, and we seek to generalize across cultures and historical periods when we examine such phenomena as the Immortals.

Why did particular individuals find this group attractive? Followers responded to the positivity and confidence missing in their own lives. Confident, successful, and friendly people attract those who are less so. Positive thinking is always attractive, and optimism is welcomed not only when you are depressed or dejected. The secret of the group's success might, indeed, have been its positive message, amplified by the leaders' confidence and likability.

In a 1994 TV appearance, we can hear Shmulik Ben-Dror explaining the group's success and stating that rich, successful people feel that something is missing from their lives. "They got everything, yet they do lack something. They die of boredom, or they commit suicide." The implication was that the group offered that something with its positivity. Another implication, quite astounding, was that the group gave members reasons not to commit suicide.[8]

What characterized most Immortality followers was a playful openness to building up the self through support, belonging, and positivity, even if expressed in absurdities. This was their search, and they were ready to settle for much less than salvation.

Highlights

- A failed minister and singer named Charles Paul Brown (1935–2014) decided in the 1960s that humans could live forever. It was just a matter of a conscious decision, which would affect all body cells. Together with his wife and her lover, he tried to sell this message, but humanity refused to listen. They somehow managed to make a living.
- Hundreds of individuals in Israel were attracted to an absurd message of eternal life in the body they already know so well. Of course, the message was no more absurd than popular religious ideas about resurrection, reincarnation, and an eternal soul.
- The group leader was a wealthy heiress who was open to salvation messages. Most members were single professional and entrepreneurial women. The men included highly successful and creative individuals.
- The groups ascendance happened between 1987 and 1995, but the group is still fondly remembered in Israel as an early manifestation of New Age culture.
- Participant observation by the author, together with the evidence of many video recordings, lead to the conclusion that the group's

[8] See www.youtube.com/watch?v=XQ1a4VmD8Wo

message of positivity, transmitted by the local leaders, attracted followers who were mostly habitual joiners of self-enhancement groups.

References

Ariel, Y. (2010). Paradigm shift: New religious movements and quests for meaning and community in contemporary Israel. *Nova Religion: The Journal of Alternative and Emergent Religions, 13,* 4–22.

Barzel Cohen, M. (2015, June 4). *Rebirthing, healing and sound healing workshop on the topic of "the phoenix—physical immortality, constant renewal"* [event]. Facebook. [Hebrew] https://www.facebook.com/events/1602868249929864/.

Baumeister, R. F. (1991). *Meanings of life.* Guilford.

Beit-Hallahmi, B. (1992). *Despair and deliverance: Private salvation in contemporary Israel.* SUNY Press.

Beit-Hallahmi, B. (Ed.). (2010). *Psychoanalysis and theism: Critical reflections on the Grünbaum Thesis.* Jason Aronson.

Beit-Hallahmi, B. (2011). The ambivalent teaching, and painful learning, of the facts of life. In V. Talwar, P. Harris, & M. Schleifer (Eds.), *Children's understanding of death: From biological to supernatural conceptions.* Cambridge University Press.

Beit-Hallahmi, B. (2015). *Psychological perspectives on religion and religiosity.* Routledge.

Beit-Hallahmi, B., & Argyle, M. (1997). *The psychology of religious behaviour, belief, and experience.* Routledge.

Berkowitz, A. E. (2017, November 9). Mystic rabbi describes how will Messiah be revealed to world. *Breaking Israel News.* https://www.breakingisraelnews.com/97595/mystic-leader-reveal-messiahs-identity/

Bin-Nun, B. (2006, December 9). Israel's 40 richest, 11: Michael & Raya Strauss. *Forbes.* https://www.forbes.com/lists/2006/81/biz_06israel_Michael-Raya-Strauss_HWNX.html

Brown N. J., & Wong, P. T. (2015). Questionable measures are pretty meaningless. *American Psychologist, 70,* 571–573.

Cahaner, L., & Leon, N. (2013). Returning to religious observance on Israel's non-religious kibbutzim. *Journal of Israeli History, 32,* 197–218.

Collie, K., & Long, B. C. (2005). Considering "meaning" in the context of breast cancer. *Journal of Health Psychology, 10,* 843–853.

Davidman, L., & Greil, A. L. (1993). Gender and the experience of conversion: The case of "returnees" to modern orthodox Judaism. *Sociological Analysis, 54,* 83–100.

Dechesne, M., Pyszczynski, T., Arndt, J., Ransom, S., Sheldon, K. M., van Knippenberg, A., & Janssen, J. (2003). Literal and symbolic immortality: The effect of evidence of literal immortality on self-esteem striving in response to mortality salience. *Journal of Personality and Social Psychology, 84,* 722–737.

Deshen, S. (2018). *Israeli Judaism: The sociology of religion in Israel.* Routledge.

148   BENJAMIN BEIT-HALLAHMI

Driskell, R. L., & Lyon, L. (2011). Assessing the role of religious beliefs on secular and spiritual behavior. *Review of Religious Research, 52*, 386–404.

Ebaugh, H. R. F., & Vaughan, S. L. (1984). Ideology and recruitment in religious groups. *Review of Religious Research, 26*(2), 148–157.

Ellwood, R. S. (1973). *One way: The Jesus Movement and its meaning.* Prentice-Hall.

Eskridge, L. (2013). *God's forever family: The Jesus people movement in America.* Oxford University Press.

Farias, M., Claridge, G., & Lalljee, M. (2005). Personality and cognitive predictors of New Age practices and beliefs. *Personality and Individual Differences, 39*, 979–989.

Fauset, A. F. (1944). *Black gods of the metropolis.* University of Pennsylvania Press.

Fredriksen, P. (1978). Augustine and his analysts: The possibility of a psychohistory. *Soundings, 51*, 206–227.

Gazit, M. (2008, May 1). Time flies when you're having fun—and also when you're not. Haaretz. https://www.haaretz.co.il/misc/1.1321850

Heelas, P. (1996). *The New Age movement: The celebration of the self and the sacralization of modernity.* Blackwell.

Heelas, P., & Woodhead, L. (2005). *The spiritual revolution: Why religion is giving way to spirituality.* Blackwell.

Heintzelman, S., & King, L. A. (2014). Life is pretty meaningful. *American Psychologist, 69*, 561–574.

Hood, R. W., Jr., & Williamson, W. P. (2008). *Them that believe: The power and meaning of the Christian serpent handling tradition.* University of California Press.

James, W. (1902/1961). *The varieties of religious experience.* Collier.

Janoff-Bulman, R. (2010). *Shattered assumptions.* Simon and Schuster.

Klinger, E. (1998). The search for meaning in evolutionary perspective and its clinical implications. In P. T. P. Wong & P. S. Fry (Eds.), *The human quest for meaning: A handbook of psychological research and clinical application* (pp. 27–50). Lawrence Erlbaum Associates.

Marwell, G., Oliver, P. E., & Prahl, R. (1988). Social networks and collective action: A theory of the critical mass. *American Journal of Sociology, 94*, 502–534.

McDermott, R. (Ed.). (1963). *The essential Aurobindo.* Schocken Books.

Melchior, S., & Sharot, S. (2010). Landmark in Israel: Recruitment and maintenance of clients in a human potential organization. *Nova Religion: The Journal of Alternative and Emergent Religions, 13*, 61–83.

Meyer, D. (1980). *The positive thinkers.* Pantheon Books.

Mizrahi, S. (2011, September 27). Raya Strauss falls victim to fraud: "Donated" 36 million NIS. *The Marker.* https://www.themarker.com/law/1.1484926

Neimeyer, R. A. (2000). Searching for the meaning of meaning: Grief therapy and the process of reconstruction. *Death studies, 24*, 541–558.

Oishi, S., & Diener, E. (2014). Residents of poor nations have a greater sense of meaning in life than residents of wealthy nations. *Psychological Science, 25*, 422–430.

Park, C. L. (2010). Making sense of the meaning literature: An integrative review of meaning making and its effects on adjustment to stressful life events. *Psychological Bulletin, 136*, 257–301.

People Unlimited Inc. (2014). http://peopleunlimitedinc.com/home

Persico, T. (2014). Neo-Hasidic revival: Expressivist uses of traditional lore. *Modern Judaism, 34*, 287–308.

Rubinstein, G. (2005). Characteristics of participants in the forum, psychotherapy clients, and control participants: A comparative study. *Psychology and Psychotherapy: Theory, Research and Practice, 78,* 481–492.

Schimel, J. L. (1973). Esoteric identification processes in adolescence and beyond. *The Journal of the American Academy of Psychoanalysis, 1,* 403–415.

Sharabi, A. (2012). "Teshuvah baskets" in the Israeli teshuvah market. *Culture and Religion, 13,* 273–293.

Sharabi, A. (2014). Deep healing: Ritual healing in the Teshuvah movement. *Anthropology & Medicine, 21,* 277–289.

Sharot, S. (1999). Traditional, modern or postmodern? Recent religious developments among Jews in Israel. In K. Flanagan & P. C. Jupp (Eds.), *Postmodernity, sociology and religion* (pp. 118–133). Palgrave Macmillan.

Shedler, J., Mayman, M., & Manis, M. (1993). The illusion of mental health. *American Psychologist, 48,* 1117–1131.

Shmueli, A., Igudin, I., & Shuval, J. (2010). Change and stability: Use of complementary and alternative medicine in Israel: 1993, 2000 and 2007. *European Journal of Public Health, 21,* 254–259.

Simchai, D. (2014). Ethno-national identity and the New Age world view in Israel. *Israel Studies Review, 29,* 17–38.

Simchai, D., & Keshet, Y. (2016). New Age in Israel: Formative ethos, identity blindness, and implications for healthcare. *Health, 20,* 635–652.

Simchai, D., & Shoshana, A. (2018). The ethic of spirituality and the non-angry subject. *Ethos, 46,* 115–133.

Snow, D. A., Zurcher, L. A., Jr., & Ekland Olson, S. (1980). Social networks and social movements: A microstructural approach to differential recruitment. *American Sociological Review, 45,* 787–801.

Steger, M. F., Frazier, P., Oishi, S., & Kaler, M. (2006). The meaning in life questionnaire: Assessing the presence of and search for meaning in life. *Journal of Counseling Psychology, 53*(1), 80–93. https://doi.org/10.1037/0022-0167.53.1.80

Steger, M. F., Kashdan, T. B., Sullivan, B. A., & Lorentz, D. (2008). Understanding the search for meaning in life: Personality, cognitive style, and the dynamic between seeking and experiencing meaning. *Journal of Personality, 76,* 199–228.

Steger, M. F., Kawabata, Y., Shimai, S., & Otake, K. (2008). The meaningful life in Japan and the United States: Levels and correlates of meaning in life. *Journal of Research in Personality, 42,* 660–678.

Streib, H., & Hood, R. W. (2011). "Spirituality" as privatized experience-oriented religion: Empirical and conceptual perspectives. *Implicit Religion, 14,* 433–453.

Streiker, L. D. (1991). *New Age comes to Main Street: A non-hysterical survey of the New Age movement.* Abingdon Press.

Taylor, S. E., & Brown, J. D. (1988). Illusion and well-being: A social psychological perspective on mental health. *Psychological Bulletin, 103,* 193–210.

Tel Aviv University. (2017, May 15). TAU Honorary Doctorates 2017. https://english.tau.ac.il/news/honorary_doctorates_2017

Tolstoy, L. (1869/1966). *War and peace* (G. Gibian, Ed., L. Maude & A. Maude, Trans.). Norton.

Tschannen, O. (1991). The secularization paradigm: A systematization. *Journal for the Scientific Study of Religion, 30,* 395–415.

Viterna, J. S. (2006). Pulled, pushed, and persuaded: Explaining women's mobilization into the Salvadoran guerrilla army. *American Journal of Sociology*, *112*, 1–45.

Walter, T. (2012). Why different countries manage death differently: A comparative analysis of modern urban societies. *The British Journal of Sociology*, *63*, 123–145.

Werczberger, R., & Azulay, N. A. (2011). The Jewish renewal movement in Israeli secular society. *Contemporary Jewry*, *31*, 107–128.

Werczberger, R., & Huss, B. (2014). New age culture in Israel. *Israel Studies Review*, *29*, 1–16.

Williamson, W. P., & Hood R. W., Jr. (2015). Poison-drinking in obedience to the faith: A phenomenological study of the experience. *Mental Health, Religion & Culture*, *18*, 196–206.

Wood, M. (2016). *Possession, power and the New Age: Ambiguities of authority in neoliberal societies*. Ashgate.

Woodhead, L. (2010). Real religion and fuzzy spirituality? Taking sides in the sociology of religion. In S. Aupers & D. Houtman (Eds.), *Religions of modernity: Relocating the sacred to the self and the digital* (pp. 31–48). Brill.

7

Aging in the Shadow of Trauma

Meaning in Life as a Resource for Older Adults in Israel

Amit Shrira, Yuval Palgi, and Dov Shmotkin

In view of the recent, extensive increase in life expectancy, there is a growing need to understand the factors that shape aging. Exposure to traumatic events and the ensuing posttraumatic reactions can accelerate the aging process and increase the risk for early mortality. In contrast, surviving into old age and surviving calamities may mark a double triumph reflecting increased inoculation and growth. What renders vulnerability or resilience among older adults who have been exposed to trauma? In this chapter, we propose that *meaning in life* (MIL) is a cardinal factor in coping with the fusion of aging processes and traumatic experiences. Thus, the absence of MIL may catalyze all sorts of health declines whereas the presence of MIL may protect from deterioration and promote successful aging.

The chapter includes three main sections. The first section focuses on Israeli older adults. This population is largely inflicted by numerous traumatic events, and therefore research of Israeli older adults is pertinent to cardinal questions about late-life susceptibility to and endurance of traumatic events. The second section enumerates seminal as well as fresh theoretical notions regarding the pivotal function of MIL in the adaptation to aging and trauma. It further presents evidence and related insights from studies on Israeli older adults who have been exposed to massive traumatic events. The third section dwells on perceptions of meaningful aging and their role in adaptation to traumatic adversity.

Aging under Fire: Israeli Older Adults Cope with Trauma

The Israeli Perspective

Older adults (age 65+) roughly constitute 11% of the population in Israel. Life expectancy at birth in Israel is one of the highest in the world. Accordingly,

Amit Shrira, Yuval Palgi, and Dov Shmotkin, *Aging in the Shadow of Trauma* In: *Finding Meaning.* Edited by: Ofra Mayseless and Pninit Russo-Netzer, Oxford University Press. © Oxford University Press 2022.
DOI: 10.1093/oso/9780190910358.003.0007

the proportion of older adults in the general population has doubled since the 1950s and is expected to reach 14% by 2045, demonstrating an increase rate of more than twice that of the general population's growth rate in this period (Shnoor & Be'er, 2019). The majority of the older population is composed of immigrants who had to flee or endure the Holocaust in Europe, had to flee persecution in North Africa and the Middle East, or immigrated from the former Soviet Union after its collapse. In addition, many older adult Israelis experience the amalgam of distal and proximal traumatic events, such as recent exposure to warfare and terrorism (Palgi, Shrira, & Shmotkin, 2015; Solomon & Ginzburg, 1998).

A recent attempt to assess the extent of traumatic exposure among Israeli older adults has been made in the Israeli component of the Survey of Health, Ageing and Retirement in Europe (SHARE-Israel), a national survey of Israelis aged 50 or older. The survey looked at events that followed the *Diagnostic and Statistical Manual of Mental Disorders* (DSM; American Psychiatric Association, 2013) definition of traumatic events, which refers to events that evoke a threat to the life or physical integrity of oneself or others (e.g., being wounded in war or in a terrorist attack). Yet this survey also adopted a wider approach by including events that may be considered potentially traumatic, meaning that they evoke a threat to psychological integrity (e.g., experiencing severe economic deprivation) (cf. Robinson & Larson, 2010). Findings from SHARE-Israel showed that 75.9% of Israeli older adults reported to have experienced at least one traumatic or potentially traumatic event (Shmotkin & Litwin, 2009). It is hard to compare this prevalence across countries as different studies used less or more comprehensive lists of adverse events, but prevalence among community-dwelling older adults may reach up to 90% as indicated in American studies that used more detailed accounts of exposure (e.g., Ogle et al., 2013).

Although exposure to traumatic and potentially traumatic events is most common, the main psychopathological response to such events, notably symptoms of posttraumatic stress disorder (PTSD), appears in a minority of individuals. PTSD currently incorporates four syndromes, including intrusive thoughts and nightmares, persistent avoidance from trauma-related stimuli, negative alterations in cognition and mood (e.g., dissociative amnesia, persistent negative beliefs and expectations), and alterations in arousal and reactivity (e.g., irritability and exaggerated startle response; American Psychiatric Association, 2013).

The general rate of PTSD in Israel is rather low, and some estimate its life-time prevalence to be as low as 1.5% (Levinson et al., 2007). Among Israeli older adults living in Jerusalem lifetime prevalence rates for PTSD were found to be 8.4% (Andreas et al., 2017). However, PTSD rates are higher, ranging up to 40%, among highly affected groups of older adults including Holocaust survivors (24–39%; Shmotkin, Shrira, Goldberg et al., 2011; Shmotkin, Shrira, & Palgi, 2011), war veterans (36%; Avidor, Benyamini, & Solomon, 2016), and civilians exposed to prolonged periods of warfare and terrorism (up to 10% according to Bleich et al., 2005, and as high as 25% according to Palgi, 2015). In addition, it should be noted that a significant number of older adults also experience subclinical levels of PTSD (Bleich et al., 2005) as well as other psychological symptoms such as depression and anxiety following traumatic exposure (Shrira et al., 2017).

To recapitulate thus far, individuals living in Israel are exposed to nu-merous traumatic and potentially traumatic events; these events catalyze clinical and subclinical symptoms of distress. As old age is often accom-panied by physical frailty and reduced social support availability, living in circumstances that demand continuous coping with past trauma or with on-going adversity may heavily tax older adults' dwindling resources. Next, we briefly mention major challenges related to old age.

The Challenges of Old Age

Age-related physical atrophy and dysfunction present an increasing chal-lenge to older adults' resources. With regard to individuals who survived to very old age, Baltes (1997) maintained that the last stage of life represents an incomplete segment in the architecture of human development as optimal functioning is doomed to disruption by irreparable biological dysfunctions. In addition to the increasing risk of physical deterioration and debilitating functional impairment, older adults are required to cope with additional challenges, such as cognitive impairment, the death of loved ones, decreased social support, and possible economic deprivation.

Nevertheless, despite the need to cope with the twofold burden of old age and traumatic aftereffects, it seems that most Israeli older adults do not suffer from clinical levels of distress, and others who show subclinical distress usually function relatively well. Moreover, even among Israeli older adults who have been exposed to massive trauma, the majority do not present clinical levels of distress. This brings us to propose that processes related to the search, generation, and preservation of MIL, as well as processes related to more hedonic experiences (e.g., satisfaction and happiness), help individuals regulate the challenges of old age and trauma. The next section dwells on these processes and their importance in old age and following trauma.

Staying Alive While Preserving Meaning: Meaning in Life, Old Age and Trauma

The Definition of Meaning in Life

Modern research on MIL mainly originates from humanistic and existentialistic psychology. MIL essentially refers to a personal, desirably consonant, combination of cognitive schemas that connect different time points and contexts throughout one's life (Baumeister, 1991). These schemas encompass comprehension or coherence, purpose, and mattering or significance (George & Park, 2016; Martela & Steger, 2016). Comprehension, or coherence, refers to the degree to which individuals perceive a sense of understanding regarding their lives (e.g., feeling that things make sense). Purpose refers to the extent to which individuals experience life as being directed and motivated by valued life goals (e.g., feeling a clear sense of direction). Mattering, or significance, refers to the degree to which individuals feel that their existence is of significance in the world (e.g., feeling that one's life and actions are consequential). An adaptational model of MIL has been formulated in Ryff's conception of psychological well-being (e.g., Ryff, 2014), which refers to positive functioning and life pursuits in the face of challenge. In this conception, meaningful life has both psychosocial and biological underpinnings and thus constitutes an essential part of positive health at large (Ryff et al., 2016).

Meaning in Life at Old Age

Erikson emphasized the importance of MIL at old age. In his comprehensive theory (Erikson 1968, 1982), he proposed that, across the life span, individuals go through a course of stages, in each of which they need to resolve a distinct crisis. In the eighth stage of old age, age-related losses and the relative proximity of death press the issue of sustaining personal integrity. As a result, aging individuals tend to review their lives and attempt to balance life successes and failures, arriving predominantly either at ego integrity or despair. *Ego integrity* is achieved when older adults are able to comprehend their life story and affirm its worth, further blending the personal story within a greater narrative of one's cultural group. The failure to do so results in dread and despair in view of the approaching end. The increased importance of MIL at old age was affirmed by ample evidence connecting MIL and numerous indices of successful aging, including preserved physical health and longer survival (Ryff et al., 2016).

Erikson suggested that MIL at old age may be achieved via reconciliation, or, in his own words, through the "acceptance of one's one and only life cycle as something that had to be and that, by necessity, permitted no substitutions" (Erikson, 1968, p. 139). Still, reconciliation seems less probable in view of adverse and traumatic events, which are most common among Israeli older adults (cf. Danieli, 1981). In this context, Lomranz and Benyamini (2016) suggested that MIL could exist without the full acceptance and reconciliation of all life events. They termed this condition as *aintegration*—the capability to feel well while holding complex, dialectical cognitions and emotional experiences, thus acknowledging that life is full of inconsistencies, discontinuities, absurdity, and paradoxes. This other form of acceptance, as Lomranz and Benyamini (2016) proposed, should be more relevant to older adults who have been exposed to trauma.

Meaning in Life and Trauma

Frankl (1963, 1969) developed a theoretical conceptualization of MIL that directly included one's attitude toward tragedy and suffering. He suggested that humans are equipped with a powerful, innate drive, termed the *will to meaning*. Frankl believed that the desire to search for meaning is hardwired into our makeup (Wong, 2014). He depicted three routes to discover MIL through creative, experiential, and attitudinal pathways. Thus, individuals can be creative in contributing to their society, they can experience encounters with their world, and they can implement a positive attitude toward unavoidable suffering. These capabilities are loomed over by trauma, which sets an inner struggle with existential issues, aiming at the reconstruction of one's disrupted world assumptions (Wong, 2014).

More recent MIL literature shows that most people formulate meaningful life through the adoption of positive assumptions, beliefs, and expectations about themselves and the world around them. Thus, people generally conceive their world as benevolent and predictable and their self as worthy (Janoff-Bulman, 1992), even if such conceptions have a moderately illusory nature. In accordance with Frankl's ideas, as exposures to trauma challenge these assumptions, a meaning-making process is initiated in order to let individuals resolve the inconsistencies between the implications of the traumatic events and their worldviews, thus regaining one's sense of controllability and comprehensibility of the world (Park, 2010). Meaning-making takes place through automatic as well as deliberate memories and thoughts and may be expressed either as assimilation of meaning attributed to the traumatic event into one's general worldviews or as accommodation of those worldviews to this trauma-based meaning (Park, 2010).

The Model of the Pursuit of Happiness in a Hostile World

Although MIL is a major psychological resource vis-à-vis aging (Erikson, 1968, 1982) and adversity (Frankl, 1963, 1969), it may interact with other major resources. Indeed, the interaction of MIL with *subjective well-being* (the latter often expressed in terms of satisfaction and positive affect) is at the heart of the *pursuit of happiness in a hostile world* model, proposed by Shmotkin (2005, 2011) and further developed by Shmotkin and Shrira (2012, 2013). MIL and subjective well-being respectively reflect the eudaimonic and hedonic aspects of well-being (Keyes, Shmotkin, & Ryff, 2002) and are considered by the model as complementary systems of adaptation. These systems are designed to cope with the *hostile-world scenario*—a personal image of actual or potential threats to one's life or, more broadly, to one's physical and mental integrity. Nourished by the individual's beliefs about catastrophes and afflictions (e.g., natural disasters, war, bereavement, violence, crime, family breakups, deprivation, oppression, accidents, illness, facing own death), the hostile-world scenario functions as a system of appraisal that scans for any potential negative condition or for an even worse condition when a negative one already prevails. Thus, in the SHARE-Israel longitudinal survey of older adults, the scanning function of the individual's hostile-world scenario was manifested by its unique capability to detect changes in physical and mental health occurring in the recent past (Lifshitz et al., 2020) as well as to predict changes in similar health outcomes occurring in subsequent years (Shmotkin, Avidor, & Shrira, 2016). Thus, when activated adaptively, the hostile-world scenario helps individuals remain vigilant and prudent in the struggle to remain safe and well, but an extreme hostile-world scenario generates a continuous sense of a disastrous world. The model assumes that MIL and subjective well-being distinctively engage with the hostile-world scenario. Thus, MIL can make the adversity represented by the hostile-world scenario more interpretable by letting individuals conceive their lives in comprehensible terms, whereas subjective well-being can make such adversity more manageable by letting individuals evaluate their lives positively even in negative conditions.

According to the model, MIL and subjective well-being interact in complementary modes of amplification and compensation (Shmotkin & Shrira, 2013). In the amplification mode, the two resources become closely associated with each other as adversity intensifies. Thus, a meaningful reconstruction of the hostile-world scenario facilitates resilient self-perceptions and beneficial engagements that may summon a stronger subjective well-being (Baumeister, 1991; Steger, 2009). In parallel, by regulating the hostile-world scenario, subjective well-being constitutes a favorable psychological environment that facilitates the generation and awareness of MIL (King et al., 2006). The other complementary mode of compensation follows the presumption that individuals may find redemption in the reestablishment of MIL when reality makes it hard for them to rely on subjective well-being or, conversely, may seek experiences that boost subjective well-being when MIL proves deceptive and senseless. Accordingly, studies found that when one resource (either MIL or subjective well-being) was low, the other resource (either subjective well-being or MIL) served to mitigate the effects of trauma and adversity on health (Shrira, Palgi, Ben-Ezra, & Shmotkin, 2011; Shrira et al., 2015). For example, in the SHARE-Israel survey of older adults, when subjective well-being was *low* (but not when it was high), the negative association between MIL and functional problems (physical symptoms, disability, depressive symptoms) was *stronger* for those who reported life adversity compared to those who reported no adversity (Shrira et al., 2011).

To conclude this section, we have shown that major theoretical frameworks view MIL as well as subjective well-being as pivotal resources when one is coping with the double burden of aging and trauma. These frameworks serve as a theoretical background in an attempt to understand the unique experience of many Israeli older adults in coping with aging and trauma through MIL. The next section returns to those Israeli older adults who have been exposed to massive trauma with the aim of demonstrating how MIL serves to ameliorate suffering even following (or amid) such horrific events.

Meaning in Life Among Holocaust Survivors

Holocaust survivors constitute a relatively large group of Israeli older adults and are estimated to constitute nearly one-third of the 70+ age group (Shnoor & Be'er, 2019). Literature reviews (Shmotkin, Shrira, Goldberg, & Palgi, 2011; Shmotkin, Shrira, & Palgi, 2011), as well as a comprehensive meta-analysis study (Barel et al., 2010), concluded that Holocaust survivors typically present general resilience alongside specific vulnerabilities. That is, relative to their counterparts who were not directly exposed to the Holocaust, Holocaust survivors suffer from higher rates of PTSD symptoms and expressions of distress, yet they do not fare worse in many other aspects of functioning in their lives. Most important in this conclusion is the notion that evident resilience often coincides with painful vulnerabilities within the same individual sphere of the survivor (Shmotkin, Shrira, Goldberg, & Palgi, 2011).

In an attempt to explain the survivors' general resilience, several scholars proposed that MIL was a vital resource for surviving the Holocaust and its aftermath. Frankl (1963, 1969), a Holocaust survivor himself, was one of the first to highlight the importance of MIL to survival. During the Holocaust, many survivors found relief in dwelling on relatively demarcated themes of meaning, such as maintaining their self-decency, adhering to their religious faith, or vowing to serve as a voice for those who perished (Armour, 2010). Following the Holocaust, the survivors' postwar familial and professional adjustment, as well as frequent social successes, served as an ultimate proof that the demonic Nazi plan to annihilate the Jewish people was thwarted (Kahana, Harel, & Kahana, 2005). In later life, it is possible that many survivors found meaning in the very fact that they survived into old age, especially when they successfully preserved good physical health (Elran-Barak et al., 2018).

In accordance with Erikson's (1968, 1982) notion of integrity via a sense of belongingness to something that is greater than the self, many Holocaust survivors derived meaning from taking part in the collective effort of building and shaping the state of Israel. Relatedly, the aforementioned meta-analysis found that Holocaust survivors living in countries other than Israel showed less well-being and social adaptation than did their comparisons, but no difference in these specific markers was found between Holocaust survivors and comparisons living in Israel (Barel et al., 2010). The authors suggested that, unlike many of their counterparts who lived elsewhere, Israeli Holocaust survivors could extract meaning from both individual and social sources.

Further resting on Eriksonian notions, some researchers tried to understand how Holocaust survivors review and narrate their life story. The life review task ought to be a laborious challenge for survivors who have lived in irreconcilable worlds of normalcy and trauma. As expected, when assessing anchor periods—subjectively delimited fragments of time that are outstandingly meaningful in one's life (i.e., "the happiest period," "the most miserable period")—survivors depicted more suffering in negative periods. Nevertheless, these narrative segments seemed to remain encapsulated from positive anchor periods that contained happiness and satisfaction to the same extent as nonsurvivors (Cohen & Shmotkin, 2007; Shrira & Shmotkin, 2008). Similarly, the reminiscence of Holocaust survivors was more characterized by bitter memories and memories of significant persons who had been lost, but, at the same time, survivors recollected memories in order to find worth and meaning to the same extent as nonsurvivors (King et al., 2015). Even when survivors reminisced bitter memories, they frequently accompanied these memories with important life lessons they wished to transfer to the next generations (O'Rourke et al., 2015). The preservation of memories of those who perished could also promote the survivors' sense of meaning and coherence (Zeidner & Aharoni-David, 2015).

Also related to Erikson's (1968, 1982) concept of integrity versus despair is the issue of forgiveness. *Prima facie*, forgiveness seems impossible in view of the horrific acts perpetrated against these survivors. Still, some Holocaust survivors aimed toward forgiveness as a way to accept the past and attain a sense of inner peace (Hantman, 2010). For example, the case of Eva Kor, one of the remaining Mengele twins, became famous when she publicly forgave the Nazis for what they had done to her and her family (Diamond & Ronel, 2019). On the other hand, some survivors preserved meaning in life by withholding forgiveness. Maintaining repulsion and vengeful feelings can be seen as an expression of self-respect, a respect for the greater moral order, and an ethical stance taken on behalf of those who perished (Krystal, 1981). In this context, a notable example is the case of Simon Wiesenthal, who decided to withhold absolution from a dying Nazi soldier who felt haunted by his crimes (Wiesenthal, 1998). Thus, the option of forgiveness among Holocaust survivors appears to be another important route empowering MIL and should be further explored.

Following Frankl (1963, 1969), who proposed that trauma creates an existential crisis, and Janoff-Bulman (1992), who suggested that trauma shatters one's world assumptions, several studies directly assessed Holocaust survivors' worldviews. Although clinical groups of survivors generally held a fragile assumptive world (Brom, Durst, & Aghassy, 2002), community-dwelling survivors showed a surprisingly mixed pattern: some views were less positive relative to those of comparisons, others were similar, and some were even more positive (Brom et al., 2002; Prager & Solomon, 1995). Palgi, Shrira, and Ben-Ezra (2011) looked at world assumptions among Ultra-orthodox religious and secular Holocaust survivors and comparisons. They found that, compared to the other groups, secular Holocaust survivors generally held less favorable views. The authors concluded that Ultra-orthodox survivors could replenish MIL through a sense of belonging to the religious community, spiritual support and guidance offered by religious author-ities, and through the meaning embedded in religious beliefs. In any case, the literature on Holocaust survivors suggests that an existential crisis may be resolved by reconstructing assumptions that regard the social world in a more intricate manner and the self as strengthened. These constituents also relate to posttraumatic growth (Calhoun & Tedeschi, 2014), seen in many survivors who succeeded in regaining self-reliance and who flourish in fa-milial and professional domains (Lev-Wiesel & Amir, 2003).

Meaning in Life Among Ex-Prisoners of War

Relative to Holocaust survivors, meaning-related concepts were assessed to a lesser extent among older adult Israeli war veterans. Such works mainly focused on ex-prisoners of war (ex-POWs). One of the most traumatic wars in Israel's history was the 1973 Yom Kippur War, which resulted in nu-merous Israeli dead and wounded. There were also approximately 300 Israeli POWs. In many cases, the captivity experience included severe tortures and humiliations that undermined the basic sense of self-integrity and prior beliefs in a just and safe world (Solomon, 1993). Solomon and her colleagues found that ex-POWs' world assumptions were less positive than combatants who were not captured. Even more startling was the fact that, across the years and up to 35 years after the war, ex-POWs' world assumptions became even more negative with time (Dekel, Peleg, & Solomon, 2013). The authors suggested that aging-related losses (e.g., physical decline, disability, loneliness) possibly triggered suppressed traumatic memories, which in turn aggravated PTSD symptoms and the succeeding meaning crisis among those war veterans. For example, hypervigilance might generate selective attention on threat cues, and increased symptoms might bring veterans to perceive themselves as totally inept. Consequently, negative views of the world and of oneself could become deeply entrenched in the veterans' meaning system.

Older adult ex-POWs further showed high levels of posttraumatic growth (Lahav, Bellin, & Solomon, 2016). There is much debate, however, whether reports of posttraumatic growth indeed reflect a genuine process of meaning reconstruction or perhaps reflect illusionary defenses, which may be beneficial in the short term but maladaptive in the long term. According to the *Janus-face model* of posttraumatic growth (Zoellner & Maercker, 2006), positive wishful thinking could comfort survivors that their suffering was not in vain. However, the preservation of illusion over long periods, as might be in the case of older adult war veterans, could increase self-disintegration as the façade of fortitude remains split-off from other parts of the self (Lahav et al., 2016). Methodological constraints make it hard to establish whether or when posttraumatic growth is genuine or primarily illusory and, still, the Janus-face model entertains the possibility that meaning systems may be more ingrained among some older adults who have been exposed to trauma and less among others.

Meaning in Life Among Older Adult Civilians Exposed to Ongoing Missile Attacks

Older adult civilians exposed to the ongoing Israel–Gaza conflict constitute another group of older adult Israelis who grapple with massive trauma. Unlike the two previous groups, who were exposed to their focal trauma in early life, these individuals experienced the focal event and its related existential crisis at older age. Older adults living in the southern part of Israel have been subjected to ongoing missile attacks due to the continuous conflict. Since 2001, thousands of rockets and mortar attacks were launched from Gaza on towns and villages in southern Israel in vacillating intensities. These attacks resulted in hundreds of casualties and the creation of a widespread sense of horror and grave disruption of daily life (Israeli Ministry of Foreign Affairs, 2015).

PTSD is relatively prevalent among older adults exposed to the ongoing Israel–Gaza conflict (Palgi, 2015) and is even higher relative to counterparts who were exposed to a time-limited warfare event (Shrira et al., 2017). Moreover, physical mobility and cognitive capacity are particularly related to PTSD symptoms following ongoing exposure, possibly because the survival of older adults living in this continuously dangerous reality heavily depends on these vital health resources (Shrira et al., 2017).

Various concomitants of MIL were found to be related to lower levels of PTSD symptoms and psychological distress in individuals exposed to missile attacks. Among these concomitants were a greater sense of coherence and a tendency to accept the situation and use positive reframing (Braun-Lewensohn & Mosseri Rubin, 2014). Reflecting insights from the literature on Holocaust survivors, lower PTSD was also related to a greater tendency to forgive (Gil et al., 2015). Although MIL may become increasingly important at old age, there is a lack of research as to whether the associations between concomitants of MIL and PTSD strengthen among exposed older adult civilians. Relatedly, one study found that, compared to other age groups, exposed older adults (age 60 and older) showed a tendency to report the lowest sense of coherence (Braun-Lewensohn & Mosseri Rubin, 2014). The authors also found that middle-aged individuals were the most resilient age group, possibly because they accomplished many developmental tasks and had more stable resources than either younger or older individuals (Braun-Lewensohn & Mosseri Rubin, 2014). Similarly, it was shown that the age of exposed older adults was negatively correlated with the will to live, a concomitant of the worthiness of life (Palgi, 2017).

Related to the notion of integrity via belongingness to something greater than the self (Erikson, 1968, 1982), older adults with a greater sense of belonging to the community were less affected by ongoing exposure to missile attacks. This was exemplified by comparing Israeli older adults living in urban versus rural communities. A staggering difference emerged in this context: PTSD was found in 30–40% of older adults living in an urban community, but only in 5–7% among those living in rural communities (Nuttman-Shwartz, Dekel, & Regev, 2015; Palgi, 2015). Indeed, older adults living in urban communities surrounding the Gaza Strip are largely of a lower socioeconomic status, whereas those in rural communities are living in kibbutzim, characterized by a higher socioeconomic status (Nuttman-Shwartz et al., 2015). Still, those in rural communities maintained higher resilience even after accounting for sociodemographic variables. Therefore, it seems that older adults in rural communities are protected against ongoing exposure due to a greater sense of belonging and solidarity—factors that augment their MIL.

Following our review of three groups of older adults who have been exposed to massive trauma (i.e., Holocaust survivors, ex-POWs, and older adults exposed to continuous missile attacks), we may conclude that the evidence converges to indicate that MIL serves as a major resource in all three groups. MIL is one major factor that helps explain the fact that many of these individuals function well despite the horrendous circumstances they lived through. In addition to MIL, there are more specific aspects of meaning, such as the meaning of old age itself, that may help regulate the challenges of old age and trauma. The next section dwells on the specific meaning of aging among older adults who have been exposed to trauma.

You're Only as Old as You Feel: The Meaning of Aging and Adaptation to Trauma

The Meaning of Aging

A developmental perspective on MIL at old age encompasses the meaning of aging itself. The meaning of aging includes various perceptions that individuals hold regarding the way they age, their age identity or the age they feel, and other perceptions they have regarding old age and old people in general (Diehl et al., 2014). Recent years have seen an outburst of research on the different ways in which older adults experience their aging. This welcome development is related to a gradual shift from attempts to define successful aging using strict objective criteria as fixed by experts to attempts that give voice to older adults' own accounts of how successfully they age (Martin et al., 2015).

Two frequently investigated perceptions in this context are subjective age and subjective nearness to death. *Subjective age* refers to the individual's evaluation of how old one perceives oneself to be, and *subjective nearness to death* refers to the individual's evaluation of how much time one has until death. The popularity of these two constructs is probably because these are two brief, straightforward ratings with an impressive predictive validity. Feeling younger than one's age or feeling further away from death predicts better future functioning and longer survival (Kotter-Grühn, Kornadt, & Stephan, 2016; Perozek, 2008). Together, these perceptions provide an integrative view of two time perspectives—one that focuses on time since birth and another that concerns time left until death. In light of the vast literature connecting these perceptions and health, it seems likely that these perceptions should also be relevant to adaptation to trauma.

The Meaning of Aging and Coping with Trauma

Several theoretical works hypothesized that the above-mentioned perceptions are especially relevant to older adults coping with traumatic events. The relationship between subjective age and traumatic symptoms was previously proposed by the *subjective weathering hypothesis* (Benson, 2014). Accordingly, experiencing trauma at early developmental stages may later lead to an older subjective age if one's emotional/cognitive maturity is not on par with current demands. Drawing on this theory, it is possible that dealing with the demands of trauma exposure in addition to coping with simultaneous aging difficulties would relate to an older age identity (Palgi, 2016). Related to subjective nearness to death, the *terror management theory* (Pyszczynski & Kesebir, 2011) suggests that developing PTSD might impair one's ability to employ anxiety-buffering mechanisms in general and, specifically, the employment of buffers against death anxiety. Individuals suffering from PTSD may thus be more pessimistic and believe that their death is closer (Palgi, 2016). It is important to add that reciprocal effects probably exist between PTSD and the above-mentioned perceptions, so that PTSD may catalyze less favorable meanings of aging while less favorable perceptions, in turn, maintain or even aggravate PTSD.

Accordingly, older adult former POWs (Avidor et al., 2016; Solomon et al., 2009) as well as older adult civilians exposed to ongoing missile attacks (Palgi, 2016) who felt older experienced higher PTSD symptoms. Similarly, feeling closer to death was related to higher posttraumatic distress in these two groups who have been exposed to massive trauma (Avidor, Palgi, & Solomon, 2017; Palgi, 2016). Moreover, favorable perceptions mitigated the negative effect of PTSD, as even when ongoing missile attacks resulted in probable PTSD, there were no other conspicuous effects of PTSD on health and aging when survivors successfully maintained a youthful age identity (Shrira et al., 2016). In addition, favorable perceptions (i.e., feeling younger or further away from death) resulted in a strengthened positive association of PTSD symptoms with posttraumatic growth (Palgi, 2016) as well as in a strengthened positive association of PTSD symptoms with the will to live (Palgi, 2017). In other words, even when posttraumatic distress is high, perceiving aging as meaningful increases the likelihood of finding meaning and positive change amid suffering.

Conclusion

Overall, this chapter provided both theoretical and empirical frameworks for the central role of MIL in the struggle of older adults against the twofold burden of aging and traumatic adversity. We saw that seminal theoretical works (e.g., Erikson, 1968, 1982; Frankl, 1963, 1969) received much support by research presenting MIL as essential to the management of aging and traumatic exposure. The integrative model, proposed by Shmotkin (2005), formulates the roles of MIL and subjective well-being in tandem, thus capturing interacting eudemonic and hedonic resources against the threats of aging and traumatic events that largely dwell within individuals' hostile-world scenario.

A further review of the evidence suggested that concomitants of MIL mitigate the effects of distal as well as proximal massive traumatic exposure on older adult Israelis. MIL may be derived from reconstructing more intricate life narratives or worldviews. Feeling one is part of something greater than the self seems to be another important pathway to a stronger sense of meaning (Wong, 2016). Such pathways may be fostered by adherence to religious, spiritual, or ideological beliefs or otherwise via affiliation to a supportive community. Other relevant concepts, such as posttraumatic growth and forgiveness, were assessed to a lesser extent among Israeli older adults exposed to massive trauma, but even more striking is the fact that a direct assessment of MIL is still scarce. Moreover, although MIL interacts with subjective well-being (Shmotkin & Shrira, 2012, 2013; Shrira et al., 2011, 2015), it is still less known if and how these mutual systems operate in groups that have been exposed to massive trauma. Therefore, the manifestations and effects of MIL and some of its less-examined constructs in these groups await further clarification. In addition, as some individuals cope with both distal and proximal events (Martin, da Rosa, & Poon, 2011), it is necessary to take a deeper look into this combined burden (cf. Shrira, Palgi, Ben-Ezra, & Shmotkin, 2010) and how it is mitigated by MIL.

Finally, the developmental perspective on the meaning of aging has brought additional important insights into ways whereby Israeli older adults cope with massive traumatic events. More specifically, the vitality of a youthful age identity together with an expanded future perspective, embedded in the feeling that death is far away, provide strength and hope in a hostile environment shaped by trauma- and age-related losses. As individuals hold various perceptions of aging and dying (Shrira, Bodner, & Palgi, 2014), future efforts should assess patterns whereby these perceptions of aging and dying interact with each other in determining posttraumatic reactions in later life.

As a final note, although this chapter has focused on MIL in the lives of Israeli older adults, insights gathered from the literature regarding this population may indeed be relevant to older adults coping with traumatic events elsewhere. Indeed, as mentioned earlier, human efforts to search and formulate MIL are universal, and these efforts are pronounced among older adults who have been exposed to trauma all around the world (e.g., Krause, 2012).

Highlights

- Older adults mobilize meaning in life and subjective well-being in order to manage the double burden of aging and traumatic adversity.
- Meaning in life (MIL) and its concomitants mitigate the effects of distal (e.g., Holocaust and Israeli wars) as well as proximal (e.g., terrorism) massive traumatic exposures on Israeli older adults.
- The beneficial role of MIL may operate via various pathways such as adherence to religious, spiritual, and ideological beliefs, as well as affiliation with a supportive community.
- A favorable meaning of aging, reflected by a youthful age identity and feeling farther away from death, provides strength and hope for Israeli older adults who have been exposed to trauma.

References

American Psychiatric Association. (2013). *Diagnostic and statistical manual of mental disorders* (5th ed.). APA.

Andreas, S., Schulz, H., Volkert, J., Dehoust, M., Sehner, S., Suling, A., Ausín, B., Canuto, A., Crawford, M., Da Ronch, C., Grassi, L., Hershkovitz, Y., Muñoz, M., Quirk, A., Rotenstein, O., Santos-Olmo, A. B., Shalev, A., Strehle, J., Weber, K., . . . Härter, M. (2017). Prevalence of mental disorders in elderly people: The European MentDis_ICF65+ study. *The British Journal of Psychiatry, 210*(2), 125–131. https://doi.org/10.1192/bjp.bp.115.180463

Armour, M. (2010). Meaning making in survivorship: Application to Holocaust survivors. *Journal of Human Behavior in the Social Environment, 20*, 440–468. doi:10.1080/10911350903274997

Avidor, S., Benyamini, Y., & Solomon, Z. (2016). Subjective age and health in later life: The role of posttraumatic symptoms. *The Journals of Gerontology Series B: Psychological Sciences and Social Sciences, 71*, 415–424. doi:10.1093/geronb/gbu150

Avidor, S., Palgi, Y., & Solomon, Z. (2017). Lower subjective life expectancy in later life is a risk factor for posttraumatic stress symptoms among trauma survivors. *Psychological Trauma: Theory, Research, Practice, and Policy, 9*, 198–206. doi:10.1037/tra0000182

Baltes, P. B. (1997). On the incomplete architecture of human ontogeny: Selection, optimization, and compensation as foundation of developmental theory. *American Psychologist, 52*, 366–380. doi:10.1037/0003-066X.52.4.366

Barel, E., Van IJzendoorn, M. H., Sagi-Schwartz, A., & Bakermans-Kranenburg, M. J. (2010). Surviving the Holocaust: A meta-analysis of the long-term sequelae of a genocide. *Psychological Bulletin, 136*, 677–698. doi:10.1037/a0020339

Baumeister, R. F. (1991). *Meanings of life*. Guilford.

Benson, J. E. (2014). Reevaluating the "subjective weathering" hypothesis: Subjective aging, coping resources, and the stress process. *Journal of Health and Social Behavior, 55*, 73–90. doi:10.1177/0022146514521214

Bleich, A., Gelkopf, M., Melamed, Y., & Solomon, Z. (2005). Emotional impact of exposure to terrorism among young-old and old-old Israeli citizens. *American Journal of Geriatric Psychiatry, 13*, 705–712. doi:10.1097/00019442-200508000-00010

Braun-Lewensohn, O., & Mosseri Rubin, M. (2014). Personal and communal resilience in communities exposed to missile attacks: Does intensity of exposure matter? *The Journal of Positive Psychology, 9*, 175–182. doi:10.1080/17439760.2013.873946

Brom, D., Durst, N., & Aghassy, G. (2002). The phenomenology of posttraumatic distress in older adult Holocaust survivors. *Journal of Clinical Geropsychology, 8*, 189–201. doi:10.1023/A:1015944227382

Calhoun, L. G., & Tedeschi, R. G. (2014). *Handbook of posttraumatic growth: Research and practice*. Psychology Press.

Cohen, K., & Shmotkin, D. (2007). Emotional ratings of anchor periods in life and their relation to subjective well-being among Holocaust survivors. *Personality and Individual Differences, 43*, 495–506. doi:10.1016/j.paid.2006.12.018

Danieli, Y. (1981). On the achievement of integration in aging survivors of the Nazi Holocaust. *Journal of Geriatric Psychiatry, 14*, 191–210.

Dekel, S., Peleg, T., & Solomon, Z. (2013). The relationship of PTSD to negative cognitions: A 17-year longitudinal study. *Psychiatry: Interpersonal and Biological Processes, 76*, 241–255. doi:10.1521/psyc.2013.76.3.241

Diamond, S., & Ronel, N. (2019). From bondage to liberation: The forgiveness case of Holocaust survivor Eva Mozes Kor. *Journal of Aggression, Maltreatment & Trauma, 28*, 996–1016. doi:10.1080/10926771.2018.1468376

Diehl, M., Wahl, H. W., Barrett, A. E., Brothers, A. F., Miche, M., Montepare, J. M., Westerhof, G. J., & Wurm, S. (2014). Awareness of aging: Theoretical considerations on an emerging concept. *Developmental Review, 34*, 93–113. doi:10.1016/j.dr.2014.01.001

Elran-Barak, R., Barak, A., Lomranz, J., & Benyamini, Y. (2018). Proactive aging among Holocaust survivors: Striving for the best possible life. *The Journals of Gerontology Series B: Psychological Sciences and Social Sciences, 73*, 1446–1456. doi:10.1093/geronb/gbw136

Erikson, E. H. (1968). *Identity, youth, and crisis*. Norton.

Erikson, E. H. (1982). *The life cycle completed: A review*. Norton.

Frankl, V. E. (1963). *Man's search for meaning: An introduction to logotherapy*. Washington Square Press.

Frankl, V. E. (1969). *The will to meaning: Foundations and applications of logotherapy*. New American Library.

George, L. S., & Park, C. L. (2016). Meaning in life as comprehension, purpose, and mattering: Toward integration and new research questions. *Review of General Psychology, 20*, 205–220. doi:10.1037/gpr0000077

Gil, S., Weinberg, M., Or-Chen, K., & Harel, H. (2015). Risk factors for DSM 5 PTSD symptoms in Israeli civilians during the Gaza war. *Brain and Behavior, 5*, e00316. doi:10.1002/brb3.316

Hantman, S. (2010). Holocaust survivor typology and forgiveness. *Journal of Human Behaviour in the Social Environment, 20*, 507–524. doi:10.1080/10911350903275226

Israeli Ministry of Foreign Affairs. (2015). The 2014 Gaza conflict: Factual and legal aspects. http://www.mfa.gov.il

Janoff-Bulman, R. (1992). *Shattered assumptions: Towards a new psychology of trauma*. Free Press.

Kahana, B., Harel, Z., & Kahana, E. (2005). *Holocaust survivors and immigrants: Late life adaptations*. Springer.

Keyes, C. L. M., Shmotkin, D., & Ryff, C. D. (2002). Optimizing well-being: The empirical encounter of two traditions. *Journal of Personality and Social Psychology, 82*, 1007–1022. doi:10.1037/0022-3514.82.6.1007

King, D. B., Cappeliez, P., Carmel, S., Bachner, Y. G., & O'Rourke, N. (2015). Remembering genocide: The effects of early life trauma on reminiscence functions among Israeli Holocaust survivors. *Traumatology, 21*, 145–152. doi:10.1037/trm0000040

King, L. A., Hicks, J. A., Krull, J., & Del Gaiso, A. K. (2006). Positive affect and the experience of meaning in life. *Journal of Personality and Social Psychology, 90*, 179–196. doi:10.1037/0022-3514.90.1.179

Kotter-Grühn, D., Kornadt, A. E., & Stephan, Y. (2016). Looking beyond chronological age: Current knowledge and future directions in the study of subjective age. *Gerontology, 62*, 86–93. doi:10.1159/000438671

Krause, N. (2012). Meaning in life and healthy aging. In P. T. P. Wong (Ed.), *The human quest for meaning: Theories, research and application* (2nd ed., pp. 409–432). Routledge.

Krystal, H. (1981). The aging survivor of the Holocaust: Integration and self-healing in posttraumatic states. *Journal of Geriatric Psychiatry, 14*, 165–189.

Lahav, Y., Bellin, E. S., & Solomon, Z. (2016). Posttraumatic growth and shattered world assumptions among ex-POWs: The role of dissociation. *Psychiatry: Interpersonal and Biological Processes, 79*, 418–432. doi:10.1080/00332747.2016.1142776

Levinson, D., Zilber, N., Lerner, Y., Grinshpoon, A., & Levav, I. (2007). Prevalence of mood and anxiety disorders in the community: Results from the Israel National Health Survey. *The Israel Journal of Psychiatry and Related Sciences, 44*, 94–103.

Lev-Wiesel, R., & Amir, M. (2003). Posttraumatic growth among Holocaust child survivors. *Journal of Loss and Trauma, 8*, 229–237. doi:10.1080/15325020305884

Lifshitz, R., Ifrah, K., Markovitz, N., & Shmotkin, D. (2020). Do past and prospective adversities intersect? Distinct effects of cumulative adversity and the hostile-world scenario on functioning at later life. *Aging and Mental Health, 24*(7), 1116–1125. doi:10.1080/13607863.2019.1597014

Lomranz, J., & Benyamini, Y. (2016). The ability to live with incongruence: Aintegration— the concept and its operationalization. *Journal of Adult Development, 23*, 79–92. doi:10.1007/s10804-015-9223-4

Martela, F., & Steger, M. F. (2016). The three meanings of meaning in life: Distinguishing coherence, purpose, and significance. *The Journal of Positive Psychology, 11*, 531–545. doi:10.1080/17439760.2015.1137623

Martin, P., da Rosa, G., & Poon, L. W. (2011). The impact of life events on the oldest old. In L. W. Poon & J. Cohen-Mansfield (Eds.), *Understanding well-being in the oldest old* (pp. 96–110). Cambridge University Press.

Martin, P., Kelly, N., Kahana, B., Kahana, E., Willcox, B. J., Willcox, D. C., & Poon, L. W. (2015). Defining successful aging: A tangible or elusive concept? *The Gerontologist, 55*, 14–25. doi:10.1093/geront/gnu044

Nuttman-Shwartz, O., Dekel, R., & Regev, I. (2015). Continuous exposure to life threats among different age groups in different types of communities. *Psychological Trauma: Theory, Research, Practice, and Policy, 7*, 269–276. doi:10.1037/a0038772

Ogle, C. M., Rubin, D. C., Berntsen, D., & Siegler, I. C. (2013). The frequency and impact of exposure to potentially traumatic events over the life course. *Clinical Psychological Science, 1*, 426–434. doi:10.1177/2167702613485076

O'Rourke, N., Canham, S., Wertman, A., Chaudhury, H., Carmel, S., Bachner, Y. G., & Peres, H. (2015). Holocaust survivors' memories of past trauma and the functions of reminiscence. *The Gerontologist, 56*, 743–752. doi:10.1093/geront/gnu168.

Palgi, Y. (2015). Predictors of the new criteria for probable PTSD among older adults. *Psychiatry Research, 230*, 777–782. doi:10.1016/j.psychres.2015.11.006

Palgi, Y. (2016). Subjective age and perceived distance-to-death moderate the association between posttraumatic stress symptoms and posttraumatic growth among older adults. *Aging & Mental Health, 20*, 948–954. doi:10.1080/13607863.2015.1047320

Palgi, Y. (2017). Matter of will: Subjective nearness-to-death moderates the association between probable PTSD and the will-to-live among older adults. *Psychiatry Research, 249*, 180–186. doi:10.1016/j.psychres.2017.01.021

Palgi, Y., Shrira, A., & Ben-Ezra, M. (2011). World assumptions and psychological functioning among ultra-orthodox and secular Holocaust survivors. *Traumatology, 17*, 14–21. doi:10.1177/1534765610395616

Palgi, Y., Shrira, A., & Shmotkin, D. (2015). Aging with trauma across the lifetime and experiencing trauma in old age: Vulnerability and resilience intertwined. In K. E. Cherry (Ed.), *Traumatic stress and long-term recovery: Coping with disasters and other negative life events* (pp. 293–308). Springer. doi:10.1007/978-3-319-18866-9

Park, C. L. (2010). Making sense of the meaning literature: An integrative review of meaning making and its effects on adjustment to stressful life events. *Psychological Bulletin, 136,* 257–301. doi:10.1037/a0018301

Perozek, M. G. (2008). Using subjective expectations to forecast longevity: Do survey respondents know something we don't know? *Demography, 45,* 95–113. doi:10.1353/dem.2008.0010

Prager, E., & Solomon, Z. (1995). Perceptions of world benevolence, meaningfulness, and self-worth among elderly Israeli Holocaust survivors and non-survivors. *Anxiety, Stress, and Coping, 8,* 265–277. doi:10.1080/10615809508249378

Pyszczynski, T., & Kesebir, P. (2011). Anxiety buffer disruption theory: A terror management account of posttraumatic stress disorder. *Anxiety, Stress, and Coping, 24,* 3–26. doi:10.1080/10615806.2010.517524

Robinson, J. S., & Larson, C. (2010). Are traumatic events necessary to elicit symptoms of posttraumatic stress? *Psychological Trauma: Theory, Research, Practice, and Policy, 2,* 71–76. doi:10.1037/a0018954

Ryff, C. D. (2014). Psychological well-being revisited: Advances in the science and practice of Eudaimonia. *Psychotherapy and Psychosomatics, 83,* 10–28. doi:10.1159/000353263

Ryff, C. D., Heller, A. S., Schaefer, S. M., Van Reekum, C., & Davidson, R. J. (2016). Purposeful engagement, healthy aging, and the brain. *Current Behavioral Neuroscience Reports, 3,* 318–327. doi:10.1007/s40473-016-0096-z

Shmotkin, D. (2005). Happiness in face of adversity: Reformulating the dynamic and modular bases of subjective well-being. *Review of General Psychology, 9,* 291–325. doi:10.1037/1089-2680.9.4.291

Shmotkin, D. (2011). The pursuit of happiness: Alternative conceptions of subjective well-being. In L. W. Poon & J. Cohen-Mansfield (Eds.), *Understanding well-being in the oldest old* (pp. 27–45). Cambridge University Press. https://doi.org/10.1017/CBO9780511920974.004

Shmotkin, D., Avidor, S., & Shrira, A. (2016). The role of the hostile-world scenario in predicting physical and mental health outcomes in older adults. *Journal of Aging and Health, 28,* 863–889. doi:10.1177/0898264315614005

Shmotkin, D., & Litwin, H. (2009). Cumulative adversity and depressive symptoms among older adults in Israel: The differential roles of self-oriented versus other-oriented events of potential trauma. *Social Psychiatry and Psychiatric Epidemiology, 44,* 989–997. doi:10.1007/s00127-009-0020-x

Shmotkin, D., & Shrira, A. (2012). On the distinction between subjective well-being and meaning in life: Regulatory versus reconstructive functions in the face of a hostile world. In P. T. P. Wong (Ed.), *The human quest for meaning: Theories, research, and applications* (2nd ed., pp. 143–164). Routledge.

Shmotkin, D., & Shrira, A. (2013). Subjective well-being and meaning in life in a hostile world: Proposing a configurative perspective. In J. A. Hicks & C. Routledge (Eds.), *The experience of meaning in life: Classical perspectives, emerging themes, and controversies* (pp. 77–86). Springer. doi:10.1007/978-94-007-6527-6_6

Shmotkin, D., Shrira, A., Goldberg, S., & Palgi, Y. (2011). Resilience and vulnerability among aging Holocaust survivors and their families: An intergenerational overview. *Journal of Intergenerational Relationships, 9,* 7–21. doi:10.1080/15350770.2011.544202

Shmotkin, D., Shrira, A., & Palgi, Y. (2011). Does trauma linger into old-old age: Using the Holocaust experience as a paradigm. In L. W. Poon & J. Cohen-Mansfield (Eds.), *Understanding well-being in the oldest old* (pp. 81–95). Cambridge University Press. doi:10.1017/CBO9780511920974.007

Shnoor, Y., & Be'er, S. (Eds.). (2019). *The elderly in Israel—the 2018 statistical abstract.* JDC-Brookdale Institute and JDC-ESHEL.

Shrira, A., Bodner, E., & Palgi, Y. (2014). The interactive effect of subjective age and subjective distance-to-death on psychological distress of older adults. *Aging and Mental Health, 18,* 1066–1070. doi:10.1080/13607863.2014.915925

Shrira, A., Palgi, Y., Ben-Ezra, M., Hoffman, Y., & Bodner, E. (2016). A youthful age identity mitigates the effect of post-traumatic stress disorder symptoms on successful aging. *American Journal of Geriatric Psychiatry, 24,* 174–175. doi:10.1016/j.jagp.2015.07.006

Shrira, A., Palgi, Y., Ben-Ezra, M., & Shmotkin, D. (2010). Do Holocaust survivors show increased vulnerability or resilience to post-Holocaust cumulative adversity? *Journal of Traumatic Stress, 23,* 367–375. doi:10.1002/jts.20524

Shrira, A., Palgi, Y., Ben-Ezra, M., & Shmotkin, D. (2011). How subjective well-being and meaning in life interact in the hostile world? *Journal of Positive Psychology, 6,* 273–285. doi:10.1080/17439760.2011.577090

Shrira, A., & Shmotkin, D. (2008). Can the past keep life pleasant even for old-old trauma survivors? *Aging & Mental Health, 12,* 807–819. doi:10.1080/13607860802428018

Shrira, A., Shmotkin, D., Palgi, Y., Hoffman, Y., Bodner, E., Ben-Ezra, M., & Litwin, H. (2017). Older adults exposed to ongoing and intense time-limited missile attacks: Differences in symptoms of posttraumatic stress disorder. *Psychiatry: Interpersonal and Biological Processes, 80,* 64–78. doi:10.1080/00332747.2016.1178028

Shrira, A., Shmotkin, D., Palgi, Y., Soffer, Y., Hamama Raz, Y., Tal-Katz, P., Ben-Ezra, M., & Benight, C. C. (2015). How do meaning in life and positive affect relate to adaptation to stress? The case of firefighters following the Mount Carmel Forest Fire. *Israel Journal of Psychiatry and Related Sciences, 52,* 68–70.

Solomon, Z. (1993). *Combat stress reaction: The enduring toll of war.* Plenum Press.

Solomon, Z., & Ginzburg, K. (1998). War trauma and the aged: An Israeli perspective. In J. Lomranz (Ed.), *Handbook of aging and mental health: An integrative approach* (pp. 135–152). Springer.

Solomon, Z., Helvitz, H., & Zerach, G. (2009). Subjective age, PTSD, and physical health among war veterans. *Aging & Mental Health, 13,* 405–413. doi:10.1080/13607860802459856Steger, M. F. (2009). Meaning in life. In S. J. Lopez & C. R. Snyder (Eds.), *Oxford library of psychology. Oxford handbook of positive psychology* (pp. 679–687). Oxford University Press.

Wiesenthal, S. (1998). *The sunflower: On the possibilities and limits of forgiveness.* Schocken Books.

Wong, P. T. P. (2014). Viktor Frankl's meaning seeking model and positive psychology. In A. Batthyany & P. Russo-Netzer (Eds.), *Meaning in existential and positive psychology* (pp. 149–184). Springer.

Wong, P. T. P. (2016). Meaning-seeking, self-transcendence, and well-being. In A. Batthyany (Ed.), *Logotherapy and existential analysis: Proceedings of the Viktor Frankl Institute* (Vol. 1, pp. 311–322). Springer.

Zeidner, M., & Aharoni-David, E. (2015). Memories of Holocaust-related trau-
    matic experiences, sense of coherence, and survivors' subjective well-being in late
    life: Some puzzling findings. *Anxiety, Stress, & Coping, 28,* 254–271. doi:10.1080/
    10615806.2014.954244
Zoellner, T., & Maercker, A. (2006). Posttraumatic growth in clinical psychology—A crit-
    ical review and introduction of a two component model. *Clinical Psychology Review,
    26,* 626–653. doi:10.1016/j.cpr.2006.01.008

8

In Search for Meaning Through Survivors' Memoirs

Intergenerational Healing Processes in Families of Holocaust Survivors in the Israeli Context

Adi Duchin and Hadas Wiseman

The long-term effects of the Holocaust, which took place more than 70 years ago, continue to resonate in the lives of many individuals and families in Israel today. In many families, the story of a family member who survived the Holocaust is part of the family fabric, whether it was spoken about or not. The impact that different family members attribute to the Holocaust story of the survivor and the roles they ascribe to it are many and varied. Indeed, the resonance of the story can be felt for each family member both within intergenerational family relations and outside of the family. The search for meaning as a resource for coping with traumatic life events was described in Viktor's Frankl's book *Man's Search for Meaning* (1946), in his words about his experience as a Holocaust survivor.

> The purpose of my words was to find a full meaning in our life, then and there, in that hut and in that practically hopeless situation. I saw that my efforts had been successful. When the electric bulb flared up again, I saw the miserable figures of my friends limping toward me to thank me with tears in their eyes. (p. 133)

Meaning in life has been defined as the extent to which one's life is experienced as making sense, comprising goals, and mattering in the world (Steger 2009; Steger & Park, 2012). Massive trauma harms severely the traumatized individual's comprehension and making sense of the world. Therefore, constructing meaning following massive traumatic

Adi Duchin and Hadas Wiseman, *In Search for Meaning Through Survivors' Memoirs* In: *Finding Meaning*. Edited by: Ofra Mayseless and Pninit Russo-Netzer, Oxford University Press. © Oxford University Press 2022. DOI: 10.1093/oso/9780190910358.003.0008 experiences is crucial for the ability to cope and experience posttraumatic growth (Calhoun & Tedeschi, 2013; Tedeschi & Calhoun, 2004). The search for meaning in the context of massive trauma concerns the discrepancy between meaning frameworks and experience, which causes distress (Dalgleish, 2004). In the families of Holocaust survivors, passing on the family legacy (Danieli, 2007) may involve an attempt to cope with this discrepancy in order to create meaning for the survivor and the next generations.

Writing a memoir has been a widespread phenomenon among Holocaust survivors. One way in which survivors can tell their traumatic stories to themselves, their children and grandchildren, and to the world, is by writing a memoir about their personal narrative and publishing it as a book (Duchin & Wiseman, 2019). Writing about a traumatic event enables the creation of a cohesive narrative and provides a way to fill in the gaps that often accompany traumatic memory (Herman, 1992; Laub, 2005; Pennebaker, 1989). The processes involved in writing the traumatic narrative contribute to creating coherency and comprehension that enable meaning-making.

This chapter focuses on "intergenerational encounters" between the writing of the traumatic story of a survivor family member, on one hand, and the reading of the story by the second and third generations, on the other, highlighting the encounters within each family. Writing and reading are a means of searching for meaning in which the survivors' writing (Duchin & Wiseman, 2019) is considered the first link in the familial search for meaning, followed by the reading responses of the children and grandchildren. The meanings accorded to writing the memoir by the survivor, together with those accorded to reading it by the family members—the second and third generations—are at the heart of our chapter.

The chapter is based on a study of 12 families in which the survivor wrote a memoir and published it as a book. In each family, the survivor-writer was interviewed (Duchin & Wiseman, 2019), as well as representatives of the second and third generations. The analysis of interviews with the family members gave rise to three family types. It is important to emphasize that we invoke these narratives and the search for meaning in the context of the Israeli scene, in which the resonance of the Holocaust trauma is felt to this day even more than 70 years later.

Intergenerational Transmission in Families of Survivors

Intergenerational transmission in the family vis-à-vis a traumatic Holocaust story has been frequently described in the literature, both relating to the survivor generation and other generations in the family (Danieli, 2007; Shmotkin et al., 2011). Holocaust survivors have been characterized as experiencing what is known in the literature as "survivor syndrome" (Niederland, 1968), but also as achieving high functioning and impressive success in their lives (Felsen, 1998; Sagi-Schwartz, 2015; Shmotkin et al., 2011). The children of survivors, called the "second generation" (Solomon, 1998), often report being close emotionally to the story of their parents' survival and to feeling that they live in the shadow of their parents' trauma (Bar-On, 1995; Hass, 1996). In this context, "disorganized attachment" (i.e., relationships characterized by confusion and difficulty in creating a coherent narrative) have been found to characterize members of the second generation. In addition, it has been found that they have a great need to satisfy the needs of their parents in a way that sometimes makes their own functioning difficult (Scharf & Mayseless, 2011).

The literature on intergenerational transmission in relation to the third generation—the grandchildren of the survivor, the children of second-generation family members—has focused on the meanings they attribute to their grandparents' stories and their impact on their lives (Bar-On, 1995; Chaitin, 2003; Duchin & Wiseman, 2016; Scharf & Mayseless, 2011). In relation to both the second and third generations, Dan Bar-On (1995) used the term "relevance of the survival story" to describe to what extent a family member feels the Holocaust story is germane to his or her life. It was found that second-generation children believed their parent-survivors' stories were relevant to their lives in numerous ways and that they identified strongly with their parents. The third generation, however, was found to identify less, and, while the story is relevant to them, the ways in which it is relevant differ from those of their parents (Bar-On, 1995; Chaitin, 2003). A qualitative study of the members of the third generation explored their ability to ask themselves whether and how their grandparents' story is relevant to their lives. It was found that that they engage in dialogue with their grandparents' story more freely than was possible for their parents, the second-generation sons and daughters (Duchin & Wiseman, 2016).

Intergenerational Communication in Families of Survivors

Familial communication patterns between survivor parents and their children concerning the Holocaust story are key to the process of intergenerational transmission in the families of the survivors. Bar-On (1995), who was the first to examine the life stories of families of Holocaust survivors, coined the term "double wall" to describe the difficulties many survivors had in relating what happened to them to their children. On the part of the parents this difficulty stemmed from their desire to protect their children from horrific stories; simultaneously, children experienced difficulty in asking questions, mainly because they feared this would cause their parents further suffering. In cases where the survivor parents or their children dared to try to break through the wall and talk about what happened, the reaction from the other side was often severe and distressful, which led to renewed isolation on the two sides of the wall. This dynamic, as expressed in interpersonal narratives of the second generation, was termed "mutual overprotection," in which the parents' tendency to overprotect their children was met with the children's tendency to be overprotective of their parents (Wiseman, Metzl, & Barber, 2006).

However, while in some families the story was dominated by silence and the survivor family member did not share it with family members for many years, in other families it was a topic of conversation and preoccupation (Bar-On, 1995; Greenspan, 1992; Krell, 1985; Wiseman & Barber, 2008). An additional family communication pattern termed "knowing-not knowing" refers to families in which the parents' story was nonverbally present in the home yet had never been fully, verbally told to the second generation (Wiseman & Barber, 2008; Wiseman et al., 2006).

Contrasting communication patterns between survivors and members of the second generation to those of the third generation, Bar-On wrote

> Still, within the families of the survivors, the echoes of the original social silencing is still present, as many survivors had their own subjective needs not to tell their children about what they went through in order "to save" them from that past. It suggested more their lack of psychological thinking, not understanding that silencing is one of the most effective ways of transmission of trauma. In many of these families the grandchildren were the

ones who opened windows in the "double wall" as I formulated as an image of the inability of survivors and their descendants to talk openly on the burden of the past." (Bar-On, in Wiseman & Barber, 2008, foreword p. xii).

The Memory of the Holocaust Vis-à-Vis the Israeli Family

The role that the traumatic story plays in families of Holocaust survivors must also be examined within the general Israeli context. By and large, Israeli society is characterized as collectivistic, with great emphasis on the family unit and the importance of close relations within it (Mayseless, 2001). The strong emphasis on close family relations in Israel is also reflected in the intergenerational relations within the family, between parents and children, between siblings, and between grandparents and grandchildren. Family cohesion is described as positive interactions between family members that include showing affection and warmth, mutual help, and concern (Barber & Buehler, 1996). According to Olson (2000), family cohesion can range from weak, in which family members describe a strong sense of separateness relative to other family members, to strong, characterized by a robust sense of family togetherness. In Israel, it appears that commitment to the family framework and family togetherness are strong (Olson & Gorall, 2003).

In families of Holocaust survivors, it appears that family unity and cohesion take on unique hues and power. Danieli (1982) found evidence that in some families of Holocaust survivors great difficulty surrounded the separation between parents and children, and second-generation members sensed the need to compensate their parents for what and who they lost in the Holocaust (Brom, Kfir, & Dasberg, 2001; Shefet, 1994). Among other families of Holocaust survivors, the second-generation children were taught not to trust anyone outside their nuclear family (Danieli, 1982). What these families share is an emphasis on family unity as a supreme value and the message that it must remain united and cohesive in all situations. It appears that even when difficulties surround separation of survivor parents from their children and family cohesion in the classic sense in the context of family systems is not strong, the emphasis on family unity and the importance of the nuclear family is prominent (Danieli, Norris, & Engdahl, 2017).

Holocaust Memory in Families Where the Survivor's Memoir Was Published

In recent years, the number of Holocaust survivors who write and publish Holocaust memoirs in Israel and around the world, has been growing. It is estimated that in Israel alone, more than 15,000 books of this type have been published (Yad Vashem, personal communication, May 2016). A unique way to study intergenerational communication and processes of working through in families of Holocaust survivors is through the memoirs that the survivors wrote and published in book form, alongside the reactions of their sons/daughters and grandchildren. Thus, the study of meaning in this context focuses on the subjective meanings of the memoir that the three generations in the family attribute to it and the interrelations between the three generations.

Methodology

Participants

The present study comprises 12 Israeli families of Holocaust survivors and included 39 participants. The survivors (6 women and 7 men) who wrote the memoirs ranged in age from 77 to 90 ($M = 84$) at the time of the interview. The majority were young children during the war (born between 1927 and 1939) and immigrated to Israel around 1945. Also interviewed were 13 second-generation family members (7 women and 6 men), ranging in age from 54 to 62, and 13 third-generation family members (6 women and 7 men) ranging in age from 15 to 30. In 11 families, representatives from all generations were interviewed. In one family, no representative of the third generation was interviewed due to the refusal of the parents. However, in one family two representatives of the second generation and two of the third generation were interviewed.

The interviewees were recruited for the study through the survivors' published books; that is, the first author read the books and later located and contacted the writers (for more details, see Duchin & Wiseman, 2019). During the initial contact with those survivors who agreed to be interviewed, contact details regarding a second- and third-generation representative who could be potentially interviewed were obtained.

The Interview

All interviews were semi-structured and were conducted by the first author. The interviewing approach was in keeping with an emphasis on
the participant–researcher relationship in the relational approach to
interviewing for qualitative inquiry (Josselson, 2013). In all families the survivor was interviewed first, following the reasoning that the book and the
story are, first of all, his or hers. Before meeting a survivor, the interviewer
read their book. Telling survivors at the beginning of the interview that the
interviewer had read their book was an important entry point for establishing
a relationship with survivors and to communicate a sense of recognition and
appreciation for their book.

Interviews with the survivors were opened with a request to describe their
books and the process of writing, emphasizing that anything that came to
mind would be relevant. Clarification questions followed regarding issues
that had been raised in the first part of the interview, such as, for example,
the motives behind writing and how the story connected to their interpersonal relationships (Duchin & Wiseman, 2019). The interviews with the
second- and third-generation family members were opened with a request to
describe their encounter with the book written by the parent or grandparent
and later involved clarification questions regarding the reading/non-reading
and its connections to familial relationships.

Narrative Analysis

All 39 interviews were audiotaped and transcribed verbatim. The interview
material was analyzed employing qualitative methodology and followed
three major complementary steps. First, a holistic analysis was conducted
in which each interview was read and analyzed as an independent text. The
second step was a categorical analysis of each interview, during which the
main themes were identified and formulated. Each interview was treated as
a unique story, and the themes were formulated to preserve the meanings
that emerged from the interviewees' words, as understood by the researcher
(Josselson, 2011; Lieblich, Tuval-Masiach, & Zilber, 1998). The third step
was a cross-analysis in which the common themes in the interviews were
extracted and labeled (for details, see Duchin & Wiseman, 2019). Each interview was analyzed, first in relation to its generational reference group

(survivors/second generation/third generation) and, second, within families and across families, thus leading to the family classification.

Findings

Qualitative analysis of the interviews led to the identification of two primary axes of meaning along which the families could be classified. The first is the axis of cohesion, referring to the sense of emotional bonding regarding the familial Holocaust story. The second is the axis of family communication patterns about the Holocaust (i.e., the tension between speech and silence). Mapping the families along these two axes led to a typology of three family types, referring to a constellation of patterns among the three generations.

Classification of Families According to Cohesion and Communication Patterns

In mapping the families, we considered the interaction between the degree or lack of cohesion in the family and the familial communication process in passing down the story to later generations in the family. We also analyzed the principal message or legacy that unfolded generationally.

Mapping the various families by family cohesion yielded three types. Families characterized by *strong cohesion* are those in which the narratives of each of the family members interviewed about the family story have common threads with those of other family members. In contrast, families characterized by *weak cohesion* are those in which each of the family members interviewed attributes different significance to the story. Thus, it seems that in families characterized by strong cohesion, family members over three generations attribute to the story a similar place in their lives, whereas, in families characterized by weak cohesion, family members interviewed from each of the generations differed in the place the story plays in their personal identities and narratives. A third type of family is one characterized by strong cohesion between the survivor and his or her third-generation grandchildren, but where the second generation (the survivors' children) does not accord the family story similar meanings. Therefore, how the latter situate the Holocaust story of their survivor parents in their own life stories is different from the way their parents and their children (the grandchildren) situate the story in their lives. We characterized these families as being *partly cohesive* regarding the family Holocaust story.

Mapping the various family types by communication patterns yielded three categories. The first category comprises families generally characterized by open communication regarding the family story, whereby speech is more common than silence, although the story told is sometimes incomplete and may not incorporate its full emotional aspects. The second category comprises families in which the story is largely surrounded by silence and large sections of it, especially those tied to the emotional world, are not expressed verbally or openly. The third category comprises families in which the family communication pattern is characterized by disparate modes of communication between the various generations. In this case, silence is more dominant between survivors and their second-generation children, but there is more open communication between them and their grandchildren.

Classification of the 12 families according to cohesion and communication yielded three types: three families in first type, four in the second type, and five in the third type. We illustrate the three types through four families (two from the first family type, one from the second, and one from the third). Each of these families serves as a sort of "exemplar" of familial patterns of the meanings the various family members accord the family Holocaust story, the role it plays in their lives, and how the story unfolds between the various generations. Nonetheless, it should be noted that each family is unique, a world unto itself, and we do not claim that the two dimensions are the only ones at work in the family; there are no doubt subtypes within this classification.

Type 1: High Family Cohesion and Open Communication

In the Levy family (all names are pseudonyms), the survivor, Sara, spent the war as a young girl and adolescent in the ghetto. She survived in the ghetto with her mother, but lost her father and brother. After the war, Sara immigrated to Israel, married, and had three children, two of whom, a son and daughter, were interviewed, along with two grandchildren. When Sara described the process of writing the memoir she published, she attributed her main motivation as intending it for her grandchildren.

> It is really thanks to my grandchildren that I wrote so quickly. At that time they were teenagers. They weren't so young that I needed to babysit them, but because their parents work they would come to me to eat lunch. . . .
> After I began writing the book, I started to read to them what I'd written

during the week. They would correct it and add to it. They would criticize me, and if I hadn't made enough progress they would scold me. They would say, "Grandma, you didn't do anything this week. You were lazy, you were unproductive." . . . And so, I actually finished writing in less than a year. It was like a serialized story and they were eager for the next installment.

Sara described a writing process that was shared with her grandchildren and said, "Everyone had the same feeling that this was important. That what I was writing is important to everyone. That it is meaningful for everyone."

When Sara's son, Ofer, referred to his mother's writing process, he said,

I knew what was happening there and that they [the grandchildren] were reading what she was writing. She let me read after she completed it. I was very pleased to know that it was a joint project and I felt my job was to allow it to take place.

Yael, Ofer's daughter and Sara's granddaughter, related,

There was a period of time when I would really be looking forward to those afternoons with Grandma, when she would read to us what she had written during the week. We would comment on it and she would make corrections. It was a joint project for all of us.

It is evident that Sara and her family members were united around the joint project, and it appears that they all shared the perception that the writing and publishing were meaningful.

When Ofer and Yael were asked if they were familiar with Sara's story before it was written, both answered yes immediately and without hesitation. Ofer added,

I always knew my mother's story. Our home was not like those where nobody speaks or talks about it. . . . My mother always talked about it, even when it was difficult, and we always listened. We had the feeling that it was very important and also belonged to us.

In a way that echoes her father's words, Yael said that "every Holocaust Remembrance Day [the grandchildren] would have a race to see who would be the first to ask Grandma to lecture at their school, or in the army." She added,

> Grandma's story is a part of me, a part of who I am. It is my history and like when I was a child, I always loved to hear her talk about her childhood and her family, so it was important for me that she would write it down and still today her book has been with me in all the apartments I've lived in.

Sara's daughter, Yehudit, also related in her interview that

> Mom's stories have stayed with me since I was a child. They are a part of me. Even though I didn't know my grandfather or my aunts and uncles, I know them from the stories. They really lived with us in the house.

Yehudit's son, Ronen, related that when he was younger he loved to come to his grandmother's house every week and hear her read what she had written. "My grandmother and what she went through had a great impact on who I am today. She is a source of inspiration and I admire her."

In the Levy family, Sara's story is meaningful and of great importance for family members of all generations. It is evident that Sara has injected her story into the life of the family over the years in various forms, and the communication surrounding it is open and enabling and evolved further over the years during the process of writing the book. Interestingly, Sara included in her book letters written to her by her children in which they tell her how much her stories affected them during childhood. They referred to the book as a "family treasure that must be guarded." Moreover, Yehudit added that she wrote in her letter for her mother's book

> All these years we have known these characters in the book well. They are our family members. Even if they weren't with us. . . . Thank you, Mom, for making them alive for us, even after they were taken from us by the Nazi animal.

Open Communication as a Process: "Healing and Recovery"

The Rosenbergs also belonging to Type 1 families, although their open communication evolved through the years. The survivor, Avraham, survived the

Holocaust in Auschwitz as an adolescent. His daughter and granddaughter, as well as a grandson (the son of daughter who was not interviewed) participated. Avraham wrote and published his book after he retired, when he was in his sixties. His daughters were part of the writing process and greatly assisted him in publishing the book. Some 20 years after the book was originally published, Avraham and his family decided to publish a new edition in which his children and grandchildren ask him questions that appear in the book and Avraham answers them. Therefore, the new edition of the book includes not only Avraham's story as he wrote it, but also the questions and observations that arose among his family. The interviews took place while the family was working together on the second edition of the book.

Avraham described a long process of healing and recovery from the war, referring to different stages.

> The catalysts to end the repression and the willingness to open up and share the memories were the Eichmann trial,[1] the integration of Holocaust survivors in Israel, the growing awareness of the Holocaust among people in Israel, raising my children, my insatiable curiosity, and the effect of time on healing and alleviating inhibitions. It was equally important to recognize and accept the wounds of the past that have slightly healed but will never be forgotten . . . the way to start was writing.

Avraham's daughter, Rachel, described how her father originally wrote the book some 20 years previously, and her involvement in the process.

> Each time he finished a chapter he gave it to me to read and I believe also to my sister. I read it and was moved by the beautiful writing, the literary phrases. I read a lot, and because of its poetics, its simplicity and minimalism, it was so short and powerful, I began printing it. . . . He never spoke a lot about what had happened to him and when he sat down to write I was very glad. I understood it was a process that had to happen, that was good for him . . . the writing was therapy for him. Until then he had really been in post-trauma, and after he wrote, it was alleviated.

---

[1] Adolph Eichmann was a senior Nazi officer who was captured in 1960 and executed in 1962, after a public trial in Israel. The Eichmann Trial (1961–1962) is considered a turning point in Israeli society vis-à-vis its attitude toward Holocaust survivors.

It appears Rachel and her father attributed to the writing a similar meaning: healing and recovery. Rachel added, "It wasn't only therapeutic for him, but for me as well. As a young girl I would wake up every night to his screaming, and, after I read what he had written, I understood. Something within me relaxed."

Rachel said that before her father began to write she and her sister knew the story, but not in detail, and not from their father, but more from their mother, who was also a survivor and told them both of their stories. She read the story for the first time in full when she typed what her father had written by hand, and in this sense the process of writing and publishing the book brought the whole story to light and led to a change in family communication patterns that became more open as a result.

Rachel's daughter, Galit, Avraham's granddaughter, described in her interview how reading the book her grandfather had written revealed the story in full, and "Now I know what happened to him and what was with him and I can also talk to him about it freely." Avraham's oldest grandson, Roey, also said that, to a great extent, the book changed his communication with his grandfather surrounding the story.

> It's a book that he wrote after many years of silence and of blocking out his memories and what he had experienced, when I know he didn't really talk about things, he spoke very little, and this was his way of getting it all out . . . I knew a few things, a number of details, but I discovered the more colorful and in-depth details from the book. . . . I think it affected me emotionally, both as a book on a moving and difficult topic and as a book that my grandfather wrote that made me proud. It still makes me proud, and I enjoyed reading it, I found it moving and interesting. I also think that in fact it was a way to connect to him because he's not really talkative. Even after the book it's not always easy for me to get close to him, and for this reason, and surely for other reasons, for me it was a way to get into his head and connect to him in a deeper way than I could have. (Duchin & Wiseman, 2016, pp. 124–125)

It appears that the cohesion of the Rosenberg family reflects the shared meanings attributed to the book by the various family members, and the book is conceived as causing a real change in family communication, making it more open and enabling. The decision to publish a new edition of the book that includes the words of both the second and third generations reflects strong cohesion, open communication, and a sense of empowerment.

Type 2: Low Family Cohesion and Silence

In the Ron family, the grandfather, Shlomo, is a survivor who was a child during the Holocaust and was hidden during the war, first without his family and later with his sister. After the war, Shlomo immigrated to Israel with his mother and sister and began an impressive military and managerial career, until his retirement as a senior ranking officer. Shlomo's son, Omer, is also a high-ranking officer in the military. Yuval, Omer's son and Shlomo's grandson, was interviewed just before beginning his compulsory army service in the Israel Defense Forces.

When Shlomo described the role his Holocaust story played in his life he said,

> For me, the story is everything. The Holocaust is a chapter, I don't want to say the most important chapter, of our lives, but it is a very weighty one. Weighty. Very weighty. . . . Who I am today, everything I have accomplished, is first of all because of what I went through during the Holocaust. Everything begins and ends there. Whenever I begin to talk about things related to it, they [the children] stop me. They stop me. They got tired of it. . . . They divert the conversation to other channels.

While for Shlomo "the Holocaust is all I am," for his children, as he himself experienced them, the picture is different. Shlomo feels his children are no longer interested in listening to his story and what he went through and that they do not accord it the same role and meaning in their lives as he does. Omer, Shlomo's son, indeed is tired of listening to his father.

> I don't have the strength for it any longer, to hear him talk about what he went through. I can't connect to it. I'm much more able to identify with what he went through in Israel, in the kibbutz. . . As a father I'm very different from him. I'm 180 degrees different. So, just as I'm not interested in hearing his remarks about how I raise my children, I'm also not interested in hearing why I should be such and such because of what he went through while in hiding.

Omer explicitly says that he does not feel that what his father went through in the Holocaust has anything to do with his own identity today. Moreover, he ties what his father went through to the complete difference between them vis-à-vis fatherhood.

Yuval, Omer's son and Shlomo's grandson, painted a different picture about the significance he accords to his grandfather's story. Yuval said,

> Grandpa tells me a lot about what he went through, and I also read his book. I love Grandpa a lot and I'm very connected to him, but sometimes I don't have the strength to listen to him. It's exhausting. Mom and Dad are also cynical sometimes about Grandpa's stories, and tell him, "Enough, leave the kids alone," and I'm glad because I really don't have the strength to listen, but I also see that it upsets him and then I get upset for him.

For Yuval, his grandfather's story is significant for his relationship with him. He feels the tension between his father and grandfather, and it appears that he asks himself what role the story plays for him. He finds it difficult to separate the story from relationships within the family in general. The meanings Yuval accords his grandfather's story is ambivalent in light of his father's stance. Yuval sometimes ponders the subject and feels that "it's as if sometimes I need to choose whose side I'm on, Dad's or Grandpa's, and I don't want to choose, so I simply abstain."

Omer does not really feel that he knows what his father went through emotionally.

> He opened up for the first time with my son, later he told us a bit more . . . he gave a lecture at my other son's school. Slowly, slowly he opened up the story, but he is still telling the same stories. He doesn't go into the specifics, the small nuances, the emotional aspects.

These words are echoed in those of Yuval.

> When Grandpa mentions what happened to him, it's always anecdotes, never a complete story. Even when I try to ask him more about what he went through he tells me about it, but it's only as if he's telling me something new. He never actually talks about how it felt. And so it's very exhausting to listen to him. . . . Even when I tried to talk to him after I read the book he wasn't willing to tell me more. He said to me—"Read." But I had already read it, and I wanted to talk to him, and he simply was not capable of talking.

It appears that the book written by the survivor and the reading reactions of his son and grandson reflect divergent narratives of each generation vis-à-vis the survivor's story. The reactions of the son to the book seem to express to some degree the unfinished business the son has with his survivor father. The reaction of the grandson, who is aware of the tensions between his own father and grandfather, is expressed in his ambivalent reaction to his grandfather and the book. The significance the story is accorded and the various narratives surrounding it do not converge into something shared, but rather reflect complex communication patterns. It appears that each family member in their own way feels they are not fully understood by the others, and the difference between the narratives emerges alongside the lack of open communication between the generations.

Type 3: Partial Cohesion and Survivor–Third Generation Open Communication; "Knowing-Not Knowing" in the Second Generation

In the Oren family, Moshe, the survivor, escaped Germany and wandered throughout Europe during the war with his mother until they immigrated to Israel. Moshe explained that he wrote his story in installments. He began while fighting in one of Israel's wars in Lebanon, when his life was in danger. After the war he stopped and only continued after he went through a serious medical emergency in which his life was again in danger. Moshe described the circumstances that led him to write as follows:

> The distance between life and death is the few millimeters where the bullet whistles by. I want my children, the children and grandchildren, the coming generations, to remember my story. I therefore need to write it down and it doesn't matter to me if I know or don't know how to write literature, but it must be documented. . . . It was a very, very dramatic experience and when I finished writing all eight chapters after a week, I felt like . . . relief, a kind of exhaustion like after you work a lot in the garden and you want to sleep a bit, a healthy sleep. I felt relief and was happy that the story exists. Because it's a story about victory and self-fulfillment and it is important that it will be read. It is important to me that it will reach as many people as possible.

His grandson, Alon, talked about the book his grandfather wrote and its significance for him with great excitement.

> It is an amazing book that tells an amazing story. My grandfather is no less than a hero, and he overcame all that happened to him. . . . I read parts

of the book on Holocaust Remembrance Day in school, and he also came himself to tell his story. I am really proud of him, I feel that his story is also mine, truly.

It is evident that the grandfather and the grandson accord the story similar significance and share feelings of pride.

In contrast, Daphna, Moshe's daughter, does not share these feelings with her father and son. She said,

> I was pleased that my father was writing, but it didn't make me very proud or anything like that. . . . I was familiar with his story from before, and just as he never spoke to me about the more difficult and painful parts of the story, he also didn't write about them in the book. So for me, it is he who thinks he is victorious and not me. . . . It's like I understand that the very fact that he is alive means he triumphed, but still.

Daphna sensed that there are additional and more important aspects of the story that do not find expression in communication with her father surrounding the story, and she regrets it.

Moshe referred in his interview to communication patterns with his children in contrast to those with his grandchildren.

> Occasionally . . . occasionally . . . whether on Independence Day, the 29th of November, historic events like that, or Holocaust Remembrance Day, I would tell the story to my children. I don't remember exactly when, but I know that the stories would emerge occasionally. . . . The grandchildren asked me about it a lot more than my children did and I told them more and I also went to their school when they asked me and I told the story.

Daphna described a different picture.

> He never told us very much, and we also never asked. It's like, I know the facts well enough to relate them to you correctly, but I don't think it was because we asked. He was the one who brought it up, and again, just like the book he wrote, it was always without referring to why it is difficult and why it is sad. It was always the same story with always the same message—I triumphed. From very early on I already didn't have the patience to hear it.

The disparate narratives in the Oren family reflect partial cohesion in that the grandfather and grandson accord similar meanings of victory and self-fulfillment to the story, and they evidently feel closer through the story, in contrast to Daphna, who does not feel the same toward the story and does not share the sense of closeness that emerges from the narratives of the grandfather and grandson.

Cohesion between the grandfather and grandson is reflected in the communication patterns between them surrounding the story. While the grandfather feels comfortable in telling his grandson the story and the grandson feels comfortable asking questions, Daphna focuses on what she feels is absent from the communication between her and her father and feels that emotional aspects of their communication are missing.

Discussion

Studying three generations in families of Holocaust survivors in which the survivor wrote and published a memoir is a unique way to shed light on the meanings the different generations attribute to the familial story in the context of a family history of massive trauma. Based on analysis of the meanings that emerged in each of the three generations and their interrelations in 12 families, we identified three types of families of Holocaust survivors. Our findings are discussed in relation to the interactions between the overt and covert layers of the familial legacy related to massive trauma transmitted between the generations.

Covert Versus Overt Layers in the Familial Legacy

The three family types described are distinguished according to their family cohesion in relation to the story of the Holocaust and the overt/covert nature of intergenerational communication in relation to it. We suggest observing the typology by way of the tension between the overt and covert legacies transmitted through the generations. In some families, the two layers are intertwined; in others, they do not converge, and there is a gap between them. The degree of integration is what colors the significance of the family Holocaust story as part of the process of searching for the general meaning of life, as described later.

The first type of family is described as having "strong family cohesion and open communication." It is characterized by the story being attributed similar meanings for all three generations and by communication that is open and overt. In this type of family, the story is an integral part of the life of the family, of its personal and family identity, and of intergenerational communication. It is evident here that the family members underwent a process that is reflected in the book, and they reached a place in which the family story is part of the family and its personal legacy, an element in the process of building the identity of its members. In this type of family, integration is expressed in the significance attributed to the story and the part the story plays in the process of creating personal and familial meaning. These families are similar to the families Danieli (1988) described as those in which the unity of the family is important (Chaitin, 2003; Litvak-Hirsch & Bar-On, 2007) but also coupled with open communication in the family (Wiseman & Barber, 2008).

The second family type is described as having "weak cohesion and silence." It is characterized by tension between the personal level and the familial legacy of the story. On the personal level, each member of the family situates the story differently in their lives and identity, yet, at the covert family level, it seems to be similar for each generation (e.g., "It is important to be strong"; "there is no room at all for expressing weakness, especially emotional weakness"). These messages are similar to the legacy that Danieli described in the families she called "those who made it" (Danieli, 1988). Nevertheless, in our typology, the focus is on the interplay between these messages and the communication patterns. In families of this type, the lack of integration between the overt parts of the legacy and its covert emotional parts is conspicuous. The process of creating meaning from the story and its role in the identity and personal stories of each family member is characterized by tension between the two layers.

The third family type is described as having "partial cohesion and survivor–third generation open communication, and 'knowing-not knowing' in the second generation." Integration occurs through the legacy passed from the generation of survivors to the third generation. The second generation largely stands between these two generations, even if this is not openly discussed, and finds it difficult to engage in an open dialogue with the survivor, thus making it difficult to find a place for the legacy, especially on the personal level. On the family level, members of the second generation appreciate and welcome the relationship created between the grandparent and grandchild and its contribution to preserving the familial legacy. On the overt level, the significance given to the story is the same for the survivor generation and the third generation. At the covert level, the second generation recognizes the significance and feels part of it, even if its members feel they are outsiders to the open communication between grandparent and grandchildren.

The Search for Meaning, Familial Communication, and the Legacy

The findings show that there is a connection between gaps in the familial legacy and the process of creating and finding meaning for the story as part of the search for meaning in life. Family atmosphere and involvement are of great importance in intergenerational transmission processes, in the role the Holocaust story plays in the lives of the family members, and in its prominence among the families of survivors (Palgi, Shrira, & Ben-Ezra, 2015). In addition, there is a strong sense among many families of Holocaust survivors that the family is of utmost importance and that family members should stick together, no matter what (Danieli, 1982). We argue that family communication patterns are central to understanding these processes. When emotional communication surrounding the family story is more open and enabling, the resulting meaning is also more integrative. In these cases, the discrepancy between the meaning frameworks and the experience that characterizes the process of meaning creation in light of massive trauma (Dalgleish, 2004) is reduced. Family cohesion is also important to the process of creating meaning and the role that the traumatic story plays within that process. Olson (2000) argues that open family communication is a means by which family cohesion can be a positive and protective factor for various family members. In the present study, when emotional family communication is open and enabling, family cohesion surrounding the story is strong, the integration of the overt and covert layers of the legacy is greater, and the traumatic story seems to acquire coherent meaning for the various family members. In contrast, when emotional communication is limited and strained, especially between the survivors and the second generation, cohesion is weaker and there is less integration.

In the Israeli context, the school project called "Family Roots" ("Shorashim") that has been active in the past 30 years requires Grade 7 pupils (age 13) to write their family history. This project has contributed to opening lines of communication, especially between survivors and their grandchildren. This school project often serves as a catalyzer for the third generation to ask and for the survivor to tell his or her personal story (Duchin & Wiseman, 2016). With the change in the public image of survivors from victims to those who against all odds triumphed, the survivor feels more accepted and wins admiration from the Israeli public and, more importantly, from their families.

The process of searching for meaning and finding a place for the traumatic story within the general life story was examined in our study through the meanings accorded to the writing and reading of the traumatic story by family members. The search for meaning has become increasingly present as in old age these survivors feel the urgency to tell their story before it is too late, as part of their need to create a meaningful and coherent life story (McAdams, 2013). Their children and grandchildren face this inevitable pressure of running out of time as they painfully realize that soon they will be the last to have had an intimate relationship with survivors and that it is up to them to carry on the familial legacy. In facing this difficult and at times confusing mission, families' successful coping and resilience, as opposed to less successful coping and vulnerabilities, deserve further research (Shmotkin et al., 2011). Helping families of survivors discover the significance of the family story for them and coherently position it in their lives is an important task for psychotherapy practitioners. The process of searching for meaning as the heart of the psychotherapeutic process is at the center of Frankl's (1959) logotherapy and for many other clinicians (Yalom, 1980) as well. We suggest that writing the story, on the one hand, and reading it, on the other, encourage the creation of the narrative and its meanings, thus constituting an important psychotherapeutic channel for families facing the mission of dealing with the legacy and searching for meaning.

Highlights

- Survivor's writing a memoir about their traumatic Holocaust experiences contributes to a comprehension that enables meaning-making that may enhance passing on a more coherent family legacy.
- Shared meanings attributed to the book by the second and third generations in the family reflect strong family cohesion and open

communication between the survivor and their children and grandchildren.

- Families characterized by weak cohesion and silence may need help in resolving the tensions between the overt and covert layers of the meaning of the familial legacy as experienced by the survivor and the second and third generations in the family.
- Soon to be the last ones to have intimately known a survivor, the grandchildren are often more open to listen to the grandparent survivor who, in old age, is eager to tell their story to them. In the Israeli context, this is facilitated through the "Family Roots" school assignment and the change in survivors' public image from victims to those who have, against all odds, triumphed.
- Survivors' writing their story and their children and grandchildren reading it enhance the creation of the narrative and it meanings, constituting an important psychotherapeutic channel for families facing the mission of dealing with the legacy and searching for meaning.

References

Barber, B. K., & Buehler, C. (1996). Family cohesion and enmeshment: Different constructs, different effects. *Journal of Marriage and Family, 58*, 433–441.

Bar-On, D. (1995). *Fear and hope: Life-stories of five Israeli families of Holocaust survivors, Three generations in a family.* Harvard University Press.

Brom, D., Kfir, R., & Dasberg, H. (2001). A controlled double-blind study on children of Holocaust survivors. *Israel Journal of Psychiatry and Related Sciences, 38*, 47–57.

Calhoun, L. G., & Tedeschi, R. G. (2013). *Posttraumatic growth in clinical practice.* Routledge.

Chaitin, J. (2003). "Living with" the past: Coping and patterns in families of Holocaust survivors. *Family Process, 42*(2), 305–322.

Dalgleish, T. (2004). Cognitive approaches to post traumatic stress disorder: The evaluation of multirepresentational theorizing. *Psychological Bulletin,130*, 228–260.

Danieli, Y. (1982). Families of survivors of the Nazi Holocaust: Some short and long term effects. *Stress and Anxiety, 8*, 405–421.

Danieli, Y. (1988). The heterogeneity of post war adaptation in families of Holocaust survivors. In R. L. Braham (Ed.), *The psychological perspectives of the Holocaust and of its aftermath* (pp. 109–127). Social Science Monographs.

Danieli, Y. (2007). Assessing trauma across cultures from a multigenerational perspective. In J. P. Wilson & C. So-kum Tang (Eds.), *Crosscultural assessment of psychological trauma and PTSD* (pp. 65–89). Springer-Verlag.

Danieli, Y., Norris, F. H., & Engdahl, B. (2017). A question of who, not if: Psychological disorders in Holocaust survivors' children. *Psychological Trauma: Theory, Research, Practice, and Policy, 9*(S1), 98–106.

Duchin A., & Wiseman, H. (2016). The third generation's encounter with their survivor grandparents' Holocaust memoirs. In E. Jilovsky, J. Silverstein, & D. Slucki (Eds.), *In the shadows of memory* (pp. 113–134). Vallentine Mitchell.

Duchin, A., & Wiseman, H. (2019). Memoirs of child survivors of the Holocaust: Processing and healing of trauma through writing. *Qualitative Psychology, 6*(3), 280–296.

Felsen, I. (1998). Transgenerational transmission of effects of the Holocaust: The North American research perspective. In Y. Danieli (Ed.), *International handbook of multi-generational legacies of trauma* (pp. 43–69). Plenum.

Frankl, V. E. (1946). *Man's search for meaning.* Beacon Press.

Frankl, V. E. (1959). The spiritual dimension in existential analysis and logotherapy. *Journal of Individual Psychology, 15*(2), 157–165.

Greenspan, H. (1992). Lives as text: Symptoms as modes of recounting in the life histories of Holocaust survivors. In G. C. Rosewald & R. L. Ochberg (Eds.), *Storied lives: The cultural politics of self understanding* (pp. 145–165). Yale University Press.

Hass, A. (1996). *The aftermath: Living with the Holocaust.* Cambridge University Press.

Herman, J. L. (1992). *Trauma and recovery.* Basic Books.

Josselson, R. (2011). Narrative research: Constructing, deconstructing, and reconstructing story. In K. Charmaz, L. McMullen, R. Josselson, R. Anderson, & E. McSpadden (Eds.), *Five ways of doing qualitative analysis* (pp. 224–242). Guilford Press.

Josselson, R. (2013). *Interviewing for qualitative inquiry: A relational approach.* Guilford Press.

Krell, R. (1985). Child survivors of the Holocaust: 40 years later. *Journal of the American Academy of Child Psychiatry, 24*(4), 378–380.

Laub, D. (2005). Traumatic shutdown of narrative and symbolization: A death instinct derivative. *Contemporary Psychoanalysis, 41*(2), 307–326.

Lieblich, A., Tuval-Mashiach, R., & Zilber, T. (1998). *Narrative research: Reading, analysis, and interpretation.* Sage.

Litvak-Hirsch, T., & Bar-On, D. (2007). Encounters in the looking-glass of time: Longitudinal contribution of a life story workshop course to the dialogue between Jewish and Arab young adults in Israel. *Peace and Conflict Studies, 14*, 23–46.

Mayseless, O. (2001). The relationships between parents and adolescents in Israel during the transition to adolescence. *Megamot*, XLI (1-2), 180–194. [Hebrew]

McAdams, D. P. (2013). The positive psychology of adult generativity: Caring for the next generation and constructing a redemptive life. In J. D. Sinnott (Ed.), *Positive psychology: Advances in understanding adult motivation* (pp. 191–205). Springer.

Niederland, W. (1968). Clinical observations of the "survivor syndrome." *International Journal of Psychoanalysis, 49*, 313–315.

Olson, D. H. (2000). Circumplex model of marital and family systems. *Journal of Family Therapy, 22*(2), 144–167.

Olson D. H., & Gorall, D. M. (2003). Circumplex model of marital and family systems. In F. Walsh (Ed.), *Normal family processes* (pp. 514–547). Guilford Press.

Palgi, Y., Shrira, A., & Ben-Ezra, M. (2015). Family involvement and Holocaust salience among offspring and grandchildren of Holocaust survivors. *Journal of Intergenerational Relationships, 13*, 6–21.

Pennebaker, J. W. (2002). What our words can say about us: Toward a broader language psychology. *Psychological Science Agenda, 15*, 8–9.

Pennebaker, J. W., Barger, S. D., & Tiebout, J. (1989). Disclosure of traumas and health among Holocaust survivors. *Psychosomatic Medicine, 51*, 577–589.

Sagi-Schwartz, A. (2015). Does extreme trauma transfer? The case of three generations of the Holocaust. In K. E. Cherry (Ed.), *Traumatic stress and long-term recovery—coping with disasters and other negative life events* (pp. 133–150). Springer.

Scharf, M., & Mayseless, O. (2011). Disorganizing experiences in second and third generation Holocaust survivors. *Qualitative Health Research, 21*, 1539–1553.

Shefet, R. (1994). Filial commitment as an impossible task in the children of Holocaust survivors. *Sihot-Dialog, 9*, 23–27. [Hebrew]

Shmotkin, D., Shrira, A., Goldberg, S. C., & Palgi, Y. (2011). Resilience and vulnerability among aging Holocaust survivors and their families: An intergenerational overview. *Journal of Intergenerational Relationships, 9*, 7–21.

Solomon, Z. (1998). Transgenerational effects of the Holocaust: The Israeli research perspective. In Y. Danieli (Ed.), *International handbook of multigenerational legacies of trauma* (pp. 69–85). Plenum.

Steger, M. F. (2009). Meaning in life. In S. J. Lopez (Ed.), *Oxford handbook of positive psychology* (2nd ed., pp. 679–687). Oxford University Press.

Steger, M. F., & Park, C. L. (2012). The creation of meaning following trauma: Meaning making and trajectories of distress and recovery. In T. Keane, E. Newman, & K. Fogler (Eds.), *Toward an integrated approach to trauma focused therapy: Placing evidence-based interventions in an expanded psychological context* (pp. 171–191). APA.

Tedeschi, R. G., & Calhoun, L. G. (2004). Posttraumatic growth: Conceptual foundations and empirical evidence. *Psychological Inquiry, 15*, 1–18.

Wiseman, H., Metzl, E., & Barber, J. P. (2006). Anger, guilt, and intergenerational communication of trauma in the interpersonal narratives of second generation Holocaust survivors. *American Journal of Orthopsychiatry, 76*(2), 176–184.

Wiseman, H., & Barber, J. P. (2008). *Echoes of the trauma: Relational themes and emotions in children of Holocaust survivors.* Cambridge University Press. Yalom, I. D. (1980). *Existential psychotherapy.* Basic Books.

PART IV
STRUGGLING FOR IDENTITY

9

The Zionist Absurd

Israel's Politics of Fear, Freedom, and Bad Faith

Uriel Abulof

"I cannot forecast to you the action of Russia," Winston Churchill said at the start of World War II, "It is a riddle, wrapped in a mystery, inside an enigma." The same can be said of Israel on any given day. To be sure, for comparativists such as myself, Israel is unique, but not unique in being unique. Other societies and countries are all baffling in their own ways. Yet, platitudes aside, Israel, and the movement that begot it—Zionism—do push the bar of sociopolitical exceptionalism. They defy common expectations and familiar patterns, creating antinomies that often seem paradoxical.

The Zionist antinomies seem omnipresent. Consider, for example, the movement's hate–love relations with the international community, with imperialism, with the Jewish diaspora, and with Judaism. Zionism saw the world as harboring almost innate anti-Semitism, yet sought to secure its goal—a Jewish state—through "public legal" approval from the international community. Zionism defied imperialism and colonialism, yet relied heavily on the British Empire's political and military might. Zionism rejected diasporic existence as dangerous, even corrupting, yet has constantly sought its support. Zionism heavily criticized Jewish tradition and religion, yet has increasingly turned to them for legitimacy. The Zionist antinomies go further into the realms of security and identity: a superpower in its region, one of nine states with a nuclear arsenal, Israel remains fearful for its survival. Identity-wise, though aligning ideologically and politically with the West, the Jewish state—an ethnonational and partly religious state—does not sit well with contemporary liberal and secular ideals and practices.

This chapter is a modest attempt to explain the Zionist–Israeli enigma, focusing on the latter two antinomies. What may explain these, and perhaps, *inter alia*, other antinomies, too? A clue lies in the very notion of antinomy, derived from ancient Greek: *anti* "against" and *nomos* "law."

Uriel Abulof, *The Zionist Absurd* In: *Finding Meaning*. Edited by: Ofra Mayseless and Pninit Russo-Netzer, Oxford University Press. © Oxford University Press 2022. DOI: 10.1093/oso/9780190910358.003.0009

Nomos is not just formal legality (Cover, 1983; Schmitt, 2003); it signifies a morally meaningful social order, providing public justification for the very existence of that order. The creation of nomos—the process of *nomization*—is effectively "existential legitimation": justifying *why* a certain society and its politics *ought* to exist. Each society, I propose, strives to develop one. For nomization to work, however, it must resonate both within the society and outside it; otherwise, *anomy* (the lack of nomos) awaits.

Zionism, I submit, is nomization; it is a moral meaning-making project on a social-political scale. Decoding this process may help us explain the trajectory of Zionism and, indeed, its antinomies. After all, what is the meaning of Israel? If meaning is definition, the answer is plain: Israel is a modern state. Dig deeper, and another meaning quickly surfaces: Israel is a Jewish state. Dig yet deeper, to the existential heart, and I propose the following: Israel itself is a protean product of a meaning-making project, currently facing an impasse. Israel is not merely the "scene" where the search for meaning happens: it epitomizes that very search, the human quest for justifying life and death: *Why ought we breathe, breed, and bleed?*

I expound my argument in four steps. First, I outline my theoretical propositions, going back to human motivations in order to evince the importance of the "fear factor" and how it might lead to both freedom (an active, reasoned choice) and "bad faith" (forgetting or forfeiting freedom). I suggest that this process is not merely individual, but entwined deeply with sociopolitical processes with far reaching implications. Second, I start my investigation of the Zionist case by exploring how Israeli Jews have been engulfed in existential fears that may go far beyond what their objective (in)security merits. Third, I propose that Zionism has partly dealt with its existential anxiety by existential legitimation (*nomization*): imbuing the dream and reality of the Jewish state with moral meaning—righteousness, rights, and *raison d'être*.

Finally, I argue that, in recent years, the Zionist nomization has reached an impasse of moral meaning bringing it closer to anomy and to meeting the *political absurd*: a creeping belief that all its legitimating efforts are doomed. The result, I propose, is the rise of bad faith politics, substituting freedom with a sense of a "chosen people" having "no choice": holding Zionism as innately just, often divinely so, without real alternatives to its identity (Jewish), polity (a Jewish state), policy (favoring Jews, sustaining occupation), and authority (a religious right-wing coalition).

Nomization: The Pursuit of (Political) Meaning as Existential Legitimation

Churchill did not settle for recognizing the Russian enigma; seeking to decode it, he quickly added: "but perhaps there is a key. That key is Russian national interest." This may be so, but explaining sociopolitical riddles through "national interest" only begs the questions. What is the national interest? Why and how is it thus defined? Kicking the causal can again and again eventually leads us to basic human motivations: Why do we do the things that we do?

Fear is one answer. This primal instinct is ingrained in all mammals (Panksepp, 1998), perhaps beyond (Bekoff, 2007), and it certainly drives humans (Witte, 1996). Fear is deeply imbedded in our evolution. Prompting us to quickly identify and effectively react to threats, fear has helped us survive—and our species thrive. Fear is the visceral hidden hand of the "selfish gene," fusing two images of man: the *Homo biologicus* and the *Homo psychologicus*, driven by evolutionary forces and emotions, respectively. The threefold reaction to fear is well-known: fight, flee, or freeze. We may wrestle with the danger, try to avoid it, or become paralyzed, like deer in the headlights.

The *Homo sociologicus* also partakes in reaction to fear. For example, recent studies indicate that women may be more prone to fear and stress (Campbell, 2013) and, in response, "tend-and-befriend": protect offspring and connect with others (Taylor, 2002). Still, tend-and-befriend may be but social, rather than solitary, means to fend off fearful threats—to fight or flee them together.

What is peculiar about the "fear factor," however, is that there's nothing particularly human about it. Many animals, especially mammals, share this bio-psychological drive. What distinguishes humans is that, apart from the triad "fight-flight-freeze," they have a fourth option: think. For some, thinking amounts to rationality, invoking an image of man driven by material cost-benefit calculations (Abulof, 2015a). However, the *Homo economicus* is also not distinctively human; animals, low and high, and certainly machines, do it, too, often more effectively than people.

Thinking from a distinctively *human* perspective means something else: critical reflection, and—in the realm of conscience—trying to make moral sense of yourself and the world around you (Abulof, 2017). Critical reflection is the bedrock of human freedom: our unique capacity to choose, reason our choices, act upon them, and take responsibility for them. Unlike liberty, which is all about "who controls what," freedom depends on us alone: we are always free, always have a choice, however circumscribed by circumstances (Sartre, 1965).

Importantly, reflective freedom does not necessarily ameliorate fear; it may well turn it into anxiety. While fear is a physical response to concrete, present dangers, anxiety is a psychological response that summons past and potential threats, often unidentified, holding great insidious sway on our mind (LeDoux, 2015). Facing a shark while diving in the ocean can trigger fear, watching *Jaws* before going to the beach may trigger anxiety. Both fear and anxiety can become existential, a question of life and death. Existential fears indicate acute dangers to our survival. Existential anxiety suggests doubts about the quality and meaning of our life: Are we happy (will we ever be)? What's the point?

Consider this: standing on the edge of a cliff, we fear the fall—fear for our (healthy, happy) life. We can fight this fear by taking safety measures, sometimes with the help of others; we can flee by walking away from the edge and sometimes we just freeze, wishing the fear, and its cause, will somehow go away. But going beyond fight-flight-freeze to freedom, a creeping thought prompts a deeper terror: it is not merely that we might fall; we may also jump.

Contemplating suicide goes to the very heart of human freedom: the conscious choice between our own life and death. This existential anxiety is deeply unsettling, and it becomes yet more daunting facing its implication: justifying our choice, making meaning/sense of our existence. Ultimately, the inevitability and availability of death (we know we are going to die and that we may actively opt to) are the wellspring of our fearful sense of freedom—the daunting, haunting realization of fundamental choice between life and death. Thus, on the edge of life's gaping abyss, we become explorers in seeking meaning that transcends our transient life. No other animal asks itself "why ought I/we live?" Humans do, and their answers have erected, and razed, cultures and civilizations.

What then is the meaning of the "meaning of life"? For one, it is not about definition. If a friend tells us she wants to end her life because it's meaningless, we probably won't offer her a dictionary. What she seeks—in searching for meaning—is the *purposeful choice* behind things, a *raison d'être* for her own existence. She becomes *Homo telos*—at long last, distinctively human. Whether we think of the meaning of the universe, Earth, or our own private life, we want to uncover their purpose. We do not settle for knowing *why* they are there; we want to grasp *for what*. Since purpose requires a conscious, perhaps conscientious, choice, in searching for meaning, we effectively try to "free the world": endow it with freedom—a reasoned choice, and a purposeful one at that. Thus, the phenomenology (the lived-experience) of the "search for meaning" is effectively the experience of "looking for a human" (Tymieniecka, 2010). No wonder then that in seeking the meaning of the many things beyond human choice and control, humans have turned to anthropomorphized entities, deities, to solve these great riddles. And yet, as far as we know, humans are the only creatures capable of making meaning—first and foremost, of their own life and death.

"There is only one really serious philosophical question, and that is suicide," Camus (1955, p. 3) famously suggested, "Judging whether life is or is not worth living amounts to answering the fundamental question of philosophy." I propose a revision. There are *three* truly serious—life-and-death—philosophical problems: suicide, birth, and homicide—judging whether life is or is not worth living, creating, or ending. Why breathe? Why breed? Why bleed? This triple quandary summons us to exercise our freedom to its fullest: justify the decision to continue living, once we become aware of the possibility of suicide; justify the decision to make new lives, once we recognize we don't have to; and justify taking the lives of others, morally reasoning what, if anything, is worth dying and killing for. Throughout, one may wonder what's worth our sacrificing, as suffering underpins this triple quandary.

The existential quandary is not merely personal, but also guides, however grudgingly, our public life, demanding us to answer *why* our politics *ought* to be this way rather than another: Why ought we subscribe to this social identity, that polity, that authority, and that policy—and not others?

When the *why* and the *ought* surface in public discourse a fascinating convergence transpires between three processes: legitimation, justification, and valuation. Though much related, these are discrete concepts. Legitimation is public, political, validation; justification is communicative reasoning; and valuation is moral meaning-making. Thus, for example, while legitimation is predominantly public, justification is often private, and while justification involves reasoning, legitimation not necessarily so. If you order, "Obey!" and I reply "Okay," you have effectively, albeit facilely, legitimated your power over me (attaining a Weberian "authority"). But if instead I ask "why?" and you answer, for example, "Because I was elected," justification commences. Adding to the mix valuation—making, not merely determining, value (e.g., "democracy is good")—brings us to *publicly reasoning the moral meaning in, of, by, and for, politics.*

I offer *nomization* as a useful shorthand for this coalescence. Ultimately, as Berger (1967, pp. 21–23) suggests, "every nomos is an area of meaning carved out of a vast mass of meaninglessness," and thus "the most important function of society is *nomization*," evincing the "human craving for meaning that appears to have the force of instinct." *Nomization* fuses the philosophical *ought* and the sociological *is*, further appending them with communicative reasoning (Abulof, 2016). *Nomization* is effectively an existential legitimation—seeking to imbue the sociopolitical order with moral meaning. Importantly, since people have ascribed diverse, dynamic meaning to politics, we effectively inhabit a *polynomic* world—a world of many moral meanings.

Nomization always faces a potential failure—the specter of *anomy*, moral meaninglessness on a mass, societal scale. If the very awareness of choice, making it, reasoning it, and taking responsibility for it, is not enough to make the burden of freedom so overwhelming, there comes the Absurd: the realization that the choice and its reasoning are in fact quite feeble and can hardly be built on any universally sound foundation. We are searching for meaning in a meaningless universe, and, in politics, may realize the vanity of seeking eternal, universal, moral absolutes.

Thus, freedom and its moral corollary—justifying *why ought* we exist and realizing our answers can ultimately fall short—may itself trigger freeze/flight/fight reactions. We may become paralyzed by the sheer weight of the looming Absurd; we may escape from it, often by replacing *nomos* with *habitus*, habituated, reproduced practices etched on bodies and minds by a given culture; or we may face the Absurd, and, like Sisyphus, struggle with the heavy lifting of the rock.

But why should we make this Sisyphean effort? Friedrich Nietzsche (2005, p. 157) argued that "if you have your 'why?' in life, you can get along with almost any 'how?'" Perhaps so, but if meaning-making is just a means to having *good life*, rather than truly realizing what (your) *life is good for*, it may—much like "the pursuit of happiness"—become self-defeating, elusive as chasing the horizon. Meaning-making helps living, and thriving, especially as a byproduct, when it involves pursuing a purpose greater than our individual selves, when one breathes, breeds, and bleeds for something greater than oneself. This is where the role of the collective becomes pivotal. We ought not anthropomorphize the collective but should consider the latter's crucial role in mitigating the individual's sense of mortality.

Ernst Becker (1975, p. 4; 1973, p. 170; 1975, p. 63) suggests that "what man really fears is not so much extinction, but extinction with insignificance," and thus seeks to "earn his immortality" through meaningful sociomoral orders, "seen as structures of immortality power." Death, life's only certitude, is a creative force, urging us to love and innovate, to hate and kill. Humans seek to transcend their transient existence by finding symbolic immortality in a meaningful perpetuation project, a *causa-sui*, to gain justification and purpose in the semblance of eternity.

Becker (1973, pp. 116–117, 187) also recognized the absurd—that the *causa-sui* is "a lie that must take its toll," for "in back of the *causa-sui* project whispers the voice of possible truth: that human life may not be more than a meaningless interlude in a vicious drama of flesh and bones that we call evolution." Ultimately, our *causa-sui* is a fiction of our imagination and has no existence without it. Still, while "there is a great deal of falseness and self-deception in the cultural *causa-sui* project. . . . Cultural illusion is a necessary ideology of self-justification, a heroic dimension that is life itself to the symbolic animal. To lose the security of heroic cultural illusion is to die" (Becker, 1973, p. 189). Or not—perhaps, to avoid dying in the face of the absurd, instead of holding fast to our freedom, we turn to bad faith.

Sartre (1965) employed the concept of "bad faith" to denote times when we forget, or else forfeit, our freedom: we come to believe there is "no choice," when in fact there is always choice. Bad faith may draw on three fallacies: essentialism (one is innately prone to something), determinism (the past preordains the future), and fatalism (the future is sealed, often from above). With essentialism and determinism, freedom looks like illusion, even delusion; forces beyond your reason dictate your actions. With fatalism, an *Appointment in Samarra* worldview, freedom is meaningless: whatever you mean, you will end up where you were meant to. In daily discourse, bad faith transpires in thinking "I must," instead of "I choose," saying, "I cannot" instead of "I refuse." We all occasionally flee from freedom to bad faith, though some, and sometimes, more than others.

Here we complete the circle of fear, freedom, and bad faith since fear can greatly facilitate bad faith, partly through biology. Acute fear may numb critical thinking, essential to freedom. Our brain operates a delicate balance and an intricate connection between distinct systemic functions, employing various regions. The *amygdala* (Greek for "almond" and thus shaped), a mass of nuclei deep in the temporal lobe, detects and responds to emotional triggers, notably fear (our personal "911 operator"). The *ventromedial prefrontal cortex* (vmPFC) helps regulate risk and fear and allows thinking, decision-making, and real-life moral evaluation (Motzkin et al., 2015). The *hippocampus* is critical for long-term memory, creativity, and imagination (Hassabis et al., 2007). When we face an imminent, often corporeal, danger the amygdala takes over: our heart rate, sweat, and stress hormones surge, but our capacity for critical reflection dwindles. Ongoing fears and anxiety may have a more insidious, lasting, effect, severing our capacity to think freely: arguably, they not only augment the amygdala but shrink the hippocampus, impairing our capacity for imagination (Suzuki & Fitzpatrick, 2015).

Imagination is critical for freedom and meaning-making because it allows people to consider possible trajectories of extant options as well as creatively conceive of novel options from which to choose. Furthermore, imagination can help mitigate fear itself via "threat extinction" (Reddan, Wager, & Schiller, 2018) and foster hopeful outlook—seeking a better life, at times by taking risks, not merely avoiding dangers (Boland, Riggs, & Anderson, 2018). Finally, by constantly fearing for our (healthy, happy) life, we may care less about figuring out what we live for. Thus, through both distraction and dullness, fear can undercut freedom and the search for meaning.

Against this backdrop, political psychologists argue that death anxiety and fear of threat and loss bolster conservative beliefs and behavior (Jost et al., 2003), often mediated through anger and authoritarianism (Jost, 2019). Yet conservatives have no monopoly over the politics of fear and bad faith. Liberals, too, may employ fearmongering to depict their (often conservative) rivals as dire dangers and subscribe to liberalism as a given, not a possible choice that requires reasoning.

Still, lest we, too, succumb to bad faith, neither biology, nor psychology, nor even sociology dictate the destiny of people and peoples. The "nature versus nurture" debate sadly neglects human freedom: neither genes, nor social circumstances preordain what we might turn into a dilemma, what choices we construct, and what we end up choosing (and then perhaps change our mind).

I develop some of these arguments in my treatise on *The Mortality and Morality of Nations* (Abulof, 2015b). Nations, I suggest, are modern pyramids—constructs of "symbolic immortality," built for masses, not monarchs. We must never forget, however, a pyramid is a vast tomb. "Small nations," who lack "that felicitous sense of an eternal past and future" (Kundera, 1995) are the falling bricks that reveal the tomb (the fear of collective death)—and the best and worst in us. They see before them existential threats, consider options, and weave beneath their polity of choice a security net made of existential threads of rights and purpose—but then they may they yield to bad faith. Such is the case of Israel.

Fear and Trembling in Zion

Zionism, the ethnonational movement that created Israel, is *causa sui*, a meaning-making "perpetuation project." But as the preceding theoretical sketch suggests, we cannot truly understand this project without realizing the "death dread" that drives it.

Few peoples and states have faced mortal dangers more than the Jewish people and the Jewish state. From the biblical narrative of slavery in Egypt, through the destruction of the First and Second Temples, exiles and pogroms, subjugation and discrimination, to the extermination camps of the Holocaust. And yet, since the end of World War II, the Jewish people, in diaspora and homeland, have become increasingly secure. In the diaspora, while anti-Semitism, discrimination, and hate crimes still abide, their scope and scale have greatly dwindled, and most Jews have increasingly enjoyed the peace and prosperity of Western countries. In the old-new homeland, too, Jews have become more prosperous and powerful than ever before.

Zionism, the Jewish national movement of late modernity, achieved in 1948 its primary goal: establishing an independent statehood for the people. In its War of Independence (1947–1949), Israel defeated both Palestine's Arabs and its Arab states. Less than a decade later, Israel had swiftly captured, and relinquished, the Sinai Peninsula. In 1967, Israel Defence Forces (IDF) defeated the armies of Egypt, Jordan, and Syria (aided by Iraq and Lebanon) in a stunning six days, taking hold over Sinai, the Golan Heights, the Gaza Strip, the West Bank, and all of Jerusalem. Even the surprise attacks by Egypt and Syria on Yom Kippur 1973 did not succeed, and the IDF soon regained the upper hand.

At the same time, Israel has developed a sizeable and diverse nuclear arsenal, sustaining a nuclear monopoly in the region by attacking Iraq (1981) and Syria (2007), and indirectly through Western diplomacy vis-à-vis, Iran (2015). Israel has forged an effective alliance with a global superpower, the United States, which became hegemonic in the early 1990s. It attained peace treaties with two of its fiercest enemies, Egypt (1979) and Jordan (1994), and was even recognized by the Palestinian Liberation Organization (PLO) before negotiating for a settlement (1993–). The Second Palestinian Intifada (2000–2004) failed to force Israel's withdrawal from the occupied territories yet contributed to the political disintegration of Palestinian society. More recently, in the wake of the Arab Spring (2010–2012), Israel's Arab neighbors, especially Syria, have greatly weakened, with Sunni leaders holding fast to the conciliatory Arab Peace Initiative (2002, 2007).

From its inception and throughout, Israel's economy has grown dramatically, becoming robust enough to contain the ill-effects of the Second Intifada and the global financial crisis. With recent gas discoveries, Israel has also become more energy self-reliant than ever. To sum, Israel has become safer and stronger, its survival more assured than ever before.

All this makes much sense but is simultaneously out of touch with the actual experiences of Israeli Jews. The chronicles of Zionism and the Jewish state present a perplexing paradox: the safer Israel has become, the more anxious Israelis have gotten. Recently, after speaking to advisers to US President Donald Trump, former Israeli PM Ehud Barak commented that "The people close to Trump cannot fathom why the government of Israel explains to them that the formation of a tiny, demilitarized Palestinian state would be an existential threat to Israel" (Hoffman, 2017). Many are baffled by the same puzzle. As indicated earlier, since the Holocaust, the Jewish people, both within and outside Israel, have gradually gained strength and security. Israel has never been more prosperous and powerful. Yet Israelis have increasingly opted for fearmongering politicians, opting for conservative, religious, and ethno-nationalist policies. Why?

Surely, part of the answer is that some objective security dangers still linger, occasionally intensifying. Israel's history is riddled with vicious wars, military operations, and terror attacks, and Israel ranks third in the world in active military per capita (21:1,000, after North Korea and Eritrea). Israel's enemies are not entirely weak, and some are getting stronger. Its precarious nuclear monopoly notwithstanding, Israel is much smaller—geographically and demographically—and strategically more vulnerable than its current and potential rivals. Turkey, under a hostile, and increasingly hegemonic, Recep Erdoğan, is a military powerhouse. It ranks eighth in the Global Firepower (2017) index worldwide and first in the Middle East. Its military budget, aircraft, and military personnel outstrip Israel's; its tanks and navy are on par with Israel's. Saudi Arabia's military budget, Syria's tanks, Egypt's navy and aircraft, Iran's personnel—all have an advantage over Israel's (Gould & Szoldra, 2017). Facing such a "nightmare coalition," Israel might not be the last one standing. Non-state actors, too, pose grave military threats. Hezbollah, in particular, has turned from a strong terror group to an effective army, with about 45,000 fighters (half in regular service), tens of thousands of rockets, hundreds of long-range missiles (with a range that covers all of Israel), hundreds of drones, advanced surface-to-sea missiles and anti-aircraft systems, and thousands of anti-tank missiles (Harel & Cohen, 2016). And within, Israeli Arabs have increasingly defied the very notion of Israel as a Jewish state (Abulof, 2008).

Objective security threats notwithstanding, it is equally important to trace intersubjective "securitization": the social construction of security often through discourse. *Securitization theory* becomes especially pertinent to Israel when it embraces its existentialism—figuring out how societies construct threats as endangering the very existence of the people and their state (Abulof, 2014a). In the case of Israel, one can trace the antecedent of such processes in the deep history of the Jewish people. "The world has many images of Israel," argued Simon Rawidowicz (1986, p. 54), "but Israel has only one image of itself: that of an expiring people, forever on the verge of ceasing to be."

Rawidowicz made this observation in 1948, when the Jewish state was founded, Zionism seemingly realized. Still, despite its incessant attempt to quell the perils of Jewish life on the verge of the abyss, Zionism has continuously seen itself living on the edge, longing for the ostensible eviternity of self-assured nations while wallowing in the mire of collective mortality (Abulof, 2015b). Generations after Rawidowicz, journalist Ari Shavit (2013) thus began his popular personal narrative, *My Promised Land*: "For as long as I can remember, I remember fear. Existential fear. The Israel I grew up in—the Israel of the mid-1960s—was energetic, exuberant, and hopeful. But I always felt that beyond the well-to-do houses and upper-middle-class lawns of my hometown lay a dark ocean." To be unsafe is to risk annihilation, as PM David Ben-Gurion (1955) explained: "Our security problem means the problem of our survival. Physical survival in its simplest sense . . . they [the Arabs] intend, as many of them openly say, to throw us all into the sea; in plainer words—to destroy the Jews in Israel."

Elites and public alike have partaken in the construction of existential threats, signaling that survival and safety are not, perhaps can never be, assured. Importantly, these discourses do not merely reflect but also affect material reality, especially when the speakers are decision-makers. The Jewish–Palestinian conflict has been a century-long object of securitization, one framed as endangering the Jewish State. For example, at the height of the Second Intifada, Chief of Staff of the Israel Defense Forces (IDF) Moshe Ya'alon referred to the conflict as a "cancerous existential threat" (*Ha'aretz*, August 30, 2002). Some weeks later, the former (and future) PM, Binyamin Netanyahu, expanded on this lethal clinical language to refer to the Islamic movement in Israel (YNET, September 21, 2002). Similarly, Zionism's struggle to obtain and sustain a Jewish majority has translated into the "demographic demon" discourse, shaping and justifying key policies against the Palestinian threat (Abulof, 2014a).

For many Israeli Jews, their military and economic superiority is but a finger in a dam. Geography and demography (Israeli Jews vis-à-vis the Arab-Muslim world), geology (mainly the role of oil), and alarming military developments (the Iranian nuclear project, Hezbollah's and Hamas's armaments) are perceived as waves converging to a tsunami, against which the Israeli-Jewish dam may be too weak to hold. We should note, however, that while the survival of the Jewish state is perceived to be at stake, the community's Jewish identity—however troubled by rivalry between distinct "tribes" (secular and religious, Mizrahi and Ashkenazi, left-wing and right-wing)—typically provides a strong anchor of identification for the overwhelming majority of Israeli Jews. They may debate whether they are "more Israeli or Jewish"—and the latter has been gaining ground—but rarely dispute they are both (Golan, 2014; Rosner & Fuchs, 2018). Herzl's proclamation at the outset of *The Jewish State*, "We are a people—one people [ein Volk]," still resonates.

Freedom: Justifying Israel

Staring at the abyss below, so full of (real and perceived) dangers, Zionists have woven a security net made not only of material threads but of moral fabric as well. Here I focus on the latter. The eminent Zionist thinker Ahad Ha'am (1948, p. 15) wrote: "Our national sentiment is the reason for our existence, but our heart . . . cannot find peace knowing the reason alone. It also yearns for an underlying purpose to our existence . . . [The Jew must know] that he lives and suffers not only because he cannot die but because he must live."

Finding "an underlying purpose to our existence" became all that more essential, and harder, as Jews found Zionism to be just one among several options to lead political life in modern times. Jews have created and cast multiple existential anchors of moral meaning onto the turbulent seas of modernity. These nomization projects sought to project and perpetuate Jewish ethnic identity through various polities (charted in Figure 9.1): some polities remained a dream, others were realized, growing in geodemographic scale (reflected in the points' size); some polities evolved in the diaspora (the lower arc), others in Palestine (the upper arc); some polities were closer to the pole of sovereignty, seeking ethnic domination; others accepted subjugation; and still others sought the middle point of equality.

Thus, for example, in the diaspora, some proposed to reject Jewish ethnicity and assimilate, some sought sovereignty outside Palestine (territorialism), but most wanted equality—and, in the West, have largely attained it. Meanwhile, in Palestine, some tried to substitute Canaanite for Jewish identity, others wanted to reach binationalism, and still others, a growing majority—the Zionists—wanted to erect Jewish sovereignty. Modern Jews wondered about, and wandered between, these existential possibilities, hotly debating their moral and practical justifications. Here was a clear case for freedom's four pillars: choose, reason, act, and take responsibility.

The annals of Zionism abound with attempts to morally reason the Jewish state, to find and found—through rights and *raison d'être*—legitimacy for this implausible political enterprise. Ze'ev Jabotinsky, the leader of the revisionist movement, provides a vivid case in point. In his most influential treatise, *The*

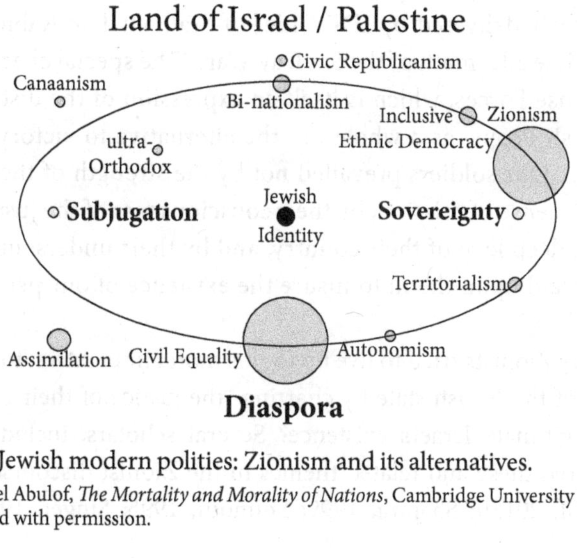

Figure 9.1 Jewish modern polities: Zionism and its alternatives.

Copyright Uriel Abulof, *The Mortality and Morality of Nations*, Cambridge University Press, 2015. Reprinted with permission.

Iron Wall, Jabotinsky (1937 [1923]) opined that Palestine's Arabs are "indigenous people" and as such naturally seek to get rid of the Zionist newcomers. The only remedy lies in presenting the Arabs with the *fait accompli* of a Jewish majority and polity, inducing them, in the long run, to compromise. Tellingly, Jabotinsky quickly followed this essay with a second treatise: "The Ethics of the Iron Wall" (Abulof, 2014b). Morality, declared Jabotinsky (1941 [1923]), "comes before everything else," even if necessitating the use of force, and the Zionist cause is "moral and just" since it subscribes to "national self-determination" as a "sacred principle."

Jabotinsky was certainly not alone in wrestling with the moral foundations and implications of Zionism. On the other side of the political aisle, PM Ben-Gurion reiterated the ideas that "the fate of Israel depends on two factors: her strength and her rectitude," and the "the state of Israel will not be tried by her riches, army, or techniques, but by her moral image and human values" (cited in *The New Yorker*, October 14, 1996, p. 91).

Zionist thinkers mostly did not claim absolute justice for their cause, merely that it was the "lesser evil." This moral line of thought was formulated by Martin Buber (2005, pp. 169–170) in his principle of the "demarcation line": it is just to aspire to the greatest possible fulfillment of Zionism while limiting as far as possible any damage done to opposing parties; "We cannot live without doing injustice—no community can. Yet every hour anew we have to examine to see that we take on no more guilt for ourselves than we must."

That military might may not suffice without a sound moral foundation is most clearly delivered by IDF Chief-of-Staff Yitzhak Rabin (1967) in the immediate aftermath of the Six Day War: "The special character of the Israel Defense Forces, which is itself an expression of the distinctiveness of the Jewish People as a whole . . . the alternative to victory was annihilation. . . . Our soldiers prevailed not by the strength of their weapons but by their sense of mission, by their consciousness of the justice of their cause, by a deep love of their country, and by their understanding of the heavy task laid upon them: to insure the existence of our people in their homeland."

How have Zionists tried to live up to this moral imperative, to "insure the existence" of the Jewish state by charting "the justice of their cause" to effectively legitimate Israel's existence? Several scholars, including myself, have explored these and related themes in the Zionist discourse and practice (Abulof, 2015b; Shapira, 1999; Shimoni, 1995; Singer, 1990). Before specifying the actual legitimating strategies, I propose we discern such strategies along two axes (Table 9.1).

First, we should distinguish between virtue and value legitimation. Legitimation always involves articulated reasoning, whether practical or moral. In the moral realm, we legitimate through the virtues and values we ascribe to actors and acts, respectively. The distinction between virtues and values is elusive yet useful as it grounds legitimation in either "being" or "doing," respectively. We can claim something is legitimate because we (or others) embody certain moral characters or else because what we (or others) do resonate with certain moral conduct. Importantly, while faulty actions can tarnish value legitimation, virtue legitimacy is less vulnerable to misconduct.

Second, we should distinguish between three core rationales of legitimation: righteousness (often religiously inspired), rights (emanating from social contracts), and *raison d'être* (forward-looking purpose). A sense of righteousness is the least susceptible to reasoned contestation; its holders often profess infallibility. Taken to the extremes, such forceful legitimation may transcend justification into the realm of sanctification, rendering its object sacred. Righteousness and *raison d'être* (as an ultimate purpose) tend to be more particularistic than rights, which are often either universal or universalizable.

We may locate Zionism's legitimations strategies along this 2 × 3 matrix. Notably some strategies figure in more than one "box." Religion is a clear case in point. For many, Judaism justifies Zionism and the Jewish state since the Bible clearly prescribes the "promised land" to the "chosen people." But this maxim could be interpreted in divergent ways. If the "chosen people" stress their contract with God, they effectively appropriate a sense

Table 9.1 Zionism's moral lifelines (legitimation strategies)

	Righteousness	Rights	Raison d'être
Virtue (being)	"Chosen people" (covenantal)	Peoplehood, survival	"Chosen people" (missionary), culture, self-actualization, homeland, survival
Values (doing)	Tradition, religion, regime	History, law, justice, compromise, force	Expedience, democracy, peace

From Uriel Abulof, *The Mortality and Morality of Nations*, Cambridge University Press, 2015. Reprinted with permission.

of self-righteousness (we are always divinely sanctioned); if, however, they underscore their mission onto other peoples, they employ a religious *raison d'être*, imbuing their very being, and occasionally their doings, with a transcendental purpose. Moreover, religion, like most traditions, could also legitimate certain actions, not only actors, as inherently righteous: seeing, for example, the settling of the land of Israel as inherently good (though believers may employ the more secular language of "rights" to introduce their religious creed).

To the religious legitimation, we may add 10 more strategies, used in Zionist discourse to justify the Jewish state.

- *History*: The early Jewish presence in Palestine, and the people's forced expulsion thereof, merit restitution in the reconstruction of that historical national home.
- *Culture*: Hebrew is the lifeline of the Jewish people as well as one of their greatest contribution to civilization and may only revive by becoming a national language.
- *Self-actualization*: Diasporic Jews, restricted to lesser occupations, have lost much of their bodily and spiritual vigor; their redemption goes through "Hebrew labor," especially the cultivation of the land—to build, and be built by, it.
- *Homeland*: Jews are not colonizers in Palestine, but native to the place; it is, and always will be, where they can feel, intuitively, truly at home.
- *Regime (democracy)*: The Jewish state is a front fortress of Western ideals and institutions, carrying the torch of democracy, liberalism, and socialism (later capitalism) to a region where these are rarely to be found.
- *Law and justice (peoplehood)*: Zionism subscribes to universal precepts, especially those espoused by the West, as well as to global norms and international law; UN resolution 181 and the right of all peoples to national self-determination justifies the Jewish state (e.g., by *virtue of being a people*, Jews have the right to political independence).
- *Expedience*: The Jewish state does not only help Jews in Israel and outside it, but also aids the global community through scientific/technological innovations, humanitarian assistance, new ideas, and a revived age-old culture.

- *Survival*: Israel is essential for the very (physical and spiritual) survival of Jews worldwide and certainly the survival of Jews in Palestine/Israel; without Jewish sovereignty, there will be either subjugation or worse, a second holocaust.
- *Peace and compromise*: Israel seeks peace with its neighbors, near and far, and is willing to make substantial compromises to make it happen.
- *Force*: While peaceful, Israel is strong, stronger than its foes, repeatedly proving by being victorious on the battlefield that it's here to stay and not another "Crusader Kingdom." All the same, the IDF maintains the "purity of arms"—conducting itself ethically.

Faith and Bad Faith: The "Chosen People Has No Choice"

The Zionist nomization has faced numerous challenges. While all Zionists nominally choose a Jewish state, they hotly debate its moral reasoning. Religious Zionism's emphasis on divine ordinance, for example, has occasionally clashed with the democratic legitimation more prevalent among secular Zionists. Different justifications often prescribe different choices— mainly of authorities and policies, but occasionally of polities and identities, too. If, for example, one regards international law as a moral linchpin for the Jewish state, one should readily delimit its territory to conform to legal decrees and resolutions by the international community.

The inner-Zionist moral debate has fostered doubt—constant uncertainty about *why* the Jewish state *ought* to exist, which, for some, dangerously bred doubts about *whether* it should exist. This debate has been both exhilarating and exhausting, invigorating the society to find its path while concomitantly bringing it ever closer to the "Zionist absurd": the realization that there may be no common moral ground on which to base the Jewish state.

This creeping moral doubt was always there. Thus, for example, Eliyahu Golomb (1944), a leader of the Haganah military organization in Mandatory Palestine, discerned that "some of the Jewish youth doubt the justice behind our arrival in *Eretz Israel*, the justice of Zionism . . . and view our actions with that same doubt. This is most dangerous . . . if we do not sense the justice of coming to an open land, which has space for the development of an additional people—we will also lack the fortitude to carry out this endeavor."

Some three decades later, PM Golda Meir responded to "The Letter from 12th-Graders" criticizing Israel's policies: "I am shocked that there are those among us who cast doubt on the just nature of our cause" (cited in Mann, 1998, p. 37). Still three decades later, Author Aharon Megged (2003, p. 325), following another "conscientious letter," bewailed the "weakening of the internal belief in the justice of the cause regarding our very existence here in the Land."

The Israeli–Palestinian conflict has spawned the moral doubt and can thus help illuminate it and the response to it. Zionist nomization was based, early on, on the above-mentioned "Iron Wall" rationale: patient vigilance in face of an understandable hostility would, ultimately, see it subside. The Arabs will recognize the Jewish state, eventually advancing peace. This rationale has faced mounting challenges, but where do challenges to national nomization come from?

Since nomization involves both self and other, both principles and practices, I suggest we discern delegitimating challenges to nomization along two distinctions—internal/external and principled/practical—creating a 2 × 2 matrix of ideal-types (Table 9.2). From within the nation, its nomization may suffer from moral contradictions (*coherence*) or seem spoiled by the nation's own practices (*integrity*). From without, national nomization may fail to live up to certain supranational principles (*validity*) or become unsustainable considering external practices (*viability*). Importantly, these challenges are intersubjective; what matters is how the nation perceives them.

In the case of Israel, these ideal-types can help us grasp the troubles of the Iron Wall, especially after 1967 (Table 9.3).

Table 9.2 Challenges to national nomization

Challenges	Internal	External
Principled	*Incoherence* (internal contradictions)	*Validity* (clash with global principles)
Practical	*Integrity* (deviational behavior)	*Viability* (clash with global practices)

From Uriel Abulof, *The Mortality and Morality of Nations*, Cambridge University Press, 2015. Reprinted with permission.

Table 9.3 Key challenges to the Zionist Iron Wall ethics

Challenge	Internal	External
Moral	*Reciprocal self-determination?* Demanding rights for Jews while denying them to Palestine's Arabs (the original formulation and after 1967, more so since 1987)	*Israel—Jewish and democratic?* Western liberalism challenges the ethnonational character of Zionism and Israel (esp. since the 1980s)
Practical	*Corrupting occupation?* Trampling the "lesser evil" by employing excessive force against the Palestinians (esp. since 1987)	*Two states for two peoples?* "Arab rejectionism" framed by Zionists as innate (esp. since 2000)

From Úriel Abulof, *The Mortality and Morality of Nations*, Cambridge University Press, 2015. Reprinted with permission.

1. *Incoherence*: Have Israeli Jews morally reasoned their case equitably? Zionism struggled to reason why it champions the *universal* principle of self-determination on behalf of the Jewish people but refuses to extend it to the Arab people already resident in Palestine (Gans, 2008). Moral coherence warrants the equal application of that right to both peoples (Halwani & Kapitan, 2008).

2. *Integrity*: Have Israeli Jews practiced what they preach when it comes to the Palestinians? The demographic transformation in the wake of the 1967 War and the growing recognition of Palestinian nationalism, especially following the First Intifada (1987–1991), cast that in doubt. The conduct of both Israeli society and military created a sense that "the occupation corrupts," practically trampling the "lesser evil" principle (discussed earlier) by employing excessive force against the Palestinians.

3. *Validity*: Has Zionist nomization resonated with the moral precepts of Western liberal democracies? From the 1970s onward, and especially since the 1990s, Western societies have increasingly rejected ethnonationalism (Brown, 1999). Zionism, however, has always been the national movement of the ethnic Jewish people, and many liberal observers have begun to doubt whether Israel's claim to be both Jewish *and* democratic could ever be valid.

4. *Viability*: Does the hopeful Zionist Iron Wall ethics remain sound? The Second Intifada (2000–2004) crushed, in the eyes of many Israeli Jews,

the belief that the Palestinians want their state alongside the Jewish state. Most Israeli Jews began to see the Palestinians as bent on their politicide, even genocide, casting a great shadow over the Iron Wall rationale of patiently awaiting Arab recognition.

The mounting challenges to Zionist nomization increasingly become an impasse of moral meaning. In the last generation, we may speak of "the transvaluation of Zionism," the revaluation of its underpinning moral meaning. Facing the Zionist absurd—the possibility that nothing can persuade all Jews and non-Jews of Israel's legitimacy—many Zionists have sought refuge in bad faith. The three fallacies of bad faith clearly surfaced.

- *Essentialism*: (Israeli) Jews are virtuous and righteous, the Arabs bent on their destruction, while the rest of the world, at best, looks the other way. There is "no partner" for peace, and there can never be one.
- *Determinism*: The Jewish past, especially the hatred and persecution of Jews, preordains the way others will treat Jews in the future. Thus, for example, Israeli Minister of Foreign Affairs Israel Katz's argument that "Poles suckle anti-Semitism from their mothers' milk" (Hacohen, 2019).
- *Fatalism*: The destiny of the Jewish people is sealed, probably from above; they have no choice but to follow it through.

Bad faith politics forfeits freedom of both self and others, Jews and non-Jews: the former have no choice but to opt for combative Zionism; the latter have no choice but to hate the former. Thus, rather than seeing Zionism as a possible choice that merits constant moral reasoning, which may be contested (typically drawing on rights or *raison d'être*), many turned to view Zionism's righteousness as a given that must never be morally debated, holding those daring to cast doubts as traitors to the (un-reasoned) cause. "The alternative," as PM Menachem Begin said of the 1982 Lebanon War, is "Auschwitz" (cited in Schiff, Yaari, & Friedman, 1984, p. 92). Israel is a "villa in the jungle," hated innately for what it is (a Jewish state), not for what it does (e.g., continuous occupation), rendering morality itself meaningless, even dangerous. Through this prism, debating Israel's policies, indeed its authorities, is treacherous; doubting its (current) narrative is courting annihilation. This perspective effectively turns Zionism teleological to tautological, from seeking meaning (purposeful choice) to surviving for survival's sake.

A telling sign of this transformation is former IDF Chief of Staff Moshe Ya'alon. Upon leaving his post, he effectively admitted failure: "After four-and-a-half years of war against Palestinian terror, we haven't succeeded in persuading even Fatah to recognize that the Jewish state will exist here forever." Now Ya'alon identified a new kind of existential threat: "We are retreating without having a narrative. . . . The combination of terror and demography, along with the question marks hanging over the justice of [Israel's] course of action, are a recipe for disaster for the Jewish state" (Ha'aretz, June 1–2, 2005).

But what infallibility could ever obliterate these treacherous "questions marks"? Not human, but divine infallibility was the answer of many: Judaism as a source, rather than a mere resource, for justifying Zionism. In the latter's discourse, the concept of the Land of Israel as a means to an end gave way to the idea of the Land constituting an end in itself, championing the "Chosen People over the Promised Land" legitimation. Bad faith entwines with Godly faith: believing that, in facing a hostile world, the only justification one needs comes from up above. Equipped with such inherent righteousness, one can let go of guilt and regret. Against this background it is easier to understand the remarkable electoral achievement of the Jewish House Party in 2013—gaining 12 seats in the Knesset under the slogan "No more apologies!"

Importantly, while the appeal of such (bad) faith is plain, there is no need to not practice Halakha to subscribe to bad faith. While about a quarter of Israeli Jews are observant, in a 2013 survey nearly two-third proclaimed that the Jews are "the chosen people" (Hermann, 2013, pp. 62–73). Religious faith is thus conductive, but unessential, for fostering and sustaining the politics of bad faith.

As suggested earlier, the politics of fear may also facilitate bad faith, and this is certainly true in the case of Israel. The more people immerse themselves in fears and anger, as Israeli society has in recent years (Helliwell, Layard, & Sachs, 2018), the less they are prone to search for a communal moral vision that can endow their collective existence with meaning—a purposeful choice. Combating enemies, real or imagined, supersedes the deliberative struggle for moral meaning. Fearmongering here thus becomes the "solution" to existential anxiety that saw reflective freedom yielding to the absurd, completing a sad circle on our argument.

Conclusion: The Zionist Sisyphus?

Five years before the 1967 War, Hebrew poet Yehuda Amichai wrote of the wrongs of righteousness and the worth of doubt: "From the place where we are righteous/Flowers will never grow/In the spring./The place where we are righteous/Is hard and trampled/Like a yard./But doubts and loves/Dig up the world/Like a mole, a plow./And a whisper will be heard in the place/Where the ruined/House once stood." Three years after the War, Hebrew poet Nathan Alterman wrote of the devil scheming to get rid of the Jewish people: "The Devil then said: How do I overcome/This besieged one?/He has courage/And talent, /And implements of war/And wits . . . Only this shall I do/I'll dull his mind/And cause him to forget/The justice of his cause./Thus spoke the Devil/And skies paled in horror/As the Devil ascended/To pursue his plot."

Zionism—a modern meaning-making project—has wavered between these two poems: questioning "the justice of the cause" and giving it better answers, on the one hand, and demonizing those who dare to forget it is not a question but an absolute imperative, on the other. At no period did Zionism wholly subscribe to either: always somewhat fearful, it neither fully followed freedom nor completely succumbed to bad faith.

Refining Nietzsche's dictum, Zionism's secret of success, its ongoing vitality in the face of constant dangers, may have been exactly that delicate balance between the two positions, two poems. The doubt dug deep to find— and cultivate—new creative ways of making moral meaning out of this pioneering political project; the certainty helped the community cast a strong anchor in the land, withstand adversities, and not wallow in the mire of self-doubt.

While the recent generation has seen the scales tip toward bad faith, many Zionists, individually and collectively, still hold fast to freedom as the engine of meaning-making—insisting that Israel faces real, and potentially reviving, choices: to sustain or stop its long 50-year occupation of another people, to follow vulgar capitalism or recreate social-economic solidarity, to turn to divine salvation or cultivate humanism.

Zionism is a rocky journey. Like the mythical Sisyphus, Israel has been trying to lift the rock—the burden of endowing its existence with meaning, a justifiable purpose—to a secure plain just to see it roll down before reaching the top. The gods condemned Sisyphus to his task, and one may only hope he could find some occasional happiness in it. But if humans, not gods, partly determine their own destiny, Zionism may yet embrace freedom and take responsibility for making its (good) fate better.

Highlights

- Israel is not merely the "scene" where the search for meaning happens, it epitomizes that very search, the human quest for justifying life and death: *Why ought we breathe, breed, and bleed?*
- Each society strives to develop "existential legitimation" (*nomization*): justifying *why* it and its politics *ought* to exist. Failed nomization may end in an impasse of meaning, a *political* absurd.
- Fear might lead to both freedom (an active, reasoned choice) and "bad faith" (forgetting or forfeiting freedom). Israeli Jews have been engulfed in existential fears that go far beyond what their objective (in)security merits.
- Zionism has partly dealt with its existential anxiety by existential legitimation (*nomization*): imbuing the dream and reality of the Jewish State with moral meaning—righteousness, rights, and *raison d'être*.
- Recently, the Zionist nomization has reached an impasse of moral meaning bringing it closer to anomy and to meeting the *political* Absurd: a creeping belief that all its legitimating efforts are doomed. The result is the rise of bad faith politics.

References

Abulof, U. (2008). Back to the future: A comparative ethical look at Israeli Arab future vision documents. *Israel Studies Forum*, 23(2), 29–54. http://www.ingentaconnect.com/content/berghahn/isf/2008/00000023/00000002/art00002 http://dx.doi.org/10.3167/isf.2008.230202

Abulof, U. (2014a). Deep securitization and Israel's "Demographic Demon." *International Political Sociology, 8*(4), 396–415. doi:10.1111/ips.12070

Abulof, U. (2014b). National ethics in ethnic conflicts: The Zionist "Iron Wall" and the "Arab Question." *Ethnic and Racial Studies, 37*(14), 2653–2669. doi:10.1080/01419870.2013.854921

Abulof, U. (2015a). The malpractice of rationality in international relations. *Rationality and Society, 27*(3), 358–384.

Abulof, U. (2015b). *The mortality and morality of nations.* Cambridge University Press.

Abulof, U. (2016). Public political thought: Bridging the sociological–philosophical divide in the study of legitimacy. *The British Journal of Sociology, 67*(2), 371–391. doi:10.1111/1468-4446.12192

Abulof, U. (2017). Conscientious politics and Israel's moral dilemmas. *Contemporary Politics, 23*(1), 34–52.

Amichai, Yehuda. (2000). *A Touch of Grace.* Translated by B. Harshav and B. Harshav: Jerusalem: Museum on the Seam.

Altarman, Nathan. (1970). Molad, vol. 3 (15–16) (224–225) (June 1970) 131. Reprinted in Aharon Ben- Ami (ed), The Book of Greater Israel (Tel-Aviv).

Becker, E. (1973). *The denial of death.* Free Press.

Becker, E. (1975). *Escape from evil.* Free Press.

Bekoff, M. (2007). *The emotional lives of animals: A leading scientist explores animal joy, sorrow, and empathy—and why they matter.* New World Library.

Ben-Gurion, D. (1955). *Induction speech to the Israeli government, 2 November 1955.* Knesset Protocols.

Berger, P. L. (1967). *The sacred canopy: Elements of a sociological theory of religion.* Doubleday.

Boland, J., Riggs, K. J., & Anderson, R. J. (2018). A brighter future: The effect of positive episodic simulation on future predictions in non-depressed, moderately dysphoric & highly dysphoric individuals. *Behaviour Research and Therapy, 100,* 7–16. doi:https://doi.org/10.1016/j.brat.2017.10.010

Brown, D. (1999). Are there good and bad nationalisms? *Nations and Nationalism, 5*(2), 281–302.

Buber, M. (2005). *A land of two peoples: Martin Buber on Jews and Arabs* (P. R. Mendes-Flohr Ed.). University of Chicago Press.

Campbell, A. (2013). The evolutionary psychology of women's aggression. *Philosophical transactions of the Royal Society of London, Series B, Biological sciences, 368*(1631), 20130078. doi:10.1098/rstb.2013.0078

Camus, A. (1955). *The myth of Sisyphus, and other essays* (1st American ed.). Knopf.

Cover, R. M. (1983). Nomos and narrative. *Harvard Law Review, 97*(1), 4–68. http://search.ebscohost.com/login.aspx?direct=true&db=aph&AN=7734400&site=ehost-live

Gans, C. (2008). *A just Zionism: On the morality of the Jewish state.* Oxford University Press.

Global Firepower. (2017). *2017 World Military Strength Rankings.*

Golan, A. (2014, April 28). 60% feel equally Jewish and Israeli [BINA survey]. *NRG.* https://www.makorrishon.co.il/nrg/online/1/ART2/575/608.html?hp=1&cat=351&loc=30

Golomb, E. (1944). *Hevyon Ez* (Vol. 2). Aynot. [Hebrew]

Gould, S., & Szoldra, P. (2017, March 15). The 25 most powerful militaries in the world. *Business Insider.*

Ha'am, A. (1948). *At the crossroads* (Vol. 1). Dvir.

Hacohen, H. (2019, February 18). Chief Rabbi of Poland: Katz offended Polish Jews with Holocaust comment. *The Jerusalem Post.*

Halwani, R., & Kapitan, T. (2008). *The Israeli-Palestinian conflict: Philosophical essays on self-determination, terrorism, and the one-state solution.* Palgrave Macmillan.

Harel, A., & Cohen, G. (2016, July 12). Hezbollah: From terror group to army. *Ha'aretz.*

Hassabis, D., Kumaran, D., Vann, S. D., & Maguire, E. A. (2007). Patients with hippocampal amnesia cannot imagine new experiences. *Proceedings of the National Academy of Sciences of the United States of America, 104*(5), 1726–1731. doi:10.1073/pnas.0610561104

Helliwell, J. F., Layard, R., & Sachs, J. (2018). *World Happiness Report 2018.* Sustainable Development Solutions Network, United Nations.

Hermann, T. (2013). *Israeli Democracy Index 2013.* Israeli Democracy Institute.

Hoffman, B. (2017, June 20). Trump advisers don't understand Israel's fear of Palestinian state. *The Jerusalem Post.* http://www.jpost.com/Israel-News/Politics-And-Diplomacy/Trump-advisers-dont-understand-Israels-fear-of-Palestinian-state-497395

Jabotinsky, V. (1937 [1923], 26 November 1937). The Iron Wall [Razsviet, 4 November 1923, No. 42/43 (80/81), pp. 2–4]. *The Jewish Herald.*

Jabotinsky, V. (1941 [1923], 5 September 1941). The ethics of the Iron Wall [Razsviet, 11 November 1923, No. 44/45 (81/82), p.3]. *The Jewish Standard.*

Jost, J. T. (2019). Anger and authoritarianism mediate the effects of fear on support for the far right—what Vasilopoulos et al. (2019) really found. *Political Psychology, 40*(4), 705–711. doi:10.1111/pops.12567

Jost, J. T., Glaser, J., Kruglanski, A. W., & Sulloway, F. J. (2003). Political conservatism as motivated social cognition. *Psychological Bulletin, 129*(3), 339–375. doi:10.1037/0033-2909.129.3.339

Kundera, M. (1995). *Testaments betrayed: An essay in nine parts* (1st ed.). HarperCollins Publishers.

LeDoux, J. E. (2015). *Anxious: Using the brain to understand and treat fear and anxiety.* Viking.

Mann, R. (1998). *Unthinkable.* Hed Artsi. [Hebrew]

Megged, A. (2003). The paradox of the Jewish people. In Department of Jewish Zionist Education Jewish Agency (Ed.), *Zionism and Israel, talks with writers and thinkers on Judaism: Jewish philosophy* (pp. 317–326). Yedioth Ahronoth; Jewish Agency. [Hebrew]

Motzkin, J. C., Philippi, C. L., Wolf, R. C., Baskaya, M. K., & Koenigs, M. (2015). Ventromedial prefrontal cortex is critical for the regulation of amygdala activity in humans. *Biological Psychiatry, 77*(3), 276–284. doi:10.1016/j.biopsych.2014.02.014

Nietzsche, F. W. (2005). *The Anti-Christ, ecce homo, twilight of the idols, and other writings* (A. Ridley Ed.). Cambridge University Press.

Panksepp, J. (1998). *Affective neuroscience: The foundations of human and animal emotions.* Oxford University Press.

Rabin, Y. (1967). *Acceptance of honorary doctorate from Hebrew University, Mt. Scopus, Jerusalem, June 28, 1967.*

Rawidowicz, S. (1986). Israel, the ever-dying people. In B. C. I. Ravid (Ed.), *Israel, the ever-dying people, and other essays* (pp. 53–63). Fairleigh Dickinson University Press.

Reddan, M. C., Wager, T. D., & Schiller, D. (2018). Attenuating neural threat expression with imagination. *Neuron, 100*(4), 994–1005.e1004. doi:10.1016/j.neuron.2018.10.047

Rosner, S., & Fuchs, C. (2018). *#IsraeliJudaism: Portrait of a cultural revolution.* Dvir. [Hebrew]

Sartre, J.-P. (1965). *Essays in existentialism* (W. Baskin Ed.). Citadel.

Schiff, Z., Yaari, E., & Friedman, I. (1984). *Israel's Lebanon war.* Simon and Schuster.

Schmitt, C. (2003). *The nomos of the earth in the international law of the Jus Publicum Europaeum.* Telos Press.

Shapira, A. (1999). *Land and power: The zionist resort to force, 1881-1948.* Stanford University Press.

Shavit, A. (2013). *My promised land: The triumph and tragedy of Israel.* Spiegel & Grau.

Shimoni, G. (1995). *The Zionist ideology.* Brandeis University Press.

Singer, M. (1990). Moral standards under pressure: The Israeli army and the intifada. *Ethics & International Affairs, 4*(1), 135–143. doi:10.1111/j.1747-7093.1990.tb00250.x

Suzuki, W., & Fitzpatrick, B. (2015). *Healthy brain, happy life: A personal program to activate your brain and do everything better.* Dey Street Books.

Taylor, S. E. (2002). *The tending instinct: How nurturing is essential for who we are and how we live.* Times Books.

Tymieniecka, A.-T. (Ed.). (2010). *Phenomenology and existentialism in the twentieth century* (Book I, II, III). Springer.

Witte, K. (1996). Fear as motivator, fear as inhibitor: Using the extended parallel process model to explain fear appeal successes and failures. In P. A. Andersen & L. K. Guerrero (Eds.), *Handbook of communication and emotion* (pp. 423–450). Academic Press.

10

Cultural Scripts, Personal Meaning, and Ethno-Class Identities Among Jews in Israel

Avihu Shoshana

Introduction

One of the central assumptions of narrative psychology is related to the close connection between collective biographies and personal biographies, or between major cultural stories and "small" life stories (Shoshana, 2013). Gergen and Gergen (1986) argue that, in this context, even if the individual can theoretically create a story that differs from the script offered to him or her by his or her culture, this cannot be redeemed in the life sphere. Furthermore, this biographical creation will not allow them to communicate with the Other, and society is likely to impose sanctions on them. These remarks echo the phenomenological claims made by Schutz and Luckmann (1974) about the construction of personal and social life-worlds and the existence of typical biographies that are culturally available to us. These typical biographies serve as cognitive frameworks and equip us with strategies of action as well as provide phenomenological definitions for our identities. In other words, these typical biographies direct, and sometimes even limit, the central aspects of meaning in life, such as the meaning of who am I? What is my identity? My self-worth? My potential developmental trajectory and my expected worldview?

This chapter proposes to connect the collective stories (or cultural scripts) that shape identities and personal identifications regarding ethnicity and class in Israel. Furthermore, this article proposes to examine this link with respect to a marked ethnic group in Israel: the Mizrahim (Jews from Arab countries). The choice to examine marked ethnic identities is related, *inter alia*, to the need for subjects to internalize the social gazes that expose them

Avihu Shoshana, *Cultural Scripts, Personal Meaning, and Ethno-Class Identities Among Jews in Israel* In: *Finding Meaning*. Edited by: Ofra Mayseless and Pninit Russo-Netzer, Oxford University Press. © Oxford University Press 2022. DOI: 10.1093/oso/9780190910358.003.0010 to dilemmas related to visibility and accountability. One of the most significant existential privileges associated with populating hegemonic social locations (whiteness for instance, or Ashkenazism in Israel; i.e., Jews from Europe and North America—see Shoshana [2016] for a detailed description) is the experience of transparency and (mainly unconscious) dissociation from oppressive social gazes.

Against this background, this chapter examines the ethnic and class identifications of adult Mizrahim (older than 30) from three different groups: Mizrahim from a low socioeconomic background (in terms of income, education, place of residence, and parental class), Mizrahim who have experienced socioeconomic mobility, and Mizrahim born to families from a high socioeconomic background. Examining the phenomenology of members of these groups can teach us about how individuals give meaning to their lives and draw their own specific existential paths. Furthermore, we can examine the relationship between different cultural scripts and personal narratives and clarify the relationships between class and ethnic identities in Israel. We can also examine the varying internal variances of different groups in the "Mizrahi" category.

The prevailing research literature generally examines the ethnic categories in Israel (Mizrahim and Ashkenazim) uniformly and prefers the empirical examination of the differences between groups (Shoshana, 2007). The examination of intragroup variance can thus deconstruct the concept of Mizrahiism and consider the differences between subgroups. Furthermore, this chapter reveals how class and ethnicity are interconnected and influence the constitution of personal scripts in relation to prevailing cultural scripts.

The chapter is divided into five parts: a review of cultural scripts and ethnic and class identities, a review of ethnic and class hierarchies in Israel and the identification of cultural scripts that may influence the existential experiences of individuals in everyday life, a description of the study design, a description of the research findings through the phenomenology of the members of three groups of Mizrahim in Israel, and a discussion about the associations between cultural scripts and personal identities.

Cultural Scripts and Ethnic and Class Identities

One of the principal assumptions in social sciences identity research is that individuals do not develop self-understandings and personal narratives in isolation but are influenced by the public-cultural narratives available to them (Somer, 1994). These cultural narratives not only help to grant existential meaning to and provide order within everyday experiences, but also are also critical to the psychological and social processes associated with our transformation into subjects. Different scholars define these narratives in various ways, such as *cultural repertoires* (Small, Harding, & Lamont, 2010), *scripts* (Simon & Gagnon, 1986), and *stories* (Ewick & Sibley, 2003). All these concepts are proposed in order to depict units of organized symbolic meanings or the cultural sources that help individuals to give meaning to their lives and self-comprehension (for a description of the differences between the concepts, see Lamont et al., 2016, pp. 21–22). I prefer the concept of *cultural scripts* to describe the set of existential assumptions available to individuals to construct their life spheres and crystallize their own senses of self. In fact, these scripts act as cognitive and social resources for navigating everyday life.

The research literature also distinguishes between strong cultural scripts (what Lamont et al., 2016, p. 75 calls "ready-made") and weak (or smaller) ones. The strong scripts are more readily available for individuals to understand reality, their interpersonal relationships, their selves, and their emotions. The psychological-therapeutic script[1] and the neo-liberal script[2] (Rose, 1996), for example, are widely described as the most dominant cultural scripts in Western culture available for establishing subjectivity in everyday life. Moreover, several studies describe how the discursive alliance between these scripts strengthens their cultural dominance (Rose, 1996; Shoshana, 2014).

Many researchers also describe how cultural scripts establish specific ethnic identities. Cultural scripts associated with neo-liberalism, for example, encourage color blindness (Bonilla-Silva, 2012). This script, which is widely described as favored by various official social actors (such as state organizations, schools, and popular media), actually encourages assimilation

[1] The psychological script is an area of knowledge that feeds on psychological knowledge and includes a special interest in the private self (compared to traditional social arrangements or collectivist cultures), emotions (especially their verbalization), and the formulation of problems in clinical or pathological terms (Nolan, 1998).

[2] The neo-liberal script is a political-economic discourse that promotes values of free market, entrepreneurship, privatization of the state from social fields, and the establishment of free and entrepreneurial individuals. Importantly, this discourse does not only refer to the political or economic sphere, but also to the promotion of specific cultural values (hence the promotion of specific subjectivity) such as competitiveness, merit, choice, self-control, self-reliance, and, briefly, *Homo economicus*.

into the dominant culture and dissociation from other scripts of ethnicity that prefer strategic assimilation (Lacy, 2004, voluntary ethnicity (e.g., symbolic ethnicity; see Gans, 1979), assimilation to minority culture, and critical awareness (postcolonialism) (Pieterse, 2001).

These cultural scripts about ethnicity change in relation to various national contexts as well as within each specific culture. For example, some researchers describe how class positions within the same culture supply specific scripts about ethnic identities and their relation to class identities (Bettie, 1995). Lacy (2004) describes how the ethnic identities of middle-class African Americans are associated with the space in which they live (homogenous or racially heterogeneous neighborhoods) and with exposure to middle- and upper-class white scripts. These scripts of ethnicity are based, *inter alia*, on boundaries, which Alba (2005) defines as bright versus blurred. The distinctions involved in bright boundaries "are unambiguous, so that individuals know at all times which side of the boundary they are on. Others are 'blurry,' involving zones of self-presentation and social representation that allow for ambiguous locations with respect to the boundary" (Alba, 2005, p. 22).

Through comparative studies, Lamont (2000) reports on differences in the mental maps, or the phenomenological boundary work of working-class and middle- and upper-class subjects in France and the United States. The concept of *boundary work* refers to the way in which individuals distinguish themselves from others. Lamont describes in detail how this phenomenological boundary work is linked to specific cultural-state scripts. Her findings reveal, for example, that blacks in the United States, as opposed to whites, explain poverty in structural and nonpersonal terms. They also express more compassion and social solidarity toward the poor. In addition, unlike white American workers, anger toward the poor was hardly mentioned by French workers. "Republicanism and a well-entrenched socialist tradition," Lamont (2000, p. 239) explains, "played key roles in diminishing boundaries toward the poor, given the ideals of social justice, equality, solidarity, and civil rights." The hegemony of neo-liberal repertories may explain the personal attributions by Americans.

A recent study (Lamont et al., 2016), which compares three countries (the United States, Brazil, and Israel) and five different (ethnic, racial, and national) groups from two different classes (middle-class and working-class), offers an impressive application of the associations between state cultural scripts and local scripts, ethno-racial identities, and self-understandings.

These comparisons have helped researchers not only to expose subjective interpretations of national cultural scripts, but also different degrees of groupness (strong among blacks in the United States and Palestinians in Israel, and weaker among Mizrahim in Israel and black Brazilians) and different relations between national and racial identities. In Brazil, for example, there is less strain between racial and national identities. In the United States, on the other hand, national identity is weaker than racial identity. These studies also reveal different relationships between racial and class identification (class stigmatization is higher in Brazil and lower in the United States) and different manifestations of ethno-racial identification (cultural vs. political, or self-identification through skin color vs. participation in critical consciousness organizations).

The highly salient racial identities among African Americans in the United States (and the relatively low awareness of class stigmatization) are explained by Lamont and her colleagues (2016) through strong cultural scripts (such as civil rights). On the other hand, blacks in Brazil express racial identifications (mainly skin color) and are aware of white superiority, but do not grant this unique content. These descriptions, referred to by the researchers as the "thinness of meaning" (Lamont et al., 2016, p. 142), echo the descriptions of Sansone (2003) about "blacks without ethnicity" in Brazil.

The institutional exclusion of Palestinians in Israel and their dissociation from the national-Jewish script (Zionism) and the cultural script of assimilation is described in the study as creating a strong groupness and a phenomenology of strong boundaries among them. The study also describes how members of two Jewish groups in Israel (Ethiopians and Mizrahim) prefer national identity and abide by the strong cultural script of assimilation, but for other reasons. The Ethiopians, whose inclusion in Israeli nationalism is based on their Judaism (or religionization), reduce the experience of otherness (and discrimination) as a means of establishing a sense of belonging to the Israeli-Jewish collective. The Mizrahim, who express low levels of groupness and prefer definitions that minimize ethnic marking (such as "Israeliness"), prefer dissociation from ethnic (i.e., Mizrahi) identities in order to avoid the negative stigma affiliated with Mizrahiism in Israel. In other words, the strong national script in Israel, the lack of institutional and legal legitimacy to raise claims on the basis of ethnic identity (see Bitton, 2011, in this context), and the dominance of neo-liberal discourse (which actually promotes apoliticism) are offered as explanations for the ethnic identifications by Mizrahim and Ethiopians in Israel.

These descriptions underscore the effects of state cultural scripts on ethnic identities and self-comprehension. My study focuses on the Israeli culture and extends previous research of ethnic and class identities within a specific ethnic group. This examination may enhance our understanding of the effects of cultural scripts on the subjective meanings produced in everyday life.

Before doing so, I would like to describe the cultural hierarchical orders in Israel and the sociohistorical development of discourse on ethnicity and class. This description can assist in garnering a complex understanding of the subjective meanings that individuals grant themselves and the influence of cultural scripts on these subjective meanings.

Cultural Scripts and Discourse on Ethnicity and Class in Israel

The main symbolic distinction of ethnic identities in Israel is between Mizrahim (Jews from Arab countries) and Ashkenazim (Jews of Europe and North America). These two categories act as something of an umbrella identity (Shohat, 1999, p. 13), which constitutes a large difference between, and low variance within, the two groups. In other words, the local subjective or collective identifications such as Polish, Kurdish, or Tunisian are hardly discussed in the various types of discourse addressing ethnicity in Israel. While Mizrahi identity is described as ethnic, Ashkenazi identity is described as non-ethnic or Israeli (Sasson-Levy, 2008). Like other countries in the world, the "black" (African American, Latin) or "yellow" (Asian) identity is marked, while the white (European American) identity is neutral, transparent, and unmarked (Frankenberg, 1993). The issue of markedness and cultural visibility has many implications for the meanings people grant to reality and their self-worth. The marked ethnic identity is described as based on "irrational" culture, attached to the traditional past and giving preference to continuity with the past rather than being future-oriented (Perry, 2001).

White identity is also described as the normative, self-evident identity, the default identity (McDermott & Samson, 2005) to which other groups are compared. Moreover, these normative qualities of whiteness also mean cultural construction that emphasizes that this category is not worthy of discovery, investigation, or intervention. The marked identities (Mizrahi, poor, and women, for example) are described, on the other hand, as problematic categories and are, therefore, worthy of research and intervention, which in turn increases their visibility.

To discuss the ways in which different spaces relate to ethnicities (Mizrahi and Ashkenazi) in Israel, I would like to describe three main scripts: state scripts, academic scripts, and current research reports on the phenomenology of the ethnicity discourse through interviews with various subjects. I call these "everyday scripts," and they are very important in light of their influence on subjective meanings.

State Scripts: Modernization, Assimilation, and Multiculturalism

The state script on ethnic identities that predominated during the first two decades following the establishment of the Jewish state is anchored in the logic of the functionalist theory and the modernization discourse. The assumptions of social equilibrium and structural integration, which underlie functionalist theory, dictated an absorption policy that encouraged immigrants to adopt the new national culture (Israeli) and abandon the premodern traditions, which were defined as deviation from the norm. The dynamics of a "melting pot" and the evolutionary transition from traditional to modern have been described as having the power to maintain a stable social order. "Modernity" was defined as a whole set of advanced technological capabilities in a capitalist economy; a method that promotes values of rationality and linear progress and (Western) values of democracy and equality (Shohat, 1999). Against this backdrop, the policy of "absorption through modernization" was developed. The cultural capital of the Jews of the Arab countries was particularly troubling to the leaders of the state, who sought to establish a state in the spirit of Western culture. The education system, as well as many academics at the time, played a central role in the culturalization of the Mizrahim and in the national attempt to distance them from Arab cultural capital in order to adopt Western cultural capital.

It is important to emphasize that the state script encouraged the cultural assimilation of ethnic groups into a common national (Israeli) identity. National or civic identity was offered as a substitute for particular identities in the form of ethnic identities. Ethnic identities were described as cultural heritage, or a pre-modern form of collective. Moreover, the cultural assimilation perspective, or the melting-pot policy, explicitly suggested that the individual achievement identity is preferable to social ascription or ethnic identities. Assimilation, according to this perspective, means reducing the use of ethnic distinctions and socioethnic consciousness (for a detailed description of the state discourse, see Shohat, 1999).

Beginning in the mid-1990s, and following pressure from social activists, state authorities began to adopt a multiculturalism policy that, in turn, provided an alternative to social and personal meanings. This alternative proposes to avoid the negative tagging of ethnicity that characterized the previous decades in Israel. Multiculturalism emphasizes the contribution that different communities make to the possibility that the individual will lead a meaningful life. In other words, this policy emphasizes the importance of collective identities in establishing a personal identity. Moreover, this policy (or cultural script) seeks to establish subjects who are equal and separate from one another (Taylor, 1994).

Academic Scripts on Ethnicity in Israel: From Binary to Hybrid

The dominant academic script on ethnic identities, which began in the early 1980s, was mainly used in the critical discourse of Said (1978). In parallel, since the beginning of the 21st century, there has also been a cultural import of theoretical models (primarily Bhabha, 1994) addressing the experience of hybridity. Said's Orientalism (1978) is described as one of the cornerstones of critical academic scripts on ethnicity in Israel. Shohat (1999) offers one of the first essays that connects Said's thinking with the ethnic discourse in Israel. The ruling Zionist story describes Shohat's claim that European Zionism saved the Mizrahim from "primitive conditions" of poverty and superstition and introduced them to modern Western culture characterized by democracy. The result of this Orientalist discourse, Shohat stresses, is that Mizrahim can see themselves only through the eyes of the West.

Analysis of the academic script on ethnicity in Israel since the beginning of the 2000s shows a binary movement toward hybridity. If the binary approach in which the East was linked to the West was previously emphasized in other binary contradictions (nature/culture, emotional/rational) (Shohat, 1999), the beginning of the 21st century saw a turning point. The current emphasis is on hybrid sites and experiences capable of tolerating the voices of Oriental conformity, resistance, and modeling at the same time

(Shenhav, 2006). Mizrahi identity, or identity under postcolonial conditions, is described as a mixed, ambivalent, fluid, hyphenated-identity—Arab and Jewish, conformist and subversive.

Hybridity, therefore, refers to a mixed product that characterizes intercultural encounters and cross-boundary experiences as well as encompassed identities such as a Jewish-Arab identity (Shenhav, 2006). Bhabha's debate about hybridity, for example, sees hybrid agents as cultural brokers who speak (or make noise) from at least two places simultaneously. The same life arena that seeks to dissociate itself from all the fetishism of boundaries in turn produces camouflage and heresy (Bhabha, 1994, p. 193). The Israeli hybrid script describes Mizrahi identity as a site in which the qualities of multiplicity and fragmentation exist (Shenhav, 2006). It is important to note that the identities proposed by academic discourse do not necessarily permeate into everyday life, as I illustrate.

The Script on Ethnicity in Everyday Life: Cognitive Dissociation from Ethnic Identities

In 1982, Sari Rosen published her research on couples of mixed ethnic origins in Israel. Rosen called the Mizrahi partners "Super-Orientals" (middle-upper socioeconomic status, higher education, liberal views). These Super-Orientals described their past as characterized by a liberal and Ashkenazi lifestyle, which in turn influenced their claim to marriage with an Ashkenazi spouse. This lifestyle has also been described through constant and conscious maintenance of dissociation from Eastern culture. The couple's children even described their future preference for marrying an Ashkenazi partner, and they expressed concern about their children's dark skin color (Rosen, 1982, p. 96).

Lavee (2005) exposes similar dynamics by examining the process of formation of the daily routine and daily life of mixed ethnic couples in Israel (Mizrahi husband, Ashkenazi wife). The study shows the dominance of Orientalist discourse, which is expressed in "the dissociation of Mizrahi men from Mizrahi culture. . . . Mizrahism is considered inferior and primitive, and therefore it is necessary to be clear of identification with it" (Lavee, 2005, p. 8). This dissociation was expressed through three mechanisms: the silencing of Mizrahism, the neutralization of ethnic differences, and the use of humor. Through these mechanisms the couple not only sought to adopt an identity that was cut off from Mizrahism, but they also helped the woman to emphasize her ethnic superiority (i.e., her Ashkenazism). The process of establishing identities among mixed-ethnic individuals is also illustrated in Frenkel's study (2012). Her research examines which identity design and coping strategies are developed by mixed-ethnic people in Israeli society. The issue of the family name received special prominence in interviews. The interviewees in this study emphasize the markedness of an Eastern surname and its impact on life experiences (in this context, see Rom & Benjamin, 2011). One of the interviewees states:

> I'm glad I'm Weinberg and not a surname that's Mizrahi. It's fun for me to be Weinberg and not Elmalich. It's nicer. For instance, my sister got married and my niece is called Lior Shitrit and not Lior Weinberg, what a bummer. It sucks. It really bums me out. Like . . . I say how lucky I am to be Weinberg because now I will be treated better.

Sasson-Levy (2008) examines the meanings of Ashkenazism through interviews with Ashkenazim. The findings of her research show that one of the characteristics of the Ashkenazi category is that its members avoid ethnic self-definition. The definition of Israeli, for example, leaves the group transparent in its own eyes. Moreover, similar to the study of whiteness elsewhere in the world, her interviewees marked the Ashkenazi self as "devoid of culture" (not in the sense of uncultured, but in the sense that it is culturally transparent). The Mizrahi self, on the other hand, is marked by "Orientalist marking" (Sasson-Levy, 2008, p. 114).

The use of Orientalist discourse helped the interviewees mark cultural differences between themselves and Ashkenazim. "In many interviews," Sasson-Levy emphasizes, "Ashkenazism was linked to ambition, higher education, success, emotional restraint, rationality, politeness, secularism, high culture, leftism, middle class and upwards, emotional coldness, and arrogance. In an almost perfect reversal, Mizrahism was identified with noise (mentioned often), emotionalism and externalization of emotions, passivity, belligerence and violence, whiny music, lying, feelings of deprivation and inferiority, religiosity or traditionality. At the same time, many Ashkenazim identified Mizrahism with true joy, with family values, and with emotional warmth. There is no need to elaborate on the similarity between these Ashkenazi images and the Orientalist discourse described by Edward Said (2000)."

Analysis of the studies on the phenomenology of ethnicity in Israel thus demonstrates the dominance of the Orientalist scripts in everyday life. The multicultural script, or the (critical) hybrid script, does not appear in the phenomenological studies of the subjective meaning that individuals grant to their lives. One of the questions that we must ask is what are the structural-discourse conditions that maintain the stability of the Orientalist script as a basis for subjective meaning and whether this script is expressed by Mizrahim that populate different class locations. These questions will be deliberated in the Discussion section.

Study Design

The findings of this research are based on several studies I conducted over the past decade on the relationship between ethnic and class identities among Mizrahim in Israel (Shoshana, 2007, 2014, 2016). In-depth interviews with 80 Mizrahim from three different groups were conducted over this 10-year span, including interviews with Mizrahim from a low socioeconomic background, Mizrahim who experienced socioeconomic mobility, and Mizrahim born to families from a high socioeconomic background. Forty interviews were conducted with members of the first group, 20 with members of the second group, and 20 with members of the third group. All interviewees were over the age of 30 (ranging in age from 30 to 70). Choosing the age of 30 was not random. The purpose of this study was to examine the relationship between cultural scripts and subjective meanings among adults whose lives are relatively stable. All respondents were recruited using the framework of a snowball sample; I sent a message via various forums (Facebook, community centers, labor organizations) that I sought to interview Mizrahim about ethnic and class identities in Israel. All the interviews, which lasted between 1.5 and 3 hours, were held at times and places that were convenient for the interviewees (coffee shops, private homes, workplaces and offices at the university).

The interviews included five main parts: a general life story ("Tell me the story of your life. Anything that comes to mind. From my point of view there is no right or wrong response"); self-concept and self-definition ("How do you define yourself?" "What is important to you in life?"), ethnic identities and definitions ("How do you define your ethnic identity?"), class identities and definitions ("How do you define your class identity, and how do you express your class identity in everyday life?"), and perceptions of ethnic and class hierarchies in Israel ("Are there differences between Mizrahim and Ashkenazim? Does ethnic and class discrimination exist in Israel?").

All the interviews were analyzed using the processes proposed by grounded theory (Strauss & Corbin, 1998).

Three open readings were done for all the interviews. These open readings allowed me to inductively extract themes I had not considered in advance (e.g., dissociation from ethnicity, preference for class identities, discursive alliances). In addition to these open readings, focused readings were done regarding the issues that originally facilitated this study (ethnic identity, orders of discourse at the foundation of the accounts, self-concept, and life story).

Findings

Mizrahim from a Low Socioeconomic Background: Dominant Ethnic Identities and Transparent Class Identities

One of the first questions I asked interviewees was about their own self-definitions. The vast majority of respondents from the lower socioeconomic class responded in ethnic terms and did not define themselves in class terms at all. Rami, a 54-year-old truck driver, offers a representative description.

> I am first of all Mizrahi. Moroccan Mizrahi. The place you come from says a lot about a person. Those are his roots. And that is what distinguishes him from other people. Mizrahi is not Ashkenazi. And I will say even more than that, Moroccan Mizrahi is also different from Yemenite Mizrahi or Tunisian Mizrahi. Everyone thinks that all the Mizrahim here are the same, but that's nonsense.

It is interesting to note that Rami not only emphasizes the importance of the ethnic component in his self-concept, but also rejects the governmental invention of the concept of "Mizrahim" (Shohat, 1999), which unites all the Jews of the Arab countries under one category and thereby eliminates intragroup variability. I suggest considering the subjective identification of the interviewees of this group as reinforcing their ethnic consciousness, as well as a protest (or as a practice of daily resistance, in the terms of Scott,

1985) against the hegemonic cultural script suggesting that Mizrahim dissociate themselves from their Arab subidentifications. This protest is explicitly
proposed by Sami, a 58-year-old metal worker.

> This Ashkenazi country wanted to erase our roots, wanted to stop us from
> being Moroccans and to educate us as if we were puppets . . . so that we will
> be like the kibbutzniks. . . . They didn't succeed. . . . Look what's happening
> here in Dimona [a development town in southern Israel]. . . . Everyone here
> is Moroccan as if we were in Casablanca [laughs]. And we will continue to
> maintain our Moroccan identity and to annoy this racist country.

When I asked Sami about identities other than ethnic ones, such as class
identities (poverty) or spatial (living in a development town), he not only
rejected my proposal but also made it clear to me, as did other interviewees,
that all these identities are related to Mizrahiism.

> Mizrahiism is the issue here. Who lives in development towns? Only
> Mizrahim. Who are the majority of the poor? Only Mizrahim. There is no
> point in talking about other things. You say Mizrahiism, you say it all.

This description also shows that Mizrahiism is a key identity among
members of this group, one that organizes their personal identities and the
meanings they impart to experiences in everyday life. It is important to note
that these meanings are anchored in a clear political-structural discourse.
This is how Suzy, an unemployed 48-year-old, describes it.

> Everything people feel, everything they experience in this life is related to
> the conditions in which they live. . . [What conditions?] . . . The attitude of
> the state towards them, where they live, Yeruham [a development town in
> southern Israel] is not Omer [a high socioeconomic class town], do you un-
> derstand what I'm saying? The family to which you were born—you cannot
> end poverty if you were born into a poor family. I am a third generation of
> poverty. Who doesn't want to get out of poverty? But the state doesn't want
> us to stop being poor. We are their workers, and we also don't interest an-
> yone. They prefer to promote their Ashkenazim.

When I asked Suzy, "What about a person's responsibility?" she answered
me decisively and immediately.

Now you are speaking Ashkenazi. Forgive me for being blunt with you, but now you sound exactly like the social workers here. They come to us and say, "Believe in yourself and everything will work out" or "If you invest in yourself and in the education of your children everything will be fine." And I say, "You cold and spoiled Ashkenazi, only someone who was born into a family of wealthy Ashkenazim can speak like that." Don't sell me this nonsense. Only a change of conditions will bring about a change in my life. Period.

It is interesting to note a number of characteristics in Suzy's theory. Suzy prefers the political-structural discourse as a framework for the interpretations and meanings she gives to her life while rejecting the psychological and neo-liberal discourses (Shoshana, 2014) that favor internal-psychological attributions for personal lives. Moreover, Suzy explicitly connects psychological talk and Ashkenaziism, and political talk and Mizrahiism. In other words, for Suzy, as for other low socioeconomic class interviewees and for several researchers (Rose, 1996), the psychological discourse is cultural capital (in terms of Bourdieu, 1984) that provides meaning primarily to subjects who occupy hegemonic positions such as high socioeconomic class.

Another central theme that was described by and is prevalent among Mizrahim of a lower socioeconomic class is related to the keen boundary work conducted between Mizrahim and Ashkenazim and its moral basis (Lamont, 2000). The concept of boundary work refers to the distinctions that individuals make with members of other groups in order to value themselves and find specific meaning that reconciles the existential experiences of everyday life. The research literature (see Lamont, 2000; Shoshana, 2007) describes how economic, cultural, and moral capital form the basis for boundary work among members of different classes. Rina, a 51-year-old cook, describes the moral foundation that is common among the interviewees.

Ashkenazim and Mizrahim are different. Ashkenazim are colder, Mizrahim are warmer. Although they [Ashkenazim] are more educated, earn more, and run the country, they do not have the values of friendship and family. They will throw their parents into some retirement home that costs NIS 20,000 a month instead of letting them live at home with them. They have to take care of their parents, a bit of respect for the parents. This does not happen with Mizrahim. They fight with their children over inheritances.

Shameful. Vile... We Mizrahim only give to our children, what we have of course.

The basis of self- and group worth for Mizrahim of the low socioeconomic class is, therefore, mainly moral (filial piety, human warmth, and honesty). In the spirit of Lamont's findings (2000) on subjects from various economic classes in the United States and France, it can be argued that the foundations of cultural and economic capital are blocked for Mizrahi Jews of low economic status, and, therefore, the use of moral capital helps bolster their self-worth and find meaning in their lives.

Thus, the interviews with Mizrahim from the lower socioeconomic class indicate the dominance of ethnic identities, the strong boundary work between Mizrahim and Ashkenazim, and the absence of explicit phenomenological use of class identities as a basis for self-worth. Moreover, the interviewees in this group, who link Ashkenazim and wealth (and high economic status) and Mizrahiism and poverty (or low economic status), prefer to use ethnic definitions to describe class identities. Finally, respondents in this group prefer to use political-structural discourse to explain personal and social experiences.

Mobile Mizrahim: Daily Existential Reminders About Dissociation from Ethnic Identities

When I asked the interviewees of this group about ethnicity in Israel and about recent data offered by the popular media regarding discrimination against Mizrahim in relation to Ashkenazim in Israel, the prevailing responses included strong opposition and refusal to recognize the claim that discrimination against Mizrahim still exists, combined with an emphasis that we are in a new era ("liberal," "democratic," and more "egalitarian") and that everything depends on the will of the individual.

Eyal, a 40-year-old accountant, expresses these views well.

I don't accept it. I really think that we are in a different era, more liberal and democratic. It may have existed in the early years [of the establishment of the state], but today everything is open. Those who want to—succeed. This preoccupation with Mizrahiism can ruin you and prevent your progress in life.

This depiction resonates with post-racial accounts in other places in the world, which place emphasis, *inter alia*, on the fact that current society "transcends the disabling racial divisions of the past" (Bobo, 2011, p. 14). Moreover, this description emphasizes the incidental character of ethnic and racial identities and everyday racism (Rollock et al., 2015). When I asked Yuval, as I did all the interviewees, about his personal Mizrahi identity, he gave a representative reply.

I do not define myself in Mizrahi terms. I'm beyond that story. It doesn't exist for me. I'm beyond that story. Why would you think that I define myself as Mizrahi, just because I am Mizrahi? I'm glad I'm not there anymore. I moved on. I'm in a much better place and it's because I do not engage in my Mizrahi identity.

When I insisted a little and asked Yuval if "Mizrahiness" absolutely does not exist for him, he replied,

I try not to let it. It is dangerous and can hurt my chances to progress. I remind myself over and over again that I'm not part of it. It's primitive to still engage in it. . . . There are quite a few Mizrahim today who are still primitive, but I'm not like that. There are also other Mizrahim.

This depiction of dissociation from Mizrahiism appeared unequivocally among many interviewees. An analysis of these descriptions indicates two characteristics: the use of Orientalist script (Shohat, 1999) toward Mizrahiism in Israel and an emphasis on dissociation by means of self-reminders about this dissociation. Eran, a lawyer, describes this as follows:

When I come to visit my family, I am shocked by their primitiveness. It disgusts me. Instead of embracing modern culture, they behave as if we are still in some dark world. . . . I keep reminding myself to stay away from it. [From what?] This Mizrahiness, this cultural poverty.

These findings on strategic ethnic dissociation are also recounted among black Caribbean parents in England (Rollock et al., 2015), Dutch parents who educate their children in international schools (Weenink, 2008), and middle-class parents in Fiji (Brison, 2011). The strategic dissociation in all these descriptions, including those of this study, is depicted as a practice that can promote social mobility or obtain cultural privileges associated with hegemonic positions.

In light of the fact that my interviewees in this group refused to define themselves as Mizrahim, I asked them how they choose to define themselves. The answer was "Israeli." This is described by Ran, a client portfolio manager at a communications company/

> I am Israeli. I don't have any other definition. I am Israeli, and this means that I am first of all an individual and not a group. An Israeli is someone who thinks in contemporary terms and not in archaic ones such as Mizrahi or Ashkenazi. Israeli is a modern identity. An Israeli is an individual who thinks in personal terms and not in group terms. An Israeli is someone who knows how to work hard and advance himself and not to shout discrimination and prejudice at every opportunity.

It should be noted that Ran's description highlights three main components associated with "Israeliness." The first component emphasizes the nonethnic nature of Israeliness; that is, this category is described as excluding ethnic distinctions. In this sense, their definition fits the model of assimilation that prevailed during the early years of the state of Israel, which emphasized the desire of the country's leaders to establish a new Jewish model that is Israeli (like Americanism in the United States) (Shohat, 1999). The second component describes Israeliness as a "disciplined self" that emphasizes ethics of hard work, responsibility, initiative, and future orientation (Lamont, 2000). The third component stresses that Israeliness is indeed a collective-local identity, but one that demands self-identity that is experienced by the individual and sidesteps a structural, social, and political consciousness. In other words, "Israeliness" is based on a collective of individuals.

One of the additional self-definitions that appeared, "a private person," resonates with the ideal subjectivity of neo-liberalism that emphasizes self-reliance, initiative, and self-control (Rose, 2009). Eyal, a software engineer, describes this.

> I am a private individual who is responsible for himself and his achievements. I do not need connections to roots in order to define myself. I am an individual who knows what he wants of himself, maps out goals and achieves them. I am the master of my destiny and responsible for my life

successes. I do not complain to the state. In general, I prefer to define myself in terms of class and not in terms of ethnicity.

When I ask Eyal to expand on the latter issue, he replies,

Class is preferable over Mizrahiness. Class takes into account that you can reach achievements, and Mizrahiness wallows in the past because you think in traditional terms and you think how the state can help you, and not how you can help yourself.

This self-definition through class identity can teach us about the relationship between class and ethnic identity that also emerges in other studies (Bettie, 1995; Lamont et al., 2016). The interviewees in this group prefer class identity over ethnic identity because it distances them from the marking and labeling entangled in Mizrahiism in Israel. Class identity is actually perceived as ethnically cleansed and experienced as cultural capital that can bolster social mobility. Moreover, as Eli, a 38-year-old engineer reports, class identity (and dissociation from ethnic identity) is proffered as a measure or sign of mobility.

As far as I'm concerned, the change I made [mobility] is thanks to the fact that I stopped thinking in terms of Mizrahiness. I remember periods when I told myself I must not think in terms of Mizrahiness, discrimination and deprivation, and when that succeeded, I understood that I did it. . . . I'm on top. . . . I made a big change from the situation in which I was born.

Because of the phenomenological dissociation from ethnicity that the Israeli interviewees stress, it can be argued that they fit the classic assimilation model (Warner & Srole, 1945). However, the subjective ethnic identifications of the interviewees indicate that the ethnic distinctions continue to exist over time, in the form of constant reminders on the part of the subject to her- or himself that they are not ethnic, or that they are "beyond the Mizrahi story" and that they prefer the meritocratic story and the neoliberal ethos identified with the middle and upper classes, which is portrayed as someone who is nonethnic. In this sense, the ethnic identity of the mobile Mizrahim is closer to what Fordham (1988) calls "raceless persona"; subjective attempts by individuals to reduce relations with the ethnic or racial community or to become "un-black" (Fordham,1988, p. 58). These attempts are accompanied by a strong belief in the dominant ideology that emphasizes the meritocratic ethos as a critical variable for contemporary living conditions and social mobility. At the same time, unlike Fordham's (1988) description, the ethnic identity of the mobile Mizrahim chronicles the strategic dissociation of the agent from ethnic identities as well as regular phenomenological engagement in internal conversations about this dissociation. These internal conversations or phenomenological reminders, therefore, do not make your ethnicity transparent and self-evident, such as white or Ashkenazi (Sasson-Levy, 2008). In other words, one of the "privileges" of being middle or upper class is to avoid thinking about ethnicity and race (Perry, 2001). This privilege does not appear among the mobile Mizrahim. In this sense, it is an identity that lacks the natural and comfortable feel (Bourdieu, 1984) that appears among individuals who were born into the upper class. It will be interesting now to clarify whether this entitlement appears among Mizrahim born to high economic status.

Mizrahim from a High Socioeconomic Background: Class Identities

The members of this group are Mizrahim born to families of a high socioeconomic status in terms of parents' education, income, and place of residence. All the interviewees in this group were born and educated in high socioeconomic localities with an absolute majority of Ashkenazim in their communities. Furthermore, they are all second-generation higher education students. Their parents are employed in white-collar professions (engineers, doctors, senior management, CEOs, and academic professors). In light of the correlation that has existed since the establishment of the state of Israel (and continues to this day) between ethnic origins and socioeconomic class (in terms of education, income, and place of residence), the members of this group are particularly intriguing. It is crucial to examine the relationship between ethnic and class identity and the cultural scripts that help Mizrahim in this group interpret and provide meaning in their lives.

The most striking finding that characterizes this group is their extensive reporting of the agentic choice (even when they were children and encouraged by their parents) "not to engage in Mizrahiness" (Tamar, aged 31) or "to choose to be ethnically transparent" (Omer, aged 34).

Unlike the mobile Mizrahim, members of this group describe other foundations to justify their dissociation from ethnicity and preference for class identity. Before I describe them, it is important to emphasize that members of this group, unlike the mobile Mizrahim, are less phenomenologically preoccupied with their ethnic identities. The frequent cognitive reminders about dissociation from ethnicity (such as identities that might undermine mobility or other life successes) are less prevalent, though they also maintain Orientalist perceptions of Mizrahim ("the Mizrahim are more emotional and less rational than the Ashkenazim"— Amir, age 30).

Contrary to neo-liberal discourse, the ethos of meritocracy[3] and self-definitions of Israeliness (all of which encourage dissociation from ethnicity) proposed by mobile Mizrahim who were born into a high socioeconomic class make extensive use of psychological discourse and the cosmopolitan ideal.[4]

The psychological discourse, which is attributed mainly to Western and secular cultures, is characterized by placing the self at the center (as opposed to the transcendental being or the community in traditional or religious societies), the preference for personal attribution to reality, verbalization of feelings, and particular engagement in values of self-fulfillment, separatism, and individualism (Nolan, 1998). The cosmopolitan ethos, attributed primarily to elitist subjects and groups, emphasizes the importance of internationalism, global (as opposed to local) aesthetics, and intercultural movement (such as temporary migration or relocation for academic or occupational purposes) (Weenink, 2008). In addition to the preference of these cultural scripts, members of this third group display a preference for definitions associated with professionalism.

What is common to all these discursive justifications is not only the dissociation from ethnicity and the preference for class identity, but also apoliticism that, in turn, provides an experience of ethnic transparency rather than marked Israeli Mizrahiness. Irit, a 30-year-old doctoral student in neuroscience, describes this as follows:

---

[3] Meritocracy suggests that personal capacities and qualities, rather than structural characteristics (such as socioeconomic status), are responsible for personal achievement and social order. In other words, according to this ethos, every individual who wants and is willing to invest can succeed.

[4] The cosmopolitan ethos emphasizes the global and international nature of contemporary identities that, in turn, establishes identities that are influenced by many cultures. Moreover, this ethos emphasizes the distance from local nationalism and the preference of transnationalism.

My ideal is to be attentive to my inner voice, to be authentic especially to myself. All this talk about Mizrahiness and discrimination is irrelevant to me. I make goals and conquer them. I choose how my life will be. I do not allow any external definition [Mizrahiness] to sabotage my successes. I am a biologist by training and soon I will have a doctorate in neuroscience. That is what matters. My professional achievements define me more than any external and terrible definition like Mizrahiness. We live in another era... [Which?] ... A technological, international, cosmopolitan age where everyone can choose their self-definition. Each person is responsible for their own actions, not the state, not the background from which you came. I prefer to be defined on the basis of my professional identity and not where my parents were born. As I see it, it is very archaic to talk about ethnic background as life-determining.

It is interesting to note several processes illustrated by Irit, who accurately represents the accounts of Mizrahim born into a high economic class. First, Irit frequently uses psychological discourse to anchor her self-concept and assign meaning to her life. In this context, she emphasizes her preference for internal attributes (and even psychological essentialism) over structural attributions. Personal responsibility, initiative, and authenticity as life values are preferable, in her view, to social identities (such as ethnicity). Second, Irit associates Mizrahiness with negative characteristics such as protesting and making social demands (discrimination). Throughout the interview, she did not raise the possibility that Mizrahiness (or strong ethnic identity) may be associated with existential resources and positive outcomes. Third, Irit, like many interviewees in this group, repeatedly emphasized her professional identity and status as providing more meaning for her than ethnic or other identities. In other words, she favors achieved identities (perceived as personal and the responsibility of the subject) over ascribed identities that she perceived as external to the individual and not under his or her control, and she feels that adopting these undermines the chances of professional success and mental well-being. Finally, Irit accentuates the cosmopolitan era and the accompanying capital (such as preference of international perspectives over local identities; see Weenink, 2008, in this context) as encouraging identities that are dissociated from ethnicity. She also highlights the superfluousness of any political-social engagement in daily life.

Yonatan, a product manager at an international high-tech company, describes this easily.

All my travels abroad have taught me that we live in a cosmopolitan era. This is really fun. I'm glad I live in this age. And in such an era, any engagement in Mizrahiness is unnecessary and marginal. More than that, I feel that it is perhaps suited to a small country such as Israel and not to those who live an international lifestyle.

These descriptions of cosmopolitanism and international identity resonate with the findings of other studies that report how cosmopolitan capital (Weenink, 2008) is portrayed as bringing the subject closer to a hegemonic location (a location that is experienced as transparent or unmarked) and dissociates it from marked ethnic identities (in terms of ethnicity and low socioeconomic status). As Brison (2011) describes parents in Fiji who cultivate their children's educational mobility (through ethnic dissociation), "Preserving ethnic languages and cultures becomes associated with being lower class" (Brison, 2011, p. 230). Cosmopolitan capital is actually perceived as equipping the subject with a class asset and a competitive edge (Weenink, 2008).

It is important to note that, similar to Weenink's (2008) study of Dutch parents who educate their children in international schools, Mizrahim who were born into high socioeconomic class do not make "genuine" use of cosmopolitanism (Hannerz, 2000); that is, they do not describe "an orientation, a willingness to engage with the Other. It entails an intellectual and aesthetic openness toward divergent cultural experiences, a search for contrasts rather than uniformity" (Hannerz, 2000, p. 103).

The interviewees, in fact, described "cosmopolitanism" as unique content related to ethnic transparency, invisibility, dissociation from structural-critical awareness, and the absence of ethnicity. In other words, the experience of cosmopolitanism equips the interviewees with the psychological and cultural capital (in Bourdieu's terms, 1984) affiliated with hegemonic positions. Moreover, like Froyum's study (2013), professionalism is described as placing emphasis on rationality, efficacy, and even dissociation from emotions identified with ethnicity (such as anger).

Mizrahim born to the upper economic class, therefore, offer accounts anchored in cultural scripts associated with neo-liberalism (Rose, 1996), professionalism (Froyum, 2013), and cosmopolitanism (Weenink, 2008). In the next section, I argue that members of this group rely on these scripts (even if they selectively choose distinct elements from them) to establish class identities (mainly in term of cosmopolitan orientation) and maintain identities that are dissociated from ethnicity.

Discussion

This chapter adds further theoretical and empirical contributions with respect to the way in which adults phenomenologically interpret their lives. This research task was executed by attempting to comprehend whether and how different cultural scripts influence self-understanding and the phenomenology of ethnicity and class (Lamont et al., 2016). With this in mind, I interviewed Mizrahi Jews from three different groups. The premise of the study was that examining different class locations of subjects belonging to the same socially "marked" ethnic group could expand our understanding of the relationships between identity and class in view of exposure to different cultural scripts.

The findings reveal how life under three different structural locations is not only expressed through the identification of different meaning-making, but also by a different ethnic identity. The interviewees of the low socioeconomic class define themselves in ethnic terms, maintain strong ethnic identities, and carry out keen boundary work between ethnic groups. Furthermore, sociopolitical discourse is offered as key to anchoring their accounts and interpreting their lives in Israel. The mobile Mizrahim make extensive use of an Orientalist discourse to describe Mizrahiness, to emphasize their choice to distance themselves from any engagement in ethnicity, to describe the preoccupation with ethnicity as undermining their chances for mobility, and to favor identities that are ethnically transparent ("Israeliness," "class"). The main discourses that support these choices and identifications are neo-liberal and meritocratic ethos. The Mizrahim who were born to families of high economic classes also dissociate themselves from ethnic identities and favor class identities (in the form of international and cosmopolitan preferences) but anchor their choices in other justifications. Psychological and cosmopolitan discourses support their decisions to dissociate from ethnic identities and provide them with experiences of existence that do not require the use of sociopolitical interpretations of everyday life. This dissociation from the ethnic and the political actually distances the ethnic (Mizrahi) subject from the visibility and accountability associated with marked identities and equips him or her with the same sense of transparency affiliated with hegemonic positions.

The phenomenological preoccupation with ethnicity (even among Mizrahim who claim that they are beyond the "ethnic story" while at the same time often reminding themselves of this) can be explained by what Bourdieu (1984) called the habitus of necessity versus the habitus of freedom from structural limitations, or the habitus of choice. The daily experience of structural limitations and the associated pain (such as the fact that Mizrahiness is a stigmatic identity) may encourage a constant awareness of taking the oppressive structure into account (and relating to social gazes). In this Bourdieusian logic, dissociation from structural limitations, and the ability to choose between alternatives, encourages an experience of freedom and psychological essentialism. A similar explanation is offered by Kraus et al. (2012) with regard to the dominance of contextual attributions among members of low economic classes and dispositionism (or psychological essentialism) among members of the upper classes. The contextual explanations are offered as a product of experiencing a low sense of control (or a higher level of uncertainty). The sense of control (and the ability to choose between alternatives and think in terms of "self-accuracy") promotes internal control among members of the upper classes.

I suggest explaining the discursive stability of dissociation from ethnic identities on the part of these two groups via the existence of strong cultural scripts (or what Lamont and her colleagues [2016] call *ready-made repertories*), such as psychological and neo-liberal discourses. These two orders of discourse, which are described in the research literature as most available in Western culture for understanding our selfhood, promote achieved identities and dissociate from ascriptive identities (Shoshana, 2014). Moreover, these two orders of discourse favor a nonpolitical subjectivity that distances itself from critical explanations of everyday life and favors solipsism. In this context, I would like to emphasize the stability of Orientalist discourse about Mizrahim in Israel that is also reported in other studies (Grosswirth-Kachtan, 2017) and, in turn, encourages dissociation from ethnic identities among Mizrahim who experience mobility or among those in high economic classes (Shoshana, 2016).

Alongside the emphasis on these powerful cultural scripts in Israel, I would also like to highlight that the discursive alliance (Shoshana, 2014) among the Orientalist, neo-liberal, and psychological scripts promotes a similar subjectivity. This subjectivity gives preference to dissociation from Mizrahiness while approximating meritocratic and class identities. As well as encouraging psychological attributions over ethnic claims, achieved statuses over ascriptive ones, and engagement in the future (and control over it by accumulating personal resources) and avoidance of engaging in the past and traditional practices (Perry 2001), it also promotes color blindness (Bonilla-Silva, 2012) and apoliticism. Moreover, this discursive alliance experiences political talk as sabotaging the chances that individuals from subaltern groups will be upwardly mobile. In other words, this chapter suggests that, for the purpose of complex phenomenological comprehension of personal identities, it is important to examine the dominant discourse and cultural scripts as well as their alliances (or clashes) with other discourses and scripts. These relationships between cultural scripts and personal identities require additional research, not only because they expose the connections between structure and agency in the everyday life worlds of individuals living under different conditions, but also because they allow for the identification of creative translations of cultural scripts within agentic everyday decisions.

In this context, it is important to emphasize the unique case of Israel. Despite the multiplicity of different cultural scripts in relation to ethnicity and class that encourage, *inter alia*, the establishment of personal meanings and critical alternatives (such as multiculturalism and hybridism), the Orientalist script still maintains long-standing stability. This stability grants personal meaning to the identities of the members of the three different groups of Mizrahim who were interviewed in this study, as well as to Ashkenazim from different groups (Sasson-Levy, 2008). One of the structural-discursive explanations that can be suggested relates to the discursive alliance of the Orientalist script with the two most dominant scripts in contemporary Israeli culture: the neo-liberal script (Shoshana, 2016) and the psychological script (Shoshana, 2014). The preference for personal attributions (or even psychological essentialism), an experience of personal freedom, distance from traditional-collective identities (such as ethnic identity), and encouragement of nonpolitical personal identity such as class identities or cosmopolitan identities is common to these three orders of discourse (for more, see Shoshana, 2016). This alliance, between three dominant cultural scripts thus establishes a unique relationship between personal choices (and subjective meanings) and structural living conditions that we must continue to explore in different (cross-)cultural contexts.

Conclusion

This chapter examines the relationship between cultural scripts and subjective meanings through ethnic and class identities in Israel. Against the backdrop of the cultural hierarchies and the marking of Mizrahism as stigmatized in Israel, in-depth interviews were conducted with three groups of Mizrahim (Mizrahi of low socioeconomic class, mobile Mizrahim, and Mizrahim born and educated in the upper socioeconomic class). Thus, this article encourages empirical examinations of the differences within ethnic groups, which are not common in Israeli and global research literature, as compared to the widespread studies of the differences between ethno-racial groups. The findings show that while the Mizrahim of the lower socioeconomic class possess strong ethnic identities, Mizrahim of the other two groups dissociate themselves from ethnic identities, which they experience as stigmatic, and prefer identities phenomenologically perceived as "clean" of ethnicity (e.g., class identities, Israeli identity, and cosmopolitan identity). The explanations for these findings are related, *inter alia*, to the manner in which structural conditions (such as class) encourage subjective meanings in the absence of control over life or the experience of structural limitations (such as in the case of Mizrahim from the lower socioeconomic class), or freedom from structural limitations. This is followed by a preference for psychological essentialism, which emphasizes dissociation from ethnic identities (as in the case of the mobile Mizrahim and Mizrahim from the upper socioeconomic class). Furthermore, this study suggests that the discursive alliances between the three cultural scripts in Israel (the Orientalist script, the psychological script, and the neo-liberal script) encourage specific subjective meanings.

Highlights

- This chapter examines the phenomenological relationship between cultural scripts and the subjective meanings for individuals in everyday life.
- This examination was conducted in relation to ethnic and class identities in light of the hierarchical cultural order in Israel
- The research populations are Mizrahim (older than 30) from three different groups: Mizrahim from a low socioeconomic background,

Mizrahim who have experienced socioeconomic mobility, and Mizrahim born to families from a high socioeconomic background.
- Research findings show that while Mizrahim of low socioeconomic class hold strong ethnic identities (and weak class identities), Mizrahim of the other two groups prefer to dissociate themselves from ethnic identities and favor class identities that are perceived as "transparent"
- The research findings illustrate how the basic dissociation from ethnicity is achieved differently by mobile Mizrahim and Mizrahim who were born into upper economic classes.
- The discussion section reveals the relationships between specific cultural scripts and the phenomenology of individuals.

References

Alba, R. (2005). Bright vs. blurred boundaries: Second-generation assimilation and exclusion in France, Germany, and the United States. *Ethnic and Racial Studies*, 28(1), 20–49.

Bettie, J. (1995). Class dismissed? Roseanne and the changing face of working- class iconography. *Social Text* 14(4), 125–149.

Bhabha, H. (1994). *The location of culture*. Routledge.

Bitton, Y. (2011). Mizrahim and the law: Absence as existence. *Mishpatim*, 41(3), 455–516. [Hebrew]

Bobo, L. (2011). Somewhere between Jim Crow and post-racialism: Reflections on the racial divide in America today. *Daedalus*, 140(2), 11–36.

Bonilla-Silva, E. (2012). The invisible weight of whiteness: The racial grammar of everyday life in contemporary America. *Ethnic and Racial Studies*, 35(2), 173–194.

Bourdieu, P. (1984). *Distinction*. Harvard University Press.

Brison, K. (2011). Producing "confident" children: Negotiating childhood in Fijian kindergartens. *Anthropology and Education Quarterly*, 42(3), 230–244.

Ewick, P., & Silbey, S. (2003). Narrating social structure: Stories of resistance to legal authority. *American Journal of Sociology*, 108(6), 1328–1372.

Fordham, S. (1988). Racelessness as a factor in Black students' school success: Pragmatic strategy or pyrrhic victory. *Harvard Education Review*, 58(1), 54–84.

Frankenberg, R. (1993). *White women, race matters: The social construction of whiteness*. University of Minnesota Press.

Frenkel, A. (2012). *The establishment of ethnic-gender identities of descendants of ethnic mixed families* (doctoral dissertation). Bar-Ilan University. [Hebrew].

Froyum, C. (2013). "For the betterment of kids who look like me": Professional emotional labor as a racial project. *Ethnic and Racial Studies*, 36(6), 1070–1089.

Gans, H. (1979). Symbolic ethnicity: The future of ethnic groups and cultures in America. *Ethnic and Racial Studies*, 12(1), 1–20.

Gergen, K., & Gergen, M. (1986). Narrative form and the construction of psychological science. In T. R. Sarbin (Ed.), *Narrative psychology: The storied nature of human conduct* (pp. 22–44). Prager.

Grosswirth Kachtan, D. (2017). "Acting ethnic"—Performance of ethnicity and the process of ethnicization. *Ethnicities, 17*(5), 707–726.

Hannerz, U. (2000). *Transitional connections: Culture, people, places.* Routledge.

Kraus, M., Piff, M., Mendoza-Denton, R., Rheinschmidt, M., Keltner, D. (2012). Social class, solopsism, and contextualism: How the rich different from the poor. *Psychological Review, 119*(3), 546–572.

Lacy, K. (2004). Black spaces, black places: Strategic assimilation and identity construction in middle-class suburbia. *Ethnic and Racial Studies, 27*(6), 908–930.

Lamont, M. (2000). *The dignity of working men: Morality and boundaries of race, class, and immigration.* Harvard University Press.

Lamont, M., Moraes Silva, G., Guetzkow, J., Welburn, J., Mizrachi, N., Herzog, H., & Reis, E. (2016). *Getting respect: Responding to stigma and discrimination in the United States, Brazil, and Israel.* Princeton University Press.

Lavee, E. (2005). *The process of formation of the marital routine among mix couples* (master's thesis). Bar-Ilan University. [Hebrew]

McDermott, M., & Samson, F. L. (2005). White racial and ethnic identity in the United States. *Annual Review of Sociology, 31*, 245–261.

Nolan, J. (1998): *The therapeutic state.* New York University Press.

Perry, P. (2001). "White means never having to say you're ethnic": White youth and the construction of "cultureless" identities. *Journal of Contemporary Ethnography, 30*(1), 56–91.

Pieterse, J. (2001). Hybridity, so what? The anti-hybridity backlash and the riddles of recognition. *Theory, Culture & Society, 18*, 219–245.

Rollock, N., Gilborn, D. Vincet, C., & Ball, S. (2015). *The colour of class: The educational strategies of the Black middle classes.* Routledge.

Rom, M. & Benjamin, O. (2011). *Feminism, family, and udentity in Israel: Women's marital names.* Palgrave MacMillan.

Rose, N. (1996). *Inventing ourselves: Psychology, power, and personhood.* Cambridge University Press.

Rosen, S. (1982). Intermarriage and the "blending of exiles" in Israel. *Research in Race and Ethnic Relations, 3*, 79–102.

Said, E. (1978). *Orientalism.* Vintage Books.

Sansone, L. (2003). *Blackness without ethnicity: Constructing race in Brazil.* Palgrave.

Sasson-Levy, O. (2008). "But I do not want an ethnic identity for myself": Social boundaries and their erasure in the contemporary discourses of Ashkenazim. *Theory and Criticism, 33*, 101–129. [Hebrew]

Schutz, A., & Luckmann, T. (1974). *The structure of the life-world.* Heinemann.

Scott, J. (1985). *Weapons of the weak: Everyday forms of peasant resistance.* Yale University Press.

Shenhav, Y. (2006). *The Arab Jews: A postcolonial reading of nationalism, religion, and ethnicity.* Stanford University Press

Shohat, E. (1999). The invention of the Mizrahim. *Journal of Palestine Studies, 29*(1), 5–20.

Shoshana, A. (2007). The phenomenology of a new social category: The case of "gifted disadvantaged" in Israel. *Poetics, 35*(6), 352–367.

Shoshana, A. (2013). Translating a national grand narrative into personal story: Alternative biographies among siblings in everyday life. *Narrative Inquiry*, 23(1), 171–191.

Shoshana, A. (2014). Discursive alliances and discursive clashes in everyday life. *Sociological Spectrum*, 34(2), 99–113.

Shoshana. A. (2016). "Ethnicity without ethnicity": Reeducation and (new) ethnic identity. *Social Identities*, 22(5), 487–501.

Simon, W., & Gagnon, J. (1986). Sexual scripts: Permanence and change. *Archives of Sexual Behavior*, 15(2), 97–120.

Small, M., Harding, D., & Lamont, M. (2010). Reconsidering culture and poverty. *Annals of the American Academy of Political and Social Science*, 629(6), 6–27.

Somers, M. (1994). The narrative constitution of identity: A relational and network approach. *Theory and Society*, 23, 605–649.

Strauss, A., & Corbin, J. (1998). *Basics of qualitative research*. Sage.

Taylor, C. (1994). The politics of recognition. In A. Gutmann (Ed.), *Multiculturalism: Examining the politics of recognition* (pp. 25–74). Princeton University Press.

Warner W., & Srole, L. (1945). *The social systems of American ethnic groups*. Yale University Press.

Weenink, D. (2008). Cosmopolitanism as a form of capital: Parents preparing their children for a globalizing world. *Sociology*, 42(6), 1089–1106.

11

On Secular and Religious Politics
of Belonging

What Does It Mean to Be an Arab-Palestinian
Citizen in Israel?

Ayman K. Agbaria, Mohanad Mustafa, and Sami Mahajnah

Introduction

Belonging is an ambiguous term, with various meanings ranging from a personal feeling to the sense of attachment to a social group or certain place, and it often serves as a political resource to establish regimes of social demarcations and distinctions (Antonsich, 2010). Research has established that, psychologically, a sense of belonging is central for finding meaning in life (Lambert et al., 2013), including collective notions of belonging and identity such as nationalism (Guibernau, 2013; Smith, 1986) and religion, among others such as cosmopolitanism or feminism (Yuval-Davis, 2011). Therefore, the search for belonging or a national, religious, or other collective identity constitutes also a search for meaning, which is central to the cohesion of a community (Cantle, 2008).

This chapter focuses on the search for meaning and belonging of the Arab-Palestinian[1] minority in Israel by discussing how belonging is debated and advocated in Arab politics in Israel. More specifically, the chapter maps and analyzes three narratives in the Arab politics of belonging: the romantic, the practical, and the visionary. The first advocates belonging to what we term a "lost paradise" of Palestine and Islam. This nostalgic type of belonging yearns for idealized places, times, and characters in the history of Palestine and Islam. The second narrative, the practical, defines belonging first and

---

[1] The literature refers to this group in many ways: "Palestinians in Israel," "Arabs in Israel," "Arab citizens of Israel," "the Palestinian Minority," and "1948 Palestinians."

Ayman K. Agbaria, Mohanad Mustafa, and Sami Mahajnah, *On Secular and Religious Politics of Belonging* In: *Finding Meaning*. Edited by: Ofra Mayseless and Pninit Russo-Netzer, Oxford University Press. © Oxford University Press 2022.
DOI: 10.1093/oso/9780190910358.003.0011

foremost as a developmental act, practiced at the community level through voluntary and charity programs. The third, the visionary, promotes belonging as an ideological position to be articulated and educated for at the national level. These three concepts are circulated and mobilized by both secular Arab political and Muslim religious actors but in different versions and to different extents. As it will be demonstrated, based on these three narratives, these actors seek to cultivate complex meaning and a political vision for Arab-Palestinian citizens in Israel through their politics of belonging.

Before presenting these politics of belonging and discussing their similarities and differences, we first provide the political background of some of the complexities of being a "Palestinian" by nationality and "Israeli" by citizenship. Second, we outline the politics of identity and belonging as a theoretical framework for analyzing the status of Arab-Palestinian citizens of Israel. Finally, we will discuss the politics of belonging as practiced by secular and religious groups, respectively.

Palestinians in Israel: Political Background

The Arab-Palestinians in Israel are a national minority whose minority status was determined involuntarily and unwillingly (Kymlicka, 1995). Following the *Nakba* (the Palestinian term for "catastrophe," describing the 1948 war and its aftermath), the Palestinians who remained within the newly created state of Israel became Israeli citizens. Since then, they form a substantial indigenous national minority. In 2015, there were around 1.5 million Palestinians in Israel, or, alternatively, 18% of the population.[2] They are affiliated with three religions: the majority, around 80%, are Muslims, living in most of the Palestinian villages and cities throughout Israel, while the Christian minority accounts for 10%, of whom most are living in the Galilee. They belong to several denominations, mainly Catholic, Orthodox, Maronite, Armenian, and several Protestant groups. The Druze constitute another 10% of the Palestinian population and live in the Galilee and the Carmel region (see Abu-Saad, 2019). While some parts of the population live in mixed cities, these cities are largely internally segregated, and thus most Arabs and Jews in Israel live separately.

---

[2] These data are more reliable as they do not include the Palestinians in East Jerusalem or the residents of the Golan Heights (Abu-Saad, 2019).

The granting of formal citizenship in Israel equips Arab-Palestinians with individual social, political, and economic rights and opportunities, yet, as a group, they face discrimination by the state and its society, being allocated only "second-class citizenship" (Jabareen, 2006, p. 1055), which affects them in the areas of income, education, infrastructure, employment, and quality of social services (Rabinowitz, Ghanem, & Yiftachel, 2000). For example, in the case of education, Arab-Palestinian citizens experience discrimination through unequal allocation of state resources, lack of recognition of the Palestinian minority's cultural needs, and marginalization of the Arab leadership's influence on education policy (e.g., Abu-Asbe, 2007; Abu-Saad, 2004; Agbaria, 2013).

Notwithstanding other historical developments (see more in Ghanem, 2001), the signing of the Oslo Accords in 1993 between the Palestinian Liberation Organization (PLO) and the state of Israel signaled a moment of revelation and reflexivity for Arab-Palestinians in Israel. The Accords manifested that they do not share any feasible political future with the rest of the Palestinian people. The future status of Arab-Palestinians in Israel was not considered, neither by the Palestinian representatives nor their Israeli counterparts, as an issue for discussion and settlement between the parties, at least not officially. Thus, Rabinowitz (2001) describes them as a "trapped minority," referring to their double marginalization: on the one hand, they are marginalized by the Jewish majority in Israel and, on the other hand, by the majority of Palestinians who are not Israeli citizens.

This "double marginality" (al-Haj, 1997) became intensified with the faltering of the Israeli-Palestinian "peace process" in the late 1990s (Ghanem, 1996). During this period, Palestinian politics in Israel witnessed the rise of two political powers: the National Democratic Assembly and the Northern Islamic Movement. The former, a secular political force by definition, emphasizes the interdependence between individual and collective rights and advocates a vision of "a state for all its citizens" (Bishara, 1993), while the latter, a religious-political actor, calls for a boycott of the Israeli Parliament (the Knesset) elections and advocates a vision of an "independent society" (Al-Mujtama' Al-Esami). According to the Northern Islamic Movement, Palestinians in Israel should have separate, nationally elected bodies and self-reliant civil society organizations to reduce the dependence of the Palestinian society on the institutions of the state in terms of education, culture, religion, and the like (Ali, 2006; Abu-Raiya, 2005).

Nevertheless, since the mid-1990s, as Israeli politics has become more divided, the economy more privatized, and civil society more diverse, the central government's capacity to impede the Palestinian minority's mobilization for equality and recognition has considerably diminished (Haklai, 2011). In the Israeli citizenship regime, which is described as hierarchical, deferential, and serving the political interests of the Jewish majority (Shafir & Peled, 2002), Arab citizens are recognized as an aggregate of individuals entitled to selective individual liberal rights but not as an indigenous national minority that is eligible for collective rights.

Consequently, the Arab-Palestinian minority in Israel has become more proactive in linking civic equality to national recognition, placing more emphasis on its indigenous status as a national minority to justify demands for collective rights (Jamal, 2006), proposing new forms of governance, remedial mechanisms of state funding, and parallel historical narratives (Agbaria, Mustafa, & Jabareen, 2015). In doing so, Jamal (2007) argues that these are attempts by Arab-Palestinians in Israel to reinvent their citizenship as a maneuvering space for resistance and as a resource for political mobilization.

Theoretical Framework: The Politics of Belonging, Identity, and Contention

The politics of belonging is connected to a range of concepts that we briefly address in this section: collective identity, nationalism, citizenship, and the politics of contention. As mentioned earlier, an important concept from which people infer meaning and which underpins the politics of belonging is identity. More specifically, *collective identity* has been defined as the "shared definition of a group that derives from members" common interests, experiences, and solidarity' (Taylor & Whittier, 1995, p. 170). Collective identity is central to nationality and citizenship: nationality as a cultural concept connects people through this shared identity (McCrone & Kiely, 2000), while citizenship is a political practice and a legal status, yet also (at least formally) tied to a particular identity (Heater, 2004; Isin & Wood, 1999). Nationalism and citizenship are connected in a sense that citizenship and its associated rights are realized in the nation-state through promoting a sense of national belonging and loyalty (Yuval-Davis, 2011). According to Yuval-Davis, the idea of a homeland is usually the physical embodiment of these national imaginations. While citizenship and the concept of homeland allow the possibility for the inclusion of different ethnic groupings through a rudimentary commitment to ethnic and/or cultural diversity, the concept of *autochthonic politics* is rather exclusionary. The notion of autochthony plays a crucial role in the formation of belonging as "some sort of primordial claim" (Geschiere, 2011, p. 175), a claim of being indigenous to a particular territory. While autochthony is a racist discourse, drawing on religion, culture, and origin as definitions of rigid boundaries of belonging and identity (Yuval-Davis, 2012), it can also be used by indigenous groups for their claims of recognition and belonging (Castells, 1997).

Yet modern nation-states have also constituted different categories of citizens through their ideologies, policies, and practices, in addition to this particular identity (Shafir & Peled, 2002; Turner, 1993). These categories, in turn, produce diverse political identities and models of membership for the citizens in their polity (Soysal, 1998).

Nevertheless, minorities might feel that states do not sufficiently recognize their collective identities (Fraser, 2000). According to Fraser (2000), misrecognition may involve cultural domination (being subjected to patterns of interpretation and communication that are associated with another culture and are alien and/or hostile to one's own), nonrecognition (being rendered invisible by means of authoritative representational, communicative, and interpretative practices), and disrespect (being routinely maligned or disparaged in stereotypic public cultural representations and/or in everyday life situations).

As indicated earlier, minorities (e.g., indigenous groups, LGBTQ communities, racial and ethnic groups, national and cultural groups) in the United States, Europe, Latin America, and other places (Alcoff et al., 2006) have raised demands toward their states to adopt public policies that would ensure "unhindered representation, recognition without marginalization, acceptance and integration without "normalizing" distortion" (Pakulski, 1997, p. 80).

The process of raising these demands may involve civic actions, such as demonstrations, strikes, etc. These activities, however, usually fall within the confines of the dominant political system, in the spaces granted by the state for political maneuvering (McAdam, Tarrow, & Tilly 2001). Yet we argue that to gain access to venues for negotiation, minorities need to challenge the state's structure, identity, and policies using a form of politics of contention. Tilly (2008, p. 5) defines politics of contention as "interactions in which actors make claims bearing on someone else's interest, in which governments appear either as targets, initiators of claims, or third parties." Through contentious politics, political actors not only create new connections among individuals, organizations, networks, and coalitions but also redraw boundaries separating one actor from another and creating collective stories about the two sides (Tilly & Tarrow, 2006).

"Identity politics" is an example of the politics of contention employed by minorities. It refers to political mobilization of minorities that demand public recognition of particular identities based on gender, ethnic, racial, religious, or sexual orientation through the allocation of group-specific rights (Alcoff et al., 2006).

Specific strategies used by minorities to demand recognition of their collective identity are (1) practices that seek to direct the public's attention to an identity-related difference that has been neglected, distorted, or silenced by the majority and (2) demands for the acknowledgment of this mis/nonrecognized identity (Maclure, 2003).

Minorities may also utilize the "politics of becoming" (how we have been represented and how we might represent ourselves) as a tool for mobilizing a collective consciousness in response to dominant groups who impose a hegemonic narrative and seek to naturalize imbalanced power relations in society (Hall, 1996). In their struggle for citizenship, belonging, and group-differentiated rights, minorities might employ fixed identity constructions (Gamson, 1995), in the sense of autochthone politics or nationalism, for example, to legitimize their collective claims. By reference to the example of secular and religious Palestinian movements in Israel, we will discuss how the discourses of belonging, identity, nationalism, and citizenship are adopted by both movements to form narratives of belonging that can be categorized into three narratives: the romantic, the practical and the visionary. Based on the literature, the romantic refers to a nostalgic dimension of belonging that seeks to the define a collective identity by drawing on a common historical narrative, culture, and connection to the land and history of struggle. In contrast, the practical narrative focuses on the politics of contention and citizenship, such as demanding recognition and collective rights for one's community or group. Finally, the visionary narrative also draws on these concepts but outlines a vision of a future national society or group and its role and function.

Secular Politics of Belonging Among
Palestinian Citizens in Israel

At the end of 2006, the National Committee of the Heads of Arab Local Authorities,[3] which constitutes more than 80% of the membership of the High Follow-up Committee for the Arab Citizens of Israel,[4] presented the Committee's collective vision for the future of Arab-Palestinians in Israel in a published document. This document was widely considered as foundational in Arab politics in Israel, highly debated by the public, and widely studied in the academy (see, e.g., Abulof, 2007; Agbaria & Mustafa, 2012; Peleg & Waxman, 2008). The document's introduction reflects the attempt to articulate a collective identity.

> It is clear that we, the Arab Palestinians in Israel, need to synthesize our various self-definitions in order to produce a lucid, integrated, and homogenous vision of our self-identity, the relations with our Palestinian people and with the state, a clear self-definition that relates to all existential areas—political, cultural, economic, educational and social, developed by all streams of our political, cultural and research professionals. (Rekhess, 2007)

The future document presents a secular vision of belonging and identity. Its publication was a historic event in the annals of the Arab-Palestinians in Israel and in their relationship with the Jewish majority and the state of Israel, on the one hand, and their interaction with the Palestinian national movement, on the other. The document, written by activists from all political currents among Arab-Palestinians in Israel, delineates what is necessary to ensure a positive future relationship between the majority and the minority in the state of Israel, including the definition of the character of the state. It is important to note that these documents seek to appeal to all Arab and Palestinian groups in Israel, including Muslims, Christians, Druze, and Bedouins.

---

[3] The National Committee of the Heads of Arab Localities (NCALC), the sole nonpartisan organization representing the Arab minority in Israel, constitutes the main party in the High Follow-Up Committee (see National Committee, 2006).

[4] The High Follow-up Committee for the Arab Citizens of Israel was established in 1982 as an extra-parliamentary organization that acts as a national coordinating and representative body for Arab-Palestinian citizens of Israel.

After the publication of the Future Vision document, two additional sem-inal documents were published by Palestinian civil society organizations in Israel: the "Haifa Declaration" was collectively authored by a group of prom-inent Palestinian intellectuals in Israel through Mada al-Carmel, the Arab Center for Applied Social Research (Mada al-Carmel, 2007; the Haifa dec-laration). Adalah, the Legal Center for Arab Minority Rights in Israel, also published another vision document entitled the "Democratic Constitution" (Adalah, 2007; the Democratic Constitution). These three documents were published by secular groups comprised of academics, social activists, and politicians.

Agbaria and Mustafa (2012) stated that these documents appeal to the failed political inclusiveness of Israel as a "Jewish and democratic" state and the need to recognize the collective identity of the Arab-Palestinian people. Moreover, while the Arab civil society adheres in these documents to the ex-isting Israeli citizenship framework, they also seek "to change its nature from within" (p. 718), for example, in regard to the "Right of Return,"[5] which con-tinues to act as one of the stumbling blocks for Arab-Palestinians in the peace process (Agbaria & Mustafa, 2012). These documents contain three different narratives of belonging, which we discuss in detail.

Romantic Narrative

The romantic narrative contains concepts such as a collective identity by drawing on a common historical narrative, culture, and connection to the land and history of struggle and by drawing partly on primordial notions of nationality. For example, the introductory chapter of the Future Vision doc-ument asserts that Israel was established as a Western colonial project in an attempt to find a solution to the "Jewish Question" in Europe. They claim that the Zionist founders devised a national project grounded on Jewish religious and ethnic foundations, linking biblical stories about the Jews' presence in the "Land of Israel" to the modern phenomenon of nationalism. In this doc-ument, it is argued that the project of settling and colonizing Palestine was

---

[5] The Right of Return is a political demand or position by Palestinian refugees (first generation and their descendants) to be granted the right to return to their previous homes in Israel and the Occupied Territories and have the property returned that they left behind when they left or were forced to leave.

catalyzed by the decline of the Ottoman Empire, the Balfour Declaration,[6] and the British Mandate. This narrative continues after the 1948 war and the Palestinian Nakba by stating that Israel emerged as an ethnocratic state that is formally democratic yet devoted to Judaizing the land and the public sphere by exercising control over its Arab-Palestinian citizens. The Haifa Declaration describes these citizens as the "sons and daughters of the Palestinian Arab people who remained in our homeland despite the Nakba, who were forcibly made a minority in the State of Israel after its establishment in 1948 on the greater part of the Palestinian homeland" (Mada al-Carmel, 2007, p. 7). Similar to the future document, the Haifa Declaration, defines the Zionist settlement of Palestine as a colonial one, it continues,

> Subsequently, in concert with world imperialism and with the collusion of Arab reactionary powers, it succeeded in carrying out its project, which aimed at occupying our homeland and transforming it into a state for the Jews. In 1948, the year of the Nakba of the Palestinian people, the Zionist movement committed massacres against our people, turned most of us into refugees, totally erased hundreds of our villages, and drove out most inhabitants of our cities. (Mada al-Carmel, 2007, pp. 11–12)
>
> Arab and Palestinian national identity is connected to an Arab cultural space.
>
> Our national identity is grounded in human values and civilization, in the Arabic language and culture, and in a collective memory derived from our Palestinian and Arab history, and Arab and Islamic civilization. It is an identity that grows ever more firm through active and continuous interaction with these values. It is continuously nourished by our uninterrupted relationship to our land and homeland, by the experience of our constant and mounting struggle to affirm our right to remain in our land and homeland and to safeguard them, and by our continued connection to the other sons and daughters of the Palestinian people and the Arab nation (Ibid., pp. 7–8).

Therefore, the concepts of belonging that fall under this narrative invoke meaning from a common historical narrative and the experience of nationhood and belonging as well as collective cultural and religious identities.

---

[6] The Balfour declaration was issued in 1917, as a statement by the British government that declared support for the establishment of a national home for the Jewish people in Palestine, who constituted a minority in this area at that time.

Practical Narrative

The practical narrative promotes a political discourse of Palestinians in Israel that has moved from being about individual achievements to one that emphasizes collective rights and identity as a basis for political action, marking a change over the past two decades.

The Future Vision documents are based on the concept of recognition (Taylor, 1989). A primary objective of Palestinian politics of belonging in Israel is to achieve the recognition of Arab-Palestinians as a national group, and the documents propose that this can be achieved through the following policies:

1. Strengthening Palestinian political participation in national and local politics.
2. Building representative national institutions, such as the High Follow-up Committee for the Arab Citizens of Israel.
3. Strengthening the role of Palestinian civil society.

Similarly, the Haifa Declaration emphasizes as its goals the strengthening of the Palestinian society and its national institutions to form a resistance against discrimination, develop a political and social agenda that promotes human and national identity, instill respect of political action, and create a credible political authority. This endeavor aims to develop an alternative consciousness, moral standards, and a different culture that will transform existing social structures and serve to connect national parties with local civil and communal institutions. Thus, this practical narrative promotes concepts such as active citizenship and political action, mainly within the frame of Israel's existing political system, while also seeking to extend the political system through collective cultural and national rights and spaces for Arabs-Palestinians in Israel.

Vision Narrative

Finally, the vision narrative includes concepts that define the goals of the politics of belonging and the aspired future collective community, its role in Israel's society, and its political system as well the vision of living together with the majority population. The secular groups' vision is constituted on several focal points: first, the recognition of Arab-Palestinians in Israel as a national group with collective rights and individual equality; second, changing the national-ethnic character of Israel from a Jewish state to a state for all its citizens; and, third, recognizing the Arab-Palestinians' right to self-determination through cultural autonomy without denying the right of Jews to self-determination.

This vision refers to the model of constitutional democracy as a form of power-sharing in societies with significant internal divisions that seeks to maintain stability by including representatives from all groups, with clear liberal elements (Agbaria & Mustafa, 2012).

What is revolutionary in these documents is the recognition of the right of Jewish-Israelis to self-determination. The Future Vision document sees Israel as the shared homeland of the Jews and Palestinians, who should live together in a consensual democratic framework.

> The State should acknowledge that Israel is the homeland for both Palestinians and Jews. Relations between the Palestinians and Jews in Israel should be based on attainment of equal human and citizenship rights based on international conventions and the relevant international treaties and declarations. The two groups should have mutual relations based on a consensual democratic system. (Future Vision, p. 11)

The Haifa Declaration, too, recognizes the right of Israeli Jews, alongside the right of Arab-Palestinians in Israel, to self-determination. This reciprocal recognition is seen as part of a reconciliation process between Arab-Palestinians and Jewish-Israelis.

> This historical reconciliation also requires that we, Palestinians and Arabs, recognize the right of the Israeli Jewish people to self-determination and to live in peace, dignity, and security with the Palestinians and the other peoples of the region. (Mada al-Carmel, 2007, p. 15)

This also includes granting equal national and citizenship rights to both Jewish-Israelis and Arab-Palestinians and thus goes beyond the current definition of Israel as the state of the Jewish people only. Both documents propose a new citizenship model that is stripped of ethnic superiority, ensuring national and civil equality for both groups. Additionally, the Future Vision document also demands to address the historical injustices that were committed against the Palestinian people, urging Israel to adopt a "corrective justice" (p. 11), for example, by restoring those parts of their land that were confiscated by Israel not for public use and by dedicating equal parts of its resources for Arab-Palestinians.

Religious Politics of Belonging Among Palestinian Citizens

The Islamic Movement is the main body representing religious politics of belonging among Arab-Palestinian citizens of Israel. Since its emergence, the Islamic Movement has presented a different political discourse on issues of identity and belonging based on the religious dimension and its integration into the national composite. In this discourse, Islam is the baseline that determines the concept of belonging to the community and the land. The Islamic Movement has established dozens of institutions and civil society organizations that have cared for community issues in various fields: education, health, rights, welfare, holy sites, and the land (Agbaria & Mustafa, 2014). The aim of these institutions, as indicated by the Islamic Movement, is to promote the concept of belonging through labor, so that it is not limited to identification with the religious body, cultural practices, and religious politics.

The Nakba outcomes and the establishment of Israel, which imposed military rule on the Palestinian communities, limited the activity of political Islam. In fact, one cannot point to any such organization among the Palestinian citizens of Israel during the 1950s, '60s, or '70s. After 1967, the situation changed as a result of renewed contact between the Palestinians in Israel and Palestinians in the occupied West Bank and Gaza Strip, due to the existence of fundamentalist organizations and religious seminaries in those areas. As a result, new conditions were created for the development of political Islam among the Palestinians in Israel (Mayer, 1989).

A number of young people who completed high school and were attracted to an Islamic environment continued their studies in the Islamic colleges and institutes that prepared them for the title of "sheikh." These young men began to preach religion in their home communities and other Muslim communities as an unorganized activity, giving sermons in the mosques and at meetings held during Muslim festivals (Mayer, 1989). Their activity paved the way for the Islamic community to organize in the form of political and social associations.

The younger generation began to organize in almost every community where there were Muslims, establishing voluntary associations to both promote social activity and raise funds for them. They also began to organize on a countrywide basis, enrolling new members and preaching for a return to their religious roots.

Romantic Narrative

The Islamic Movement framed the concepts of the romantic narrative based on two dimensions: the practical, which we discuss in detail in the next section, and the moral. The latter is based on a morality that stems from a specific Arab-Islamic heritage.

Sheikh Raed Salah (2015), the Head of the Northern Muslim Movement, linked Islamic morality to nationalism. In an article entitled, "Uncontrolled Nationalism," he considers nationalism as not being confined to the land, the geographical borders of the homeland and a specific political entity, which he calls "soil" nationalism; rather, Palestinian nationalism is continuous with Arab and Islamic heritage, history, civilization, and values, extending beyond narrow borders.

He claims that a secular form of "soil" nationalism even supports the Zionist project of relinquishing Palestinian heritage and history by omitting its Islamic moral dimensions.

Another Islamic scholar, Kamal Khatib, agrees with Raed Salah on his argument that the concept of belonging of the Palestinian people requires a return to the Islamic heritage, and he criticizes secular concepts as being primitive, superstitious, or even fanatic. To conclude, the Islamic movement frames belonging and nationalism as being based on Islamic values and heritage, as opposed to the secular version that emphasizes its geographical dimensions.

Practical Narrative

The Islamic Movement promotes a form of practical nationalism, associated with labor. The concept of labor is exemplified in their literature by voluntary work, the renovation of demolished homes, and through providing financial aid to those affected by poverty or by unjust government policies such as the demolition of unlicensed Arab homes. Sheikh Kamal Khatib (1993), the Deputy Head of the Islamic Movement, described the Movement's activism as the following:

> We demonstrate, when protests are called for, we have sit-ins when there is a call for them, and we shout against the oppressor and with the highest voice. We fully and strictly abide by the call for strikes. However, with all this, we combine between all this and work, giving, spending money and exhausting the body in the service of our people.

The Movement translates the concept of practical belonging into the establishment of a large network of institutions and social, educational, and civil rights organizations that provide services to the Palestinian community, mostly free of charge (Agbaria & Mustafa, 2014). These institutions operate at a local or national level and support needy individuals, poor families, or even entire population groups, such as the residents of the Naqab (Negev) and the mixed cities, such as Acre, Lid/Lod, Haifa, Ramleh/Ramla, Jaffa, and Jerusalem. These institutions not only inculcate awareness and advocacy of collective rights but also provide direct and personal services of a practical and concrete nature based on Islamic moral values.

Rabinowitz (2001) argued that whereas the Movement is alienated from the Israeli state, it has the potential to reinforce civil activity from within and extend it even beyond religious institutions.

Another practical strategy, coined by Sheikh Raed Salah (2001), of the religious movement is to create a "self-reliant society" that is independent of non-Muslim funding and donations, which are seen as "impure" (Ali, 2006) and pose the risk of dependency on foreign entities.

Vision Narrative

Over the years, the Islamic Movement has partly achieved the cultivation of such a "self-reliant society" through the establishment of Arab institutions independent from state resources in all areas, including private education. This idea has become popular among members of the Islamic Movement, which has framed the Islamic Northern Faction as an external movement that refuses to integrate into parliamentary politics. Instead, the movement believes that building a self-reliant Arab Muslim community is the only solution for the emancipation of the Arab-Muslim minority in Israel. Indeed, the Movement rejects all other proposed political solutions to regulate the majority–minority relationship, such as a state of all its citizens, a binational state, or various other proposals for autonomy (Ghanem & Mustafa, 2009).

The overall Arab-Islamic dimension plays an important role in the autonomous "self-reliant society" project. Sheikh Salah argues that the establishment of such a society or community requires that the relationship between the Arab world and the Muslim nation at large has to be further cemented. This may indicate that the external parliamentary Islamic movement sees itself as part of the Muslim nation not only in symbolic-cultural terms but also in a practical sense. The ideological orientation of the movement extends beyond the particularity of the condition and status of Muslims in Israel and instead perceives their status to be an integral part of political Islam in general, as constituting a part of an ideal Muslim society seeking to resurrect the idea of an enlightened and guided caliphate (in Arabic: *Al-Khilafah Al-Rashedah*).

At the same time, however, the parliamentary movement believes that Muslims in Israel are in a unique situation and that political Islam in Israel is context-specific, requiring special attention.

Conclusion

Under the influences exercised by the forces of globalization that have given rise to new identities or the renewed importance of religious and ethnic identities (Bokser-Liwerant, 2002), combined with the state's efforts to downplay the national component in their collective identity, Arab-Palestinians in Israel provide various answers to the question: "What does it mean to be a Palestinian citizen of Israel?" In their responses, the politics of belonging is revealed in its full complexity. On the whole, their answers or proposed solutions reflect a genuine search for meaning and a political vision to restructure, reframe, and reconcile the entangled relationships and contradictions between their Palestinian nationality, Israeli citizenship, and Islam in Israel. To varying degrees, these three components are central to the collective identity of Arab-Palestinians in Israel and are part and parcel of their sense of belonging and search for meaning.

Drawing on Yuval-Davis's framework (2011), the politics of belonging among Arab-Palestinians revolves around their belonging to the state of Israel, to the Palestinian people, and to the land. Indeed, these concepts partly refer to much broader politics of belonging, including collective identities and envisioned societies or communities of Arabs, Palestinians, and Muslims. Yet these aspirations are constrained by the current nation state framework and their minority status, even if the religious movement tries to circumvent these constraints in their visionary narrative. In an attempt to find an integrative framework for these three narratives of belonging, Arab-Palestinian political actors in Israel have envisioned a political future for congruent belonging to Israel as a nation state, the Palestinian people as a nation, and the Arab-Palestinian minority in Israel as a differentiated national group. These visions address the ramifications of belonging to a nation state, to a nationality, and to an indigenous community. These cycles of belonging diverge and converge in the lives of the Arab-Palestinians in Israel, creating tensions and rival forms of patriotism.

Generally, there are three different narratives envisioned by the major sociopolitical actors in Palestinian politics and civil society in response to our opening question regarding the meaning of being Palestinian citizens of Israel. These narratives are the romantic, the practical, and the visionary. Each reveals a different synthesis or blend of the three components of nationalism, citizenship, and religiosity.

The first, the romantic narrative, is shared by both secular and religious political groups. This concept strongly invokes the past and is oriented to retrieve and restore it by promoting nostalgia and memory. In Arab secular politics, this concept is evident in the growing emphasis on Palestinian tradition and indigeneity and by celebrating Palestinian literature, folklore, culinary art, customs, and history as reflecting the special attachment to the homeland and the distinctive identity of Palestinians in Israel as an indigenous group. In Arab Muslim politics, the romantic narrative and its concepts are particularly evident in those discourse, writing, and activities that advocate for character education and the refinement of desired ideal behaviors, morals, and virtues. These are depicted as Islamic and as having been practiced by Muslims in their renowned history of glory and fame. Through the emphasis on religious heritage, they seek to invoke the past and make it the basis of the politics of belonging that extends beyond modern notions of nationalism. Whereas their practice is presented as an unattainable standard of morality, these Islamic deeds and virtues are described as conditional and foundational to any notion of true belonging to the local Palestinian community and the Islamic Ummah (nation).

The second narrative, the practical, signifies a process preoccupied with presentism and is geared toward finding practical solutions to the demand for successful integration and improved living conditions. In this process, the politics of identity, contention, and activism are dominant. In secular Arab politics, the practical concept is embodied by state-centered politics since Arab secular actors place heavy emphasis on identifying inequality and misrecognition in the allocation of the state's material and symbolic resources. Thus, in practice, these politics refer to court litigations and advocacy work at the ministerial level, involving senior officials, parliamentary lobbying, and drafting position papers and policy statements, as well as proposing new mechanisms to achieve more substantial equality. In contrast, in Arab Muslim politics, the emphasis on belonging as a practice is more evident in its community-centered politics. Here, belonging is used as a basis for a pragmatic strategy to improve the living conditions of the local community through voluntary work and community development projects in education, welfare, and medical services.

The third narrative, the visionary, defines belonging as an ideological position. The ultimate expression of belonging as a practical act of development can be seen as full involvement and systematic participation in voluntary community programs and societal initiatives to improve the living conditions for Arab-Palestinians. The lucid reflection of belonging as an ideological position is visible among the secular groups as a shared historical consciousness of the collective national identity of the Palestinians and as a shared aspiration to constitute an ideal Muslim society. This concept places heavy emphasis on educating and mobilizing the public to believe in the feasibility of a different vision that would ensure a shared identity and political fate. In the religious politics of belonging, the visionary stance promotes an apocalyptic awareness, according to which the end of days is approaching and Islam will ultimately prevail, ruling globally through a just caliphate. The vision of the secular politics of belonging is less spiritual but still ambitious in its demand for a secular state for all its citizens at times of growing racism and hatred in Israeli society.

The religious agenda gives priority to belonging to the local Muslim community, while the secular agenda prioritizes belonging to Palestinian nationality. At the center of the former is the ideal of a religious society, while at the heart of the latter is the idea of homeland. Both seek not only to shape the sentiment of belonging to the Palestinian people but also the experience of Israeli citizenship. Moreover, both approaches compete over gaining dominance in Arab politics in Israel. For the Muslim religious groups, belonging remains incomplete and unfulfilled as long as it is only an ideology, a feeling, or a position that is not supported with actual deeds and tangible actions that deal with real-life problems. They argue that advocating belonging with no action leaves society alienated and detached from politics.

For secular and national groups, belonging cannot be reduced to welfare programs, religious affinities, or development projects. Without a political compass and an ideological vision, they argue, belonging will remain limited, short-sighted, and historically decontextualized without citizenry discourse in Israel. In contrast, the concepts that underpin the romantic, practical, and visionary narratives of belonging render it meaningful, which is central for the internal cohesion of the Arab-Palestinian community in Israel.

Highlights

- The Arab-Palestinian minority in Israel has become more proactive in linking civic equality to national recognition while placing more emphasis on narratives of belonging.
- Secular and religious politics of belonging provide different answers to the question: "What does it mean to be a Palestinian citizen of Israel?"
- In their search for the meaning of their citizenship and national identity, Palestinians in Israel use the political domain to articulate and advocate three narratives of politics belonging: the romantic, the practical, and the visionary.
- Each narrative reflects a different synthesis of nationalism, citizenship, and religiosity.
- These narratives reflect a genuine search for meaning and a political vision to reconcile the entangled relationships and contradictions among their Palestinian nationality, Israeli citizenship, and religion of Islam in Israel.

References

Abu-Asbe, K. (2007). *Arab education in Israel: Dilemmas of a national minority.* Floersheimer Institute for Policy Studies. [Hebrew]

Abulof, U. (2007). Homework abroad. *Eretz Acheret, 39,* 62–67. [Hebrew]

Abu-Raiya, I. (2005). Concrete versus abstract religiosity: The case of the split within the Islamic Movement in Israel. *Megamot, 43*(4), 682–698. [Hebrew]

Abu-Saad, I. (2004). Separate and unequal: The role of the state educational system in maintaining the subordination of Israel's Palestinian Arab citizens. *Social Identities, 10*(1), 101–127.

Adalah: The Legal Center for Arab Minority Rights in Israel. (2007). *The Democratic Constitution.* https://www.adalah.org/uploads/oldfiles/Public/files/democratic_constitution-english.pdf

Agbaria, A. K. (2013). Arab civil society and education in Israel: The Arab Pedagogical Council as a contentious performance to achieve national recognition. *Race Ethnicity and Education, 18*(5), 675–695.

Agbaria, A. K., & Mustafa, M. (2012). Two states for three peoples: The 'Palestinian–Israeli' in the Future Vision Documents of the Palestinians in Israel. *Ethnic and Racial Studies, 35*(4), 718–736.

Agbaria, A. K., & Mustafa, M. (2014). The case of Palestinian civil society in Israel: Islam, civil society, and educational activism. *Critical Studies in Education, 55*(1), 44–57.

Agbaria, A. K., Mustafa, M., & Jabareen, Y. (2015). In Your Face Democracy: Education for Belonging and its Challenges in Israel. *British Educational Research Journal, 41*(1), 143–175.

Alcoff, L. M., Hames-García, M., Mohanty, S. P., & Moya, P. M. L. (Eds.). (2006). *Identity politics reconsidered.* Palgrave-Macmillan.

Al-Haj, M. (1997). Identity and orientation among the Arabs in Israel: A situation of double periphery. *State, Government and International Relations, 41*(42), 103–122. [Hebrew]

Ali, N. (2006). "Religious Fundamentalism as Ideology and Practice: The Islamic Movement in Israel in Comparative Perspective." Doctoral dissertation, University of Haifa.

Ali, N. (2007). The Islamic movement's perception of the "independent community." In A. Reches (Ed.), *The Arab minority in Israel at the elections for the 17th Israeli Parliament* (pp. 100–110). Tel-Aviv University. [Hebrew]

Antonsich, M. (2010). Searching for belonging—An analytical framework. *Geography Compass, 4*(6), 644–659.

Bishara, A. (1993). On the question of the Palestinian minority in Israel. *Theory and Criticism, 3,* 7–20.

Bokser-Liwerant, J. (2002). Globalization and collective identities. *Social Compass, 49*(2), 253–271.

Cantle, T. (2008). *Community cohesion: A new framework for race and diversity.* Palgrave Macmillan.

Castells, M. (1997). *The power of identity.* Wiley-Blackwell.

Fraser, N. (2000). Rethinking recognition: Overcoming displacement and reification in cultural politics. *New Left Review, 3*(3), 107–120.

Gamson, J. (1995). Must identity movements self-destruct? A queer dilemma. *Social Problems, 42*(3), 390–407.

Geschiere, P. (2011). Autochthony, citizenship, and exclusion paradoxes in the politics of belonging in Africa and Europe. *Indiana Journal of Global Legal Studies, 18*(1), 321–339.

Ghanem, A. (1996). The Palestinians in Israel, part of the problem and not of the solution: The question of their status in the era of peace. *State, Government and International Relations, 41*(42), 132–156. [Hebrew]

Ghanem, A. (2001). *The Palestinian Arab minority in Israel: A political study.* SUNY Press.

Ghanem, A., & Mustafa, M. (2009). Coping with the Nakba: The Palestinians in Israel and the "future vision" as a collective agenda. *Israel Studies Forum, 24*(2), 52–66.

Ghanem, A., & Khalaile, M. (2015). *Palestinian Arab Localities un Israel and Their Local Authorities.* Shafaamr: The Galilee Society.

Guibernau, M. (2013). *Belonging: Solidarity and division in modern societies.* Polity.

Haklai, O. (2004). Palestinian NGOs in Israel: A campaign for civic equality or "ethnic civil society"? *Israel Studies, 9*(3):157–168.

Haklai, O. (2011). *Palestinian Ethnonationalism in Israel.* University of Pennsylvania Press, Philadelphia.

Hall, S. (1996). Introduction: Who needs "identity"? In S. Hall & P. du Gay (Eds.), *Questions of cultural identity* (pp. 1–17). Sage.

Heater, D. (2004). *A history of education for citizenship.* Routledge Falmer.

Isin, E. F., & Wood, P. K. (1999). *Citizenship and identity.* Sage.

Jabareen, Y. T. (2006). Law and education: Critical perspectives on Arab Palestinian education in Israel. *American Behavioral Scientist, 49*(8), 1052–1074.

Jamal, A. (2006). The Arab leadership in Israel: Ascendance and fragmentation. *Journal of Palestine Studies, 35*(2), 6–22.

Jamal, A. (2007). Strategies of minority struggle for equality in ethnic states: Arab politics in Israel. *Citizenship Studies, 11*(3), 263–282.

Khatib, K. (1993). The Islamic movement and secular movements face to face. *Voice of Truth and Freedom,* 7 May: 5.

Kymlicka, W. (1995). *Multicultural citizenship: A liberal theory of minority rights.* Clarendon Press.

Lambert, N. M., Stillman, T. F., Hicks, J. A., Kamble, S., Baumeister, R. F., & Fincham, F. D. (2013). To belong is to matter: Sense of belonging enhances meaning in life. *Personality and Social Psychology Bulletin, 39*(11), 1418–1427.

Maclure, J. (2003). The politics of recognition at an impasse? *Identity Politics and Democratic Citizenship Canadian Journal of Political Science, 36*(1), 3–22.

Mada al-Carmel—The Arab Center for Applied Social Research. (2007). *The Haifa declaration.* http://mada-research.org/en/files/2007/09/haifaenglish.pdf

May, S., Modood, T., & Squires, J. (Eds.). (2004). *Ethnicity, nationalism and minority rights.* Cambridge University Press.

Mayer, T. (1989). *The awaking of Muslims in Israel.* The Institute of Arab Studies. [Hebrew]

McAdam, D., Tarrow, S., & Tilly, C. (2001). *Dynamics of contention.* Cambridge University Press.

McCrone, D., & Kiely, R. (2000). Nationalism and citizenship. *Sociology, 34*(1), 19–34.

National Committee of the Heads of Arab Local Authorities in Israel. (2006). *The future vision of the Palestinian Arabs in Israel.* https://www.adalah.org/uploads/oldfiles/newsletter/eng/dec06/tasawor-mostaqbali.pdf

Pakulski, J. (1997). Cultural citizenship. *Citizenship Studies, 1*(1), 73–86.

Peleg, I. (2007). *Democratizing the hegemonic State: Political transformation in the age of identity.* Cambridge University Press.

Peleg, I., & Waxman, D. (2008). *Israel's Palestinians: The conflict within.* Cambridge University Press.

Rabinowitz, D. (2001). The Palestinian citizens of Israel, the concept of trapped minority and the discourse of transnationalism in anthropology. *Ethnic and Racial Studies, 24*(1), 64–85.

Rabinowitz, D., Ghanem, A., & Yiftachel, O. (2000, November). *After the rift: New directions for government policy towards the Arab population in Israel: An emergency report by an inter-university research team, submitted to Mr Ehud Barak, prime minister of Israel.* Hamachpil.

Rekhess, E. (2007). The evolvement of an Arab-Palestinian national minority in Israel. *Israel Studies, 12*(3), 2–28.

Salah, R. (2001). Towards an Independent Society. *Sawt al-Haq wal-Huriyya,* July 13, 2001, p. 5.

Salah, R. (2015). Uncontrolled nationalism. *Voice of Truth and Freedom,* 19 June: 4.

Shafir, G., & Peled, Y. (2002). *Being Israeli: The dynamics of multiple citizenship.* Cambridge University Press.

Smith, A. D. (1986). *The ethnic origins of nations.* Blackwell.

Soysal, Y. N. (1998). Toward a postnational model of membership. In G. Shafir (Ed.), *The citizenship debates: A reader* (pp. 189–217). University of Minnesota Press.

Taylor, C. (1989). *Sources of the self: The making of the modern identity.* Harvard University Press.

Taylor, V., & Whittier, N. (1995). Analytical approaches to social movement culture: The culture of the women's movement. In Hank Johnston and Bert Klandermans (Eds.), *Social movements and culture.* Minneapolis: University of Minnesota Press.

Tilly, C. (2008). *Contentious performances.* Cambridge University Press.

Tilly, C., & Tarrow, S. (2006). *Contentious politics.* Paradigm Publishers.

Turner, B. (1993). Contemporary problems in the theory of citizenship. In B. Turner (Ed.), *Citizenship and social theory* (pp. 1–18). Sage.

Yuval-Davis, N. (2011). *The politics of belonging: Intersectional contestations.* Sage.

Yuval-Davis, N. (2012). An autochthonic scent of memory? *Feminist Review, 100*(1), 154–160.

12

The Quest for Meaning and Fulfillment Among Haredi Women in Israel

Menachem Keren-Kratz

Introduction

The adjective and noun "Haredi" (originally from the Hebrew word *Hared*, namely "fearful" [of God]) indicate people who closely observe the Halakhah (religious Jewish laws) as well as many traditional customs and are also referred to as Ultra-orthodox. This chapter focuses on the current quest for meaning and fulfillment among Haredi women in Israel and adopts a historical perspective to understand the specific ways by which contemporary Haredi women carve their distinct way for a meaningful life. In such pursuits they combine intrinsic adherence to a Haredi identity and tradition while also adopting other ways of behaving with personal agency to pursue meaning in their life.

The names of two outstanding Haredi women appeared regularly in the pages of Israeli newspapers and on internet sites in the early years of the 21st century. The first is "Rebbitzin" Beruria Zevuluni, a mother of eight, the daughter of kabbalist Rabbi Shalom Ifargan and the sister of the kabbalist Rabbi Ya'acov Israel, whose reputed knack of diagnosing hidden illnesses earned him the moniker "The Roentgen," or "the X-Ray Man." Most unusually for a Haredi woman, many individuals, poor and rich, and even leading businessmen and politicians, visit her home in Jerusalem to seek blessing and advice. The story that attracted the most media attention at the time was Zevuluni's role as a mediator in disputes between criminals, an activity that she turned into a profession. In 2012, *Forbes* magazine estimated her wealth at more than NIS20 million NIS (close to $US6 million).

The second woman, Beruria Keren, became known as "Mother Taliban." She earned this nickname after promoting the idea that every Jewish woman should cover her face and body in several layers of clothes. Although this

Menachem Keren-Kratz, *The Quest for Meaning and Fulfillment Among Haredi Women in Israel* In: *Finding Meaning.* Edited by: Ofra Mayseless and Pninit Russo-Netzer, Oxford University Press. © Oxford University Press 2022. DOI: 10.1093/oso/9780190910358.003.0012 notion initially aroused considerable opposition among rabbis who condemned it as being too innovative and untraditional, it was soon adopted by a group of women who began roaming the streets of Jerusalem and Beit Shemesh wearing their striking outfits of all black, multilayered clothes. Keren gained notoriety after she was convicted of maltreating her own children while claiming that she had only sought to educate them properly (Doron, 2016).

Interestingly, both women are called Beruria, a name that in Jewish tradition expresses the very essence of an independent woman and her tragic fate. The Talmud (from the Hebrew word *Limud*; namely "study") is the central text of Rabbinic Judaism and is the primary source of Jewish religious law its traditions. It tells the story of Beruria, wife of Rabbi Meir. She was renowned as an outstanding Torah scholar who actively participated in Talmudic discussions in which all the other debaters were men. Wishing to curb her outrageous exploits, her husband, so the Talmud relates, sent one of his handsome students to seduce her. Beruria's failure to resist his advances led her husband to reveal his stratagem and expose her disloyalty. Thus shamed, Beruria took her own life and her sorrowful husband migrated to another land. Outstanding and independent women, so the Talmud tells us, have no room in Jewish society (Bacon, 2002).

This derogatory perception of women in Jewish tradition was expressed by scholar Rachel Elior as follows:

> The [religious] perspective . . . deprives a woman of sovereignty and in-dependent standing; instead, she is a virgin in her father's possession, as a property until she is wed, at which time she passes to the possession of her husband . . . only in old age, after her husband's death and the exhaustion of her reproductive potential, can she become independent. . . . The woman is viewed in religious law as the property of her father or her husband, as chattel, as livestock, as still life, as a piece of property that can be bought and sold. (Elior, 2010, p. 396)

While this whole volume deals with the quest for a worthy purpose and a significant meaning in life, one should remember that such terms have different connotations in the general secular world than in a religious context. While in a nonreligious society meaning- and purpose-seeking is optional and each individual is free to define his own goals in life, this is not the case in a religious environment. A religious lifestyle indicates, *inter alia*, everyone's meaning and purpose in life, which are basically to fear God and follow his commands. Moreover, all monotheistic religions consider the "limited life in this world" to be meaningless compared to "the eternal life thereafter." Namely, the value of one's existence in this world can only be appreciated with respect to its consequences regarding his or her "life after death." This notion stands in acute contrast with nonreligious thought in which individuals have only one limited life span to live, which is exactly the reason why they should seek purpose and meaning in that life.

This chapter will examine how religious women, committed to life's predetermined divine meaning and purpose, seek meaning and purpose in their secular interpretation. In their eyes, unlike the opinion of many men and especially rabbis, the two sets of values can coexist and even strengthen one another. For example, a conservative rabbi may rule that a Haredi woman who is successful at work attracts too much attention and is therefore not modest. The woman, on the other hand, may claim that her greater income allows her husband to spend more time in Talmud studies, which is his religious obligation. Consequently, her pursuit of a meaningful career and greater value in this world also means she earns more credit points to the life thereafter.

The Roller Coaster of Jewish Women's Status

The social status of Jewish women has undergone several upheavals over the past millennium. Because until the Holocaust Ashkenazi Jews comprised almost 90% of the Jewish people, most studies focused on women from Central and Eastern Europe. Yet historical data about Sephardi women in Jewish communities in Africa and the Middle East indicate that their status was not significantly different. Scholar Avraham Grossman maintains that owing to improved economic conditions in the 11th–13th centuries, Jewish women enjoyed a higher social status during that time than in the previous or ensuing periods (Grossman, 2004). The following two centuries were a time when Jews suffered severe persecution, most notable of which was their expulsion from Spain in 1492. This resulted in a decline in the social status of women.

Scholar Jacob Katz explains that with the advent of greater economic opportunities in the 16th–18th centuries in Europe, women were once again granted greater freedom and allowed to go out to work in order to augment their families' income. Earning money and venturing out of their homes enhanced their social status and their independence (Katz, 2000, pp. 20–21, 151). This situation, however, changed following the appearance of the Sabbatean and Frankist messianic movements. Their popular and radical leaders exempted Jews from some of the religious commands, sponsored sexual promiscuity, and allowed women greater freedom (Rapoport-Albert, 2007). Traditional Jews reacted by adopting a stricter lifestyle that allowed no room for lenience, and women were once again driven back to the privacy of their homes. This was especially evident within the Hasidic movement. This mid-18th-century revolutionary social trend put greater emphasis on the spiritual experience than on study and religious compliance yet allowed no place for women (Wodziński, 2013). Consequently, in European Jewish society of the late 18th and early 19th centuries, Jewish women were left far behind their non-Jewish counterparts whose public position steadily improved during the same period. All this began to change in the mid-19th century.

During the second half of the 19th century, Jews gained wider civil rights and moved up the social ladder, seeking greater integration with non-Jewish society in the cultural, economic, and political spheres. Jewish women, by now less restricted in terms of their educational curriculum and their use of free time, began exploring new horizons. Consequently, even many religious women attended schools and received general education in fields such as science, music, and foreign languages (Chovav, 2009). The circle of the most observant Jews who still denied their daughters a wider education was constantly shrinking.

Among the many changes Jewish society underwent after World War I was a reassessment of the desirable social role of observant woman and the education they required to fill it. Consequently, the interwar period was in many ways a "golden era" for Jewish women in general and for observant women in particular. This was manifested in the establishment of the Beit Ya'acov school network for Haredi girls and its rapid expansion throughout the Jewish world (Oleszak, 2011; Scharfer, 2011; Weissman, 1995). Girls' schools were also established by Ha-Mizrahi, the religious-Zionist movement. Even the Old Yishuv, namely Jerusalem's most religious and conservative section of the Jewish society, established its first school for Haredi girls. Although this was an issue that sparked a social and religious confrontation, during this period Haredi women, both in Europe and in Palestine, were even accorded the right to vote (Shiloh, 2013; Weissman, 1976).

Haredi Women in Israel After the Holocaust

Back to our grandmothers, we must follow our grandmothers. Our mothers, as much as we love and cherish them, have absorbed too much European culture . . . and were enchanted by modernity . . . they, even the best of them, considered theater as an expression of culture and the ballet a form of "pure art." With all our love for our mothers we must not withhold the truth and say: our mothers took erroneous paths, they observed the creations of foreigners and enjoyed them. . . . We, the daughters of Sarah, Rivka and Rachel . . . cannot accept our mothers as a role model of supreme spiritual education. Our slogan must therefore be: "Back to the grandmother." (*Diglenu*, Heshvan 5715, November 1954, p. 11)

This exhortation, voiced at a Haredi women's and daughters' convention in 1954, represents a radical shift in the stand of the Haredi leadership toward women. To understand what brought about this change one must examine the situation of Haredi society in the years following the establishment of the state of Israel (Friedman, 1998).

The Israeli rabbis who survived the Holocaust felt an overwhelming obligation to restore Europe's ruined Torah world. This, however, was not a simple task. The economy of the new state, which was recovering from the war of independence and needed to absorb hundreds of thousands of immigrants, was unstable. Many of those who were raised in Orthodox families lost their faith following the Holocaust, while many others adopted a religious-Zionist modern lifestyle. The few remaining Haredi families were scattered in mixed neighborhoods alongside non-Haredi, traditional, and secular Jews.

The reestablishment of a European-style Haredi society required a comprehensive paradigm change: (a) whereas in the past all observant Jews had lived side by side with Gentiles and non-observant Jews, Haredi leaders now sought to establish segregated neighborhoods especially for their people. (b) While throughout Jewish history only a handful of talented Torah scholars continued their religious studies after their marriage, now pressure was put on all Haredi youngsters to continue to study in yeshivas for many years after their marriage. (c) In the past, all observant families had sought material prosperity and a good standard of living, just as all other Jews had. Now, since young men were encouraged to study in the yeshiva for many years, most Haredi families had to settle for a far lower income and accept living on the verge of poverty.

Such wide-ranging social changes could not have occurred had they not been supported by the wives, mothers, and especially the daughters—who would soon become wives and mothers themselves. What this meant was that Haredi women had to forego all the social advancement they had made prior to the Holocaust. The first step was to ban women from heading their own educational institutions. Thus, in place of Sarah Schnirer, the mythological founder of Beit Ya'acov, and an array of other women who succeeded her, a man now took the helm.

Rabbi Yosef Avraham Wolf established the most influential Haredi school for girls after the Holocaust. It paved the way for a multitude of additional institutions that educated the Haredi girl to pursue just one purpose in her life: to become a good wife to a yeshiva student. To this end the girl was given mainly religious instruction, designed to strengthen her faith. She was taught just enough secular material for her to find a decent job, preferably as a teacher. The girls were educated to believe that, unlike their mothers, they had to work so as to enable their husbands to continue their studies in the yeshiva for many years. They were also encouraged to bear as many children as possible and to educate them according to the same uncompromising principles (El-Or, 1994).

Haredi girls were furthermore taught to obey their husbands and their rabbis. They were told not to seek to broaden their cultural horizons or learn about "foreign subjects" such as art, music, or literature. Their social circle was restricted to their close family, and they were prohibited from participating in any "external" activity, such as going to the theater or the movies, or even reading secular books and newspapers, let alone listening to the radio and watching television (Brown, 2013).

The 1980s: Change Gets Under Way

Much of the credit for the transformations in Haredi society in Israel is accorded to the leaders of the "Lithuanian" camp, namely the rabbis of the non-Hasidic Ashkenazi Haredim. The first was Rabbi Avarham Yesha'aya Karelitz, also known as the *Hazon Ish*, the title of his book, who was the first to promote change in post-Holocaust Haredi society in Israel. After his death in 1953, he was succeeded by Rabbi Yitzhak Ze'ev Halevi Soloveitchik, also known as the Brisk Rabbi, who was less dominant than his predecessor. The most influential figure to shape Israel's post-Holocaust Haredi world was Rabbi Elazar Menachem Mann Shach, who was appointed to the Torah Sages' Council in 1966 and was regarded as the undisputed Haredi leader until his death in 2001.

From the 1980s onward, the Haredi world has undergone several fundamental changes. In 1977, the Likud party won the national elections and, for the first time in many years, the Haredi parties joined the coalition government. This resulted in the allocation of greatly increased budgets to the Haredi public, which enabled it to distance itself further from the general Israeli public. This, however, also led to intra-Haredi controversies, and the hitherto more or less united Haredi leadership was divided into four political wings: the non-Hasidic Lithuanians, who followed Rabbi Shach; the Hasidim, led by the rabbis of Gur and Viznitz; the religious Sephardi Jews, who followed Rabbi Ovadia Yosef; and Habad, which followed Rabbi Menachem Mendel Schneerson—the Lubavitcher Rebbe.

Another camp that began to form in those years, and which would have a significant impact on the status of Haredi women, was that of the Hozrim Be-Teshuva (repentants). This trend among secular and traditional Israelis who decided to become observant and adopt a Haredi lifestyle began after the Six-Day War in 1967 and gathered pace during the 1970s and 1980s. Secular and traditional Israeli women who were raised on Western values of equality found themselves face to face with the paternalistic and condescending Haredi way of life. Some of them, like the two above-mentioned Berurias, became significant agents of change (Doron, 2013).

The division and competition between the Haredi camps accelerated the process of inner social changes, which in turn influenced the status of Haredi women. The first sign of change was Rabbi Ovadia Yosef's acquiescence to his daughter's decision to study fashion design at a secular academic institute. The daughter, Israel Prize laureate Adina Bar-Shalom, later became a leading advocate of academic studies for Haredim in general and for Haredi women in particular.

The continuous growth of Haredi society and the lack of sufficient places of employment for women within the Haredi sector drove some of them to seek employment in the public sector and in non-Haredi businesses. The public criticism of this phenomenon, alongside the women's relatively poor salaries, which did not meet the needs of their growing families, drove their husbands to go out to work (Blumen, 2002). These processes, which coincided with the illness of Rabbi Shach, who was thus unable to confront them, led to the establishment of the Haredi College of Jerusalem, the first higher education institutions designed especially for Haredi men and women in the late 1990s (Lupu, 2003).

The 21st Century: The Great Rupture Among Haredi Women

When one examines the major social trends that the Western world has undergone in the 20th century, the feminist revolution is undoubtedly near the top of the list. Belying their conservative image, non-Haredi Jewish women in Palestine, before the establishment of the state of Israel, enjoyed a higher social status than their counterparts in many other places. Already in the Ottoman period, women pioneers worked shoulder to shoulder with men and were among the leaders of Zionist institutions and pioneer groups. Women attained the right to vote for the Jewish institutions in the early 1920s, far earlier than their counterparts in many other countries (Shilo, 2009). Women played an active role in the pre-state paramilitary organizations and fought in Israel's war of independence. After statehood, most women served in the Israeli Defense Forces (IDF), and Israel's governments numbered several women ministers. One of them, Golda Meir, served as prime minister from 1969 to 1974. Israeli women also made their way into academia, into the business and financial world, and into the judicial and medical professions. Although men still dominate Israel's public sphere, the proportion of women participating in it is constantly rising.

Throughout the 20th century, the feminist movement made no impact on Israel's Haredi society, which continued to view women as secondary to men and as a means for them to fulfill their role. This worldview, however, has changed dramatically in the 21st century, as Haredi women currently seek to close some of the gaps between them and their non-Haredi counterparts. Nowadays, many Haredi women seek to enrich their life in ways that until recently were considered undesirable and immodest. However, they do it in a unique and distinct way that conserves their identity and perspective as Haredi women. While the quest for knowledge, aesthetics, and respect and the search for one's place and purpose in life is regarded as a worthy spiritual aspiration in the secular world, this is not the case in Haredi society. There, such aspirations can only be justified by claiming that they enhance one's predeterminate goals, which are to fear God and obey his commands.

Although nowadays many Haredi women aspire for greater economic, social, and political opportunities, they are reluctant to admit that such quest has a standalone value. Therefore, what a spectator from the outside may judge as search for meaning and purpose in life, a Haredi woman may regard as new ways to implement ancient principles. The real change is that, today, women, not men, may determine the new ways to fulfill God's will. Consequently, unlike secular women who take pride in their personal achievements, Haredi women are expected to be more restricted when speaking about themselves and to attribute some of their success to their supportive husbands.

These changes can be observed in four spheres: (a) the home, (b) the workplace, (c) leisure time, (d) and Haredi politics. The following sections examine the changes in each sphere more closely.

Change in the Home

If a Haredi woman is to begin to consider finding meaning and self-fulfillment beyond her demanding daily routine, she must first strive to make progress on the following four parameters: (1) to gain some say in choosing the man with whom she is to share her life; (2) to establish her position in the home as a worthy and autonomous being who, despite her inferior *halakhic* (religious Jewish law) status, deserves to be treated with respect and dignity; (3) to gain recognition from both society and the rabbinical leadership of her right to decide on the number of children she will bear and the intervals between them; and (4) to experience intimacy, tenderness, and sexual satisfaction.

Concerning item (1), in almost all Haredi circles marriage is the outcome of a process handled by the future spouses' parents (Lehmann & Siebzehner, 2009). In the past, the future bride and groom had almost no say in the matter and were compelled to acquiesce to their parents' decision. Once married, most couples would remain so, through thick and thin, and only religious considerations, such as the infertility of the woman, could justify divorce. Divorce, however, cast a blemish on the entire family, and the couple's children as well as their unmarried brothers and sisters were consequently tainted.

This has changed during the 21st century. First, in almost all Haredi circles nowadays, a match is not concluded without the full consent of the young couple. Second, today, more than ever before, failed marriages end in divorce, and the rate of Haredi divorcees is constantly rising; in 2018, it reached 6.5%, a fivefold increase since 2000. This demonstrates a greater social acceptance of the phenomenon and suggests that a greater number of women who remain married do so of their own free choice (Barth, 2012; Cohen, 2001; Zalcberg 2012).

As for item (2), every woman is entitled to be protected from sexual, physical, or verbal abuse, at school, in the street, and at home. In Haredi society, however, cases of abuse remained, for many decades, largely unaddressed. They were either not reported or handled discretely within the community. In many instances the perpetrator was merely warned or asked to move to a different community where he often failed to change his ways. In other cases, women and parents of girls who reported sexual abuse had to endure public censure for leveling accusations of misconduct at members of the community (Steinmetz & Haj-Yahia, 2006). The plaintiffs were often accused of improper conduct that had allegedly provoked the abuser. Some were offered money or relocation in return for agreeing not to shame a public figure (Shoham, 2012).

This state of affairs began to change in the 21st century even among the most zealous communities (Rotem, 2006; Shmuely, 2001; Steinmetz, 2002). More incidences of offensive behavior toward both women and girls were reported to the police, leading to the perpetrators' arrest and trial. Other cases were discussed online, and it appears that fewer cases now remain unreported and resolved within the community (Goren, 2013). At the same time, the Bat Melekh (the king's daughter) organization established shelters for abused Haredi women and, with the help of social workers and community activists, endeavors to educate the general Haredi public on this matter (Heller, 2011; Shpigel, 2005). In 2013, Haredi lawyer Rivka Schwartz established Min Ha-Meitsar (from the strait), an organization that offers legal assistance to Haredi victims of sexual abuse (Litman, 2017).

Concerning item (3), in the past, Haredi women knew little about the process of being pregnant, giving birth, and raising a baby and the challenges associated with them. The first book on pregnancy adapted especially to the Haredi woman appeared only in 1993. Since then its authors Barukh and Malki Finkelstein have written three more books on fertility problems, postpartum depression, and on caring for babies (Kfir, 2017). Having access to medical and psychological information, Haredi women realized that bearing so many children has a hefty toll.

THE QUEST FOR MEANING 285

Today, Haredi women are more willing to approach their rabbis, who nowadays more than ever before permit them to use contraceptives for a certain duration. Whereas for many decades the number of children in a Haredi family rose steadily, reaching its peak in 2005, with an average of 7.6 children per family, since then we have witnessed a sharp decline to 6.5 children per family, and this number is expected to drop further in the years ahead (Cahaner, Choshen, & Malach, 2016, p. 28). Bearing fewer children means that a woman has more free time that she can employ for her self-empowerment.

Finally, as for item (4), today, greater numbers of Haredi women are seeking more fulfilling emotional and physical intimacy. This is achieved in various ways. First, since most Haredi men have no sexual knowledge, let alone experience, prior to their marriage they are referred to a special counselor who instructs them in the secrets of the bedroom. Today, more than ever before, young men are encouraged to respond to their wives' physical needs and to satisfy them sexually. If, however, the couple, and especially the woman, is dissatisfied with their sex life, it is not uncommon for them to seek professional counseling, either from a Haredi or a non-Haredi therapist (Peleg, 2014). Another way in which women try to boost their sex life is by wearing sexy clothes or using sex toys, all of which can now be obtained in shops especially designed for the religious and Haredi public (Cohen, 2017).

A few dissatisfied Haredi women seek love and sexual pleasure with other men (Ata'ely, 2010). Some such extramarital liaisons begin on internet forums and in chat-rooms designated especially for the Haredi public (Rotem, 2011). Thus, in order to fulfil their sexual needs, some Haredi women are prepared to breach one of the most fundamental religious laws while still purporting to lead a Haredi lifestyle.

Change at the Workplace

The first generations of Haredi women who provided for their families so that their husbands would be free to study in the yeshiva settled for low-paying jobs, mostly in the Haredi education system or in other Haredi institutions. These positions where soon filled, and the following generations of Haredi women had to find work in other, non-Haredi workplaces. In order to compete in this market they needed to acquire professional skills, including the use of computers, bookkeeping, typing, and proficiency in English. These and other vocational subjects were initially taught at Haredi girls' schools, but as the market demanded greater specialization, Haredi women turned to post high school and even academic studies (Hoori, 2010). This trend can also be discerned, although not to the same degree, among the most zealous groups (Shneler, 1978; Zalcberg, 2005). As a result, during the 21st century, the proportion of Haredi working women has risen dramatically from about 50% in 2000 to more than 75% in 2015 (Cahaner et al., 2016, pp. 142, 155).

This trend is not confined to "horizontal" growth—an increase in the number of working women—but is also manifested in "vertical" growth, namely an increase in the number of Haredi women who occupy managerial positions. In a television series about Haredi women aired in June 2016, journalist Amnon Levi interviewed several successful Haredi businesswomen and entrepreneurs. One of them, Avigail Shakovitsky, owns a large accounting and consulting firm that employs several dozen Haredi women as well as nonprofessional staff (the firm's web site is www.mishorcpa.co.il). A former manager of the Beit Ya'acov girls' school chain, Shakovitsky is also active on the Institute of Certified Public Accountants in Israel. Levi also interviewed Adina Bar-Shalom, a social activist who founded and headed the first Haredi academy, which became a multimillion NIS business.

Another field in which the participation of Haredi women is on the rise is in the high-tech industry, which employs 5% of all Haredi women (Klein, 2017). This development inspired Rachel Ganot, a Haredi woman, to found Rachip, which deals in both hardware and software solutions. The company site explicitly states that "The Rachip team is based on a carefully selected and meticulously trained group of [80] women engineers from the Ultra-Orthodox (HAREDI) community" (the firm's web site is www.rachip.com). In 2013, Ganot was chosen by *Lady Globes*, an annual special publication of Israel's leading business magazine, as one of Israel's 50 most influential women (Perets, 2013). She is joined by Nili Davidovitz, who ran the Da'at high-tech center that employs more than 40 Haredi women, and by other Haredi women entrepreneurs (Ifargan, 2015; the firm's web site is www.daatsolutions.co.il). Given such developments, it is not surprising that commercial firms began organizing conferences aimed specifically at Haredi businesswomen (Nagid-Mizrahi, 2013; the firm's web site is www. temechcon.org).

Leisure Time

With more free time, higher salaries, and fewer children to raise, Haredi women seek to expand their horizons to areas that until recently were unavailable to them. With no television in most Haredi homes, a simple way to pass the time is reading (Fisher-Roller, 1996). Consequently, an increasing number of books that target Haredi children and women are being published. Most of the novels are authored by Haredi women such as Menuha Fuchs and Sarah Pakhter (aka. Mali Green), who have written dozens of books and dominate the prose shelves in Haredi bookstores. Author Maya Keinan took Haredi literature a step forward when she published a highly successful science fiction series (Chiki-Arad, 2016).

Other recreational options are now available to mothers and children outside the privacy of their homes. These include communal centers sponsored by municipal authorities as well as privately administered arts and crafts courses (Ettinger, 2011; Rotem, 2004). During the summer, women and daughters can enjoy a swim at segregated beaches for women-only (Lajos, 1999; Schneller, 1999). Haredi women can also work out in gyms located in Haredi centers or participate in women's classes in gyms in secular neighborhoods (Getzlick, 2014). In the evenings Haredi women gather in public halls or in private. They may attend a religious lecture or watch a film or theater show especially adapted and approved by their rabbis (Vinig, 2011). Some women take acting classes while others learn arts and crafts (Amrusi, 2012). Increasingly popular are self-awareness courses taught by other Haredi women (Rotem, 2005).

Another popular way to pass the time is to go shopping. In the past most Haredi women would buy cheap clothes that were only required to meet the halakhic standards. Today, Haredi women are gaining a growing awareness of fashion. Many run their own home-stores in which they sell clothes they imported, which include major brands. Others design and sell their own Haredi-style fashion collections (Rabinowitz, 2014). Given this widespread awareness of one's appearance, it is not surprising to come across beauty events and fashion shows dedicated to Haredi women (Falah, 2017).

Taking care of their appearance does not stop at clothing. Since a Haredi woman is forbidden to expose her natural hair, the selling and grooming of wigs is a thriving business in which many Haredi women are involved (Bronner, 1993). In addition, most Haredi women and even girls regularly receive cosmetic treatments and some even turn to cosmetic surgery

(Farbzner-Bashan, 2016). As this trend gathered pace, Haredi women opened cosmetic spas even in Haredi strongholds such as Bnei Brak (Haritan, 2014).

Haredi Women in Politics

The previous sections have shown how Haredi women have branched out into new territory at home, in the work place, and in their free time. Although substantial, these achievements are confined to the individual level, as each woman pursues her own goals and seeks to exploit the new freedom and opportunities close at hand. This section addresses those women who seek to change the lives of entire sections of Haredi women wherever they may live.

Although Haredi women are generally not perceived as role models, some of the wives of great rabbis have attained a special status and are respected and revered even by Haredi men (Rubin-Schwartz, 2006). These women begin by relying on their husbands' reputation, but a few years down the road they establish their own dominant status and use it to influence other Haredi women, Such were the widows of Rabbi Yehoshua Leib Diskin of Brisk and of Rabbi Joel Teitelbaum of Satmar, and the wife of Rabbi Amram Blau. Nowadays, several of the wives of renowned Hasidic Rabbis operate discretely in the political arena (Cohen, 2012). One of the known and more active Rebbitzins was the late Bat-Sheva, wife of Rabbi Haim Kanievsky, one of the most prominent Lithuanian (namely, non-Hasidic) leaders. Most unusually for a Haredi woman, she was the subject of several books written after her death (Malka, 2011; Weinberger, Weinberger, & Indig, 2012). She was succeeded by her sister, Rebbitzin Lea Kolodetzky. Other such illustrious rebbitzins are the above-mentioned Beruria Zevuluni, who is both the sister and the daughter of famous Sephardic rabbis, and Sarah, the wife of Rabbi Yisakhar Dov Rokeach—leader of the Hassidic court of Belz—and the daughter of the former leader of the Viznitz Hasidic court.

Women leaders are today found in all major sections of Haredi society: Lithuanian, Hassidic, and Sephardic. They are highly respected by both men and women and use their elevated status to make a mark on their communities through individual counseling or by gathering and preaching to a large audience of women. Some of these rebbitzins run their own charities or educational organizations.

In recent decades, other women, unrelated to prominent rabbis, also have begun to lead women's groups. In the late 1990s, Rebbitzin Lea Kook of Tiberias began preaching to women, encouraging them to correct their ways and lead a more observant life. She was featured in a documentary film titled *Tikkun*, which was made by Talia Finkel in 2002. Rebbitzin Kook was recently joined by her daughter Bat-Sheva, and the two maintain their own internet site (www.kook-dov.co.il). At the women's gatherings she held, the ritual of Hafrashat Hala was performed. This ritual, along with lighting of the Sabbath candles and avoiding touching her husband during her menstrual period, when a woman is considered impure, are the three major mitzvoth for which women are responsible.

For many generations this ritual, the Hafrashat Hala, during which a woman takes a small piece of the dough she is preparing and burns or discards it while reciting a special blessing, was performed only in the privacy of a woman's kitchen. In recent years, however, the ritual had taken pride of place at many Haredi women's gatherings. These are performed by a new type of Rebbitzin, usually Hozrot Be-Teshuva (repentants), such as former hairstylist Lisa Dadon. She transformed this intimate ceremony into a mega-event attended by thousands of women (Ben-Haim, 2015). Although these rebbitzins were not raised in Haredi families and carry on in a most untraditional manner, they attract large crowds of Haredi women, especially Sephardis and Hozrot Be-Teshuva (Gruzman, 2017).

The most prominent Haredi female figure is the above-mentioned Beruria Keren. Her introduction of multilayered, full body coverage was revolutionary not only because of the strict modesty standards it established, but primarily because these were set by a woman. Although this innovation was met by fierce opposition by many rabbis, it has become a norm in certain groups. This trend of women who establish new norms of strict modesty is regarded by some scholars as a form of radical feminism (El Guindi, 2003). The "ultra-modest" fashion Keren introduced has influenced other groups, which have adopted a milder version of coverage using a dark and broad shawl that hides the contours of the female figure (Zalcberg-Block, 2011).

Haredi political parties claim to represent the interests of their constituency. Although allowed and even encouraged to vote and support the parties, Haredi women are not allowed to hold any official position in them. This taboo, too, is beginning to weaken as more Haredi women realize that their voices and their own interests are not well represented. In 2013, a group of Haredi women who called themselves "Not Elected—Not Voting" called on women to refrain from voting for the Haredi parties in municipal elections because no woman was included on their lists. In the same year, Mikhal

Chervovitzki formed her own "Mothers' Party" to run in the municipal election in El'ad, a Haredi town (Anonymous, 2013).

In 2015, a Hozeret Be-Teshuva named Rut Kulian, along with several other women, founded a national Haredi party named *Uvizkhutan* (i.e., "and by their rights"). Although they gained support from several rabbis, the party won fewer than 2,000 votes in the national election that year (Krakowski, 2015; Tzarfati, 2015). Kulian's struggle was documented in Israel's Channel 8 film titled *A Jewish Woman*. These efforts on the part of Haredi women to become involved in politics have aroused strong opposition not only among rabbis and Haredi men but also on the part of Haredi women as well. The party was not allowed to publicize itself in Haredi newspapers and contested the issue all the way to the Israeli Supreme Court. Despite such setbacks, upon considering other powerful trends toward change within Haredi society, it appears only a matter of time before Haredi women become a force in the sector's political institutions.

Conclusion

The status of Orthodox women has undergone many changes in history and reached its peak during the interwar period. At that time, Orthodox women were allowed to acquire both traditional and general education and enjoy the fruits of Western culture. They also helped to provide for their families, either by working with their husbands or by running their own businesses. During that period, Orthodox society rarely criticized women who read secular books, visited museums, listened to concerts, or went to the theater.

These achievements were not maintained during the post-Holocaust period in Israel as Haredi women were encouraged to bear as many children as they could and become the family's main breadwinner in order to allow their husbands to study in the yeshiva for many years. Haredi women took up this burden and, for many decades, sacrificed their well-being and health without complaint. In the 21st century, once Haredi women realized that the world of the Torah had regained and even surpassed its former glory in pre-Holocaust Europe, they sought to reclaim their previous, more advantageous pre-World War II social status.

These changes are manifested in the life and work of yet another Beruria. Rebbitzin Beruria David is the daughter of Rabbi Yitzchak Hutner, one of America's greatest rabbis and Jewish scholars, and the wife of Rabbi Yonassan

David, head of two Haredi yeshivas, one in Israel and the other in the United States. She not only obtained a doctorate in Jewish history from Columbia University, but also helped to edit her father's writings and to write his biography. Women such as Beruria David, who were raised in the more open Haredi atmosphere that exists in America, serve, after they migrate to Israel, as agents of change.

David's illustrious example serves as a model for the many female students in the post-high school institution, known as a seminary, that she established in the 1970s, in Jerusalem. Named Bais Yaakov Jerusalem, the seminary prepares Haredi girls, many from English-speaking countries, for advanced academic studies. This precedent paved the way for further Haredi girls' high schools, such as Darkei Sarah, more than 95% of whose students are eligible for academic studies.

In conclusion, in the 21st century, Haredi women from all sections seek more in their lives than simply supporting their families and bearing many children. They pursue a better and more comfortable life at home, they seek more stimulating and more rewarding jobs, and they want to be able to choose how to enjoy their spare time. These changes are also evident in the public sphere, as increasing numbers of Haredi women play leading roles as social, business, and political entrepreneurs. Judging by what transpired in the Modern Orthodox societies in both Israel and the United States, Haredi women's quest for better and more rewarding life in this world, justified by religious reasons, is here to stay and is bound to transform Haredi Judaism as we know it (Ross, 2004).

Highlights

- The social status of Orthodox women has undergone many changes in history and reached its peak between the two World Wars.
- After the Holocaust and the loss of the Torah World in eastern Europe, the surviving rabbis were determined to reestablish it in Israel.
- Haredi women became part of that effort and were encouraged to bear many children and support their families in order to allow their husbands to study in the yeshiva for many years.
- In the 21st century, the Torah World has regained and even surpassed its former scope in Eastern Europe, and Haredi women sought to reclaim their previous social status.

- Nowadays, many Haredi women seek to enrich their life in ways that, until recently, were considered undesirable and immodest.
- They seek fulfillment, meaning, and greater satisfaction within their own family and workplace, as well as in their free time and also in their public and political representation.

References

Amrusi, E. (2012 April 6). Me-Ahorey Ha-Homot (Behind the walls). *Israel Hayom*.

Anonymous. (2013, September 29). Larishona Mifleget Imahot Harediot Be-El'ad (For the first time a Haredi mothers' party in El'ad). *Yediot Aharonot*.

Ata'ely, A. (2010, June 10). Roman Yotse Dofen: Haredit U-Me'ahev Palestina'i (An unusual affair: A Haredi woman finds a Palestinian lover). *Ma'ariv*.

Bacon, B. (2002). How shall we tell the story of Beruriah's end? *Nashim*, 5, 231–239.

Barth, A. (2012). *Tension and duality: Characteristics and social construction of divorce in the Ultra-Orthodox community* (doctoral dissertation). Haifa University. [Hebrew]

Ben-Haim, A. (2015, August 21). Lisa Dadon, Kohenet Hafrashat Ha-Hala Kavsha Et Keysaria (Lisa Dadon, Hafrashat Hala's priestess conquers Caesarea amphitheater). *Nana 10*.

Blumen, O. (2002). Criss-crossing boundaries: Ultraorthodox women go to work. *Gender, Place, and Society*, 9(2), 131–152.

Bronner, L. L. (1993). From veil to wig: Jewish women's hair covering. *Judaism*, 42(4), 465–477.

Brown (Hoisman), I. (2013). Bein "teva ha-isha" le-"marut ha-ba'al": ha-ideologia ha-hinukhit ha-haredit u-gevulot ha-haskala ha-toranit le-banot. *Identities*, 3, 98–123. [Hebrew]

Cahaner, L., Choshen, M., & Malach, G. (2016). *The yearbook of ultra-orthodox society in Israel: 2016*. The Israel Democracy Institute.

Chiki-Arad, R. (2016, September 8). Mihen Ha-Sofrot ha-Haredion She-Motsi'ot Meot Sefarim Be-Shana? (Who are the Haredi women who author hundreds of books every year?). *Ha-Aretz*.

Chovav, Y. (2009). *Maidens love thee: The religious and spiritual life of Jewish Ashkenazic women in the early modern period*. Carmel. [Hebrew]

Cohen, I. (2012, February 23). Ha-Piyus Ha-Histori: Ha-Ahayot Le-Beit Satmar U-Belza Mashchu Ba-Hutim (Historic reconciliation: The sisters, the rebbetzins of Satmar and Belz, pulled the strings). *Kikar Ha-Shabat*.

Cohen, M. (2001). Shidukhim Ve-Zugi'ut Ba-Hevra Ha-Haredit. *Alma*, 9.

Cohen, U. (2017, April 4). Oneg Elohi: Hanuyot Ha-Sex La-Migzar Ha-Haredi Ve-Ha-Dati Tofsot Teutsa (Godly pleasure: Sex shops for the religious and Haredi societies are on the rise). *La-Isha*.

Doron, S. (2013). *Shuttling between two worlds: Coming to and defecting from ultra-orthodox Judaism in Israeli society*. Hakibbutz Ha-Meuhad. [Hebrew]

Doron, S. (2016). Parashat Ha-Imahot Ha-Harediyot: Mabat Aher Al Kehilot Segurot (The Haredi Mothers affair: A different look at segregated communities). In E. Shoham & S. Doron (Eds.), *Over-visibility versus transparency: The attitude to the "other" in Israeli society* (pp. 99–126). Ashkelon Academic College. [Hebrew]

El Guindi, F. (2003). *Veil: Modesty, privacy and resistance.* Berg.

Elior, R. (2010). "Present but absent," "still life," and "a pretty maiden who has no eyes": On the presence and absence of women in the Hebrew language, in Jewish culture, and in Israeli life. *Studies in Spirituality, 20,* 381–455.

El-Or, T. (1994). *Educated and ignorant: Ultraorthodox Jewish women and their world.* L. Rienner.

Ettinger, Y. (2011, August 19). Yerushalaim Matsiga: Sehiya Keshera Lemehadrin (Jerusalem presents: Extra-kosher swimming). *Ha-Aretz.*

Falah, H. (2017, January 25). Glat Maslul: La-Rishona Tetsugat Ofna Le-Nashim Harediot (Strictly kosher cat-walk: A first fashion show for Haredi women). *Kol Ha-Zeman.*

Farbzner-Bashan, Y. (2016, July 21). Lihiot Yafa Bishvil Bore Olam (Becoming pretty for God). *Mako.*

Fisher-Roller, A. (1996). *In their own words: The literature of ultra-orthodox Jewish women* (master's thesis). Hebrew University of Jerusalem.

Friedman, M. (1998). Back to the grandmother: The new ultra-Orthodox women. *Israel Studies, 1,* 21–27.

Getzlick, Y. (2014). Lihiyot Modernit Be-Darka: Nashim Harediot Be-Hadrei Kosher Ba-Migzar Ha-Hilony (Their own way of being modern: Haredi women in gyms in secular neighborhoods). *Ha-Hinukh U-Sevivo, 36,* 319–335.

Goren, Y. (2013, February 7). Be-Modi'in Ilit Mitkashim Le-Hitmoded Im Ha-Shemu'ot Al Ha-Ones" (Modi'in Ilit faces up to rape allegations). *Ma'ariv.*

Grossman, A. (2004). *Pious and rebellious: Jewish women in Medieval Europe.* Brandeis University Press.

Gruzman, M. (2017, April 25). Et Kulan Sahaf Ha-Or: Hakiru Et Ha-Rabaniot Ha-Hadashot (They were all swept away by the new light: Meet the new Rebetzins). *Makor Rishon.*

Haritan, S. (2014, December 29). Mamlekhet Ha-Ipur She-Giliti Bi-Bnei Brak (The make-up kingdom I discovered in Bnei Brak). *Walla.*

Heller, S. (2011, June 3). Kakh Metzilim Nashim Harediot Me-Alimut (The way to save Haredi women from violence). *Kikar Ha-Shabat.*

Hoori, R. (2010). *No need to be afraid anymore: Ultra-orthodox women lawyers in Israel* (master's thesis). Bar Ilan University. [Hebrew]

Ifargan, S. (2015, September 2). Mibhinati Nashim Harediot She-Lo Makshivot Le-Rabanim Hen Lo Harediot (Haredi women who do not obey the rabbis are not really Haredi). *Mako.*

Katz, J. (2000). *Tradition and crisis: Jewish society at the end of the Middle Ages.* Syracuse University Press.

Kfir, M. (2017, August 17). Lifnei 25 Shana Lo Haya Shum Homer Mutam La-Tsibur Haharedi Al Herayon Ve-Leida (25 years ago there were no books on pregnancy and birth which were adapted to the Haredi reader). *Hidabroot.*

Klein, S. (2017, March 2). Ha-Nashim Ha-Harediot Ovedot Be-Hi-Tech? Netunim Shel Mehkar Megalim Et Ha-Emet (Haredi women in hi-tech? New data reveals the truth). *Haredim10.*

Krakowski, T. (2015, March 17). Head of Ultra-Orthodox Women's Party answers haters. *Forward*.

Lajos, B. (1999). *Defusei Sh'eot Ha-Penai Shel Ne'arot Ba-Zerem Ha-Hasidi Be-Israel (Leisure time patterns of Haredi Hassidic teenage girls in Israel)* (master's thesis). Bar Ilan University.

Lehmann, D., & Siebzehner, B. (2009). Power, boundaries and institutions: Marriage in ultra-Orthodox Judaism. *European Journal of Sociology, 50*(2), 273–308.

Litman, S. (2017). Rivka Schwartz Nilhemet Be-Tofa'at Ha-Pegiot Ha-Mini'ot Ba-Hevra Ha-Haredit (Rivka Schwartz fights sexual abuse in Haredi society). *Ha-Aretz*.

Lupu, J. (2003). *A shift in Haredi Society: Vocational training and academic studies*. Jerusalem: The Floresheimer Institute for Policy Studies. [Hebrew]

Malka, Y. (2011). *Ha-Rabanit Kanievsky: Toldot Hayeha* (The life of Rebbetzin Kanievsky). Bene Brak (no publisher).

Nagid-Mizrahi, Y. (2013, June 4). Al Titasku Itan: Karieristiot Harediot (Don't mess with them: Haredi career women). *Ma'ariv*.

Oleszak, A. (2011). The Beit Ya'akov school in Kraków as an encounter between east and west. *Polin, 23*, 277–290.

Peleg, Y. (2014, January 9). Sex Be-Me'a Shearim: Hatsatsa Le-Hayei Ha-Min Ba-Olam Ha-Haredi (Sex in Mea Shearim: A glimpse into sex life in Haredi society), *Mako*.

Perets, N. (2013, September 9). Kavod La-Migzar: Raheli Ganot Nivhera Le-Ahat Mi-50 Ha-Nashim Ha-Mashpi'ot Be-Israel (Respect for the Haredi society: Raheli Ganot was elected one of Israel's 50 most influential women). *Be-Hadrei Haredim*.

Rabinowitz, B. (2014, August 11). Kakh Hafkha Avigail Lorenzi Le-Me'atsevet Ofna Le-Harediot Be-Gil 20 (This is how Abigail Lorenzi became a designer of Haredi women's clothes at the age of 20). *Kikar Ha-Shabat*.

Rapoport-Albert, A. (2007). "Something for the female sex": A call for the liberation of women, and the release of the female libido from the "shackles of shame," in an anonymous Frankist manuscript from Prague c. 1800. In J. Dan (Ed.), *Gershom Sholem (1897–1982): In Memoriam* (Vol. II, pp. 77–135). Hebrew University of Jerusalem.

Ross, T. (2004). *Expanding the palace of Torah: Orthodoxy and feminism*. Brandeis University Press.

Rotem, T. (2004, November 7). Ha-Haredim Kovshim Et Ha-Mat'nas (Haredim are taking over the community center). *Ha-Aretz*.

Rotem, T. (2005, 7 April). Shitat Ha-Megerot Ovedet (The "drawers method" works). *Ha-Aretz*.

Rotem, T. (2006, July 6). Bimkom Makot Mi-Mishmerot Ha-Tzeniut" (Instead of getting beaten-up by the "Chastity brigades"). *Ha-Aretz*.

Rotem, T. (2011, November 6). Ke-She"Hasid Nasui" Pogesh Et "Meta Al Ha-Kadosh Barukh Hu" (When "married Hasid" meets "I'm crazy about God"). *Ha-Aretz*.

Rubin-Schwartz, S. (2006). *The Rabbi's wife: The Rebbetzin in American Jewish life*. New York University Press.

Scharfer, C. (2011). Sarah Schenirer, founder of the Beit Ya'akov movement: Her vision and her legacy. *Polin, 23*, 269–275.

Schneller, R. (1999). Controlled adoption of modern leisure culture: An abiding challenge to the ultra-Orthodox community in Jerusalem. In Y. Rich & M. Rosenak (Eds.), *Abiding challenges: Research perspectives on Jewish education* (pp. 303–341). Freund Publishing House.

Shilo, M. (2009). Feminism and nationalism: the case of women's suffrage in Mandatory Palestine 1917-1926. In I. Sulkunen, S. Nevala-Nurmi, & P. Markkola (Eds.), *Suffrage, gender and citizenship: International perspectives on parliamentary reforms* (pp. 357–372). Cambridge Scholars.

Shilo, M. (2013). *Ha-Ma'avakₕAl Ha-Kol: Neshot Ha-Yishuv U-Zekhut Ha-Behirah 1917-1926*. Yad Ben Zvi.

Shmuely, S. (2001, March 26). Amarti Amen Aharei Kol Maka" (I said Amen after each beating). *Yediot Acharonot*.

Shneler, R. (1978). Tsmihato Ve-Hitpathuto Shel Hinukh Ha-Banot Ba-Edah Ha-Haredit (The development of girls' education in the Edah Ha-Haredit). In G. Stern & E. Stern (Eds.), *Michtam Le-David: Sefer Zikaron Ha-Rav Oks* (pp. 321–342). Bar Ilan University Press.

Shoham, E. (2012). *A glimpse behind the walls: Violence towards women in segregated communities*. Ben Gurion University.

Shpigel, H. (2005, October 27). Nehnakh Miklat Le-Nashim Harediot Mukot (The establishment of a shelter for abused Haredi women). *Be-Hadrei Haredim*.

Steinmetz, S. (2002). *Emdotav Shel Tzibur Ha-Gevarim Ba-Migzar Ha-Haredi Kelapei Be-Ayot Ha-Alimut Shel Be'alim Neged Nashim* (Views of Haredi men on husbands using violence against their wives) (master's thesis). Hebrew University of Jerusalem. [Hebrew]

Steinmetz, S., & Haj-Yahia, M. M. (2006). Definitions of and beliefs about wife abuse among ultra-Orthodox Jewish men from Israel. *Journal of Interpersonal Violence, 21*(4), 555–565.

Tzarfati, O. (2015). Mi-Nashim Shekufot Le-Nashim Nokhehot: Ma'avakan Shel Nashim Harediot Al Yitzugan Be-Kneset Ha-20 (From transparent to present women: Haredi women's struggle for proper representation in Israel's 20th Knesset). *Migdar, 4*, 1–29.

Vinig, M. (2011). *Orthodox cinema*. Resling. [Hebrew]

Weinberger, N., Weinberger, N., & Indig, N. (2012). *Rebbetzin Kanievsky: A legendary mother to all*. Mesorah Publications.

Weissman, D. (1976). Bais Ya'acov: A historical model for Jewish feminists. In E. Koltun (Ed.), *The Jewish woman: New perspectives* (pp. 139–150). Schocken Books.

Weissman, D. (1995). Bais Ya'akov as an innovation in Jewish women's education: A contribution to the study of education and social change. *Studies in Jewish Education, 7*, 278–299.

Wodziński, M. (2013). Women and Hasidism: A "non-sectarian" perspective. *Jewish History, 27*(2-4), 399–434.

Zalcberg, S. (2005). *The world of the Hassidic women of Toldot Aharon* (doctoral dissertation). Bar Ilan University. [Hebrew]

Zalcberg, S. (2012). Gender differences in the involvement of young people in the matchmaking process in an extreme ultra-Orthodox community. *Journal of Jewish Identities, 5*(2), 27–50.

Zalcberg-Block, S. (2011). Shouldering the burden of the redemption: How the "fashion" of wearing capes developed in ultra-Orthodox society. *Nashim: A Journal of Jewish Women's Studies & Gender, 22*, 32–55.

13

Transcending Locality

From Embodied Meaning to Universal Identification in Vipassana Meditation Practice in Israel

Michal Pagis

When Daniel reached the age of 32, he started having fantasies about living in a peaceful place where there are no worries or stress. He felt that his life in Israel had become a burden. He had dreams about India, a place he never visited but nonetheless envisioned as the opposite to Israel—a place where the rhythm is slow, where everything is simple, where spirituality comes before the pursuit of money. In spite of his wife's dissatisfaction, he left his high-salary high-tech job, started practicing Yoga, and seriously considered leaving his wife and traveling to India. He was looking for a different kind of life, a peaceful life. This was the emotional state that accompanied him to his first 10-day vipassana meditation retreat in Israel. He spent those 10 days in almost complete silence, in the company of 60 other Israelis he had no previous acquaintance with, with no email or phone connection to the external world, meditating for 10 hours a day. When the retreat ended, the first thing Daniel did was call his wife and tell her: "It's OK, I don't have to travel to India. . . . I found what I was looking for."

What did Daniel find that quenched his desire to leave Israel? In this chapter, I illustrate how, in periods of search, doubt, and uncertainty, when the social world no longer supplies an anchor and meaning, the embodied meaning that is found in meditation supplies an anchor for selfhood that transcends the specific local political or economic context in which practitioners live. I argue that in the embodied experience that meditation produces, considered by practitioners as the most personal, "private" withdrawal into the self, Israeli vipassana practitioners find a bridge to a universal identification with humanity at large that transcends their specific worries, doubts, and fractures in life.

Michal Pagis, *Transcending Locality* In: *Finding Meaning*. Edited by: Ofra Mayseless and Pninit Russo-Netzer, Oxford University Press. © Oxford University Press 2022. DOI: 10.1093/oso/9780190910358.003.0013

Daniel is one of the many vipassana practitioners I met and followed while conducting fieldwork. Between 2005 and 2011, I conducted participant observation in Israeli and American meditation centers belonging to the same global meditation organization, Vipassana Meditation as Taught by S. N. Goenka. This is the largest global vipassana meditation organization, with more than a hundred meditation centers worldwide, all of which offer courses free of charge. I participated in meditation courses, volunteered in meditation centers, and observed meditation group sittings around Israel and Chicago. I spoke with practitioners in both formal and informal conversations and observed them in meditation retreats. During this period, I conducted in-depth interviews with 60 meditators, 20 in North America and 40 in Israel. In addition, I conducted three to five follow-up interviews with each of 12 Israeli practitioners and interviewed their family members as well.

The search for meaning on which this chapter focuses is a search for self-identity. From a sociological perspective, the self is a reflexive process through which one gives meaning and signification to himself as an object (Mead, 1934). This process offers answers and anchors to the question "Who I am?," answers that take the form of identities (Glaeser, 2000). Following recent advances in theories of identity, I understand identity as emerging in specific moments of identification that provoke awareness of the self (Glaeser, 2000; Pagis, 2016; Tavory, 2010). However, the notion of moments of identification does not imply an inherent fluidity of identities. To the contrary, these moments of identification can grant stability and coherence to the images we carry of ourselves.

In this chapter, I illustrate that vipassana meditation offers practitioners new moments of bodily based identifications and thus influences their perceptions of self and identifications with others. I illustrate how the practice shifts the experience of the self from being anchored in local social relations and roles to being anchored in embodied experience. I suggest that this experience, produced by what practitioners perceive as the "universal body," offers a bridge to identification with universal-global society at large.

I first review the popularization of Buddhist meditation practice in the world and, within this phenomenon, the specific Israeli attraction to Buddhist thought and practice. I then enter the specific fieldwork I conducted among practitioners of vipassana meditation as taught by S. N. Goenka. After introducing the search for self that brings people to meditation, I illustrate the double, mutually supportive processes of withdrawal inward and universal identification that take place in meditation practice and how practitioners perceive and interpret these processes as connected to shifts in self-identity.

The Popularization of Buddhist Meditations: Israel and Beyond

Vipassana meditation is a part of the tradition of Theravada Buddhism, the predominant form of Buddhism in Southeast Asia. Until the 20th century, this meditation was practiced mainly by monks as a way toward enlightenment. In the Theravada tradition, enlightenment is anchored in the realization that the self is not a permanent entity but an impersonal, substanceless, ever-changing phenomenon of mind and matter. To realize this nature of the self, the monk was required to detach from all his bondages in life, live a renounced life, and become mindful of his body and mind in the present, moment after moment, realizing the impermanent and impersonal nature of thoughts and sensations.

Before the end of the 19th century, the spaces we know today as "Buddhist meditation centers" did not exist, either in Buddhist or non-Buddhist locations (Gombrich, 1983). In Buddhist locations, one could learn to practice meditation if one went to the monastery. However, it was quite uncommon for lay people—those not ordained as monks—to practice meditation seriously. Even in Thailand or Burma, where there is a long history of temporary ordination of boys for a short period, meditation practice was not common.

From the beginning of the 20th century, we witness a transformation in the practice of Buddhism in general and with it the practice of vipassana meditation. This transformation can be tracked back, in different Theravada countries, to around the same time: the British occupation of Burma in 1885, the opening of the Southeast Asia to the "West," the modernization and urbanization of Southeast Asia, and the entrance of Western tourists who showed interest in Buddhism and meditation practice (Gombrich, 1988; Gombrich & Obeyesekere, 1988; Jordt, 2007). Following British colonial rule, with the translation of Pali texts into English and local languages and rising percentages of literacy, the urbanized middle class gained direct access to Buddhist doctrine and meditation. This led to a decline in the classical distinction between monks and laity: laity no longer only supported the monk toward his enlightenment through giving donations; they could now practice directly toward their own enlightenment.

This process was pushed by different evangelic Buddhist movements that propagated meditation to the laity (Jordt, 2007). Vipassana meditation was no longer seen as a pure monastic practice. While traditional Buddhist monks claimed that vipassana should only be learned after years of practicing concentration meditations (referred to as *Samadhi*), the new movements of meditation claimed that one could start directly with vipassana. Since vipassana is oriented toward enlightenment, but at the same time offers common "daily benefits" such as reducing anxiety and increasing feelings of inner peace, it easily gained popularity among the urban and intellectual strata (Gombrich & Obeyesekere, 1988, p. 237; Spiro, 1970, p. 273).

While the first interest in the practice of meditation was limited to counterculture groups, this is no longer the case. In the contemporary world, meditation practice at large, vipassana included, is propagated to business people, doctoral students, and the educated strata in general (Fronsdal, 1998; Heelas, 2008). Meditation became a way to calm oneself, improve health, improve relations, increase self-awareness, or regain emotional balance. Though the ultimate goal of meditation—enlightenment—had never been forgotten, the majority of people who practice meditation today have little interest in enlightenment. Meditation has been turned into a modern self-reflexive tool, a part of the modern culture of the self (Kucinskas 2018; Pagis 2019).

The interest in meditation practice is evident in Israel. In the past 20 years, we are witnessing a growing interest in Israel in different practices and traditions that connect body and mind. This includes, among others, alternative medicine, Yoga, alternative healing, Eastern marshal arts, and a variety of Buddhist-based meditation practices (Feraro & Lewis, 2016; Simhai & Tavory, 2007; Werczberger & Huss, 2014). This flourishing scene attracts mainly Israelis who identify themselves as Jewish-secular, though similar attraction was recently noted also in more religious Jewish groups (Klin-Oron & Ruah-Midbar, 2010; Persico, 2014a). In this spectrum of alternative body-mind practices, vipassana meditation, also known as *insight meditation*, gained popularity. "Vipassana," "insight," and "mindfulness" all refer to the same Buddhist practice: the open nonjudgmental awareness of body and mind phenomenon.

The contemporary practice of Buddhist-based meditations in Israel has many variations, starting from 10-day silent meditation retreats and ending in mindfulness meditation practice in hospitals and psychological clinics. In some teaching traditions, we find more emphasis on Buddhism or Dharma (the teachings of the Buddha), while others uprooted the practice from its Buddhist context. Some manifestations also include hybrid combinations of Jewish meditation practice, similar to the hybrid combinations found in the United States (Sigalow, 2019). Out of this variety, this chapter focuses on vipassana meditation as taught by S. N. Goenka, a teaching school that offers relatively long 10-day meditation courses. This teaching school holds mediation centers around the world and has gained popularity in the Israeli meditation scene.

Arrivals to Vipassana: Self-identity and Meaning

To understand the kind of "meaning" for which meditation practitioners search, we need to understand the reasons that people provide when asked why they began to meditate. For many of my informants, life before meditation was characterized by a blockage, a loss of place in the world, or a search for an answer to the question, "What is next?" The kind of meaning they were searching for was not mystical or religious but connected to "this-worldly" difficulties and concerns.

One common theme that arose in the interviews was a rupture or transition in life. I met people who were motivated to meditate after going through divorce, separations, or the death of a family member. Others, like Daniel who we met in the opening of the chapter, were feeling estranged with their work, searching for a new venue in life. Young adults after military service or after completing their bachelor's degrees were also asking questions about the next station in their life, experiencing uncertainty regarding their position in the "adult" world.

Another common theme that drove people to vipassana was long-standing unhappiness with one's emotional state. I met people who suffered from depression, anxiety, obsessive thoughts, or stress. These emotional states were frequently accompanied by doubts regarding the meaning of life and with dissatisfaction with one's self-identity. The third description I encountered portrayed a period of self-exploration for frames of meaning that included alternative forms of spirituality. Here, people explicitly said that they were "searching" for something—be it meaning, direction, or an otherworldly experience—that would ground or center their life.

These motivations were not static and changed over time. As one of my informants told me, "Right now, I am too happy to meditate. But when things get tough, I know I can always go back." For example, Doron, a 33-year-old engineer, first encountered vipassana when traveling in India as a young adult, during a period of his life characterized by uncertainty after he completed his bachelor's degree and was wondering what to do next. In India, he participated in two vipassana retreats, and he later participated in another retreat in Israel. He then got married, had three children, and completely stopped meditating. His divorce led him back to meditation practice. Finding himself again in period of rupture, this time also accompanied by a mild feeling of depression, he thought that meditation could help him to find the center and heal the rupture.

The narratives offered by practitioners reveal that meditation is not a mere hobby or a simple technique for relaxation. For all of them, meditation represented a possible solution to the fractures and blockages they experienced. I suggest that these fractures led them to search for something different, a space outside of their local identities and social roles. In what follows, I demonstrate how vipassana came to represent such a space, and I examine what kind of self-identity it offers practitioners.

Against Particularism: Distancing from Local and Religious Connotations

An important channel through which I realized the desire to gain distance from local identifications was silence. When I began my ethnographic research among practitioners of vipassana meditation in Israel and the United States, I was expecting to uncover the unique "Israeli" elements of meditation practice. I was searching for the Israeli identity in Buddhist meditation, for the hybrid combinations that are produced when Buddhism and Israeli culture meet. I was thus surprised, and even disappointed, to find that the interviews with Israeli practitioners were almost completely silent regarding Israeli political and social context. In fact, interviews conducted with Israelis were extremely similar to those I had with American practitioners. Remove the identifying information and some of the background, and it became difficult to recognize if a particular interview transcription belongs to an Israeli or American. In contrast to what I was expecting, Israelis hardly mentioned politics, the security situation, or the Arab–Jewish conflict. In many ways, their stories were decontextualized from larger macro processes that take place in Israel.

It took me a while to realize that this silence about Israeli social and cultural context is in fact important data. This silence is both an experience and an ideology, as it becomes in itself a way of distancing certain identifications and cultivating new ones. For Israeli practitioners, meditation is both about turning inward into the self and about finding universal connections to all human beings. When doing so, they negate the local, group, ethnic identifications that are a part of their everyday social life.

For many Israelis, the encounter with Buddhist-based meditations was connected to an actual physical escape from the local when traveling away from Israel, frequently to India. In the past 20 years, India has become a major tourist attraction for young adult Israelis. The rise of India as a tourist attraction is anchored in the unique life-course of young Jewish Israelis. At the age of 18, most Jewish citizens, men and women, are required to serve in the army for a period of 2–4 years. This obligatory military service produces a break between graduation from high school and the start of higher education, a break that does not exist in other developed countries. Due to this obligatory service, the stage to which David Brooks (2007) gave the name the "Odyssey years," the stage between adolescence and the starting of a work career, is prolonged. After leaving the army, at the age of 21 or 22, contemporary young Israelis do not rush to begin their life-long careers or even to begin college. Instead, in the past 30 years, a growing number of released soldiers have decided to work for a year and then embark on a backpacking trip to an exotic and developing country. This backpacking trip has become a common ritual of passage from the stressful period of military service to the free life of adulthood (Noy, 2004). The most popular destination for this trip is South-East Asia, specifically India and Nepal, where the cost of living is very low. In the past 10 years, especially since the local financial crisis in Israel in 2002 and the following global financial crisis in 2008, it is also common to see Israelis who have lost their high-tech jobs taking a second backpacking trip at around the age of 30.

As illustrated in Daniel's story which opened this chapter, for Israelis, India represents the opposite of Israel. In India, they become familiar with yoga workshops and meditation courses. Even though India is not Buddhist, it has become a center for Buddhist meditation retreats, vipassana included. It has become popular for Israelis travelers to join a 10-day silent vipassana retreat in India as part of their tourist adventure.

It is important to note that while vipassana certainly symbolizes the "East," this "East" is represented as an eternal universal wisdom, with every attempt made to distance it from any particular local religion (Loss, 2010). Take, for example, the way vipassana is described in the website of "vipassana meditation as taught by S. N. Goenka": "Vipassana, which means to see things as they really are, is one of India's most ancient techniques of meditation. It was taught in India more than 2,500 years ago as a universal remedy for universal ills, i.e., an Art of Living." While India is mentioned in this presentation, there is no reference to Buddhism or to the recent history of the revival of vipassana practice in South-East Asia. From this description, vipassana emerged in a mystical past 2,500 years ago and is now practiced as a universal remedy for universal ills.

This denial of the particular past of meditation practice is not unique to Israel. Previous studies on the rise of spirituality have noted that the importation of different practices from the "East" is accompanied by a process of forgetting these practices' historical biography or their previous particularism (Bender, 2010). Thus, the travel of Eastern practices to Israel can be seen as a part of the more global popularization of these practice, turning previously religious self-exploration techniques into semi-therapeutic techniques that are labeled as "universal" and frequently also "scientific."

The stance against particularism was also revealed in the deliberate denial of any connection between vipassana and religion. For my informants, religion signified specific social groups and identities. I found that, in the meeting between Jewish practitioners and a Buddhist practice, both religious localities are negated. Teachers and practitioners I interviewed stressed that vipassana has no connection to religious belief or religious community. Informants frequently said that this is what they liked about meditation— that it does not require some kind of conversion to or belief in a particular cosmology. In fact, the number of atheists I spoke to who practiced meditation in Israel was quite high.

Such understanding of vipassana as nonreligious practice is connected to what I have called elsewhere the "scientization" of meditation (Pagis, 2019). The spread of Buddhist meditations in the West was legitimized by the scientific community and is supported by a large number of scientific publications on the positive effects of meditation. The main advocators of meditation practice in the West are not religious authorities and gurus but psychiatrists, neuroscientists, and psychologists. Moreover, in Israel, the stance that meditation has nothing to do with religion is most likely intensified due to the suspicion and antagonism that secular Jews in Israel hold against religious orthodoxy in light of the Orthodox monopoly over state institutions. Unlike in the United States, where religious pluralism is the norm, when Israel was established it produced a "church-like" religious authority (Rabbinate) that is a part of the state apparatus. This move gave birth to what one scholar describes as a "politicized, institutionalized Jewish religion" that is unique to Israel as a Jewish state (Levy, 2011, p. 94). Historical circumstances, connected to what people in Israel call "the status quo," granted full authority over state religious services and institutions to Orthodox Judaism. Since more than half of Jewish Israelis do not identify themselves with Orthodoxy, Israeli society is characterized by a religious-secular conflict (Cohen & Susser, 2000; Sasson et al., 2010). Among those who identify as secular, this conflict is manifested in suspicion of and antagonism against religious institutions and representatives at large.

Take for example Roi, a doctoral student who considered himself a "rational" thinker.

> I am a very skeptical person, and very rational. I never thought of myself as spiritual or mystical. I always look around through a skeptic lens, or maybe not skeptic, but realist. I remember the feeling that vipassana was very different from anything else I touched before—of Judaism or other religions, or every Buddhism. . . . A feeling that I agree, that I cannot find something that does not work out. . . . If in the written instructions, or the opening talk, or the result-oriented approach of the teachers. It was all very minimalist. And I come from a minimalist world, so, it all felt fitting to me personally.

What Roi names as "minimalism" and "result-oriented" is in fact an outcome of the denial of particularism described earlier. Since meditation is introduced as a universal practice that has little to do with belief, skeptics such as Roi can connect to it more easily. In fact, some practitioners specifically stressed that "I never connected to this *Rochnik* [dismissive slang for spiritual] stuff," using the word "Rochnik" in order to distance themselves from the popularity of New Age in Israel and categorize meditation as a "rational" nonspiritual practice. In addition, vipassana teachers I spoke to reported that the Israeli students are very skeptical and ask a lot of questions when compared to students from other places in the world. It seems that skepticism and an antireligious stance characterize those who are attracted to vipassana meditation in Israel. For Israelis, meditation is a universal, global, nonmystical practice.

The Meditation Center as a Space Without a Place

A common distinction in sociological research is between place and space. *Place* is the unique, local configuration of a space. In contrast, "space is what place becomes when the unique gathering of things, meanings, and values are sucked out" (Gieryn, 2000, p. 465). When people move into a space, such as an apartment, or office, they produce "placements," filling the space with their own unique identifications (Glaeser, 2000). Modern global spaces, such as airports and shopping malls, are "without a place" (Sorkin, 1992); that is, they are spaces that are not endowed with local or personal meaning.

The unique configuration of vipassana meditation centers manifest such spaces without a place. Even though each center is built in a specific geographical location in a specific country, and even though the teachings in these centers are based on a specific local cultural ideas (i.e., Buddhism), the centers are purposefully emptied out from any unique, local meaning and values.

Entering a vipassana center in Israel is like entering any other vipassana center in the United States or Europe. All vipassana centers include a meditation hall, a kitchen, dining hall, and dorms. The meditation halls I visited in both Israel and the United States were painted white—there were no symbols, pictures, or any "Eastern" or Buddhist symbols. The rooms were also plain, with no pictures or symbols on the walls. There were no sculptures or pictures of the Buddha. The meditation teachers arrived from all around the world, and I met Chinese, Indian, American, and European teachers. Thus, the meditation centers radiated nonparticularism in an attempt to produce a universal standardized mold.

Except for the translation of meditation instructions into Hebrew (which follows the English instructions), when participating in a retreat in Israel I could easily forget if I were sitting for meditation in Israel or in North America. The meditation instructions were identical around the world and were all based on video and audio recordings of the head teacher, S. N. Goenka. This non-Israeli experience was intensified by the fact that, in most of the retreats I observed in Israel, the meditation teachers were not Israeli and thus spoke in English. While some Israeli Buddhist groups have incorporated some local characteristics, such as lightening candles on Friday evening, the vipassana group I studied deliberately rejected any such adaptations. It is thus relatively extreme in its stance against any adaptation to locality, seeing vipassana as a global practice.

Moreover, the structure of meditation retreats invite and encourage people to leave their local identities and social roles "outside." The retreats, usually of 10 days, are conducted in complete silent, discouraging conversations about external social roles of identification (i.e., work, family, politics, etc.). During the retreat participants are asked to refrain from any connection to the outside world, including phones, newspapers, television, or internet. They are completely disconnected from their external lives.

In the words of the anthropologist Victor Turner (1974), the retreat is a *lominoid space*, outside of social structure. It becomes a space of refuge from "who I am" in the daily world. And indeed, when talking about meditation retreats people expressed such tropes. They said that they are going to the meditation center in order to "take a break," "time out," to "take something for relaxation," or "charge the batteries." Such expressions point to an experience that is not a part of daily life. Without actually leaving the country, vipassana practitioners enter a non-place experience, one that leaves behind their local social world.

Distancing from Biographical and Social Identities

Alongside entering a space that is devoid of local identifications, the practitioners train in the reflexive practice of vipassana, a practice that is based on creating a distance, or detachment, from one's particular biographical social story. In the teaching school reviewed in this chapter, this is done through nonjudgmental observation of bodily sensations. The participants are asked to sit, close their eyes, and focus on their breath going in and out, and then on sensations in different parts of the body. The observation of sensations takes place with minimal movement, trying to achieve equanimity toward emotions, sensations, and thoughts.

I suggest that since much of our thoughts and emotions are connected to our position in the world as persons, and to our social relations, practicing vipassana means bracketing the causes and narratives that make up our identities in the social world.

To exemplify this I want to offer an ethnographic vignette taken from participant observation in a meditation course in which I volunteered as a course assistant. This is the story of Tanya, a 55-year-old women, a former immigrant from Russia. Tanya arrived in Israel with her two daughters while her larger family stayed in Russia. Her Hebrew was not good, and she did not make new friends. She arrived at the meditation course after her daughters left the house to pursue their own lives, leaving her extremely lonely and depressed. At this moment of rupture in her life, she was searching for a new anchor for her life.

Tanya found herself in tears quite often during this meditation retreat. After one night in which she could not stop crying, she was invited to speak with the teacher. As a course assistant, I accompanied her. We entered the empty meditation hall. The teacher was sitting on his small podium and Tanya was sitting on the floor in front of him. Since the teacher did not speak Hebrew, I sat next to Tanya and translated from English to Hebrew and back. Sitting there, I was sure that Tanya was going to explain why she was so sad, tell her biographical narrative. But to my surprise that did not happen. The teacher asked her how she was doing, and she said, "Not so good, I cannot stop crying." He smiled at her kindly and told her, "It is OK to cry. If you cry, cry, but cry like a vipassana meditator—feel the sensations. Tears come down, watch them. A tear is coming down, and another tear is coming down. . . . When a storm comes, do not let it overpower you."

When I later looked at my notes on Tanya's conversation with the teacher, I realized that the teacher strictly avoided encouraging her to tell her story. He was not interested in her biographical past, in the macro social circumstances that surround her life. Like many other immigrants to Israel who arrived from Russia, Tanya was lonely. Her Hebrew was poor, her children had moved away from the house, she had no supporting community. All these were considered by the teacher as unnecessary context. Instead of searching for the cause of her emotion, he encouraged her to concentrate completely on the physical aspect of her emotion. Her life story was irrelevant to the self-awareness mode practiced in meditation, a mode I named elsewhere "embodied self-reflexivity" (Pagis, 2009).

Practitioners in meditation retreats find that the concentration on sensations provides an internal space that stays away from their hectic life and identities. In the following quote, Avi describes how the outside social role of work penetrated the meditation retreat and how he used vipassana to bracket or stay away from it.

I found out that if I observe sensations time flies. If I observe sensations and don't think on what awaits at home, on all the things I want or need to do, the future that awaits me with my new job. If I don't think about it time goes faster and it is easier. And when I do think about it I get sad and sometimes cry. So when that happened I tried to observe my tears and that calmed me down again.

This example is one of many in which vipassana practitioners use concentration on the corporal body to "calm down" or, as in Tanya's story, confront the "storm." Such confrontation is not merely an inner psychological process but includes an important social dimension—it is based on reducing identification with the person I am in the world. Yoav, an Israeli BA student, put it aptly when he remarked that meditation is a time in which "I don't have the need to be in a form. Just to sit and breath and find a whole world in it." The use of the notion "form" alludes to the social self in everyday life—the social roles that are a part of who we are in the world. Of course, in meditation, Yoav is actually in a form—that of a meditator, sitting with his legs crossed and his back straight, without moving. Yet, for Yoav and other practitioners, the form of a meditator represents a place outside of structured social identities.

Connection to Humanity at Large

Even though the main practice of vipassana is based on an extreme turn inward, it still entails a connection with others. However, as part of the dislocalization of the practice, the others with whom one connects are not friends and family. The others represent a general human category, unidentified others, again, others who do not carry specific identities and social roles.

This connection to others begins in meditation retreats. Meditation retreats offer a unique form of what Schutz (1967) named "we-relationship." In the meditation retreat we find a silent community that is different from normative social structure. Participants in meditation retreats do not know each other by name, occupation, or family status. They sit in close proximity to silent strangers. And yet they share with these strangers the joint effort of looking inward. They synchronize with others in silence as 60 bodies sit still together. In the meditation center people feel the influence of others, often stating that others help them to meditate and that collective meditation sittings are stronger when compared to solitary ones (Pagis, 2010).

This unique form of togetherness leads to feelings of gratitude and kindness to others who share the meditation retreat. Take, for example, Aaron's description of an experience he had close to the end of a difficult meditation session: "I felt a feeling I never felt in my life, a feeling of deep peace . . . a feeling of kindness to everyone in the retreat." These others toward whom he felt kindness are non-familiar others. This is a group of strangers united by the mere fact that they support one another in the attempt to turn inward, away from everyday life, each to his or her own sensations.

The connection to others just described is encouraged by the teachings in vipassana courses, specifically through the practice of "metta" meditation, also named "loving kindness" or "compassion." Like vipassana, the practice of metta is also based on bodily observation. Students are asked to concentrate on the subtle sensations of flow in any part of their bodies (the ends of the hands and the head are usually the common parts to feel these subtle sensations). While concentrating on these sensations, they should feel positive feelings toward themselves and others. The words that the teacher repeats are: "May I be free, free of all the anger, ill-will, hatred, animosity. May I generate love and goodwill, peace and harmony. May all people be liberated, may all people share my love, peace and harmony. . . ." In the actual practice of metta meditation, practitioners do not repeat these words, but these words are an important part of the meditation training since they orient the meditators toward the required attitude.

Metta is an interesting kind of emotional state, one oriented toward all living creatures, enemies and friends. This kind of love, titled by the sociologist Max Weber (1946) "brotherly love" is also referred to as "world-denying love" since "as opposed to worldly love, which is always love for particular persons, [this] is love for all, without distinction—love for whoever comes, friends, strangers, enemies" (Bellah, 1999, p. 277). Indeed, practitioners referred to a feeling of being united with others, bracketing judgments and categorizations. For example, Noam, an Israeli professor who practices vipassana, said, "For me metta is a way to see things as they are, without judgments. When you see others as they are, not as good or bad, not as us versus them, you accept people as they are, that leads to compassion."

An important channel through which practitioners, especially the more serious ones, express this feeling of compassion is through volunteering in the meditation center. Such volunteering is titled "serving." Again, such serving is oriented toward a group of strangers and is supposed to be "blind" to any social categorizations and judgments; as one practitioner told me, "When I serve in the meditation center, I serve everyone equally, and that helps me to open up to all kind of people." Another practitioner added, "When I volunteer I encounter so many people, in all sizes and shapes, and they all want the same thing, to be free of suffering. There is something deeply universal in this search."

Shifts in Identifications: From the Internal to the Universal

In the previous sections I illustrated how meditation retreat and practice offer a zone outside of daily social roles, relations, and identities. I would like now to illustrate how practitioners of meditation take the practice into their life and use it in order to shift their identifications. When vipassana practitioners spoke about their practice, they did not think of it as a mere hobby or vacation. From their perspective, vipassana had an impact on who they are. Their narratives were narratives of self-transformation, and many of them used before and after narratives: as Oren said "I am a completely different person now, there is the before vipassana Oren and after vipassana."

In their reflections about their self-identities, two themes were found. The first is vipassana as offering an embodied anchor for selfhood that substitutes the social self. The second is identification with humanity at large. Vipassana thus includes a double shift, one to the most private micro, the other to the most universal macro.

I open with the shift to anchoring the self in the body. More than a few times I heard the phrase "in vipassana I found myself." Others said that vipassana helps them feel grounded in the body, or, as one meditator stated "the body is with me like it has never been before." Instead of "I think therefore I am" meditators shifted to "I feel therefore I am."

This shift to the body as an anchor for selfhood is experienced as liberating and relaxing, as the body transcends all social situations, remaining a stable source of self as we move from one situation to another (Katz, 1999; Pagis, 2019). In interviews with informants I found that practitioners of vipassana take the embodied mode of reflexivity into their life and use it to gain a distance from the worries and difficulties of local social life and identities. Like Tanya, who was advised to observe the sensations of sadness instead of narrating her life biography, so do other practitioners use meditation to stay away from the tensions, sadness, or anxiety related to their social roles and relations.

Yoel, an organization advisor, explained his meditation in the following words: "I am constantly outside, in work and with people, and I need the space to move inward or I lose myself." Yael, a teacher, said it helps her to create a distance from her emotionally draining work: "Vipassana helps me to make a separation" she said, "that there is me, and then there is Ron or Beni [her students]." Udi, a doctoral student, said that without vipassana his life would be "enslaved . . . I would become addicted to competition, to aspiration . . . to all that nonsense." Likewise, Rachel used vipassana as a way "find her center" after a romantic separation, Dina sees it as helping her coping with an unsatisfying marriage, and David found it helpful to "return to himself" after family conflicts.

The kind of self that meditators found in vipassana is not their social self, in the sense of their role and position in the social world. Through the attempt to empty the unique and personal biography, to take a pause from "being in a form," they find a self that is not contingent or dependent on social context. This was revealed in numerous examples in the interviews. As Yoni, another graduate student, described it: "Before [vipassana], I was always worried about how others see me. I tried to be someone that I was not. I wanted to impress people. I used to hide how I feel. Now I am more real . . . ." Or, as Ron said, "There is this great relief. Relief from the worries of what others think of you. I just care less. And it comes with this tremendous feeling of freedom, of liberation from something that used to haunt me."

The second theme that appeared in the interviews in regard to self-identities is identification with humanity at large. While practitioners did not say explicitly that they are citizens of the world, they spoke of moments of identifications with all others, of connecting to people when naked from their "social clothes" of collective identities. As Dana said: "There is something very fundamental in the realization that everyone suffers. It connects people. And with this comes compassion. For everyone." They spoke about the fact that everyone shares a body and that this body leads to the same shared experiences; as Shai said, "you sit in meditation and you have all this pain, but you are not alone, everyone has pain, it is a part of life." In such examples, practitioners refer in a nonexplicit way to the Buddhist tenet of suffering (*dukkha*), which in Buddhist thought represents the constant state of all living creatures who are not enlightened. Even though this is a particular cultural Buddhist trope, the practitioners I spoke to rarely mentioned its connection to Buddhism, thus ignoring its original cultural and historical emergence.

Many practitioners spoke of feeling closer to other human beings—not specifically to their partners, families, or ethnic or national group. They spoke of universal love, for people at large, to all nonidentified others. They used expressions such as "heart-opening" or "falling in love with everyone." Some even stressed that previously their approach to people was dislike and now "I like people, even in the supermarket, I can see their suffering." As Tanya told me. "The meditation helps me. I am a different person. I love people now. I feel I have so much strength in my hands, I want to help people."

Some also spoke of a feeling of "oneness" as, for example, expressed by Yuval: "I find comfort in an experience that I sometimes reach in meditation that I am not separated, that I am a part of a whole, I get to a feeling of oneness with everyone." Sharon offered a likewise perception when saying "we are all the same, everyone in the world is searching for the same thing." Such expressions illustrate that vipassana represents a space outside of local form and identity, a space through which people tap into what they believe is a universal human condition without actually leaving their local dwelling.

Discussion

I opened this chapter by asking what is it in vipassana practice that quenched the desire to escape the stressful life in Israel. Our tour through the stories and experiences of Israeli vipassana practitioners illustrates how, in moments of fractures and blockages, vipassana offers an alternative source for self-identity, one that reduces the importance of local and personal identities while at the same time creating a bridge to a universal conception of humanity. Through the presentation of vipassana as a universal global practice stripped from any particular local or religious connotations, through the unique configuration of the meditation center as a space without a place, through the turn of attention inward while detaching from collective identifications and biographical narratives, and through a cultivation of compassion for humanity at large, Israeli practitioners find an anchor for selfhood that is not based on local social context.

The growing Israeli interest in spiritual and mind-body practices is frequently interpreted as part of the departure of Israeli culture from collectivism and a move toward individualization (Persico, 2014b; Tavory &

Goodman, 2009). Indeed, practices of inward looking, such as meditation practice, are focused on the self, pushing the social and political world to the background. However, as sociologists have pointed, individualization is not necessary an asocial process that merely rejects collective identities (Pagis, 2016). While the focus on the individual may indeed break or reduce local identifications, at the same time it creates a channel to connect to universal, cosmopolitan identities that are based on beliefs regarding universal humanity (Levitt, 2007; Pagis, Cadge, & Tal, 2018).

The focus on feeling the body while trying to keep a nonjudgmental, detached mode of attention offers a bridge to universal views regarding the human condition which unites all living creatures, thus enabling identification with people who might hold very different religious and political views. This is what makes vipassana both a very private and intimate experience and, at the same time, an experience of oneness with all others. I suggest the turn to the body provides a way to create universal identifications in a highly divided and multicultural society, a very intimate and private experience that can connect the practitioner to universal brotherhood, jumping over the specific national, political, religious, professional, or familial identities that divide practitioners. When people meditate together they do not hold the same political or religious views. They do not hold the same beliefs. They may have different motivations for why they meditate. But they all breath in and out the same air in the same meditation hall, they all feel pain in the uncomfortable positions. By zooming into the body they encounter the universal human condition that can easily be attached to what Weber named brotherly love, a universal compassion toward all others.

The people I met were not "cosmopolitans" in the usual sense of the word. They did not hold dual nationalities, they did not live outside of their home countries, and they did not have a diverse global social network. They lived a "normal" local social life. They had a job, a family, many had romantic partners and children. The Israelis I met served in the army, read the news, some were politically active. They were a part of the local, particular Israeli context. Yet, even though vipassana is practiced by local people, for its Israeli practitioners, it carries a bridge to universal identification. It provided a world which they interpreted as devoid of particularism and locality, a world distanced from personal biography and social context, a world in which they can connect to humanity at large, bracketing categorizations and judgments. In this sense, the practice of meditation produces a bridge to a nonlocal existence, one that transcends their hectic local life in Israel.

Highlights

- Vipassana meditation is a previously Buddhist monastic practice turned into a popular embodied self-reflexive modern technique.
- Israelis arrive to vipassana in periods of biographical rupture, loss of self-identity, and search for life meaning.
- The practice is perceived by Israelis as disembedded from particular social and cultural contexts, as manifested both in the discursive representations of vipassana and in the unique non-place configuration of the meditation center.
- The meditative reflexive mode entails a shift away from local roles and social identities while focusing exclusively on the body.
- In the collective atmosphere of the meditation center, and in the practice of loving-kindness, practitioners experience connection to nonidentified others.
- Practitioners report two mutually supportive shifts in self-identity: anchoring the self in the embodied realm and identification with humanity at large.
- The focus on the universal body produces a bridge to a nonlocal existence, one that transcends the hectic local life in Israel.

References

Bellah, R. N. (1999). Max Weber and world-denying love: A look at the historical sociology of religion. *Journal of the American Academy of Religion, 67*(2), 277–304.

Bender, C. (2010). *The new metaphysicals: Spirituality and the American religious imagination.* University of Chicago Press.

Brooks, D. (2007). The odyssey years. *The New York Times*, October 9.

Cohen, Asher, and Bernard Susser. (2010). "Reform Judaism in Israel: The Anatomy of Weakness." *Modern Judaism* 30 (1), 23–45.

Feraro, S., & Lewis, J. R. (Eds.). (2016). *Contemporary alternative spiritualities in Israel.* Springer.

Fronsdal, G. (1998). Insight meditation in the United States: Life, liberty and the pursuit of happiness. In C. S. Prebish & K. Kenneth (Eds.), *The faces of Buddhism in America* (pp. 163–182). University of California Press.

Gieryn, T. F. (2000). A space for place in sociology. *Annual Review of Sociology, 26,* 463–496.

Glaeser, A. (2000). *Divided in unity: Identity, Germany, and the Berlin police.* University of Chicago Press.

Gombrich, R. (1983). From monastery to meditation center: Lay meditation in contemporary Sri Lanka. In P. Denwood & A. Piatigorsky (Eds.), *Buddhist studies ancient and modern* (pp. 20–34). Curzon Press.

Gombrich, R. (1988). *Theravada Buddhism: A social history from ancient Benares to modern Colombo*. Routledge & Kegan Paul.

Gombrich, R., & Obeyesekere, G. (1988). *Buddhism transformed: Religious change in Sri Lanka*. Princeton University Press.

Heelas, P. (2008). *Spiritualities of life: New Age, romanticism and consumptive capitalism*. Blackwell.

Jackson, P. A. (2003). *Buddhadasa, Theravada Buddhism, and modernist reform in Thailand*. Silkworm Books.

Jordt, I. (2007). *Burma's mass lay meditation movement: Buddhism and the cultural construction of power*. Ohio University Press.

Katz, J. (1999). *How emotions work*. University of Chicago Press.

Klin-Oron, A., & Ruah-Midbar, M. (2010). Secular by the letter, religious by the spirit: The attitudes of the Israeli new age to Jewish law. *Israeli Sociology, 12*(1), 57–80. [Hebrew]

Kucinskas, J. (2018). *The mindful elite: mobilizing from the inside out*. Oxford University Press.

Levitt, P. (2007). *God needs no passport: Immigrants and the changing religious landscape*. The New Press.

Levy, G. (2011). "Secularism, Religion and The Status Quo." In J. Barbalet, A. Possamai and B. S. Turner (Eds.), *Religion and the State: A Comparative Sociology* (pp. 93–121). London: Anthem Press.

Loss, J. (2010). "Buddha-Dhamma in Israel: Explicit non-religious and implicit non-secular localization of religion." Nova Religio 13.4: 84–105.

Mead, G. H. (1934). *Mind, self, and society: From the standpoint of a social behaviorist*. Chicago: The University of Chicago press.

Noy, C. (2004). This trip really changed me: Backpackers' narratives of self-change. *Annals of Tourism Research, 31*(1), 78–102.

Pagis, M. (2009). Embodied self-reflexivity. *Social Psychology Quarterly, 72*, 265–283.

Pagis, M. (2010). Producing intersubjectivity in silence: An ethnography of meditation practices. *Ethnography, 11*, 309–328.

Pagis, M. (2016). Fashioning futures: Life-coaching and the self-made identity paradox. *Sociological Forum, 31*(4), 1083–1103.

Pagis, M. (2019). *Inward: Vipassana meditation and the embodiment of the self*. University of Chicago Press.

Pagis, M., Cadge, W., & Tal, O. (2018). *Translating spirituality: Universalism and particularism in the diffusion of spiritual care from the United States to Israel*. Sociological Forum, 33(3), 596–618.

Persico, T. (2014a). Hitbodedut for a new age: Adaptation of practices among the followers of Rabbi Nachman of Bratslav. *Israel Studies Review, 29*(2), 99–117.

Persico, T. (2014b). Neo-Hasidism & Neo-Kabbalah in Israeli contemporary spirituality: The rise of the utilitarian self. *Alternative Spirituality and Religion Review, 5*(1), 31–54.

Sasson, Theodore, E. Tabory, and D. Selinger-Abutbul. (2010). "Framing Religious Conflict: Popular Israeli Discourse on Religion and State." *Journal of Church and State,* 52(4), 662–685.

Schutz, A. (1967). *The phenomenology of the social world*. Northwestern University Press.

Sigalow, E. (2019). *American JUBU: Jews, Buddhists, and religious change in the United States.* Princeton University Press.

Simhai, D., & Tavory, I. (Eds.). (2007). *Dancing in a thorn field: The new age spirituality in Israel.* Hakibbutz Hameuchad.

Sorkin, M. (1992). *Variations on a theme park: The new American city and the end of public space.* Macmillan.

Spiro, M. E. (1970). *Buddhism and society: The great tradition and its Burmese vicissitudes.* Harper & Row.

Tavory, I. (2010). Of yarmulkes and categories: Delegating boundaries and the phenomenology of interactional expectation. *Theory and Society, 39*(1), 49–68.

Tavory, I., & Goodman, Y. C. (2009). "A collective of individuals": Between self and solidarity in a rainbow gathering. *Sociology of Religion, 70*(3), 262–284.

Turner, V. (1974). Liminal to liminoid, in play, flow, and ritual: An essay in comparative symbology. *Rice Institute Pamphlet-Rice University Studies, 60*(3), 43–92.

Weber, M. (1946). Religious rejections of the world and their directions. In *From Max Weber: Essays in sociology* (pp. 323–359). Oxford.

Werczberger, R., & Huss, B. (2014). New Age culture in Israel. *Israel Studies Review, 29*(2), 1–16.

PART V
BETWEEN RELIGIOSITY AND SECULARISM

14

Contemporary Spirituality in Israel

The Search for Meaning and the Privatization of Judaism Following the Decline of the Secular Zionist Meta-Narrative

Tomer Persico

Herbert Weiner was a Reform Rabbi who visited the young state of Israel in the late 1950s, in a quest for displays of spirituality. He found very little. After a visit to the Ultra-orthodox neighborhood of Mea Shearim, Ben Gurion's house, Rabbi Zvi Yehuda Kook's near-empty yeshiva, and Martin Buber's home he concludes by observing that

> there is a lack of religious interest among non-Orthodox Jews in the Holy Land today. . . . The Present conditions of life in Israel . . . make it difficult to find time or energy for anything except the absolutely vital and necessary. A "hothouse" religion which may flourish in suburban America . . . is a kind of luxury religiosity that cannot find roots in a land which only has time for the absolutely necessary. (Weiner, 1963, p. 257)

While Weiner's words reflected the reality in Israel up to the end of the 1980s, today they are a forgotten part of history. The lack of interest in religion that Weiner discovered among the non-Orthodox has long passed. From the 1990s on, Israeli Jewish society is brimming with a colorful display of "hothouse" religions (or "boutique" religions, as the current Israeli slang would put it). From luxurious yoga halls to private colleges that supply a diploma in alternative medicine, contemporary spirituality in Israel carries not only new religious content, but new religious forms and, with them, new religious identities for those who seek meaning and fulfillment through such a course. And while these forms of religiosity have greatly increased in presence within Israeli society since the 1990s, there has also been a growth in specifically new *Jewish* religious movements. So much so that these new

Tomer Persico, *Contemporary Spirituality in Israel* In: *Finding Meaning*. Edited by: Ofra Mayseless and Pninit Russo-Netzer, Oxford University Press. © Oxford University Press 2022. DOI: 10.1093/oso/9780190910358.003.0014

Jewish religious identities and practices have encompassed proportion-
ally an increasingly greater part of Israeli contemporary spirituality (Ruah-
Midbar, 2014).

In this chapter, I focus on the sociological reasons underlying the evident
growth of alternative Jewish religious and spiritual identities. Taking the collapse of the Secular Zionist meta-narrative as my point of departure, I explain
the bourgeoning of contemporary spirituality circles as a response to a need
for alternative meaning, shaped by the post-collectivist, individualistic ethos.
"Meaning" here is of course not meant in the simple sense of the content of a
message, but in the existential sense of personal significance, position toward
reality, and self-understanding. Accordingly, meaning is closely correlated
to identity, and the search for meaning is thus understood as the search for a
stable, viable identity that draws legitimation from its relationship, positive
or negative, to common horizons of meaning. As such, meaning is always
socially dependent, though the individual searching for meaning can find
meaning by constructing her identity through adopting, changing, or rebel-
ling against what is commonly held as "true," "good," or "proper" meaning. In
this chapter, the rise of a specifically Jewish "New Age" will be attributed to
the lack of a coherent Jewish identity, a situation created by that same Secular
Zionist collapse. I will clarify why this search for identity and meaning does
not regularly end in becoming observant Orthodox Jews, and following that,
how this process fits in with different trends of secularization.

Forms of Jewish Identity at Israel's Founding

Whereas "New Age" spirituality became a significant social phenomenon in
the United States in the 1960s, in the state of Israel, as noted earlier, it would
take three more decades to do so. The reasons for that, however, were not restricted, as Weiner suggests, to economic factors, but were deeply connected
to Israeli social structure at that time. As is widely accepted, in its formative years, Israeli society was strongly collectivistic, with a consensual ethos
which placed national well-being and an ideal of self-sacrifice at its center.
These were considered essential for state-building and for the formation of a
Jewish socialist model society (Galnoor & Blander, 2013; Kimmerling, 2004;
Shafir & Peled, 2002). In this republican worldview one's identity was not her
or his own to make, but a derivative of the community's. Following that, a

person's religious character was again defined through participation in a certain social group.

Significantly, Jewish Israeli society was then divided very distinctly between the majority secular population (together with the more traditional, but not observant, public, close to 90% of all Israelis) and the minority religious (both Religious-Zionists and Ultra-orthodox), with clear roles agreed upon for each sector. While the secular would build the state, protect it, and make it prosperous (both economically and morally), the religious would delegated a "priestly" role, being in charge of life-cycle ceremonies (weddings, funerals, etc.) and a minimum of traditional symbolic capital (Kosher laws, blessings on holy days).

This division of roles came into being because in wishing for a Jewish state, secular Israelis could not completely cut away from the Jewish religious tradition, which was essential to the Jewish identity. In particular, the Halakhic laws (traditionally seen as divinely sanctioned observances mandatory for Jews) that decreed how a person becomes a Jew were of importance as the new state could not form another way for deciding this very important question. The Rabbis would thus be in charge of the borders of the Jewish people and, following that, the citizenship of the Jewish state. Because Reform and Conservative Judaism were all but nonexistent in Israel at the time of its founding, the hegemonic form of religious Judaism in the young state was Orthodox Judaism, and the Orthodox Chief Rabbinate (founded 1921) was given monopolistic control of the administration of religious rites.

The Breakdown of the Secular Zionist Collectivist Ethos

As demonstrated in various studies, since the 1980s changes in economic thought and structure, the political system, the justice system, and Israeli demographics led to abandoning the republican ethos that characterized Israeli society under the rule of Mapai (the Secular Zionist socialist party that founded the state) and encouraged the rise of the liberal ethos, on the one hand, and ethno-nationalism, on the other (Kimmerling, 2004; Ram, 2007). Following the adoption of neo-liberal economics, extensive privatization processes, increased global impact on the economy, and the rise of high-tech manufacturing industries Israel developed a postindustrial and hypercapitalist economy.

Developments in the economic sphere were accompanied by parallel adjustments in social and cultural fields. Globalization brought not only products but also Western (especially American) ideals and social trends. The introduction of utilitarian logic and consumerism affected the ideological and ethical fields in Israel, and privatization was not restricted to the economy. Economic globalization brought not only goods but ideas and, with them, the individualistic ethos of self-fulfillment. The choice of a place to live or even to live in Israel or abroad, for example, which until the 1990s was saturated with ideological considerations, was now thought of as a private matter, not the business of anyone but a person's self and family (Meyers, 2001). Ideas and ideals incorporated through globalized economic conditions were the most significant reason underlying the change from a collectivist to an individualistic ethos. The rise of an ideal of individual self-fulfillment simultaneously created the conditions for the fall of the collectivist Zionist ethos and presented the ethos that was to replace it. The Israeli individual now saw herself not as an integral part of the people, drawing values and goals from the collective, but as an autonomous unit standing apart from society and, indeed, before it, both ontologically and ethically.[1]

These developments allowed the privatization of the spiritual quest: the individual was empowered as sole authority in matters concerning her spiritual path and even religious identity. The various elements to fill her spiritual world were gathered from the spiritual marketplace that grew around her (Roof, 2001). For the first time since the establishment of the state of Israel the religious and spiritual field was diversified and woven into numerous parallel channels. Some of these channels have completely ignored Jewish tradition, and some engaged it with a new multifaceted and versatile discourse (for an analysis of the different ways contemporary Jewish Spirituality engages Halakha, see Ruah Midbar & Klin Oron, 2010). This discourse, sometimes called (depending on the speaker) "pluralistic," "spiritual," or "neo-Reform," was no longer based on the premise that the Jewish Orthodox establishment faithfully represented authentic Jewish tradition. Quite the opposite, it wanted to reclaim Jewish heritage—especially Talmudic, Kabbalistic, and Chassidic[2]—as a part of secular Israeli identity (Sheleg, 2010). This

---

[1] Such a view naturally emphasizes the rights of the individual, and comprehensive discussion of human and civil rights had indeed become dominant (in part also because of the activity of the Supreme Court in Israel) since the 1970s and particularly from the 1980s and 1990s.

[2] The Talmud is a many-volumed compendium recording Halakhic discussions among Jewish sages from the first centuries CE. Kabbalah is a complex esoteric lore developed since the 13th century that explains the workings of the divine realms and the connection of the Halakha to them.

reclaiming, in turn, is a significant part of the search for meaning because it allowed its participants to construct a needed and novel Jewish identity for themselves.

The Flowering of Contemporary Spirituality in Israel

A significant growth of interest in the tradition and practice of Judaism can be witnessed since the early 1990s. The first pluralistic seminaries ("Beit Midrash") for the study of Talmud, the "Hamidrasha" School at the Oranim Academic College near the city of Haifa, and the "Elul" Beit Midrash in Jerusalem, were both established in 1989. A few years later special events on the eve and night of the Shavuot holiday began, in which observant as well as secular Jewish Israelis were invited to take part in fluid, multifaceted all-night studies of traditional texts. In 1997, two "festivals" of Jewish learning were introduced, one in Kfar Blum (*Lo Ba'Shamayim*; tr. "not in the heavens") and one in Efal (*Hakhel*), and, a few years after that the first secular prayer communities were founded (*Nigun Ha'Lev*; tr. "melody of the heart"; and *Beit Tefilah Israeli*; tr. "Israeli house of prayer"). Closer to general Western New Age culture were the mass festivals (Shantipi, Bereshit, Boombamela), which, at their peak in the late 1990s, attracted tens of thousands. These events were held during the three traditional pilgrimage Jewish holidays and combined general contemporary spirituality (e.g., Reiki, mindfulness meditation, Tarot) with traditional Jewish symbols (including having a Jewish "House of Prayer" in the center of the festival's compound).

The first decade of the millennium signaled the diversity of the phenomenon and its branching off into different cultural avenues and alternative communities, both ideological and social. It is then that Israel witnessed popular New Age phenomena such as a flowering of "channelers" and the huge popularity of rabbis who advise the rich and famous, both expressing the search for meaning and certainty while shaking off any old secular hesitation of seeking advice from the mystical (Ruah-Midbar, 2014). With these came trends such as the adopting of traditional customs by different artists and celebrities who are "on a journey to find themselves, and bring spiritual meaning to their lives" and who construct "a new perception of citizenship,

---

Hasidism is the first modern religious renewal movement of Judaism, founded in the 18th century and emphasizing a personal, heart-felt connection with the divine.

in which spirituality is the main component of Israeli-ness" (Lebovitz, 2016, p. 4, 17). This era also witnesses the formation of distinct social circles by formally-observant Jews ("Datlash"; Gal Getz, 2011), creating small communities of like-minded Israelis with an affinity, though not strict devotion or deference to tradition. A growing interest in Kabbalah and neo-Kabbalah was also observed, with groups like Bnei Baruch and the Kabbalah Centre attracting a large and diversified body of students in Israel (Huss, 2007; Myers 2007). Bnei Baruch, led by Rabbi Michael Laitman, is probably the most successful new religious movement in Israel, offering a popular version of Rabbi Yehuda Ashlag'a Kabbalah to tens of thousands of committed students (Ben-Tal, 2010).

Israel is also the home for novel Jewish spiritual paths such as the courses in "Jewish Meditation," in which mindfulness-based techniques are applied to connect to the God of Abraham (Persico, 2016) or the Yemima method (sometimes called "Conscious Thinking"), a spiritual path based on the instructions of Yemima Avital (1929–1999), which combines psychological insights with Kabbalistic language and offers students introspective practice designed to enable a release from psychological distress. We need also note the rising popularity of alternative religious services which are not part of the Israeli Chief Rabbinate (such as conducting independent wedding ceremonies; Prashizky, 2014). All these are manifestations of the same basic impetus, which is the search for meaning through the formation of a new Jewish identity based on internal, autonomous authority.

Of significant importance is that, for the first time since the founding of the state of Israel, this subversive move toward tradition enjoyed wide public legitimacy. Seminaries founded by secular and religious alike brought a new discourse to Talmud and Halakha study and a willingness to challenge the assumptions taken as first principles in any religiously observant study of canonical sources. Secular prayer communities expressed a desire to get closer to the annual circle of Jewish holy days, but in their own way and on their own terms. Non-orthodox Jewish movements significantly expanded their ranks, so that currently no fewer than 7% of Israel's Jewish population identify as either Reform or Conservative (Gutman-Avi Chai, 2013).[3] Even the Baal Teshova movement, in which secular Jews "return" and become observantly Orthodox, has changed its character and is full of seekers of

---

[3] It must be noted, however, that a minute fraction of these numbers visit Reform and Conservative schuls regularly.

emotional satisfaction and spiritual experiences (and therefore leads many of the newly observant to Hasidic communities such as Breslov (Persico, 2014; Weinstock, 2011) or partial returnees, for whom the adoption of observance is taken according to personal choice and appeals to personal taste.

Factors Contributing to the Search of Meaning Through Contemporary Jewish Spirituality

If this short account of conditions that allowed the transition from a collectivist framework of state-endorsed Judaism to a private and autonomous spiritual search and individualized Jewish identity is correct, we need to describe the factors that led to its creation. Even allowing for the preceding elaboration and historical description, we must still examine the reasons so many secular Israelis who did not have any real connection with past tradition turned to an intellectual and spiritual search specifically via Jewish sources.

Apparently, the answer is clear: Judaism is accessible and "natural" for Jewish Israelis. Jewish tradition, we can assume, is the first place they will look for meaning. But this is not a satisfactory answer for two reasons: first, the Zionist movement spurned large parts of Jewish tradition, and an anti-religious sentiment was embraced by the Israeli secular public. The same sentiment persists, preventing any rapprochement with tradition and directing those interested in scholarship to the faculties of philosophy and those interested in spirituality to the arts or the global spiritual culture of the New Age. Second, one must distinguish the specific parts of tradition that receive current focus: namely, Talmud, Kabbalah, and Hasidism. No great return to the classic interest of the Zionist movement with the Bible is seen here, and there is also no interest in Halakha. In other words, not all of Jewish tradition is appropriated by secular Israelis at this time, and, in any case, what we are witnessing is not a wholesale "natural" affirmation of "Judaism" but the careful selection, whether conscious or unconscious, of different parts of the tradition.

What, then, motivates and creates this phenomenon? A few interlocking forces can be discerned. Without a doubt, the collapse of the Secular Zionist collectivist ethos and the rise of a neo-liberal (economic and social) mindset created a crisis of values that required restoration. The disintegration of the Zionist (and with it, the socialist) meta-narrative created not only an opening for different and divergent voices, some of them silenced before, to be heard, but also a search for an alternative narrative with which to fashion a meaningful worldview. The vacuum of values that the demise of the Zionist movement left had to be filled, and the search for meaning in contemporary spirituality presented one way to fill it.

In addition, it must be remembered that this search desires not only a substitute for a missing meaningful worldview. The Zionist ethos provided not only that, but purported to formulate a distinct *Jewish* identity, creating, as it were, a "new Jew" who presumably enjoyed historical legitimacy and who was presented as an alternative to traditional, "diasporic" Jewish life. The Zionist Jew was secular, patriotic, nationalist, "manly," "biblical," and socialist, with the particular goal of establishing a model society in the land of his forefathers through adhering to the "ethics of the [Jewish] prophets" (as it is written in Israel's Declaration of Independence). With the breakdown of that Jewish character it became necessary to establish an updated relationship between the nonobservant Israeli and her legacy. In other words, former Zionist Israelis had to seek a new answer to the question "How am I Jewish? What makes me a Jew?" What was needed was a new conception of living meaningfully *as an Israeli of Jewish ancestry.*

These two vectors—the search for meaning in contemporary spirituality and the search for a new Jewish identity—merged perfectly in the flourishing of contemporary Jewish spirituality, giving one answer to these two seemingly different demands.

A secondary reason for this move is connected to the social profile of many of the members of the Jewish revival, at least at its beginning. In general, those who led the "Jewish Renaissance" then were older, more affluent, and better educated than the average Israeli, and almost all were of Ashkenazi descent (Sheleg, 2010).[4] These were Israelis who came mainly from the socioeconomic layers that enjoyed economic prosperity on the one hand, and, on the other, witnessed the beginning of the decline of their status as a cultural and political hegemony in Israel (Ariel, 2011; Kimmerling, 2001; Werczberger 2011). Some members of this group felt the need to turn to new paths of accumulation of symbolic capital and had, in their eyes, the legitimation and

[4] Notwithstanding this, the Jewish awakening eventually became very diverse, as different parts of it attract different parts of the Israeli collective. Movements of Neo-Kabbalah, for example, attract many veteran immigrants from the former Soviet Union; pursuit of "Piyut," poetical prayers, appeals to many Sephardic Jews; and so on. As the movement developed, the communities taking part in it have increased and diversified, and today it would be wrong to restrict this social movement to a single segment of the population.

authority to shape their own relationship with tradition and, to a large extent, to shape tradition itself. Thus the interest in tradition is also related to the attempt to maintain a hegemonic position of superiority through appropriation of cultural capital.

Finally, and in a manner that places the collapse of the Zionist ethos in an ironic light, the augmentation of national feelings also took part in this renewed appeal to tradition. The dissolution of the Zionist meta-narrative also brought with it a withdrawal from vision of the establishment of a liberal democracy, a state that respects the rights of "all its citizens irrespective of religion, race or sex" (again, as written in the Israeli Declaration of Independence). Here, not the establishment of a model, democratic socialist, society is placed in the center of the Israeli identity, but the simple "Jewishness" of the people, the inhabitants of the Land of Israel. The Zionist republican common denominator is replaced by a Jewish ethnic one (Pedahzur, 2012).

At the same time, the rise and fall of negotiating a peace agreement with the Palestinians led to an increment in nationalist sentiments, emphasizing the connection between the nation of Israel and the Jewish religion. The Oslo Agreement threatened to take the West Bank out of Israel's control, and this in itself raised awareness of the historic and religious significance of these lands in the chronicles of Judaism. The collapse of the Oslo process in the Second Intifada brought many more Israelis to adopt a perspective that places Israeli ethnos (and its existence, well-being, and rights) first on the scale of values (Pedahzur, 2012), leading to a wave of ethnic nationalism. These processes thus also led to an interest in tradition, fulfilling a wish to charge an ethno-national ethos with content.

The Extension of Secularization Thorough Other Means

Yet it is imperative to understand what form the new interest in tradition and Jewish spirituality takes. As stated earlier, the protagonists of this process do not become observant Orthodox Jews. In fact, many of them do not even accept the Orthodox ruling regarding the definition of Judaism itself. While 51% of respondents in the Guttman-Avi Chai survey of 2009 indicated that their identity is "Jewish" before "Israeli" (41% said the opposite), many define Jewish identity as "belonging to the Jewish people" and not "the Orthodox position on the question 'Who is a Jew'" (3.3 on a scale of 1–4 versus 1.9;

Guttman-Avi Chai, 2009). It is also almost needless to state that many of those involved in this phenomenon are also practicing activities deemed heretic by Orthodox standards (from Hindu yoga, through Buddhist meditation and up to the common and obvious playing of music on the Sabbath; Persico, 2016) The return to Jewish tradition is, therefore, emphatically not the adoption of Jewish Orthodoxy. As noted earlier, interest is centered on the Talmudic texts, Kabbalah, and Hasidism—not Halakha.

If the interest in Jewish tradition comes as a search for meaning after the collapse of the Zionist worldview and a quest for a renewed answer to the question "what makes me Jewish?," why won't those who seek meaning and a connection with "Judaism" simply embrace a religiously observant way of life? The reason for this is simple: the Jewish spiritual awakening is taking place already within the confines of a liberal and individualistic consciousness that struck down the collectivist Secular Zionist meta-narrative and that led to the search for meaning in the first place. There is no retreat here from the liberal, individualist worldview and the creation of a new collectivist structure to replace Zionism, but a manifestation of the spirit of self-fulfillment in other ways. Talmud, Kabbalah, and Hasidism (as opposed to Halakha and Torah), the most widespread interests of the current search, allow the development of personal religious identity, culturally and spiritually, without any commitment to a different lifestyle or to a community (Sheleg, 2010). It is no accident, thus, that they are chosen as the building blocks of the new individualistic Jewish identity. In other words, it is the individualized cast of the current search for meaning and advance toward tradition that produces the privatized Judaism that is displayed and not an implementation of a Halakhic way of life.

Finally, it is important to note that while these processes might be interpreted as a religious revival in Israel, they are not contradictory to the process of modern secularization. While secularization is connected to the loss of faith and the withdrawal from religious activity, it has more fundamentally to do with the removal of power, influence, and authority from established religion and their channeling into other institutions, such as the secular state or the scientific world (Casanova, 1994; Taylor, 2007). A situation in which large parts of the public engage in a religious tradition in order to produce meaning through individual, autonomous, tailor-made religiosity is primarily the extension of secularization thorough other means.

Far from the concerned—indeed, at times hysterical—voices in Israeli public and media talking about the increasing religious radicalization of Israeli society, these processes are not signaling a move toward fundamentalism, which is always a collective project, but toward the individual religion of spiritual seekers (indeed, at times of religious reformers).[5] It is no coincidence that the past few years have highlighted an unprecedented negativity held by the Israeli public toward the religious (Jewish Orthodox) Israeli establishment. The legitimacy of the Chief Rabbinate is at an all time low (only 9.4% of secular Jews in Israel say that they trust the institute; Hermann et al., 2015), and, more than ever before, Israeli citizens are conducting their marriages without registering through it (even though there is no way to be legally married in Israel without going through the Rabbinate, except by flying abroad and getting married in another country; Prashizky, 2014). It is quite clear that the current interest in tradition is far from being an interest in traditional authorities.

Compared with similar trends abroad, the contemporary Jewish spiritual search in Israel may be analogous to what Robert Putnam and David Campbell call "the rise of the Nones" (Putnam & Campbell, 2012, p. 123). Putnam and Campbell identify a surge in the numbers and share in population of those who identify with no religious denomination, although most are not atheist. This group has increased its share in American (and European) society over the past 20 years, culminating at about 23% of the population, from about 13% at the beginning of the 1970s (Putnam & Campbell, 2012, p. 122). As this privatization of religion decreases the power of religion in the public sphere and its influence on the modern state, and indeed challenges each religion's own institutions and traditions, it should be considered one of the primary manifestations of the secularization process of our time. While I don't believe the end of religion will be complete and total privatization, as Steve Bruce (2002) holds, this is, nevertheless, a significant phenomenon.

The current privatization of Judaism in Israel thus signals a new phase in the character of Judaism in Israel. It stands as a departure from the Secular Zionist model, which divided sectors of Israeli society into a secular majority

---

[5] This is not to deny the rise of ethnocentric nationalism. There is indeed in Israel at this time, as mentioned, a wave of ethnic nationalism which often uses traditional Jewish symbols (e.g., the sanctity of the land, the idea of Jewish chosenness and superiority, etc.), but that is a national phenomenon at its root, not a religious one, and thus a different but parallel issue.

estranged from tradition and a religious minority that performs the collective religious rites and enjoys the stamp of authenticity and the state's legitimacy. What we are presented with now is a much more diversified society in which the secular public is significantly more involved in its relationship with the Jewish tradition, takes individual paths in forming idiosyncratic Jewish interpretations, and has partly withdrawn its granted legitimacy from the Jewish Orthodoxy as the single bearer of authentic Jewish tradition. As a result of the breakdown of the Secular Zionist ethos and the introduction of a neo-liberal conception of individual self-fulfillment, this search for meaning is manifested in the formulation of a privatized Jewish identity, one constructed within the Jewish subdivision of the contemporary culture of New Age spirituality.

Highlights

- Contemporary spirituality, flowering in Israel since the 1990s, presents increasingly Jewish characteristics.
- Since the 1980s, changes in the economy, political system, justice system, and Israeli demographics led to a breakdown of the collectivist Secular Zionism meta-narrative.
- Correspondingly, Israel witnessed the rise of an individualist ethos of self-fulfillment.
- The collapse of the Secular Zionist meta-narrative left secular Israelis without the secular Jewish identity it had provided.
- Out of that arose a quest for meaning, in this case Jewish identity.
- Shaped by the postcollectivist, individualistic ethos, it expressed itself as Jewish contemporary spirituality.
- This individual, autonomous, tailor-made Judaism is itself a form of secularization.

References

Ariel, Y. (2011). Jews and new religious movements: An introductory essay. *Nova Religio*, *15*(1), 5–21.

Ben-Tal, S. (2010). Bnei-Baruch: The story of a new religious movement. *Akdamot*, *25*, 149–169. [Hebrew]

Bruce, S. (2002). *God is dead: Secularization in the west*. Blackwell.

Casanova, J. (1994). *Public religions in the modern world*. University of Chicago Press.

Gal Getz, P. (2011). *Leaving religion behind: A journey into the world of ex-Orthodox Jews*. Am Oved. [Hebrew]

Galnoor, I., & Blander, D. (2013). *The political system of Israel*. Am Oved & The Israel Democracy Institute. [Hebrew]

Guttman-Avi Chai. (2012). Israeli Jews—A portrait: Beliefs, observing tradition and values among Jews in Israel 2009. [Hebrew] https://www.idi.org.il/media/1026914/%D7%93%D7%95%D7%97%20%D7%90%D7%91%D7%99%D7%97%D7%99%20%D7%94%D7%9E%D7%9C%D7%90.pdf

Hermann, T., Heller, E., Cohen, C., Be'ery, G., & Lebel, Y. (2015). *The Israeli democracy index 2014*. The Israel Democracy Institute.

Huss, B. (2007). The new age of Kabbalah: Contemporary Kabbalah, the New Age, and postmodern spirituality. *Journal of Modern Jewish Studies, 6*(2), 107–125.

Kimmerling, B. (2001). *The end of Ashkenazi hegemony*. Keter. [Hebrew]

Kimmerling, B. (2004). *Immigrants, settlers, natives: Israel between plurality of cultures and cultural wars*. Am Oved. [Hebrew]

Lebovitz, A. (2016). "Jew Age" among Israeli celebs: Jewish spirituality as discourse of citizenship. *Celebrity Studies, 7*(2), 182–202.

Meyers, O. (2001). A home away from home? Israel Shelanu and the self-perceptions of Israeli migrants. *Israel Studies, 6*(3), 71–90.

Myers, J. (2007). *Kabbalah and the spiritual quest: The Kabbalah Centre in America*. Praeger.

Pedahzur, A. (2012). *The triumph of Israel's radical right*. Oxford University Press.

Persico, T. (2014). Neo-Hasidic revival: Expressivist uses of traditional lore. *Modern Judaism, 34*(3), 287–308.

Persico, T. (2016). *The Jewish meditative tradition*. Tel Aviv University Press. [Hebrew]

Prashizky, A. (2014). The invention of Jewish rituals: Non-Orthodox weddings and funerals in Israel. In G. Katz, S. Ratzabi, & Y. Yadgar (Eds.), *Beyond Halakha: Secularism, traditionalism and new age culture in Israel* (pp. 242–282). The Ben-Gurion Research Institute & Ben-Gurion University Press. [Hebrew]

Putnam, R. D., & Campbell, D. E. (2012). *American grace: How religion divides and unites us*. Simon and Schuster.

Ram, U. (2007). *The globalization of Israel: Mc'World in Tel Aviv, Jihad in Jerusalem*. Routledge.

Roof, W. C. (2001). *Spiritual marketplace: Baby boomers and the remaking of American religion*. Princeton University Press.

Ruah Midbar, M. (2014). A channeler, healer and shaman meet at the rabbi's: A roadmap of Israeli Judaism(s) in the New Age. In G. Katz, S. Ratzabi, & Y. Yadgar (Eds.), *Beyond Halakha: Secularism, traditionalism, and New Age culture in Israel* (pp. 498–528). The Ben-Gurion Research Institute & Ben-Gurion University Press. [Hebrew]

Ruah Midbar, M., & Klin Oron, A. (2010). Jew Age: Jewish praxis in Israeli New Age discourse. *Journal of Alternative Spiritualities and New Age Studies, 5*(1), 33–63.

Shafir, G., & Peled, Y. (2002). *Being Israeli: The dynamics of multiple citizenship*. Cambridge University Press.

Sheleg, Y. (2010). *The Jewish renaissance in Israeli society: The emergence of a New Jew*. The Israel Democracy Institute. [Hebrew]

Taylor, C. (2007). *A secular age*. Belknap—Harvard University Press.

Weiner, H. (1963). *The wild goats of Ein Gedi*. Doubleday.

Weinstock, M. (2011). *Uman: The Israeli journey to the Tomb of Rabbi Nachman of Bretslov*. Yedioth Sefarim. [Hebrew]

Werczberger, R. (2011). *When the New Age entered the Jewish bookshelf: Jewish spiritual renewal in Israel* [doctoral dissertation]. The Hebrew University of Jerusalem. [Hebrew]

15

Judaism Is the New Orient

How Experiencing the Far East Helps Israelis Find Meaning in Their Jewish Tradition

Marianna Ruah-Midbar Shapiro

As long as deep in the heart,
The soul of a Jew yearns,
And forward to the East to Zion, an eye looks, Our hope will not be lost,
The hope of two thousand years . .

Excerpt from HaTikva, by Naftali Herz Imber,
Israel's National Anthem

The Question: "To the East" or "To Zion"?

Over the past 150 years, the East has increasingly inflamed the imagination and stirred the hope of a wide range of social and religious movement scholars. The 19th century's Romantic Orientalism starred the East as a source of remedy and a promise of redemption for Westerners (Jews included; see Huss, 2010). The reverence for the East that formed during the Modern era began within somewhat small circles, comprised of intellectual elites and thinkers, and has since gradually expanded to form new religious movements that have spread out from the East and seeped into Western societies from the Theosophical Society, through the disciples of the Rajneesh Movement, to Mindfulness.

The past few decades have seen an increasing number of quests in search of meaning. Namely, in the face of the descent of traditional religions as "total institutions" (Goffman, 1961) which provide all private and social human aspects with guidance and meaning, individuals are at their wit's end, faced with a loss of values, competing offers for lifestyles, and a multitude of

Marianna Ruah-Midbar Shapiro, *Judaism Is the New Orient* In: *Finding Meaning.* Edited by: Ofra Mayseless and Pninit Russo-Netzer, Oxford University Press. © Oxford University Press 2022. DOI: 10.1093/oso/9780190910358.003.0015 fragmented identities that deepen alienation, as well as the inflation of data, the media, and symbolic systems in general. In the face of this confounding situation, individuals started searching for alternative sources of wisdom (or rather, a final, total one), that might serve as a recipe for daily living and self-understanding. This widespread phenomenon was termed "a generation of seekers" (Roof, 1993). In their quest for meaning, many seekers believed the answers would, in fact, be found in the East. For many of them, the East represents a right and natural way of living and an expression of a forgotten truth and a pure essence, as will be shown hereinafter.

Thus, the exotic interest that individuals and elite groups have in the East has become an entire generation's desire. Among extensive sectors of "progressive" Western societies, backpacking to India is common. In the West, many identify with Tibetan teachings, use traditional Chinese practices, and so on. Often, this adoption of practices and beliefs begets the formation of an Eastern or syncretistic identity among Westerners. The flourishing of alternative spirituality (often referred to as "New Age") in contemporary Western society is fertile ground for the expansion of such trends.

Jews are clearly prominent in this pro-Eastern movement within Western society (Roper, 2003). This chapter focuses on a more specific case study: Israeli Jews[1] and their distinct pursuit of the East as part of their quest for meaning. To do so, I analyze Westerners' enthusiastic interest in the East, later projected upon the Jewish-Israeli context. However, the presented research framework will in fact provide insights into wider contexts than just these local groups.

If we have so far evoked the question of what Israelis look for in the East and what it gives them, an even more surprising question surrounds the phenomenon of Israelis' return to Judaism following their Eastbound journey. Unexpectedly, many Israelis who have shown indifference—and even opposition—to Jewish tradition (Ruah-Midbar & Klin Oron, 2010), show a renewed interest in it precisely after experiencing the Eastern alternative.

The words to Israel's national anthem were written in Europe during the last quarter of the 19th century as an expression of the Jewish-European sentiment of Zionistic longing aimed Eastward, to Jerusalem (also see Huss, 2013). Remarkably, having returned to Zion, we are once again witnessing

---

[1] For convenience's sake, the remainder of this chapter will often refer to these simply as "Israelis," rather than Jewish-Israelies. This sector makes up approximately 80% of the Israeli population. Notably, this interest in the East is not as prevalent in the Arab sector as it is in the Jewish one.

Jews whose longing for the East (now referring to the Far East) paradoxically leads many of them to return to the bosom of Jewish tradition.

This study seeks to examine this phenomenon: How does the Far East aid Israelis in finding meaning in their lives, and, moreover, how does it eventually enable their reconciliation with Jewish tradition and the rehabilitation of their Jewish identity? How does the East, of all things, convert Israelis' hearts, indifferent and estranged from Judaism as they may be, so much that they discover excitement and meaning in their own tradition?

Our exploration will reveal that the question regarding Israelis' attraction to the East and the question regarding their return to Judaism share an explanatory framework. Moreover, this shared explanation is greatly relevant to a broader understanding of contemporary Western society. Therefore, this study should be viewed as a case study of contemporary liberal culture—its motives, desires, images, developments, struggles, and identity formation.

The chapter begins with an exposition on cultural context: New Age spirituality and its draw to the East, a review of the fruits of the study on Israelis' interest in the East, and a description of common narratives regarding a return from the East to the bosom of Judaism. Further on, I present the prevalent explanation of the draw of the East—the thesis according to which the Western paradigm is profoundly challenged by the East and, accordingly, the deep cultural transformation in the contemporary West. Then, I examine the critique of the Easternization Thesis, following which I offer my own explanation for the draw of the East, as well as for the subsequent attraction to Judaism, and present a conclusion.

Exposition: Israeli-Jews Turn Eastward

While during the 1980s the pursuit of the East was considered peripheral, dangerous, and weird, nowadays it has become widespread, legitimate, and desirable. Today, tens of thousands of Israelis go backpacking through the East every year (in addition to other tens of thousands who go on shorter trips), with ever-rising numbers. In Israel itself, an abundance of centers offer workshops on various Buddhist traditions. New religious movements, from the International Society for Krishna Consciousness to Transcendental Meditation, built local communities in Israel. Even in Israeli establishments, the introduction of Eastern methods is evident: acupuncture and Ayurveda has been formally added to Israel's extended state healthcare, and state schools commonly incorporate yoga and mindfulness.

Often, sights must be set upon the journey itself more so than the destination, as it is an expression of a sociopsychological need (as well as the promoter of a sociopsychological process). For Israelis, the journey to the East has become one of the popular stepping-stones on the track to social initiation—a part of the socialization process. After high school, most Israelis go on to complete their compulsory service in the army, after which they prepare for their "big post-army trip," which constitutes a sort of rite of passage into Israeli adulthood (Noy, 2012). Despite this youthful image the journey has gained eastbound journeys are common across various age groups. The journey to the East serves a different purpose for each age group, in accordance with travelers' social needs and their biographical state (Maoz, 2007). This journey is especially common among the large nonreligious sector (approximately 80% of the Jewish population) in Israel, however, over the past several years it has spread among religious sectors as well (Peretz, 2015).

I therefore begin by presenting the wider cultural context of this interest in the East. In fact, this trend is widespread among current alternative culture. Activists in contemporary alternative spirituality (i.e., New Age) are often called "seekers" (Roof, 1993) due to their constant journey in search of wisdom and meaning across a variety of locations—and undoubtedly beyond Western traditions. In their search, New Agers feel comfortable drawing inspiration from and even mixing different traditions out of a perennialistic outlook according to which all religions and cultures can be traced to a shared and ancient kernel of truth. The religions known throughout Western societies in their current forms (particularly the Judeo-Christian tradition) are seen as the outcome of that kernel's distortion or misunderstanding, while Other cultures—indigenous or Eastern—are seen as having preserved the religious truth in its purest form.

Therefore, the Israeli-Jewish context also sees the perennialistic belief expressed through a narrative which links Judaism and Eastern religions by way of a join ancient source. And yet Judaism, having traveled such a long historical road, is perceived as one that has lost essential pieces, much like other Western religions. According to this outlook, these pieces may be restored or amended through the study of indigenous and Eastern traditions (Ruah-Midbar, 2007).

Indeed, many Israelis, upon returning from a trip to the East and having undergone a myriad of religious and spiritual experiences during their journey, believe they have encountered there the pieces Judaism has lost (Ruah-Midbar, 2015). They sometimes mention the biblical story of Abraham's gifts to his concubines' sons before sending them to the East (Gen. 25:6) and explain that these gifts are spiritual secrets and tools, passed down from *Abraham*, the father of Judaism, to *Brahma*, the Hindu God of Creation.[2] The doctrines found at the basis of original Judaism are presented as *Yeda*, meaning knowledge, passed down to the Indian *Veda*; thus no wonder there's a connection between *Yehudi* (Jew) and *Hodi* (Indian). Therefore, according to these beliefs, the East holds formerly Jewish treasures that should be restored.[3]

Others take note of the role that the encounter with Chabad House (a Jewish Orthodox establishment) in the East plays as a moment of profound revelation (Maoz & Bekerman, 2010). Another widespread story claims that Eastern gurus send Jews back to their native tradition, whether by preaching loyalty to their ancestral tradition or by acknowledging the superiority of Judaism over the teachings of the East (Persico, 2012).

Seeing that many Israelis find meaning in the East that they have not found in Judaism, some do not see any sense in returning to search Judaism once they have found what they were searching for in Eastern teachings (Loss, 2010). Others abandon the East and dive back into Judaism, understanding that "home" holds brighter treasures. And some find a renewed interest in Judaism, discover layers within it, and casually combine it with Eastern teachings and practices (Elhanan, 2006). Thus, a syncretistic sphere is created comprising a wide variety of phenomena: "Aleph-Bet Yoga," Jewish Reiki, "Jubu," and many others.[4] This chapter delves into the common basis for all

---

[2] Brahma is the god that created the universe in Hinduism. He is eternal and infinite, the source of all things and a part of them. Some people in contemporary Jewish-Israeli spirituality even link the goddess Sarasvati with Sarah, Abraham's wife.

[3] This contemporary myth of the Jewish-Abrahamic source of Hindu and Eastern wisdom, common within Israeli-Jewish reverence for the East, was preceded by an illustrious line of Hellenistic pagan myth incarnations from ancient history and the Jewish myths that followed. The prevalent myths of ancient Greece (which passed into Jewish traditions) pointed at Eastern wisdom as the source of all scientific branches. Some of these myths revolved around Indians (*Indoi*) and some around Jews (*Ioudaioi*), and some linked the two peoples—whether claiming that Jews are descendant from Indians, that Abraham discovered Monotheism under the influence of Indian perceptions, or in other ways (see more in Melamed, 2010, ch. 1–2). If so, the West's reverence for India (and for the East) and the contemporary spiritual yearning for ancient pre-Jewish teachings both originate in an ancient pagan myth that was probably unknown to the inventors of these modern traditions. Another way in which Orientalism brings Jews back to search ancient Jewish traditions is presented in Boaz Huss's research (Huss, 2010).

[4] The Reiki method uses symbols based on ancient Japanese letters for healing, while Jewish Reiki uses Jewish symbols. Similarly, the Aleph-Bet yoga method adjusts yoga positions to the shape of

these approaches—namely, searching the East, of all places, for meaning—
while addressing an issue other researchers have yet to discuss: people's
increased interest in their native tradition following their journey to the East.
We shall discover why non-religious Jews who have experienced no interest
in, identification with, or sense of nostalgia toward Judaism prior to their
trip to India enthusiastically adopt, in its wake, the lost secrets of Abraham's
tradition.

Discussion: The East as the Answer to the Quest for Meaning

The question of the East's attractiveness in the eyes of the Western quest for
meaning has already been raised by contemporary Western society scholars.
Many want to get to the core of the unique answer which lies in the East and
is absent from the source culture of those Westerners who pursue the East.
Naturally, this answer was likely to be found in the characteristics of Eastern
thought and culture and in the differences between them and Western characteristics. Therefore I later present the contradictions between these two
paradigms, West and East.

   In representing this thesis, I provide Colin Campbell's arguments regarding the West's Easternization, with its direct and blunt wording that
some might even call simplistic and Orientalist. His basic assumption is
that an oppositional "West" and "East" exist.[5] Campbell is therefore an
easy target for his opponents, whether they wish to push these pseudo-
New-Age claims or seek to refine the dichotomous Orientalist approach
to reach more complex insights. After presenting the criticism of the
thesis, I open a breeding ground for discussion on the Israeli-Jewish
case study.

Hebrew letters. These methods are, of course, founded on the assumption regarding the sanctity
of letters and symbols. "Jubu" is an identity-doctrinal combination of Judaism and Buddhism and
seems to be more common in the Diaspora than in Israel.

   [5] In writing this chapter, I avoided using quotation marks as much as possible when using the
terms "West" and "East" since I deal with these entities as perceived by Campbell or spiritual
spokespersons. As I later explain, these words are worthy of quotation marks throughout the
whole chapter.

The Easternization Thesis

In his book, British sociologist Colin Campbell (2007, relying on a 1999 article) composed his "Easternization of the West" thesis. Campbell, who dealt with contemporary cultural change processes from the 1960s counter-culture to the New Age, confirms with this thesis claims made by alternative-spiritual discourse regarding a profound paradigmatic change Western society has undergone over the past decades under the (welcome) influence of Eastern cultures. This is not a matter of importing goods, ideas, or practices (rice, fabrics, Feng-Shui, meditation) from the East, but rather a profound fundamental transformation which has generated a true revolution in Western meaning systems—in beliefs, in the value system, in the manner of contemplation, in social structures, and in the private and public way of life.

As accepted in the study of Western contemporary spirituality, Campbell, too, focuses on an outlined field of research as a representative example of the West. He provides a line of evidence for the change occurring in Britain: the rise of the ecological trend, a growing emphasis on "awareness" and "consciousness," and a shift in religious beliefs. This last change is evident throughout several trends: the weakening of the belief in a personal god alongside the strengthening of the belief in god as "some sort of spirit or life-force" and a weakening belief in the Christian doctrine of Heaven and Hell alongside a strengthening belief in reincarnation, which is considered heresy by Christianity. In seeking out a theory that would bind together all these cultural changes, Campbell indicates the rise of a particular religious form in the West that may be characterized as spiritual/mystical and includes, among other things, immanent theology,[6] belief in spiritual evolution,[7] an antinomian approach,[8] and perennialism.

Campbell suggests understanding this mysticalization as a process of Easternization of the West. Toward this aim, he sets a series of oppositional alignments between East and West, the latter based on the concept of sin and

---

[6] According to immanent theology, the divine dwells within the world and manifests in nature, from the inanimate to the living. This approach stands in opposition to transcendental theology, according to which god is above and beyond our world, beyond the physical dimension, beyond space and time, and, of course, beyond the sphere of humanity.

[7] According to the belief in spiritual evolution, the world is undergoing a process of gradual development. This conjecture is applied to the universe and everything in it—humanity, civilizations, and individuals—and even god.

[8] An antinomian approach opposes the law (Latin: *Nomus*), which usually means god's law.

redemption, a dichotomy between the natural and the supernatural, and a personal divinity, while the Eastern outlook sees the spirit as permeating all things—namely, an impersonal divinity and personal deification, spiritual wholeness. Campbell also contradicts the Western concept of a Church of believers with an Eastern band of seekers guided by a spiritual leader (a guru).

In the tables Campbell provides, the East is identified with a union between man and nature, body and mind, avoiding analysis, doubting the progress offered by science and technology, and attributing meditation with importance, while the West is concordantly identified with discerning between man and nature and between body and mind, acknowledging god as superior to man, attributing importance to rationalism and analysis toward problem-solving, viewing science and technology as a life-improving factor, and viewing competitiveness and initiative as important. The generalizations are sometimes even more crude, contrasting synthesis, subjectivity, intuition, morality, affiliation, and ecstasy (the East), with analysis, objectivity, reason, legalism, power, and order (the West).

Campbell identifies the buds of the Easternization process in the West as far back as the first decades of the 20th century; however, in the contemporary West, he recognizes a *profound and total* paradigmatic Easternization. The downfall of the Western paradigm has occurred, in his opinion, due to the collapse of optimism in regard to science and technology. This has weakened the modern Western paradigm while Eastern thought is immune to this wave of criticism due to its radical individualism and the relativistic status of truth. Thus, the attack of secular humanism on the modern West has itself (ironically) brought about the undermining of the status of Western science and promoted Eastern mystical claims.

In summation, Campbell claims that, after two thousand years of ruling the roost, the Western paradigm's effectiveness has waned and has made way for the Eastern paradigm. Unlike the old paradigm represented, to his view, by the Great Chain of Being metaphor of the 18th century, he believes the new paradigm is best represented by the Gaia Hypothesis metaphor[9]—Earth Mother and all its living creatures as an interconnected web, linking nature and spirit as one system.

---

[9] The Gaia Hypothesis was formulated by British scientist James Lovelock (1979) and claims that the earth, from its very core to the rims of the atmosphere, is a super-organism. All things on the earth—living or inanimate—are parts of a whole, greater organism and linked by their interconnectedness with the rest of the planet earth. This controversial hypothesis was published during the 1970s. Many scientists saw in it a pseudo-scientific theory, though that did not prevent neo-pagan and ecologic-spiritual movements from using it as a recurring and founding argument.

Criticism of the Thesis

Indeed, Campbell's thesis holds more than a grain of truth. There are some claims in the spiritual discourse that are being academically organized and theorized. Thus they are re-presented as academic theories.

Campbell is aware of the generalization evident in the presentation of his arguments. He himself raises as self-criticism the "Instrumental Activism" problem. In spite of the Easternization process, he admits, the West has yet to show substantial signs of abandoning the activist paradigm in favor of an Eastern-style fatalistic surrender. The West continues to show a real interest in this world and in the tools to alter and fix it. The Western approach is characterized by world affirmation, as expressed by its interest in success, enjoyment, family, business, politics, physics, and so on. This approach still overpowers Eastern attitudes of abstention, denial, and rejection of this world.

As mentioned, Campbell's Easternization thesis has been widely criticized. Here, I present criticisms that combine the insights of a series of critical studies on East–West relations (whether regarding Campbell's thesis or prior to its inception) with my own analysis (see Dawson, 2006; Diem & Lewis, 1992; Hamilton, 2002; Hammer, 2001a; Hanegraaff, 1998; Said, 1995).

First and foremost, Campbell's own criticism may be expanded on for it is no small reservation. Can one truly claim that the West has been Easternized while it is up to its neck in this-worldly matters? The West is characterized by a significant worldliness—in its business activities, social values, and ideals. Even when we look, for example, at the rise of ecological awareness (an awareness Campbell attributes to the Taoist influence of the Easternization process), still, the Western activism which characterizes this trend does not allow for its interpretation as an expression of Easternization.

To further expand on this criticism, one may wonder whether the process which takes place in the West's convergence with Eastern notions is indeed an Easternization of the West or rather a Westernization of the East. Do Eastern concepts not, in fact, undergo a drastic and destructive adaptation process which transforms them into remarkably Western concepts, so much so that the West consumes the East without trace? In this spirit, I may provide a more complex interpretation of the conceptual-cultural change process taking place in the West and claim it is mutual and reciprocal relations and a complex synthesis of East and West.

And perhaps this is too mild a criticism. Studies have shown how elements and pieces of Asian traditions chosen selectively have been redesigned into a purely Western framework. In fact, this is an issue of Asian tradition invention (Hobsbawm & Ranger, 1983) to suit Western needs. As Dawson wrote (2006), "East is East, except when it's West." Inter-Western considerations have driven Western thinkers and activists to use India—with its revered exotic image—to explain or excuse the change they believe the West requires.

For example, instead of presenting Western sources (Greek, Judeo-Christian, and so on) for the concept of peace of mind, or alternative Western descriptions of the perception of divine punishment, these ideas are presented using terms such as "Shanti" and "Karma." Sometimes, the elements taken from the East are put to use at face value, as mere terminology. For instance, we can supposedly view the West's common belief in reincarnation as Eastern, yet the New Age form of the concept of reincarnation is far removed from that of Hinduist or Buddhist tradition (Perry, 1992).

Like Jewish tales of the knowledge the sons of Abraham have taken with them to the East, New Age Christians tell of how Jesus visited India and of his meeting with Buddha as a call to restore past glory and go back to the true and original Christianity, which is in line with Buddhism. More than these stories reflect New Age values, they remain loyal to Christianity and Buddhism's ancient traditions (Hanegraaff, 1998). (Respectively, in what follows, I address the image of Judaism to which Israelis return after their Eastern experience.)

Thus, the East is used as a "Significant Other" (Hammer, 2001a) toward inner growth within Western conceptual frameworks—whether ignorance begets such ideal descriptions (Hammer, 2001b) or whether a conscious choice is made with the "Oriental fantasy." While concepts, values, and practices that appear in the West as new trends are presented in the Easternization thesis as the adoption of Eastern elements, apparently these elements did not really originate in the East, but are actually often Western or Westernized.

This Western trend of revering the East and clinging to Eastern notions in order to promote a Western agenda is not new: the Easternization thesis is but a contemporary reincarnation of romantic Orientalist adoration of the mysterious and exotic East that was so prevalent in the 19th century. The end of that century saw many British Orientalists translate a series of Hindu scriptures, molding them into an ideal image of India while portraying the Golden Age of ancient India. It goes without saying that the production of historical knowledge on India by relying on religious texts—let alone a selection of them—is not at all reliable. However, this is an excellent tool for creating that same ideal image that serves Westerners as a "significant other." As it turns out, "a rich Western imagination" also exists. Indian reformers coming as missionaries to the West at the start of the 20th century have also contributed to this very trend: they have preached Hinduism in the spirit of the invented tradition and presumed to be its embodiment. For example, Vivekananda, one of Ramakrishna's eloquent disciples, relied on Hindu scripture in telling his Western disciples that, during the Golden Age of ancient India, no Hindu ever spoke a lie (Diem & Lewis, 1992).

Western Enlightenment thinkers, such as Voltaire, found similarities between the Golden Age of India and those of ancient Greece and China. This triple parallelism was also used by Western thinkers who opposed the claim of enlightenment regarding Western progress. They claimed that not only is the cultural world not advancing, but, on the contrary, we are witnessing an obvious decline compared with ancient times. Moreover, these thinkers have miraculously found similarities not only among the ancient thought of India, Greece, and China, but between these and their own modern thought as well. A later significant example of this parallel genre is a book written by physicist Fritjof Capra (1975), *The Tao of Physics: An Exploration of the Parallels Between Modern Physics and Eastern Mysticism*. In it, the author claims that the supreme wisdom of ancient Eastern mysticism increasingly verifies the new discoveries made in physics.

Turn-of-the-century British Orientalists depicted ancient India's Golden Age as contrary not only to the Western movement they opposed, but also to the India of their day, which they deemed as decadent and lacking in any remnant of past glory. They considered modern Indian decadence parallel to modern European decadence. Similarly, Indian nationalists have posited that contemporary India's decline is an outcome of Western occupation, which has hindered Hinduism from best expressing itself as it did in the distant past. The idealization of historic India, which involved its juxtaposition with contemporary India, further manifests in the claim that ancient Hinduists were monotheistic, unlike current Indian polytheists. This approach enables contemporary fans of the East (backpackers and tourists included) to selectively design the Eastern image they encounter in reality to suit the ideal of their own making.

This analysis raises further issues embedded in the Easternization thesis: its latent juxtaposition between East and West is actually based on images from different eras. The East usually symbolizes an ancient

344 MARIANNA RUAH-MIDBAR SHAPIRO

traditional society, while the West symbolizes a contemporary modern society. In other words, we could have just as well concluded the complete opposite had we painted a picture of an idealistic ancient Greece as an expression of the West and modern decadent India as an expression of the East.

An example of the problematics of the Easternization thesis is contemporary American Buddhism, which we may as well call "Protestant Buddhism." Studies have shown that Americans who embrace Buddhism think it right to purify it of the contamination and decadence they believe have clung to it over the years. To do so, they downplay its emphasis on suffering and stress the possibility of achieving enlightenment in this world; of bringing out its philosophical and psychological motifs and concealing its ritualistic aspect, which they consider folkish, tacked on, and removed from the pure essence of tradition. Some even claim that, originally, the Indians were monotheistic. Another example is US neo-Hinduism, which does not present meditation as a path to transcending the ordinary self, time, and existence but rather as a wonder-remedy for the ills of modern urban culture and as a way of keeping up with intense modern life without drastically changing it (Hamilton, 2002). These examples illustrate once again how the West selectively appropriates Eastern teachings and practices and invents an ideal image of the ancient East remarkably suited to modern Western lifestyles and thought patterns. The realization that the East imitated by the West is no more than a Western invention that "purifies" the East of its Eastern properties under the guise of restoring past glory and adds another layer to the problematics of the Easternization thesis.

Yet another surprising twist in the history of Western reverence for the East (and especially for India), took place during the 1960s and later, with the rise of New Age culture. This time, Western romantic sentiments actually turned toward present-day India, painted in the image of the imagined Indian Golden Age. Needless to say, India's current image among New Age culture matches the New Age's own values and ideals (Hammer, 2001b), much like its description by 19th-century thinkers who found in it a validation of their own views.

Another criticism of the Easternization thesis claims that the "East" is an idealistic generalization. Orientalist reverence for the East attributes it with permanent special qualities, as an essentialist being with defined characteristics. Is there truly an Eastern essence, or is that a crude stereotype? Can such a vast array of cultures really be bound together as one group under the definition of "East" when they each come from different times and places, and have many complexities and blatant differences? Can China, India, Indonesia, Korea, the Philippines, Mongolia, and Japan all truly represent one particular tendency? And, in the event that we consider India alone, can we truly uncover an Indian essence which exemplifies all of the movements that were formed in India, ever? These pointed questions undermine all talk of the "East" as a unitary and permanent being.

Finally, we must complicate the matter further by asking whether the changes that the Western world is indeed undergoing (if there truly is such a thing as a "Western world") do indeed stem from an Asian-Eastern influence or from another source. For example, do the "green" trend and new attitude toward nature indeed stem from Eastern influences or instead from the new nature religions and the Western neo-Pagan movement? Is it true that the rise of immanent theology is the result of Eastern influence, or rather of the feminist wave sweeping the West (which, by the way, has not been flourishing to the same extent in the East)? Additionally, we may even suggest that these new ideas originated in the rise of postmodernism or the disclosure of Kabbalistic texts. The global world in which we reside is characterized by a fast transference of concepts between cultures and places. As eclecticism grows and the source of any one cultural change becomes harder to trace, we may as well speak of mutual affinities or *zeitgeist*, rather than unidirectional influences.

Moreover, we must wonder whether the depicted changes are indeed a unidirectional and unambiguous development or rather an expression of different movements and directions which inhabit, at all times, a large cultural space that contains various tendencies. Such criticisms and more have been thrown at the Easternization thesis and similar Orientalist approaches. So, what is left of the well-constructed theory of the Easternization of the West: Has the East made any contribution to the changes taking place in Western culture over the past few decades? What part has the East played in these transformations? And, if it had no real part in them, why does the *emic* discourse (that of believers, of spiritual activists) claim the East has contributed significantly to the change in consciousness and values which they call for? And, within the Israeli context, if the East does not provide all that Israeli admirers find in it, why do they still journey there and adopt Eastern teachings, practices, and even identities? And how do all these affect their attitude toward Jewish tradition? I discuss this in the following section.

Judaism is the New Orient

As we have witnessed, the explanation according to which Israelis are drawn to the East and change their whole setting of meaning systems, namely—their way of life, values, and views—due to certain Eastern content is especially dubious. Still, Israelis continue to pine for the East, travel there, talk about Eastern teachings—with or without Judaism. I have no other recourse but to conclude that the East is their "significant Other" (Hammer, 2001a), the Other which actually *enables* them to understand and construct themselves. The East is used as an object onto which Israeli (and overall Western) wants and needs are then projected to appease their source-culture's local discontent, which holds together the general Western crisis of meaning with which this chapter began and, in particular, Jewish Israeli identity problems.

I'd like to argue that, in an Israeli-Jewish context, the draw of the East teaches us more of Israeli sense of discontent toward Jewish tradition and Western-Israeli culture than of appreciation of the East itself. This is especially true of the secular sector in Israel which holds negative views of Judaism. The attitude toward Judaism across this sector includes indifference, alienation, and vast censure (Ruah-Midbar & Klin Oron, 2010). The journey to the East brings Israelis together with religion and spirituality in an entirely different context—a non-Judeo-Christian one—that allows them to take a new look at how rituals, beliefs, and metaphysics contribute to a meaningful life. The openness and empathy these seekers experience toward Eastern religions gives them a new perspective on Judaism as well. Just as they could see Eastern religions through the selective spiritual glasses constructed by an idealization of the East, later they can identify meaningful layers in Judaism as well and even redesign Judaism with similar selectiveness. In this "New Age-y" reconstruction, Judaism is not so different from the West-designed "East."

These Israelis search the East for values and experiences that fit their quest for meaning, such as peace of mind, human fraternity, mystical experiences, closeness to nature, well-being, and openness to a variety of lifestyles and faiths—all things that current Eastern residents do not necessarily possess yet that Israelis perceive as an expression of the East, having consumed its New Age image. As they backpack their way through their journey, these same Israelis successfully ignore a series of obvious Eastern characteristics: poverty, India's traditional stratified social structure which prevents social mobility and includes an "Untouchables" caste, the extreme oppression of women throughout traditional societies, environmental pollution, a life expectancy often shorter than in Israel, the acute theological differences between the various Eastern religions, and more. Accordingly, Israelis who visit the East tend to selectively adopt its local traditions and values. For example, they avoid the prevalent ascetic traditions, such as abstaining from material pleasures or affirming self-love, and opt for those that affirm worldliness, enjoyment, empowerment, and so on.

These Israelis have experienced empathetic attitudes toward religious beliefs and practices, as well as religion's potential contribution to the quest for meaning. They have also acquired skills in the selective design of the image of Eastern culture. Therefore, they may now choose the imagined East over the negative Judaism they have left behind (though it is no less imagined). Another path chosen by some is the projection of similar images on their source culture, Judaism (similarly to Orientalist 19th-century thinkers and the spiritual seekers of the 1960s, who found in the East confirmations of their own doctrines).

This change of heart toward Judaism is but an aspect of a larger spiritual transformation wherein these individuals gradually take on a new set of values, discourse, and lifestyle as their spiritual quest deepens. The details of these processes extend beyond the scope of my research, but I shall nevertheless identify the points along this journey that attest to this transformation and may shed light on the novel attitude these Israelis have toward Judaism. These phases are as follows: first, abstaining from or defying Judaism, which then leads to estrangement and a yearning for the admired exotic Orient and a geographical and cultural spiritual journey. Second, overlooking some problematic aspects of the Oriental sphere when confronted with them by employing a selective state of mind which preserves a reverence of spiritual Eastern values, namely an imagined East. Last, a return to the homeland and the application of this "reverent" selectiveness to Jewish heritage (Ruah-Midbar, 2015). The result is a reimagination and reshaping of Judaism in the likeness of the Eastern traditions that were redesigned by Western and New Age values (sometimes even a syncretistic blend of East and Judaism; see Altglas, 2014; Stambler, 2004). In one of my studies, I named this process the "exotization of Judaism" (Ruah-Midbar, 2014).

Thus, a certain group of Israelis uses the East in affirming those aspects of Jewish tradition they like by reconstructing and reimagining Judaism along the same lines that Westerners reconstruct and reimagine the East. Others go even further, as mentioned, and abandon the (imagined) East once they have realized that Judaism affords them everything they found there and even more.

In order to found my argument, I must mention that, unlike its common image, Judaism may extend beyond its 20th-century orthodox form—its prevalent image throughout Israeli society (Goodman, 2016). In fact, the same ideas and values sought after by the seekers of alternative culture, commonplace across the East, can also be found in abundance in Jewish tradition. Jewish tradition contains great amounts of ideas, approaches, and practices that might provide meaning of the same kind found in the wide and diverse "Eastern" sphere as well as in New Age thought: belief in reincarnation and in the assigned destiny of each incarnation, ways to cope with suffering, immanent theology, and even an emphasis on the divine's feminine aspects, the sanctification of sexual intercourse, exercises and tools for meditation and mystical experiences, body-based practices, and a variety of esoteric doctrines (see, e.g., Niculescu, 2012; Persico, 2016; Vallely, 2006).

Notably, Jews are especially comfortable adopting such concepts, common throughout the East (as imagined by spiritual activists), due to the uniquely rich nature of Jewish tradition. Here is a short example. Adopting the belief in incarnation among a quarter or a fifth of the Western population seems extraordinary to Western scholars of religion because, according to conventional Christian doctrines that emphasize the question of the doctrine/faith's precision, those who believe in reincarnation are condemned to Hell. On the other hand, a similar finding in Israel will evoke no wonder. Issues of doctrinal faith in Jewish tradition are more flexible and varied, and belief in reincarnation may even be interpreted as an adoption of Jewish tradition, rather than foreign. Another example is the heavy emphasis on suffering in Buddhist doctrine—which many Jews who adopt a Jubu identity consider natural (Altglas, 2014; Stambler, 2004).

Much like the above-mentioned development regarding the East, we see a contradiction between two types of Judaism: original/ancient/true/pure Judaism versus current/distorted/twisted Judaism. The Judaism Israelis know and are closest to before they journey to the East is, according to them, unattractive: it reflects establishment and conservatism, lacks an emotional and physical experience, deals with a zealous and petty god, boring, and even repugnant. Its external form—dress, language, music, tastes—also reflects the same undesirable qualities. It belongs to an entirely "other" sector (the religious sector) and holds no relevance for them.

However, the history of this ancient-new pure Jewish tradition is, of course, similar to descriptions of the ancient Indian Golden Age (Ruah-Midbar, 2007). This new Judaism is exotic, saturated with content of inner exploration, deals with experiences of the body, is rich in spiritual secrets waiting to be deciphered, and, most of all, it is remarkably similar to the idealized India and sometimes even transcends it. The new Judaism has a wide variety of meditative and ecstatic techniques and an interest in healing and its tools; it contains chanting, is open to sexual techniques, interreligious camaraderie, and the sense of curiosity that stems from a perennialistic spirit; and it presents spiritual teachers whose paradoxical teachings (much like Zen teachers, as well as Hassidic leaders) lead to enlightenment. The interest that new Judaism shows in the specifics of day-to-day life is not prescriptive-Halachic as it is in traditional Judaism, but rather an attitude that finds it enchanting and meaningful. In this Judaism, Israelis feel "at home," and it is as much theirs as it is other sectors'. In fact, they feel as if they discover, know, and represent Judaism in its truest form, more so than people of the religious and Haredi sectors, whom Israeli society usually views as the authentic representatives of tradition.

This understanding that Judaism can provide seekers with the same things the East provides them by satisfying their need for meaning is at the heart of the journey I have described. Even unconceptualized and unconsciously done, redesigning the East as well as Judaism in a selective manner suited to the needs of the seekers is performed spontaneously and has a variety of expressions. This development often requires an *exotization* of Judaism, its transference from the known and irrelevant image to a new image in a way that will make it attractive and meaningful (Ruah-Midbar, 2014). These Israelis, after encountering the East, view Judaism as their new object upon which they may project their own needs and desires and as a new sphere in which they may search for the answers they seek. Transforming Judaism from a loathsome object to a desirable one, transforms Judaism into the new Orient.

Epilogue: Discontents and Criticism

Every disciple must know, that by visiting the Tzaddik
And the Rabbi, he shall know that treasure may not be found

At the Rabbi's home alone, and when he goes to his home—he shall search

And excavate as far as his hand extends, and seek and ye shall find

Believe the word is very nigh unto thee, in thy mouth, and in thy heart, that thou mayest do it [see Deut. 30:14], right there with him.

And you must understand.

Rabbi Simcha Bunim of Peshischa (*Simchat Yisrael*, 25)

I have analyzed a process that involves the invention of tradition (Hobsbawm & Ranger, 1983) performed twice in a diachronic manner: first, in regard to the East and finally with Judaism—both in the spirit of contemporary alternative spirituality. While the journey to the East portrays the first step on the "Hero's Journey" (Campbell, 2008) in which the seeker travels far-far-away, the return to Judaism expresses the second stage of his journey—the understanding that the treasure he was seeking was already waiting for him at home. Thus, Israelis leave home and contemporary decadent Judaism and travel far, following the Brahmins. There, of all places, they find the road back to the ancient legacy of Abraham.

In fact, the reason that put them on their journey to the East is the same reason they return to Judaism—the same search for meaning in the spirit of contemporary spirituality. Sometimes, one must leave in order to come back and find the answers at home. The treasure does not glimmer but from afar. One must go far to discover it. The exercise that calls for traveling to the East enables Israelis to observe their own traditions anew, with a fresh gaze, and discover in it an attractive face or find within themselves a new passion for their tradition. We must distance ourselves in order to become close, much like the advice of Hasidic tradition. The exoticization of Judaism that this process leads to is a condition for finding at home the very treasure they sought in exile.

Our analysis has demonstrated how a joined explanation framework addresses those who remain indifferent or hostile toward Judaism, those who combine the East with Judaism, and those who abandon the East in favor of Judaism. As clearly arises from the analysis, these conclusions are also greatly true of other Westerners who are not Israeli nor Jewish.

In conclusion, I should nevertheless address the pressing need to embark upon that far-away journey. The prevalent use of the East to meet (Western/Jewish) internal needs testifies to the weakness of Western culture and its intellectual, religious, and "secular" traditions. The need to find inspiration in other sources and to make a stand that is not perceived as traditional reveals a sense of discontent with the source culture (Ruah-Midbar Shapiro & Ruah Midbar, 2017). In fact, we have witnessed that many seek a way to preserve the achievements of the Western cultural framework while assimilating significant changes into the system. Yet a question remains that cannot be answered herein: Does the heart of the matter lie in a need for self-improvement by way of initiating true change within the Western/Jewish-Israeli setting, or is this entire trend no more than another expression of a prominent system characteristic, a sort of "immune deficiency"—self-criticism. In other words: Does criticism of Judeo-Christian tradition stem from an honest desire to deviate from the system, or is it an expression of the affirmation of the critical system? It seems that the built-in critical character of Westerners/Israeli-Jews is what pushes them to their imagined Asian Other, in a journey to find answers and relief from their home-based anguish. To paraphrase the anthem's words, the yearning yet critical (Western) soul always looks forward to some Other, or to the Orient, with a hope that has not been lost for thousands of years––to find meaning out there, in the distance.

Highlights

- In the face of the decline of traditional religions, individuals are at their wit's end: losing meaning and values, having their identities fragmented, and experiencing a deepening sense of alienation.
- Israeli secular Jews view Judaism as a tradition missing its essential pieces, much like other Western religions. Thus, like their Western counterparts, they pursue the East as part of their quest for meaning since the Asian context enables a positive outlook on rituals, beliefs, and metaphysics.
- The West is not going through an Easternization process, as it might seem. Apparently, elements of Asian traditions were selectively chosen and redesigned to fit a Western framework, overlooking some problematic aspects and thus enabling the perseverance of reverence toward this imagined East.
- Like the East, Judaism becomes an object onto which Israelis may project their own needs and desires and a sphere in which they may search for meaning. Judaism becomes their "new Orient." This is a reimagined Judaism, one made in the likeness of the Western

redesign of Eastern traditions and New Age values, thus achieving the "exotization of Judaism."
• The far-away journey is needed to meet internal needs. The built-in critical character of Westerners/Israeli-Jews is what pushes them toward their imagined Asian Other, in a journey to find answers and relief from their home-based anguish.

Acknowledgments

This article was supported by Zefat Academic College.

References

Altglas, V. (2014). *From yoga to Kabbalah: Religious exoticism and the logics of Bricolage.* Oxford University Press.

Campbell, C. (2007). *The easternization of the west: A thematic account of cultural change in the modern era.* Paradigm Publishers.

Campbell, J. (2008). *The hero with a thousand faces.* New World Library.

Capra, F. (1975). *The Tao of physics: An exploration of the parallels between modern physics and eastern mysticism.* Shambhala Publications.

Dawson, A. (2006). East is east, except when it's west: The easternization thesis and the western habitus. *Journal of Religion and Society, 8,* 1–13.

Diem, A. G., & Lewis J. R. (1992). Imagining India: The influence of Hinduism on the New Age movement. In J. R. Lewis & J. G. Melton (Eds.), *Perspectives on the New Age* (pp. 48–58). State University of New York Press.

Elhanan, N. (Ed.). (2006). *Me'Hodu Ve'ad Kan: Hogim Israelim Kotvim al Hodu Ve'Ha'Yahadut Shelahem* (From India to here: Israeli thinkers write about India and their Judaism). Ruben Mass.

Goffman, E. (1961). *On the characteristics of total institutions.* Holt, Rinehart, and Winston.

Goodman, Y. (2016). Ha'Kesher Ha'Gordi Beyn Datiyut Le'Hiloniyut Be'Yisrael: hachala, hadara ve'shinuy (The Gordian Knot between religiosity and secularism in Israel: Containment, exclusion, and change). In Y. Fischer (Ed.), *Secularization and secularism (interdisciplinary perspectives)* (pp. 197–221). Van Leer Institute.

Hamilton, M. (2002). The easternisation thesis: Critical reflections. *Religion, 32*(3), 243–258.

Hammer, O. (2001a). *Claiming knowledge: Strategies of epistemology from theosophy to the New Age.* Brill.

Hammer, O. (2001b). Same message from everywhere: The sources of modern revelation. In M. Rothstein (Ed.), *New Age religion and globalization* (pp. 42–56). Aarhus University Press.

Hanegraaff, W. J. (1998). *New Age religion and western culture: Esotericism in the mirror of secular thought*. Brill.

Hobsbawm, E., & Ranger T. (Eds.). (1983). *The invention of tradition*. Cambridge University Press.

Huss, B. (2010). The Sufi Society from America: Theosophy and Kabbalah in Poona in the late nineteenth century. In *Kabbalah and Modernity* (pp. 167–194). Brill.

Huss, B. (2013). Forward, to the east: Naphthali Herz Imber's perception of Kabbalah. *Journal of Modern Jewish Studies, 12*(3), 398–418.

Loss, J. (2010). Buddha-Dhamma in Israel: Explicit non-religious and implicit non-secular localization of religion. *Nova Religio, 13*(4), 84–105.

Maoz, D. (2007). Backpackers' motivations: The role of culture and nationality. *Annals of Tourism Research, 34*(1), 122–140.

Maoz, D., & Bekerman, Z. (2010). Searching for Jewish answers in Indian resorts: The postmodern traveler. *Annals of Tourism Research, 37*(2), 423–439.

Melamed, A. (2010). *Rokchut Ve'Tabachut: Hamitos al Mekor Ha'Chochmot* (Pharmacy and cookery: The myth of the source of wisdom). University of Haifa and Magnes Press.

Niculescu, M. (2012). I the Jew, I the Buddhist: Multi-religious belonging as inner dialogue. *Crosscurrents, 62*(3), 350–359.

Noy, C. (2012). *Israeli backpackers: From tourism to rite of passage*. SUNY Press.

Peretz, S. (2015). *With God in my backpack: Religiously observant Israeli backpackers in northern India* (master's thesis). Ben-Gurion University of the Negev.

Perry, M. (1992). *Gods within: Critical guide to the New Age*. SPCK.

Persico, T. (2012 April 16). Ha'Dalai Lama Ke'Mahzir Bi'Teshuva: Le'Gilguleya Shel Bedaya (The Dalai Lama returns Jews to Judaism: The reincarnations of a myth). *Lula'at Ha'el*. https://tomerpersico.com/2012/04/16/shama_lama_ding_dong.

Persico, T. (2016). *Meditatzya Yehudit: Hitpathutan shel Tirgolot Ruhaniyot Be'yahadut Zmaneinu* (Jewish meditation: The development of spiritual practices in contemporary Judaism). Tel-Aviv University.

Roof, W. C. (1993). *A generation of seekers: The spiritual journeys of the baby boom generation*. Harper Collins.

Roper, D. (2003). The turbulent marriage of ethnicity and spirituality: Rabbi Theodore Falcon, Makom Ohr Shalom and Jewish mysticism in the western United States, 1969–1993. *Journal of Contemporary Religion, 18*(2), 169–184.

Ruah-Midbar, M. (2007). Be'Hazara Le'Gan Ha'Eden Be'Mahshevet Ha'Idan Ha'Hadash—Dimuyim Shel Avar Ide'ali Be'Toldot Am Israel (Return to paradise in New-Age thought—Images of an ideal past in the history of the people of Israel). In I. Tavory (Ed.), *Dancing in a thorn field: The New Age spirituality in Israel* (pp. 28–59). Hakibutz Hameuhad Press.

Ruah-Midbar, M. (2014). Metaksheret, Hilerit Ve'Shaman Nifgashim Etzel Ha'Rav: Mapat Ha'Drachim shel Hayahad(iy)ut Ha'Yisre'eli(yu)t Ba'Idan Ha'Hadash (A medium, a healer and a shaman meet at the Rabbi's: A roadmap of New-Age Judaism and Israeliness). In G. Katz, S. Ratzabi, & Y. Yadgar (Eds.), *Beyond Halacha: Secularism, traditionalism and "New Age" culture* (pp. 498–528). Sde Boker: The Ben-Gurion Research Institute for the Study of Israel & Zionism.

Ruah-Midbar, M. (2015). Hodu La'Adonai Ki Tov—Mabat al Israelim (Ye)Hudim Le'or Tezat Mizruah Ha'Ma'rav (Thank God for India—A look at Jewish Israelis in light of the easternization of the west thesis). *Theory and Criticism, 44*, 311–325.

Ruah-Midbar, M., & Klin Oron, A. (2010). Jew age: Jewish praxis in Israeli New Age discourse. *Journal of Alternative Spiritualities and New Age Studies, 5*(1), 33–63.

Ruah-Midbar Shapiro, M., & Ruah-Midbar, O. (2017). Outdoing authenticity: Three postmodern models of adapting folklore materials in current spiritual music. *Journal of Folklore Research, 54*(3), 199–231.

Said, E. W. (1995). *Orientalism: Western conceptions of the Orient*. Penguin Press.

Stambler, D. (2004). *Blades of grass in sidewalk cracks: A narrative study of Jewish Buddhist teachers* (doctoral dissertation). Tel Aviv University.

Vallely, A. (2006). Jewish redemption by way of the Buddha: A post-modern tale of exile and return. *Jewish Culture and History, 8*(3), 22–39.

16

Jewish Spiritualization as "Meaning Injection"

An Ethnography of a Rabbinic Seminar in the Israeli Military

Udi Lebel, Batia Ben-Hador, and Uzi Ben-Shalom

Introduction

The Israeli Defense Forces (IDF) holds a unique status in Israeli society, being not only a security-providing institution but also one of symbolic capital, around which the entire Israeli society is organized in a unique form of cultural militarism. However, toward the end of the millennium, Israel's elites, similarly to other neo-liberal communities in the Western world (Ruckert, 2006) began experiencing what has been referred to as the "civil-military gap"—a dissociation from the military ethos in particular and from the collective-patriotic one in general in favor of a new, post-modern, individualistic ethos.

This new ethos has contributed to the army's transition into a phase defined by Edward Luttwak (1996) as "post-heroic" and by Charles Moskos (1977) as a transition from "institution" to "occupation." As a by-product, the army has become increasingly similar to civil organizations in terms of its organizational culture, which has been relying more and more on financial and other quantitative parameters, management theories and constant control, and, above all, on a dominant judicial discourse. This has been achieved in parallel to a decline in the impact of what used to be called "fighting spirit," which tended to rely on more qualitative, traditional parameters.

But, despite these transformations, the army has been unable to successfully cope with the motivational crisis experienced by elite groups in Israeli society. Moreover, changes in the military resulted in an alienation among soldiers and commanders. The height of the crisis concerns the army's

Udi Lebel, Batia Ben-Hador, and Uzi Ben-Shalom, *Jewish Spiritualization as "Meaning Injection"* In: *Finding Meaning.* Edited by: Ofra Mayseless and Pninit Russo-Netzer, Oxford University Press. © Oxford University Press 2022. DOI: 10.1093/oso/9780190910358.003.0016 non-heroic components—soldiers, and especially standing army personnel serving in "blue collar" positions. They will not be able to convert their military capital to a civil or business one, and, moreover, during their service, they do not enjoy a prestigious position or attractive pay (Sason-Levy, 2003). These are the classic roles among which high levels of alienation are experienced toward the workplace (Ames & Janes, 1987; Dubin, Champoux, & Porter, 1975).

Psychologists such as Fromm (1962) acknowledged alienation as a fundamental risk that is detrimental to mental health and results in stress, depression, and anxiety. Sociologists such as Seeman (1959) and Durkheim (1968) believed that alienation is a social disease that may result in the disintegration of communities. Hence, alienation in organizations is considered a negative phenomenon, detrimental to employees and their performance. One of the ways in which organizations deal with alienation is by embedding spiritual content into their messages to employees (Jurkiewicz & Giacalone, 2004).

The current study, however, focuses on an aspect not examined yet: the institutionalized effect of an internal military unit—the "Jewish consciousness unit" (a unit within the IDF's Military Rabbinate corps), which, relying on Jewish spiritual practices, is dedicated to spreading among soldiers a sense of meaning and intent as well as recognition and appreciation.

The *raison d'être* of this "Jewish consciousness" unit is that, as opposed to the alienated, privatized army, with its formal organizational culture, its representatives are perceived as working to instill the army with "good old values," aimed at restoring it to its "good old days." The result of this work has been a return to a nostalgic discourse for an era in which the army was in its heroic state (as opposed to "post-heroic"): free of civil control, eager to go to war, and instilled with patriotic and religious justifications or meaning for its actions. De facto, the "Jewish consciousness" unit at the Military Rabbinate makes excessive use of spiritual practices aimed at pushing military commanders to adopt a conservative-republican ideology. This in itself is an innovation, as, contrary to the perception of spirituality as belonging to post-modernistic worlds (Wexler, 1996), here it is used and even coopted in favor of promoting conservative-republican values, alongside an intensive use of the religious-Zionist discourse that links religious reason with nationalistic ideologies while viewing the achievement of political and military goals as fulfillment of religious precepts. Albeit being a spiritual discourse, it promotes operative targets in the physical world while equipping combatants with an old-new meaning to their military operations.

The inductive study outlined in this chapter relies on content and discourse analysis of lesson plans, conversations, and interviews with "Jewish consciousness" representatives and an ethnography study conducted during the sessions of a "Managerial Skills in Biblical Spirit" seminar organized by the "Jewish consciousness" unit. The Jewish consciousness activity, as shall be illustrated, is infused with spiritual practices aimed at promoting conservative insights. Participants learn that the post-heroic army is failing and that military management principles that have existed since biblical times (but nevertheless are presented as modern) are the solution for restoring the army to its previous glory.

Background: The Jewish Consciousness Unit

With the establishment of the state of Israeli in 1948, and in parallel to the establishment of the IDF and its compulsory service model, the need arose for an internal body that would provide religious services while developing a line of religious thinking that would establish the *raison d'être* within Jewish religious law for religious soldiers serving in the army. For this purpose, the Military Rabbinate Corps was established, consisting mainly of military rabbis in their compulsory and reserve service, as well as providers of various religious services.

In 2001, the Chief Military Rabbi decided to transform the roles and target audiences of the Military Rabbinate—a process during which the Military Rabbinate would become involved in the army's "fighting spirit," and as such serve as an active and relevant agent for all serving soldiers and not only religious ones. According to his vision, the Rabbinate would take an active educational role in the formation of the Israeli soldier's spiritual world (Kampinski, 2009). To this end he inaugurated a new unit at the Rabbinate, which he coined "Jewish Consciousness," stating that it would be responsible for instilling values, motivation, and empowerment among combat soldiers in the context of Jewish discourse and origins.

In parallel to this transformation in the role and definition of the military Rabbinate corps, the army in general experienced a transformation in its sociodemographic context. During most of its years of existence, the vast majority of the IDF's combat forces and in particular its combat commanders belonged to secular-socialist sectors in Israeli society. However, ever since these communities began experiencing neo-liberal and demilitarization processes (Lebel & Hatuka, 2016), inciting in them what is known as the "civil-military gap" (Lebel, 2010), religious-traditionalist groups began to fill combat roles, including junior and intermediate officer ranks (Libel & Gal, 2015).

As more and more religious soldiers started serving in combat divisions and units, and most of all as growing numbers of religious soldiers became commanders, the services of the Jewish Consciousness unit grew in demand and popularity, its Rabbis being routinely invited to visit combat units to deliver lectures, seminars, and empowerment talks. This has resulted in the unit, very shortly after its establishment, becoming one of the main factors contributing to the formation of the army's "fighting spirit"—the motivational and empowerment discourse of its warriors. Consequently, and by definition, this process also included the injection of Jewish religious thought as an inseparable part of these discourses.

While the official purpose of the Military Rabbinate is to provide religious services within the army, the "Jewish consciousness" unit injects spiritual meaning that is not necessarily religious.

1. *Approaching new target audiences—secular soldiers.* Although the Military Rabbinate was established to provide religious services to religious soldiers, the newly defined unit embarked on a precedential process by which it develops services and content that are intended for all soldiers, regardless of their religious inclinations. Moreover, judging from its internal discourse, the unit's preferred target audience is a secular one.

2. *Priest anointed for the conduct of war—a transformation in the identity of the military Rabbi.* By emphasizing and preaching the idea of fighting spirit and not only the provision of religious services, the military Rabbi has become more similar to the biblical notion of a "Priest anointed for the conduct of war" (Deut. 20:1–9). This biblical priest accompanies the army in order to encourage the soldiers prior to going into battle by incorporating a religious, belief-based rhetoric (Benedict, 1970). This is similar to the role of the chaplains—religious officers in ancient armies of the Christian world who served as religious authorities granting theological justifications for battle and, in doing so, contributed to soldiers' motivation and fighting spirit (Otis, 2010).

3. *Warrior Rabbi.* The Jewish Consciousness unit recruited Rabbis who had previously served as combat officers and thus possessed first-hand

knowledge and experience of the challenges of being a warrior. These Rabbis accompany soldiers in their operational work during routine times as well as during wartime. Moreover, in recent years, the military Rabbi has become an organic part of combat units, being available to commanders and soldiers for counseling purposes and taking part in the formation of the unit's culture during daily military routine (Kampinski, 2009).

The evolved role of the IDF's Rabbis involves the creation of a "Discourse Community," one that perceives reality through a specific spectrum while providing a unique language with which to experience this reality within a community that shares the same images, metaphors, and perceptions (Duszak, 1997).

The Opposition

The work of the Jewish Consciousness unit was met by much opposition by internal military politics—because it took over activities that were previously performed solely by the IDF's Education corps—as well as for ideological-political reasons. While the Education corps relied mostly on academic lecturers on reserve duty, most of whom came from universities' humanities and social sciences departments and therefore were mostly identified with the neo-liberal left, for the first time educational discourses and activities toward the formation of soldiers' fighting spirits are now being carried out by Rabbis—most of whom are identified with the neo-conservative right wing. Opponents warned of the army's theocratization and religionization.

Opposition was also expressed in Israel's academic discourse in the narrow context of research on the Jewish Consciousness unit, as well as in the wider context of military-religion relationships. Researchers holding neo-liberalist views have warned of the danger of this process to the status of women in the army, to the willingness of religious soldiers to obey orders perceived as contrary to Jewish law, and to the effect of the process on warriors' combat ethics and on the military culture, which will become increasingly influenced by nationalistic-religious sources as opposed to universalistic-cosmopolitical ones. The body of studies pertaining to this warning style of writing has been referred to in Israel's academic discourse as "the religionization discourse. (in Hebrew: "Hadata")" This critical paradigm incorporates political sociology models and methods of analysis toward framing the range of processes described as a "social problem" (Hervieux & Voltan, 2018), warning of its spread and following its outcomes (Drori, 2015; Levy, 2013). De-Facto it is a "Moral-Panic" against the ongoing Constant recruitment national-religions soldiers to the military which used to be a secular island (Lebel, 2015; Lebel, 2016).

The Purpose of the Current Study and Its Contribution

We propose to examine the work of the Jewish Consciousness unit within the IDF as a practice of "meaning injection," or the ability to establish a routine reframing within a spiritual-Jewish climate where daily work would be perceived as meaningful and recognizable, thereby leading to the necessary empowerment and increased motivation to persist in the work. A more spiritual climate, and in this case a Jewish-spiritual one, enhances the ability to position and frame daily routine in a way that would lead to an increased sense of satisfaction and self-reward, as expressed in Klerk's pioneering paper "Spirituality, Meaning in Life, and Work Wellness: A Research Agenda" (Klerk, 2005).

Further to Klerk's studies, increasing numbers of studies have shown that spiritual discourse in organizations leads to ascribing meaning to work among workers. In particular, studies have suggested the use of the injection of spiritual discourse as an effective practice for minimizing workers' sense of alienation within the work organization, which in turn leads to an empowerment of the sense of commitment and motivation at work (Kashdan & Nezlek, 2012). In addition it was found that spiritualism helps workers identify with their organization and its management and contributes to the perception of organizational goals as the personal goals of each individual worker, leading to a competitive advantage for the organization among its competitors (Cunha, Rego, & D'Oliveira, 2006).

Some studies even emphasize the advantage of meaning injection through a spiritual-religious discourse serving as a frame that paints secular-rational practices with an ethos that relies on a sense of mission, commitment, and recognition of the effort and sacrifice—specifically contributing toward a sense of meaning that is so lacking in an era controlled by rational organizations (Moran, 2017).

Our use of the term "meaning injection" is actually borrowed from the school of thought on "policy injection," originally "policy diffusion" (Boushey, 2016; Marsh & Sherman, 2009; Quin & Keun, 2005; Sugiyama, 2008). These are processes by which policy communities have adopted a unique strategy to ensure that institutions would eventually adopt their preferred policy: the injection of a unique discourse into a field or an organization (such as for instance the "green discourse" or "human rights discourse"). Of course, such discourse also involves the creation of an ideology, values, and unique perceptions for experiencing and judging reality (Buhrs, 2003; Smith, 1978; Wittberg, 1989), for instance, the transformation that has taken place in the military organization over the past decades by which the army has undergone a process of "organizational alienation" involving a spiritual-emotional nullification and the loss of a sense of meaning (Kathuria, Joshi, & Porth, 2007).

In light of these trends, the possibility to ascribe a spiritual aspect to their daily work essentially leads to an empowered sense of consciousness and esteem among soldiers as well as an elevated sense of organizational commitment and increased motivation to achieve their goals (Rego & Chuna, 2008). Our decision to use this conception to assess the contribution of the Jewish Consciousness unit to the injection of meaning among soldiers is not a deductive one. It relies on ethnographic research and phenomenological analysis of the unit's activities, as further elaborated in the section on methodology.

Our ethnographic study opens a new direction in the discourse on religion and the military in Israel in general and in the discourse on the work of the Jewish Consciousness unit in particular. While previous studies have examined the effect of the religious discourse within the IDF on the religionization-secularization continuum from within the assumption that, in its work, the Jewish Consciousness unit pushes military culture toward its religious extremity, we propose to assess the unit's work on a different continuum, one of meaning-alienation. We argue that the unit's work brings soldiers' experiences closer to the spiritual extremity. By doing so we have been able to identify three innovatory methodological practices:

1. *A shift of the discourse from the sociopolitical to the cultural-organizational.* We do not intend to contribute to the macro-sociological level, within which it may be possible to use the work of the Jewish Consciousness unit to deduct more general conclusions about social processes in

Israel relating to religion and the state; instead, we wish to contribute to the micro-sociological level in order to assess how macro processes are expressed in a well-defined field: a case study of the Jewish Consciousness unit in the IDF. We assume that the permeation of the discourse to the "field" may impact the cultural-organizational context and be perceived by it in unexpected ways, even for those directly involved in its operation.

2. *A discourse community.* We will not make do with assessing the political thought promoted by the examined case study, but also will assess its level of acceptance. Hence, this is not a normative study but a phenomenological one that examines the impact of the promoted discourse on the military service experience and the way it is perceived by its consumers. In this context we define military personnel exposed to the content taught by the Jewish Consciousness unit as "active agents," or a "discourse community." Specifically, as illustrated by Koos (2012), this group can be identified as an interpretive community whose members experience a process of political consumerism.

3. *Spirituality in the service of conservatism.* Extensive research has been published on New Age movements and their contribution to the injection of meaning that alleviates our existence in an alienated, post-industrial world. Most of these studies perceive these new social movements as being in conflict and in opposition with the modern-nationalistic discourse, undermining the social order and adopting a discourse intended to promote a political deconstruction and an ideological alternative to the hegemonic social order (Welton, 1993). We propose that at a time in which the extent of meaning provided by the military is weakened, the spiritual discourse can be used to explain the process of the establishment, empowerment, and reproduction of a conservative, modern, nationalistic-religious social order. In this cooptation of spiritualism, a sense of meaning is empowered and implemented by the two ultimate totalitarian and conservative institutions: religion and the military (Scott, 2010).

During the seminar that we observed, we saw how a basic function of religion—the fact that it is a system of ascribing meaning—is utilized. As described by Silberman in her seminal paper: "Religion as a Meaning System: Implications for the New Millennium" (Silberman, 2005), and as elaborated later, the spiritual process leads its consumers on a nostalgic journey and ignites a passion to connect to modern-conservative practices and values. While spirituality as an experience has been largely identified with the New Age (i.e., with post-modernism), here we expose how it serves as no less than a catalyst for empowering components that are in opposition to post-modernism, leaving us with spirituality as a post-modern practice in the service of modernism.

Methodology and Structure

This study is a phenomenological attempt to uncover the subjective experiences of individuals exposed to "spiritual" injections of meaning in the army (Lincoln & Guba, 1985).

We used content and discourse analysis methodologies from organizational studies (Fairclough, 2005) to analyze lesson plans produced by the Jewish Consciousness unit and made available to army commanders so that they may use them to guide and instruct their soldiers; popular books published by the unit's reserve personnel, which they use when presenting their lectures to soldiers and commanders; conversations and interviews held with the unit's personnel and with those exposed to its work; and, most of all, an ethnography which we carried out during the seminar entitled "Management in Biblical Spirit," presented by the Jewish Consciousness unit to career soldiers in the army—a seminar which incorporated in it most of the materials outlined earlier.

"Management in Biblical Spirit" is a military seminar participated in by commanders of various ranks who have registered for the seminar of their own accord in order to be eligible for promotion and higher wages. The seminar is held during one week, from Sunday to Thursday, ending at 17:00 every day, at which time the participants return home. Twenty-five career soldiers, officers, and non-commissioned officers participated in the seminar that we observed. About 50% were religious and about 25% of the participants were women. The seminar consisted of frontal lectures presented by various lecturers. The formal aims of the seminar were to inform participants of the Bible's contributions to military management skills relevant to our time. The three researchers were present throughout the entire seminar, documenting both the formal discourse and the informal one (conversations between participants and between them and the lecturers).

In addition to participation in the seminar, we also conducted four interviews: with the military rabbinate commander in charge of the seminar, with the military rabbinate administrative coordinator of the seminar, and with two seminar lecturers.

It should further be noted that we obtained all necessary approvals from relevant army officials to be present during the course as ethnographers, without having to present our findings or research outputs to the army.

In the findings section of this chapter we outline the range of themes that we identified from the various texts, interviews, and ethnography conducted, all of them components of our examination of the process of spiritual meaning injection in the military. In the following sections we provide an organizational/historical context which may serve to clarify why this meaning injection process is effective while understanding the military void in terms of meaning. Finally, we attempt to reach some conclusions from our analysis by outlining the military and social implications of the processes examined.

Findings

We chose to describe a process of infiltration of a spiritual discourse into a military context, which leads to the injection of meaning. This meaning injection process includes actions, content, and messages which can be summarized into the following three themes:

1. *Injection targeted mainly at combat soldiers and combat situations.* "You are the continuation of our past"; spirituality for warriors and warfare
2. *Injection targeted mainly at combat support units (administrative positions operative during routine times):* "Every military action has national implications," a message to supporters of warfare during routine times
3. *A specific analysis of the seminar lecturers and instructors while identifying the messages that they provide,* as a product of their personality as well as their instruction and teaching methods

You Are the Continuation of Our Past: Spirituality for Warriors and Warfare

One of the main recurring messages of the seminar is that all IDF soldiers are descendants of Biblical leaders, as well as of courageous and revered commanders from the IDF's formative years. The seminar lecturers illustrated the principles taught by demonstrating their relevance in the decision-making processes of famous IDF commanders—with nearly all of the examples used involving commanders who, after completing their military service, were identified with the political right wing. Their work was compared to military and leadership decisions made by Biblical warrior figures such as Gideon, King David, Jephthah (Yiftach), Samson, and Joshua. In some cases actual comparisons were made between battles in the Bible and the ways in which revered IDF commanders conducted their modern-day battles. It was clearly explained that these commanders had in fact adopted solutions which had been part of the "Biblical toolbox."

A further message has been to explain the uniqueness of the Israeli military case, emphasizing that it has been around much longer than the other warring nations of the world. For instance, in a lesson plan entitled "The Chain of Generations," the lecturer is required to ask the soldiers "What do we know about our nation?" The lecturer is then required to explain to his students that the IDF's battle heritage did not commence in 1948 (with the establishment of the modern state of Israel) but thousands of years ago. For instance, students who may have believed that the 1948 War of Independence is the first in which a small Jewish force overcame a multitude of Arab armies are in for a surprise. According to the lesson plan, "The first war in which a small Jewish force defeated an international power . . . [took place] about 2200 years ago during the Maccabean Revolt against the Greek rule" ("The Chain of Generations," pp. 3–4). It is then further clarified that the IDF's modern-day wars took place at the same sites as many Biblical battles and moreover were fought against the same enemy, thereby comparing the Palestinians to the Philistines or the Amalekites.

A return to Jewish origins can be noted even in the discussion of bravery, by the explanation that both the IDF's forefathers and the modern-day warrior-heroes have absorbed their perception of bravery from the Bible.

In the seminar which we observed, the lesson was concluded with an answer to the question, "Why is it that soldiers from the Zionist-religious sector—such as Roi Klein (an officer who died during the 2006 Lebanon War after jumping on a grenade to save his fellow soldiers) are those who nowadays excel in military work and possess extraordinary bravery?" The discussion ignored the fact that their demographic presence increases the probability that when bravery is required, it would be shown by those who in any case are serving in the army, opting instead to focus on the conscientious aspect.

A recurring didactic principle in the seminar involves discussing a military problem currently on the public agenda while explaining that the solution to the problem can be found in the Bible. For instance, one of the lesson plans is titled: "The Commander in the Lead—A Lesson Plan on Personal Example—From Jewish Sources." In the seminar that we attended, the lecturer began the lesson by asking general questions regarding the importance of this issue.

Many of the participants mentioned the lessons of the Second Lebanon War (2006) in which the IDF fought against the Hezbollah and that was perceived by the Israeli public as a war in which Israel was defeated (Kober, 2008). Following pressure from protest movements, an investigating committee had been appointed, concluding, among other things, that many commanders conducted battles from afar, using technological command and control systems, rather than being present in the battlefield to lead their soldiers. The lecturer agreed with the students and showed a slide containing a quote from the investigating committee's report stating that "It is difficult to give soldiers a message of the importance of fighting and getting the job done, if their commanders are sitting behind . . . we find in this phenomenon a deep ethical failure" (Winograd et al., 2008).

The lecturer explained that the IDF's well-known call of "Follow me" is an expression of symbolic-mythical value in Israeli society and among the IDF's typical characteristics in its days of glory, when it fought victorious wars that elevated its commanders and warriors to places of public reverence. As an example, the lecturer presented the well-known quote of former Chief of Staff Haim Bar-Lev, who was asked whether it is not folly to position army commanders before their soldiers, thereby making them vulnerable to the enemy's fire. Bar Lev's response is presented on a slide to the class: "The fact that our senior commanders go together with their men to places of danger is first and foremost an expression of human character and moral level and not the result of a utilitarian decision . . . the willingness of our commanders to always stand in the lead is the source of moral power that they need in order to make decisions . . . by personal example . . . they form the character of the army and nurture its spirit." With this slide in the background, the lecturer returns to the Bible and describes the battle principles embodied by Gideon, who said to the people of Israel, "Watch me, and do likewise." Over and over the message is conveyed that the source of the term "Follow me"—a term expressing a military culture yearned for by the Israel public in the aftermath of the Second Lebanon War—originates from ancient Jewish history.

Every Military Action Has National Implications:
A Message to Supporters of Warfare During
Routine Times

Many of the lessons have been devised for soldiers and permanent service personnel who are not combatants, but who work in administrative, technological, or logistic positions and therefore do not enjoy the benefits of heroic glorification granted to those serving in combat units—a fact which may result in a sense of frustration in the absence of recognition and appreciation for their work. The "spiritual journey" embarked upon by the "Jewish Consciousness" unit attempts to also help these soldiers perceive their roles differently. For instance, a lesson plan entitled "A Journey of Observation" is in fact an attempt at reframing soldiers' conceptualizations of their roles and of themselves—a common practice in support groups for elevating participants' self-esteem (Rochat & Zahavi, 2011). The message conveyed to the soldiers is that every soldier can decide how to perceive his task and his role. And if he would manage to understand the importance of the tasks for which he is responsible, he would feel more satisfaction and pride and would also perform in a better way.

The next lesson was entitled "To Be a Free Man." This lesson attempts to make every participant realize that he is free, that he should not complain of a tedious or boring routine, as in fact he is performing an important and meaningful role and should know that it is appreciated and remind himself that he has chosen this role. The lesson plan emphasizes that the unit's role is "to show the soldier that although he is part of a total organization, and obligated to follow orders, he is free" ("To Be a Free Man," p. 1). It is suggested that lecturers ask the students why they think that the Passover holiday is relevant to this lesson. The students state that this holiday reminds us that the Jewish people used to be slaves in Egypt, and then the lecturer shows a slide containing a long list of historical periods in which Jews were persecuted and oppressed, from the period of servitude in Egypt through to modern waves of anti-Semitism. The following slide presents soldiers in various roles, mostly noncombat ones, and in the center the words "IDF Service." The lecturer explains that simply service in the IDF, in whichever role, even if it entails frustration, orders, and lack of vacation time, has by definition the implications of liberty and freedom.

After a short discussion on the importance of responsibility on the battlefield, the lecturer explains that there is no difference between the responsibility of a commander not to return with his company until his combat task has been completed, even if this means sacrificing his life, and someone who would not dare leave his base or his office until he is convinced that all his tasks have been completed and that all noted deficiencies have been repaired. Participants then give examples of situations in which only thanks to the responsible work performed by combat support units would the warriors themselves be able to achieve victory in battle.

The seminar lecturer then explained that "The world is divided into those who show responsibility and those who ignore it. . . . would the State of Israel continue to exist if not for responsible people?" The lecturer asked the participants to recall their nonoperational routine work days, imploring them to adopt a rule of daily soul-searching: "Am I completely loyal to the decisions of the commanders of my unit? Or of the army? Do I care even about things that are not under my direct responsibility? Do I perform my tasks just because I have to, or do I care about the quality of my work? Do I make an effort to save and avoid waste of army and State resources? Do I look for the good in each of my companions? Am I appreciative enough of what the army and the country have given me? Am I aware of times when I am cynical, arrogant, or critical? Do I dedicate my own time to contribute to the community and to charity?" ("Soul Searching," p. 11).

The lesson ends with the phrase "Every one of us is a leader" and the message that every role and every period is an opportunity to achieve recognition and appreciation for courage, leadership, and caring.

The Seminar Lecturers and Their Methods of Work

We chose to discuss the biographical and psycho-political identity of the lecturers as emanating from their worldviews regarding life, the military, and Israeli society. It seems that their identities as well as their teaching methods are essential components in achieving the seminar's goals.

Who then are these lecturers?

They are all men who in their past were combat soldiers and commanders, and all of them still volunteer for reserve duty despite the fact that most are beyond the required age.

All are married, with an average of seven children each. Despite their relatively young ages, some already have grandchildren—meaning that they were married no later than their early twenties.

All are religious, and nearly all are ordained Rabbis.

All lecturers are in contact with current or former army commanders or reserve ones, are well-informed of daily activities in the army, invite lone soldiers to stay at their houses, and have contributed to all military operations—whether through reserve duty or by volunteering to help. Their children are raised to become warriors and contribute to the army in the best ways they can. One of them even established a highly reputable pre-military academy and a "Yeshivat Hesder"[1] whose students tend to become IDF commanders—and in which the period of serving is twice as long as in other arrangement yeshivas.

Nearly all of the lecturers live in settlements—community villages characterized by a religious lifestyle and located in Judea and Samaria, beyond the "green line." Some have taken part in the establishment of new settlements/strongholds in Judea and Samaria, and some have even been evacuated in the past from settlements from which the state of Israel had retreated.

From this, we can easily conclude that all lecturers, by definition, belong to the Israeli right wing and are identified with the acceleration of the religious-nationalist trend that has become prevalent over the past decades both in Israel and internationally. This trend, which can be characterized from a theological perspective as religious devoutness, joins nationalist devoutness (patriotism, republicanism, militarism) and both serve a single hybrid religion (Fox, 2001) whose founders perceive themselves as authentically in charge of national and moral existence and as being exclusively identified with working for the general good, including giving their lives for the nation, thus posing an alternative to the old founding elites who have tired of carrying the burden and have undergone bourgeoisification, cosmopolitanization, and globalization processes which have alienated them from the national-collective ethos (Lebel, 2013).

Moreover, all lecturers are involved in collective work and volunteer for various social causes, and their personal stories include exceptional sacrifices and giving. It appears that even the way in which their personal stories are presented is the result of well-formulated planning, a "performance" that ignites emotion and a heartfelt excitement among listeners. In fact, a majority of the lecturers did not come to the seminar in order to give a "lesson

[1] An "arrangement" yeshiva—a yeshiva that has an arrangement with the IDF by which its students enlist together in the same unit.

plan" but rather to tell about themselves and share their experiences, their daily lives, and their volunteering channels.

Three main recurring themes have been identified as central impressions made on participants by their lecturers.

1. *Belief, persistence and humility—Jewish values:* The seminar lecturers were perceived as men who, due to the strength of their belief, their religiosity, and their education, are meticulous with every demand, be it religious, social, or familial. They do not "cut corners," they are perfectionists and therefore can be trusted. They are able to perform daring and courageous acts, and these would be carried out with faith and professionalism.

2. *Religion and nationalism:* The social identity of the lecturers is known in Israel as religious-nationalist or Zionist-religious. Its members uphold a hybrid national and religious discourse. They perceive military service, as they do all other "Zionist precepts" (such as settlement on the land), as extensions of religious precepts, thereby granting members of this community a much stronger meaning for their military service than ascribed to it by their secular counterparts (Eastwood, 2016).

3. *Family and relationships:* The lecturers adhere to the traditional family model, in which women carry out mostly domestic roles, and, if they do enter the public sphere, it is in volunteering positions. All of them have many children, and repeat the message that "Thanks to my wife being at home I am able to fight for the people of Israel." It was emphasized a number of times that a religious Jewish family life is critical as the engine that enables a complete, full, and productive life and that a military man cannot truly fulfill his role in the absence of a family backing him, and especially a wife as a "help meet for him" (Genesis 2:18).

Participants' Feedback

At the end of the seminar, a 2-hour feedback session was held in which participants expressed their views on their experience. Most participants felt that the seminar had met or exceeded their expectations. As a chief sergeant in the IT Corps said, "The seminar is fascinating. I chose to attend because it sounded interesting to me and I really learned a lot. The content of the seminar connects to my daily life at work."

Many participants expressed a desire to continue with these courses and implement their content in their military units and offices. Some related to the values of connection to the land and its people. For example, a female lieutenant said, "I serve in a base at Ha'Ela valley, where the fight between David and Goliath took place. I never attached much importance to it, but the seminar made me proud to serve in this base."

Another male sergeant said, "I don't believe in god, but it is important to me to remember again and again that what I'm doing relies on our tradition and history."

As mentioned, although the seminar was arranged and instructed by the Jewish Consciousness unit, about half of the participants were not religious. One participant (male lieutenant) expressed his feelings as follows: "When I came to the seminar I was afraid that the lecturers will try to pull me into religion. Not only did that not happen, but I feel closer to Judaism now."

One captain even said, "I wish my wife had been here, I bet it would make her better understand the importance of my work."

Many career soldiers spend long days away from home and consequently miss a lot of their family's everyday life. Even those who serve at bases near their homes typically work many hours and participate in training and exercises, resulting in a very fragile work–family balance. The captain's wish that his wife would better understand the importance of his work indicates that the meaning injection has been successful.

It is interesting to note that no feedback was received regarding the family values emphasized in the seminar. During one break, we asked the female participants if they had noticed a masculine bias or were bothered by the seminar lecturers ignoring the fact that many female soldiers also fight on the battlefield, but they replied that they did not notice it at all.

Discussion

The contents of the seminar that we have analyzed and the instructors and lecturers presenting them point to a process of "meaning injection" for military personnel.

In their daily work, seminar participants often experience a reality that is perceived by them as gray and boring. They hold what can be referred to as

a "secular viewpoint" toward their military place of work, often feeling critical, cynical, estranged, and even antagonistic toward it. But the seminar has
enabled them to ascribe sanctity to their work, to frame their daily tasks as
meaningful and substantial. The seminar's meaning injection process has
enabled them to create what has been coined by Ross (1996) as a "spiritual
dimension" of their military routine.

In our examination of the imprint of the religious-Zionist movement on
military culture in general and of the work of the Jewish Consciousness unit
in particular, we have noted a "positioning" with the following challenge: the
provision of spiritual components to an organization that has recently undergone a process of social alienation, secularization, and rationalization. This
positioning offers an opportunity for military personnel to feel part of a military "spiritual journey," framing their actions in a way that would increase
their motivation, commitment, and self-satisfaction, thus empowering their
sense of public appreciation and granting them the acknowledgment which
they desire.

While formally the Military Rabbinate and the Jewish Consciousness
unit should be about religion, we did not necessarily see a religious positioning, but rather a spiritual one involving the provision of meaning to
IDF soldiers.

There are various epistemic communities that act to promote the injection of meaning into professional or organizational discourses (Scarbrough
& Swan, 2001). These are rhetorical processes that lead to a change of consciousness or policy, causing the discourse to become "greener," more feminist, or enhancing a sense of serviceability, well-being, religiousness, or
nationalism (Green, 2004). The injection of such components eventually
affects organizational and personal behaviors, modes of conduct, satisfaction levels, extent of organizational commitment, and the motivation of all
employees because this is the strength of the discourse. As written by Day
(1998) in his pioneering paper, in order to achieve organizational change, a
transformational discourse is needed. In our case, the Jewish Consciousness
unit is an agent responsible for the injection of spirituality into daily military
work. Religious Jewish sources relying on biblical examples are the didactic
means for inflaming a sense of spirituality, and it can be assumed that, for
audiences who were not brought up on traditionalism or who are not Jewish,
other sources would be needed to create such psycho-conscious injections
of meaning. It should be noted in this context that most of the seminar

participants chose to take part in it and arrived with a predisposition to the subject matter.

Russo-Netzer and Mayseless (2014) explained that a spiritual change marks a multidimensional process of personal transformation, especially in individuals' capacity to self-transform the meaning of their lives or their work and to experience renewed emotions in their daily lives. We examined the evolution of this process among seminar participants and found that the Jewish Consciousness unit representatives act as spiritual guides working to create what Lynn and her colleagues referred to as "work-faith integration" (Lynn, Naughton, & Vander Veen, 2010). Our interviews with seminar participants showed that they experienced a process which transformed their attitudes and perceptions regarding their daily military lives. This process has previously been identified as an organizational resource. The extensive literature on spirituality in the workplace, most of which centers on sense-making processes affected by the penetration of spirituality into an organization, also emphasizes the various functions of spirituality aimed at increasing the productiveness of employees in the organization. It was found that spirituality in the workplace encourages effort and creativity as well as persistence, enhanced quality of life, increased productivity, reduced fatigue, increased motivation, and an increased sense of belonging and caring for one's colleagues (Crossman, 2016; Scheitle & Adamczky, 2016).

Next, we discuss two main functions that are relevant to the military context in general and to the seminar participants in particular.

Sense of Free Choice

The contribution of spiritual meaning injection in the military organization is in enhancing soldiers' sense of choice as alienation often results in soldiers feeling that their daily military routine is being forced upon them and is a burden. Russo-Netzer and Mayseless have found that, in the organizational context, the spiritual constructs that result from the meaning injection process create a sense of self-mastery and choice (Russo-Netzer & Mayseless, 2014). Similar findings have been described by other researchers who found that sense of choice, control, activeness, and freedom are all central contributors of spirituality to the organization, as the sense of alienation consists first and foremost of perceiving work reactively and not proactively—as a constraint and not a prerogative (Adams et al., 2000; Sagy & Antokovsky, 1996; Zika & Chamberlin, 1992).

It is important to note a further insight made by Russo-Netzer and Mayseless, which is that we are not referring to the absence of criticism by the individual toward his work, but rather to his repossessing a sense of choice in his work despite its shortcomings and enhancing his sense of responsibility regarding these shortcomings, as well as his commitment to act to improve them (Russo-Netzer & Mayseless, 2014).

Enhanced Sense of Recognition and Personal and Social Appreciation

The process of meaning injection within the organization enhances the ability of those carrying out tasks to accredit themselves with a status, whether this is in their own eyes or in their ability to imagine how their work is perceived by society (Russo-Netzer & Mayseless, 2014). Here, too, we are dealing with the opposite of alienation, which is the disengagement from community and society, while appreciation and acknowledgment provide a sense of belonging to a community.

Conclusion

The IDF is still perceived today as an organization that needs a "meaning injection." For instance, Padan and Ben Shalom (2012) expressed their opposition to what they referred to as "the increased involvement in material matters while neglecting the human-social aspect" in the IDF's strategic policy, warning that the army "would make a grave mistake by relying solely on its material force and technological ingenuity." They argued that such an attitude toward manpower development relies on managerial theories rather than leadership ones and on providing commanders with physical and intellectual tools while ignoring their need to "influence the spirit of their soldiers" (Padan & Ben Shalom, 2012).

Charles Moskos, one of the world's most influential military sociologists, has criticized the liberal West, which, during the years following the Vietnam

War, had nearly completely abandoned the military's ideological component, specifically in relation to the training of soldiers. Moskos criticized the fact that Western armies stopped investing in what he referred to as "latent ideology": the emotional faith-laden component that connects the warrior to society and provides him with a sense of justification, purpose, and meaning for his actions (Moskos, 1970). Other researchers have found that soldiers who did not identify with the goals of their military's actions, or were at least neutral toward them, were at a higher risk for experiencing frustration, ambivalence, and alienation toward their tasks and their commanders and that this was eventually translated into an avoidance of fulfilling tasks as well as to reduced professionalism (Lebel, 2014).

Public criticism toward alienation in the IDF focused on combat situations, but the need for meaning injection or fighting spirit exists throughout the entire army. The practices used by the Military Rabbinate's Jewish Consciousness unit as reviewed in this chapter are one possible way of injecting spiritual meaning into the army or of preventing the spread of alienation in the army.

While we cannot ignore the widespread criticism expressed in the media as well as in academia toward the increased impact of religion on the Israeli army (Levy, 2011), these criticisms are motivated by ideological opinions, and we do not intend to take part in this cultural-political controversy.

Whatever the impact of the religious-nationalist community on the military, our contribution is in marking the ways in which it makes its impact and the strategies by which it may gain a foothold among IDF soldiers. We have outlined a spiritual-religious discourse injecting meaning to the military service, which in turn enhances individuals' sense of service and of wellness in their services, as well as granting them a sense of acknowledgment and recognition of their daily work. However, to achieve these feelings, soldiers are required to position themselves within the spiritual-religious discourse because only within its principles, languages, myths, and ethos is the reframing process of their daily work made possible. It is, in fact, a ruse that involves positioning oneself within the religious discourse in order to qualify for obtaining the desired sense of meaning and recognition. Spirituality is seen here as a tool that serves the two most traditional and total institutions—the military and religion. We are dealing with a cooptation of spiritualism—the use of the post-modern practice of spiritualism for the reproduction of a modern hegemony of religion in the army.

Highlights

- A military seminar aims to infuse among soldiers a sense of "Jewish spirit" to empower and enhance motivation to serve.
- The main aim of the seminar is to "inject meaning" into the military service of noncombat officers who lack "symbolic capital" and experience alienation in their military work environment.
- We argue that the seminar has succeeded in positioning these soldiers' military service as attractive, productive, and meaningful by infusing in them a Jewish-spiritualistic discourse and language.
- The use of the language of Judaism, and its linking to a spiritual discourse parallel to the "New Age" discourse, has enabled the soldiers to imagine their daily service in a more meaningful way.
- The Jewish-spiritual discourse allows them to identify sources of acknowledgement and recognition of their contribution, as well as to adopt a spiritual language that masks the alienation, routine, and marginality of their daily work.
- This spiritual meaning injection is carried out within a military organization that has recently undergone a process of social alienation, secularization, and rationalization.
- Finally, the post-modern motif of spiritualism is used to promote the reproduction of a modern hegemony of religion in the army, and participants are ultimately drawn closer to the Jewish-nationalist discourse because only from this perspective is it possible to ascribe to their daily work such a strong sense of meaning, mission, and recognition.
- Use of faith language in favor of organizational behavior (motivation creating)

Acknowledgment

The authors would like to thank Ms. Yael Nachumi for her constructive comments and professional editing assistance, and we thank the anonymous reviewers and the volume's editors for their comments and suggestions which improved and upgraded the chapter. A big thank you to the editor of Oxford

Publishing Ms. Poonguzhali Ramasamy for her professional and kind work and supervision in producing the chapter.

References

Adams, T. B., Bezner, J. R., Drabbs, M. E., Zambarano, R. J., & Steinhardt, M. A. (2000). Conceptualization and measurement of the spiritual and psychological dimensions of wellness in a college population. *Journal of American College Health*, 48(4), 165–173.

Ames, G. M., & Janes, C. R. (1987). Heavy and problem drinking in an American blue-collar population. *Social Science and Medicine*, 25(8), 949–960.

Benedict, M. (1970). Notes on the service of the priest anointed for the conduct of war and his deputy. *Moriya*, 33(2014), 1–3.

Boushey, G. (2016). Targeted for diffusion? *The American Political Science Review*, 110(1), 198–214.

Buhrs, T. (2003). From diffusion to defusion. *Environmental Politics*, 12(3), 83–101.

Crossman, J. (2016). Alignment and misalignment in personal and organizational spiritual identities. *Identity*, 16(3), 154–168.

Cunha, M. P., Rego, A., & D'Oliveira, T. (2006). Organizational spiritualties: An ideology-based typology. *Business and Society*, 45(2), 211–234.

Day, M. T. (1998). Transformational discourse: Ideologies of organizational change in the academic library and information science literature. *Library Trends*, 46(4), 635–667.

Drori, Z. (2015). The "religionizing" of the Israel Defence Force: Its impact on military culture and professionalism. *Res Militaris*, 5(1), 1–21.

Dubin R., Champoux, J. E., & Porter, L. W. (1975). Central life interests and organizational commitment of blue-collar and clerical workers. *Administrative Science Quarterly*, 20(3), 411–421.

Durkheim, E. (1968). *Suicide, a study in sociology*. Free Press.

Duszak, A. (1997). Cross cultural academic communication: A discourse-community view. In: A. Duszak (Ed.), *Trends in linguistics* (pp. 11–39). Mouton De Gruyter.

Eastwood, J. (2016). Meaningful service: Pedagogy at Israeli pre-military academies and the ethics of militarism. *European Journal of International Relations*, 22(3), 671–695.

Fairclough, N. (2005). Discourse analysis in organization studies. *Organization Studies*, 26(6), 915–939.

Fox, J. (2001). Religion as an overlooked element of international relations. *International Studies Review*, 3(3), 53–73.

Fromm, E. (1962). Alienation under capitalism. In E. Josephson & M. Josephson (Eds.), *Man alone: Alienation in modern society* (pp. 56–73). Dell.

Green, S. E. (2004). A rhetorical theory of diffusion. *Academy of Management Review*, 29(4), 659–689.

Hervieux, C., & Voltan, A. (2018). Framing social problems in social entrepreneurship, *Journal of Business Ethics*, 151(2), 279–293.

Jurkiewicz, C. L., & Giacalone, R. A. (2004). A values framework for measuring the impact of workplace spirituality on organizational performance. *Journal of Business Ethics*, 49(2), 129–142.

Kampinski, A. (2009). The military Rabbinate and the question of its double loyalty. *Emdot*, 1, 161–184. [Hebrew]

Kashdan, T. B., & Nezlek, J. B. (2012). Whether, when, and how is spirituality related to well-being? Moving beyond single occasion questionnaires to understanding daily process. *Personality and Social Psychology Bulletin, 38*(11), 1523.

Kathuria, R., Joshi, M. P., & Porth, S. J. (2007). Organizational alignment and performance: Past, present and future. *Management Decision, 45*(3), 503–517.

Klerk, J. (2005). Spirituality, meaning in life, and work wellness: A research agenda. *The International Journal of Organizational Analysis, 13*(1), 64–88.

Kober, A. (2008). The Israel defense forces in the second Lebanon War: Why the poor performance? *Journal of Strategic Studies, 31*(1), 3–40.

Koos S. (2012). What drives political consumption in Europe? *Acta Sociologica, 55*(1), 37–57.

Lebel, U. (2010). "Casualty panic": Military recruitment models, civil-military gap, and their implications for the legitimacy of military loss. *Democracy and Security, 6*(2), 183–206.

Lebel, U. (2013). Postmodern or conservative? Competing security communities over military doctrine—Israeli national-religious soldiers as counter [strategic] culture agents. *Political and Military Sociology: An Annual Review, 40*, 23–57.

Lebel, U. (2014). Blackmailing the army—military strategic refusal as policy and doctrine enforcement: Israeli warfare at Lebanon, Samaria, and Gaza. *Small Wars and Insurgencies, 24*(5), 297–328.

Lebel, U. (2016). "The 'Immunized Integration' of Religious-Zionists within Israeli Society", *Social Identities* 22(6), 642–660.

Lebel, U. (2016). The "immunized integration" of Religious-Zionists within Israeli society. *Social Identities, 22*(6), 642–660.

Lebel, U., & Hatuka, G. (2016). De-militarization as political self-marginalization: Israeli Labor Party and the MISEs (members of Israeli security elite) 1977–2015. *Israel Affairs, 22*(3-4), 641–663.

Levy, Y. (2011). The Israeli military: Imprisoned by the religious community. *Middle East Policy, 18*(2), 67–83.

Levy, Y. (2013). The theocratization of the Israeli military. *Armed Forces & Society, 40*(2), 269–294.

Libel, T., & Gal, R. (2015). Between military–society and religion–military relations: Different aspects of the growing religiosity in the Israeli defense forces. *Defense & Security Analysis, 31*(3), 213–227.

Lincoln, Y., & Guba E. (1985). *Naturalistic inquiry.* Sage.

Luttwak, E. (1996). A post-heroic military policy: The new season of bellicosity. *Foreign Affairs, 75*(4), 33–44.

Lynn, M., Naughton, M., & Vander Veen, S. (2010). Connecting religion and work. *Human Relations, 64*(5), 675–701.

Marsh, D., & Sherman, J. (2009). Policy diffusion and policy transfer. *Policy Studies, 30*(3), 269–288.

Moran, R. (2017). Workplace spirituality in law enforcement: A content analysis of the literature. *Journal of Management, Spirituality and Religion, 14*(4), 343–364. doi: 10.1080/14766086.2017.1376287.

Moskos, C. (1977). From institution to occupation. *Armed Forces and Society, 4*(1), 41–50.

Moskos, C. C. (1970). *The American enlisted man: The rank and file in today's military.* Sage.

Otis, P. (2010). An overview of the US chaplaincy. *Faith and International Affairs, 7*(4), 3–15.

Padan C., & Ben Shalom, U. (2012, November 29). The place of military leadership in Israel in light of the IDF's strategy. Retrieved from Polak, U., "Kipah" Website, *The Military Rabbinate during Operation Pillar of Defense: Judaica and reinforcement talks for warriors.* [Hebrew]

Quin, M., & Keun, L. (2005). Knowledge diffusion, market segmentation, and technological catch-up. *Research Policy, 34*(6), 759–783.

Rego, A., & Chuna, M. (2008). Workplace spirituality and organizational commitment. *Journal of Organizational Change Management, 21*(1), 53–75.

Rochat, P., & Zahavi, D. (2011). The uncanny mirror: A re-framing of mirror self-experience. *Consciousness and Cognition, 20*(2), 204–213.

Ross, L. (1995). The spiritual dimension. *Nursing Studies, 32*(5), 457–468.

Ruckert, A. (2006). Towards an inclusive-neoliberal regime of development: From the Washington to the post-Washington consensus. *Labour, Capital and Society/Travail, Capital et Société, 39*(1), 34–67.

Russo-Netzer, P., & Mayseless, O. (2014). Spiritual identity outside institutional religion: A phenomenological exploration. *Identity, 14*(1), 19–42.

Sagy, S., & Antonovsky, H. (1996). Structural sources of the sense of coherence: Two life stories of Holocaust survivors in Israel. *Israel Journal of Medical Sciences, 32*(3-4), 200–205.

Sason-Levy, O. (2003). Masculinity and citizenship: Tensions and contradictions in the experience of blue-collar soldiers' identities. *Global Studies in Culture and Power, 10,* 319–345.

Scarbrough, H., & Swan, J. (2001). Explaining the diffusion of knowledge management. *British Journal of Management, 12*(1), 3–12.

Scheitle, C. P., & Adamczyk, A. (2016). Divine callings: Religious sensemaking in the organizational founding process. *Journal of Management, Spirituality & Religion, 13*(2), 94–116.

Scott, S. (2010). Revisiting the total institution. *Sociology, 44*(2), 213–231.

Seeman, M. (1959). On the meaning of alienation. *American Sociological Review, 24*(6), 783–791.

Silberman, I. (2005). Religion as a meaning system: Implications for the new millennium. *Journal of Social Issues, 61*(4), 641–663.

Sugiyama, N. B. (2008). Ideology and networks: The politics of social policy diffusion in Brazil. *Latin American Research Review, 43*(3), 82–108.

Welton, M. (1993). Social revolutionary learning: The new social movements as learning sites. *Adult Education Quarterly, 43*(3), 152–164.

Wexler, P. (1996). *Holy sparks: Social theory, education, and religion.* St Martin's Press.

Winograd, E., Gavison, R., Dror, Y., Nadel, C., & Einan, M. (2008). *Final report of the commission of inquiry into the events of military engagement in Lebanon 2006.* State of Israel. [Hebrew]

Wittberg, P. (1989). Feminist consciousness among American nuns: Patterns of ideological diffusion. *Women Studies, 5,* 529–537.

Zika, S., & Chamberlain, K. (1992). On the relation between meaning in life and psychological well-being. *British Journal of Psychology, 83*(1), 133–145.

17

Religious Sense-Making, Purpose-Making, and Significance-Making Among Jewish, Druze, and Muslim Young Adults in Israel

Nurit Novis-Deutsch, Peter Nynäs, and Sawsan Kheir

Introduction

The "human effort after meaning" (Bartlett, 1932/1995), is a key distinctive feature of people and societies. Our basic conative need to know and understand our self and surroundings is neurologically hardwired (Baumeister & Vohs, 2002; Rolls, 2018), while the needs for being valued, belonging, and self-actualizing generate a search for purpose and significance throughout life (Batson & Stocks, 2004; Wong, 2013). With such powerful motivators for meaning-making, it is no wonder that engaging in meaning is as universal as culture itself, with some researchers using the terms "culture" and "meaning-making" interchangeably (e.g., Oyserman, 2011). Meaning-making plays an integral role in the development of one's sense of self and identity, which can explain why so much of it takes place during adolescence and emerging adulthood, as self and identity gain coherence (Kunnen & Bosma, 2000; McLean & Pratt, 2006). It has also been found to play a significant role in subjective well-being, leading to higher levels of psychological adjustment and happiness (George & Park, 2016; Hamby et al., 2017; Park, 2005, Park 2010; Park, 2013) although this link is not uniformly agreed upon (e.g., Singer, 2004) or culturally consistent (e.g., Alea & Bluck, 2013).

"Meaning" is a noun. It refers to a system of explanations which individuals inherit, receive, internalize, or reject. "Meaning-*making*" is a verb: a highly personal, dynamic, and ongoing activity of the individual. While the former involves internalization and identification with an external system and implies a finite process, the latter involves ownership, discovery, and boundless construction, or, as Postman and Weingartner (1969, p. 91) put

Nurit Novis-Deutsch, Peter Nynäs, and Sawsan Kheir, *Religious Sense-Making, Purpose-Making, and Significance-Making Among Jewish, Druze, and Muslim Young Adults in Israel* In: *Finding Meaning.* Edited by: Ofra Mayseless and Pninit Russo-Netzer, Oxford University Press. © Oxford University Press 2022. DOI: 10.1093/oso/9780190910358.003.0017 it: "The meaning maker . . . continues to create new meanings." People usually make use of external meaning systems such as religions, ideologies, and philosophies to inform and shape their meaning-making activity, but, over time, they tend to make these meaning systems uniquely their own, and, as a result, no two people adhering to the same external meaning system will interpret and understand it in fully the same way (Seitz & Angel, 2015). At the same time, culture plays a key role in meaning-making, so that meaning-making differences are apparent not only between individuals but also between groups. This can be boiled down to two related questions: Is meaning "discovered" or "constructed" (Baird, 1985; Baumeister, 1991)? And is it primarily a project of the individual or of their culture? We keep both broad questions in mind as we describe our study and return to them in the discussion.

We begin this chapter by delineating its theoretical framework. First, we locate the concept of meaning-making within the broader spectrum of meaning research. Then, we present a typology of meaning-making activities which will be used in this study, making a note of how it compares to related typologies. Last, we review findings on the relation between meaning-making, religiosity,[1] and culture.

In the empirical part of the chapter, we report a study of Israeli emerging adults who belong to three faith traditions, Jewish, Muslim, and Druze. We identify several socially recognized paths for pursuing meaning through religion and spirituality, one socially agreed-upon narrative of secularity, and a few less socially sanctioned narratives of religious meaninglessness. In the discussion, we analyze our findings in terms of meaning-making, subjective well-being, and Israeli subcultures. Finally, we discuss some of the implications of these findings for the study of meaning, religiosity, and culture.

The Place of Meaning-Making Within Meaning Research and Some of Its Subconstructs

The broad field of meaning research spans several constructs ranging from *meaning in life*, *meaning-making*, and *meaning maintenance*, all of which

---

[1] Throughout this chapter, unless otherwise noted, we use the term "religiosity" or "religious" to connote religiosity and/or spirituality.

directly address meaning, to broader related constructs such as goals, worldviews, identity, and existential anxiety (George & Park, 2016). Perhaps as a result of the ubiquitous use of "meaning" in psychological research, the field has suffered from definitional ambiguities and lack of integration (Heintzelman & King, 2014; Martela & Steger, 2016). This has led in recent years to a concerted effort to define "meaning," partition it, and relate its subconstructs to one another. This section locates meaning-making in relation to other concepts and explores some of the ways in which it has been typologized.

There is a broad range of ways to study meaning in individuals' lives: we can examine to what extent people feel that their lives are meaningful (typically explored in *meaning in life* studies); we can explore people's meaning frameworks, or the relationships they perceive and expect in the world (Baumeister, 1991); and we can explore how these meaning systems are maintained, created, or modified in light of experiences and challenges in life through the *meaning maintenance model* (Heine, Proulx, & Vohs, 2006) or using the *meaning-making* framework (Parks, 2011). This last term refers to "the activity of composing a sense of the connections among things: a sense of pattern order, form, and significance" (Parks, 2011, p. 19). We follow Kroger (2004) in considering meaning-making to be the idiosyncratic and evolving way in which people actively organize their own experiences. It is often construed in the form of an insightful personal narrative (McLean & Pratt, 2006). A similar situation might have entirely different meanings for different people, or even for the same person at different points in their life (Kunnen & Bosma, 2000).

Meaning-making has been divided by scope (Janof-Bulman, 1992; Park, 2013) into *global meaning systems*, which make sense of life in general, and *situational meaning-making*, which relate to specific events and experiences. When an event threatens the integrity of individuals' global meaning, they engage in an appraisal of the discrepancy between the two. The more discrepant they are, the more stress is generated. To alleviate this stress, people make meaning-making efforts which result, through various coping strategies, in either "meaningfulness" or in "meaninglessness" (Park, 2013). Two major paths to restore meaning are *assimilative meaning-making*, which involves changing the situational appraisal that preserves global meaning intact, and *accommodative meaning-making*, which involves modifying global beliefs to reflect the situation. When global meaning is either restored or revised, a sense of well-being is expected to prevail, although empirical data are not fully conclusive, as we will show.

Recent studies on the related construct of *meaning in life* (MIL) have adopted Martela and Steger's (2016) tripartite model which partitions meaning in life into *coherence* (the degree to which individuals perceive a sense of coherence and understanding regarding their lives; also termed comprehension), *purpose* (the extent to which individuals experience life as being directed and motivated by goals which they value), and *significance* (the degree to which individuals feel that their existence is of importance and value in the world). This last component is also termed *mattering* (George & Park, 2014, 2016). Researchers of the Terror Management Theory point out that a sense of significance can involve deriving "symbolic immortality" from internalized cultural worldviews (Greenberg & Arndt, 2012). Living in light of a grander scope of meaning than that available to any single human mitigates the fear of death and provides a sense of equanimity in the face of its inevitability.

A Typology of Three Meaning-Making Activities

While the MIL typology of coherence/comprehension, purpose and signif-icance/mattering (Heintzelman & King, 2014; Martela & Steger, 2016) has been related to the construct of meaning-making (George & Park, 2016), it has not been directly applied to it. We suggest a modified version the MIL typology to connote three central psychological activities involved in meaning-making. Meaning making can involve any or all of the following three psychological activities: *sense-making* is the act of making sense of re-ality. Maslow (1954) highlighted people's "conative needs" as a basic need, running parallel to the needs for survival and safety. Questions such as how the world works, what happens after death, and why people suffer seek and gain answers in the process of sense-making. Sense-making paves the way to *purpose-making*, which involves crafting a sense of subjective purpose and agency in life. Here the meaning is not "of the world," but "in the person" as it is the individual as subject who is at the center of this meaning-making endeavor. For this activity, sense-making questions are turned inward: Why am *I* here? Why did this happen to *me*? What does *my* life mean? Finally, *significance-making* reflects an attempt to understand and feel that reality *matters beyond one's own monadic life*, an act which goes beyond conferring a purpose to individual life or making sense of reality. Significance, as opposed to importance, involves connecting with something larger than oneself and, in the process, losing one's self-boundaries. Examples include merging with a group (e.g., in war, Graham & Haidt, 2009), serving an ideal or briefly assimilating with the ultimate in "unio-mystica" (James, 1902/2003).

The three meaning-making activities are interconnected. For example, the feeling of illumination arising from making sense of the world can be powerful enough to confer a sense of purpose or even of significance on the life of the person experiencing it. Similarly, experiences of significance can also make sense of the world, as they are often noetic (James, 1902/2003). Despite being interconnected, however, each meaning-making activity involves a different psychological activity: Sense-making implies turning one's gaze outward toward reality, purpose-making involves turning it inward toward the self, and significance-making dissolves the borders between inner and outer. Another distinction is that sense-making (similar to coherence) is primarily a contemplative, cognitively motivated activity which results in understanding, purpose-making is an experiential and affectively motivated activity which results in goals, while significance-making, which is not fully explainable by either emotion or cognition, results in connection. Thinking about meaning in this way can lead to some interesting hypotheses. We might speculate, for example, that the three aspects of meaning-making are developmentally sequential; sense-making precedes purpose-making which in turn precedes significance-making both within the development of individuals and in the cultural development of human societies.

Two notes before turning to our own study. First, we offer this typology as an integration of previous studies since each of the three meaning-making activities has been discussed separately elsewhere (see Davis et al., 1998, on "sense making"; Park & Folkman, 1997, on the "search for significance" and Baumeister & Vohs, 2002, on "personal purpose-seeking"). Second, the meaning-making typology does not fully map on to MIL typology, although the two share significant commonalities. Table 17.1 sums their shared aspects as well as their differences.

Religion, Spirituality, and Meaning-Making

Meaning-making in all three subtypes is wide-ranging in scope. People can make sense of reality through science, myth, or philosophy. They can seek

Table 17.1 The meaning-making typology in relation to the meaning in life (MIL) typology

Meaning-making typology	Meaning in life typology	Shared aspects	Differences
Sense making: an activity aimed at making sense of reality by learning, exploring, and discovering the world.	*Coherence* (or comprehension): a perceived sense of coherence regarding one's life.	Both involve the conative aspect of meaning; both involve cognitive processes.	Sense making applies to the order of reality; coherence applies to one's life. Sense making is an activity; coherence is an index of how much sense one's life makes.
Purpose making: an activity aimed at identifying the purpose, goals and meaning of one's own life.	*Purpose*: experiencing life as goal and value-directed.	Both involve motivational aspects of meaning; relate to affect; are focused on the self.	These two constructs directly map onto each other in two spheres: having a sense of purpose and seeking or actively creating purpose.
Significance making: the act of forgoing the focus on the self in favor of merging with a larger cause, ideal, or entity.	*Significance* (or mattering): feeling that one's existence is of importance and value in the world.	Both address existential concerns.	Significance making is an activity which involves sacrificing self-boundaries; promotes humility. Significance assuages existential fears by assuring individuals of their everlasting importance.

and find purpose to their lives through social activity, art, nature, work, or love (Hamby et al., 2017). They can attain significance through offspring, altruism, or nationalism. Without discounting the importance of these myriad sources of meaning, religion and spirituality (as well as their counterparts, secularism and atheism) have a special link to meaning-making.

Religion is construed as a "meaning system" above all its other attributes. It has been defined as a meaning structure within the human cognitive system which includes attitudes and beliefs, values, goals, self-definition, and some locus of ultimate concern (Paloutzian & Park, 2014). Batson and Stocks go so far as to define religion as "whatever a person does to deal with existential questions" (2004, p. 141), implying that the terms "religion" and "meaning-making" are synonymous.

Religion and spirituality are uniquely suited for the job of making meaning as they involve four important attributes which promote it. First, they are comprehensive, offering all-encompassing global meaning systems; second, they are culturally universal (Brown, 2000), so they are widely accessible; third, they make direct claims that translate meaning into actions; and finally, they involve the transcendent, which allows them to easily relate to "significance" and "ultimate meaning" (Hood, Hill, & Williamson, 2005; Park, 2013).

In terms of the above-suggested typology, religious sense-making would mean the use of religious cosmology and theology to make sense of the world; religious purpose-making would imply the use of religious practices, beliefs, and values to craft a sense of personal purpose in the world; and religious significance-making would mean using religious ideas, techniques, and experiences to transcend the boundaries of the self and connect with what lies beyond. While many other meaning systems can provide sense and purpose to life, "no other system of meaning is so bold in its proclaimed ability to provide a sense of significance" (Hood, Hill, & Spilka, 2009, p. 16).

The Role of Culture and Social Norms in Meaning-Making

Although meaning-making and the use of religion and spirituality to guide it are universal, they are also culturally contingent (Tarakeshwar, Stanton, & Pargament, 2003). Culture affects meaning-making processes in several ways.

First, it shapes the content and range of acceptable options for making meaning. As Triandis (2007) put it, culturally appropriate situations seem right; culturally inappropriate situations seem wrong or off-key. Some societies offer many viable paths to meaning, others offer very few, raising more of a challenge for those who cannot identify with the accepted meaning systems.

Second, cultures affect the frequency, style, and intensity of engaging in meaning-making. Although every society engages in meaning-making on a cultural level and promotes its meaning-systems, meaning-making as an individual activity may be encouraged or discouraged, depending on, among other factors, the importance ascribed in a given society to values of authority, traditionalism, autonomy, and openness. It may also be constrained by forms of social exclusion. Thus, we should not expect meaning-making to take place at similar levels of intensity among members of all groups and cultures.

Third, culture can affect the psychosocial outcomes of meaning-making. In societies where individuals are socialized to accept inherited meaning systems, a prolonged process of meaning-making may be associated with decreased well-being. In others, individuals may be encouraged to continually reinvent their meaning systems, leading to enhanced well-being for individuals who engage in ongoing meaning-making. For example, the robust finding that meaning-making activity that produces a restored or revised global meaning system leads to more subjective well-being (Barry & Abo-Zena, 2014) is more ambiguous and at times completely absent in non-Western societies (Alea & Bluck, 2013).

To sum, we have defined meaning-making and highlighted the importance of the spiritual-religious domain within it. We have subdivided meaning-making into sense-making, purpose-making, and significance-making and considered each in terms of religious-spiritual activity. We noted that although universal, meaning-making is also culturally contingent, such that its relation to well-being, identified in Western countries, is in need of further cross-cultural exploration.

This chapter presents a modest cross-cultural analysis of religious meaning-making using the sense-, purpose- and significance-making typology in a specific cultural context: that of Jewish, Muslim, and Druze Israeli emerging adults. The questions which guided our exploration are listed here.

1. To what degree and manner do emerging adults in Israel (ages 18–30) engage in religious-spiritual meaning-making?
2. How does this activity relate to their sense of emotional well-being?
3. To what degree do they engage differentially in religious sense-making, purpose-making, and significance-making?
4. Can we discern any differences in religious meaning-making by faith tradition (Judaism, Islam, and Druze) in this sample?

Method

To explore these questions, we conducted an analysis of a subset of the data deriving from a large international study on the values and religiosity of young adults globally (the YARG study; Nynäs et al., 2021, http://www.abo.fi/

fakultet/yarg). This international mixed-method study includes Israel as one of its 13 locations. A total of 4,964 participants were surveyed, and 546 of them were interviewed in depth as well. The interviews lasted for 1–3 hours and included a tool called the Faith-Q-Sort (FQS interview; Wulff, 2019).

Participants

A total of 754 young Israeli adults ages 18–30 (329 Jewish, 199 Muslim, and 226 Druze) completed The YARG Survey which probed for values, beliefs, social attitudes, social belonging, subjective and social well-being, religiosity, and demographic information. The sample, which was not random but rather purposeful, was recruited by advertising at multiple colleges and universities throughout Israel. Participants were invited to complete the survey and then, if interested, apply to participate in the FQS interview. Of the Israeli survey participants, 42.7% of the respondents were male, 57.2% were female, and 0.1% described themselves as "other." Of the total, 24.1% were 18- to 20-year-olds, 54.0% were 21- to 25-year-olds, and 21.1% were 26- to 30-year-olds. 44.5% of the respondents reported belonging to some religious, spiritual, or philosophical community. The interview sample (n = 90) was purposefully chosen from among the willing survey participants to maximize demographic and value-profile diversity. It included 45 Jews, 22 Muslims, and 23 Druze of varying levels of religiosity.

Tools

The Faith Q-Sort
The YARG project implemented a Q-sort tool, the FQS (Wulff, 2019). Q-methodology in general provides a foundation for a systematic study of subjectivity and a person's viewpoints, opinions, beliefs, and attitudes (Watts & Stenner 2012). The FQS instruments was designed to account for diversity in religious subjectivities and explores religion in a way that allows for observing the complexity of contemporary religiosities. Participants are asked to sort 101 cards containing statements regarding religion, faith, praxis, and core values into groups according to their importance to them. These statements stem from a broad variety of sources in the history of religion, psychology, and sociology of religion in order to account for different

religious traditions and forms of religiosities (Wulff, 2019).[2] During the session, participants are asked to arrange their card-sorting along a normal distribution ranging from +4 for the 5 most representative cards to −4 for the 5 least representative cards, with all the others falling in a normalized curve in between. This array of statements makes up a participant's *Q-sort*. Each Q-sort is unique, but it is possible to discern shared patterns in the sorts, known as *prototypes*. Each prototype reflects a socially shared viewpoint about religion and spirituality. It important to stress that prototypes are not groups of people, but rather coherent and culturally sanctioned worldviews or states of mind. For this sort of analysis, the robustness of the pattern is not a function of the number of participants who express it but rather of the coalescence of items in each perspective. To generate prototypes from the individual Q-sorts, each national/ethnic set of Q-sorts is factor-analyzed separately. Thus, in our study, all Jewish Q-sorts were analyzed separately, as were Muslim and Druze ones. Factor analysis of Q-sorts (known as *Q-methodology*) differs from standard factor-analysis (R-method) in that R-method involves correlating variables across subjects, while the Q-method involves clustering subjects across variables and reducing many individual viewpoints to a few shared ways of thinking.

The Meaning-Making in Religion Scale

We created a Meaning-Making in Religion scale (MMR) scale using 24 of the 101 FQS items. We chose these items by identifying statements which attest to (1) the use of religious or spiritual frameworks to make sense of the world (the sense-making subscale, 8 items, Cronbach's alpha = .74); (2) statements which refer to the use of religion or spirituality to guide one's personal purpose in life (the purpose-making subscale, 8 items, Cronbach's alpha = .78), and (3) statements which attest to attempts to transcend the self and connect to the beyond (the significance-making subscale, 8 items, Cronbach's alpha = .75). Reliability of the full 24-item MMR scale was .90. The three subscales were intercorrelated (.74 to .75), indicating a shared underlying construct. As a sort of validity test, each subscale distinguished those belonging to a religious or spiritual group from those who didn't (p <.00). Here are examples of items (i.e., FQS statement cards) which contributed to each index of meaning-making[3]:

---

[2] For all full list of the 101 statements in English, Hebrew, or Arabic, please contact the authors.
[3] For a full list of the 24 items comprising the Meaning-Making in Religion (MMR) scale, please contact the authors.

Religious sense-making:
- Spends much time reading or talking about his or her convictions.
- Has a thorough knowledge of religious scriptures or texts
- Views all events in this world within a religious or spiritual framework.

Religious purpose-making:
- Centers his or her life on a religious or spiritual quest.
- Actively works toward making the world a better place to live.
- Feels adrift, without direction, purpose, or goal (reverse-coded)

Significance-making:
- Seeks to intensify his or her experience of the divine or some other-worldly reality.
- Has experienced moments of intense divine, mysterious, or supernatural presence.
- Willingly gives up worldly or bodily pleasures for religious or spiritual reasons.

Additional tools in this part of the YARG study included the Positive Affect Negative Affect Scale (PANAS) and the Subjective Well-Being Scale (SWBS), which were distributed to all survey participants.

Procedure and Analytic Plan

After individually completing the FQS with a trained researcher (40 minutes to 1 hour), each participant was interviewed in depth (a further 1–2 hours) about their sorting and the background to this in terms of, for example, their religious identity and development.

We first analyzed the correlations between the MMR scale and subscales, and various demographic and well-being information for each of the 90 participants. Next, we used the 12 FQS prototypes which were generated by the Q-analysis and compared the average scores on each meaning-making subscale for each prototype. Then, we used data from in-depth interviews with participants who loaded strongly on a specific prototype ("defining sorts") to explore cultural aspects of the narratives referring to meaning-making activities.

Findings

General Findings

One-way ANOVA tests between the three religious groups revealed that the Jewish sample was significantly less religious than the Muslim and Druze (p <.00) and that the Druze were significantly less religious than the Muslims (p <.01.) Scores on the scale measuring subjective well-being (SWBS) were modestly but significantly higher for Muslims and for Druze than for Jews (p <.05 and p <.01, respectively).

When analyzing differences on meaning-making on an individual level, no significant gender differences were found on any of the meaning-making subscales. A significant correlation between younger age and meaning-making was found for the full MMR scale (r = .24, p <.05) and for the sense-making subscale (r = .27, p <.01). An ANOVA showed significant differences in religious meaning-making by religion (see Table 17.2). Post hoc tests found that Muslims were significantly more engaged in religious meaning-making activities than the Druze, and that the Druze were more engaged than the Jews.

Surprisingly, no significant relation was found between SWBS scores which measured subjective well-being and MMR scores measuring religious meaning-making. The only modest significant correlation was between significance-making and positive life orientation (r = .23, p <.05).

The FQS Prototypes

The picture shifts when examined at the resolution of the 12 extracted prototypes, rather than at level of faith traditions. Each individual loaded differently on the prototypes of their group (i.e., Jewish, Muslim, or Druze), with some loading very high on one prototype and being considered a "defining sort" and fewer double-loading on several prototypes or not loading high on any of them. The analysis of meaning-making by prototype reveals that worldview plays as important a role in meaning-making as the faith traditions themselves.

To delve into the meaning-making processes by prototype we briefly describe the 12 prototypes that were extracted from the Q-analysis. The

Table 17.2 Differences in three subtypes of meaning-making and overall meaning-making, by religion (Jewish, Muslim, Druze): ANOVA

		Sum of squares	df	Mean square	F	Sig.
Sense-making	Between groups	24.974	3	8.325	6.742	.000
	Within groups	106.187	86	1.235		
	Total	131.161	89			
Purpose-making	Between groups	11.874	3	3.958	2.930	.038
	Within groups	116.182	86	1.351		
	Total	128.056	89			
Significance-making	Between groups	17.353	3	5.784	5.273	.002
	Within groups	94.343	86	1.097		
	Total	111.695	89			
Full Meaning-Making in Religion (MMR) scale	Between groups	17.192	3	5.731	5.799	.001
	Within groups	84.993	86	.988		
	Total	102.185	89			

following summaries incorporate the wording of statements which each prototype either strongly identified with or strongly rejected. An asterisk (*) following a sentence indicates that this aspect distinguishes the prototype from all others, at a significance level of p <0.01.

In the Q-analysis of the 45 *Jewish* Israeli Q-sort arrays, 4 prototypes emerged. Thirty-two of the 45 Q-sorts were "defining sorts," which means that they loaded heavily on one prototype and not on the others.

Prototype 1: The Socially Concerned Rationalist: This perspective is characterized by a combination of forcefully rejecting religiosity and strongly embracing a moral and socially active outlook. Religious ideas that conflict with scientific and rational principles are rejected*, while individual freedom of choice in matters of faith and morality is supported*. At the core of this prototype lies an atheist view of divinity which sees religion as the illusory creation of human fears and desires*. However, this narrative is not only about disbelieving and rejecting. It also sets great store on being caring, empathic, morally involved, and socially engaged, and it actively seeks to change societal structures and values*.

Prototype 2: The Institutionally Committed Socially Engaged Adherent: This prototype reflects a religious worldview which involves belief in a divine being with whom a personal relationship can be had; strongly identifying with religious texts and teachings* which are considered to be clear and true*, engaging regularly in religious or spiritual practices in private and in public,* and actively working toward making the world a better place to live as part of what it means to be religious*. Alongside a religious commitment, this prototype reflects some progressive thought. For example, it supports individual freedom of choice in matters of faith and morality and actively endeavors to change societal structures and values. This prototype also involves a positive outlook on life, characterized by inner peace and a sense of internal conviction.

Prototype 3: The Security-Oriented Unengaged Traditionalist: This is a perspective of a nonpracticing believer-of-sorts. Lacking religious knowledge and experience, it reflects religious disengagement, but the "synagogue not attended" is traditional. This prototype involves believing in some way, but not in a way that would count as "religious."* The deity ascribed to is similarly disengaged—a deep mystery that can be pointed to but never fully understood*. This faith is not accompanied by religious activity, public or private* although it does involve becoming more religious at times of crisis or need*. A vague and shifting religious outlook is also reported*. There is a clear sense of discomfort with religion, partly attributable to a lack of religious knowledge and partly resulting from disengagement. Still, the continuity of ancient religious traditions is deemed important.

Prototype 4: The Experience-Oriented Spiritual Seeker: This is a strongly spiritual perspective*. It involves a deeply held belief of a personal nature leading to moments of profound illumination*. This prototype involves further seeking to intensify experiences of the divine or some otherworldly reality* by acquiring knowledge and by using consciousness-altering methods*. Spiritual self-realization is a primary goal in life*, and the idea that particular religious claims are true is rejected*. Rather, elements from various religious and spiritual traditions are embraced*. Finally, this prototype is not one of contemplative spiritual retreat from the world, but rather an active endeavor to make the world a better place to live, blending spirituality with social action.

Muslims constitute 17.5% of the Israeli population, making them the largest minority group in Israel (CBS, 2016). The Muslim community in Israel has absorbed significant Western secular trends leading to changes in the role of religious values since the establishment of the state, but is still considered a traditionalist society. Today, Muslims in Israel experience the pull of two powerful processes: the return to religion and secularism (Al-Haj, 2004).

In the factor analysis of the 22 Muslim Israeli Q-sort arrays, 5 prototypes emerged. Fourteen of the 22 Q-sorts were "defining sorts," loading clearly on one of the four prototypes, but not on the others. Following is a brief description of each prototype:

Prototype 1: The Committed Institutionally Anchored Believer: This prototype involves a strong and firmly held belief in Islam, God, and Islamic scriptures. Religious faith is viewed as a never-ending quest* for a deeper, more confident faith*. Faith is reflected behaviorally in religious and spiritual practices such as prayer and strictly observing the religious commandments*. Uniquely, this prototype involves a belief that religion should play the central role in the ruling of the nation*, and it is the only one to reject individual freedom of choice in matters of faith and morality*.

Prototype 2: The Institutionally Unattached Universalist: This prototype reflects a sense of comfort with faith and its use mainly for personal comfort in times of need*. God and religion are taken as given, the level of involvement is deemed just right, there is little guilt for not living up to ideals*, and there is a strong sense of inner peace*. This is a prototype which values stability. For example, existing social structures and values are supported*. There is a spiritual side to this prototype, too, as it involves the experience of moments of profound illumination*. The insights of religion are a source of comfort and support, but this is not reflected in daily religious practices other than engaging in charitable acts or social action*

Prototype 3: The Religiously Uninterested but Culturally Committed: This prototype is characterized by a powerful sense of distance from religion and from God*. It expresses modern Western precepts of individualism, and religion does not seem to occupy a major role in it, possibly due to daily responsibilities, which leave little or no time for spiritual matters*. There are signs of religious doubt, which have been felt for a long time*, yet this prototype avoids exploring or expressing this doubt*, perhaps due to fear of being criticized for secularity or due to a general disengagement with religion. Rather than a sense of peace in the face of life's difficulties* there is a disquieting sense of guilt for not living up to ideals*.

Prototype 4: The Experientially Inclined Committed Believer: This prototype expresses a strong belief in God, who is perceived to be a compassionate and spiritual mystery* as well as a sheltering and nurturing parent*.

However, organized religion does not play a role for this prototype, nor does being an active, contributing member of a religious or spiritual community*. This faith is of a personal sort rather than communal, and it does not lead to a sense of affinity with those who share the same faith or outlook*. The effect of modernization on religiosity is evident in this prototype, which embraces Western individualistic views that detach morality from religion and support freedom of choice in religious matters.

Prototype 5: The Scripture- and Institution-Oriented Traditionalist: This is a highly traditional religious perspective. It involves the belief that it is important to maintain continuity of the religious traditions of family and ancestors* and that one should remain loyal to the religion of one's nation in an uncritical manner. Religion is considered a central means for becoming a better and more moral person, but it is also a key to flourishing in the world to come, and earthly life is spent in conscious anticipation of the life hereafter. Religious dictums such as preserving one's purity, gender essentialism, offering charity, and giving up worldly or bodily pleasures are observed, yet no sense of personal closeness to God is reported; spiritual experiences are not an important part of this prototype.

The *Druze* are an ethno-religious community concentrated mainly in the Middle East with religious practices and ideas which diverged from Shiite Islam in the 11th century. Most of the Druze live in Syria, Lebanon, and Northern Israel. At the end of 2016, they made up 1.6% of the Israeli population and 8% of its Arab population (CBS, 2016). Druze is an esoteric, philosophically oriented religion with few rituals and a focus on moral commandments. Its core principles of faith are kept in great secrecy, and only some tenets such as an abiding faith in the unity of God and a belief in destiny and in reincarnation, are known to outsiders. Conversion to the Druze religion is forbidden and even within the Druze community, only an elite minority of initiates known as Uqqāl ("The Wise") have access to religious teachings and services (Falah, 2002). The distinction between Uqqāl and Juhal ("The Ignorant") is sharp. Shifting from one to the other can never be revoked and requires a rigorous initiation process. Druze communities are conservative, and the family is at the nucleus of society (Abu-Rukun, 2006; Ben-Dor, 1996). However, they, too, have been undergoing a process of transition from traditionalism to modernization (Al-Haj, 2004; Azaiza, 2004; Lavee & Katz, 2002).

In the factor analysis of the 23 Druze Israeli Q-sort arrays, 3 prototypes emerged. Thirteen of the 23 Q-sorts were "defining sorts" which loaded clearly on one of the prototypes and not on the others. It is worth noting that 22 of the 23 interviewees were "Uqqāl" or Druze religious initiates. This is a typical situation for young Druze adults.

Prototype 1: The Confident Religious Traditionalist: This prototype is characterized by a strong sense of religiosity* and a deeply held belief in the Druze religious convictions and traditions, such as affirming the idea of reincarnation, the cycle of birth and rebirth. However, since it is a nonreligious prototype in the Druze sense of the term (not *uqqāl*), religion does not fully dictate this worldview nor is it reflected in religious practices per se, which cannot apply to it. One might say that this prototype reflects orthodoxy but not orthopraxis.

Prototype 2: The Socially Emphatic Ambivalent Conformist: This prototype embraces both the traditions of the Druze community and the values of Western modernity. There is a strong belief in God and in the core tenets of Druze religion, such as reincarnation, but, at the same time, the Western worldview of striving for social change* is supported. The mixed effects of incorporating traditional and modern elements are expressed by observing some traditional proscriptions (e.g., not using forbidden substances), while disregarding others such as personal prayer.

Prototype 3: The Privately Detached Adherent: This prototype reflects a shift toward secularity and Western values of universalism, autonomy, and nonreligious morality. It involves some sort of belief but does not involve being religious*. This prototype is the only one in the Druze sample to support individual freedom of choice in matters of faith and morality* and to believe that one can be moral without being religious*. Living in a strict and conservative community, this is a privately held prototype which is considered best kept to oneself*.

The Relation Between Prototypes and Religious Meaning-Making

We compared these 12 prototypes on religious meaning-making using the MMR scale we devised. In each of the three religious groups we examined, some prototypes seemed to involve more meaning-making activities than others. Figure 17.1 outlines the 12 prototypes by each

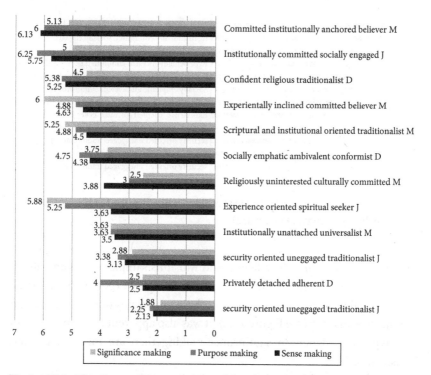

Figure 17.1 Meaning-making activities of the 12 prototypes in the Israel sample (M = Muslim, J = Jewish, D = Druze).

subtype of meaning-making activity. The proportions of sense-, purpose-, and significance-making vacillated as well. We identified religiously cross-cutting patterns in the subtypes of meaning-making, as follows:

Sense-making: In all three faith traditions, the prototypes which most strongly reflected institutionalized religion (e.g., following religious dictates and traditions, belonging to a religious community etc.) were those who engaged in the most religious sense-making. The secular prototypes tended to be the lowest on religious sense-making, as did the spiritual prototypes (see Figure 17.2).

Purpose-making: Similarly to sense-making, the more institutionally committed religious prototypes were those who engaged in religious purpose-making most often. However, the prototypes that were characterized by high levels of spirituality also used religious purpose-making, more than they use religion for sense-making.

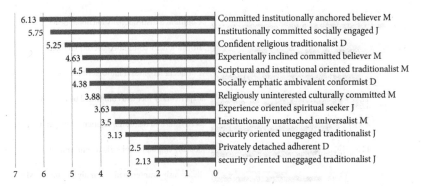

Figure 17.2 Sense-making subscale scores by Faith-Q-Sorts (FQS) prototype (M = Muslim, J = Jewish, D = Druze).

Significance-making: The Jewish and Muslims samples each generated a single distinctly spiritual prototype, which was highly experiential, mystical, and personal in its religious worldview. These prototypes were the highest on significance-making (see Figure 17.2). It was also apparent that most Muslim prototypes are higher on significance-making than are most Druze and Jewish ones.

To sum, across faith traditions, the institutionally committed prototype tended to be higher on religious sense-making, while the spiritual-experiential prototype tended to be highest on religious significance-making (Figure 17.3), and both types were high on purpose-making (Figure 17.4). The secular or detached prototypes were low on all three subtypes of religious meaning-making.

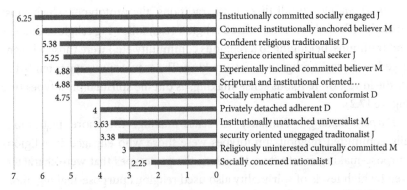

Figure 17.3 Significance-making subscale scores by Faith-Q-Sorts (FQS) prototype (M = Muslim, J = Jewish, D = Druze).

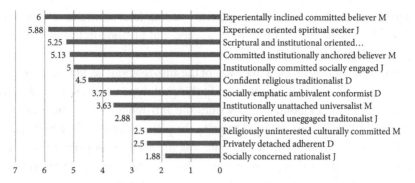

Figure 17.4 Purpose-making subscale scores by Faith-Q-Sorts (FQS) prototype (M = Muslim, J = Jewish, D = Druze).

An In-Depth Analysis of Narratives: Prototypes and Meaning-Making

A closer look at the narratives of the defining sorts for each prototype uncovered a third and more nuanced layer of meaning-making and meaninglessness in this sample of young Israeli adults. The narrative analysis pointed to the role of culture as socially sanctioning or frowning upon nonreligious meaning-making. We describe the Jewish case study in some depth and touch briefly on the other two faith traditions due to space constraints.

Among the Jewish sample, religious meaning was confined to the religious and spiritual prototypes, but the Socially Concerned Rationalists clearly engaged in a different sort of meaning-making. In contrast, the Security Oriented Unengaged Traditionalist prototype stood out as very low on meaning-making of any kind.

The Socially Concerned Rationalist prototype matches the attitudes of anti-religious secularity in Israel. Unquestionably, religion is not a sense-making framework for this prototype, but there is a clear alternative: science and rationality. This is further supported by survey data in which the self-reported average level of religiosity among the defining sorts of this prototype was the lowest of all four prototypes: 1.24 (standard deviation [SD] = 1.6) on a 0–10 scale.

Noa,[4] one of the defining sorts for this prototype, says, "I am a pure atheist. . . . I'm, like, I have a lot of criticism toward religion. Uh—especially

---

[4] All names and identifying details were changed.

regarding the state, but also in general" adding later how she feels about faith: "I really despise it. I believe in science, and I believe in things you can prove, things that can be tested."

Socialist Kibbutzim are a mainstay of the anti-religious secularism. A sizeable proportion of participants who fit this prototype were raised or live on kibbutzim. Elli, a kibbutznik, describes the anti-religious sentiment on his kibbutz: "Yom Kippur, we used to go to the plantations to have a barbecue. When I was a child, when the kibbutz was still really a cooperative kibbutz and such, so on Yom Kippur there was—there was like a party of the kibbutz, and a barbecue of a huge pig." An "anti" stance may not provide enough positive meaning in life. However, these narratives also positively embrace humanism and social involvement. Kobi says: "I know a lot of people who are religious and are not moral, and I know a lot of people who are moral and are not religious at all. I try to be one of them. We all have our moral conscience." This is in marked contrast to the reputation of the anti-religious seculars in Israel, who are often portrayed in the media (and by religionists) as hedonistic, egocentric, and empty of values. Clearly, this is not the case for this prototype. Science provides this worldview with an alternative to religious sense-making, and humanistic activism offers a sense of purpose in life. What seems lacking is a venue of connecting to something greater than themselves, now that social communism is not a viable option. As Ella says: "For me life is as it stands. We will all die, be buried, become dust. That's it."

The narrative of the Institutionally Committed Socially Engaged prototype is indicative of moderate Religious Zionism in Israel and reflects a mixture of traditional and modern values. This prototype is rated as the most highly religious of the sample, with a mean score of 7.7 (SD = 1.5) on the 1–10 religiosity scale. All three meaning-making activities were easily identifiable in these narratives. Sense-making was expressed, for example, by a strong conviction that religious scriptures are true and God-given. Eliav says: "Moses wrote the Torah from the name of the Holy One Blessed Be He. And this is something essential, I mean compared to other belief systems where one person at most wrote it, here, the whole people, many people heard it. It's a collective memory thing." At the same time, there is a clear modernist bent guiding these narratives, and sense-making is seen as a process involving critique. Yaakov says: "I have a hard time with brain-washing. . . . sometimes in religious culture, certain ideas, to certain values, and—dogmatism, and—there is some sort of intolerance toward those who question these things." Moria says: "I'm OK with criticizing my religion." In terms of inherited versus constructed meaning-making, these religious emerging adults are engaging in both internalizing and critiquing, working to take ownership of this global meaning system by personalizing it.

For this prototype, religion is also instrumental in providing a sense of purpose. Moshe says, "The connection to God, the religion that—I truly believe in that. That—is something important to me. . . . The thing is that it really has a deep meaning in my life. It's the force that keeps me going to this day." But religion informs purpose-making in another way, too: it fosters social activism and voluntarism. This prototype has the highest levels of voluntarism and benevolence on the survey. Dovrat explains: "You came to this world to improve it. Like, when you really boil it down. That is what is required from you, and you should act accordingly."

Significance-making via self-transcendence of any sort was reported less frequently in these interviews. Some participants described communicating with God, but most did not, with one stating clearly: "I am not mystical."

The Security Oriented Unengaged Traditionalist prototype matches the "traditional secular" perspective in Israel. Interestingly, all the defining sorts for this prototype were female and most were immigrants from the former USSR. Being Jewish in the former USSR was at times dangerous and typically allowed for very little knowledge and practice. Marina describes being Jewish in the Ukraine: "No, it's very difficult. Nearly impossible. I don't remember any store near us being Kosher in the Ukraine . . . as a child it was very difficult," later adding: "It's dangerous. It is dangerous to be there now. Especially for Jews, and for anyone who looks very Jewish," but Jewish identity did not become much easier after emigrating to Israel: "They [local Israelis] pushed me out. That wasn't easy at all." Involvement with Judaism was similarly disappointing: "I didn't keep Kosher. I tried, I tried fasting, OK, I tried. And then I stopped again." Similarly disengaged although born in Israel, Rona describes the role of Judaism in her life: "When I look back at my life, it's not something that I, like, relate to or engage with. I mean, it's kind of always there, but I don't, I simply don't think about it." Still, this prototype does not reflect principled atheism. Sveta says: "I do believe there is a God but I'm not really in touch with him"

This prototype involved very little meaning-making of any sort, religious or otherwise. Rona says: "No one truly knows what is right. . . . Like, purpose, what's the purpose? what is the purpose and the direction?" Natasha says: "Most of the time I'm like a robot that functions. . . . I feel, I know I'm not the only one that is constantly chasing something, but I, like, don't understand it. . . . It's, like—is it even worth all the energy put into all this time?" Correspondingly, the defining sorts who made up this prototype had the lowest Positive Life Orientation score (2.25), the highest depression score (19.5), and the lowest meaning-making score (2.71) of all 12 prototypes in our study.

The Experience-Oriented Spiritual Seeker prototype was in many ways the most active meaning-maker of all 12 prototypes. Principled spiritualism is a relatively new player on the Israeli religious scene, breaking-down the pervasive "secular–religious" dichotomy. This was a minority narrative in the sample, but its voice was loud and clear. Yuval describes the process of seeking and actively making meaning for himself: "It started about 3 years ago, when I started meditating with a mentor, and then I really started, I found it very interesting. I became exposed to all of this Buddhism, that entire field, of seeing what it is exactly." Eilon describes his religious eclecticism: "I am interested in all kinds of religions. . . . I'll take from the religious traditions what is useful to me. And if it's in—in the Buddhism, the meditation, and holy texts in the Christianity or in the Kabbalah." This prototype engages in considerable significance-making by means of self-transcendence but is just as involved in social action. In this it challenges the Israeli stereotype of the New-Ager as self-centered and disengaged from society. Eliana[5] says: "I donate to Greenpeace every month and . . . if we go camping, and we arrive to a dirty camp site, we will take trash bags and pick up the trash. Um—and I was a girl-scout, and that is something that is very important to me." She says she is active in "many groups. Social justice, Free Israel, all that stuff." Tuval volunteers in a center for Jewish and Arab children: "A tough neighborhood. It's some sort of a house that kids come to at noon to meet other kids. So, I'm there to help them with it." Correspondingly, this Active Spiritualists prototype had the highest score of all prototypes on Positive Life Orientation (4.25).

The Muslim and Druze Prototypes and Meaning-Making Activity

The narrative patterns of meaning-making were somewhat different for the Muslim and Druze samples. Each group displayed one prototype with low levels of engagement, low levels of well-being, and low levels of meaning-making. However, among the two Arab samples this converged with secularism—the Religiously Uninterested but Culturally Committed

---

[5] Eliana loaded high on the Active Spiritualist, although not one of its defining sorts.

among the Muslims and the Privately Detached Adherent among the Druze—whereas among the Jews it was the Security-Oriented Unengaged Traditionalist prototype that exhibited this lowered level of meaning-making, in contrast to the highly secular Jewish prototype which had come into its own humanistic meaning-making system.

Muslim participants reflecting the Religiously Uninterested but Culturally Committed prototype, such as Hanan, feel religion does not make sense to them, but they are not able to search elsewhere for meaning. Telling of being encouraged to study the Quran by a religious leader, Hanan recalls: "So he said to me: 'Now you come and try and listen to the Quran,' so here, to be honest, I felt a strong feeling of rejection, like 'No, I do not *want* to listen to the Quran!' And Uh—and it is that also when I talk about the thing, I talk about the thing with a lot of sensitivity. Because I do not like to say things like 'What is that Quran? And what is that? This is Nonsense!'" In effect, Hanan says that she cannot, or will not, voice her private views on the Quran.

All other Muslim and Druze prototypes reflected faith narratives of sorts, at times ambivalent but fully within the normative bounds of conformity. Most of these interviews indicated deep and unwavering faith, but the meaning was of the inherited meaning form rather than actively meaning-making. Mona, a Druze who reflects the Confident Religious Traditionalist prototype, says, "Religion is—yes, it has a role of the first order, very powerful, especially the Druze religion, I trust and believe in it very, very much. It is what gives you—it guides you to the right way, like, it makes you walk right." Similarly, Shirin, a female Muslim who was one of the defining sorts of the Committed Institutionally Anchored Believer said, "I think that religion should play the central role in the ruling of the nation. . . . I am of course talking about *my* religion. I mean, we should follow, in my opinion, my religion that I believe in. In Islam for example, if you follow it, everything will surely be fine, if I follow it one hundred percent, as in the Quran, according to the Sunnah of our Prophet Mohammed, so yes, surely everything will be right, and the biggest proof is that our Prophet Mohammed, for example, he was the cleverest man in the world, and there were studies about that and it was written, so whoever follows his way, according to our belief, will definitely do well." Raya, A female Muslim who reflected the Institutionally Unattached Universalist prototype, also expresses a strong sense of certainty in the inner sense of the world: "God is managing human matters. Of course, God is the one who also knows what will happen to me, he is the—like, this faith, faith which is what lets me know, as they say, what is written is written. Our faith in what is written is—that is the thing which, like, you and I, in the future, we do not know what will happen to us. That is managed by the Almighty God." There is little doubt in these narratives that the self-critical note of the Jewish Institutionally Committed Socially Engaged prototype is missing here. Thus, we conclude that there was more *inherited* meaning, particularly of the sense-making variant, among the Muslim and Druze participants that we interviewed than there was personal meaning-making, which seemed to be more acceptable among the Jewish participants, religious and secular alike.

Things were less simple for Arab believers in terms of purpose-making via religion. For some, religion plays a clear and important role in conferring purpose. Shirin, a Muslim female says: "I constantly think that . . . yes, what is this life, like, at the end surely there is a hereafter, death will surely come. So as much as possible I try to correct myself every time I make a mistake. . . . So I always, yes, I set in front of me the hereafter, paradise and hell, and think to myself that I want to be at the highest level in paradise, God willing, and that is it, actually the most important thing." However, purpose-making can be challenging for other believers since they may wish to pursue self-realization and feel that religion inhibits their exploration. This might be a gendered quality. Siham, a Druze woman says: "Many things are becoming *Haram, Haram, Haram* [forbidden by religious law]. . . . In our religion it is not written that it is *Haram* that a girl sleeps outside her home but I was forbidden by the sheiks to sleep outside of the home. . . . I want to build myself, I want to build—I want to study and finish my studies and become educated, I don't want only to be called religious."

Reported significance-making was relatively rare in the interviews of all three faith traditions, but we found it especially noteworthy that is was nearly entirely absent from the Druze narratives. This is surprising as the Druze is a deeply spiritual and even mystical religion. It would seem that for these Druze participants, the very idea that a person who is not Uqqāl could have a mystical experience is perceived as impudent. The implicit message was: The ancient prophets experienced God, but who am I, a modern ignoramus, to have such an experience? The one type of significance-making which we identified in the interviews was a merging of individual and community. Sari, a Druze, says, "I love to participate in things, many activities. Anything for the sake of the village, I will throw myself into it. I love making improvements, changes for the good of my community in general because I feel the thing—the thing belongs to me."

Finally, although sample sizes were too small to compare statistically, three prototypes stood out as exceptionally low on well-being and high on depression: The Jewish Security Oriented Unengaged Traditionalist, the Muslim Religiously Uninterested but Culturally Committed, and the Druze Privately Detached Adherent. This can be taken as an indication of how the cultural sanctioning or prohibition of nonreligious paths to meaning affects subjective well-being, perhaps more than the actual role of religion and spirituality in meaning-making, among this sample of emerging adults in Israel.

Discussion

We began this study with the theoretical construct of meaning-making and subdivided it into three categories of meaning-making activities—sense-making, purpose-making, and significance-making—which are comparable but not parallel to the Meaning in Life typology (George & Park, 2016; Martela & Steger, 2016). From this model we derived the 24-item (Cronbach's alpha = .90) MMR scale and used it to explore how religious meaning-making is expressed in the FQS and interviews of 90 emerging Israeli adults in three faith traditions. We analyzed meaning-making levels and patterns on four levels: (1) overall in the sample; (2) a quantitative faith-tradition comparison of Jews, Muslims and Druze; (3) a more nuanced quali-quantological comparison of 12 religious prototypes which emerged from the FQS; and (4) an in-depth qualitative analysis of religious meaning-making patterns, based on the interviews. Throughout, we considered how meaning and meaninglessness are culturally sanctioned and how this relates to the affect and subjective well-being of the participants. Our main findings were as follows:

1. Overall, being religious and/or spiritual was related to more religious meaning-making, serving as a sort of validity-check for the MMR. Subjective well-being was unrelated to meaning-making on this level.
2. When compared by faith tradition, Muslims were significantly more engaged in all three subtypes of religious meaning-making activities than the Druze, who in turn, were more engaged in them than the Jews.
3. When comparing the 12 emerging FQS prototypes on MMR scores, worldviews were found to play as much of a role in meaning-making as faith traditions. Across religious groups, prototypes reflecting organized religion were highest on sense-making, while prototypes reflecting

a spiritual outlook were highest on significance-making. Each faith tradition had one detached prototype. Among the Jews, these were the traditionalists, while among the Muslims and Druze, these were the secularists. These prototypes had the lowest levels of meaning-making and, correspondingly, the lowest levels of subjective well-being.

4. A qualitative analysis pointed to the role of culture as socially sanctioning or frowning upon nonreligious meaning-making. Thus, secular Muslims and Druze had less of an outlet for secular meaning-making activities and ended up with a sense of meaninglessness. In comparison, Jewish seculars reflected high levels of purpose-making based on social action, indicating that they have come into their own culturally sanctioned forms of nonreligious meaning-making activities.

We would like to expound on this last finding. In allowing meaning studies and psychology of religion to illuminate each other, our study found that secular humanism did a good job of allowing for meaning to emerge, both in terms of sense and purpose. Thus, sense-making and purpose-making needs can be met by religion, spiritual teachings, science, humanism, or social action. However, this was true only of the Jewish sample, whereas secular prototypes in the Arab samples had a harder time constructing meaning. This indicates how important it is to have multiple culturally sanctioned routes to meaning-making to allow as many individuals as possible to find meaning in life.

In fact, one of the important findings in this study was that not all emerging adults in Israel have found or are actively seeking meaning: in each religious group, we found one prototype of detached young adults who engage very minimally in meaning-making and express low levels of well-being. Whereas among the Arab samples these were the (often closeted) seculars, who may feel a sense of discrepancy between their society and their own personal beliefs and may not have the possibility of exploring other meaning venues, among the Jews these were in fact traditionalists, whose support for tradition has become disconnected from personal meaning, possibly due to lack of in-depth knowledge of tradition.

We also found that a certain type of explorative, questing, and self-critical meaning-making characterized the Jewish religious sample more than the religious Muslim or Druze. While the basic process of meaning-making is a universal cultural attribute and is clearly practiced across cultures (Oyserman, 2011), a personal search for meaning reflects cultural expectations and values about seeking and openness, tradition and submission to authority. Muslim and Druze societies in Israel endorse tradition and authority values (Novis-Deutsch et al., in press), and this may mean that for many individuals in these groups, meaning-making is more of a process of internalization than of creative modification and construction.

Another possible interpretation is that, for the Arab groups, being minorities in a Jewish state and experiencing difficult identity conflicts may mean less meaning creation and more meaning internalization since new meaning construction might highlight the impossible conundrums in which they live. In the Israeli context of a powerful Jewish majority and a marginalized Arab minority, we see a set of young adults who have not completed a transformation to a Western mindset or, perhaps, do not desire to do so, but this leaves them in some respects "stuck" between cultural tropes. This is particularly noteworthy as this study explores an internal psychological process, which shows how at least some Arab young adults turn to a practical, day-by-day mindset and give up on attempts to make meaning altogether.

This study also demonstrated the importance of spirituality in religious meaning-making. Although the four most institutionally committed religious prototypes across all three faith traditions involved high engagement in sense-making, spiritual seekers, although few and far between in our sample, fared better at engaging in significance-making, and their levels of well-being were the highest in the survey. This last point—the paucity of spiritual seekers in our sample—deserves further pondering: Across samples, significance-making did not seem have much place in the lives of these emerging adults. There are various possible explanations of this. First, it may be less common in this specific sample (and might surface in larger samples). Second, it may be due to participants' developmental stage in life: busy emerging adulthood may not necessarily be the time for transcending the self. It is also possible that significance-making should be formulated more broadly. In line with Czordas's (2004) discussion about alterity, significance-making might better be expressed as making meaning from a position of strong identification with an "other" (deity, group, or individual) which has a relevant, decisive, and productive impact and relevance on one's life, implying a shift from "ego" to "alter." Future studies should explore this alternative formulation of significance-making.

This study has pointed us on the route to exploring the extent to which social and cultural constraints implicitly affect engagement with meaning-making activities, religious, spiritual and other, but some of our finding require further exploration:

First, the MMR scale doesn't explore forms of meaning such as love, family, friends, and work. Culturally shaped meaning-making both constrains and enables perception and reasoning (Nisbett & Noranzayan, 2002; Shweder, 1984). Further studies might allow us to engage in depth with this issue by including these forms of meaning and provide empirical indications as to when we are witnessing low levels of meaning-making and when meaning-making is merely subtler and rooted in everyday life. To fully understand the place of religious meaning-making in the larger scheme of personal meaning systems, we need nuanced and comparable measures of nonreligious meaning-making.

Second, our finding that religious meaning-making did not relate directly to higher levels of subjective well-being does not match previous findings about meaning-making and well-being (Hamby et al., 2017; Park, 2013) and instead supports Alea and Bluck's (2013) findings that this relationship does not hold in non-American settings. This small-scale study provides yet another indication that the SWB-meaning relation is in need of further cross-cultural attention.

Third, to further test our argument about the cultural contingency of meaning-making, additional studies should use larger and more representative cross-cultural samples.

Finally, let us return to the pair of questions posed in the Introduction: Is meaning created or discovered, and by whom? Geertz (1973, p. 31) once famously noted that "man is an animal suspended in the webs of significance he himself has spun . . . I take culture to be those webs, and the analysis of it to be . . . an interpretive one in search of meaning." For meaning to inform an individual's life, it must be the product of subjective effort, and, in that sense, it must involve ongoing acts of agentic appropriation, adaptation, and even invention. At the same time, meaning is made in social and cultural context. Attempting to set apart the invented aspects of meaning from its inherited ones is akin to trying to disentangle a spider from its web. We conclude that although cultural values play an important role in determining the relative weight of meaning constructed and meaning discovered, ultimately it involves both processes; it is the shared venture of individuals and their social network. Nowhere is this more apparent than in the domain of religion, where meaning can be transmitted across the generations, perhaps indefinitely, yet cannot survive for even a single generation unless it is adapted and reinvented by its individual adherents, every lifetime afresh.

Highlights

- In a sample of 90 Israeli students (18–30 years old) from three faith traditions, being religious and/or spiritual was related to more religious meaning-making activity.
- Among the three faith traditions, Muslims were significantly more engaged than the Druze in three subtypes of religious meaning-making activities (sense-making, purpose-making, and significance-making). The Druze were more engaged in them than the Jews.
- Subjective well-being was unrelated to overall levels of meaning-making but was found to relate positively to significance-making.
- When comparing the 12 faith prototypes (derived from a Q-sort measure) on meaning-making across religious groups, prototypes reflecting institutionalized religion were highest on sense-making, while prototypes reflecting a spiritual outlook were highest on significance-making.
- Each faith tradition had one detached prototype. Among the Jews these were the traditionalists, while among the Muslims and Druze these were the secularists. Detached prototypes had the lowest levels of meaning-making and subjective well-being.
- Culture was important in socially sanctioning or frowning upon meaning-making paths. Secular Muslims and Druze had less of an outlet for humanistic meaning-making than did Jewish seculars. The former often expressed a sense of meaninglessness, while the latter expressed high levels of purpose-making based on social action.
- Social and cultural constraints implicitly affect engagement with meaning-making activities, religious, spiritual, or otherwise.
- Although cultural values play an important role in determining the relative weight of meaning constructed and meaning discovered, ultimately meaning-making involves both processes.

References

Abu-Rukun, S. (2006). *Druze identity in Israeli society* [unpublished doctoral dissertation]. University of Haifa. [Hebrew]

Alea, N., & Bluck, S. (2013). When does meaning-making predict subjective well-being? Examining young and older adults in two cultures. *Memory, 21*(1), 44–63.

Al-Haj, M. (2004). *Immigration and ethnic formation in deeply divided society: The case of the 1990 immigrants from the former Soviet Union in Israel.* Brill.

Azaiza, F. (2004). Patterns of labor division among Palestinian families in the West Bank. *Global Development Studies, 3*(3), 203–220.

Baird, R. M. (1985). Meaning in life: Discovered or created?. *Journal of Religion and Health, 24*(2), 117–124.

Bartlett, F. C. (with Kintsch, W.). (1932/1995). *Remembering: A study in experimental and social psychology.* Cambridge University Press.

Barry, C. M., & Abo-Zena, M. M. (Eds.). (2014). *Emerging adults' religiousness and spirituality: Meaning-making in an age of transition.* Oxford University Press.

Batson, C. D., & Stocks, E. L. (2004). Religion: Its core psychological functions. In J. Greenberg, S. L. Koole, & T. Pyszczynski (Eds.), *Handbook of experimental existential psychology* (pp. 141–155). Guilford Press.

Baumeister, R. F. (1991). *Meanings of life.* Guilford Press.

Baumeister, R. F., & Vohs, K. D. (2002). The pursuit of meaningfulness in life. In C. R. Snyder & S. J. Lopez (Eds.), *Handbook of positive psychology* (pp. 608–618). Oxford University Press.

Ben-Dor, G. (1996). The Druze community in Israel in the late 90s. In H. Hershkowitz & M. Amiel (Eds.), *The Druze community in Israel towards the twenty-first century* (pp. 53–56). Jerusalem Center for Public Affairs. [Hebrew]

Brown, D. E. (2000). Human universals and their implications. In N. Roughley (Ed.), *Being humans: Anthropological universality and particularity in transdisciplinary perspectives.* (pp. 156–174). Walter de Gruyter.

CBS. (2016). *The population in Israel, by selected years, religion, and population group.* The Israeli Central Bureau of Statistics.

Czordas, T. (2004). Asymptote of the ineffable: Embodiment, alterity, and the theory of religion. *Current Anthropology, 45*(2), 163–185.

Davis, C. G., Nolen-Hoeksema, S., & Larson, J. (1998). Making sense of loss and benefiting from the experience: two construals of meaning. *Journal of Personality and Social Psychology, 75*(2), 561.

Falah, S. (2002). *The Druze in the Middle East.* Druze Research & Publications Institute.

Geertz, C. (1973). *The interpretation of cultures.* Basic Books.

George, L. S., & Park, C. L. (2014). Existential mattering: Bringing attention to a neglected but central aspect of meaning? In A. Batthyany & P. Russo-Netzer (Eds.), *Meaning in positive and existential psychology* (pp. 39–51). Springer.

George, L. S., & Park, C. L. (2016). Meaning in life as comprehension, purpose, and mattering: Toward integration and new research questions. *Review of General Psychology, 20*(3), 205–220.

Graham, J., & Haidt, J. (2009). Planet of the Durkheimians, where community, authority, and sacredness are foundations of morality. In J. Jost, A. C. Kay, & H. Thorisdottir (Eds.), *Social and psychological bases of ideology and system justification* (pp. 371–401). Oxford University Press.

Greenberg, J., & Arndt, J. (2012). Terror management theory. In P. M. Van Lange, A. W. Kruglanski, & E. Higgins (Eds.), *Handbook of theories of social psychology* (Vol. 1, pp. 398–415). Sage.

Hamby, S., Segura, A., Taylor, E., Grych, J., & Banyard, V. (2017). Meaning-making in rural Appalachia: Age and gender patterns in seven measures of meaning. *Journal of Happiness and Well-being, 5*(2), 168–186.

Heine, S. J., Proulx, T., & Vohs, K. D. (2006). The meaning maintenance model: On the coherence of social motivations. *Personality and Social Psychology Review, 10*, 88–110.

Heintzelman, S. J., & King, L. A. (2014). Life is pretty meaningful. *American Psychologist, 69*, 561–574.

Hood R. W., Jr., Hill, P. C., & Spilka, B. (2009). *The psychology of religion: An empirical approach*. Guilford Press.

Hood, R. W., Hill, P. C., & Williamson, W. P. (2005). *The psychology of religious fundamentalism*. Guilford Press.

James, W. (1902/2003). *The varieties of religious experience: A study in human nature*. Routledge.

Janoff-Bulman, R. (1992). *Shattered assumptions: Towards a new psychology of trauma*. New York: Free Press.

Kroger, J. (2004). *Identity in adolescence: The balance between self and other*. Routledge.

Kunnen, E. S., & Bosma, H. A. (2000). Development of meaning-making: A dynamic systems approach. *New Ideas in Psychology, 18*(1), 57–82.

Lavee, Y., & Katz, R. (2002). Division of labor, perceived fairness, and marital quality: The effect of gender ideology. *Journal of Marriage and Family, 64*(1), 27–39.

Martela, F., & Steger, M. F. (2016). The three meanings of meaning in life: Distinguishing coherence, purpose, and significance. *The Journal of Positive Psychology, 11*(5), 531–545.

Maslow, A. H. (1954). *Motivation and personality*. Harpers.

McLean, K. C., & Pratt, M. W. (2006). Life's little (and big) lessons: Identity statuses and meaning-making in the turning point narratives of emerging adults. *Developmental Psychology, 42*, 714–722.

Nisbett, R.E. and Norenzayan, A. (2002). Culture and Cognition. In *Stevens' Handbook of Experimental Psychology*, H. Pashler (Ed.). Wiley.

Novis-Deutsch, N., Lassander, M., Sztajer, S., Keysar, A., Beit-Hallahmi, B., & Klingenberg, M. (in press). Rhetorics of conservative and liberal values in relation to religiosity among Y-generation university students. In M. T. Lassander, P. Nynäs, M. Shterin, B. W. Kwaku Golo, P. Stenner, & S. Sjö (Eds.), *Young adults in higher education and religion: A global perspective on the worldviews and values of the next generation in charge*. Routledge.

Nynäs, P., Kontala, J. & Lassander, M., (2021) The Faith Q-sort: In-Depth Assessment of Diverse Spirituality and Religiosity in 12 Countries. In: Ai, A. L., Wink, P., Paloutzian, R. F. & Harris, K. A. (eds.). Assessing spirituality in a diverse world. Springer, pp. 553–573.

Oyserman, D. (2011). Culture as situated cognition: Cultural mindsets, cultural fluency, and meaning-making. *European Review of Social Psychology, 22*(1), 164–214.

Paloutzian, R. F., & Park, C. L. (2014). *Handbook of the psychology of religion and spirituality*. Guilford Press.

Park, C. L. (2005). Religion as a meaning-making framework in coping with life stress. *Journal of Social Issues, 61*(4), 707–729.

Park, C. L. (2010). Making sense of the meaning literature: An integrative review of meaning-making and its effects on adjustment to stressful life events. *Psychological Bulletin, 136*(2), 257–301.

Park, C. L. (2013). Religion and meaning. In R. F. Paloutzian & C. L. Parks (Eds.), *Handbook of the psychology of religion and spirituality* (2nd ed., pp. 357–379). Guilford Press.

Park, C. L., & Folkman, S. (1997). Meaning in the context of stress and coping. *Review of General Psychology, 1*(2), 115–144.

Parks, S. D. (2011). *Big questions, worthy dreams: Mentoring young adults in their search for meaning, purpose, and faith* (10th anniversary ed.). Jossey-Bass.

Postman, N., & Weingartner, C. (1969). *Teaching as a subversive activity.* Delacorte Press.

Rolls, E. T. (2018). The neuroscience of purpose, meaning, and morals. In G. D. Caruso & O. Flanagan (Eds.), *Neuro-existentialism: Meaning, morals and purpose in the age of neuroscience* (pp. 68–86). Oxford University Press.

Seitz, R. J., & Angel, H. F. (2015). Psychology of religion and spirituality: meaning-making and processes of believing. *Religion, Brain & Behavior, 5*(2), 139–147.

Shweder, R. A., Le Vine, R. A., LeVine, R. A., & Economiste, R. A. L. (Eds.). (1984). *Culture theory: Essays on mind, self and emotion.* Cambridge University Press.

Singer, J. A. (2004). Narrative identity and meaning-making across the adult lifespan: An introduction. *Journal of Personality, 72*(3), 437–460.

Tarakeshwar, N., Stanton, J., & Pargament, K. I. (2003). Religion: An overlooked dimension in cross-cultural psychology. *Journal of Cross-Cultural Psychology, 34*(4), 377–394.

Triandis, H. (2007). Culture and psychology: A history of their relationship. In S. Kitayama & D. Cohen (Eds.), *Handbook of cultural psychology* (pp. 59–76). Guilford Press.

Watts, S., & Stenner, P. (2012). *Doing Q methodological research: Theory, method and interpretation.* Sage.

Wong, P. T. P. (Ed.). (2013). *The human quest for meaning: Theories, research, and applications* (2nd ed.). Routledge.

Wulff, D. M. (2019). Prototypes of faith: Findings with the Faith Q-Sort. *Journal for the Scientific Study of Religion, 58*(3), 643–665.

PART VI

CONCLUSION

18

Meaning in Life at the Crossroads of Personal Processes and Cultural Crisis

Pninit Russo-Netzer and Ofra Mayseless

Conceptual Background on Meaning in Life

This chapter takes a broad look at individuals' meaning in life (MIL) at the cross-roads of personal processes and cultural crisis. The quest for meaning is considered a central and unique human motivation. The meaning this book addresses is not the meaning *of* life, or ultimate meaning, which relates to a broad theological issue concerned with the "big questions of life" and universal human concerns. Rather, the book is concerned with MIL, which refers to the personal experience of one's meaning of life. In the words of Viktor Frankl, "what matters is not the meaning in life in general, but rather the specific meaning of a person's life at a given moment" (1963, p. 131).

Throughout the history of mankind, people have been extensively preoccupied with existential questions, such as "Why are we here? What is my purpose?" These universal questions deal with the core concern of what it means to be human and have inspired various myths, religions, arts, and philosophies in different cultures around the world and across time and traditions. Answers to these questions are embedded at the heart of human existence and comprise the force that motivates people—from the first question children ask—"Why?"—to make sense of themselves and the world.

A significant well-known theoretical and applied conceptualization of MIL is Viktor Frankl's existential analysis and logotherapy (Frankl, 1966). Frankl (1969) posited that human beings have a "will to meaning," which he defined as a powerful drive to find significance and meaning in their lives. According to this perspective, human psychology cannot be understood solely in terms of learning history or drives, but essentially through existential concerns such as freedom, meaning, and purpose. He saw the search for MIL as the main motivation for living, and he argued that people can

Pninit Russo-Netzer and Ofra Mayseless, *Meaning in Life at the Crossroads of Personal Processes and Cultural Crisis*
In: *Finding Meaning*. Edited by: Ofra Mayseless and Pninit Russo-Netzer, Oxford University Press. © Oxford University Press 2022. DOI: 10.1093/oso/9780190910358.003.0018

find meaning even under the most difficult circumstances. Frankl based his model on the notion of nonreductionism as a heuristic principle, implying that each aspect or dimension of a human being—the physiological, the psychological, and the noetic (or spiritual)—represents a layer of properties and functions that interact with each other but nonetheless are ontologically separate and independent of each other (Frankl, 1966). However, each of these is an aspect of what constitutes a human person and therefore none can be discarded or ignored in our quest to truly align psychology with what it means to be human (cf. Russo-Netzer, Schulenberg, & Batthyany, 2016). Several subsequent scholars similarly suggested that people have an inherent need to find MIL (Baumeister, 1991; Heine, Proulx, & Vohs, 2006; Klinger, 2012; Maslow, 1968).

The existential tradition, traced to Kierkegaard (1843/2016) and Nietzsche (e.g., 1888/2007), has also assumed the existence of an existential need for meaning that relates to the question of how a person can find or create meaning in a seemingly meaningless and random universe. Existential thought refers to several overarching existential universal concerns or "givens," which include death, freedom, isolation, and meaninglessness. Each of these concerns may reflect a potential source of anxiety for the individual (e.g., Yalom, 1980). The four concerns may evoke death anxiety, freedom anxiety, isolation anxiety, and meaninglessness anxiety (Wong, 2010). A lack of meaning, for example, may lead to boredom, anxiety, and disengagement, described as an existential vacuum (Frankl, 1977). This may be reflected in hopelessness, futility, emptiness, fragmentation of personal identity, mental health problems, depressiveness, and overall adjustment disorders (e.g., Batthyany & Guttmann, 2005; Bruce et al., 2011; Damon, 2008). In a similar vein, Becker (1975) and exponents of terror management theory (TMT) have viewed meaning as a fundamental ingredient that buffers existential anxiety and mortality salience (e.g., Grant & Wade-Benzoni, 2009; Landau, Kosloff, & Schmeichel, 2011; Pyszczynski, Greenberg, & Solomon, 1999).

Baumeister and colleagues (1991; Baumeister & Vohs, 2002) suggested that MIL involves four basic needs: purpose, values, a sense of efficacy, and self-worth. According to this conceptualization, *purpose* enables people to find meaning in their life events from their connection to possible future events, mainly goals and fulfillments. *Values* refer to justification for one's past, present, and future actions. *Efficacy* affords people with a sense of being in control and capable of making a difference. *Self-worth* refers to people's need to feel that they are worthwhile. This model of four needs for meaning has been suggested as a framework for understanding how people make sense of their lives (e.g., Baumeister, 1991; MacKenzie & Baumeister, 2014).

Within current conceptualizations of well-being, MIL has become a central component. Current conceptualizations discuss the distinction between hedonic and eudaimonic well-being (e.g., Friedman, 2012; Ryan & Deci, 2001; Ryff & Singer, 1998; Ryff, Singer, & Dienberg Love, 2004; Waterman, 1993). *Hedonia* involves pursuing happiness, positive affect, life satisfaction, and reduced negative affect (Huta & Waterman, 2014; Ryan, Huta, & Deci, 2008). *Eudaimonia* supports the idea that well-being is achieved when individuals live in accordance with their "true selves," which includes experiencing self-actualization, meaning, virtuous purpose, and growth at the individual level (Ryan & Deci, 2001; Ryff et al., 2004; Waterman, 1993) as well as commitment to shared goals and values at the social level (Massimini & Delle Fave, 2000). Although distinct, both theoretically and empirically (e.g., Huta & Ryan, 2010), they are considered to have complementary functions, and both are required for well-being and happiness (Huta, 2016). In line with the purported centrality of eudaimonia to well-being, extensive research has provided evidence that the presence of meaning is beneficial and central to various aspects of well-being and happiness (e.g., Park et al., 2010; Ryff, 1989; Steger, 2012; Steger, Kashdan & Oishi,2008). Thus, interest in and research on MIL has steadily grown during the past three decades.

Meaning in Life: Current Conceptualization and Research

The current common integrative conceptualization offers a conception of MIL that includes three central dimensions: comprehension, purpose, and mattering (George & Park, 2016; Martela & Steger, 2016; Steger, 2012). Specifically, MIL "may be defined as the extent to which one's life is experienced as making sense, as being directed and motivated by valued goals, and as mattering in the world" referring to these three dimensions respectively (George & Park, 2016; p. 2). Based on this conceptual foundation, mounting empirical research in recent decades supports the theoretical and philosophical foundations indicating the centrality of MIL to human experience and underscores its importance as a contributing factor for human flourishing and as a coping mechanism for adjustment to life's adversities and suffering (e.g., Czekierda et al., 2017; Damon, 2008; Janoff-Bulman & Yopyk, 2004; Linley & Joseph, 2011; Melton & Schulenberg, 2008; Ryff & Singer, 1998;

Steger, 2012; Steger, Oishi, & Kashdan, 2009). For example, people high in MIL report more positive future orientations (Steger, Kashdan, Sullivan, et al., 2008), hope, and optimism (e.g., Mascaro & Rosen, 2006; Steger & Frazier, 2005; Steger et al., 2006) and enjoy their work more (e.g., Bonebright, Clay, & Ankemann, 2000). They also appear to cope better with life's challenges, demonstrating less avoidance coping and more emotion-focused coping (Edwards & Holden, 2001) as well as less depression (e.g., Mascaro, Rosen, & Morey, 2004) and vulnerability to psychopathology (Debats, 1999). Higher levels of MIL have also been found to be longitudinally associated with preventive behaviors such as physical activity among older individuals (Lampinen et al., 2006).

Recent years have further witnessed a growing sophistication in assessing MIL (e.g., George & Park, 2016; Martela & Steger, 2016) and new conceptualizations regarding the place of MIL within general models of well-being (Huta & Ryan, 2010; Keyes, Shmotkin, & Ryff, 2002). As part of this surge in research, increased attention has been given to the understanding, assessment, and practice of MIL in numerous arenas and contexts, such as psychotherapy, education, and organizations (e.g., Batthyany & Russo-Netzer, 2014; Hill, 2018; Park & George, 2018; Russo-Netzer et al., 2016; Vos, 2018; Wong, 2014). So, how do we go about pursuing meaning, which is so central in our lives?

The Construction and Sources of Meaning in Life

As discussed earlier, searching for meaning is conceived as fundamental to human life and hence there is a natural motivation (will to meaning) to pursue this important and central human endeavor (e.g., Frankl, 1963). However, other scholars also view the search for meaning as a warning sign that meaning has been lost (e.g., Baumeister, 1991). Empirical research has found that searching for meaning is associated with less life satisfaction (e.g., Park et al., 2010) and greater anxiety, depression, and rumination (e.g., Steger, Kashdan, Sullivan & Lorentz, 2008). Yet studies have also shown that searching for meaning is also associated with positive outcomes such as open mindedness, drive, and absorption (Steger et al., 2006 Steger, Kashdan, Sullivan & Lorentz, 2008). It has been suggested that search for meaning may operate as a schema, helping the individual to identify and arrange information relevant to making accurate meaning-in-life judgments (Steger, Oishi, & Kesebir, 2011).

Furthermore, meaning can be constructed through a process of meaning-making, in particular in the face of challenging life circumstances such as adversity, crisis, and trauma (e.g., Park, 2010; 2013). According to the meaning-making model, perceived discrepancies between appraised meaning of a particular situation and global meaning (i.e., general orienting systems of beliefs and goals) create distress, which generates meaning-making efforts to reduce it. Meaning can also be prioritized as a value in itself. In this sense, prioritizing meaning reflects individual differences in the extent to which meaning is implemented via the decisions individuals make about where to invest effort in the context of everyday life (Russo-Netzer, 2018). Such prioritizing has been found to be connected with happiness, life satisfaction, and gratitude among adults. This suggests that focusing on and prioritizing engagement in activities that are inherently value-congruent may serve as a tangible and concrete mechanism for instilling life with meaning and increasing well-being.

Varied conceptualizations regarding sources of MIL have been offered, and these share commonalities as well divergence. For example, Emmons (1999) identified five such sources: personal strivings, achievement, intimacy, religion/spirituality, and generativity. Wong and Ebersole, respectively, each pointed to somewhat similar factors: a personal meaning profile, achievement, relationships, religion, and self-transcendence (Wong, 1998); and life narratives, life work, relationships, religious beliefs, and service (Ebersole, 1998). Furthermore, across empirical studies, personal relationships have been found to be a central source of meaning (e.g., Debats, 1999; O'Connor & Chamberlain, 2000).

Interestingly, the sources of meaning vary throughout the life span (e.g., Lambert et al., 2010; Prager, 1998; Schnell, 2009) and vary according to demographic factors such as gender and socioeconomic status (e.g., Debats, 1999; Schnell, 2009). Furthermore, meaning has been argued to carry different functions for different individuals, and, in particular, three main broad functions have been suggested: recognition and discerning of signals and patterns in the environment; communication, as part of language and sharing of information; and controlling oneself, which involves self-regulation of emotion and behavior through considering possibilities and cultural expectations (see MacKenzie & Baumeister, 2014).

Despite the burgeoning research and emerging understanding of MIL, its sources, and its contribution to human functioning, knowledge is still to a large extent focused on the individual from a psychological point of view. Yet the experience of meaning and its manifestations may evoke different understandings in different cultures, and sources and processes of MIL are probably moderated by culture (Steger, Kawabata, Shimai & Otake, 2008).

Meaning and Culture

Culture affects individuals through language, norms, symbols, rituals, values, the experience of time, schemas, beliefs, and more. Essentially almost all aspects of meaning-making, from the way we perceive and interpret ourselves and our life circumstances and events, to the way we construct our goals and values or turn to different sources for MIL, are embedded in a sociocultural context. This underscores the interplay between individuals and the sociocultural context in which they live and operate (Baumeister, 2005; Chao & Kesebir, 2013; Chiu & Hong, 2007). The uniquely human search for meaning is shaped and influenced by forces and frameworks embedded in culture, and, in turn, individuals' search for meaning also simultaneously recreates and affects culture (Chao & Kesebir, 2013). The dynamic interplay between meaning and culture is evident when a shared network of meaning is being constructed, distributed, and reconstructed among a collective of interconnected individuals which constitute a given culture (Chiu & Hong, 2007). Culture, thus, represents a framework or a web of meaning and enables individuals to function in a given ecology (Fiske, 2000).

It has been suggested that the interplay between meaning and culture can be characterized broadly through two main perspectives (Chao & Kesebir, 2013): *Comprehensibility ("small-m-meaning"),* and *mattering, significance, or worth (capital-M-meaning).* Comprehensibility ("small-m-meaning"), emphasizes a feeling of life that "makes sense" and that it represents a coherent whole (George & Park, 2016; Heintzelman & King, 2014; Martela & Steger, 2016). Detecting connections, associations, and regularities in the environment is an adaptive capacity shared by all creatures (e.g., Geary, 2004). For example, a series of laboratory studies found that the feeling of meaning often emerges when reliable patterns exist in environmental stimuli (Heine et al., 2006; Hicks, Schlegel, & King, 2010). It was also found that exposing people to examples of discrepancy and incoherence in nature or society decreased their sense of purpose in life (Heintzelman, Trent, & King, 2013), as well as their willingness to engage in purposeful pursuits and goal-directed actions (Kay et al., 2014). In this sense, culture plays a critical role in enabling individuals to organize fragmented daily experiences, detect links and patterns, and integrate them into a coherent narrative of self and life (e.g., Chao & Kesebir, 2013; Heine et al., 2006).

The second perspective relates to the dimension of *mattering, significance, or worth (capital-M-meaning)*, which refers to "the degree to which individuals feel that their existence is of significance, importance, and value in the world" (George & Park, 2016, p. 206; see also Martela & Steger, 2016; Mascaro et al., 2004). It relates to ultimate meaning (e.g., Frankl, 1969) and has to do with the "big questions of life" that relate to humans' universal concerns about the fragility and limitations of life and their value (e.g., Greenberg, Solomon, & Pyszczynski, 1997). In this sense, culture can provide individuals with a moral and value-related compass or framework for such exploration and a connection to entities beyond oneself and beyond one's daily existence. Individuals' sense of belonging and individuals' sense of identity both rely on the interplay of these two aspects of culture to provide individuals with MIL that is strongly embedded in symbolic creations of a specific culture. The two perspectives interact as "small-m-meaning" involves lower level, more concrete everyday connections, such as through language and norms, while "capital-M-meaning" addresses more complex and abstract connections, such as values and beliefs (e.g., values, beliefs about the self and the universe and the place of the self in this universe), both reflecting the importance of the mutual relationships between meaning and culture (e.g., Chao & Kesebir, 2013).

Empirical research has started to examine cultural differences related to MIL. For example, while the search for meaning was found to be negatively related to the presence of meaning among US participants, it was positively related to the presence of meaning among Japanese individuals (Steger, Kashdan, & Oishi, 2008). This suggests that the search for meaning may evoke different understandings in different cultures (Steger, Kawabata, Shimai & Otake, 2008). Similarly, individuals in collectivist cultures tend to prioritize goals in their lives that take the larger community into account and are attuned to others, while people in individualist societies tend to emphasize more personal goals and preferences (e.g., King & Watkins, 2012).

Beyond specific cultural differences, the general sociohistorical context that includes worldwide global processes and values also affects the individual search for meaning and the specific MIL that individuals adopt. Such a general cultural context is often referred to as *Zeitgeist* (the spirit or time of an age) and it provides a sociocultural framework for the human and universal questions of MIL in addition to the effects of specific cultures. Such is the current *zeitgeist*—the post-modern context. The current post-modern context has brought with it new challenges for the human quest for meaning. Individuals today operate in an increasingly diverse and dynamic reality, so that life is less predictable than in previous centuries (International Labour Organization, 2016) and hence *comprehensibility ("small-m-meaning")* is more difficult to attain. In addition, processes of cultural and traditional deconstruction and fragmentation are taking place, causing people to experience increased feelings of loneliness, meaninglessness, and alienation (Sperry & Shafranske, 2005) and making the universal human quest for MIL, the *mattering, significance or worth (capital-M-meaning)* aspect more flexible, open, and free yet perhaps also more challenging.

The Post-Modern Sociocultural Context

The contemporary pluralist and complex post-modern sociocultural context has challenged existing processes of continuity, socialization, and certainty as well as the transmission of traditional patterns (Buxant, Saroglou, & Tesser, 2010). The post-modern challenge to notions of truth has led to a deep questioning of existing meaning structures including values, moralities, norms, and expectations as well as distinctions between natural and supernatural, science and faith (Toit, 2006). This is characterized by a gradual weakening of traditional structures, increased secularization, and the "disembedding of social institutions" (Giddens, 1991, pp. 16–21). Instead, the post-modern context emphasizes individualism and more specifically reflects a "massive subjective turn" (Taylor, 1991, p. 26) from an externally influenced life to one that is more attuned to a person's inner experience.

In addition, forces and processes such as industrialization, urbanization, and the decline in the moral authority of religion (Cushman, 1990) have left people more alienated and exposed than before. Against this background, ontological certainties that rely on cultural meanings have weakened as fundamental structures and are often now "particularized" and "mutable" (Moules, 2000), setting the stage for disengagement, a deconstruction of values, and a loss of meaning. This may create an "empty self" that yearns to compensate for what has been lost (Cushman, 1990) and that hungers for personal meaning, a void that contemporary meaning-making systems are attempting to fill. Individuals are faced with the challenge of personally searching for and constructing their own life meaning with less clear guidance of traditions and modern social structures.

The dismantling of established rules and stable institutions and values, as well as the emphasis on relativism, fragmentation, and self-selection has led to fundamental uncertainties concerning what is right and wrong, real and unreal, good and bad, and meaningful versus meaningless. Conversely, "fast-pace," "instant," fluid, and boundless have become dominant motifs in our post-modern discourse. Such fluidity, relativism, and uncertainty rupture individuals' sense of purpose and value in life and often culminate in a void in individuals' meaning systems (Crescioni & Baumeister, 2013).

This void may be associated with distress and anxiety but it can also pave the way for changes, transformations, and creativity (Bauman, 1998; Lyon, 2000). This void further propels the people of today to search for meaning in an attempt to address such existential concerns as "Who am I?," "What is the purpose of my life?," and "What can make my life worth living?," "Where can I belong"?, and "Should I belong?" Such searches are reflected in a host of communal as well as personal ways, such as engaging in searching processes within institutional religions, turning to radical movements, engaging in self-led secular processes of spiritual transformation, getting involved in service to society, advocating for sustainability and environmentalism, joining new religious movements, and more. People may also cope with such voids of meaning by escaping through behaviors such as consumerism, substance abuse, or addiction to the fast pace and intensive shower of stimuli (Gur-Ze'ev, 2010).

In this chapter we suggest that, instead of major overarching cultural schemes, institutions, or narratives for MIL which used to be prominent and dominant, such as religion, contemporary societies offer a large variety of narratives, termed here *master narratives of meaning* that individuals may adopt and adapt to fulfil their need for MIL and have clarity and stability and, specifically, to satisfy their need for comprehension, purpose, and mattering.

Master Narratives of Meaning in a Post-Modern Context

Scholars have suggested that the significant role of the sociocultural context in affecting individuals' functioning is evident in the construction of master narratives, largely defined as "culturally shared stories that guide thoughts, beliefs, values, and behaviors" (McLean & Syed, 2015, p. 323). As such, they may serve as frameworks for common ground around cognition, emotion, and actions (Hammack, 2008; McAdams, 2006; McLean & Syed, 2015; Thorne & McLean, 2003) providing guidance and direction for individuals' personal developmental processes as well as social power. McLean and Syed (2015) suggested several core principles that characterize master narratives, such as utility, ubiquity, invisibility, compulsory, and rigidity. In this sense, master narratives are often invisible (they are cast as natural and followed without noticing them), ubiquitous (they permeate many realms in one's life and in society), compulsory (individuals in society are strongly expected to follow them and deviation is often associated with risks), and rigid (resistant to change) and hence exert strong social power on individual lives. Accordingly, master narratives may inform how one's story may unfold (utility); imbue various aspects of society, family life, and institutions (ubiquity); appear natural and rarely noticed by the individual (invisibility); possess an adherence that is anticipated by the members of a given society or culture (compulsory); and demonstrate a resistance to change in order to preserve the current system (rigidity).

A clear example of master narratives is institutionalized religion. Within institutionalized religions, master narratives may be maintained and facilitated through religious rituals and shared activities, beliefs, and traditions (e.g., Pargament & Mahoney, 2009). In such contexts, individuals can often rely on clear structures (e.g., ideologies, practices, coping resources, symbols, and context) and established spiritual agents (e.g., pastors, priests, rabbis, and imams) to foster a sense of coherence and security (Haslam, Reicher, & Platow, 2011; Kinnvall, 2004; Ysseldyk, Matheson, & Anisman, 2010). These appear to contribute to an individual's sense of control, life purpose, and security, and to positive psychological outcomes and well-being (Emmons, 2005; Park, 2007; Silberman, 2005) as well as coping in challenging and stressful times (Park, 2013; Park, Edmondson, & Hale-Smith, 2013). Furthermore, religions provide a coherent and organized view of life and a set of values, standards, and guidelines for living life in a meaningful and worthy way (Krok, 2014; Spilka et al., 2003), all of which promote a sense of control, certainty, and efficacy (Park, 2005). By offering an agreed-upon system of beliefs and worldviews that involve guiding global moral meaning systems from birth to death and beyond, as well as knowledgeable authorities, religions provide clear guidelines about what is true and valid as well as how to live one's life.

In the grand sociocultural context of the post-modern era today this situation might be different in master narratives of meaning, including religious ones. Contemporary master narratives of meaning are often not perceived as compulsory and are less rigid and often only partially invisible. Namely, individuals in a given society can identify and notice them and embrace or oppose them. They are not automatically followed, and they may be changed by individuals to suit their own version of the narrative.

Thus in post-modern contexts, predictability, comprehensibility, and stability, which often grant a sense of overarching direction to one's life, may be more difficult to attain (Park et al., 2013). We suggest that in such contexts different kinds of sociocultural master narratives are available and can become "master narratives of meaning" by serving as meaning systems for individuals and groups. Such master narratives are not assumed to be ubiquitous or compulsory, and they are much less invisible and rigid. They serve as optional master narratives of meaning because they offer venues for comprehension, purpose, and mattering—the three common components of MIL. Specifically such master narratives should afford individuals a sense of coherence and the capacity to make sense of their life (i.e., comprehension), provide them a sense of being directed and motivated (i.e., purpose), and a sense of value and significance in the world (i.e., mattering). We suggest that this multiplicity of potential narratives is the case in Israel, which in this volume served as a case study of search for meaning in a post-modern world.

Master Narratives of Meaning in a Post-Modern Context: The Case of Israel

Israel has unique cultural characteristics, in particular the prominence of existential threats resulting in a sense of collective vulnerability, uncertainty, and insecurity, together with dialectic identity and worldviews as part of a multicultural immigrant society (e.g., Ezrachi, 2004).

The Zionist narrative that was taken for granted among most of the Jewish citizens of Israel until the past two or three decades served as a meta-narrative, an overarching framework and *raison d'être* (i.e., "reason for existence" or overarching purpose) since the late 19th century. However, as described by Abulof (Chapter 9 in this volume) this narrative has been gradually weakened, leading to various alternative narratives which provide a personal and shared sense of meaning. Abulof claims that as such process unfolded "finding 'an underlying purpose to our existence' became all that more essential, and harder, as Jews found Zionism to be just one among several options to lead political life in modern times. Jews have created, and cast multiple existential anchors of moral meaning onto the turbulent seas of modernity. . . . In the last generation, we may speak of 'the transvaluation of Zionism,' the revaluation of its underpinning moral meaning" (Abulof, Chapter 9). Part of the process included the transition to an individualistic worldview and the deepening of social, cultural, and ideological crises of identity and belonging. Although several concurrent master narratives of meaning existed along with the Zionist meta-narrative, its fragility legitimized the search for alternative sources for meaning.

As the various chapters in this volume suggest, a variety of alternative, often competing, master narratives have surfaced in response to the collapse of the dominant master narrative. These appear to characterize the meaning-making processes of different subgroups within a given multicultural mosaic of the Israeli scene. Here we delineate several central processes in forming or adopting and adapting such alternative master narratives.

1. One direction concerns the *turn to the east and other spiritual-religious traditions* as delineated in some of the chapters (Persico, Chapter 14; Ruah-Midbar Shapiro, Chapter 15). The collapse of the Zionist master narrative and the descent of traditional religion and collectivist ethos have led to a turn to the Far East and Asian traditions: "an increasing number of quests in search of meaning. . . . Individuals started searching for alternative sources of wisdom . . . that might serve as a recipe for daily living and self-understanding. . . . For Israelis, the journey to the East has become one of the popular stepping-stones on the track to social initiation, a part of the socialization process" (Ruah-Midbar Shapiro, Chapter 15). This state of affairs is also demonstrated in the bourgeoning of contemporary spiritualities: "From luxurious yoga halls to private colleges that supply a diploma in alternative medicine, contemporary spirituality in Israel carries not only new religious content, but new religious forms and, with them, new religious

identities for those who seek meaning and fulfilment through such a course. . . . The Israeli individual now saw herself not as an integral part of the people, drawing its values and goals from the collective, but as an autonomous unit standing apart from society and, indeed, before it, both ontologically and ethically" (Persico, Chapter 14). Interestingly, many of these seekers eventually also adopt certain aspects of Judaism, yet reconstruct for themselves a new individualized combination of East and West, blending Judaism with Buddhism, Zen, Chinese philosophy, humanistic perspectives, Hinduism, or a combination of these. Despite being individualized, these seekers are often part of certain social circles or social groups which provide a context of belonging with their unique language and culture, even though these social structures are often quite loose and fluid. Such self-initiated processes within the fluid, eclectic, and deregulated arena of alternative spirituality (Bruce, 1996; Sutcliffe, 2000) are for the most part voluntary (Roehlkepartain et al., 2006) and idiosyncratic (Kwilecki, 1999). Thus, individuals are faced with the challenge of personally constructing their own worldview and identity with less clear guidance from traditions and the support of stable structures and designated authorities to guide this process.

2. Another direction which emerges as an alternative to the central master narrative is the *personalization of the religious narrative* that has been broadened and reshaped to carry various individual and flexible versions of connection to faith, subject to personal experience and interpretation. This is evident in various flexible adaptations, nuances, and structures to a rigid traditional framework which emphasizes social norms and a clear script of institutionalized religion within which one can search for his or her own personal meaning. For example, Orthodox women who integrate self-development as part of their religious way of life: "in such pursuits [for a meaningful life] they combine intrinsic adherence to a Haredi identity and tradition while also adopting other ways of behaving with personal agency to pursue meaning in their life. . . . In their eyes, unlike the opinion of many men and especially rabbis, the two sets of values can coexist and even strengthen one another" (Keren-Kratz, Chapter 12).

Another way of constructing connection to Jewish identity in a flexible manner, from a different perspective and setting, involves instilling a connection to spiritual roots and legacy in the army: "the Jewish Consciousness unit representatives act as spiritual guides working to create. . . a spiritual-religious discourse injecting meaning into the military service, which in turn enhances individuals' sense of service and wellness in their services, as well as granting them a sense of acknowledgment and recognition of their daily work" (Lebel, Ben-Hador & Ben-Shalom, Chapter 16). These examples and others suggest that various groups are constructing and reconstructing forms of religious affiliations that are no longer hegemonic, rigid, or communal, but rather ones that enable more space for individual connection.

Unmediated connection with the transcendent may embody qualities of more intimate presence "right here," rather than "out there." This may resemble the suggestions of contemporary scholars with regard to the changing perception of God, especially outside organized religions: from traditional images of a being that is external, distant, and removed from the world to a more accessible and more personal higher power that is both transcendent or "beyond" but still present in individuals' everyday lives and experiences (Roof, 1999). Luhrmann (2004) described a rather similar phenomenon among evangelical congregants who, as part of the contemporary social-cultural influences of the post-modern condition, built an intimate interpersonal relationship with God. Such a relationship is essentially experienced as tangibly more vivid and personal than the God of their fathers (Wuthnow, 1998). In the context of this volume, this is evident in the renovation of secularized Judaism through individual, autonomous, tailor-made Judaism, which serve as a master narrative of meaning.

The first two narratives reflect an increased interest in and move toward spiritual and metaphysical venues of meaning in Israeli society (Beit-Hallahmi, 1992). Such spiritual yearnings have been manifested in religious circles where individuals who upheld the Jewish tradition started to also search for spiritual experiences and for a personal developmental path that would give them meaning in addition to adherence to expected religious behaviors (*mitzvot*). Being mostly a secular country, such spiritual yearning also provided an impetus for secular Israelis to search for spiritual meaning outside religious contexts through autonomous and individual processes (Russo-Netzer, 2018).

3. A third direction outlined in this volume is the *missionary or radical religious and/or ethnic master narrative*. This master narrative

emphasizes the importance of historical and\or ethnic background and is often involved with fundamentalism or delegitimization of alternate narratives and sometimes also with aggression and dehumanization. An example of such a master narrative of meaning can be seen in the case of the Hilltop Youth's extremist ideology and messianic activism which opposes mainstream political and religious structures: "the case of the Hilltop Youth demonstrates a vigorous blend of meaning and purpose: an individual pursuit of identity and content coupled with shouldering of social roles and responsibilities bestowed by a higher being or a social group.... The Hilltop Youth epitomize a revitalized extremist group driven by a fervent desire to usher in a holistic new future on the ruins of what is perceived by them as a totally failing system" (Peleg, Chapter 5).

In a different context, a master narrative that has some missionary tones and involves delegitimization of alternate narratives can also be found among the ethno-class identity of Mizrahim (Jews of Arab origin) from a low socioeconomic class who hold strong ethnic identities and harbor intense anger at the dominant majority (see Shoshana, Chapter 10). A somewhat radical master narrative of meaning among Arab-Palestinian citizens in Israel is the "visionary" narrative, which "defines belonging as an ideological position.... In the religious politics of belonging, the visionary stance promotes an apocalyptic awareness according to which the end of days is approaching, and Islam will ultimately prevail, ruling globally through a just caliphate" (Agbaria, Mustafa, & Mahajnah, Chapter 11). These examples demonstrate belonging to a distinct and defined ethnic, national, religious, or cultural identity which serves as a central core anchor of identity and meaning, often with delegitimization of alternate narratives to varied extents.

4. Another unique master narrative of meaning relates to the *significance of death and symbolic immortality*. This master narrative comes in different forms and relates in Israel to the prominence of existential threats and the salience of death and mortality. The Holocaust and its modulations in the first, second, and third generation appear to reflect a shared national trauma as can be seen, for example, in the case of the survivors' memoirs as intergenerational healing processes: "the search for meaning has become increasingly present as in old age the survivors feel the urgency to tell their story before it is too late.... Their

children and grandchildren face this inevitable pressure of running out of time as they painfully realize that soon they will be the last to have had an intimate relationship with survivors and that it is up to them to carry on the familial legacy" (Duchin & Wiseman, Chapter 8). This is also evident in the manner in which MIL serves as a resource for older adults in Israel in the shadow of trauma: "concomitants of MIL mitigate the effects of distal [e.g., the Holocaust and Israeli wars] as well as proximal massive traumatic exposures [e.g., terrorism] on older adult Israelis" (Shrira, Palgi, & Shmotkin, Chapter 7). Another demonstrative example is that of the centrality of the movement to include more casualties (e.g., from terror attacks) in the "national bereavement discourse" and the "family of bereavement" to ensure that they have not died in vain: "the many families of Israelis killed and wounded in organized terror attacks against civilians in the aftermath of the Oslo Accords and the 2000 Intifada began to function as a 'memory community' aiming to include their loved ones among the country's national fallen—a category referred to as 'Israeli casualties of war. . . . In order to obtain the resource that they value most—national meaning for their loss and trauma—the families of terror victims did not ask to establish a unique or separate victimized identity for themselves but rather to be perceived as an inseparable part of the 'families of Israeli casualties of war,' a community recognized by the Israeli public as holding a meta-frame that leads to the perception of their loved ones as having died during productive operational action" (Lebel & Ben-Gal, Chapter 4). This is also the case in the Physical Immortality group, which has been small yet salient in Israel and believed that they could control their death and in fact live forever (Beit-Hallahmi, Chapter 6). These may serve as characteristic examples of human universal existential needs by offering a framework for "symbolic immortality" (see Kesebir & Pyszczynski, 2014; Tomer, 2014) which serves as a master narrative of meaning.

5. Another contemporary master narrative of meaning includes a *quest for self-fulfillment* and personal development, often shaped through the penetration of therapeutic, self-fulfillment, and self-actualization discourse into the Western cultural narrative (e.g., Illouz, 2008), where "psychology has become the secular successor to religion" (Fuller, 2001, p. 123). An example of such a master narrative can be seen among mobile Mizrahim: "the ethos of meritocracy and self-definitions of

Israeliness (all of which encourage dissociation from ethnicity) proposed by mobile Mizrahim who were born into a high socioeconomic
class make extensive use of psychological discourse and the cosmopolitan ideal. The psychological discourse, which is attributed mainly to
Western and secular cultures, is characterized by placing the self at the
center (as opposed to the transcendental being or the community in
traditional or religious societies), the preference for personal attribution to reality, verbalization of feelings, and particular engagement in
values of self-fulfilment, separatism, and individualism" (Shoshana,
Chapter 10). This process of self-fulfillment appears to be self-oriented
and less community-oriented or prosocial.

6. The *universalist master narrative* outlines a perspective of multiculturalism or a "citizen of the world" manifested in a sense of interconnected to humanity in general rather than belongingness to a specific
ethnic, national, or religious group. The focus is on the commitment
to humanity, which involves a prosocial perspective, untied to specific
cultural constrains or definitions. This may appear to be undermining
the value of relatedness and belonging yet it provides a sense of com-
petence and autonomy and may be more prevalent among upper mobility individuals (Jews and Arabs) as well as those adopting a Buddhist
Vipasana stance, perceived as reflecting a connection to humanity as a
whole, disconnected from particular identifications: "vipassana offers
an alternative source for self-identity, one that reduces the importance
of local and personal identities while at the same time creating a bridge
to a universal conception of humanity. Through the presentation of
vipassana as a universal global practice stripped from any particular
local or religious connotations, through the unique configuration of
the meditation center as a space without a place, through the turn of
attention inward while detaching from collective identifications and
biographical narratives, and through a cultivation of compassion for
humanity at large, Israeli practitioners find an anchor for selfhood that
is not based on local social context" (Pagis, Chapter 13).

7. Finally, a general master narrative of meaning relates to *identification
with one's nation as a unique and special nation* but without delegitim-
izing other narratives. For example, Doron (Chapter 2) suggests that
for Jewish Israelis the "Startup Nation" of Israel provides a "deep sense
of worth and significance through a 'special compensation mechanism'
that connects each Israeli to its Jewish past, its 'start-up nation' present,

and the unique Israeli free spirit and self-expression." Despite the weakening of the meta narrative of Zionism, Jewish Israelis are proud to be Israeli and have a cultural ethos for the Jewish state of Israel that gives them meaning, belonging, and worth (Doron, Chapter 2). Some similarity to such master narratives of meaning is the "romantic" narrative among some of the Arab-Palestinian citizens in Israel (Agbaria, Mustafa, & Mahajnah, Chapter 11): "the romantic narrative . . . is shared by both secular and religious political groups. This concept strongly invokes the past and is oriented to retrieve and restore it by promoting nostalgia and memory. In Arab secular politics, this concept is evident in the growing emphasis on Palestinian tradition and indigeneity and by celebrating Palestinian literature, folklore, culinary art, customs, and history as reflecting the special attachment to the homeland and the distinctive identity of Palestinians in Israel as an indigenous group."

Major Trends in Israeli Narratives and Their Relevance to Other Cultures

Several trends can be observed in the master narratives just described.

1. The centrality of religious and spiritual narratives—self-spirituality within and outside established religions.
2. The still important role of national identity based on tradition and ethos as well as current achievements, such that citizens feel pride in their national belonging
3. A turn to radical messianic narratives (often religious ones) associated with delegitimation of other narratives and aggression
4. A humanistic stance with a focus on self (self-actualization and self-fulfillment) and/or on humanity at large (citizen of the world) with prosocial perspectives.
5. Search for symbolic immortality.

We suggest that different versions of such processes may also be observed in other cultures today. For example, Lu and Yang (2020) distinguish between cultures with religious polarization (a more dogmatic perspective) and cultures with religious fractionalization (multicultural perspective) and highlight the existence of different effects on health for each of them.

Similarly, Heelas (1996) and others (e.g., Hood, 2003) discussed self-spirituality and the blurring of boundaries between secular and religious in different cultures more than two decades ago. Future sociological research on processes of meaning-making in other countries and cultures may shed light on these issues.

What do these master narratives tell us about processes of search for meaning in a post-modern context?

We suggest that meta-narratives adopted by a very large number of people with qualities of master narratives (e.g., ubiquity, invisibility, compulsory, and rigidity; McLean & Syed, 2015) are less prevalent today, and instead cultures may offer a variety of master narratives of meaning that provide comprehension, purpose, and worth and probably also belonging and identity. Such narratives are often visible, and hence individuals feel moderately free to choose among them as well as adopt several concurrently or adapt them to their needs.

Additionally, we want to underscore several broad processes or dimensions of the search for meaning that became clear as we analyzed the variety of master narratives of meaning that unfolded in the Israeli scene. Although arising in the Israeli scene, we suggest that these general dimensions might be relevant to other cultures that are embedded within the post-modern sociocultural context as well.

First, a central aspect of processes of search is the mix-and-match quality of narratives that are constructed individually to fit each person but are still quite similar to those of others and allow belonging to social circles and groups. (See similar insights by other scholars; e.g., Hamilton, 2000; Rindfleish, 2005; Wuthnow, 2007).

Second, the narratives uncovered the centrality of the dimension of legitimation of a variety of narratives versus the delegitimation of other narratives and the upholding of a dogma with absolute truth.

Third, in search processes an important dimension relates to a somewhat selfish and self-focused process versus the focus on belonging to a community or becoming a citizen of the world with responsibility to make it a better place.

Fourth, despite the emergence of searching for a variety of ways to accrue symbolic immortality in the chapters of the book, these were less prevalent. We believe that such searches may not be unique to this era as people have been engaged in such processes for millennia (e.g., by erecting buildings and tombs, composing or writing, having children, etc.). Search for MIL through symbolic immortality may be somewhat invisible as death might still be a major taboo in many cultures.

Conclusion, with an Eye to the Future

Cultures facilitate the gratification of humans' psychological needs, such as a sense of self-worth (Wan et al., 2011) or an epistemic and existential sense of order, stability, controllability, and connection (e.g., Chao & Kesebir, 2013), thus buffering against possible threats and uncertainties (e.g., Greenberg et al., 1997; Heine et al., 2006). The post-modern context has challenged the static, single, and continuous structures of self and society and called for a self that is fluid, multiple, and fragmented, and which constantly comes into being or is "becoming" (e.g., Rindfleish, 2005). Disconnected from sustaining overarching frameworks, individuals are challenged to construct their own personal guiding narratives of meaning and address fundamental existential issues on their own. Indeed, in many cultures today, individuals are no longer obligated to fixed, culturally given structures and are faced with the freedom to form their own identities through conscious and autonomous choices (Adams, 2003). This state of affairs, while liberating, also leaves individuals vulnerable in the face of their existential human condition. For some, this leads them to be guided by their inner reflection, choice, and observation for validation and judgment purposes. Others try to rely on a more rigid narrative with absolute truths that often involve delegitimization of other narratives, and both may also rely on tradition and the legacy of their culture/nation.

To conclude, while several core principles of master narratives have been outlined in the literature, such as utility, ubiquity, invisibility, compulsory, and rigidity (McLean & Syed, 2015), we suggest that, with the turn of post-modern processes, the variety and options of alternative master narratives which provide a sense of meaning appear to be more visible than before and more readily "mixed and matched." The numerous alternatives to master narratives of meaning have taken the place of a central hegemonic, invisible, and rigid one, accompanied by individuals' agency and autonomous choice. This demonstrates the dialectic between the committed sense of identity, MIL, and purpose and a continuous, fluid, and flexible process of "becoming," of shaping one's meaning through reevaluation and continuous exploration. The post-modern era offered opportunities for the search for meaning and thus the creation of new identities: plural rather than unitary, relational and contingent rather than self-contained and absolute (Rattansi & Phoenix, 1997). The post-modern perspective views identity as dynamic, multiplistic, relativistic, fluid, context-specific, decentered, and fragmented (Rattansi & Phoenix, 1997). Post-modernism's wealth of choices spurred the creation of other identity structures, such as multiracial identities (Sanchez, Shih, & Garcia, 2009), the fragmentation of self (Strauss, 1997), and hybrid identities (Linzer, 1996). The relatively prevalent notion of identity hybridization reflects the individual's ability to borrow and mix different elements from a range of religious, gender, or ethnic identities (Rattansi & Phoenix, 1997). Along these lines, the master narratives of meaning described here reflect a central element of choice between options, given that traditional master narrative and the societal expectations, norms, and sanctions have declined and are less rigid.

The increased freedom to choose also involves weaker commitment and, perhaps, sense of belonging. With no clear guidelines, social markers, or absolute truths that have been accepted and taken for granted, as well as with the increasing exposure to a multitude of alternatives and options, there is an increased tendency to rely on internal touchstones and self-constructed guidelines as sources of validity and ultimacy. *Ultimacy*, in this sense, refers to experiences of deep truth, or what has been described as embodying the "absolutely true, absolutely real," which thus provides "tremendous authority and legitimacy" (Lomax & Pargament, 2011, p. 82). This may represent a potential way of coping with the post-modern challenges of pluralism, freedom, and choice, with individuals utilizing these very same qualities to navigate their journeys.

However, while a shift has occurred from an essentialist and committed identity to a more fluid and dynamic one, the beneficial aspects of the freedom of choice and decategorization may come with a price. In line with social identity theory (Tajfel & Turner, 1986; Tajfel & Turner, 1979), which postulates that one's own identity and subsequent self-esteem derive in part from the affiliation with distinct social groups, it is possible that a lack of distinct commitment may affect the sense of significance, continuity, and unique identification.

Given the important role of culture in establishing people's values, assumptions, and needs (Markus & Kitayama, 1991), human processes and patterns may carry different manifestations across cultures. Open questions with regard to the cultural facilitators which trigger change or instead maintain one's adoption of a master narrative remain: What allows a master narrative or script to "stick" as a meaning framework in a particular culture? Can we find a matrix or combination of master narratives of meaning in a given culture? What is the role of the *zeitgeist* (spirit of times) in the manner in which individuals choose their master narratives? Can we find processes similar to that of New Age discourse suggesting eclectic and idiosyncratic "pick-and-mix" (Hamilton, 2000) or "take-it-or-leave-it" experimental approach (Rindfleish, 2005) or "tinkering" (Wuthnow, 2007)?

Epilogue

This book was conceived and written between 2016 and 2019, but 2020 brought with it the corona virus pandemic (COVID-19), a crisis that affected most nations and cultures in the world. A major aspect of COVID-19 is not just the fear for one's health but the social distancing it entailed and the strong and encompassing uncertainty about what will happen, how to cope, and what could be the consequences. This uncertainty and the ways in which political leaders coped further shattered many well-established and central national structures such as education systems, work arenas, and economic stability. Where this will lead us and what kind of master narratives of meaning we, as the human species, will adopt is still hard to tell. Will new master narratives emerge? Will new citizens of the world arise? How will this time affect the interplay between individuals and cultures? These are open questions yet to be discovered and explored.

References

Adams, M. (2003). The reflexive self and culture: A critique. *The British Journal of Sociology, 54*(2), 221–238.
Batthyany, A., & Guttmann, D. (2005). *Empirical research in logotherapy and meaning-oriented psychotherapy.* Zeig, Tucker, & Theisen.
Batthyany, A., & Russo-Netzer, P. (Eds.). (2014). *Meaning in positive and existential psychology.* New York: Springer.
Bauman, Z. (1998). *Globalization: The human consequences.* Columbia University Press.
Baumeister, R. F. (1991). *Meanings of life.* Guilford.
Baumeister, R. F. (2005). *The cultural animal: Human nature, meaning, and social life.* Oxford University Press.

Baumeister, R. F., & Vohs, K. D. (2002). The pursuit of meaningfulness in life. In: S. Lopez (Ed.), *The Oxford Handbook of positive psychology* (pp. 608–618).

Becker, E. (1975). *Escape from evil*. Free Press.

Beit-Hallahmi, B. (1992). *Despair and deliverance: Private salvation in contemporary Israel*. Suny Press.

Bonebright, C. A., Clay, D. L., & Ankenmann, R. D. (2000). The relationship of workaholism with work–life conflict, life satisfaction, and purpose in life. *Journal of Counseling Psychology, 47*(4), 469.

Bruce, A., Schreiber, R., Petrovskaya, O., & Boston, P. (2011). Longing for ground in a ground (less) world: A qualitative inquiry of existential suffering. *BMC Nursing, 10*(1), 1–9.

Bruce, S. (1996). *Religion in the modern world: From cathedrals to cults*. Oxford University Press.

Buxant, C., Saroglou, V., & Tesser, M. (2010). Free-lance spiritual seekers: Self-growth or compensatory motives? *Mental Health, Religion & Culture, 13*(2), 209–222.

Chao, M. M., & Kesebir, P. (2013). Culture: The grand web of meaning. In *The experience of meaning in life* (pp. 317–331). Springer.

Chiu, C., & Hong, Y.-Y. (2007). Cultural processes: Basic principles. In E. T. Higgins, & A. E. Kruglanski (Eds.), *Social psychology: Handbook of basic principles* (pp. 785–806). Guilford Press.

Crescioni, A. W., & Baumeister, R. F. (2013). The four needs for meaning, the value gap, and how (and whether) society can fill the void. In J. A. Hicks & C. Routledge (Eds.). *The experience of meaning in life* (pp. 3–15). Springer, Dordrecht.

Cushman, P. (1990). Why the self is empty: Toward a historically situated psychology. *American Psychologist, 45*(5), 599.

Czekierda, K., Banik, A., Park, C. L., & Luszczynska, A. (2017). Meaning in life and physical health: Systematic review and meta-analysis. *Health Psychology Review, 11*(4), 387–418.

Damon, W. (2008). *The path to purpose: Helping our children find their calling in life*. Free Press.

Debats, D. L. (1999). Sources of meaning: An investigation of significant commitments in life. *Journal of Humanistic Psychology, 39*(4), 30–57.

Ebersole, P. (1998). Types and depth of written life meanings. In T. P. Paul Wong & S. Prem Fry (Eds.), *The human quest for meaning: A handbook of psychological research and clinical applications* (pp. 179–191). Lawrence Erlbaum.

Edwards, M. J., & Holden, R. R. (2001). Coping, meaning in life, and suicidal manifestations: Examining gender differences. *Journal of Clinical Psychology, 57*(12), 1517–1534.

Emmons, R. A. (1999). *The psychology of ultimate concerns: Motivation and spirituality in personality*. Guilford Press.

Emmons, R. A. (2005). Striving for the sacred: Personal goals, life meaning, and religion. *Journal of Social Issues, 61*(4), 731–745.

Ezrachi, E. (2004). The quest for spirituality among secular Israelis. In U. Rebhun & C. I. Waxman (Eds.), *Jews in Israel: Contemporary social and cultural patterns* (pp. 315–328). University Press of New England.

Fiske, A. P. (2000). Complementarity theory: Why human social capacities evolved to require cultural complements. *Personality and Social Psychology Review, 4*, 76–94.

Frankl, V. E. (1963). *Man's search for meaning: An introduction to logotherapy.* Washington Square Press.

Frankl, V. E. (1966). Logotherapy and existential analysis—a review. *American Journal of Psychotherapy, 20*(2), 252–260.

Frankl, V. E. (1969). *The will to meaning: Foundations and applications of logotherapy.* World Publishing.

Frankl, V.E. (1977). The Unconscious God. London: Hodder and Stoughton.

Friedman, E. M. (2012). *Well-being, aging, and immunity.* In S. C. Segerstrom (Ed.), *Oxford library of psychology. The Oxford handbook of psychoneuroimmunology* (pp. 37–62). Oxford University Press.

Fuller, R. C. (2001). *Spiritual, but not religious: Understanding unchurched America.* Oxford University Press.

Geary, D. C. (2004). *Origin of mind: Evolution of brain, cognition, and intelligence.* APA.

George, L. S., & Park, C. L. (2016). Meaning in life as comprehension, purpose, and mattering: Toward integration and new research questions. *Review of General Psychology, 20*(3), 205–220.

Giddens, A. (1991). *Modernity and self-identity: Self and society in the late Modern Age.* Stanford University Press.

Grant, A. M., & Wade-Benzoni, K. A. (2009). The hot and cool of death awareness at work: Mortality cues, aging, and self-protective and prosocial motivations. *Academy of Management Review, 34*(4), 600–622.

Greenberg, J., Solomon, S., & Pyszczynski, T. (1997). Terror management theory of self-esteem and cultural worldviews: Empirical assessments and conceptual refinements. In M.P. Zanna (Ed.). *Advances in experimental social psychology* (Vol. 29, pp. 61–139). Academic Press.

Gur-Ze'ev, I. (2010). *Diasporic philosophy and counter-education. Educational futures re-thinking theory and practice.* Sense Publishing.

Hamilton, M. (2000). An analysis of the festival for Mind-Body-Spirit, London. In S. Sutcliffe & M. Bowman (Eds.), *Beyond new age: Exploring alternative spirituality* (pp. 188–200). Edinburgh University Press.

Hammack, P. L. (2008). Narrative and the cultural psychology of identity. *Personality and Social Psychology Review, 12*(3), 222–247.

Haslam, S. A., Reicher, S. D., & Platow, M. J. (2011). *The new psychology of leadership: Identity, Influence, and Power.* Psychology Press.

Heelas, P. (1996). *The new age movement: The celebration of the self and the sacralization of modernity.* Blackwell.

Heine, S., Proulx, T., & Vohs, K. (2006). The meaning maintenance model: On the coherence of social motivations. *Personality and Social Psychology Review, 10*, 88–110.

Heintzelman, S. J., & King, L. A. (2014). (The feeling of) meaning-as-information. *Personality and Social Psychology Review, 18*(2), 153–167.

Heintzelman, S. J., Trent, J., & King, L. A. (2013). Encounters with objective coherence and the experience of meaning in life. *Psychological Science, 24*(6), 991–998.

Hicks, J. A., Schlegel, R. J., & King, L. A. (2010). Social threats, happiness, and the dynamics of meaning in life judgments. *Personality and Social Psychology Bulletin, 36*(10), 1305–1317.

Hill, C. E. (2018). *Meaning in life: A therapist's guide.* American Psychological Association.

alra5e5

Hood, R. W. (2003). The relationship between religion and spirituality. In A. L. Greil & D. Bromley (Eds.), *Defining religion: Investigating the boundaries between the sacred and the secular. Vol. 10: Religion and the social order* (pp. 241–265). Elsevier.

Huta, V. (2016). Eudaimonic and hedonic orientations: Theoretical considerations and research findings. In: J. Vitters (Ed.), *Handbook of eudaimonic well-being* (pp. 215–231). Springer.

Huta, V., & Ryan, R. M. (2010). Pursuing pleasure or virtue? The differential and overlapping well-being benefits of hedonic and eudaimonic motives. *Journal of Happiness Studies, 11*, 735–762.

Huta, V., & Waterman, A. S. (2014). Eudaimonia and its distinction from hedonia: Developing a classification and terminology for understanding conceptual and operational definitions. *Journal of Happiness Studies, 15*(6), 1425–1456.

Illouz, E. (2008). *Saving the modern soul: Therapy, emotions, and the culture of self-help.* University of California Press.

International Labour Organization. (2016). Non-standard employment around the world: Understanding challenges, shaping prospects. Geneva: ILO

Janoff-Bulman, R., & Yopyk, D. J. (2004). Random outcomes and valued commitments: Existential dilemmas and the paradox of meaning. In J. Greenberg, S. L. Koole, & T. Pyszczynski (Eds.), Handbook of experimental existential psychology (pp. 122–138). Guilford Press.

Kay, A. C., Laurin, K., Fitzsimons, G. M., & Landau, M. J. (2014). A functional basis for structure-seeking: Exposure to structure promotes willingness to engage in motivated action. *Journal of Experimental Psychology, 143*(2), 486–491.

Kesebir, P., & Pyszczynski, T. (2014). Meaning as a buffer for existential anxiety. In A. Batthyany & P. Russo-Netzer (Eds.). *Meaning in positive and existential psychology* (pp. 53–64). Springer.

Keyes, C. L., Shmotkin, D., & Ryff, C. D. (2002). Optimizing well-being: The empirical encounter of two traditions. *Journal of personality and social psychology, 82*(6), 1007.

Kierkegaard, S. (1843/2016). *Fear and trembling.* New York: Penguin

King, R. B., & Watkins, D. A. (2012). "Socializing" achievement goal theory: The need for social goals. *Psychological studies, 57*(1), 112–116.

Kinnvall, C. (2004). Globalization and religious nationalism: Self, identity, and the search for ontological security. *Political Psychology, 25*(5), 741–767.

Klinger, E. (2012). *The search for meaning in evolutionary goal-theory perspective and its clinical implications.* In P. T. P. Wong (Ed.), *Personality and clinical psychology series. The human quest for meaning: Theories, research, and applications* (p. 23–56). Routledge/ Taylor & Francis Group.

Krok, D. (2014). The religious meaning system and subjective well-being: The mediational perspective of meaning in life. *Archive for the Psychology of Religion, 36*(2), 253–273.

Kwilecki, S. (1999). *Becoming religious: Understanding devotion to the unseen.* Bucknell University Press.

Lambert, N. M., Stillman, T. F., Baumeister, R. F., Fincham, F. D., Hicks, J. A., & Graham, S. M. (2010). Family as a salient source of meaning in young adulthood. *The Journal of Positive Psychology, 5*(5), 367–376.

Lampinen, P., Heikkinen, R. L., Kauppinen, M., & Heikkinen, E. (2006). Activity as a predictor of mental well-being among older adults. *Aging and Mental Health, 10*(5), 454–466.

Landau, M. J., Kosloff, S., & Schmeichel, B. J. (2011). Imbuing everyday actions with meaning in response to existential threat. *Self and Identity*, *10*(1), 64–76.

Linley, P. A., & Joseph, S. (2011). Meaning in life and posttraumatic growth. *Journal of Loss and Trauma*, *16*(2), 150–159.

Linzer, J. (1996). *Torah and Dharma: Jewish seekers in Eastern religions*. Jason Aronson.

Lomax, J. W., & Pargament, K. I. (2011). Seeking "sacred moments" in psychotherapy and in life. *Psyche en Geloof*, *22*(2), 79–90.

Lu, Y., & Yang, X. Y. (2020). The two faces of diversity: The relationships between religious polarization, religious fractionalization, and self-rated health. *Journal of Health and Social Behavior*, *61*(1), 79–95.

Luhrmann, T. M. (2004). How God becomes intimate in contemporary US Christianity. *American Anthropologist*, *106*(3), 518–528.

Lyon, D. (2000). *Jesus in Disneyland: Religion in postmodern times*. Polity

MacKenzie, M. J., & Baumeister, R. F. (2014). Meaning in life: Nature, needs, and myths. In A. Batthyany & P. Russo-Netzer (Eds.). *Meaning in positive and existential psychology* (pp. 25–37). Springer.

Markus, H. R., & Kitayama, S. (1991). Culture and the self: Implications for cognition, emotion, and motivation. *Psychological Review*, *98*(2), 224.

Martela, F., & Steger, M. F. (2016). The three meanings of meaning in life: Distinguishing coherence, purpose, and significance. *The Journal of Positive Psychology*, *11*, 1–15.

Mascaro, N., & Rosen, D. H. (2006). The role of existential meaning as a buffer against stress. *Journal of Humanistic Psychology*, *46*(2), 168–190.

Mascaro, N., Rosen, D. H., & Morey, L. C. (2004). The development, construct validity, and clinical utility of the spiritual meaning scale. *Personality and Individual Differences*, *37*(4), 845–860.

Maslow, A. H. (1968). *Toward a psychology of being*. (2nd ed.) Van Nostrand.

Massimini, F., & Delle Fave, A. (2000). Individual development in a bio-cultural perspective. *American Psychologist*, *55*(1), 24.

McAdams, D. P. (2006). The redemptive self: Generativity and the stories Americans live by. *Research in Human Development*, *3*(2-3), 81–100.

McLean, K. C., & Syed, M. (2015). Personal, master, and alternative narratives: An integrative framework for understanding identity development in context. *Human Development*, *58*(6), 318–349.

Melton, A. M., & Schulenberg, S. E. (2008). On the measurement of meaning: Logotherapy's empirical contributions to humanistic psychology. *The Humanistic Psychologist*, *36*(1), 31–44.

Moules, N. J. (2000). Postmodernism and the sacred: Reclaiming connection in our greater-than-human worlds. *Journal of Marital and Family Therapy*, *26*(2), 229–240.

Nietzsche, F. (1888/2007). *Thus spoke Zarathustra*. Penguin Classics.

O'Connor, K., & Chamberlain, K. (2000). Dimensions and discourses of meaning in life: Approaching meaning from qualitative perspectives. In G. T. Reker & K. Chamberlain (Eds.), *Exploring existential meaning: Optimizing human development across the life span* (pp. 75–91). Sage.

Pargament, K. I., & Mahoney, A. (2009). Spirituality: The search for the sacred. In S. J. Lopez & C. R. Snyder (Eds.), *Oxford library of psychology. Oxford handbook of positive psychology* (pp. 611–619). Oxford University Press.

Park, C. L. (2005). Religion as a meaning-making framework in coping with life stress. *Journal of Social Issues*, *61*(4), 707–729.

Park, C. L. (2007). Religiousness/spirituality and health: A meaning systems perspective. *Journal of Behavioral Medicine, 30*(4), 319–328.

Park, N., Park, M., & Peterson, C. (2010). When is the search for meaning related to life satisfaction?. *Applied Psychology: Health and Well-Being, 2*(1), 1–13.

Park, C. L. (2010). Making sense of the meaning literature: An integrative review of meaning making and its effects on adjustment to stressful life events. *Psychological Bulletin, 136*(2), 257–301.

Park, C. L. (2013). The meaning making model: A framework for understanding meaning, spirituality, and stress-related growth in health psychology. *European Health Psychologist, 15*(2), 40–47.

Park, C. L., Edmondson, D., & Hale-Smith, A. (2013). Why religion? Meaning as motivation. In K. I. Pargament (Ed.), *APA handbook of psychology, religion and spirituality* (Vol. 1, pp. 157–171). American Psychological Association.

Park, C. L., & George, L. S. (2018). Lab-and field-based approaches to meaning threats and restoration: Convergences and divergences. *Review of General Psychology, 22*(1), 73–84.

Prager, E. (1998). Observations of personal meaning sources for Israeli age cohorts. *Aging & Mental Health, 2*(2), 128–136.

Pyszczynski, T., Greenberg, J., & Solomon, S. (1999). A dual-process model of defense against conscious and unconscious death-related thoughts: an extension of terror management theory. *Psychological review, 106*(4), 835.

Rattansi, A., & Phoenix, A. (1997). Rethinking youth identities: Modernist and postmodernist frameworks. In J. Bynner, L. Chisholm, & A. Furlong (Eds.), *Youth, citizenship and social change in a European context* (pp. 121–150). Ashgate.

Rindfleish, J. (2005). Consuming the self: New age spirituality as "social product" in consumer society. *Consumption, Markets and Culture, 8*(4), 343–360.

Roehlkepartain, E. C., King, P. E. E., Wagener, L. E., & Benson, P. L. (2006). *The handbook of spiritual development in childhood and adolescence.* Sage.

Roof, W. C. (1999). *Spiritual supermarket: Baby boomers and the remaking of American religion.* Princeton University Press.

Russo-Netzer, P. (2018). Prioritizing meaning as a pathway to meaning in life and general well-being. *Journal of Happiness Studies, 20*(6), 1863–1891.

Russo-Netzer, P., Schulenberg, S. E., & Batthyany, A. (Eds.). (2016). *Clinical perspectives on meaning: Positive and existential psychotherapy.* Springer.

Ryan, R. M., & Deci, E. L. (2001). On happiness and human potentials: A review of research on hedonic and eudaimonic well-being. *Annual Review of Psychology, 52*(1), 141–166.

Ryan, R. M., Huta, V., & Deci, E. L. (2008). Living well: A self-determination theory perspective on eudaimonia. *Journal of Happiness Studies, 9*(1), 139–170.

Ryff, C. D. (1989). Happiness is everything, or is it? Explorations on the meaning of psychological well-being. *Journal of Personality and Social Psychology, 57*(6), 1069.

Ryff, C. D., & Singer, B. (1998). The contours of positive human health. *Psychological Inquiry, 9*(1), 1–28.

Ryff, C. D., Singer, B. H., & Dienberg Love, G. (2004). Positive health: Connecting well-being with biology. *Philosophical Transactions of the Royal Society of London. Series B: Biological Sciences, 359*(1449), 1383–1394.

Sanchez, D. T., Shih, M., & Garcia, J. A. (2009). Juggling multiple racial identities: Malleable racial identification and psychological well-being. *Cultural Diversity and Ethnic Minority Psychology, 15*(3), 243.

Schnell, T. (2009). The Sources of Meaning and Meaning in Life Questionnaire (SoMe): Relations to demographics and well-being. *The Journal of Positive Psychology*, 4(6), 483–499.

Silberman, I. (2005). Religion as a meaning system: Implications for the new millennium. *Journal of Social Issues*, 61(4), 641–663.

Sperry, L. E., & Shafranske, E. P. (2005). *Spiritually oriented psychotherapy*. American Psychological Association.

Spilka, B., Hood, R. W., Hunsberger, B., & Gorsuch, R. L. (2003). *The psychology of religion: An empirical approach*. Guilford.

Steger, M. F. (2012). Experiencing meaning in life. In P. T. P. Wong (Ed.), *The human quest for meaning* (pp. 165–184). Routledge.

Steger, M. F., & Frazier, P. (2005). Meaning in life: One link in the chain from religiousness to well-being. *Journal of Counseling Psychology*, 52(4), 574.

Steger, M. F., Frazier, P., Oishi, S., & Kaler, M. (2006). The meaning in life questionnaire: Assessing the presence of and search for meaning in life. *Journal of Counseling Psychology*, 53, 80–93.

Steger, M. F., Kashdan, T. B., & Oishi, S. (2008). Being good by doing good: Daily eudaimonic activity and well-being. *Journal of Research in Personality*, 42, 22–42.

Steger, M. F., Kashdan, T. B., Sullivan, B. A., & Lorentz, D. (2008). Understanding the search for meaning in life: Personality, cognitive style, and the dynamic between seeking and experiencing meaning. *Journal of Personality*, 76, 199–228.

Steger, M. F., Kawabata, Y., Shimai, S., & Otake, K. (2008). The meaningful life in Japan and the United States: Levels and correlates of meaning in life. *Journal of Research in Personality*, 42, 660–678.

Steger, M. F., Oishi, S., & Kashdan, T. B. (2009). Meaning in life across the life span: Levels and correlates of meaning in life from emerging adulthood to older adulthood. *The Journal of Positive Psychology*, 4(1), 43–52.

Steger, M. F., Oishi, S., & Kesebir, S. (2011). Is a life without meaning satisfying? The moderating role of the search for meaning in satisfaction with life judgments. *The Journal of Positive Psychology*, 6(3), 173–180.

Strauss, A. L. (1997). *Mirrors and masks: The search for identity*. Transaction Publishers.

Sutcliffe, S. (2000). "Wandering stars": Seekers and gurus in the modern world. In S. Sutcliffe and M. Bowman (Eds.), *Beyond New Age: Exploring alternative spirituality*. Edinburgh University Press.

Tajfel, H. (1979). Individuals and groups in social psychology. *British Journal of Social and Clinical Psychology*, 18(2), 183–190.

Tajfel, H., & Turner, J. C. (1979). An integrative theory of inter-group conflict. In W. G. Austin & S. Worchel (Eds.), The social psychology of inter-group relations (pp. 33–47). Monterey, CA: Brooks/Cole.

Tajfel, H., & Turner, J. C. (1986). The social identity theory of intergroup conflict. In S. Worchel & W. G. Austin (Eds.), *Psychology of intergroup relations* (pp. 7–24). Chicago, IL: Nelson-Hall

Taylor, C. (1991). *The ethics of authenticity* (Vol. 30). Harvard University Press.

Thorne, A., & McLean, K. C. (2003). Telling traumatic events in adolescence: A study of master narrative positioning. In: Fivush, R., Haden, C. (Eds.) *Connecting culture and memory: The development of an autobiographical self* (pp. 169–185). Mahwah, NJ: Lawrence Erlbaum.

Toit, G. (2006). The significance of postmodern theories of interpretation for contractual interpretation: A critical analysis (doctoral dissertation). University of Stellenbosch.

Tomer, A. (2014). Meaning in terror management theory. In A. Batthyanny & P. Russo-Netzer (Eds.), *Meaning in positive and existential psychology* (pp. 65–79). Springer.

Vos, J. (2018). *Meaning in life: An evidence-based handbook for practitioners.* Macmillan International Higher Education.

Wan, C., Dach-Gruschow, K., Hong, Y. Y., & No, S. (2011). *Self-definitional functions of culture.* Cambridge University Press.

Waterman, A. S. (1993). Two conceptions of happiness: Contrasts of personal expressiveness (eudaimonia) and hedonic enjoyment. *Journal of Personality and Social Psychology, 64*(4), 678.

Wong, P. T. (2010). Meaning therapy: An integrative and positive existential psychotherapy. *Journal of Contemporary Psychotherapy, 40*(2), 85–93.

Wong, P. T. (2014). Viktor Frankl's meaning-seeking model and positive psychology. In A. Batthyanny & P. Russo-Netzer (Eds.), *Meaning in positive and existential psychology* (pp. 149–184). Springer.

Wong, P. T. P. (1998). Implicit theories of meaningful life and the development of the personal meaning profile. In P. T. P. Wong & P. S. Fry (Eds.), *The human quest for meaning* (pp. 111–140). Erlbaum.

Wuthnow, R. (1998). *After heaven: Spirituality in America since the 1950s.* University of California Press.

Wuthnow, R. (2007). *After the baby boomers: How twenty- and thirty-somethings are shaping the future of American religion.* Princeton University Press.

Yalom, I. (1980). Existential psychotherapy. BasicBooks.

Ysseldyk, R., Matheson, K., & Anisman, H. (2010). Religiosity as identity: Toward an understanding of religion from a social identity perspective. *Personality and Social Psychology Review, 14*(1), 60–71.

Index

For the benefit of digital users, indexed terms that span two pages (e.g., 52–53) may, on occasion, appear on only one of those pages.

Figures and tables are indicated by *f* and *t* after the page number.

boutique religions, 319–20
Brahma (Hindu god), 336–37, 337n.2
Brisk Rabbi, 280–81
British Empire, 199, 261–62
Brooks, David, 302
Brown, Charles Paul, 124, 146
Buber, Martin, 56, 212
Buddhism
    discussion, 11, 144–45, 298–300
    Judaism syncretistic beliefs and, 335–
        38, 337nn.2–3, 337–38n.4
    pro-Eastern master narrative and, 342–
        45, 425–26
Buddhist meditation
    centers and retreats, 298–99
    connection to humanity via, 308–10
    discussion, 296–98, 312–14
    identity distancing and, 306–8
    needed distance provided, 301–4
    origins, 298–300
    popularization, 298–300
    search for meaning via, 300–1
    self-identification via, 301–4
    as space without place, 305–6
    universal identification via, 310–12, 431
Bunim, Simcha, 350
Burma, 298–99

Campbell, Colin, 338–45
Campbell, David, 329
Canaanism, 211f, 211
Cantril Ladder, 26–28
Capra, Fritjof, 343
Carnegie, Dale, 139, 144
casualties of war category
    discussion, 64–65, 86–88
    framing theory in analyzing, 65–67
    in loss reframing, 83–86
    reserved for IDF soldiers, 81–82
category blurring, 52–54
causa sui, 205, 207
CBJ (Chuck, Bernie, and Jim) group,
    124–25, 127. See also Physical
    Immortality group
ceremonies, 83
Chabad House, 337
Chassidic movement
    Halakhah and, 322–23n.2, 335

political wing, 281, 288
    women in, 277–78, 288
Chervovitzki, Mikhal, 289–90
China
    education system, 23–24
    pro-Eastern master narrative and, 342–
        45, 425–26
    traditional practices, 334
Chosen People identity
    excellence and, 38, 39
    in Judaism, 19–20, 29
    master narrative, 431–32
    sense of belonging to, 29
Christianity
    among Arab-Palestinian
        minority, 255
    immortality delusions in, 128–30
    New Age spirituality and, 342
Chuck, Bernie, and Jim (CBJ) group,
    124–25, 127. See also Physical
    Immortality group
Churchill, Winston, 199, 201
chutzpah quality, 34–37, 39
civic republicanism, 211f, 211
civilian casualties
    discussion, 63–65
    meaning attribution of, 70–71
civil-military gap, 355, 357–59
coherence typology
    discussion, 154, 383–84, 385t
    in meaning in life, 420–22
collective identity, 257–59
collective memory studies, 64–65
collective stories, 225–26. See also specific
        scripts
communal perspective, 5, 6, 7–258. See
        also kibbutzim
"Community as a Key to Healing After
        a Death of a Child" (Hastings,
        Musambira, & Hoover), 68
compensation mechanism
    active citizenship and, 19–23
    Chosen People identity and, 29
    discussion, 37–39
    master narratives of meaning, 431–32
    outline of, 20–21, 28
    self-expression and, 34–37
    Startup Nation identity and, 30–34